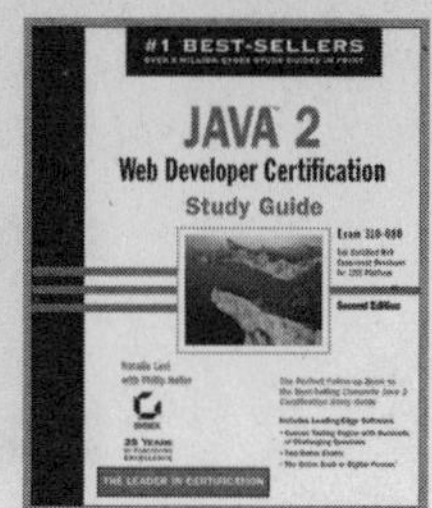

Java™ 2 Web Dev
Certification S

Natalie Levi

ISBN: 0-7821-4202-8 57

An invaluable tool for any experienced Java Programmer preparing for the Sun Certified Web Component Developer for J2EE Platform exam, the *Java 2 Web Developer Certification Study Guide* covers all enterprise-level topics comprising the objectives for the exam. You'll learn about servlets, exception handling, session management, security, JavaServer Pages (JSP), and creating custom tags and more. It contains all the new features of Sybex's market-leading *Study Guides*, including *Exam Essentials* sections to reinforce key concepts and real-world scenario sidebars with practical programming assignments. The companion CD-ROM has an assessment test, bonus practice exams, chapter-ending review questions, and a fully searchable electronic edition of the book.

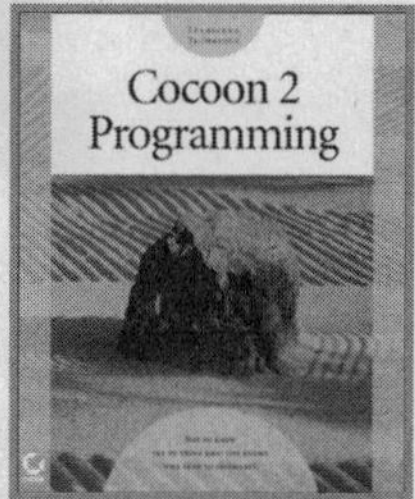

Cocoon 2 Programming: Web Publishing with XML and Java™

Bill Brogden, Conrad D'Cruz, and Mark Gaither

ISBN: 0-7821-4131-5 384 pages US $39.99

Cocoon 2 Programming: Web Publishing with XML and Java clearly explains the value of Cocoon and helps you build on your familiarity with XML and Java Servlets as you design, build, and implement a range of Cocoon applications. You'll begin by learning to control presentation for various platforms, both wired and wireless. Then you'll move on to Cocoon's capabilities for logic control and content management, using both sitemaps and XSP to create a site dynamically generated from a variety of data sources and types. As you'll see, Cocoon also supports powerful organizing techniques known as design patterns, and you'll master their use in both presentation and content generation. These are essential tools for the planning of your site, and after its implementation, you'll command powerful techniques for site management and optimization.

Mastering™ JSP™

Todd Cook

ISBN: 0-7821-2940-4 688 pages US $49.99

Mastering JSP is an essential tool in building the skills you need to design and develop a wide range of JSP-based web applications, beginning with a basic, dynamically generated website. From there, you'll build apps that read from and write to databases, create your own custom tags, and process and present XML. Throughout, you're helped by detailed, completely illuminated examples.

ENTERPRISE JAVA™ 2, J2EE™ 1.3 COMPLETE

SAN FRANCISCO ▸ LONDON

Associate Publisher: Joel Fugazzotto

Acquisitions Editor: Diane Lowery

Developmental Editor: Tom Cirtin

Compilation Editor: Victor Peters

Freelance Editor: Susan Hobbs

Production Editor: Lori Newman

Technical Editor: Robert Castaneda

Book Designer: Maureen Forys, Happenstance Type-o-Rama

Graphic Illustrator: Tony Jonick

Electronic Publishing Specialist: Interactive Composition Corporation

Proofreaders: Emily Hsuan, David Nash, Laurie O'Connell, Nancy Riddiough, Monique van den Berg

Indexer: Nancy Guenther

Cover Designer: Design Site

Cover Photographer: Don Farrall, PhotoDisc

Library of Congress Card Number: 2002111960

ISBN: 0-7821-4145-5

Manufactured in the United States of America

10 9 8 7 6 5 4 3 2 1

CONTENTS AT A GLANCE

Introduction *xxv*

Part I Java Web Applications 1

Chapter 1 An Introduction to J2EE 3
Written for Enterprise Java™ 2, J2EE™ 1.3 Complete by Vince E. Marco

Chapter 2 The Basic Servlet API 11
Updated from Java™ Developer's Guide to Servlets and JSP by Bill Brogden
ISBN 0-7821-2809-2 $49.99

Chapter 3 The Basic JSP API 37
Updated from Java™ Developer's Guide to Servlets and JSP by Bill Brogden
ISBN 0-7821-2809-2 $49.99

Chapter 4 Servlet Web Applications 71
Adapted from Java™ 2 Web Developer Certification Study Guide, Second Edition by Natalie Levi
ISBN 0-7821-4202-8 $59.99

Chapter 5 Introducing JavaBeans 93
Adapted from Mastering™ JSP™ by Todd Cook
ISBN 0-7821-2940-4 $49.99

Chapter 6 Session Management 139
Adapted from Java™ 2 Web Developer Certification Study Guide, Second Edition by Natalie Levi
ISBN 0-7821-4202-8 $59.99

Chapter 7 Using Custom Tags 167
Adapted from Java™ 2 Web Developer Certification Study Guide, Second Edition by Natalie Levi
ISBN 0-7821-4202-8 $59.99

Part II **Naming Services, Databases, and Security** **209**

Chapter 8 Java Naming and Directory Interface (JNDI) 211
Written for Enterprise Java™ 2, J2EE™ 1.3 Complete by Victor Peters and Michael Ernest

Chapter 9 Database Connectivity (JDBC) 243
Updated from Java™ 2 Developer's Handbook™ by Philip Heller and Simon Roberts
ISBN 0-7821-2179-9 $59.99

Chapter 10 Advanced Database Programming 285
Adapted from Mastering™ JSP™ by Todd Cook
ISBN 0-7821-2940-4 $49.99

Chapter 11 Secure Web Applications 327
Adapted from Java™ 2 Web Developer Certification Study Guide, Second Edition by Natalie Levi
ISBN 0-7821-4202-8 $59.99

Part III **XML, SOAP, and Messaging** **353**

Chapter 12 XML for Data Description 355
Adapted from Java™ Developer's Guide to E-Commerce with XML and JSP by Bill Brogden and Chris Minnick
ISBN 0-7821-2827-0 $49.99

Chapter 13 Presenting XML With JSP 391
Adapted from Mastering™ JSP™ by Todd Cook
ISBN 0-7821-2940-4 $49.99

Chapter 14 Understanding XML Messaging 429
Adapted from SOAP Programming with Java™ by Bill Brogden
ISBN 0-7821-2928-5 $49.99

Chapter 15 A Survey of SOAP 443
Adapted from SOAP Programming with Java™ by Bill Brogden
ISBN 0-7821-2928-5 $49.99

Chapter 16 A SOAP Server Example 459
Adapted from SOAP Programming with Java™ by Bill Brogden
ISBN 0-7821-2928-5 $49.99

Chapter 26 Building a High-Volume Spider 801

Adapted from Programming Spiders, Bots, and Aggregators in Java™ by Jeff Heaton

ISBN 0-7821-4040-8 $59.99

Chapter 27 Building a Bot 849

Adapted from Programming Spiders, Bots, and Aggregators in Java™ by Jeff Heaton

ISBN 0-7821-4040-8 $59.99

Appendix Setup 901

Adapted from Mastering™ JSP™ by Todd Cook

ISBN 0-7821-2940-4 $49.99

Glossary 915

Adapted from Cocoon 2 Programming: Web Publishing with XML and Java™ by Bill Brogden, Conrad D'Cruz, and Mark Gaither

ISBN 0-7821-4131-5 $39.99

Index *931*

CONTENTS

INTRODUCTION

Enterprise Java 2, J2EE 1.3 Complete is a one-of-a-kind computer book—valuable both for the breadth of its content and for its low price. This thousand-page compilation of information from some of the very best Sybex books provides comprehensive coverage of the hottest topics in Java enterprise programming today. This book, unique in the computer book world, was created with two goals in mind:

- To offer a thorough guide covering all the aspects of J2EE programming at an affordable price
- To acquaint you with some of our best authors—their writing styles and teaching skills, and the level of expertise they bring to their books—so you can easily find a match for your interests as you delve deeper into Java programming

Enterprise Java 2, J2EE 1.3 Complete is a thorough reference to all of the technologies that form Java 2 Enterprise Edition (J2EE). This book will help you utilize the incredible power of J2EE to create effective, scalable, maintainable, and adaptable enterprise applications to solve an extremely wide range of problems. Java servlets and Java Server Pages (JSP) will be discussed in detail to allow you to create powerful web applications. Enterprise JavaBeans (EJB) will be discussed in detail to allow you to take advantage of this technology to greatly increase the power and scalability of your business logic. The increasingly popular XML and web services technologies will be discussed so that you are better able to have your system communicate with other systems. Supporting J2EE technologies, such as JDBC, JNDI, JMS, and JCA, will also be discussed to round out your knowledge of the power that J2EE can bring to your application development efforts. This book provides the vital information you'll need to further your J2EE programming knowledge, while also inviting you to explore greater depths and wider coverage in the original books. If you've read other computer "how-to" books, you've seen that there are many possible approaches to the task of showing how to use software effectively. The books from which *Enterprise Java 2, J2EE 1.3 Complete* was compiled represent a range of the approaches to teaching that Sybex and its authors have developed—from the specific *Developer's Handbook* style to the wide-ranging, thoroughly detailed *Mastering* style. These books also address readers at different levels of computer experience. As you read various chapters of this book, you'll discover which approach works best for you.

You'll also see what these books have in common: a commitment to clarity, accuracy, and practicality.

You'll find in these pages ample evidence of the expertise of Sybex's authors. Unlike publishers who produce "books by committee," Sybex authors are encouraged to write in individual voices that reflect their own experience with the software at hand and with the evolution of today's personal computers. Nearly every book represented here is the work of a single writer or a pair of close collaborators, and you are getting the benefit of each author's direct experience.

In adapting the various source materials for inclusion in *Enterprise Java 2, J2EE 1.3 Complete,* the compilers preserved these individual voices and perspectives. Chapters were edited only to minimize duplication and update or add cross-references, so that you can easily follow a topic across chapters. A few sections were also edited for length so that other important information could be included.

Who Can Benefit from This Book?

Enterprise Java 2, J2EE 1.3 Complete is designed to meet the needs of any Java programmer who wants a complete reference to building applications for intranets and the Web. The contents and index will guide you to the subjects you're looking for.

How This Book Is Organized

Enterprise Java 2, J2EE 1.3 Complete has five parts, consisting of 27 chapters, an appendix, and a glossary:

Part I: Java Web Applications These first seven chapters discuss the details of developing web applications using Java servlets, Java Server Pages (JSP), JavaBeans, and custom tags.

Part II: Naming Services, Databases, and Security These four chapters discuss how J2EE applications can access data stored in databases and directory services. This part also discusses how to make secure J2EE web-based applications.

Part III: XML, SOAP, and Messaging The six chapters in this part begin by describing how XML works and how it can be used. This will lead into studying how XML web services can be used to send messages between applications. Finally, the part will conclude with using the Java Messaging Service (JMS) to send messages between applications or inside of an application.

Part IV: Remote Communications and Enterprise JavaBeans The seven chapters in this part begin by describing how RMI and CORBA can be used to communicate across networks and possibly between programming languages. The part will then discuss the Enterprise JavaBeans (EJB) technologies.

Part V: Spiders and Bots The three chapters in this part will provide an intriguing conclusion to our tour. These three chapters discuss how to write Spiders and Bots that can automatically explore web sites. Although these are not J2EE-specific issues, this material will be very useful to many J2EE web developers.

A Few Typographical Conventions

When a Windows operation requires a series of choices from menus or dialog boxes, the ➢ symbol is used to guide you through the instructions, like this: "Select Programs ➢ Accessories ➢ System Tools ➢ System Information." The items the ➢ symbol separates may be menu names, toolbar icons, check boxes, or other elements of the Windows interface–anyplace you can make a selection.

`This typeface` is used to identify Internet URLs and code, and **boldface type** is used whenever you need to type something into a text box.

You'll find these types of special notes throughout the book:

TIP

You'll see a lot of these—quicker and smarter ways to accomplish a task, which the authors have based on many years of experience working with Java.

NOTE

You'll see these notes, too. They usually represent alternate ways to accomplish a task or some additional information that needs to be highlighted.

WARNING

In a few places you'll see a warning like this one. When you see a warning, do pay attention to it.

YOU'LL ALSO SEE "SIDEBAR" BOXES LIKE THIS

These boxed sections provide added explanation of special topics that are noted briefly in the surrounding discussion, but that you may want to explore separately. Each sidebar has a heading that announces the topic, so you can quickly decide whether it's something you need to know about.

For More Information

See the Sybex web site, `www.sybex.com`, to learn more about all the books that went into *Enterprise Java 2, J2EE 1.3 Complete.* On the site's Catalog page, you'll find links to any book you're interested in. Also, be sure to check the Sybex site for late-breaking developments about the sample code and applications.

We hope you enjoy this book and find it useful. Good luck in your J2EE programming endeavors!

Part I

Java Web Applications

Chapter 1

An Introduction to J2EE

The Java2 Enterprise Edition (J2EE) is a powerful collection of technologies that sit on top of the Java2 Standard Edition (J2SE) environment. This base of Java2 provides a stable and reliable application environment that runs on many different operating system (OS) platforms. The cross-platform compatibility lifts both application and server environments above the dependencies of specific OS and hardware platforms.

The enterprise technologies that extend the Java2 environment are focused upon providing standard interfaces, which J2EE application server vendors can implement while providing a robust environment for server-based solutions; not only are J2EE enterprise solutions free from OS and hardware dependencies, but also achieve a high degree of portability between application servers. It is precisely this standards-based approach that continues to attract enterprise systems development. Before a picture of J2EE is laid out, let's take a look at the demands of enterprise applications.

Written for *Enterprise Java™ 2, J2EE™ 1.3 Complete*
by Vince E. Marco

Enterprise Applications

Functional requirements of enterprise applications are typically more expansive than many traditional applications. Their functional requirements often include extensive access to a varied array of data sources, and accessibility from a wide array of user interfaces. Enterprise applications also usually have more demanding non-functional requirements including availability, scalability, security, and maintainability. Availability largely refers to an application's capability to process client requests. Enterprises collect and process information using a distributed environment consisting of clients and servers. Enterprise applications include server-based components that desire to provide constant availability to client requests. Application servers restrict the free use of resources (such as threads) to prevent an application from starving a server and preventing clients from accessing needed services.

Scalability refers to the capability of an application to support a wide range of numbers of users. This includes effectively supporting just a handful of users to millions of users by merely changing the deployment environment. In the past, enterprise development was performed on large and expensive mainframes. While this did support large-scale applications, it wasn't effective at deploying small or medium scale applications, and it certainly was costly to maintain a mainframe just for development of the application.

Maintainability involves the management of software complexity. Because Java2 is an object-oriented language, objects are the method for managing this complexity. Objects provide a means for building small software units that interact to provide an entire application. This object technology is extended with components. Components add features such as distributed access, transactions, security, and lifecycle management to objects, and are ideal for server-side objects supporting many clients over a network. As an example, both JavaBeans and Enterprise JavaBeans (EJBs) provide component technology by defining component properties and definition.

J2EE addresses these enterprise application requirements by providing a standard for Java-based application servers. These J2EE application servers are then provided by vendors, each providing the standard J2EE application server functionality, but competing on specific implementation and extended behavior. These servers utilize clustering to provide availability and scalability, enabling enterprise applications to be deployed into a cluster of machines of various sizes.

NOTE

`http://java.sun.com/j2ee` is the homepage for J2EE and contains links for a plethora of J2EE learning and development resources.

Java2 Enterprise Edition (J2EE)

J2EE is a collection of several different technologies, each of which helps developers meet the requirements of enterprise applications. Figure 1.1 is a diagram of these technologies.

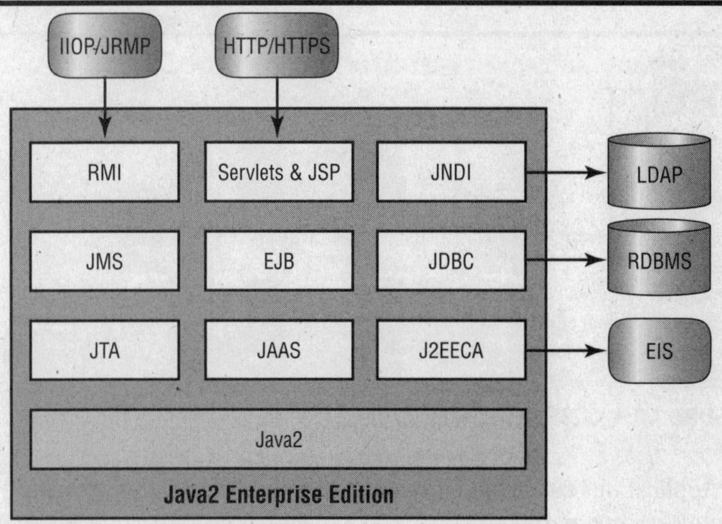

FIGURE 1.1: J2EE technologies

The foundation starts with the standard Java2 environment. This provides a base environment that is cross-platform, and fully supports and leverages the Java2 language and features. A set of technologies is added to this with each technology addressing an enterprise application need. Each technology is composed of an application programming interface (API), and a contract for behavior. The API is composed of a set of Java2 interfaces and classes that define constant values and methods (member functions) for objects not yet implemented. Vendor implementations of these interfaces provide the actual classes that provide J2EE behavior. The behavioral contract is in the form of a specification document, which describes exactly what each technology implementation must do to be compliant with the J2EE specification.

J2EE Technologies

Each J2EE technology focuses on a set of functionality needed by server-based applications. These technologies address the enterprise application demands of availability and scalability through the use of *clustering*.

Clustering is the configuration of multiple servers, each identical in the service provided and enabling client access to be effectively distributed across many servers rather than one large server (see Figure 1.2). This provides effective availability and scalability.

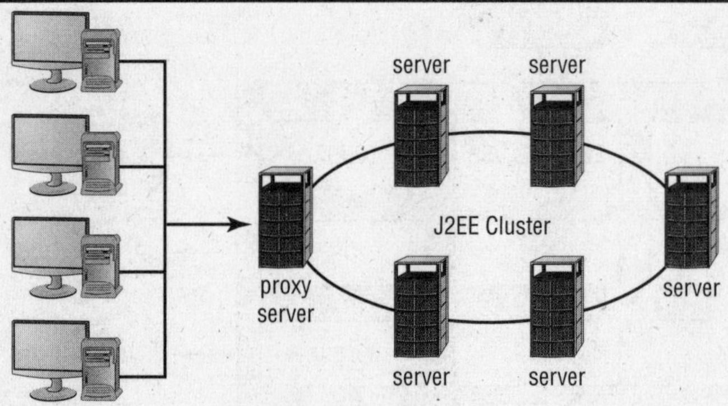

FIGURE 1.2: Clustering of J2EE servers

Applications can be built on one machine as small as a laptop and then deployed to as many servers as needed. Some of these can even be main-frames. Application maintenance is enhanced by using object-oriented and component-based framework development. Also important to J2EE development is multi-tiered development and the separation of technologies. The following describes each technology.

Remote Method Invocation (RMI) RMI provides a way to access distributed Java objects running on a remote server on the network. It can use the Java Remote Method Protocol (JRMP), which supports RMI, or the Internet Inter-Orb Protocol (IIOP), which supports both RMI and CORBA distributed method calls (see Chapter 18, "Persistence and Remote Method Invocation").

Java Database Connectivity (JDBC) JDBC provides a Java-based, standardized API for executing SQL-92 queries and statements on database servers from different vendors (see Chapter 9, "Database Connectivity [JDBC]").

Java Naming and Directory Interface (JNDI) JNDI provides a uniform and standardized Java-based naming and directory services interface for accessing various types of naming providers such as LDAP and DNS (see Chapter 8, "Java Naming and Directory Interface [JNDI]").

Java Authorization & Authentication Service (JAAS) JAAS provides a uniform interface for managing enterprise-wide security (see Chapter 22, "EJB Transactions and Security").

Java Transaction API (JTA) JTA is a standard Java interface for supporting local and distributed transactions (see Chapter 22).

Java Management Extensions (JMX) Java Management Extensions is a framework for managing Java-based services supporting web and external tool integration.

Java Messaging Service (JMS) JMS is an interface that allows standardized access to Message Oriented Middleware servers that can provide asynchronous messaging, through reliable point-to-point and publish-and-subscribe messaging models (see Chapter 17, "Java Messaging Service [JMS]").

Enterprise JavaBeans (EJBs) A container-based component model that allows for distributed and container managed Java components. A developer creates Java components, called beans, which are placed in an EJB server that provides life-cycle management and services to the bean, such as security, transactions, and object pooling. EJBs can be an excellent technology to create business components that need to be very scalable or support other typical enterprise characteristics (see Chapter 20, "EJB Architecture and Clients"; Chapter 21, "Session, Entity, and Message-Driven EJBs"; Chapter 22; and Chapter 23, "EJB Environment, Client, and Design Issues").

Servlets and JSPs A model for container managed components that process client requests to a server. They are most commonly used for handling HTTP or HTTPS web requests. Java Server Pages (JSPs) provide an abstraction of servlets that makes it easier to create servlets which predominantly produce dynamic web content such as HTML or XML content. Together servlets and JSPs provide the web interface behavior for J2EE (see Chapter 2, "The Basic Servlet API"; Chapter 3, "The Basic JSP API"; Chapter 4, "Servlet Web Applications"; Chapter 5, "Introducing JavaBeans"; Chapter 6, "Session Management"; and Chapter 7, "Using Custom Tags").

JavaMail and JavaBeans Activation Framework (JAF) An API that enables the sending of email from Java applications. The JavaBeans Activation Framework is used by JavaMail and enables the support of MIME content within email messages.

JavaIDL An API that enables J2EE application components to invoke external CORBA objects via the IIOP protocol. These CORBA objects may be written in a wide variety of languages and run on any CORBA platform (see Chapter 19, "Java IDL and CORBA Connectivity").

J2EE Connector Architecture (J2EECA) This is a standard Java-based architecture for connecting transactional J2EE applications to existing Enterprise Information Systems (see Chapter 24, "J2EE Connector Architecture").

Multi-Tiered Applications

Enterprise applications are characterized by their distributed and scalable nature. These applications encompass both client and server components, and include web applications and services. The explosion of the Internet has led to the need to access and manage large amounts of information within these enterprise applications. Meeting the requirements of modern enterprise application requires not only robust technologies but effective architectural patterns and recommended guidelines for most effectively using these technologies. This has identified the need to separate business logic from the technologies used within these applications. Sun has provided a guideline for building J2EE applications called the J2EE Blueprint. This blueprint organizes enterprise applications into multiple tiers to manage the complexity.

These tiers provide a means of managing the dependencies between the J2EE technologies and reducing the accidental complexity added by the technologies themselves. The base tier includes enterprise information systems and databases. The business model containing the business logic and functionality required by the application sits above the base tier. The user interface sits above the business model, and consists of Java clients such as Java-based applications or applets as well as web clients supported through servlets and JSPs. These tiers separate the aspects of an enterprise application as well as the business logic so that each tier can change at its own rate while minimizing the change to the entire application.

NOTE

The J2EE Blueprints are available online at `http://java.sun.com/j2ee/blueprints`.

WHAT'S NEXT

The Java2 Enterprise Edition defines a new standard for enterprise applications and the servers used to deploy them. The J2EE specification provides several technologies for the building and deploying of enterprise applications. Not every enterprise application will use every technology, but these applications now have a standard framework of tools as well as a market of vendors supporting the environment.

This market extends from application servers to frameworks of EJBs to integrated development environments (IDEs) and tools. The J2EE frameworks provide the J2EE developer with many tools for building cross-platform applications for today's informational enterprise.

The following chapters will detail each technology, and present a complete understanding of how they operate and how to use them. As you cover each chapter, the full picture of the Java2 Enterprise Edition will become complete.

Chapter 2

The Basic Servlet API

Servlets are one of the most essential technologies in J2EE. Along with JSP pages, servlets provide the best mechanism for J2EE applications to provide a web interface. This chapter will introduce you to the essential concepts of developing servlets.

In 1993, messages sent in the Hypertext Transfer Protocol (HTTP) format used by web servers were only a minute portion of the traffic on the Internet. HTTP's tremendous functionality led to a rapid expansion in both the number and capabilities of web servers. Essentially, it was HTTP that made the World Wide Web possible.

Originally, a basic web server simply returned a text page when it got a correctly formatted request message; however, it did not take programmers long to discover that great things were possible if some extra functionality was added, such as forms and graphics capabilities.

Updated from *Java™ Developer's Guide to Servlets and JSP* by Bill Brogden
ISBN 0-7821-2809-2 $49.99

The Common Gateway Interface (CGI) standard enables the user of a web browser to submit data from a web page to a server for further processing. Programming with Java servlets and JavaServer Pages builds on this universal standard and makes it easier to use. To understand how this works, you must understand how a web server processes HTTP transactions, and how these transactions are related to the servlet Application Programming Interface (API).

Featured in this chapter:

- How a web server handles HTTP requests
- How an HTTP request is passed to the servlet engine
- How to get input data from a `Get` or `Post` operation
- How to create web page output with Java
- Understanding the implications of the servlet thread model
- Setting up a system for servlet development

How a Web Server Handles HTTP Requests

The current standard for web servers, HTTP version 1.1, is maintained by the World Wide Web Consortium (W3C) organization (`www.w3.org`). A simple HTTP transaction between a web browser and a web server takes place in several steps. If you enter `http://java.sun.com/jsp/simplepage.html` into a browser connected to the Internet, the following actions occur:

1. The browser establishes a TCP/IP (Transmission Control Protocol/Internet Protocol) connection to the server represented by java.sun.com.
2. The browser sends a request message for the page represented by jsp/simplepage.html to the server.
3. The server sends a response message that includes either the text of that page or an error report.
4. The TCP/IP connection is closed.

In this case, the server has to locate only the text file represented by the jsp/simplepage.html part of the request, which it does by using conventions the webmaster has set up to map from requests to the local file system. The text file contains all the HTML markup needed to create the page display on the browser, so it is passed through unaltered by the web server.

Request Message Contents

The request message from browser to web server starts with one or more text lines terminated by carriage return–line feed (crlf) characters. The first line specifies a method, a Uniform Resource Identifier (URI), and an indicator of the HTTP version being used. The standard methods in the HTTP 1.1 protocol are `OPTIONS`, `GET`, `HEAD`, `POST`, `PUT`, `DELETE`, `TRACE`, and `CONNECT`. The request for a plain HTML page uses the `GET` method. With JSP and Java servlets, the most important methods are `GET` and `POST`. The following sections describe the process with JSP and Java servlets.

The GET Method

The `GET` method is used to request a resource, such as an HTML page. When you type a request, such as `http://www.someserver.com/index.htm`, the request message to the server specifies the `GET` method, and the URI is index.htm. In this case, the requested resource is an HTML page, but it can also refer to a process that creates data on the fly. A `GET` request can include some additional information appended to the URI string as a query string. You have undoubtedly seen this in action at web shopping sites.

The server process is passed this query string when it is executed. Because of restrictions on the size of the request header that servers can handle, the total of URI and query string should be less than 240 characters. Listing 2.1 is a simple HTML form that uses the `GET` request.

Listing 2.1: An HTML page with a form

```
<html><head>
<title>Chapter 2 GET example</title>
</head>
<body><font size="4">
<center>Please enter your name and password
then press Start<br>
<form method="GET" action="http://localhost/servlet/GetDemo">
Name: <input name="uname" value="" type="text" size="20"><br>
```

```
Password:
<input name="userpw" value="" type="password" size=10>
<input type="submit" value="Start" ><br>
</form></center>
<hr></body></html>
```

The resulting page will be rendered as shown in Figure 2.1, where the user has filled in the fields. Note that because the password type is used for the second field, the browser shows "****" instead of the actual characters.

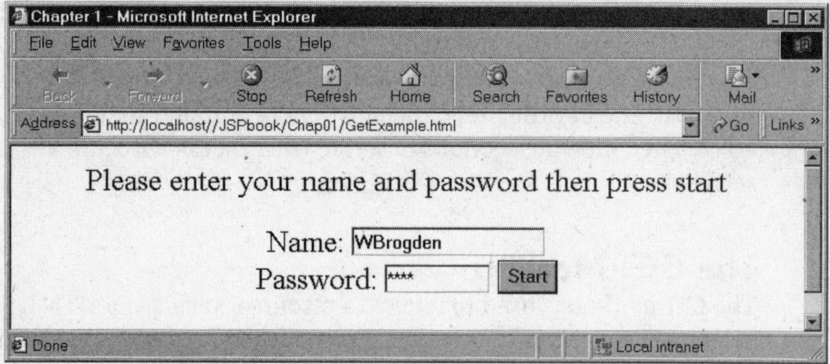

FIGURE 2.1: Browser rendering of the GET example HTML page

NOTE

A note about HTML tags. Although most browsers can parse both upper- and lowercase letters, you are probably used to seeing HTML tags and attributes such as <FORM> in uppercase. The reason lowercase tags and attributes are used in this chapter is because the HTML 4.0 standard uses them, and we all might as well get used to it.

When the Start button is clicked, the browser submits a GET style request line that includes the form data in the URL. The first line is followed by several lines that take the following form:

```
keyword: value
```

These lines define various bits of optional information about the browser and are followed by blank lines. Listing 2.2 is the complete request (note that certain lines are wrapped in this display).

NOTE

Please note that some lines of code in this text are broken for print purposes only.

Listing 2.2: The request generated by the example form

```
GET /servlet/GetDemo?uname=WBrogden&userpw=java HTTP/1.1
Accept: application/msword, application/vnd.ms-excel,
    image/gif, image/x-xbitmap, image/jpeg, image/pjpeg, */*
Accept-Language: en-us
Accept-Encoding: gzip, deflate
User-Agent: Mozilla/4.0 (compatible; MSIE 5.0;
  Windows NT; DigExt)
Host: localhost
Connection: Keep-Alive
```

The web server has been set up to associate the use of `servlet` in the URL with the servlet engine so this request is passed to the servlet engine for processing. The servlet engine creates a Java object that implements the `HttpServletRequest` interface and an object that implements the `HttpServletResponse` interface. It passes references to these objects by means of a mechanism (see "Inner Workings of a Servlet Engine" later in this chapter) to the doGet method of an instance of the `GetDemo` servlet. Listing 2.3 shows the Java code for the `GetDemo` servlet.

Listing 2.3: Source code for the GetDemo servlet

```
// demonstrates handling of a GET request
import java.io.*;
import javax.servlet.*;
import javax.servlet.http.*;

public class GetDemo extends HttpServlet
{
  public void doGet(HttpServletRequest req,
        HttpServletResponse resp)
  throws ServletException, IOException
  {
    resp.setContentType("text/html");
    PrintWriter out = resp.getWriter();
    String username = req.getParameter("uname");
    String password = req.getParameter("userpw");
```

```
    out.println("<HTML>");
    out.println("<HEAD><TITLE>GetDemo</TITLE></HEAD>");
    out.println("<BODY>");
    out.println("Hello " + username + "<br>");
    out.println("Your password was: " + password + "<br>");
    out.println("</BODY>");
    out.println("</HTML>");
    out.close();
  }

}
```

Note how the `getParameter` method is used to get the values of the uname and userpw parameters that were in the URL from the `HttpServletRequest` object. Having these parameters parsed out of the GET request by the servlet engine vastly simplifies servlet programming.

The following steps describe how the output that goes back to the browser is created using the `HttpServletResponse` object:

1. The `setContentType` method sets the MIME type of the response that will be sent to the browser. The response creates all the other header lines using default values.
2. The `getWriter` method returns a `PrintWriter` object named `out` so that we can output plain text.
3. The various calls to `out.println` send text creating the HTML page to the output stream.
4. Finally, the call to `out.close` flushes the output stream buffer and then terminates the sending of the response.

Response Message Contents

The response message from web server to browser always starts with a status line composed of the protocol being used, a numeric status code, and a text version of the status code. This is followed by various lines of additional information in the `keyword: value` format, followed by a single blank line. The `HttpServletResponse` object takes care of creating these lines, but the servlet has control over the values that are returned. The response continues with the data that were written to the output stream by the servlet. Listing 2.4 shows the complete response text generated by the GetDemo servlet. Note the blank line that is required to terminate the header area.

Listing 2.4: The text of the GetDemo response

```
HTTP/1.0 200 OK
Server: Microsoft-PWS/2.0
Date: Sat, 26 Feb 2000 22:34:04 GMT
Content-Type: text/html

<HTML>
<HEAD><TITLE>GetDemo Output</TITLE></HEAD>
<BODY>
Hello WBrogden<br>
Your password was: java<br>
</BODY>
</HTML>
```

When the browser receives this data, it decides what to do with it on the basis of the response code and content type. In this case, the content is displayed as an HTML page, as shown in Figure 2.2. Note that the `userpw` parameter value is readable in the browser's address field for the URL request sent to the server, making GET a less secure way to send sensitive information than the POST method.

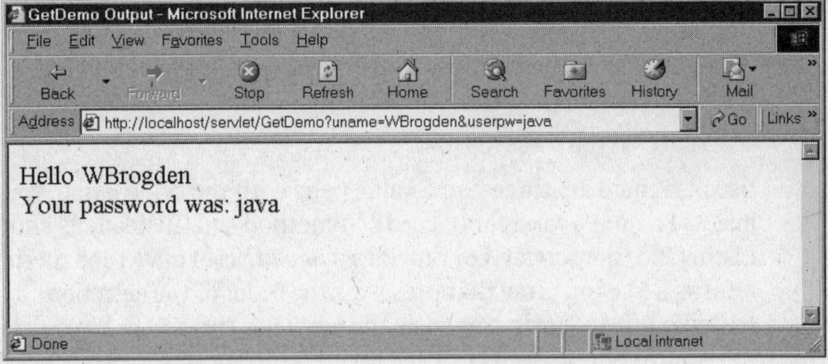

FIGURE 2.2: The browser display generated by the `GetDemo` servlet

The POST Method

When the method specified in a request is POST, the request can contain any amount of information because it is sent as lines of text, and the URL contains only the name of the servlet to process the request. Listing 2.5 provides an example of an HTML form using the POST method.

Listing 2.5: An HTML page with a form using the POST method

```
<html><head>
<title>Chapter 2</title>
</head>
<body><font size="4">
<center>Please select topics of interest<br>
<form method="post"
    action="http://localhost/servlet/MultiDemo" >
<select name="topic" multiple >
<option value="a">APL
<option value="b">Basic
<option value="c">C++
<option value="e">Eiffel
<option value="f">FORTH
<option value="j">Java
<option value="p">Pascal
</select><br>
<input type="submit" value="Submit Selection" >
<input type="submit" value="Cancel" ><br>
</form></center>
<hr></body></html>
```

If the user selected APL, Eiffel, and FORTH in the list box and then clicked either of the buttons, the transmitted request would include the following text:

```
topic=a&topic=e&topic=f
```

Because there are three name-value pairs with the same name, you can't just use a `getParameter("topic")` method call. Instead, as shown in Listing 2.6, the servlet API provides a `getParameterValues` method that returns a `String` array that preserves the order of the selections as presented on the page. In this case, the array has three `String` objects, with the values "a," "e," and "f."

Listing 2.6: The doPost method handles POST requests

```
public void doPost(HttpServletRequest req,
     HttpServletResponse resp)
     throws ServletException, IOException
  {
    resp.setContentType("text/html");
    PrintWriter out = new
        PrintWriter(resp.getOutputStream());
```

```
    String[] topics = req.getParameterValues("topic");
    out.println("<HTML>");
    out.println(
      "<HEAD><TITLE>MultiDemo Output</TITLE></HEAD>");
    out.println("<BODY>");
    out.println("Selected " + topics.length +
      " topics<br>");
    for(int i = 0; i < topics.length; i++){
      out.print( topics[i] + " " );
    }
    out.println("</BODY>");
    out.println("</HTML>");
    out.close();
  }
```

Inner Workings of a Servlet Engine

You can think of the servlet engine as acting like a container for the servlet code, just as a web browser is a container for applet code. The servlet engine performs many tasks that greatly simplify the programmer's job. Here are the stages of the lifecycle of a servlet that uses the standard threading model:

1. *Servlet instance creation.* The servlet engine loads the Java classes to create a servlet instance either when the engine is started, or when the first request for a particular servlet arrives. When this happens depends on settings for the particular servlet. Typically, the engine creates only a single copy of the servlet object and reuses the object for every request, even if more than one request is being processed at the same time.

   This saves the time that would be required to create a new servlet object for every request, but it requires careful planning by the programmer; however, see the Single Thread Model interface for alternatives.

2. *Instance initialization.* The engine calls the servlet's `init()` method. With this method, you would typically set up parameters that are going to be constant for the life of the servlet, such as paths to files or a pool of database connections. After

initialization, the servlet instance sits in memory until a request is directed to it.

3. *Request handling.* Each request that an engine gets is handled by a separate Java `Thread`. The engine may create a new `Thread`, or it may assign one from a pool. The `Thread` creates request and response objects as previously discussed and then calls the servlet's `service()` method. The `service` method is responsible for deciding how to handle the request.
4. *Thread management.* Any number of threads may be executing the methods of an object at the same time, each with its own request and response objects. Designing your code so that it is thread-safe is a major part of learning servlet programming.
5. *Other services.* A typical service provided by an engine is session tracking. This provides a method by which your program can keep track of data belonging to a particular user.
6. *Instance destruction.* When the servlet engine needs to shut down completely, or just to recover memory, it calls the servlet's `destroy()` method. At this point, the servlet can close files and otherwise shut down gracefully.

One of the services the servlet engine provides to servlets is management of the standard outputs, `System.out` and `System.err`. Text output to these streams will be directed to log files. The exact location of the files varies between engines. When writing information to one of these streams, remember that other servlets may also be writing data, and be sure your message is labeled so you can tell which servlet it comes from.

The Servlet API Packages

The Java servlet library is elegantly simple, considering how much power it gives the programmer. We will be concerned with the following packages:

`javax.servlet` The basic generalized servlet package

`javax.servlet.http` Specialized extensions for web pages

`javax.servlet.jsp` Classes for creating JavaServer Pages

`javax.servlet.jsp.tagext` Specialized extensions to jsp classes

The following sections cover these packages in more detail.

The javax prefix indicates that these classes are what Sun calls *standard extensions*. Although standard extensions are part of the official Java standard, developers of Java Virtual Machines (JVM) are not required to provide them. Examples of other standard extensions are the "Swing" GUI interface, Enterprise JavaBean, and the accessibility packages.

The javax.servlet Package

The javax.servlet package contains a number of interface definitions that provide the basic structure of the entire API. The interfaces you will be using most often are listed here:

`Servlet` This interface defines the methods that all servlets must implement. The `GenericServlet` class implements the `Servlet` interface.

`ServletRequest` All information about a client request is accessed through an object implementing this interface. Creating a `ServletRequest` object is the responsibility of the servlet engine.

`ServletResponse` An object implementing this interface must be created by the servlet engine and passed to the servlet's `service` method to be used for output of the MIME body to the client.

In addition to the interfaces just listed, the javax.servlet package has the following utility interfaces:

`Filter` Filters can be used to modify requests before the request is sent to resources such as servlets or JSP pages. Filters can also be used to modify responses that are sent from those resources.

`FilterChain` Multiple filters can be chained together to perform different operations on a request or response. This interface gives the developer access to the chain of filters.

`FilterConfig` Provides initialization and configuration information for the filter.

`RequestDispatcher` This powerful interface permits you to forward a request from the current servlet to another servlet or a JSP page for additional processing.

`ServletConfig` Objects using this interface are used to hold information used during servlet initialization.

`ServletContext` Objects using this interface let a servlet locate information about the servlet engine it is running in and its web application, which is composed of the related servlets and JSP pages for this project.

`ServletContextAttributeListener` This interface, and all of the listener interfaces, is analogous to the listener interfaces in Java GUI design. The `ServletContext` can store attributes that can be accessed by a group of related servlets and JSP pages that are in the same web application. A programmer would implement this interface in an object that needs to be notified when attributes are added, removed, or replaced from the `ServletContext`.

`ServletContextListener` A programmer would implement this interface in an object that needs to be notified when the ServletContext of their web application is initialized or destroyed. This can be used to write an init or destroy method for the entire web application.

`SingleThreadModel` This interface contains no methods. It is a marker that forces the servlet engine to ensure that only one `Thread` executes an instance of the servlet at one time. The servlet engine can do this either by restricting access to a single instance of the servlet or by creating a separate instance for every `Thread`.

The classes in the `javax.servlet` package provide basic bare minimum functionality. In general, you will work with classes that extend these for more specific applications.

`GenericServlet` Provides bare minimum functionality for any type of servlet

`ServletContextAttributeEvent` Event object passed to a ServletContextAttributeListener

`ServletContextEvent` Event object passed to a Servlet-ContextListener

`ServletInputStream` A class for reading a stream of binary data from the request

ServletOutputStream A class for writing a stream of binary data as part of a response

ServletRequestWrapper A subclass of ServletRequest that allows the wrapping of modified functionality around a Servlet-Request

ServletResponseWrapper A subclass of ServletResponse that allows the wrapping of modified functionality around a ServletResponse

Only two exceptions are defined in the `javax.servlet` package. These classes do not descend from `RuntimeException`, so if a method declares that it throws `ServletException`, a calling method must provide for catching it.

ServletException A general purpose exception used throughout the servlet API.

UnavailableException This exception is to be thrown when a servlet needs to indicate that it is temporarily or permanently unavailable.

The javax.servlet.http Package

When programming servlets to create web pages, you will be dealing with classes in the `javax.servlet.http` package. To give maximum flexibility to servlet engine designers, most of the package functionality is defined in interfaces.

HttpServletRequest This extension of the `ServletRequest` interface adds methods specific to HTTP requests such as typical web applications.

HttpServletResponse An extension of the `ServletResponse` interface, which adds methods specific to HTTP transactions.

HttpSession Objects implementing this interface allow the programmer to store information about a user between individual page visits or transactions. Servlet engines provide methods for keeping track of `HttpSession` objects using unique IDs. The use of these objects is discussed in Chapter 6.

HttpSessionActivationListener A programmer would implement this interface in an object that needs to be notified when an HttpSession will be activated or passivated.

HttpSessionAttributeListener A programmer would implement this interface in an object that needs to be notified when an attribute is added, removed, or replaced in an HttpSession.

HttpSessionBindingListener A programmer would implement this interface in an object that needs to be notified when it has been attached to or detached from an `HttpSession` object.

HttpSessionContext This interface is deprecated as of version 2.1 of the API due to security concerns about letting one servlet find out too much information about other servlets on the system.

HttpSessionListener Class implementing this interface will be notified when the HttpSession is created or destroyed.

The following are the classes in the javax.servlet.http package:

HttpServlet This abstract class is the one you will usually extend to create useful web servlets. The methods are discussed in detail later in this chapter.

HttpServletRequestWrapper A subclass of HttpServlet-Request that allows the wrapping of modified functionality around a HttpServletRequest.

HttpServletResponseWrapper A subclass of HttpServlet-Response that allows the wrapping of modified functionality around a HttpServletResponse.

Cookie These objects are used to manipulate cookie information that is sent by the server to a browser and returned on subsequent requests. Cookie information in a request is turned into `Cookie` objects by the `HttpServletRequest`.

HttpUtils Static methods in this class are useful occasionally.

HttpSessionBindingEvent Objects of this type are used to communicate information to `HttpSessionBindingListener` objects when they are attached to or detached from an `Http-Session` object.

HttpSessionEvent Event object passed to HttpSession listeners.

NOTE

The 2.3 version of the servlet specification added the three filter interfaces, the request and response wrapper classes, and the listener interfaces and event classes for listening to servlet contexts, servlet context attributes, HTTP session activation, and HTTP session attributes. This means that if your servlet container is older than the 2.3 specification, it may not support these methods.

Implications of the Servlet Thread Model

If you are not used to programming multi-threaded applications in Java, you will probably need to change some of your programming practices. The significant points to emphasize include:

- There is only one instance of your servlet class, and many `Thread` objects may be executing methods in this instance at any one time.
- This instance remains in the servlet engine memory for long periods of time. Any errors in memory management that might go unnoticed in a short-lived application will eventually show up.
- Because there is only one instance, all instance variables or static variables are open to modification by more than one `Thread` simultaneously.

Variable Storage Considerations

There are three ways to organize storage of variables in your servlet program: as static variables, instance variables, and local (or automatic) variables. Recall that static variables in Java belong to a class as a whole and exist independently of class instances, so they clearly should not be used for data related to a particular transaction; however, the distinction between instance variables and local variables sometimes trips up first-time servlet programmers.

The code fragment in Listing 2.7 is from the `GetDemo` servlet shown at the start of this chapter. Because the `String` variable `password` is declared inside the `doGet` method, it is a local variable. The storage location that holds a reference to the actual `String` object is on the stack belonging to the `Thread` executing the `doGet` method. If two `Thread` objects are executing `doGet`, each will have its own stack and its own `password` variable.

Listing 2.7: GetDemo with password a local variable

```
public class GetDemo extends HttpServlet
{
  public void doGet(HttpServletRequest req,
        HttpServletResponse resp)
  throws ServletException, IOException
  {
    resp.setContentType("text/html");
    PrintWriter out = new PrintWriter(
        resp.getOutputStream());
    String username = req.getParameter("uname");
    String password = req.getParameter("userpw");
    // method continues .....
```

In contrast, the code fragment in Listing 2.8 shows how we might define `password` as an instance variable. If there is no chance of more than one `Thread` executing `doGet` in the same object, this will not cause a problem. In the normal servlet environment, however, any number of requests may be processed simultaneously, and there is only one copy of the servlet object. When a `Thread` retrieves the `password` value, it could be from a different request from the one the `Thread` is working on.

Listing 2.8: GetDemo with password an instance variable

```
public class GetDemo extends HttpServlet
{
  String username ;
  String password ;
  public void doGet(HttpServletRequest req,
        HttpServletResponse resp)
  throws ServletException, IOException
  {
    resp.setContentType("text/html");
    PrintWriter out = new PrintWriter(
        resp.getOutputStream());
    username = req.getParameter("uname");
    password = req.getParameter("userpw");
   // method continues.....
```

Unfortunately, the conceptual error of using an instance variable in a servlet will probably not show up as a bug in normal testing. Because it takes multiple simultaneous requests to create the error, the problem will show up at irregular intervals and be almost impossible to duplicate—a real programmer's nightmare.

If for some reason a servlet can't be written using local variables, it can implement the `SingleThreadModel` interface. This interface does not specify any methods but rather serves as a signal to the servlet engine to ensure that only a single `Thread` can be using an instance at one time. Because this implies extra delays when handling multiple requests, the normal practice is to take the appropriate precautions for multiple `Thread` access.

Synchronized Access to Resources

In many servlet applications, you need to control access to resources that are managed outside of the servlet object. Typical examples include access to databases and files. Careful use of Java's synchronization mechanism is needed to ensure that threads managing different requests do not interfere with one another. Listing 2.9 shows a code fragment from a servlet that records comments in a guest book log file. Here, synchronizing the critical part of the code on the `gbPath` object prevents collisions between threads.

Listing 2.9: Synchronizing on the gbPath object prevents interference between Threads writing to a file

```
public class GuestBook extends HttpServlet
{
  static String gbPath = null ;
     // gbPath must be set in the init method
  static void addToLog( String usr, String cmnt )
       throws IOException{
    if( gbPath == null ) return ;
    synchronized( gbPath ){
       // open file in append mode
      FileOutputStream fos = new FileOutputStream(
             gbPath, true );
      PrintWriter pw = new PrintWriter( fos, true );
      pw.println("User: " + usr + " Says " + cmnt );
      pw.println(); // blank line
      pw.close();
    } // end block synchronized on gbPath
  }
  // class continues ....
```

One technique for resource management that you are sure to run into is object pooling. This is particularly useful with objects that are time consuming to create and/or that use scarce resources. Database connections are frequently managed in object pools.

- On servlet startup a specified minimum number of connection objects is created.
- When a servlet needs a database connection, it requests one from the pool manager. If none is available and the number in the pool is less than the maximum, a new one is created. If the pool is at maximum size and none is available, the servlet thread is blocked until a connection object becomes available.

Parts of a Basic Servlet

The life cycle of a servlet has three main phases: initialization, response to requests, and destruction. We will now take a closer look at each of these phases.

The init Method

Servlet developers should place initialization code in the `init` method, which takes no parameters, instead of a constructor. The servlet engine is guaranteed to call `init` after the servlet object is constructed and before any request is handled.

When the servlet is deployed in the servlet engine, initialization parameters can be specified. This allows the programmer or server administrator to assign a value to a name that the servlet code can look up using the `ServletConfig`. Any servlet method can access the `ServletConfig` by calling `getServletConfig()`. The `ServletConfig` provides these methods:

`getInitParameter(String name)` This method returns a `String` corresponding to the name or returns null if no such parameter exists.

`getInitParameterNames()` This method returns an `Enumeration` over all the names in the set of parameters.

`getServletContext()` This method gets the `ServletContext` that the servlet is operating in.

Listing 2.10 shows an example of an `init` method reading an initialization parameter called "language" that's value was specified in the deployment configuration of the servlet.

Listing 2.10: A code fragment from an init method

```
public void init()
    throws ServletException {
  String language =
    getServletConfig().getInitParameter("language"
  // more initialization goes here
}
```

NOTE

For more information on servlet deployment issues, such as specifying initialization parameters, see Chapter 4.

The Http Request Service Methods

As discussed earlier in this chapter, the standard methods in the HTTP 1.1 protocol are OPTIONS, GET, HEAD, POST, PUT, DELETE, TRACE, and CONNECT. Although practically all servlets deal with only the GET and POST methods, the service method in the HttpServlet class can dispatch requests to doOptions, doGet, doHead, doPost, doPut, doDelete, and doTrace methods.

Although parameters in a GET request are parsed out of the URL, and parameters in a POST method are parsed out of the body of the request, the HttpServletRequest object does not distinguish between them. So typical doGet and doPost methods have similar sequences of action:

1. Examine the request and determine what to do.
2. Set the response content type.
3. Create the appropriate output stream.
4. Perform the desired function and create the response content.

Methods in the ServletRequest Interface

Although you will typically be working with a HttpServletRequest object, the most commonly used methods are defined in the ServletRequest interface. Here are the more commonly used methods:

BufferedReader getReader() A BufferedReader would be used if you want to read and parse the request body text line by line instead of using the parsed parameters.

ServletInputStream getInputStream() The ServletInputStream class is an extension of InputStream that is capable of reading binary data.

String getContentType() The String returned gives the MIME (Multipurpose Internet Mail Extensions) type of the content.

int getContentLength() The int value returned is the number of bytes in the body of the request. You might use this as a preliminary verification that the content is what you expect. For instance, excessively long input might be due to a hacker attempting to overload the server.

Enumeration getParameterNames() The names of parameters parsed out of the request are made available as an Enumeration rather than a String array because the name-value pairs are stored in a Hashtable, and Hashtable objects return the list of all keys as an Enumeration.

String getParameter(String name) This method returns the String value corresponding to a parameter name or returns null if the name does not appear in the request. It is a wise precaution to always check the returned value versus null. If there may be more than one parameter with the same name, this method returns only the first one in the request.

String[] getParameterValues(String name) If there may be more than one value associated with a particular name, this method should be used. The String array that is returned preserves the original order of the parameters. If no parameter with this name exists, null is returned.

Methods Added by HttpServletRequest

This interface extends ServletRequest and adds a number of useful methods, most of which are related to getting at information in the HTTP header that precedes the body of the request. The GET methods that access the header information by name are not sensitive to case.

String getMethod() A call to getMethod() returns a String indicating the HTTP method used in the request, such as GET or POST. You would use this if you were implementing your own version of the service method.

Cookie[] getCookies Cookies are chunks of text sent from a server to a web browser that the browser can return on subsequent transactions. Cookie data contained in a request are parsed into Cookie objects that are available as an array. The method returns null if the request contains no cookie data.

String getHeader(String name) This method returns the String value associated with a header name. For example, the request shown in Listing 2.2 would return the String "localhost" when called with the name "Host." The method returns null if the name does not appear in the request header.

Enumeration getHeaderNames() This returns an Enumeration over all the header names in the request as uppercase strings. For example, the request shown in Listing 2.2 would return all these names: ACCEPT, ACCEPT-LANGUAGE, ACCEPT-ENCODING, USER-AGENT, HOST, and CONNECTION. Not all servlet engines support this method, however, so it may return a null.

At least one engine returns an Enumeration of names that *might* appear in a header rather than those that actually do appear; therefore, you should always test a value returned by getHeader or getHeaderNames for null before using it.

String getQueryString() This method returns the original query String that was present in the URL of a GET request. When working with this String, remember that many special characters get encoded by HTTP conventions.

HttpSession getSession() HttpSession objects are used to maintain state information between transactions with a particular user. The servlet engine can maintain sessions for the programmer automatically, and provide the object associated with a given user with this method.

MIME Content Types

A servlet response is always characterized by a MIME content type. As the name implies, content type was originally developed to facilitate transmission and interpretation of non-text data in e-mail. The concept proved so useful that it is widely used in other areas. For example, Java can use MIME types in cut-and-paste operations. A content type string takes the form type/sub-type, which results in a very flexible format.

Many MIME types are in use on the Internet; a good starting point for more details is RFC2045. Here are just a few MIME types to give you the idea:

`image/gif` An image in the 256-color gif format

`image/jpeg` An image in the more flexible JPEG format

`text/html` Normal HTML

`text/plain` Straight ASCII text

`application/pdf` Used for Adobe Acrobat

`application/java-archive` Used for Java JAR files

`application/x-zip-compressed` Used for ZIP format archives

`application/octet-stream` Used for arbitrary binary data

Methods in the ServletResponse Interface

All the data returned to a client in response to a request is managed by a single response object created by the servlet engine and passed to your servlet. Although you will typically be working with a `HttpServlet-Response` object, the most commonly used methods are defined in the `ServletResponse` interface.

`void setContentType( String type )` The response type will be one of the MIME types and may optionally include character encoding information. For example, the type for html in the "Latin-4" character set for Northern European languages would be "text/html; charset=ISO-8859-4." If the character set is not specified, the default of ISO-8859-1 (ASCII) will be used. You should set the content type before getting a text output stream because the `PrintWriter` class encodes the characters.

`void setContentLength( int len )` This sets the number in the Content-Length header line, and must be called before any content is actually sent. Use of this method is optional. To use it, you must know the exact length of the body the servlet is going to send.

`ServletOutputStream getOutputStream()` The `Servlet-OutputStream` returned by this method is suitable for output of binary data. It is an extension of `java.io.OutputStream` and can be used to create specialized output streams such as `ObjectOutputStream` or `ZipOutputStream`.

PrintWriter getWriter() This returns a PrintWriter that will encode the output stream according to the content type set earlier. It is important to remember that bytes are buffered by both PrintWriter and ServletOutputStream and are not sent as soon as they are written. You can call the flush() method to force the data out. The close() method must be called when your servlet has finished writing output, or the client may never receive anything.

Methods Added by HttpServletResponse

Most of the time, you will work with an object implementing the HttpServletResponse interface. This interface adds some useful methods specific to HTTP output and also defines a bunch of constants corresponding to the response status codes such as the infamous "404 – page not found" message. Here are some of the most commonly used methods in this interface:

void addCookie(Cookie c) Adds the content of an individual cookie to the response. This method can be called multiple times, but note that browsers may accept only 20 cookies from a given source or may be set to refuse all cookies.

void addHeader(String name, String value) and void setHeader(String name, String value) These two methods may be used to create or modify a line in the response header.

void sendRedirect(String newurl) This method redirects the user's browser to a new URL. Calling this method effectively terminates the response.

void sendError(int ecode) This method sends a header with one of those annoying error codes that are defined as constants in the HttpServletResponse interface.

Working with Cookies

Cookies were introduced by Netscape to store a limited amount of information on the user's system so that it can be returned to the server in subsequent transactions. Cookies are the basis for Amazon's "one-click" shopping and sites that "remember" your password. The cookie mechanism will return cookie information to only the host that originated it, subject to various restrictions. Cookies have the following properties:

Version Only two values are possible, version "0" is the original Netscape style, and version "1" is defined in RFC2109.

Domain The domain controls the range of servers to which the cookie is sent. By default, it is only returned to the originating domain such as `www.sybex.com`, but setting the domain to `.sybex.com` will allow the return of the cookie to servers such as `www2.sybex.com` or `ftp.sybex.com`.

Max-Age This numeric property should be used to avoid clogging up a browser with outdated information. The browser is expected to delete cookies that are older than this age in seconds. The server can force a browser to expire a cookie at once by setting Max-Age to zero. Setting a negative value instructs the browser to keep the cookie for the duration of the session but not to save the cookie when it exits.

Path This variable restricts the paths on the server to which the cookie is returned. This is the path as seen by external clients, not the file system path. A setting of "/" would allow it to be returned to all paths on a server, whereas a setting of "/servlets" would restrict visibility of the cookie to URLs starting with "servlets," including all subdirectories.

Secure If the Secure attribute is present, the browser should send the cookie only if the communication channel is secure.

Name All cookies must have a name.

Value This is the text that is returned to the server.

The `javax.servlet.http.Cookie` API provides methods for setting and getting all these properties. A `Cookie` is always constructed with a name and value `String` and is then modified as necessary.

The destroy Method

The `destroy()` method is called when a servlet engine is about to discard the servlet object, either to recover the memory or as part of an orderly shutdown. Typically you would use the `destroy` method to close files or database connections and generally save any state information.

The servlet engine will not call `destroy` if any `Thread` objects are using it. You are guaranteed that after `destroy` has been called, no more requests will be sent to the servlet. Note that just like all Java objects, the `finalize()` method will be called after the servlet object has been selected for garbage collection.

What's Next

Servlets are one of the most essential technologies for most J2EE applications. This chapter has demonstrated how servlets are used to extend the abilities of a web server by writing Java code to handle web requests. Servlets offer a very efficient, scalable, and effective way to handle web requests. However, the reader may have noted that servlets do not seem very desirable for generating dynamic web content. Placing HTML, XML, WML, or other web content into a servlet makes the servlet harder to write, read, reuse, and maintain. When the primary purpose is to generate web content, a Java Server Page (JSP) is a much better solution.

The next chapter will build on this chapter by explaining how JSP pages provide an easier way to create servlets that generate dynamic web content. It is important to understand how to write both servlets and JSP pages, since most J2EE architectures recommend using a mixture of both technologies. Future chapters will provide further detail on both servlet and JSP development.

Chapter 3

The Basic JSP API

Part I

JavaServer Pages (JSP) are a critical J2EE technology for creating web content. Although servlets are ideal for many tasks, JSP pages offer a much better alternative for generating dynamic content. This chapter will introduce you to the essential concepts of developing JSP pages.

As web servers have expanded into application servers over the last few years, there has been a great interest in special scripting languages that add functionality to plain web pages. Many proprietary languages, such as Microsoft's ASP (Active Server Pages) and Netscape's Server-Side JavaScript, have been created. With JSP and other languages, the intent for scripting in web pages is to permit the separation of presentation from content generation, thus giving web designers great flexibility while minimizing the need for involving a programmer with presentation design issues.

Featured in this chapter:

- The Role of JavaServer Pages
- The Relation of the Servlet API to JavaServer Pages

Updated from *Java™ Developer's Guide to Servlets and JSP* by Bill Brogden

ISBN 0-7821-2809-2 $49.99

- How a JavaServer Pages page is handled by a server
- The Tags used in JavaServer Pages
- The Relation of JavaServer Pages to XML

THE ROLE OF JAVASERVER PAGES

In the world of web-accessible J2EE applications, JavaServer Pages and servlets occupy a central position between web-enabled clients and application servers. You can think of JSP and servlets as working in the environment of a *web container* that provides connections and services. By means of these connections, JSP and servlets control the presentation of data derived from operations on databases to network-connected clients. This central role is suggested in Figure 3.1.

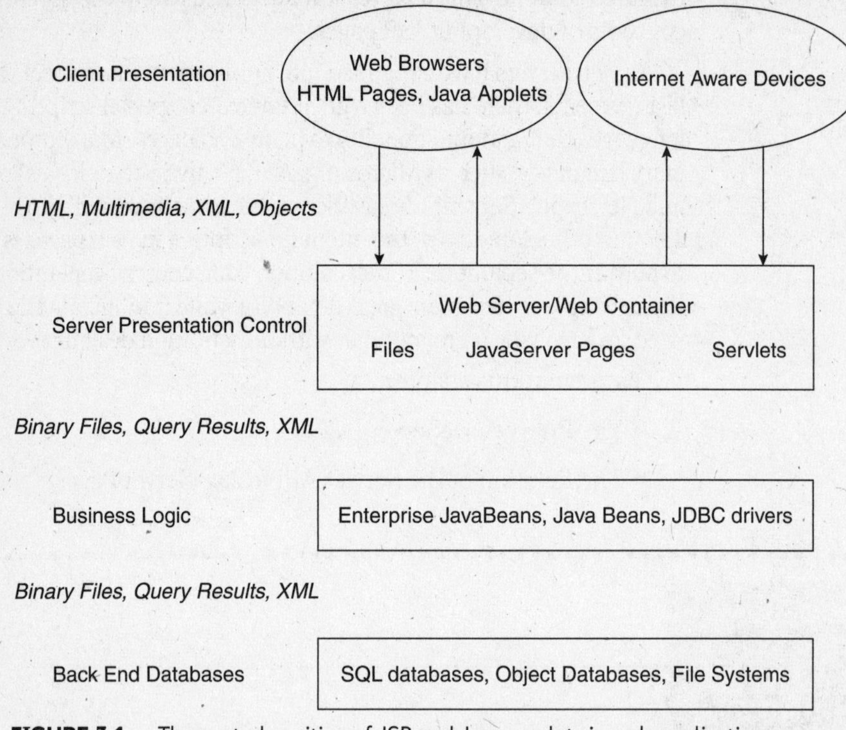

FIGURE 3.1: The central position of JSP and Java servlets in web applications

Servlets and JSP pages can be executed by any J2EE server, but they can also be run by standalone web servers and web server plug-ins. Servlets and JSPs can be run with expensive server software and hardware configurations; however, they can also be run on modest hardware inside free web containers such as Apache Tomcat.

It is important to note that JSP is not limited to generating Hypertext Markup Language (HTML) pages. The technology generates content with Extensible Markup Language (XML) markup or Extensible HTML (XHTML) formatting equally well. Some people feel that serving XML documents to browsers that then format the data according to separate style sheets is the future of the Web.

Sun's Web Application Vision

In the 2.2 version of the Java Servlet Specification, Sun uses the term *web application* for a collection of servlets, JSP pages, HTML files, image files, and other resources that exist in a structured hierarchy of directories on a server. The idea is that descriptive information in a standard XML-based format will support administration of this application in a consistent way. Distribution of a web application can be accomplished in a single Web Application Archive file that will run under any server meeting the standard. These archives use the Java Archive (JAR) format but with a file type of `.war` to indicate the intended purpose.

NOTE

It is easiest to first learn JSP development without using a formal web application. Thus, this chapter will not discuss web applications any further. The next chapter will expand on this topic by discussing how web applications are used under the Servlet 2.3 and JSP 1.2 specifications.

How JSP Is Related to Servlets

As discussed in Chapter 2, a web server essentially receives a client request and then creates a response. In the servlet processing model, the request is translated into a request object, which is passed to the appropriate servlet method. The server also provides a response object that the servlet uses to create a complete response to the client.

That is exactly the model used in processing JSP, except that instead of a servlet written entirely by a Java programmer, the servlet is written by the server engine, based on the contents of a JSP page. A JSP page looks very much like a standard HTML page, and in fact may contain nothing but standard HTML tags. A JSP page may also consist of nothing but JSP tags, but most commonly has both HTML and JSP.

You might think of a server handling a JSP request as a *page compiler*, combining template text with Java code directed by JSP elements into a single servlet that implements the `HttpJspPage` interface. The `_jspService` method in this servlet is executed to create the response. Although parsing and compiling takes a fair amount of time the first time the JSP is executed, the servlet can then be executed directly. Here are the steps involved:

1. A request naming a JSP page is directed to the JSP engine by the web server.
2. The JSP engine looks for the corresponding servlet based on the page name. If the servlet exists and is up to date, the request is passed to the servlet `_jspService` method using `HttpServletRequest` and `HttpServletResponse` objects just like with a regular servlet.
3. If the source page has been changed or has never been compiled, the page compiler parses the source and creates the equivalent Java source code for a servlet, extending `HttpJSPServlet`.
4. This code is then compiled, and the new servlet is executed. The servlet object can stay in memory, providing a very fast response to the next request.

The request and response objects are exactly the same ones used in normal servlets; the difference in this situation is that the service method is created by the JSP engine.

JSP and Components

The potential for JSP is very much enhanced by the ease of using software components in building a page. The idea of software components that would be as easy to connect as electronic components are has been kicked around programming circles for quite a while. Microsoft's Visual Basic is probably the most successful software component architecture in recent years, thus demonstrating that you don't have to use a true object-oriented language to use software components.

Java has two kinds of components: JavaBeans and Enterprise JavaBeans. Enterprise JavaBean (EJB) components are an essential part of Sun's J2EE vision, and depend on specialized server services; JavaBean components are simpler.

If you are using a modern development environment for Java, it probably provides for building graphical user interfaces (GUIs) with JavaBeans, but JavaBeans are not restricted to GUI components. A JavaBean is simply a Java class that meets the following criteria:

- The class must be public.
- The class must have a no-arguments constructor.
- The class must provide `set` and `get` methods to access variables.

If the JavaBean class is serializable, the JSP programmer has the option of either creating a new object from the class file or reading in a serialized object with variables already set.

JSP Version History

The JSP specification has gone through several versions. It is important to have some idea of the difference between the specification versions because most current JSP containers do not yet support the newest specification. As you select a JSP container, or begin to use your existing JSP container, you should consider what version of the specification it supports.

JSP Version 0.92

Development of the JavaServer Pages API has been somewhat slower than that of the Servlet API because changes in the basic Java language and the Servlet API had to be incorporated into the JSP mechanism.

JSP Version 1.0

Many aspects of JSP changed with the 1.0 release. This version is compatible with the 2.1 servlet specification, and includes many tag revisions. There is no compatibility between version 0.92 and version 1.0 JSP pages; for example, the `<%@ include` directive replaces a technology known as Server Side Includes (SSI).

Other major changes include making all tags case sensitive for compatibility with XML and XHTML, as well as adding many new directives. The final release of the 1.0 specification occurred in September 1999, but many vendors had been working on preliminary versions.

JSP Version 1.1

The final release of the 1.1 specifications was in December 1999, so it clearly was prepared in parallel with the 1.0 specification. The following are the main differences between the 1.0 and 1.1 specifications:

- The 1.1 specification was based on the Servlet 2.2 specification.
- The classes `JspException` and `JspError` were added to better unify exception reporting.
- The 1.1 specification provided for tag extensions with the `taglib` mechanism. This is intended to foster creation of portable toolkits.
- The 1.1 specification clarified the relationship between JSP pages and JSP containers.

JSP Version 1.2

JSP Version 1.2 was released in 2001. The following are the main differences between the 1.1 and 1.2 specifications:

- The 1.2 specification was based on the Servlet 2.3 specification and requires J2SE 1.2 or higher.
- The 1.2 specification defines an optional XML syntax for writing JSP pages.
- The 1.2 specification refined the extremely useful and important custom tag library capabilities that were added by the 1.1 specification.
- The 1.2 specification refined many other aspects of JSP pages, including character encoding, localization support, and output flushing issues.

Creating JSP Pages

What you create when working with JSP is, not surprisingly, a page of text that looks like plain text with HTML markup tags using the familiar angle bracket (<>) symbols in conjunction with other punctuation. A JSP engine can process a page with only text and HTML markup, a page with nothing but JSP tags, or a mixture of both. Listing 3.1 shows a simple page with a single JSP tag embedded in HTML.

Listing 3.1: A Java expression embedded in HTML with a JSP tag

```
<HTML>
<HEAD><TITLE>JRun Date Demo</TITLE></HEAD>
<BODY>
<H2>Date And Time <%= new Date().toString() %></H2>
<hr>
</BODY>
</HTML>
```

The example in Listing 3.1 uses what we might call the original style of JSP tag, in which the tag starts with special punctuation and ends with the "%>" character sequence. We discuss XML-compatible tags in the section titled "XML Compatibility Style Tags," later in this chapter.

Table 3.1 shows all the JSP tags that use this style.

TABLE 3.1: JSP tags in the original style

Tag	Used for	Example
<%-- --%>	Comments	<%-- this is never shown --%>
<%= %>	Expressions (evaluated as String)	<%= new Date() %>
<%! %>	Declarations	<%! Date myD = new Date() ; %>
<% %>	Code Fragments	<% for(int i = 0 ; i < 10 ; i++){ %>
<%@ %>	Directives	<%@ page import="java.util.*" %>

Here is a quick summary of how these tags are used, followed by greater details:

Comments Text inside the <%-- to --%> comment tags is not processed by the JSP compilation process.

Expressions The Java expression inside the tags is evaluated as a String, and is written to the output stream.

Declarations A declaration declares a variable or method that can be used in the page.

Code Fragments A code fragment can contain any valid Java code. It is executed when the request is processed.

Directives The `page`, `include`, and `taglib` directives are discussed in the section titled "Directives," later in this chapter.

Comments in JSP

Several different forms of comments are actually possible in a JSP page. These styles enable you to control where the comment can be seen.

`<%-- jsp comment text %>` This text appears in the original JSP page but is skipped over by the page compiler, so it does not appear in the resulting Java code.

`<% /* java comment */ %>` or `<% // java comment %>` These standard Java comments enclosed in code fragment tags will appear in the Java code created by the page compiler, but not in the output page.

`<!-- html comment -->` An HTML-style comment can be used anywhere in the template data; it will be transmitted with the output page but not displayed. You can generate an HTML comment that includes text generated by Java expressions.

Declarations and Member Variables

Declarations define variables and methods that will be members of the servlet that the page compiler creates and will be available in the entire page. Listing 3.2 shows an example declaration of a `String`, a `Vector`, and a `jspInit` method that reads a text file into the `Vector`. Note that we override the `jspInit` method, but call the parent class method in case it has to do any implementation-specific actions.

Listing 3.2: An example of declaring variables and methods with declaration tags

```
<%!
 String listPath = "E:\\scripts\\errata\\errcatISBN.txt";
 Vector ertLines = new Vector() ;

 public void jspInit(){
   super.jspInit();
   File f = new File( listPath );
```

```
      try {
        BufferedReader br =
          new BufferedReader( new FileReader(f));
        String tmp = br.readLine();
        while( tmp != null ){
          if( ! tmp.startsWith(":") ){
            ertLines.addElement( tmp );
          }
          tmp = br.readLine();
        }
        br.close();
      }catch(IOException e){
      }
    }
  %>
```

The Implicit Variables

Every JSP page contains reference variables pointing to objects, called *implicit objects*, that are always defined. You can use implicit variables inside your code. Many of the classes these objects implement have already been described in Chapter 2; the rest are discussed later in this chapter in the section titled "The JSP Packages." Table 3.2 summarizes the variable names and uses. Note that the `exception` variable is defined only if the page is declared an error page.

TABLE 3.2: The implicit JSP page variables

Variable Name	Type	Used For
request	A descendent of javax.servlet .ServletRequest	Represents the user's request
response	A descendent of javax.servlet .ServletResponse	Creates the output response
pageContext	A javax.servlet.jsp.PageContext object	Contains attributes of this page
session	A javax.servlet.http.HttpSession	Contains arbitrary variables attached to this user's session
application	A javax.servlet.ServletContext object	Contains attributes for the entire application; affects the interpretation of several other tags

TABLE 3.2 continued: The implicit JSP page variables

Variable Name	Type	Used For
out	A javax.servlet.jsp.JspWriter object	The output stream for the response
config	A javax.servlet.ServletConfig object	Contains servlet initialization parameter name value pairs and the ServletContext object
page	An object reference pointing to *this*	The current servlet object
exception	A java.lang.Throwable object	Only pages designated as error pages in the page directive have this object

Scope of Variables

Some of the implicit variables have a scope beyond that of a single JSP page. In addition to page scope, a variable can have request, application, or session scope.

Request Scope A request can actually be processed by several pages because of the forwarding mechanism. The request object can carry additional objects with it.

Application Scope Sun uses the term *web application* to refer to the collection of servlets, JSP, and other resources installed in a particular server address space. The `ServletContext` class is intended to let all of these resources share information by means of mutually accessible stored objects in "application scope." The application scope affects the interpretation of relative URL specifications.

Session Scope Servlets and JSP pages can save information specific to a user in an `HttpSession` object managed by the servlet engine. Objects stored this way are said to have *session* scope.

Code Fragments

Code fragments are chunks of Java code that will end up being compiled into the `_jspService` method of the servlet that the page compiler writes. The order in which code fragments appear in the page is the order in which they appear in the method. You may also see code fragments referred to as *scriptlets*. Each code fragment must be a legal Java code element, but it can be mixed in with template text, as shown in Listing 3.3.

Listing 3.3: Code fragment tags mixed with normal text

```
<% for( int j = 1 ; j <= 10 ; j++ ){
%>  count = <%= j %> <br>
<% }
%>
```

The Java code produced by the JSP engine from these tags is shown in Listing 3.4.

Listing 3.4: The Java statements created from Listing 3.3

```
for( int j = 1 ; j <= 10 ; j++ ){
        out.print("  count = ");
        out.print(j );
        out.print(" <br>\r\n");
}
```

The ability to mix code fragments with literal text is very powerful, but it also means there are a number of different ways of combining tags with literal text to create a given output. As we will see in later examples, JSP allows the possibility of writing hard-to-understand code.

Directives

There are three kinds of directives: `page`, `include`, and `taglib`. The `page` and `include` directives define conditions for the entire JSP page; a `taglib` directive acts at a particular place in the page.

Page Directive

The page directive defines attributes that apply to an entire JSP page. A typical use would be

```
<%@ page language="java" import="java.util.*,java.io.*" %>
```

which informs the JSP processor that the language of the code on the page will be Java, as well as declaring the packages that will be imported. At present, Java is the only language defined for JSP, but obviously the designers wanted to leave open the possibility of using other languages. Note that the value of an attribute must be enclosed in quotation marks. Table 3.3 shows the attributes that may appear in a page directive.

TABLE 3.3: Attributes appearing in the page directive

Attribute	Used for	Note
language	Defines the language used in code fragments.	Currently always Java.
extends	Defines the parent of the resulting servlet.	Use with caution.
import	Defines a list of classes to be imported, separated by commas.	The list becomes Java import statements.
session	Determines whether a session object will have to be defined.	Value is either "true" or "false," default is true.
buffer	Controls the size of the response output buffer.	Value can be either "none" or a size such as "12kb"; the default is "8kb."
autoFlush	If set "false," an overflow of the buffer causes an exception. If set "true," the buffer will be flushed to the output stream when full. The default value is "true."	Must not be set to "false" when the buffer value is "none."
isThreadSafe	When set "false," the JSP container must allow only one request to be processed at a time. When set "true," more than one request Thread can run at the same time.	Default is "true."
info	Defines a String value that can be accessed in the code using the getServletInfo() method.	
errorPage	If present, the value defines a URL of a resource that will be sent any Exception or Error object that is not caught in the Java code of this page.	The JSP engine will provide a default errorPage.
isErrorPage	If set "true," the current page is the target of another page's errorPage URL.	If "true," this page will have an "exception" variable defined.
contentType	This value gives the MIME content type and character encoding of the page as used in the ServletResponse setContentType method.	The default is "text/html: charset=ISO-8859-1" character encoding.

Include Directive

The include directive tells the engine to include text or output from a specified resource. The format uses the relative URL specified above. For example, the following tag would be useful to ensure that the same copyright message is included on every page:

```
<%@ include file="/JSPbook/copyright.txt" %>
```

When this tag is encountered, the text in the file will be read and processed. It can be anything that can legally appear in a JSP page.

Relative URLs for Resources When tags refer to resources, such as servlets or JSP files, they can use relative URLs that are based on the ServletContext or the current JSP page location. Consider the following examples of the include directive:

```
1. <%@ include file="/JSPbook/copyright.txt" %>
2. <%@ include file="copyright.txt" %>
```

In line 1, the leading "/" character indicates that the system should look for the file in this path relative to the ServletContext. In line 2, the system would look for the file in the same directory as the current JSP page.

This design lets each web application live in its own address space. It is intended to make it easy to install a new application in a server with a minimum of fiddling with the file system by allowing resources to be addressed relative to the application.

Taglib Directive

The `taglib` directive allows you to define a library of custom action tags that will be used in the page. This is a powerful concept that will enable you to use specialized toolkits as easily as you use the standard tags. Custom tags use interfaces and classes in the `javax.servlet.jsp.tagext` package. Due to the complexity of defining your own tag library, this directive is covered in detail in Chapter 7.

XML Compatibility Style Tags

You have no doubt noticed that web applications are all turning to XML and XML-related ideas for many functions. Java applications are no exception, but this created a problem for the further development of JSP because the original tags are not compatible with the XML standard. This incompatibility would prevent use of JSP tags in pages using the new XHTML standard, which was clearly not acceptable.

XHTML is the standard that many developers hope will finally rationalize HTML markup. The latest recommendations for XHTML are to be found at:

```
http://www.w3.org/TR/
```

To be compatible with XHTML, Sun created a complete alternate set of tags that satisfy the XML requirement for formatting. Adopting XML namespace conventions also makes JSP much more flexible and powerful because it allows you to create your own library of custom tags or to buy a custom toolkit for particular purposes.

Before the advent of JSP, many application server vendors created their own custom tag systems, such as ColdFusion for HTML markup. These vendors may now be able to fit their specialized tags into the general JSP framework as tag libraries, which will allow for wider acceptance.

Table 3.4 shows the XML equivalent tags for the basic "<%" style tags. The "jsp:" at the start of the tag identifies the namespace that the tag belongs to, in this case the standard JSP namespace. This XML convention ensures that JSP tags can be interpreted separately from other XML tags in the data. Naturally, being able to use a named tag makes this style much easier to use than the punctuation-based tag style.

TABLE 3.4: The XML equivalent for JSP tags

Tag	JSP XML Tag	Used for	Example
<%!	<jsp:declaration>	declaration	<jsp:declaration> String ver = "version 1.0"; </jsp:declaration>
<%=	<jsp:expression	expression	<jsp:expression> </jsp:expression>
<%	<jsp:scriptlet>	Java code fragment	<jsp:scriptlet> for(int i = 0 ; i < 10 ; i++){ </jsp:scriptlet>
<%@	<jsp:directive	directives	<jsp:directive.page language="java" />

There are two styles of elements in XML markup, and Table 3.5 shows both kinds. The code fragment markup uses an opening and a closing tag to enclose text. On the other hand, the directives tag style has all data enclosed in a single "<" – "/>" pair, and contains named attributes that give values in quotation marks. This is called an *empty element*.

Tags are also divided into directives and actions. Directives are messages to the JSP engine that do not produce any output. Actions such as an expression modify the output stream and create, use, or modify objects.

TABLE 3.5: XML-style JSP tags

JSP Tag	Used for	Example
<jsp:include />	Incorporates bulk text from a file	<jsp:include page="copyright.htm" />
<jsp:forward />	Forwards the request to a servlet, another JSP, or ?	<jsp:forward page="someURL.jsp" />
<jsp:param />	Used inside a forward, include, or plugin to add or modify a parameter in the request object	<jsp:param name="user" value="newName" />
<jsp:getProperty />	Gets the value of a Bean property by name	<jsp:getProperty name="nameOfBean" property="nameOfProperty"/>
<jsp:setProperty />	Sets the value of a Bean property	<jsp:setProperty name="nameOfBean" property="nameOfProperty value="somevalue" />
<jsp:useBean />	Locates or creates a Bean with the specific name and scope	See Chapter 5
<jsp:plugin />	Provides full information for a download of a Java plugin to the client web browser	<jsp:plugin type="applet" code="nameOfApplet" width="width" height="height"/>

The XML Equivalent of a JSP Page

Many JSP engines create an XML representation of the JSP page, along with the Java source code, when compiling a JSP page. In the following two listings, you can compare a JSP page in conventional JSP syntax and in XML syntax. Listing 3.5 shows a JSP page that has only two elements: one that outputs a String showing the current date and time, and one that includes a copyright message.

Listing 3.5: A simple JSP page to show current time

```
<HTML>
<HEAD>
  <META NAME="GENERATOR" CONTENT="JSPbook Chapt02" >
  <TITLE>A Simple Page</TITLE>
</HEAD>
<BODY>
<%@ page language="java" %>
<%= new Date() %>
<br><hr>
<%@ include file="/JSPbook/copyright.txt" %>
</BODY>
</HTML>
```

Listing 3.6 shows this page translated into XML by the JRun JSP page compiler. The original was in only two lines of text that have been split along logical lines for this listing.

Listing 3.6: XML representation of the page created by JRun

```
<?xml version="1.0" ?>
<jsp:root
   xmlns:jsp="http://java.sun.com/products/jsp/dtd/jsp_1_0.dtd"
   package="jsp.JSPbook.Chapt02" name="TimeNow">
  <jsp:directive.dependency
     resource="/JSPbook/Chapt02/TimeNow.jsp"/>
     <![CDATA[\r\n<HTML>\r\n
     <HEAD>\r\n  <META NAME=\"GENERATOR\"
         CONTENT=\"JSPbook Chapt02\" >\r\n  <TITLE>A Simple
  Page</TITLE>\r\n
     </HEAD>\r\n<BODY>\r\n]]>
  <jsp:directive.page language="java" /><![CDATA[\r\n]]>
  <jsp:expression><![CDATA[new Date()]]>
  </jsp:expression>
  <![CDATA[\r\n<br><hr>\r\n]]>
  <jsp:expression>
  <![CDATA["<i>Copyright &#169; 2000,
    LANWrights, Inc., Austin, TX</i><br>"]]>
  </jsp:expression>
```

```
    <![CDATA[\r\n]]><jsp:directive.dependency
    resource="/JSPbook/copyright.txt"/>
    <![CDATA[\r\n</BODY>\r\n</HTML>\r\n]]>
  </jsp:root>
```

This listing gives you an excellent chance to see XML concepts in action. Here are some important points:

The `<?xml version="1.0" ?>` line gives the XML version.

The `<jsp:root` tag and the corresponding `</jsp:root>` tag at the end of the page provide the required enclosing tag or *root* for the document. The starting tag has attributes that give the document type definition (DTD) the document follows, the name of the class that will be generated, and the package to which the class will belong.

The `<jsp:directive page` tag specifies the language attribute as called for in the JSP API.

The `<jsp:directive dependency>` tags give the names of resources involved in generating the page. This information could be used by the JSP engine to determine whether or not the generated Java class is out of date; however, note that a dependency directive is not part of the JSP 1.2 API. Presumably, it is a JRun extension.

The template data of the original JSP page end up as chunks of text enclosed in tags that start with `<![CDATA[` and end with `]]>`. XML treats this as literal character data to be written out without XML processing. Because this is data to be written by a Java servlet, you will find escaped special characters (such as the String "\r\n" that stands for carriage return) and line feed control characters.

The original JSP tag <%= is turned into `<jsp:expression>` with the Java statement enclosed as a CDATA section followed by a closing tag of `</jsp:expression>`.

The original JSP `<%@ include` tag caused the text of the copyright.txt file to be brought into the XML as CDATA and enclosed in a `<jsp:expression> </jsp:expression>` tag pair plus a dependency notation.

After looking at that, you will probably agree that the XML representation of the page would be a lot harder to edit by hand than the JSP version;

however, Java provides some nice tools for parsing and manipulating XML documents.

Finally, Listing 3.7 shows the Java source code generated for this JSP page by the JRun page compiler. Some long lines have been split for this listing.

Listing 3.7: The Java code generated by JRun for the TimeNow page

```
package jsp.JSPbook.Chapt02;

import java.io.*;
import java.util.*;
import java.net.*;
import java.beans.*;

import javax.servlet.*;
import javax.servlet.http.*;
import javax.servlet.jsp.*;

public class TimeNow
    extends com.livesoftware.jsp.HttpJSPServlet
    implements com.livesoftware.jsp.JRunJspPage, HttpJspPage
{

  public void _jspService(HttpServletRequest request,
        HttpServletResponse response)
        throws ServletException, IOException
  {
    ServletConfig config = getServletConfig();
    ServletContext application = config.getServletContext();
    Object page = (Object) this;
    PageContext pageContext =
      JspFactory.getDefaultFactory().getPageContext(this,
    request, response,  null, true,8192, true);
    JspWriter out = pageContext.getOut();
    HttpSession session = request.getSession(true);
    response.setContentType("text/html; charset=ISO-8859-1");

    out.print("\r\n<HTML>\r\n<HEAD>\r\n  <META NAME=\
    ➥"GENERATOR\"
```

```
                  CONTENT=\"JSPbook Chapt02\" >\r\n  <TITLE>A
➥Simple Page</TITLE>
                  \r\n</HEAD>\r\n<BODY>\r\n");
      out.print("\r\n");
      out.print(new Date());
      out.print("\r\n<br><hr>\r\n");
      out.print(
            "<i>Copyright &#169; 2000, LANWrights, Inc.,
➥Austin, TX</i><br>");
      out.print("\r\n");
      out.print("\r\n</BODY>\r\n</HTML>\r\n");
      out.flush();
    }
    private static final String[][] __dependencies__ = {
          {"/JSPbook/Chapt02/TimeNow.jsp", "953159826000" },
          {"/JSPbook/copyright.txt", "952623990000" }, };

    public String[][] __getDependencies()
    {
      return __dependencies__;
    }

    public String __getTranslationVersion()
    {
      return "5";
    }
  }
```

The JSP Packages

Two packages with classes are related to JSP. Both are considered standard extensions closely related to servlets, so the package names start with `javax.servlet` in both cases.

The javax.servlet.jsp Package

This package contains all the interfaces, classes, and exceptions used by standard JSP pages. This section covers the most commonly used methods in these interfaces and classes in detail.

The javax.servlet.jsp.JspPage Interface

When the JSP engine creates a servlet to handle a page, this interface defines two of the methods it must provide. JspPage extends the servlet interface, and these methods are an obvious parallel to the `init` and `destroy` methods in that interface.

`public void jspInit()` This method is the first one called by the server when the JSP-created servlet is loaded. At this point, the programmer can call the `getServletConfig` method to access initialization parameters.

`public void destroy()` This method is called just before the server destroys the servlet object. This is the programmer's chance to close files and generally release any resources held by the servlet.

The javax.servlet.jsp.HttpJspPage Interface

This extension of the `JspPage` interface defines the `_jspService` method that the JSP compiler must produce. The method parameter list is the same as that of the `doGet` and `doPost` methods in the `HttpServlet` interface.

```
public void _jspService( HttpServletRequest request,
   HttpServletResponse response )
```

The JspEngineInfo Class

Each JSP engine should provide an extension of this abstract class to provide information about itself. At the present time, the only required method is

```
public String getSpecificationVersion()
```

which returns a String giving the version of the JSP API that the engine implements. This String is in Dewey decimal-style format, such as 1.1.2, where the left digit is most significant. It is anticipated that future versions will provide information such as the vendor's name and the engine's title.

The JspFactory Class

Each JSP engine implements an extension of this abstract class to control creation of instances of the various objects needed to support the servlet. You can think of this class as a parallel to the java.awt.Toolkit class used in AWT-based graphic applications.

public static JspFactory getDefaultFactory() This static method simply returns the current default JspFactory.

public static void setDefaultFactory(JspFactory fac) This method is for use by creators of JSP servers only.

public JspEngineInfo getEngineInfo() The JspEngine Info object r can be used to determine the JSP API version the engine implements.

public void releasePageContext(PageContext pc) This method is typically called just before the _jspService method exits. The purpose is to release any resources held by the PageContext.

public PageContext getPageContext(Servlet thisServ, ServletRequest sreq, ServletResponse sresp, String errorPageURL, boolean needSession, int buffer, boolean autoflush) The getPageContext method initializes a PageContext object with the various reference variables and parameters that characterize the processing of a request. It is typically called early in the _jspService method constructed by the JSP engine so that JSP programmers don't have to create the call.

Listing 3.8 shows a bit of Java code from a generated servlet to illustrate how JspFactory and the getPageContext method are used.

Listing 3.8: The start of a service method generated by JSP

```
public void _jspService(HttpServletRequest request,
       HttpServletResponse response)
       throws ServletException, IOException
  {
    ServletConfig config = getServletConfig();
    ServletContext application =
        config.getServletContext();
    Object page = (Object) this;
    PageContext pageContext =
        JspFactory.getDefaultFactory().getPageContext(this,
            request, response,  null, true,8192, true);
    JspWriter out = pageContext.getOut();
```

The JspWriter Class

An instance of this class, called `out`, is created automatically in the `_jspService` method from a `PageContext` as shown in the preceding code listing. A `JspWriter` object is similar to a `java.io.PrintWriter` object in that it writes a character stream with a specific encoding. There is a significant difference, however, in that a `JspWriter` output method can throw an `IOException`. In the `PrintWriter` class, an `IOException` is handled internally, and the programmer has to call `checkError()` to determine if an exception was thrown.

The capability to throw an `IOException` is essential for managing the buffering behavior of the `JspWriter`. Recall that the *page* directive lets you set two attributes named buffer and autoFlush. A buffer of "8kb" and the value autoFlush = true are the defaults. With these settings, output goes to the buffer, and the buffer is flushed to the response output stream when it is full. If the buffer attribute is set to "none," all output immediately goes to the response output stream. The `JspWriter` class has three important methods related to buffer behavior.

`public void clear()` This discards the current buffer contents, but if the buffer has already been flushed, it throws an `IOException` to warn you that some output has already been sent.

`public void clearBuffer()` This method discards the buffer contents but will never throw an `IOException`.

`public void flush()` The `flush` method immediately sends the buffer contents.

To see why use of the `clear()` method might be necessary, suppose your JSP page consists of these three sections:

- Introductory text
- Table generated from a database query
- Concluding text

If an error occurs in accessing the database, you can `clear()` the introductory text and write a completely different message to the response. Naturally, you must set a large enough buffer to accommodate the introductory text.

If autoFlush is false, overflowing the buffer causes an `IOException` to be thrown. This capability probably exists to prevent a runaway process from writing an endless stream of text.

In addition to the `print( String s )` method, `JspWriter` provides a full set of methods to output primitives, including output from all or part of an array of type `char`. These methods are similar to those in the `PrintWriter` class.

The PageContext Class

The `PageContext` class is used to organize references to all of the objects involved in creating a JSP page and provide a number of utilities. As shown in Listing 3.8, the JSP compiler generates a call to the `getPageContext` method of the default `JspFactory` to create an instance of `PageContext` named `pageContext` in the `_jspService` method.

The `PageContext` class has many utility methods. Table 3.6 summarizes those that provide convenient access to the implicit objects and configuration information objects in a typical JSP.

TABLE 3.6: Some utility methods in the PageContext class

Method	Returned Reference Type	The Implicit Object Reference Returned
getOut()	JspWriter	out
getException()	Exception	exception
getPage()	Servlet	page
getRequest()	ServletRequest	request
GetSession	HttpSession	session
getResponse()	ServletResponse	response
getServletConfig()	ServletConfig	config
getServletContext()	ServletContext	-

Normally, the JSP engine writes the code that obtains the implicit objects from the `pageContext`, so you don't have to worry about that; however, many more objects are accessible through the `pageContext`. Unfortunately, the method names are rather similar and easily confused:

`findAttribute( String name )` Searches all of the contexts—page, request, session, and application—and returns any object that has been stored under this name.

getAttribute(String name) Looks only in the pageContext and returns any object that has been stored under this name.

getAttribute(String name, int scope) Searches a scope defined by the scope constant that must be one of those defined in the PageContext class, PAGE_SCOPE, REQUEST_SCOPE, SESSION_SCOPE, or APPLICATION_SCOPE.

There are also methods that place named objects in the various scopes:

setAttribute(String name, Object obj) Stores the object in the pageContext with page scope.

setAttribute(String name, Object obj, int scope) Stores the object in the scope indicated by the constant.

The combination of these methods allows the various parts of an application to communicate by means of stored objects. For example, if one page locates a file name, it can be stored in the SESSION_SCOPE context and later retrieved by another page.

The pageContext object is responsible for forwarding or including, as directed by the <jsp:forward> or <jsp:include> tags. The JSP engine normally takes care of writing this code for you.

The pageContext object is also responsible for handling exceptions that occur in the _jspService method if the *page* directive gives an *errorPage*. This is illustrated in Listing 3.9, which shows a code fragment from the end of a _jspService method that catches all exceptions.

Listing 3.9: The pageContext object handles an exception

```
} catch (Exception ex) {
   if (out.getBufferSize() != 0)
          out.clear();
          pageContext.handlePageException(ex);
} finally {
       out.flush();
      _jspxFactory.releasePageContext(pageContext);
}
```

The JspException Class

This is a generic exception for reporting errors in JSP processing, which was added in the 1.1 API. JSP engines will presumably extend this class for specific purposes. Presently, only certain methods in the tag extension package throw a `JspException`.

The JspError Class

The `JspError` class descends from `JspException` and is used to report errors in JSP processing that are unrecoverable. Note that in spite of the name, this class descends from `java.lang.Exception` and not `java.lang.Error`. The JSP engine must forward the exception to the error page where it has the default name `exception`.

The javax.servlet.jsp.tagext Package

Tagext stands for Tag Extension. Classes in this package are intended to provide a method for extending JSP capabilities with custom tags and to support authoring systems for JSP pages. The `tagext` package was added by the 1.1 JSPAPI. Custom tags are discussed in Chapter 7.

Design Considerations

Today's web designers face a tremendous number of design choices. The basic philosophy, which you will hear frequently, is that JSP pages let you separate data from presentation. In Sun's view of the Java-powered application server, JSP and servlets handle presentation, where JavaBeans and Enterprise JavaBeans handle business logic. It seems all too easy, however, to create a page that mixes presentation logic and data logic.

Too Many Alternatives?

Some serious commentators on the Java scene have suggested that the JSP approach offers too many alternatives and too many ways to write bad code. Jason Hunter, co-author of one of the first books about Java servlets, has posted an essay on this issue on his website that deserves your consideration:

```
http://www.servlets.com/soapbox/problems-jsp.html
```

Design for Debugging

Unfortunately, there are many ways for a JSP page to go wrong and produce hard-to-understand results or no output at all. Remember, for a JSP page to work, several levels of technology must cooperate, and there is a chance for error at every level. Here are a few hints for JSP debugging.

Build from Working Parts For example, check the layout of a page in HTML before you add JSP elements. Check the workings of a JavaBean in a simple test program before adding it to a JSP page.

Use Logging Statements that write to `System.out` or a log file can let you know what is going on. Learn to use the logging facilities your JSP engine offers.

Catch Those Exceptions Java's Exception mechanism can be a big help.

A Simple JSP Example

As you start programming JSP pages, you will probably be struck by the fact that there is a tremendous number of ways to accomplish the same output. This is because the programmer can combine HTML, JSP, Java servlets, and other Java technologies.

The JSP programmer must actively strive to develop a style that produces clear, easily debugged, and easily maintained code. It is too easy to whip out something that does the job, but will be incomprehensible when you look at it later.

For the purposes of this example, assume we need to create an online demonstration of the workings of the Java shift operators for a beginning Java class. The student will enter an integer into a form, click a button, and view a table that shows the number in decimal, hex, and binary form, as acted on by the different shift operators. Figure 3.2 shows the desired result.

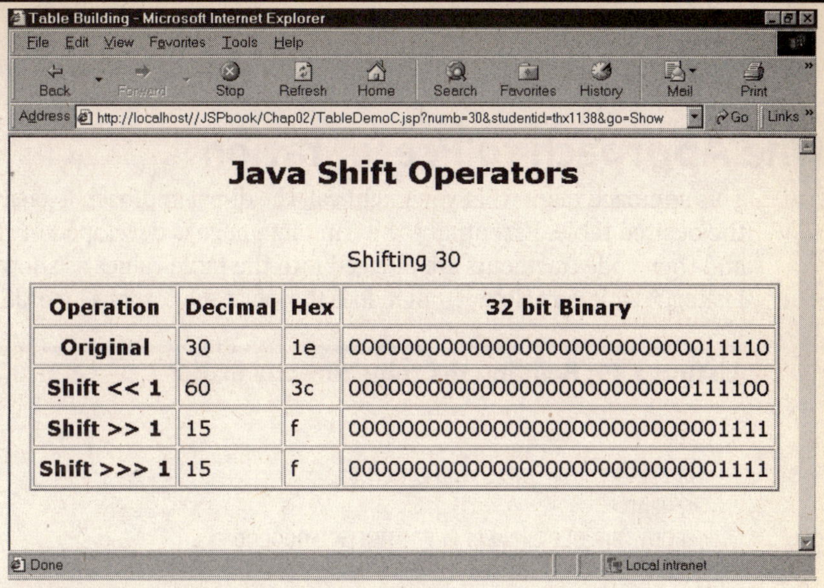

Operation	Decimal	Hex	32 bit Binary
Original	30	1e	00000000000000000000000000011110
Shift << 1	60	3c	00000000000000000000000000111100
Shift >> 1	15	f	00000000000000000000000000001111
Shift >>> 1	15	f	00000000000000000000000000001111

FIGURE 3.2: A table in an HTML page, showing the result of applying Java shift operators

The Input Form

Input is simple enough; we just need a plain HTML page with a form that sends a request to a JSP page. Listing 3.10 shows the page text.

Listing 3.10: A simple input form to get a number

```
<HTML>
<HEAD>
<TITLE>Shift Demo Number Entry</TITLE>
</HEAD>
<BODY BGCOLOR="#FFFFFF" TEXT="#000000">
<FONT FACE=VERDANA>
<H2 ALIGN=CENTER>
     Welcome to the Shift Operator Demo
</H2><BR>
<form action="TableDemo.jsp" method="GET">
Enter Number to be shifted:
<input name="numb" type="text" size="10">
<input type="submit" value="Show" name="go" ><br>
```

```
</form>
</BODY>
</HTML>
```

One Approach to Presentation

This approach takes what you might call the direct approach to creating the desired table. Essentially, the complete page is developed in HTML, and then code fragments are plugged into the table values as shown in Listing 3.11. It isn't elegant, but it does the job at the cost of a lot of JSP tags.

Listing 3.11: Building the table directly in JSP

```
<HTML>
<HEAD>
<TITLE>Table Building</TITLE>
</HEAD>
<BODY BGCOLOR="#FFFFFF" TEXT="#000000">
<FONT FACE=VERDANA>
<H2 ALIGN=CENTER>Java Shift Operators
</H2><BR>
<%@ page language="java"
    errorPage="/JSPbook/Chap02/whoops.jsp" %>
<%!
public String padBinary( int n ){
   String tmp = "00000000000000000000000000000000"
      + Integer.toBinaryString( n );
   return tmp.substring( tmp.length() - 32 );
}
%>
<%
String numbS = request.getParameter( "numb" );
int x = Integer.parseInt( numbS ) ;
int n = x ;
%>

<table align="center" border="2" cellpadding="5" >
<caption><%= "Shifting " + x + "<br>\r\n" %></caption>
<tr><th>Operation</th><th>Decimal</th><th>Hex</th><th>32 bit
   Binary</th></tr>
<tr><th>Original</th><td><%= n %></td>
        <td><%= Integer.toHexString(n)%></td>
        <td><%= padBinary( n ) %></td></tr>
```

```
<% n = x << 1 ; %>
<tr><th>Shift &lt;&lt; 1</th><td><%= n %></td>
        <td><%= Integer.toHexString(n)%></td>
        <td><%= padBinary( n ) %></td></tr>
<% n = x >> 1 ; %>
<tr><th>Shift &gt;&gt; 1</th><td><%= n %></td>
        <td><%= Integer.toHexString(n)%></td>
        <td><%= padBinary( n ) %></td></tr>
</tr>
<% n = x >>> 1 ; %>
<tr><th>Shift &gt;&gt;&gt; 1</th><td><%= n %></td>
        <td><%= Integer.toHexString(n)%></td>
        <td><%= padBinary( n ) %></td></tr>
</TABLE>
</BODY>
</HTML>
```

Debugging with this approach was rather time consuming. The only way to test it was to try to submit a number through a browser and see what happened. Because JSP parsing has to proceed without error to create a Java servlet, a single missed tag syntax tended to produce the dreaded "HTTP 500–Internal server error" message. Every time that happened, the JSP engine log had to be examined to locate the error.

The resulting Java servlet code was not particularly elegant, either. There were dozens of little `out.print()` statements.

The JavaBean Approach

As discussed earlier in this chapter, in the section titled "JSP and Components," a JavaBean is a way of creating a software component that has simple provisions for setting and getting parameters. A JSP page can get an instance of a bean with the simple `<jsp:useBean` tag, and can later refer to it by name. This is illustrated in Listing 3.12, where all the table-creating functions have been delegated to the `tableBean` bean, resulting in a much more compact JSP page.

Listing 3.12: A JSP page to create the table using a bean

```
<HTML>
<HEAD>
<TITLE>Table Building</TITLE>
</HEAD>
<BODY BGCOLOR="#FFFFFF" TEXT="#000000">
```

```
<FONT FACE=VERDANA>
<H2 ALIGN=CENTER>Java Shift Operators
</H2><BR>
<%@ page language="java"
    errorPage="/JSPbook/Chapt02/whoops.jsp" %>
<jsp:useBean id="tableBean" scope="page"
   class="JSPbook.Chapt02.ShiftTable" >
</jsp:useBean>
<jsp:setProperty name="tableBean" property="*" />
<%= tableBean.getTable() %>
</BODY>
</HTML>
```

It is particularly interesting to note how easy it is to transfer the input parameter from the request to the bean in the `<jsp:setProperty` tag. The syntax `property="*"` means that for every named value in the request, the servlet will try to locate a `set` method in the bean and then call it with the matching value. Listings 3.13 through 3.15 show the service method that the JSP engine creates from the page in the preceding listing.

Listing 3.13: The _jspService method created from the JSP in Listing 3.12

```
public void _jspService(HttpServletRequest request,
   HttpServletResponse response)
   throws ServletException, IOException
{
   ServletConfig config = getServletConfig();
   ServletContext application = config.getServletContext();
   Object page = (Object) this;
   PageContext pageContext =
   JspFactory.getDefaultFactory().getPageContext(this,
      request, response, "/JSPbook/Chapt02/whoops.jsp",
      true,8192, true);
   JspWriter out = pageContext.getOut();

   HttpSession session = request.getSession(true);
   response.setContentType("text/html; charset=ISO-8859-1");

  try {
   out.print("<HTML>\r\n<HEAD>\r\n<TITLE>Table
   Building</TITLE>\r\n</HEAD>\r\n<BODY BGCOLOR=\"#FFFFFF\"
   TEXT=\"#000000\">\r\n<FONT FACE=VERDANA>\r\n<H2
     ALIGN=CENTER>Java Shift Operators\r\n</H2><BR>\r\n");
```

```
out.print("\r\n");
JSPbook.Chapt02.ShiftTable tableBean=null;
tableBean = (JSPbook.Chapt02.ShiftTable)
pageContext.getAttribute("tableBean",
   pageContext.PAGE_SCOPE);
```

The last statement attempts to recover the `tableBean` object by name from the pageContext. A PageContext instance acts as a sort of repository of objects for a particular JSP page. If no `tableBean` is already defined, we proceed to create one.

Listing 3.14: The _jspService method continued

```
if(tableBean == null) {
   tableBean = new JSPbook.Chapt02.ShiftTable();
   pageContext.setAttribute("tableBean", tableBean,
pageContext.PAGE_SCOPE);
   out.print("\r\n");
} // end useBean initialization
out.print("\r\n");
com.livesoftware.jsp.JSPRuntime.setBeanProperties(
   tableBean, "tableBean", request);
```

The call to `setBeanProperties` transfers the values of all request parameters that have names matching properties defined by the bean by means of the `set` methods. In this example, this means that the text from the input text field named "numb" will be used to call a `setNumb` method in the bean.

After all the work of setting up the `tableBean`, generating the actual output involves a single call to the `getTable` method.

Listing 3.15: The _jspService method continued

```
out.print("\r\n");
out.print(tableBean.getTable());
out.print("\r\n</BODY>\r\n</HTML>\r\n");
out.flush();
}
catch(Throwable __exception__) {
  ((com.livesoftware.jsp.JRunPageContext)
     pageContext).handlePageException(__exception__);
  }
}
```

Note that any error or exception thrown during the operation—such as a `NumberFormatException` that might occur if the user enters text that can't be converted to an integer in the `setNumb` method–is handed to the designated error handling page. Because the output stream is buffered by default, nothing is written to the response until the `out.flush()` statement is executed, and only then if no exceptions or errors are thrown. This means that the only text displayed in the event of an error will be that generated by the error page.

The error page for our example gets the error or exceptions as the default variable `exception`. It can test the type of exception and respond accordingly, as shown in Listing 3.16.

Listing 3.16: The whoops.jsp error handling page

```
<HTML>
<HEAD>
<TITLE>Database Testing Entry</TITLE>
</HEAD>
<BODY BGCOLOR="#FFFFFF" TEXT="#000000">
<FONT FACE=VERDANA>
<H2 ALIGN=CENTER>
   Shift Operator Demo Error
</H2><BR>
<%@ page language="java" isErrorPage="true" %>
<% if( exception instanceof NumberFormatException ){
%> Only numeric characters may be entered.<br>
<% } else { %>
<%= exception %>
<% } %>
</form>
</BODY>
</HTML>
```

In a complicated application, you should consider creating a custom exception type rather than carry detailed information to the error page.

The Table Building Bean

As mentioned previously, the requirements for a JavaBean are easily stated:

- The class must be public.
- The class must have a no-arguments constructor.
- The class must provide `set` and `get` methods to access variables.

For the purposes of our example, a simple bean was created, having methods to set a variable named numb and get a variable named `table`. Note that the JavaBean naming conventions require that the method names use the variable name but with an initial uppercase character, so the methods end up named `setNumb` and `getTable`. Listing 3.17 shows the complete bean source code.

Listing 3.17: A Java class to create an HTML table

```
// simple JavaBean to create a table building String
package JSPbook.Chapt02;

public class ShiftTable extends java.lang.Object
{
  protected int numb;
  public ShiftTable(){ }

  public void setNumb(String s )
  {
    this.numb = Integer.parseInt( s ) ;
  }

  public String padBinary( int n ){
    String tmp = "00000000000000000000000000000000"
      + Integer.toBinaryString( n );
    return tmp.substring( tmp.length() - 32 );
  }

  void buildRow( StringBuffer sb, String hdr, int n ){
    sb.append("<tr><th>");
    sb.append( hdr );
    sb.append("</th><td>");
    sb.append( Integer.toString(n) );
    sb.append("</td><td>");
    sb.append( Integer.toHexString(n));
    sb.append("</td><td>");
    sb.append( padBinary( n ));
    sb.append("</td></tr>\r\n");
  }
  public java.lang.String getTable()
  { StringBuffer sb = new StringBuffer();
    sb.append("\r\n\r\n<table align=\"center\" border=\"2\"" +
       "cellpadding=\"5\" >\r\n<caption>");
```

```
        sb.append("Shifting " + numb + "<br>\r\n");
        sb.append("</caption>\r\n<tr><th>Operation</th>
           <th>Decimal</th>" +
           "<th>Hex</th><th>32 bit Binary</th></tr> \r\n" );
        buildRow( sb, "Original", numb );
        buildRow( sb, "Shift &lt;&lt; 1", numb << 1 );
        buildRow( sb, "Shift &gt;&gt; 1", numb >> 1 );
        buildRow( sb, "Shift &gt;&gt;&gt; 1", numb >>> 1);
        sb.append("</TABLE>\r\n");
        return sb.toString() ;
     }
  }
```

The convention for the base of the directory where the JSP engine looks for bean classes depends on the individual engine.

WHAT'S NEXT

This chapter has explained the basics of JSP development. The next chapters will delve into more detail on many of these topics. The next chapter will explore more robust ways to deploy servlet and JSP web applications. The following chapter will explain how to effectively remove business logic from JSP pages by using Java Beans.

Chapter 4

Servlet Web Applications

Part I

This chapter was adapted from the Web Component Developer Certification for the J2EE Platform book. This certification study guide helps Java developers learn about servlet and JSP technologies, and helps them prepare for the Sun Certified Web Component Developer Certification. The previous three chapters have introduced servlet and JSP development using a simple deployment model that allowed the reader to focus on the programming concepts rather than advanced deployment issues. Web containers that support the Servlet 2.2 or above specification provide a more robust alternative mechanism for deploying servlets and JSPs into web applications and using an XML deployment descriptor to specify deployment settings. This chapter will explain the concepts of this more robust model of deployment.

Adapted from *Java™ 2 Web Developer Certification Study Guide*, Second Edition by Natalie Levi

ISBN 0-7821-4202-8 $59.99

For an application to be accessible by a container, the many resources that make up the application must be strategically placed in a predefined directory structure. This chapter will show how to classify the various parts of a web application, and identify where these parts must be placed. The directory layout is the key behind the container's ability to locate the data it needs.

Other configuration information is stored within a file specific to each web application. The container accesses this file to determine the purpose, location, and behavior of various resources. This chapter will point out how to format this file and the tags used to communicate between the web application and the container.

Featured in this chapter:

- Description of web applications
- Web application directory structure
- WAR files
- Deployment descriptor tags

Understanding a Web Application

It takes many pieces to make a final program that is accessible through the Web. These pieces, when grouped together, are referred to as the *web application*. A single application can consist of any or all of the following elements:

- Servlets
- JSP pages
- Utility classes
- Static documents
- Client-side Java applets, beans, and classes
- A standard configuration file (required)

A standard J2EE application can contain many servlets and/or JSP pages. The utility classes help execute these server programs, and the static documents provide a more aesthetic appeal to the client application. The client application might also incorporate other Java classes, such as business objects, or applets to help deliver the desired program. Finally, all web applications must contain a standard configuration file to help the server identify each object's purpose and structure.

In addition to informing the server about the details associated with each class, it is imperative that the web application be portable. If the application is placed on a new or different server, it should execute successfully with minimal administrative work. You can ensure successful execution by creating a standard directory structure and configuration file for a web application. All the server needs to do is use the directory structure to locate the application classes in their defined directories and then use the web application's configuration file to identify any configuration settings that need to be applied to needed resources. The server can then execute the application, and in the end, portability is achieved.

Understanding a Directory Structure

Grouping web application classes and files into a structured directory hierarchy provides the web server with a map to find the appropriate resource. This hierarchical structure is defined by the servlet specification, but leaves the choice of implementation up to the vendor creating the container. While recommended by the specification, it is not required that all servlet containers adhere to this organizational pattern; however, for the servlet container to be certified by Sun, it must adhere to the servlet specification. The good news is that most servlet vendors choose to accept the defined format. This section will discuss each layer of the hierarchy and the proper placement of each web application object.

The hierarchy is made up of three significant layers. The first is the context. It is one or more directories used to locate the web application associated with the client request. Within the context exists the `/WEB-INF` directory, which marks another layer. It contains several subdirectories that help organize class files and compressed Java files. The `/WEB-INF` directory also contains a document that maps all files and defines characteristics of the entire application. This layer is hidden from the client. This means the client cannot directly access files from within the `/WEB-INF` directory. The final layer is quite the opposite. Client-viewable files are located either in the context directory itself, or in the /classes directory that is located directly within the context. This includes welcome and error pages, graphic and audio files, and so forth.

The Context

A single web server can run multiple applications. Each application is usually contained within a directory called the root, or *context*. For example, you might have a chat servlet that is made up of multiple directories containing 20 classes and files. All those files and directories will be placed in one directory called `/chatApp`. The `/chatApp` directory is then defined as the context for this web application. The name of the created directory is arbitrary; however, the location of this directory is server dependent. The server determines how to point to the context.

The Tomcat reference implementation provides an automatic directory structure, whereby all directories placed inside the *`tomcat-installation-directory`*`/webapps` directory are automatically configured as web applications. You are not forced to use this directory; you can point the context to another location, but that location must be defined in both the server and application configuration files. JRun, another web server by Macromedia, allows the developer to define the context by specifying the directory name or using a graphical user interface (GUI) wizard tool to specify the application directory. Basically, the location of the context can be customized.

TIP

The context itself is the root for a single web application.

Table 4.1 lists some context examples.

TABLE 4.1: Context Examples

SERVLET	PATH	CONTEXT
ChessServlet	`webserver/webapps/chessApp`	`chessApp/`
CalculatorServlet	`myApps/calculatorApp`	`calculatorApp/`
InstallServlet	`/installApp`	`installApp/`
MusicServlet	`/`	`/`

From this example, you can see that the parent directory can be any directory, as long as its location is communicated to the server. The context is a directory defined by the developer, and, again, its information must be mapped to the server.

WARNING

A container should be configured to reject any attempt to deploy two web applications with the same context path.

When a request is sent from the client, the container must find the appropriate web application to handle the task. In doing so, the web application finds the longest context path that matches the start of the request URL. The container then locates the servlet by using the following mapping rules in the order shown.

Assuming that the servlet path pattern defines the request URL and the incoming path defines the longest context path match, the servlet container will try to find:

Exact mapping All strings match exactly. Here is an example of a match:

Servlet path pattern: `/foo/bar`

Incoming path: `/foo/bar`

Path mapping The string begins with a forward slash (/) and ends with a forward slash and asterisk (/*). The longest match determines the servlet requested.

Here is an example of a match:

Servlet path pattern: `/programs/wordprocessing/*`

Incoming path: `/programs/wordprocessing/index.html`

Incoming path: `/programs/wordprocessing/wp2.4/start.jsp`

Extension mapping The string begins with an asterisk (*).

Here is an example of a match:

Servlet path pattern: `*.jsp`

Incoming path: `/catalog/order/start.jsp`

Incoming path: `/catalog/form.jsp`

Incoming path: `/test.jsp`

Default mapping The container provides server content appropriate for the resource request, such as a default servlet. The string begins with a forward slash (/), and the servlet path is the requested Uniform Resource Identifier (URI) minus the context path. The path info is `null`.

Here is an example of a match:

Servlet path pattern: `/sport`

Incoming path: `/sport/index.html`

NOTE

Containers often have implicit mapping mechanisms built into their systems. For example, a container might have `*.jsp` extensions mapped to enable JSP pages to be executed on demand. The keynote is that explicit mapping by a web application or servlet takes precedence over implicit mapping.

TIP

Request mapping is case sensitive.

WEB-INF

For every web application, there must be a public directory called `/WEB-INF`. This directory contains the main files for the application that are not provided to the client by the container. For example, a graphics file would not be included here because that is something provided to the client; however, a servlet used to calculate data would be stored somewhere within the `/WEB-INF` directory structure.

Through the `ServletContext` object, which the servlet acquires by using the `getServletContext()` method, a servlet can access files and code in the `/WEB-INF` directory by using the following methods:

- *`URL`* `getResource(`*`String path`*`)`
- *`InputStream`* `getResourceAsStream(`*`String path`*`)`

Typically, these methods are used to include the output from other application resources into the current application. Either a URL or

`InputStream` object is returned to the resource mapped in the path parameter. Basically, if an application developer wants to access another resource without exposing that file to the web client, they can do so by using these methods.

There are three main categories for content in the `/WEB-INF` directory:

/WEB-INF/web.xml The deployment descriptor.

/WEB-INF/classes This directory contains all the server-side Java classes, such as servlet and utility classes.

/WEB-INF/lib/*.jar The `/lib` directory contains all necessary compressed Java files that are used for the web application. These files are referred to as *Java archive files* or *JAR files*. They can consist of servlets, JSPs, beans, and utility classes.

NOTE

When loading classes from the `/WEB-INF` directory, the `ClassLoader` first loads from the `/classes` directory and then the `/lib` directory.

Web Application Archive File (WAR File)

When distributing a web application, it is convenient to deliver one file that contains all the necessary classes and resources utilizing the standard directory structure. A *web archive (WAR) file* is like a JAR in that it compresses all necessary classes and resources recursively in their directories into a single file. A JAR file is a compressed file used for a standard Java application and its related classes. A WAR file is a compressed file used for a standard web application and its related classes. The technique used to create a WAR file is the same as a JAR. You can create a WAR file by using the following command-line statement:

```
jar -cvf ShoppingCart.war *
```

or you can extract a WAR file by using the following command:

```
jar -xvf ShoppingCart.war
```

Notice that the `jar` command is used to create and extract a WAR file. The second argument is a list of options telling the command what to do and how. Generally, you should be familiar with the basic options available after the minus sign. They are outlined in Table 4.2.

TABLE 4.2: WAR Options

Option	Definition
C	Create
X	Extract
T	Table of contents
V	Verbose
F	Target file

One of the first three options (`c`, `x`, or `t`) will be used to define the action. You are looking to create (c) a WAR file, extract (x) the contents of the WAR file, or list the table of contents (t) from a specific WAR file.

The `v` (verbose) option is usually used to display the output of the command as it is taking place. The `f` (file) option denotes that the name of the WAR or JAR file will be defined in the next section of the command.

NOTE

For additional options, refer to the following site: `%JDK_HOME%/docs/tooldocs/win32/jar.html` or `$JDK_HOME\docs\tooldocs\solaris\jar.html` (where `%JDK_HOME%` and `$JDK_HOME` represent the path to the JDK installation directory).

NOTE

The minus sign in front of the options is not mandatory. It is used only as a convention carried forward from Unix. The option tags can be placed in any order.

The third item in the previous command line is the name of the WAR file. It should end with a `.war` extension. Finally, if you are creating a file, the last item consists of a single directory or multiple directories, separated by spaces, which will be compressed into the WAR file.

Syntactically, the only difference between the two files types, a JAR and a WAR, is the extension. So why make two file types? Well, their purposes are very different. A JAR file is a compressed file containing resources and classes for a Java application. A WAR file is a compressed file containing resources and classes for a web application. The distinction is significant, in that the container is designed to look for different features for a WAR file than for a JAR file. For a container to execute a WAR file, the file should be placed in the server's default or configured directory used to hold all web applications.

NOTE

Most servers provide a default directory for all WAR file applications. Placing a WAR file in this directory causes the server to automatically load the application into its context. Some vendors provide an additional feature, whereby they allow the placement of WAR files in another directory outside the default directory. Restarting the server will result in the loading of all WAR files from default and configured directories.

Because the WAR file contains all recursive directories needed to use the web application, starting with the context directory, the WAR file should be placed in the web server's application root directory—the one preceding the context.

NOTE

When developing a web application, creating a WAR file might not be practical because classes need to be recompiled, reloaded, and tested. Usually the WAR file is created during the packaging and production stages of a project.

Client-Viewed Files

All files that the container can send to the client are located in the context or subdirectories other than the `/WEB-INF` or `/META-INF` directories.

NOTE

The *//META-INF* directory is the *meta information* directory and contains, at a minimum, one file named `MANIFEST.MF` (the manifest file). The manifest file contains meta information pertinent to the classes that are included within the WAR/JAR file, such as digital signature information, version control information, and package sealing information.

NOTE

Digital signature files are also located in the `/META-INF` directory, but have the extension of `.sf`, which stands for signature file.

The default servlet starting page, usually referred to as `index.html`, is often located directly in the context directory. It is also common to have a graphics or images directory, which contains pictures to display on the web client, within the context directory. Here is a sample directory layout of the different files contained within a single web application:

```
webapps/test/index.html
webapps/test/instructions.jsp
webapps/test/comments.jsp
webapps/test/images/logo.gif
webapps/test/images/smileyFace.gif
webapps/test/WEB-INF/lib/testTabular.jar
webapps/test/WEB-INF/classes/com/
    spiderProductions/servlet/TestServlet.class
webapps/test/WEB-INF/classes/com/
    spiderProductions/util/Utilities.class
```

You can compress the files and directories of the `/test` context into a WAR file called `testApp.war`. The file will be placed in the root application directory as `/webapps/testApp.war`. The WAR file will contain everything from the test directory down.

THE BOTANICAL APPLICATION

The Botanical Market in upstate New York has developed a thriving online business by selling a variety of rare herbs to the general population. Their web site is simple, informative, and efficient. The developers focused their efforts on designing a web application that is portable because the company predicts future upgrades as their revenues grow.

In structuring the web application, the developers placed all static and JSP files in the context directory. Because they were accessing a database, which contained the inventory and order information, some servlets needed Java Database Connectivity (JDBC) calls. The drivers to the database were in JAR format, so they were placed in the *`context`*`/WEB-INF/lib/` directory. The servlets, such as the HerbServlet, OrderServlet, and UserServlet, were placed in the *`context`*`/WEB-INF/classes/` directory. After all pieces were placed in their appropriate locations, and the product was ready for production, the developers compressed the web application into

CONTINUED ⟶

a file called HerbApp.war starting at the context directory. That single file now resides in the current web server's default application directory.

The benefit of configuring the web application to meet the standard directory structure is that it will require little administrative work to relocate the application to a new web server when the company chooses to upgrade. In an ideal setting, it should be as easy as moving the WAR file to the new server's application directory.

Using Deployment Descriptor Tags

A container can contain multiple web applications. For each web application, however, there must exist only one *deployment descriptor*, also referred to as a web.xml. This file identifies and maps the resources for a single web application and is stored at the root of the /WEB-INF directory. Written in Extensible Markup Language (XML), the web.xml utilizes predefined tags to communicate resources and information for use by the web application. All commercial web servers will generate the web.xml file by using a GUI administration tool. Although this makes life a little easier for the developer, it is still the developer's responsibility to be able to understand the various tags and modify the file manually if changes or errors occur.

This section will discuss the basic tags used to construct a web.xml file. It will then identify the tags used to map a request to a servlet and transition to tags that identify a servlet and its parameters. Listing 4.1 shows you a complete web.xml (see Listing 4.1); its tags and purpose are shown in detail.

Listing 4.1: A Sample Deployment Descriptor

```
<?xml version="1.0" encoding="ISO-8859-01"?>

<!DOCTYPE web-app PUBLIC "-//SUN Microsystems, Inc.//
  DTD Web Application 2.3//EN" "http://java.sun.com/
  dtd/web-app_2_3.dtd">
```

```
<web-app>
    <display-name>Exotic Bird Encyclopedia</display-name>

    <context-param>
      <param-name>SEARCH_PATH</param-name>
      <param-value>/features/utilities</param-value>
    </context-param>


    <servlet>
        <servlet-name>Search</servlet-name>
        <servlet-class>SearchServlet</servlet-class>
        <init-param>
          <param-name>defaultType</param-name>
          <param-value>cockatiels</param-value>
          <description>default search value</description>
        </init-param>
    </servlet>

    <servlet-mapping>
        <servlet-name>Search</servlet-name>
        <url-pattern>/utilities/*</url-pattern>
    </servlet-mapping>

    <session-config>
        <session-timeout>60</session-timeout>
    </session-config>

    <mime-mapping>
        <extension>pdf</extension>
        <mime-type>application/pdf</mime-type>
    </mime-mapping>

    <welcome-file-list>
        <welcome-file>index.jsp</welcome-file>
        <welcome-file>index.html</welcome-file>
        <welcome-file>index.htm</welcome-file>
    </welcome-file-list>
</web-app>
```

This `web.xml` file begins by providing versioning information. The first tag, `?xml`, defines the version of the language being used. The character-encoding value is an ISO value and is defined as the Latin standard, which is used for American English countries. The !DOCTYPE line indicates the root XML element and the location of the document type definition (DTD) that defines the structure of the deployment descriptor. A DTD is used to specify the structure of an XML document and to validate the document. The standard for a web application is to use the DTD provided by Sun Microsystems, which designates the web-app as the root element or tag. As you can see in the example, the servlets defined within the DTD will use the 2.3 or earlier spec. This information helps the container synchronize with the provided resources.

After the format tags have been defined, you are ready to begin mapping all resources to the web application. Because the DOCTYPE tag defines the root element as web-app, you are required to start with the web-app tag to open the form. Had the DOCTYPE indicated the root element as web-app2, the XML document would begin with web-app2. In this example, all resources are defined between the opening <web-app> and closing </web-app> tags.

The first set of tags within the web application define parameters that are available to all servlets within the web application. By using the ServletContext method getInitParameter(...), you can pass in the param-name and have the param-value returned within the servlet. Remember, the value is always represented as a String. Usually, the context-param specifies database drivers, protocol settings, and URL path information. Although these tags are important, they are not mandatory. Defining the servlets of the web application is most significant.

Basic Servlet Tags

To define a servlet, the XML document uses the opening <servlet> and closing </servlet> tags. All servlet-related characteristics are defined within these tags, such as the name, class, description, and parameters. When referring to the various servlets in an application, it is sometimes convenient to do so by using an alias name–a less technical name independent of the actual servlet name that follows the *XXX*Servlet naming standard.

```
<servlet>
    <servlet-name>Search</servlet-name>
    <servlet-class>SearchServlet</servlet-class>
</servlet>
```

This example defines the alias servlet name as `Search`, while the actual servlet class name is `SearchServlet`. This enables the servlet to be referred to by a name different from the actual servlet class name. Consequently, if you later changed the alias Search to a servlet class that had a completely different name, no additional changes to source code are necessary.

Initialization Parameters

For now, complete the `servlet` tag by looking at how to define servlet parameters:

```
<servlet>
    <servlet-name>Search</servlet-name>
    <servlet-class>SearchServlet</servlet-class>
    <init-param>
        <param-name>defaultType</param-name>
        <param-value>cockatiels</param-value>
        <description>default search value</description>
    </init-param>
</servlet>
```

A servlet can contain multiple parameters, and each parameter will always be embedded between a set of `<init-param></init-param>` tags. The `init-param` tag defines a name, value, and description for a variable that the outer servlet can access. In this example, the `SearchServlet` class can use the `getInitParameter("defaultType")` method, inherited from the `GenericServlet` class, to get the value `cockatiels`.

TIP

Remember, the `ServletRequest`'s `getParameter(`*`String name`*`)` method returns data acquired from the HTML request. The Servlet's `getInitParameter(`*`String name`*`)` method returns parameters defined within the `web.xml` file.

The description is optional but helps describe the variable's purpose. It is usually only valuable to GUI tools that will use the description to enable the user to know what to enter into the field. The closing `</init-param>` tag closes the information for the one parameter. If another parameter needed to be defined, a new set of `<init-param></init-param>` tags must be defined. Finally, the closing servlet tag, `</servlet>`, marks the end of specific information pertaining to the one servlet.

Mapping the URL to the Servlet

Before the servlet container can access a servlet's parameters, it must locate the servlet. When a container is started, it reads its server's configuration file (`.../conf/server.xml`) to determine the server configuration. The `server.xml` file can list different context paths using the `Context` tag. For example,

```
<Context path="/features" docBase="c:/projects/features">
</Context>
```

The `path` attribute points to the root directory (context) for a particular web application. The actual location of this context is expressed via the `docbase` attribute.

TIP

If mapping information is not included, the container will look to default directories defined by the server's deployment descriptor to find the specified servlet. For the reference web server implementation Tomcat, the default directory for all automatically loaded web applications is the directory called *`tomcat-installation-directory`*`/webapps/`.

Placing all web applications in a default directory is simple, but is not the most organized approach. A container that is running complex applications should be able to locate web applications in designated locations outside the default directory structure. By using the `Context` and `servlet-mapping` tags (which will be discussed next), you can place a servlet in a specific location and point the container to that location.

For the container to locate a servlet it must have information on the location and display rules of the following three items: the context, the code located in the `WEB-INF` directory, and the servlet's file. Look at each item specifically.

As was just described, the `context` is usually defined within the server's configuration file using both the `path` and `docbase` attributes. Next, you must consider the default servlet directory. This value is used in place of all files located within the `WEB-INF` directory. By default, Tomcat uses the term *servlet* within servlet URLs in place of explicitly defining the location of these hidden files.

Lastly, the servlet's fully qualified name is used to locate the servlet within the /classes directory. Because the fully qualified name can be long and cumbersome, each application's web.xml file may use optional servlet-mapping tags, which allow the developer to create an alias for the fully qualified servlet name. By including the servlet-mapping tags and defining a url-pattern, you can make the final modification. Consider the following code snippet:

```
<servlet>
  <servlet-name>SearchServlet</servlet-name>
  <servlet-class>com.kci.SearchServlet</servlet-class>
</servlet>

<servlet-mapping>
  <servlet-name>SearchServlet</servlet-name>
  <url-pattern>/search</url-pattern>
<servlet-mapping>
```

Take a look at how the URL of our SearchServlet can be altered depending on the deployment descriptor tags.

Basic URI http://localhost:8080/features/servlet/com.kci.SearchServlet

Using the servlet-name tag http://localhost:8080/features/servlet/SearchServlet

Using the servlet-mapping tag http://localhost:8080/features/search

The url-pattern tag is used to alter what the user sees and what the developer requests. Instead of relying on a directory provided by the server, you can provide the servlet with a more logical path structure. Based on the information provided, you, like the container, should be able to construct a URI for the following servlet.

```
context path = /car/engines  docBase=c:/projects
alias name = TurboRacer
servlet-name = com.eei.RaceCarServlet
url-pattern = /vehicles/fast
```

By utilizing the information, you should map the servlet to the following locations:

```
http://localhost:8080/car/engines/servlet/com.eei.RaceCarServlet

http://localhost:8080/car/engines/vehicles/fast/TurboRacer
```

The container takes the url-pattern (/vehicles/fast) that is associated with the servlet alias name (TurboRacer) and then maps that name to the actual servlet class (com.eei.RaceCarServlet).

Figure 4.1 breaks down the active location of the servlet graphically.

```
c://projects/car/engines/WEB-INF/classes/com/eei/
     RaceCarServlet.class
```

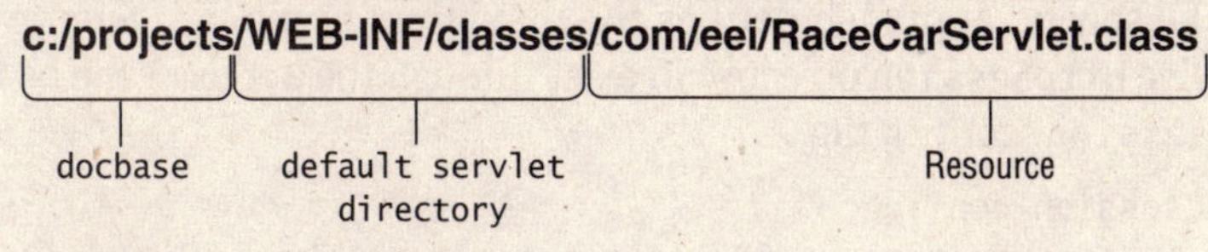

FIGURE 4.1: URL mapping

Session Configuration

After a request is mapped to a servlet, an HttpSession object may be assigned to the client; therefore, if there are 5000 users making requests, the container will maintain 5000 HttpSession objects on the server. If a portion of those users is inactive, the application is wasting memory resources. A timeout flag can be set two ways:

- Within the servlet code, in seconds, by using the HttpSession object's method, *setMaxInactiveInterval(int seconds)*
- Within the web.xml file, in minutes, by using the session-config tag

The first approach utilizes servlet code to set the maximum number of seconds a request can remain inactive. The following code snippet demonstrates how this can be done:

```
...
public void doGet(HttpServletRequest req,
                  HttpServletResponse res)
   throws ServletException, IOException {
    ...
    HttpSession session = req.getSession();
    session.setMaxInactiveInterval(60);
    ...
}
...
```

The downside to this approach is that when the number of seconds needs to be modified, the code itself must be recompiled. To solve this problem, you could use a deployment descriptor parameter value instead of hard-coding the number of seconds. Now, the question often asked is, "Why not use the second approach exclusively because it uses the deployment descriptor to define the value and exclude the code from the servlet?" A developer might opt to choose one approach over the other because the first applies the timeout value to a specific session, rather than the entire web application.

The second approach defines the maximum number of *minutes* all inactive `HttpSession` objects can exist through the `web.xml` file by using the `session-config` tag.

```
<session-config>
   <session-timeout>1</session-timeout>
</session-config>
```

Modifications to the `web.xml` file do not require the servlet to be recompiled. Instead, the container simply needs to be restarted and to reload the servlet. Unlike the setMaxInactiveInterval that takes a timeout value in seconds, the `<session-timeout>` takes a timeout value in minutes. In both examples, you set the timeout amount to one minute. Ultimately, they both achieve the same end result—the code authorizes the container to remove the inactive session from memory after its time expires.

MIME Type Mappings

When transmitting information between the client and server, both parties need to know the format of the content being transferred. The Multipurpose Internet Mail Extension (MIME) type defines the format of the request or response. A MIME type is a `String` that defines the type and subtype: *`type/subtype`*. Some common examples are `text/html`, `text/plain`, and `image/gif`.

When a servlet sends a response to a client, the browser needs to know how to render the information received. Consequently, the server can construct a response to notify the client of the MIME type using two different approaches:

- By using the `HttpServletResponse`'s method: `setContent-Type(...)`
- By using the `mime-mapping` tag in the `web.xml` file for the web application

The first approach utilizes servlet code to set the MIME type of the response. The following code snippet demonstrates how this can be done:

```
...
public void doGet(HttpServletRequest req,
                  HttpServletResponse res)
  throws ServletException, IOException {
    ...
    res.setContentType("application/pdf");
    ...
}
...
```

Again, this applies the content type to a specific servlet. To apply the content type to all public files of a specific extension within an entire web application, you can use the `mime-mapping` tag. The following example demonstrates how the context will automatically associate the `application/pdf` MIME type with all files with the extension of `.pdf`:

```
<mime-mapping>
    <extension>pdf</extension>
    <mime-type>application/pdf</mime-type>
</mime-mapping>
```

After the client receives this response, it knows it must use a tool such as Adobe Acrobat Reader to interpret the `.pdf` response.

Welcome File List

When a web site is accessed, the `index.html` file is usually the first page displayed. Typically this file is the default page for a web site or a web application. In fact, if a client enters a URL path to a servlet, usually the web server will automatically change focus to point to the welcome page associated to the application. For example, if a user enters `http://www.testWebserver.com/application`, the site switches to `http://www.testWebserver.com/application/index.html`.

The `index.html` file is the default welcome page for servlets. Including the `welcome-file-list` tag in the `web.xml` file overrides the server defaults and enables the container to search for specified welcome pages. A list of welcome files can point the web server to alternative display pages.

```
<welcome-file-list>
   <welcome-file>index.jsp</welcome-file>
   <welcome-file>start.html</welcome-file>
   <welcome-file>go.html</welcome-file>
   <welcome-file>index.html</welcome-file>
</welcome-file-list>
```

The files listed within the welcome-file-list tag apply to the web application and its subdirectories. Take a look at an example—imagine a company with a web application that resides in the root directory called /SpiderInc.com. Its subdirectories and files look similar to the following structure:

```
/SpiderInc.com
    |__index.html
    |__employees/
        |____index.jsp
```

When SpiderInc.com is accessed, the welcome page index.html is displayed by default. Now, when the employees/ link is accessed, the user might be prompted for a login and password entry. After access is granted, a welcome page could be generated dynamically to acknowledge the user's name and information. The welcome page for the employee site is called index.jsp. For the container to associate the index.jsp file to the welcome page, the file index.jsp must be defined in the web.xml file with a welcome-file tag. This entry identifies additional filenames for the container to look for when searching for the welcome page for a site. In this example, the container will first look for index.html. If it can't find it in the employees/ directory, it will look at the first filename in the welcome-file list and then search for that file next. Because index.jsp is found, the container displays that page to the client. Without the XML entry, the container would fail to display the starting page because index.html is not available within the employee directory.

TIP

The specification does not address the order in which containers will access the welcome file list. Generally, most containers start with the first file in the list when searching for a welcome page.

What's Next

This chapter covered the details associated with the web application. It began by addressing the basic directory structure for a web application. Each resource should be placed in a specific location for the container to access its information when it is needed. Because the container doesn't always find direct matches for the files it is searching, this chaper also covered the mapping rules a container will use to select the best fit. Finally, how to wrap up the entire application in a WAR file for production was described.

The second part of this chapter focused on identifying the most common deployment descriptor tags. The overall tag list is very large, and only those that are general to the web application were covered. Specifically, tags that apply to the entire application, such as the `Context`, `session-config`, `mime-type`, and `welcome-file` tags, were addressed. In addition to those, tags specific to the servlets contained within the web application itself were covered.

The web application is made up of multiple pieces. It is important that the pieces are arranged logically and their purpose is identified to the server.

Chapter 3, "The Basic JSP API," introduced the concept of using JavaBeans with JSP pages. The next chapter will elaborate on the many uses of JavaBeans, and discuss JavaBean best practices.

Chapter 5

Introducing JavaBeans

Have you ever tried to use the same piece of code twice—a snippet that worked perfectly—only to find out that it doesn't quite fit? Somehow, it got mangled between the last time you visited your secret `Code-That-Works-Because-I-Wrote-and-Tested-It-Myself` treasure chest directory and now when you need to copy and paste it into your current project. Every developer has fallen victim to this trap. You've already seen how JSP lets you get away from endless copying and pasting by reusing sections of code, such as the header at the top of a page, with the aid of the JSP file include tag (for example, `<%@ include="header.jsp" %>`). This is an excellent solution, but still vulnerable to human carelessness. For example, what if the `header.jsp` file is open on your desktop, or you've highlighted a line, or the keyboard gets bumped and part of the header disappears? Now you have something to worry about. The boss is coming to see your presentation, and the header is going to be mangled on every page. Don't laugh; these things happen.

Adapted from *Mastering™ JSP™* by Todd Cook
ISBN 0-7821-2940-4 $49.99

Fortunately, you have a way to ensure greater security and stability in your quest to reuse code: JavaBeans.

Featured in this chapter:

- Understanding JavaBeans
- Designing JavaBeans
- Learning JavaBeans scope
- Understanding JavaBeans naming conventions
- Dealing with Bugs in JavaBeans

An Overview of JavaBeans

You can use JavaBeans to package functions, processing, values, database access, and anything else you can dream up in Java code that another developer can use from inside a JSP page, a servlet, another JavaBean, an applet, or an application. You can think of JavaBeans as giving you the ability to copy and paste code anywhere, without having to worry about it changing. What's more, the code pasted in by the action of the JavaBean is in a form of shorthand, just a reference to the JavaBean and the method call–the section needed. Before we get into the mechanics of using JavaBeans, though, let's take an in-depth look at their development and requirements.

The Development of JavaBeans

Originally, JavaBeans were proposed as a standard for packaging code for reusable software components. Specifically, they were designed to help companies developing Java software components for use in an Integrated Development Environment (IDE). These components included, for example, a Grid control (represented by a little grid in an IDE toolbox window) that users could drag onto a form under development. Since their initial development, JavaBeans have expanded to become a standard component in Java web applications, and the JavaBean component framework has expanded with Enterprise JavaBeans (EJB).

In the original design, a company could compile a JavaBean source file into Java bytecode and distribute it to developers. A developer designing an application could then select, for example, a graph JavaBean, drop it on a form, and see a list of its methods and properties–all without ever having access to the original source code. Furthermore, the developer could then define the graph's property values, such as its dimensions on the form, and the IDE could save the values, which would be loaded at runtime.

JavaBean Requirements

JavaBeans are Java classes that adhere to certain coding guidelines. These guidelines extend the flexibility and scope of JavaBeans, and expose access to their internal properties and methods. By doing this, a JavaBean class can be used in the following ways:

- In an IDE whose JavaBean features let an application developer see its methods, even if the bean is compiled and the original source is not available. Think of it this way: You could write a spreadsheet control and give it–ahem–sell it to your developer friends. They could then drop it into their nifty Java application designer studio, drop it on their forms, and use it without ever having to tinker behind the scenes with the code you wrote.
- In a distributed manner by Remote Method Invocation (RMI). That doesn't sound exciting now, but it will later when we cover Enterprise JavaBeans. Basically, using RMI means that your JavaBean can run on a server in New York, and help the rest of an application running in Los Angeles or anywhere else in the world! Of course, a considerable effort is required to change a JavaBean into an EJB entity bean, but it's an option for code reuse. We'll look at how to use EJBs in Chapter 20, "Enterprise JavaBeans Architecture and Clients."
- Serialized, whereby its property values and state can be saved and stored on a disk. Serialization also allows you to move a JavaBean from one location to another. For example, your JavaBean is on a server in New York helping the rest of an application in Los Angeles. The Java application server hosting your JavaBean receives a message that the server is going down for maintenance; it then contacts another server elsewhere, and arranges for the other server to take over. Not wanting to crash out an end user using your JavaBean, the Java application server has your JavaBean save its state, using serialization, and it moves the JavaBean location and data to the new server where the saved JavaBean data is loaded again. The user continues using the application without noticing a thing.

Nifty features, but perhaps you only want to use the code reuse feature right now. That's fine, but reading through all the requirements now might prevent some future headaches should you ever want your JavaBean to grow beyond the range of web servers and browsers.

A No-Arguments Constructor

The no-arguments constructor means that a user must be allowed to create an instance of a JavaBean just by calling its name. For example, if you have a web application with a section that logs in users with a JavaBean, you must allow that JavaBean to be created as is, just like a block of concrete without any information chiseled on it. The class might look something like this:

```
public class User implements Serializable
 {
  private String id = "";
  private String pwd = "";

  public User ()
   {}
 // begin methods section
  . . .
 }
```

And you can represent creating the class as is as follows:

```
User mUserInstanceOnTheWebPage = new User();
```

If the class is written so that it requires a user's ID before creating itself as an object, it cannot be called a "legal" JavaBean; therefore, it might not behave as a JavaBean, or work in the situations described earlier in this chapter. For example, the following will *not* work:

```
public class User implements Serializable
 {
  private String id = "";
  private String pwd = "";

  public User (String strLogin, String strPwd)
   {
```

```
    id = strLogin;
    pwd = strPwd;
  }
// begin methods section
. . .
```

MULTIPLE CONSTRUCTORS

The Java language lets you define multiple constructors; therefore, the following is a legal JavaBean:

```
public class User implements Serializable
 {
  private String id = "";
  private String pwd = "";

  public User()
   {}

  public User (String strLogin, String strPwd)
   {
    id = strLogin;
    pwd = strPwd;
   }
 //begin methods . . .
```

The previous was a no-arguments constructor defined next to a constructor that takes two arguments, a login ID and a password.

In addition, the Java compiler generates a default constructor, the same thing as a no-arguments constructor, if the author of a class does not provide one; therefore, the following is also a legal JavaBean:

```
public class User implements Serializable
 {
  private String id = "";
  private String pwd = "";
  //begin methods . . .
```

Supporting a Multithreaded Environment

The basic requirement is that each JavaBean be designed so that it is responsible for the integrity of its own data. It should also be able to handle multiple requests for its data, always handing out values in an orderly fashion even if two requests grab for the same value at the same time. For example, if a JavaBean is in charge of assigning or guaranteeing unique names for people visiting a chat room, it must order the requests—to *synchronize* them—so that if two people request the same login name at the same time, the JavaBean keeps order, handing out a unique name to one and rejecting the other request. Who wins and who loses the micro-millisecond race for the login name isn't important; it's only important that the JavaBean not fail in its specific job, which in this case is guaranteeing unique chat room names. You can provide multithreading safety by using synchronization locks on sections of the class that manipulate data. Doing so is as simple as adding the `synchronized` keyword to all the functions that access data values that could change, as in the following:

```
public synchronized void setSsn(String strSsn)
 {
     if (strSsn == null)
         ssn = "";
     else
         ssn = strSsn;
 }
```

NOTE

Synchronizing a method call slows down its execution by at least four times (depending on the Java implementation); however, bugs in multithreaded code are some of the most difficult to eradicate.

TIP

Play it safe: Declare all public data access methods synchronized, and remove them only when you determine it improves performance and does not harm the data's integrity. Improperly synchronized methods can cause deadlocks, so you must use them judiciously. It's often a choice of the lesser of two evils, but it's far easier to spot deadlocks than to pinpoint data corruption arising from race conditions (for example, when one thread starts to access a piece of data and then another thread changes that stored data value before the first thread is allowed to complete its action of retrieving the data).

Supporting Persistence by Implementing Serializable or Externalizable Using the java.io Package

Each JavaBean is supposed to be responsible for its own data by being able to save and load its values. This action of saving and loading is called persistence, and it allows a JavaBean to be moved. For example, if a supporting server in a distributed application is going to be shut down, a Java application server or a Java Enterprise management system can save JavaBean values and re-instantiate them elsewhere. Because this requirement is often not enforced by IDEs and JavaServer Engines inside web servers, you can create and use JavaBeans without adding the extra code; however, technically, they aren't in accordance.

Exposure of Public Properties

A JavaBean should expose certain methods by declaring them public. Name the properties in a straightforward manner that gives unambiguous hints as to their parameters, behavior, and return values. It's important to name and expose functions that a developer who is manipulating the bean might find helpful, such as the accessor methods (*accessor* is a fancy term for methods that provide and restrict access to the data members in a class) and methods that return debug information. You'll see an example of these special, customized methods later in this chapter when we discuss the `validate` function.

When providing JavaBean methods that allow users to interact with the data, it's okay to include a basic validation check. In the following example, the incoming string parameter is checked to see if its value is null. If so, an empty string is assigned.

```
public void setId (String strId)
{
    if (strId != null)
        id = strId.trim();
    else
        id = "";
}
```

```
public String getId ()
  {
      return id;
  }
```

This design prevents a JavaBean from reporting a `null` value from a database query on a web page form. Without this code, the value is printed on the web page as a string `null`, and if the value is inserted back into the database, it is a string that says `null`.

WARNING

Do not confuse `null` values with a string that spells out null. `Null` in a database is a special value indicating an empty column; a string that says null is four characters long. See your SQL reference and database documentation for more information.

In the `setId` method, the input string is tested. If the string is not null, leading and trailing white space is removed, and the string is assigned to the variable ID. If the string is null, an empty string is assigned. Simply assigning an incoming null can cause problems when accessing a database; displaying the word null in a textbox is not acceptable to users. In addition, calling the string method `trim()` on a string with a `null` value will throw an exception, specifically a `java.lang.NullPointerException`. The code for this chapter's UserInfo JavaBean addresses this problem, as shown in Listing 5.4.

JavaBean Design Considerations

In the real world, it is often helpful to extend the design of JavaBeans beyond mere representations of objects or processes. Always consider providing the information that a web developer might want from your JavaBean in the future. For example, you can often provide masked entries for the HTML display of sensitive data, such as passwords, social security numbers, and sometimes even phone numbers. Here are some approaches:

NOTE

To enforce data, declare sensitive data access methods private, or don't declare them at all.

```
public void setPwd (String strPwd)
 {
     if (strPwd != null)
          pwd = strPwd.trim();
     else
          pwd = "";
 }

private String getPwd ()
 {
     return pwd;
 }
```

TIP

Sometimes it makes sense to provide multiple access methods to ease programming tasks and support user requirements, such as one method for data entry and another for display. For example, a social security number is a sensitive piece of information; whenever possible, display it as masked.

The following code snippet illustrates how access to a social security number can be masked for display on a web page:

```
public void setSSN(String strSSN)
{
   if (strSSN != null)
     ssn = strSSN;
   else
      ssn = "";
}

public String getSSN
{
   // for data access
     return ssn;
}
```

```
public String getSSNMasked
{
    // return masked SSN for display
    return ("xxx-xx-" + ssn.substring(8,11));
}
```

Because a well-designed JavaBean is responsible for managing its own data, it usually has several methods for generating the `insert`, `update`, and `delete` SQL statements. Chapter 9 of this book discusses database access using JDBC. Chapters 7 and 10 of *Mastering JSP* (Sybex 2002) also discuss JDBC and a utility class called QueryManager that can streamline JDBC code. This utility is briefly used here. Right now, it's important just to see how proper design can ease the tasks of managing the JavaBean's data and the handling of null and optional values. The following code snippet comes from our UserInfo JavaBean, shown in Listing 5.4. The UserInfo JavaBean is used in our example at the end the chapter. Here's the method that generates the `insert` statement:

```
public boolean InsertUser()
 {
  if (!IsValid())
      return false;
   try
    {
    StringBuffer sbUser = new StringBuffer (
                    "insert into tusers values ('");
    sbUser.append( firstName);
    sbUser.append("', '");
    sbUser.append( lastName );
    sbUser.append("', '");
    sbUser.append( userEmail );
    sbUser.append("', '");
    sbUser.append( login );
    sbUser.append("', '");
    sbUser.append( pwd );
```

```
        sbUser.append("', '");
        sbUser.append( ssn );
        sbUser.append("', '");
        sbUser.append( workPhone );
        sbUser.append("', '");
        sbUser.append( age );
        sbUser.append("', '");
        sbUser.append( getLanguagesAsString() );
        sbUser.append("') ");
        System.out.println( sbUser.toString() );
        //  QueryManager.execInsert( sb.toString());
        // implemented in Mastering JSP chapters 7 and 14
       return true;
       }
      catch (Exception e)
       {
        System.out.println("Error in Insert User");
       }
       return false;
   }
```

Using this method, the UserId JavaBean can generate the following SQL statement:

```
insert into tusers values ('Lorne', 'Daylem',
                          'lorne@cookconsulting.com',
                          'lorne', 'ambulance',
                          '123-45-6789',
                          '555 123-4444',
                          '32',
                          'English, Spanish')
```

This SQL statement executes properly even if the *age* variable is a number field in the database because values are passed over the wire as strings and the quotation delimiters separate only the values.

TIP

Oracle database SQL syntax treats empty strings as null values. Additionally, because Oracle stores numbers as character values, a quoted number is inserted as a regular number! Be sure to call `trim()` before sending values, however. Leading or trailing white space will cause the insert or update to throw an error.

This behavior significantly reduces the need for extra coding, and keeps the data-manipulation code-generating section relatively clean. It also provides a great deal of flexibility. For example, in our UserInfo JavaBean shown in Listing 5.4, *age* is an optional value; therefore, the SQL used to insert a user could easily be as follows:

```
insert into tusers values ('Lorne', 'Daylem',
                           'lorne@cookconsulting.com',
                           'lorne', 'ambulance',
                           '123-45-6789',
                           '555 123-4444',
                           '',
                           'English, Spanish')
```

This SQL statement could simply cause the *age* variable to be entered as null. If that number value placeholder is not quoted, however, it fails in the following form:

```
insert into tusers values ('Lorne', 'Daylem',
                           'lorne@cookconsulting.com',
                           'lorne', 'ambulance',
                           '123-45-6789',
                           '555 123-4444',
                           ,
                           'English, Spanish')
```

In this case, you must amend the relevant SQL generation section to the following:

```
sbUser.append("', ");
  if (age == null)
     sbUser.append( "null" );
 else
     sbUser.append( age );
sbUser.append(", '");
```

A *NULL* IN JAVA IS NOT THE SAME AS A *NULL* IN SQL

If you declare the *age* variable as an `int` inside the JavaBean, you must still deal with the issue of resolving the value because there is no default for age, an `int` can't be initialized as a `null`, and the compiler will complain if an operation is performed on the `int` value without it being explicitly initialized.

For example, consider this test program:

```
public class NullTest
 {
   public static void main (String[] args)
    {
    int i = 0;
    //int i = null;  // not a valid initialization
    String str=null;
    String strZeroedOutValue ="";
    // e.g. Simulating a user clearing a field
    //      and thereby submitting an empty string
    StringBuffer sb = new StringBuffer ("Null test:
      String
                        initialized as null=");
    sb.append(str);
    sb.append("\n String representing a Zeroed Out
      Value: ");
    sb.append(strZeroedOutValue);
8          System.out.println(sb.toString());
    }
 }
```

The NullTest program produces the following output:

CONTINUED →

Running the NullTest program proves the wisdom of the programming idiom in which an empty string is substituted for a null value for text displays and SQL inserts and updates as well as for HTML text displays. And yet, if a user wants to delete some information, by deleting text from a form's field, it's important to send the zero-length string to the database so that it's properly inserted as a null value.

Although most databases handle empty strings as null values, you'll have to write additional Java code when building your SQL insert statement, if the database you're using doesn't handle empty strings as nulls. For example:

```
if (age.length() == 0)
   {
    sb.append("null");
   }
   else
   {
    sb.append(age);
   }
```

JavaBean Scope

Scope is the lifespan of a variable. A JavaBeans scope is indicated inside the `<jsp:useBean scope="...>` tag, which creates the shorthand reference for the JavaBean. Before you can reference a JavaBean, you must instantiate it as follows:

```
<jsp:useBean id="MJSPUserPrefsBean"
  class="MasteringJSPUserPreferencesBean"
   scope="session" >
```

Here you create a shorthand reference, `MJSPUserPrefsBean`, that refers to the class `MasteringJSPUserPreferencesBean`, which would be visible to the developer as `MasteringJSPUserPreferencesBean.java`. It must be located in the JavaServer Engine's classpath. Last, the scope is declared by its own attribute, here for the session.

The <jsp:useBean ...> declaration is usually placed at the top of a page for clarity.

NOTE

The JavaServer Engine strips out the <jsp:... tag, and end users won't ever see the instantiation code by viewing the web page's source in their browser window.

There are four types of scopes: page, request, session, and application. JavaBeans most commonly use request, page, and session scope.

Session Scope Session-scoped JavaBeans are great for activities that take place over several pages and time. Some examples include filling a shopping cart, incrementally filling out information and receiving feedback, keeping track of a list of actions that a user has recently performed over a series of pages (such as a list of the last 10 houses viewed on a real estate site), and so on. A session-scope JavaBean retains a small amount of information associated with the client's session ID, which is derived from a temporary session cookie removed from the client and server when users close their browser windows.

Page/Request Scope Page and request scope JavaBeans are sometimes referred to as *form beans* because they most often process the results of a form. Form beans need to exist just long enough to process user input, usually being instantiated on the page that receives the HTTP POST or GET request with parameters. Additionally, page and request scope beans can be helpful in reducing the load on the server for a large web site on which a single process might consume excessive resources if it were held as a session bean. For example, a web application that calculates horoscopes, star charts, and numerology from a basic user input screen could require some heavy processing that only needs to be performed once. The results could then be saved in a smaller session-scoped JavaBean for easy access for the rest of the user's session without burdening the JavaServer. Most users probably want to look at the chart, maybe save something to their desktop, and move on.

Application Application scope is most often used by server components such as JDBC connection pools, application monitors, user counters, and other classes that participate indirectly with a user's activities.

Naming Conventions

Using proper naming conventions is crucial. The following sections detail the major issues. Beyond providing a no-arguments constructor, a JavaBean declares itself publicly by adhering to the following conventions:

- Access to member variables is channeled through public data access member functions.
- A member function with a signature `void getPropertyX` requests the value for the named `propertyX`; it returns the same type as variable `X`.
- A member function named `setPropertyX (type NewX)` requests the JavaBean to assign `NewX` to the named `PropertyX`.
- Member variables begin with a lowercase letter, but they're represented in the public property name's signatures with an uppercase letter.

We'll look at special cases in the next section. Overall, the JavaServer Engine expects JavaBeans to adhere to these basic standard naming conventions.

Naming Properties

Naming properties is the sole mechanism for getting a JavaBean to grab data from a web page, store it, return it to another page, and make it accessible to other server-side objects, classes, and services. The following is the archetypal naming pattern for getting and setting a property:

```
public <PropertyType> get<PropertyName>();
public void set<PropertyName>(<PropertyType> a);
```

In the previous lines, `PropertyType` refers to variable type. Here is a fleshed-out example:

```
<jsp:setProperty id="MJSPUserPrefsBean" property="bgcolor"
    parameter="white">
<jsp:getProperty id="MJSPUserPrefsBean" property="bgcolor">
```

This is the same as the short form, which uses servlet tags:

```
<% MJSPUserPrefsBean.setBgcolor("white"); %>
<%= MJSPUserPrefsBean.getBgcolor(); %>
```

Boolean properties are allowed to follow the traditional `isPropertyName` format.

```
public void setValid (boolean bValid )
 {
     bIsValid = bValid;
 }

public boolean IsValid()
 {
   return bIsValid;
 }
```

Naming Indexed Properties

An array of HTML check boxes on a form is represented to a JavaBean as an indexed property, just as it is in JavaScript. Indexed properties are represented with an additional placeholder for an array subscript:

```
public void setLanguages (String [] strLanguages )
 {
   languages = strLanguages;
 }

public String[] getLanguages ()
 {
   if ( languages == null)
      return (new String [] {""});
  //prevents error from being thrown
  // when not populated
   else
      return languages;
 }

public void setLanguages (int i, String strLanguage )
 {
   languages[i] = strLanguage;
 }
```

```
public String getLanguages ( int iLanguageNumber)
 {
   if ( languages[iLanguageNumber] == null)
      return "";
   else
      return languages[iLanguageNumber];
 }
```

It's often helpful to write a function for representing the String array to users. The following is a code snippet from the UserAuth JavaBean (Listing 5.4):

```
public String getLanguagesAsString ()
 {
   if (languages == null)
      return "";
   else
     {
       String AllLanguages ="";
     for (int ii = 0; ii < languages.length; ii++)
        {
        AllLanguages += languages[ii];
        AllLanguages += ", ";
        }
       return AllLanguages.substring(0,
                        AllLanguages.lastIndexOf(","));
     }
 }
```

If your application has many arrays, such as optional check boxes, this function might be better placed in a utility bean such as BeanTools, covered in Listing 5.5.

NOTE

By convention, HTML input tags should match the variable declaration names inside the JavaBean class. They should also begin with lowercase that matches an uppercase method name. For example, the HTML `loginName` matches a variable login name and bean methods `getLoginName` and `setLoginName(String newLoginName)`.

You can assign properties one at a time, as seen earlier, or you can use a wildcard to cycle through the properties of a bean, matching them to correspondingly named inputs from a web page, as in the following:

```
<jsp:setProperty name="MJSPUserPrefsBean" property="*" />
```

AVOIDING JAVABEAN VARIABLE NAME COLLISIONS

Cycling through properties with a wildcard can be a great coding time-saver, but it can cause problems. The wildcard asterisk causes the JavaServer Engine to cycle the parameters through the JavaBean, populating *any* variables that match and that have `getProperty` methods. Variable names should match input fields, but if multiple session beans are present at the same time, names should be different. Collisions will cause unpredictable application behavior.

If you want to maintain the same names across beans, you can do so by explicitly getting or assigning properties using the `<jsp:...>` tags. Ideally, it's best to limit the number of session-scoped JavaBeans, and use page or request scoped JavaBeans for processing HTML form data.

Nonetheless, differentiating names might make sense for your application. For example, if you are designing a web application for patient feedback to a hospital, and you might have two JavaBeans, a ScreeningBean and a MedicalProcedureBean, representing the same input, Patient Comfort Level, at different times. You would want to differentiate their names on the HTML input value name as well as inside the JavaBean. Naming the variables and `get/set` Property methods as `patientComfortLevelScrn` and `patientComfortLevelMedProc` will avoid confusion when the JavaServer Engine probes the cached JavaBeans for data assignment.

Naming Events

A JavaBean can make public the hooks for event listening. This is most often used for visual JavaBeans to become responsive in another environment, such as on a form, in an applet, or in an IDE.

```
public void add<EventListenerType>(<EventListenerType> a)
public void remove<EventListenerType>
                         (<EventListenerType> a)
```

The <EventListenerType> type here extends the `java.util.EventListener` interface. The use of an `EventListener` represents a JavaBean acting as a multicast event source for the events registered.

A developer might mark an EventListener as unicast by indicating that it throws a `java.util.TooManyListenersException`. If so, you can assume that the event source is unicast, and can tolerate only a single event listener being registered at a time. The following is a function call that adds a mouse listener:

```
public void addMouseListener(MouseListener t)
                throws java.util.TooManyListenersException;
```

This function call can then be used to remove the listener, as desired:

```
public void removeMouseListener(MouseListener t);
```

We'll work with events in greater detail in the next section.

Working with Session Events

It's possible for a JavaBean to register itself with the JavaServer Engine context by implementing `javax.servlet.http.HttpSessionBindingListener`. The coupling is handled by the following:

```
public void valueBound (HttpSessionBindingEvent event)
public void valueUnbound (HttpSessionBindingEvent event)
```

The `HttpSessionBindingEvent` has two methods:

```
public String getName();
public HttpSession getSession();
```

This feature facilitates interactions with users. Perhaps a user logged in to the system wants to be alerted if a friend is also on the system. If the login JavaBean raises a session event after the user is validated, all other live login session scope beans can hear about that new user if they are hooked into that session event.

For more on session events–what they are, how to manipulate them, and how they relate to one another and overall server processing–see Chapter 3, "JSP Processing," of *Mastering JSP* (Sybex, 2002).

JavaBean Design Guidelines

It's a good idea to separate simple checking and assignment from complex validation. You can see this principle at work in our chapter example and as shown in the code in Listing 5.4, in which password length is checked when fetching the masked field for display on the CheckInfo JSP page. The database call on the login name `CheckUnique` is relegated to the `validate` function. The `validate()` function is a good place to tally values, for example, to see if a shopping cart has too many items for the value of an electronic gift certificate, necessitating a payment. The `validate()` function might also be a good place to remind a user that if they don't enter a social security number, they won't get a check.

It is often preferable to check all values in one function, such as `validate()`. Doing so makes it easy to update the requirements. Another validation approach is to send error messages back to the user as close as possible to the site of the error. The example code in this chapter does this as shown by the UserInfo JavaBean (Listing 5.4) and the validation it returns as shown in Figure 5.4.

Overall, most users prefer to see exactly where their input caused a problem instead of being confronted by an error condition described by a paragraph printed at the bottom of the form they were filling out. The worst treatment is displaying a generic error message blocking their progress, for example, "Please fill in all required fields." Avoid this at all costs. Please the user. Users won't enjoy searching the page to find out what they have to change to proceed with the application. In this chapter's example, specifically in Listings 5.1 and 5.2 as shown in Figures 5.3 and 5.4, trying to enter a password of fewer than four letters returns an error next to the password field as well as in the validation message section. You have many options when it comes to enforcing the business logic of a company on the Presentation layer. Present the options to your project manager. Let them know what you can do; if they don't show a preference, aim to please and ease the user's tasks.

Reflection: How a JavaServer Engine or an IDE Learns about a JavaBean's Behavior

A JSP page is compiled into a servlet of Java bytecode, which is stored in a directory. When the JavaServer Engine starts, it compiles Java files, if they aren't already compiled; then the JavaServer Engine introspects the classes to see which member functions are exposed for public use. Beans rely on this behavior. Introspection is a feature of the Java language in which a class file can be dynamically loaded and probed for a list of properties, a list of methods, and their arguments. (For more information of how Reflection works, see Chapter 3, "JSP Processing," of *Mastering JSP* (Sybex, 2002).)

Developers frequently refer to JavaBeans based on their types:

Value Beans Value Beans are containers for values, objects, or processes as a whole. The `UserInfo` bean is an example.

Component Beans Component beans are classes with visual components that represent items that can be dropped onto a form in an IDE. A custom-built spreadsheet control is an example.

Utility Beans Utility beans are helper classes, providing generalized utility functions. BeanTools, covered later in this chapter, is an example (see Listing 5.5).

The business rules of your company and the requirements of the application will guide you in factoring out functions into your utility classes. For example, earlier in this chapter you saw how an indexed array of check boxes is supported by a `get/set` property and how a specialized function must be written to handle the generation of a flat, comma-delimited string representation of the array. If you commonly deal with arrays of optional values, you might find it helpful to factor out the code into functions housed in a utility class.

Bugs in JavaBeans

When you declare a JavaBean in the session scope, it caches input field values across several pages, which is good, because that helps track a user's session. However, this caching behavior is ugly if the user tries to delete a value already entered; the JavaServer Engine doesn't detect a change in the variables state, and so the change doesn't register as an update. That's right–the old value reappears like an ugly ghost.

The main problem is that the web application doesn't perform as the user would assume. Simply clicking the browser's Back button, deleting a field's value, and clicking the Submit button doesn't correct the problem, and the workaround of deleting the field and inserting a blank space is not an intuitive user action. You can solve this problem in three ways.

You can use the `initialize` function as follows:

```
public synchronized void initialize()
{
```

```
    firstName ="";
    lastName ="";
    userEmail ="";
    login ="";
    pwd ="";
    ssn ="";
    workPhone ="";
    languages = new String [] {""};
    age ="";
}
```

This function sets all strings to empty, wiping the slate clean of all cached values. Insert the function after the bean is instantiated and before the page request populates the data like this:

```
<jsp:useBean id="UserInfoBean" scope="session"
     class="webbeans.UserInfo" />
<% UserInfoBean.initialize(); %>
<jsp:setProperty name="UserInfoBean" property="*" />
<HTML>
```

The previous snippet is from the CheckUserInfo JSP, shown in Listing 5.2. The disadvantage of this solution is that it tends to wipe out all previous data and forces the user to re-enter many fields.

A second solution is to use page/request scope beans, dump the values into hidden text inputs inside a hidden form, and submit when moving to the next page. The disadvantage of this solution is that it clutters and complicates the Presentation layer, which is visible to the user if they view the page's source.

Another solution is to add a client-side JavaScript script that adds a space to all values. The assignment is trimmed even if it's quickly assigned to a number variable. The advantage of this solution is that it's a transparent flexibility for the user; the web application works as expected. The disadvantage is that this workaround is visible if the user views the page's source.

I favor the third solution because it provides users with the greatest flexibility and, given good data assignment management, it requires the least amount of code. The initial input page should already contain a JavaScript block that enforces simple client-side validation, such as proper date entry, numeric input only, and whatever the business logic and user interface standards require.

Restricting the Generation of HTML within a Bean

Theoretically, a JavaBean should not generate any HTML because that is a job for the JSP Presentation layer; however, practically it is often useful to provide some preliminary formatting for diagnostic messages. Generated HTML should be lean and returned by clearly labeled JavaBean methods.

```
public synchronized void validate ()
 {
  hTMLErrorMessage = "";
  setValid(true);
  if ( (userEmail.length() < 5)
       || ( userEmail.indexOf("@") == -1) )
      {
      setValid(false);
      hTMLErrorMessage +=
       "<br>Please enter a valid email.<br>";
      }
  if (!CheckUnique (login))
      {
      setValid(false);
      hTMLErrorMessage += "<br>Please choose another"
      + " user name that one is already taken.<br>";
      // TO DO: modify username with
      // random number generation appendage
      }
  if (workPhone.length() < 10)
      {
       setValid(false);
       hTMLErrorMessage += "<br>Your phone number"
        + " must include the area code.<br>";
      }
   if (!BeanTools.IsHyphenatedNumber(getSsn()) )
     {
```

```
        setValid(false);
        hTMLErrorMessage += "<br>Please enter only numbers "
        + " or hyphens for social security "
        + " or phone numbers.<br>";
        }
      if (pwd.length() < 4)
        {
        setValid(false);
        hTMLErrorMessage += "<br>Please choose a password "
        + "longer than four characters.<br>";
        }
    }

  public synchronized String getValidationErrorHTMLMsg()
    {
      return hTMLErrorMessage;
    }
```

In this example, `validate()` is called just prior to generating a check values and submit page. Although it might be tempting to compress the two functions and have `validate()` return an HTML string, this could severely limit the JavaBean's future flexibility. It's a bad idea because anyone using your bean would have to look inside the validation method to see what it returns. Also you can't easily customize this sort of behavior without going into the bean and changing it. Remember, a JavaBean is a special kind of permanent yet flexible container.

Here are some important dos and don'ts:

Don't ever put any font sizes into the HTML returned from a JavaBean. Not all browsers are the same, and many instances can't handle the full range of font sizes. For example, a wireless phone display can't handle a font size of 14 points.

Don't ever put any script or DHTML into the HTML returned from a JavaBean. Exporting script or DHTML straight to a page is suicidal because some browsers versions actually crash on incorrectly formed scripts (rare but nonetheless possible). If your JavaBean is dynamically pushing out complex HTML at runtime, you are courting a debugging nightmare. Additionally, exporting complex HTML will limit the lifespan and flexibility of your JavaBean. For example, full scripting language support may not be available on all handheld browsers. Similarly, if the exported HTML contains a script that pops up a message box alert or yes/no question, it could grind the whole application to a halt.

Do provide an alternative. Always provide users with an alternate approach if they are viewing your pages with a different system, such as a handheld computer. On the CheckInfo page, the JavaBean does write out a JavaScript Enabled button, but an HTML hyperlink is also provided.

White-Box Testing

Black-box software refers to a component that's obscure in its handling of data or execution procedures. With third-party tools, a certain level of obscurity about what the underlying code is doing is often unavoidable. With custom or in-house code, however, there's no excuse for depriving a fellow developer of a window into the code's internals.

White-box software refers to software that allows a developer to see what goes into it and how it changes. White-box designs allow users to look at more information to diagnose whether the software is performing as promised. Additionally, white-box designs allow developers and testers a fine-grained manipulation of the data so that intricate and thorough tests can be performed.

Some years ago an innovation in software project management and code design suggested that routines, subprograms, packages—whatever unit of code that is to be isolated—should be responsible for testing itself and guaranteeing that the code performs as required. Although this idea is common sense, few developers implemented it before it was suggested. Now, good software engineers frequently write self-testing code. Writing the extra function that self-tests a class to see that it behaves appropriately and returns the expected results does require time. Ideally, the self-testing routine mechanism should be rewritten any time the class changes in any major way so that the self-testing is appropriately thorough.

With JavaBeans, it's easy to implement white-box design by simply providing each class with a main function that instantiates itself and provides some test values and produces output. Although a JavaBean requires a default constructor that takes no arguments, you can still define another constructor that takes arguments, or subsequent calls in the program's main function can provide values for testing.

Utility beans have no excuse for providing white-box testing functionality because they should be able to stand on their own. The following is an example from this chapter's BeanTool JavaBean, shown in Listing 5.5.

```
public static void main (String[] args)
 {
  System.out.println(IsHyphenatedNumber("123-45-6789"));
  System.out.println(IsHyphenatedNumber("123-45-break"));
 }
```

This test is so simple that there isn't any excuse for not writing it in and running the test to make sure it works. It's also important to update your white-box testing code to reflect any additional changes in the code.

Another important concept in white-box testing design is to demonstrate that certain input can cause the program to log an error and recover or fail gracefully. Ideally, this should take place within every Java class, but it is often necessary to test the channels of communication between classes. For example, a Connection factory class with too short a timeout will cause dependent JavaBeans to appear hung up. You'll learn more about the Connection factory approach with the ConnectionManager class in Chapter 10, "Advanced Database Programming."

Putting It All Together

Our sample application shows how a user can enter information that is then validated by a UserInfo JavaBean. The UserInfo.jsp, shown in Figure 5.1, allows a user to enter information that is then posted to the CheckUserInfo JSP.

Listing 5.1: UserInfo.jsp

```
<HTML>
<BODY>
<H3>Please Enter User Info</H3>
(red asterisk indicates required field)<BR>
<FORM ACTION="CheckUserInfo.jsp" METHOD="POST">
<TABLE>
<TR><TD>
```

```
First Name</TD><TD><INPUT NAME="firstName" VALUE="">
</TD></TR>
<TR><TD>
Last Name</TD><TD><INPUT NAME="lastName" VALUE="">
</TD></TR>
<TR><TD>
User Email  <font color="red">*</font></TD><TD>
  <INPUT NAME="userEmail" VALUE="" SIZE="27">
</TD></TR>
<TR><TD>
Login  <font color="red">*</font></TD><TD>
  <INPUT NAME="login" VALUE="">
</TD></TR>
<TR><TD>
Password  <font color="red">*</font>
  </TD><TD><INPUT NAME="pwd" type="password" VALUE="">
</TD></TR>
<TR><TD>
Social Security Number  
<font color="red">*</font></TD><TD>
<INPUT NAME="ssn" VALUE="">
</TD></TR>
<TR><TD>
Age </TD><TD><INPUT NAME="age" VALUE="" SIZE="5">
</TD></TR>
<TR><TD>
Work Phone  <font color="red">*</font></TD><TD>
     <INPUT NAME="workPhone" VALUE="">
</TD></TR>
</TABLE>
<BR>
Please indicate the languages you speak
<BR>
<input type="checkbox" name="languages"
       value="English">English
<input type="checkbox" name="languages"
       value="Spanish">Spanish
<input type="checkbox" name="languages"
       value="French">French
<input type="checkbox" name="languages"
       value="German">German
<br>
```

```
<br>
<input type="submit" value="Submit">
</FORM>
</BODY>
</HTML>
```

Notice the absence of a `<jsp:useBean>` tag at the top of the UserInfo.jsp listing. Other than the input box naming conventions, there's no trace of JSP; the setup page could just as easily be plain HTML.

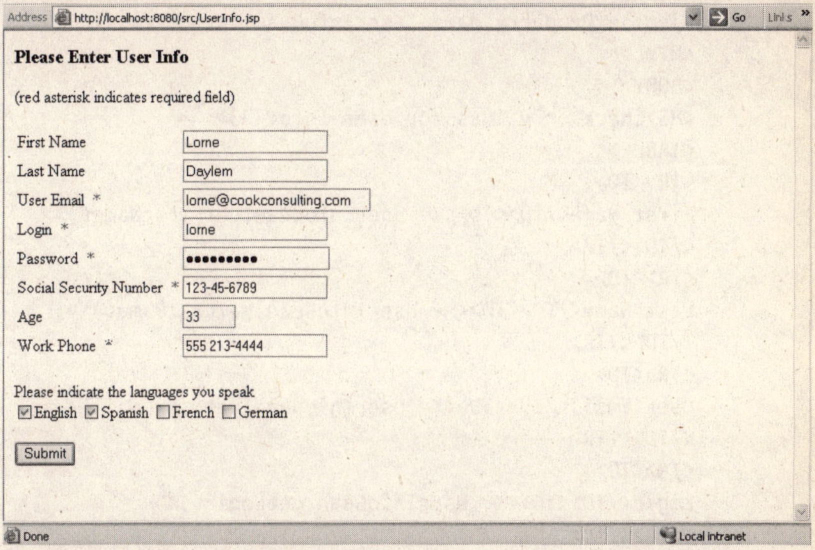

FIGURE 5.1: The UserInfo.jsp form

The CheckUserInfo JSP, shown in Listing 5.2, instantiates a JavaBean that accepts, validates, and processes information for creating a user.

The UserInfoBean is scoped on the request level, and it uses a `<jsp:forward ...>` tag to forward the request to the InsertUser JSP. If the UserInfoBean were scoped on the page level, the insert user operation would fail because the UserInfoBean would be instantiated again on the InsertUser JSP; however, it wouldn't be initialized with the previous values because the CheckUserInfo JSP doesn't send any values in an HTTP POST or GET to populate the newly instantiated page-scoped UserInfoBean. Remember, a page-scoped JavaBean doesn't cache values because its lifespan only lasts for one page.

To use a page-scoped UserInfo JavaBean, the CheckUserInfo page would have to validate the user and then immediately call the `insertUser` member function. A session-scoped bean would retain all the validation code as baggage for the length of the user's session.

Listing 5.2: CheckUserInfo.jsp

```
<jsp:useBean id="UserInfoBean" scope="request"
     class="webbeans.UserInfo" />
<% UserInfoBean.initialize(); %>
<jsp:setProperty name="UserInfoBean" property="*" />
<HTML>
<BODY>
<H3>Check on values for User Info</H3>
<TABLE>
<TR><TD>
First Name</TD><TD><%= UserInfoBean.getFirstName()%>
</TD></TR>
<TR><TD>
Last Name</TD><TD><%= UserInfoBean.getLastName()%>
</TD></TR>
<TR><TD>
User Email</TD><TD><%= UserInfoBean.getUserEmail()%>
</TD></TR>
<TR><TD>
Login</TD><TD><%= UserInfoBean.getLogin()%>
</TD></TR>
<TR><TD>
Password</TD><TD><%= UserInfoBean.getPwdMask()%>
</TD></TR>
<TR><TD>
Social Security Number</TD><TD><%= UserInfoBean.getSsn()%>
</TD></TR>
<TR><TD>
Work Phone</TD><TD><%= UserInfoBean.getWorkPhone()%>
</TD></TR>
</TABLE>
<BR>
<%
if (UserInfoBean.getLanguages(0).length() == 0)
  {
   %>You didn't select any languages.
     Although not required, this will prevent
```

```
        us from sending you documentation in
        multiple languages.<%
    }
  else
    {%>
  You selected the language(s): <%=
  UserInfoBean.getLanguagesAsString() %>
  <%}%>
  <BR>
  <BR>
  <% UserInfoBean.validate();%>
  <%= UserInfoBean.getValidationErrorHTMLMsg()%>
  <%
  if (UserInfoBean.IsValid())
  {
  %>
  <jsp:forward page="InsertUser.jsp" />
  <%
     // instead of using a forward tag with
     // a request scoped bean one could use
     // a session scoped bean with the links below.
     // See the sidebar in the text, Avoiding JavaBean
     // Variable Name Collisions for an explanation
     // of the pros and cons.
  %>
   <input type="button" value="Submit User Info"
   onClick="javascript:window.location.href='InsertUser.jsp'"
    >
   <BR>
   <BR>
   <a href="InsertUser.jsp">or click here to Submit your User
      Info</a>
  <%
  }
  %>
  </BODY>
  </HTML>
```

Notice the use of `getPwdMask` as well as the inline validation. When using UserInfo as a request scoped JavaBean, a successful series of inputs forwards the request directly to the InsertUser JSP. For illustration purposes, we've changed UserInfo to a session-scoped JavaBean (by removing the `<jsp:forward ...>` tag) so that we can see how a successful series of inputs is displayed, as shown in Figure 5.2.

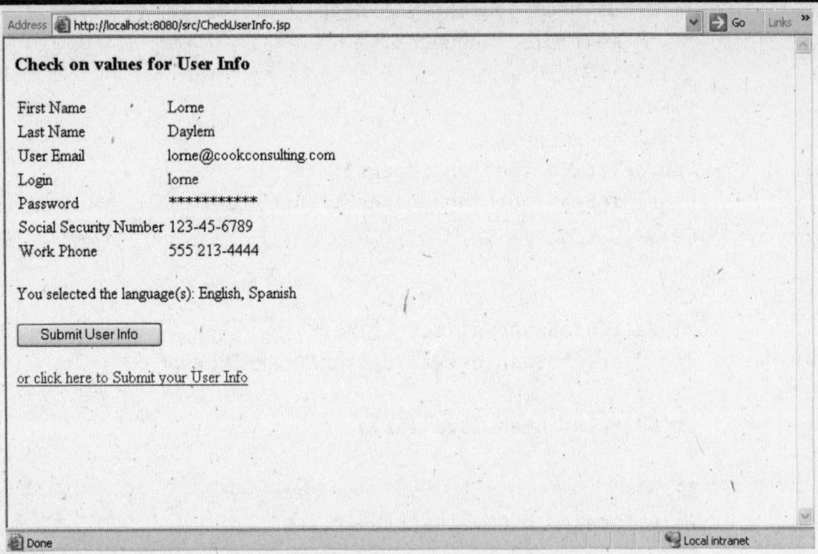

FIGURE 5.2: CheckUserInfo.jsp displays the processing results of the UserInfoBean as a session-scoped JavaBean.

If the user information passes the validation test, the user can submit the entry to a page that will then process the results. The InsertUser JSP is shown in Listing 5.3.

Listing 5.3: InsertUser.jsp

```
<jsp:useBean id="UserInfoBean" scope="request"
     class="webbeans.UserInfo" />
<html>
<head>
<title>
InsertUser
</title>
</head>
<body>
<h1>
Insert User
</h1>
<% if (UserInfoBean.InsertUser())
   {
  %>Your information has been entered. Thank you.
<% }
```

```
else
{
%>There was a problem processing your request. Please try
  again later.<%
}%>
</body>
</html>
```

Listing 5.3 produces this result:

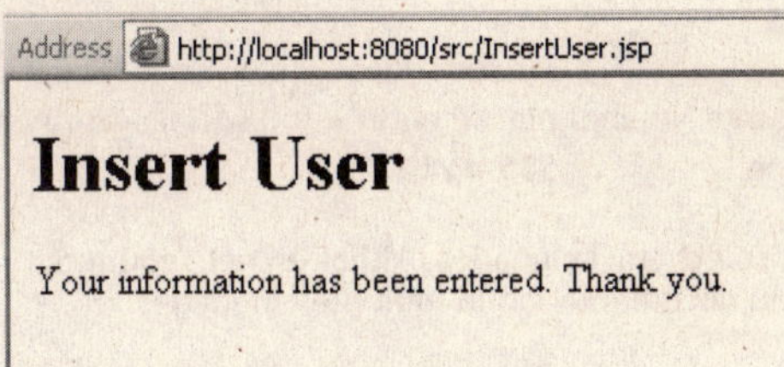
Address http://localhost:8080/src/InsertUser.jsp
Insert User
Your information has been entered. Thank you.

Likewise, Figure 5.3 shows incorrect information being entered into the UserInfo JSP:

Address http://localhost:8080/src/UserInfo.jsp

Please Enter User Info

(red asterisk indicates required field)

First Name Test
Last Name
User Email * test_at_.yahoo.com
Login * Test
Password * ••
Social Security Number * 123456789
Age
Work Phone * 555-1212

Please indicate the languages you speak
English Spanish French German

Submit

FIGURE 5.3: Incorrect information entered as input to the UserInfoBean

The UserInfo JavaBean returns error information to the CheckUserInfo page, as shown in Figure 5.4.

Check on values for User Info

First Name	Test
Last Name	
User Email	test_at_yahoo.com
Login	Test
Password	please choose a password longer than four characters
Social Security Number	please enter a full social security number as: ###-##-####
Work Phone	555-1212

You didn't select any languages. Although not required, this will prevent us from sending you documentation in multiple languages.

Please enter a valid email.

Your phone number must include the area code.

Please enter only numbers or hyphens for social security or phone numbers.

Please choose a password longer than four characters.

FIGURE 5.4: The CheckUserInfo.jsp page shows the error feedback created by the UserInfoBean.

Notice the absence of the Submit button; the application does not allow users to mistakenly enter illegal values in the database. The heart of the sample application is the UserInfo JavaBean, shown in Listing 5.4.

Listing 5.4: UserInfo.java

```
package webbeans;

public class UserInfo
 {
  private String firstName ="";
  private String lastName ="";
  private String userEmail ="";
  private String login ="";
  protected String pwd ="";
  private String ssn ="";
  private String workPhone ="";
  private String [] languages = {""};
```

```
 private String age ="";
 private String hTMLErrorMessage ="";
 private String pwdMask ="";
 private boolean bIsValid = false;

public UserInfo ()
 {}

public void UserInfo (String strLogin, String strPwd)
 {
 login = strLogin;
 pwd = strPwd;
 }

/**
 *   Get/Set Property functions
 */

public synchronized void setLogin (String strLogin)
 {
    if (strLogin != null)
         login = strLogin.trim();
    else
         login = "";
 }

public synchronized String getLogin ()
 {
    return login;
 }

public synchronized void setPwd (String strPwd)
 {
    if (strPwd != null)
         pwd = strPwd.trim();
    else
         pwd = "";
 }

private synchronized String getPwd ()
 {
    return pwd;
 }
```

```
public synchronized String getPwdMask()
 {
     switch (pwd.length())
     {
     case 0:
     return "please choose a password";
     // most efficient form,
     // note lack of break; statments
     case 1:
     case 2:
     case 3:
     case 4:
     return "please choose a password"
             + " longer than four characters";
     default:
     return "***********";
     }
 }

public synchronized void setFirstName (String
                                       newFirstName)
 {
   if ( newFirstName != null)
       firstName = newFirstName.trim();
   else
       firstName="";
 }

public synchronized String getFirstName ()
 {
  // for data access
    return firstName;
 }

public synchronized void setLastName (String
                                     newLastName)
 {
   if ( newLastName == null)
       lastName="";
   else
       lastName = newLastName.trim();
 }
```

```
public synchronized String getLastName()
 {
    return lastName;
 }

public synchronized void setUserEmail(
                                  String newUserEmail)
 {
   if ( newUserEmail != null)
       userEmail = newUserEmail.trim();
   else
       userEmail ="";
 }

public synchronized String getUserEmail()
 {
    return userEmail;
 }


public synchronized void setSsn(String strSsn)
 {
     if (strSsn == null)
         ssn = "";
     else
           ssn = strSsn;
 }

/**
 *  @return error message if an invalid
 *  social security number was asssigned
 */

public synchronized String getSsn ()
 {
     if (ssn.length() < 11)
        return "please enter a full social security"
               +" number as: ###-##-####";
     else
        return ssn;
 }
```

```
public synchronized String getSsnMasked ()
 {
   return ("xxx-xx-" + ssn.substring(8,11));
 }

public synchronized void setWorkPhone (String
                                           strWorkPhone)
 {
   workPhone = strWorkPhone;
 }

public synchronized String getWorkPhone ()
 {
   if ( workPhone == null)
      return "";
   else
      return workPhone.trim();
 }

public synchronized void setAge (String strAge)
 {
   age = strAge;
 }

public synchronized String getAge ()
 {
   if ( age == null)
      return "";
   else
      return age.trim();
 }

public synchronized void setValid ( boolean bValid )
 {
      bIsValid = bValid;
 }

public synchronized boolean IsValid ()
 {
    return bIsValid;
 }
```

```
public synchronized void setLanguages (String []
                                       strLanguages )
 {
   languages = strLanguages;
 }

public synchronized String[] getLanguages ()
 {
   if ( languages == null)
      return (new String [] {"", ""});
       //prevents error from being thrown
       // when not populated
   else
      return languages;
 }

public synchronized String getLanguagesAsString ()
 {
   if ( languages == null)
      return "";
   else
     {
      String AllLanguages ="";
     for (int ii = 0; ii < languages.length; ii++)
       {
       AllLanguages += languages[ii];
       AllLanguages += ", ";
       }
      return AllLanguages.substring(0,
                  AllLanguages.lastIndexOf(","));
     }
 }

public synchronized void setLanguages (int i,
                                 String strLanguage)
 {
   languages[i] = strLanguage;
 }

public synchronized String getLanguages (
                                 int iLanguageNumber)
 {
```

```
    if ( languages[iLanguageNumber] == null)
       return "";
    else
       return languages[iLanguageNumber];
  }

/**
 *  Procesing code
 */

 public synchronized void initialize()
  {
    firstName ="";
    lastName ="";
    userEmail ="";
    login ="";
    pwd ="";
    ssn ="";
    workPhone ="";
    languages = new String [] {""};
    age ="";
  }

 public void validate ()
  {
    hTMLErrorMessage = "";
    setValid(true);
    if ( (userEmail.length() < 5)
         || ( userEmail.indexOf("@") == -1) )
      {
        setValid(false);
        hTMLErrorMessage +=
         "<br>Please enter a valid email.<br>";
      }
    if (!CheckUnique (login))
      {
        setValid(false);
        hTMLErrorMessage += "<br>Please choose another"
        + " user name that one is already taken.<br>";
        // TO DO: modify username with
        // random number generation appendage
      }
    if (workPhone.length() < 10)
```

```
      {
       setValid(false);
       hTMLErrorMessage += "<br>Your phone number"
       + " must include the area code.<br>";
      }
    if (!BeanTools.IsHyphenatedNumber(getSsn()) )
      {
       setValid(false);
       hTMLErrorMessage += "<br>Please enter only numbers"
       + " or hyphens for social security "
       + " or phone numbers.<br>";
      }
    if (pwd.length() < 4)
      {
       setValid(false);
       hTMLErrorMessage += "<br>Please choose a password"
       + " longer than four characters.<br>";
      }
 }

public String getValidationErrorHTMLMsg()
 {
    return hTMLErrorMessage;
 }

private boolean CheckUnique (String strLogin)
{
 // call db and check to see
 // if login name already exists
   return true;
}

public synchronized boolean InsertUser()
 {
  if (!IsValid())
      return false;
    try
    {
    StringBuffer sbUser = new StringBuffer (
                 "insert into tusers values ('");
    sbUser.append(firstName);
    sbUser.append("', '");
    sbUser.append( lastName );
```

```
        sbUser.append("', '");
        sbUser.append( userEmail );
        sbUser.append("', '");
        sbUser.append( login );
        sbUser.append("', '");
        sbUser.append( pwd );
        sbUser.append("', '");
        sbUser.append( ssn );
        sbUser.append("', '");
        sbUser.append( workPhone );
        sbUser.append("', '");
        sbUser.append( age );
        sbUser.append("', '");
        sbUser.append( getLanguagesAsString() );
        sbUser.append("') ");
        System.out.println( sbUser.toString() );
        //  ConnectionManager.execInsert( sb.toString());
        // implemented in the Database chapter
        return true;
        }
        catch (Exception e)
        {
        System.out.println("Error in Insert User");
        }
      return false;
    }

      /**
        *  White box testing for this class is perhaps
        *   best done from JSPs designed for testing
        */

   public static void main (String[] args)
    {
      System.out.println("main() self test not implemented");
    }
  }
```

The BeanTools utility class referenced earlier in the text is shown in Listing 5.5. Although designed to be a general utility class for common data validation routines, it currently has only one function that checks a string to see if it's a hyphenated number. The `IsHyphenatedNumber` member function strips out hyphens from the string parameter, and the resulting string is used to construct a number. If the string contains any alphabetic characters, the test will fail. Because social security numbers cannot contain alphabetic characters, the method is an appropriate test for social security numbers.

Listing 5.5: BeanTool.java

```
package webbeans;

public class BeanTools
{
  public synchronized static boolean
       IsHyphenatedNumber(String strNum)
  {
   strNum = strNum.trim();
    //System.out.println("strNum=" + strNum);
    while (strNum.lastIndexOf("-") > -1 )
      {
      int iPos = strNum.indexOf("-");
      strNum = strNum.substring(0, iPos)
               + strNum.substring(iPos + 1);
      // System.out.println("strNum="+strNum);
      }
      try
      {
       new Integer(strNum);
      }
      catch (Exception e)
      {
      System.out.println ("problem in IsHyphenatedNumber
                  with value" + strNum);
      return false;
      }
  return true;
  }

  public static void main (String[] args)
  {
   System.out.println(IsHyphenatedNumber("123-45-6789"));
   System.out.println(IsHyphenatedNumber("123-45-break"));
  }
}
```

This utility class demonstrates white-box testing. As a bean, its main method is not normally executed, but it's there to allow developers to test it and to show which values and ranges the methods support. The simple self-testing function demonstrates that the class actually does what it promises to with a piece of sample data. To understand this utility class and see what's going on, uncomment the `System.out.println` debug lines, compile it, place it in your classpath, and execute it.

Good Practices with JavaBeans

Good practices separate simple data validation from extensive checking, limit the generation of HTML, and work together to keep the user from entering incorrect data or making a mistake.

It's almost always a good practice to avoid generating HTML within a JavaBean. If the developer can't resist, they should at least restrict the generation of HTML to clearly labeled methods, and they should make an effort to avoid potential problem areas, namely:

- Don't ever put any font sizes in the HTML returned from a Java. Not all browsers are the same, and many instances can't handle the full range of font sizes (for example, font size 14 on a wireless phone display).
- Don't ever put any script or DHTML into the HTML returned from a JavaBean. Exporting script or DHTML straight to a page is suicidal because some browser versions actually crash on incorrectly formed scripts—rare, but nonetheless possible.

When writing classes be sure to add self-testing functions that prove that the class solves the problem for which it was originally designed, or behaves the way it should. By doing this, you can be confident that the code you have isolated for reuse will perform as it should or at least raise warnings if anything has been changed. This will help strengthen all the building blocks of your future applications.

Last, session-scoped beans can display buggy behavior by cacheing values that aren't cleared out when a user zeroes out information and resubmits the form. There are three workarounds for this:

- Use an initialize function.
- Use hidden text inputs and form submission.
- Add client-side JavaScript to add a space to values (which is then trimmed in well-written `get/setProperty` methods).

All effect a change in the data state, and force an update on the member variables.

What's Next

JavaBeans extend the flexibility and functionality of JSP pages by encapsulating code for reuse. JavaBeans have grown from being simple containers for reusable components to being the standard scaffolding for Enterprise JavaBeans.

A JavaBean requires a no-arguments constructor, support for a multi-threaded environment by using the `synchronize` keyword wherever data needs to be protected from multiple requests, and support for being externalizable by implementing serializable or externalizable. Most important, a JavaBean must expose properties by declaring them public.

Several design considerations enter into the construction of Java-Beans. Data integrity is provided by the multithreaded protection mechanisms, and data security comes from displaying passwords and social security numbers as masked fields. JavaBeans should also take responsibility for data management. They can do so by preparing SQL statements to be executed by a helper class, such as a ConnectionFactory. It's also important to be aware of the differences between java null and SQL null.

JavaBeans can be declared with different scopes: from the page/request duration, which is good only for the processing of one hop (an input page leading directly to an output page), to the use of session-scope beans, which cache values for the scope of a user's session.

Handling properties goes beyond the common sense naming of the properties, and includes the responsibility for coding functions that help manage and manipulate complex HTML constructions such as the indexed properties of optional arrays. The Presentation layer can utilize helper functions for displaying indexed properties as a flat string.

JavaBeans can interact with users on a visual level by hooking into events and providing hooks to other beans on both the client and the server side. The framework is available for a full range of interaction, including the ability to hook into session events.

The last few chapters have demonstrated a wide range of techniques need for web application development in servlets and JSP pages. One question that has not been answered yet is how we can save client session state. Most complex web applications require that the servlets and JSP pages be aware of actions the user took on previous servlets and JSP pages. This is problematic since HTTP is inherently a stateless protocol. The next chapter will explore different options for overcoming this obstacle such as cookies, URL rewriting, hidden form fields, and the Java Session API.

Chapter 6
Session Management

Imagine having a conversation with a person who was unable to remember what you just said. At first, you might find this interesting; however, soon your amusement would turn to irritation as they continually asked you to repeat yourself. This is the scenario servlets would encounter if their data could not be temporarily cached during a conversation with a web application. When a client accesses a web application, they often supply information that will be used by the application at a later period during the conversation. If this information could not be retained, the application would need to ask for the information again. This is both time-consuming and inefficient. A servlet's session object is used to resolve this issue. Sessions provide various ways to monitor and maintain client data.

Knowledge of how the session works will help you manage a session object more efficiently. This chapter will begin by discussing the various ways to track a session.

Adapted from *Java™ 2 Web Developer Certification Study Guide*, Second Edition by Natalie Levi

ISBN 0-7821-4202-8 $59.99

Featured in this chapter:

- Track a client's session
- Change a session's data
- Respond to the creation or destruction of a session object and its attributes
- Invalidate a session

Tracking Sessions

When a client interacts with a server application, that client is likely to make multiple requests to achieve a particular goal. Because the HTTP protocol is stateless, it closes its connection after each request. Consequently, client data stored within a request is available for only a short period of time. For a client object with a longer lifespan, a session is used. A *session object* is usually created when a client makes its first request to an application. It is unique to a client: It can exist longer than a single request, or even longer than the life of a client. It is an object used to track client-specific data for the duration of the conversation or a specified period of time. What distinguishes one session from another is its unique ID. In fact, the container uses this ID to map an incoming request to the correct session object, which in turn is associated to a particular client. The actual client information can be transferred by using one of three session processes:

- Using hidden form fields
- Rewriting the URL
- Using cookies

This focus in this section will be to discuss the many ways to maintain a session object, and will begin by addressing how to transfer a session ID by using a form attribute type called `hidden`.

Using Hidden Form Fields

Transferring information between an HTML form and a servlet can be done in several ways. The most basic procedure is to transfer information back and forth as data values. A form can contain fields with client-cached values passed between each request. Because this information does not need to be visible to the client, it is marked by using a field type of `hidden`.

Imagine the following web application scenario:

1. A login screen is displayed.
2. The user enters their login name and password.
3. The servlet verifies the information and returns a web page for the client to utilize the company's services.
4. The new page stores the client's login name from the previous servlet. This information is not visible to the client, but is needed for checkout purposes.

By using *hidden HTML values*, you can store client data between servlets to use at a later date. The following HTML code produces the login screen used for this scenario:

```
<FORM ACTION='servlet/CarServlet' METHOD='POST'>
  <P>Enter your: </P>
  <P>Login <INPUT TYPE='text' SIZE='18' NAME='login'></P>
  <P>Password <INPUT TYPE='password' SIZE='15'
                   NAME='pwd'></P>

  <P><INPUT TYPE='submit' VALUE='GO!' NAME='button'> </P>
  </FORM>
```

After the user enters their login name and password, they trigger the request by clicking the Submit button. The servlet then verifies the information and constructs a response containing the client's information. The following code shows this process. Pay particularly close attention to the bold text. It highlights how hidden values are transferred.

```
public class CarServlet extends HttpServlet {
  public void doPost(HttpServletRequest req,
                   HttpServletResponse res)
   throws ServletException, IOException {
    String login = req.getParameter("login");
    String pwd = req.getParameter("pwd");
      ...
    //verify login and password with database
    //Use database to get customer information like
    //their firstName, lastName, address

    Customer cust = db.getCustomer(login);
    String firstName=cust.getFirstName();
    String lastName=cust.getLastName();
    String address=cust.getAddress();
```

```
        res.setContentType("text/html");
        PrintWriter out = res.getWriter();
        ...
        //generate HTML form containing car characteristics
        ...
        out.println("<FORM ACTION=
                'CheckOutServlet' METHOD='POST'>");
         out.println("<INPUT TYPE='hidden' NAME='loginName'
                VALUE='"+ login + "'>");
         out.println("<INPUT TYPE='hidden' NAME='firstName'
                VALUE='" + firstName + "'>");
         out.println("<INPUT TYPE='hidden' NAME='lastName'
                VALUE='" + lastName + "'>");
         out.println("<INPUT TYPE='hidden' NAME='address'
                VALUE='" + address + "'>");
         ...
         out.println("<INPUT TYPE='submit' VALUE='CheckOut'>");
    }
}
```

The CarServlet creates an HTML form response containing four hidden values. Each value is assigned a specific piece of client information. By clicking the Submit button, the user triggers a request to check out. This request is sent to the CheckOutServlet, which retrieves hidden values by using the ServletRequest method getParameter(*String name*).

```
public class CheckOutServlet extends HttpServlet {
    public void doPost(HttpServletRequest req,
                       HttpServletResponse res)
        throws ServletException, IOException {

        String loginName = req.getParameter("loginName");
        String address = req.getParameter("address");
        res.setContentType("text/html");
        PrintWriter out = res.getWriter();
        out.println("<HTML><BODY>");
        out.println("<P> Thanks for your order " +
                            loginName + "</P>");
        out.println("<P> Your invoice will be mailed to:
                    </P>");
        out.println("<P><I>" + address + "</I><P>");
    }
}
```

Figure 6.1 shows the hidden value output.

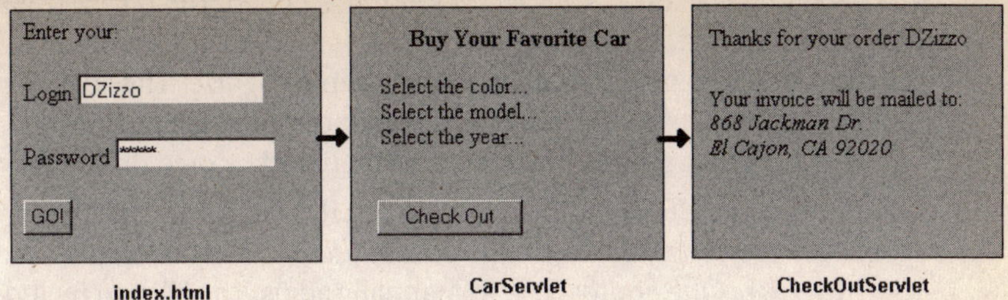

FIGURE 6.1: Hidden value output

Hidden values provide a way to transfer data to the server in a manner that prevents the client from modifying the information directly. Typically, the client does not even know the data is being sent back and forth. The disadvantages to this approach are as follows:

- Tracking each hidden value in each servlet can become tedious. Unfortunately, as the session persists and information increases, passing hidden data back and forth can become taxing.
- The session can persist only through dynamically generated pages. If there is a need to display static, e-mail, or bookmarked documents, the session will be lost.
- Hidden value transfers are the least secure method of maintaining information between pages. Because HTTP transfers all data as clear text, it can be intercepted, extracted, and manipulated. If someone were watching the transmission between client and server, they could easily read information such as the login ID and password.

Although there are many disadvantages, it is a simple approach that can be used when you are communicating a small amount of noncritical information.

Rewriting the URL

Anonymous session tracking can also be done using a technique called URL rewriting. This approach to session tracking is used when clients do not accept cookies (cookies will be discussed in the next section). *URL rewriting* is a methodology that associates a session ID to all URL addresses used throughout the session. Using the ID, a developer can map client-related data to the session object for that client. The ID is temporarily stored until the session has ended. After the session has ended, the ID and related data are discarded. Keep in mind that it is important for the session ID to have a standard name that all containers can recognize. The specification defines that name as `jsessionid`. A standardized name enables the container to associate requests to their session objects stored on the server.

Rewriting the URL to contain the session ID enables any related servlet to extract previously tracked data. There are two methodologies used to rewrite a URL. One approach is to manually adjust the URL to include the session ID; the other approach is to use provided API methods to encode the URL. Both techniques will be covered in detail.

Manual URL Rewriting

Manually rewriting a URL can be done by physically adding the ID to the constructed URL. How the ID is stored and accessed from within the URL can vary. Table 6.1 lists several ways to rewrite the URL.

TABLE 6.1: URL-Rewriting Approaches

URL	State
`http://localhost:8080/servlet/MyServlet`	Original
`http://localhost:8080/servlet/MyServlet/567`	Extra path information
`http://localhost:8080/servlet/MyServlet?jsessionid=567`	Add parameter
`http://localhost:8080/servlet/MyServlet;jsessionid=567`	Custom change

The first example in Table 6.1 shows the original path. The second approach adds the session ID to the path directly. This approach works on all servers, but isn't very effective when other information must also be added to the path of the URL. The third approach adds the ID as a parameter. To avoid naming collisions and guarantee automatic mapping, the session ID must be called `jsessionid`. The last approach uses a custom, server-specific change that works for servers that support this technique; however, even custom approaches are required to name the parameter `jsessionid`.

This section will show you how to rewrite the URL by adding a session ID to the URL path, but how the ID is generated is discussed first. The goal is to derive a value that is completely random and not shared. The Remote Method Invocation (RMI) API provides several methods that help develop such a method. The common procedure is to create a method that does the following:

```
public static String generateSessionID(){
    String uid = new java.rmi.server.UID().toString();
    return java.net.URLEncoder.encode(uid);
}
```

The `UID` class is used to create a unique identifier on the host system generating this value. For further complexity, the value is converted into MIME-type format by using the `URLEncoder`'s `encode(`*`String uid`*`)` method. Fundamentally, the goal is achieved; when called, this method generates a unique ID that can be used by a session on the existing system.

You're now ready to learn how to rewrite the URL to contain the session ID. Begin by revisiting the URL structure:

```
Request URL = contextPath + servletPath + pathInfo + query string
```

Given a request URL of `/games/Chess`, you can break the pieces into their defined categories:

Context path: `/games`

Servlet path: `/Chess`

Path info: `/null`

Query string: `/null`

If you had a session ID with the value `567`, that ID could be incorporated into the URL by adding it to the path info section, as follows:

```
/games/Chess/567
```

Literally, this can be done by concatenating the session ID to the `ACTION` value's URL. For example:

```
out.println("<FORM ACTION='/games/Bingo/"
        + sessionID + "' METHOD='POST'>");
out.println("<INPUT TYPE='submit' VALUE='Bingo'>");
```

Say the current servlet that is running is called `/games/Overview`. On the page, there is a button with the text Bingo. When the button is clicked, the current URL is switched to `/games/Bingo/567`. This new servlet page provides the session ID within the URL, which enables the developer to extract any data stored from previously accessed servlets. To access the session ID, use the `HttpServletRequest` method `getPathInfo()`. This method returns extraneous information between the servlet and the query string. The new servlet can then use utility classes to retrieve data associated with the session ID. Generally, you would expect to have a utility class for writing data and its associated session ID to a location. The class should also provide functionality to retrieve the client data based on a unique session ID. You might expect the class to contain methods similar to those listed here:

```
Import java.sql.*;
public class SessionIDUtility {
   public static String generateSessionID(){
      String uid = new java.rmi.server.UID().toString();
      return java.net.URLEncoder.encode(uid);
   }
   public static void writeSessionValue(Connection con,
            String sessionID, String name, String value) {
      // write record to database for the provided
      // sessionID
   }
   public static String[] getSessionValues(
            Connection con, String sessionID) {
      //returns the values associated to the provided
      //sessionID
   }
  public static Object getSessionValue(
            Connection con, String sessionID, String name) {
      // returns the Object associated to the name
      // for a particular session ID
   }
}
```

Given these methods, a servlet could save current data and retrieve it from any other servlet accessed during the session. Figure 6.2 shows a simple application that begins by asking the user for their name. A session ID is generated to store the name for other servlets in the application to access. When the user selects a game of choice, the new servlet accesses the session information by retrieving the ID and then getting the user's name. The application should appear as shown in Figure 6.2.

The first image is a simple HTML page that asks the user for their name. When the Begin button is clicked, the `/games/OverviewServlet` is accessed and displays two game options. Before going into the functionality details, take a look at the source code for these files. Listing 6.1 displays the HTML code necessary to launch the initial program.

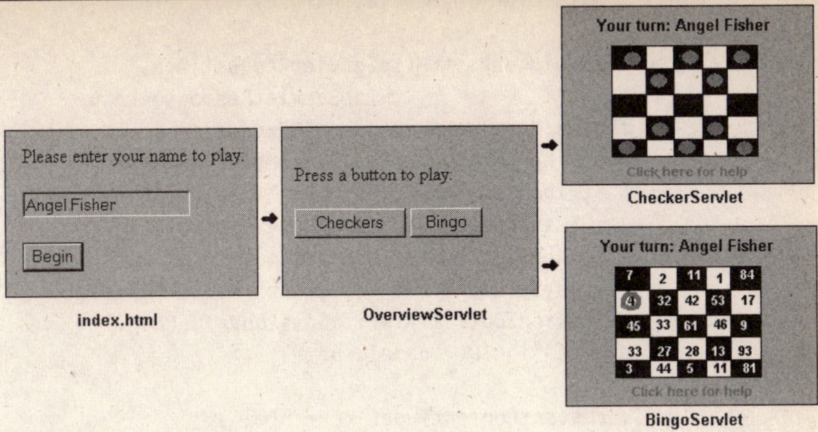

FIGURE 6.2: Sample URL-rewriting application

Listing 6.1: index.html

```
<HTML>
    <HEAD><TITLE>Welcome to the Game Center</TITLE></HEAD>
    <BODY>
        <FORM ACTION='servlet/OverviewServlet'
              METHOD='POST'>
            <P>Please enter your name to play: </P>
            <P><INPUT TYPE='text' SIZE='20'
                      NAME='name'></P>
            <P><INPUT TYPE='submit' VALUE='Begin'
                      NAME='button'></P>
        </FORM>
    </BODY>
</HTML>
```

The file `index.html` simply provides a form for the user to submit their name. When a request is triggered, the `OverviewServlet` is invoked. The code for this class is shown in Listing 6.2.

Listing 6.2: OverviewServlet.java

```
import javax.servlet.*;
import javax.servlet.http.*;
import java.io.*;
import java.util.*;
import java.sql.*;
```

```
public class OverviewServlet extends HttpServlet {

    public void doPost(HttpServletRequest req,
                        HttpServletResponse res)
        throws ServletException, IOException {
          String name = req.getParameter("name");
          String sessionID =
            SessionIDUtility.generateSessionID();
          Connection con = (Connection)
            getServletContext().getAttribute("Connection");
          SessionIDUtility.writeSessionValue(con,
            sessionID, "name", name);

          res.setContentType("text/html");
          PrintWriter out = res.getWriter();
          out.println("<HTML><BODY>");
          out.println("<H1>The Game Center</H1>");
          out.println("<P>Press a button to play:</P>");

          out.println("<FORM ACTION=' CheckersServlet/" +
            sessionID + "' Method='POST'>");
          out.println("<INPUT TYPE='submit' VALUE=" +
             "'Checkers'></FORM>");
          out.println("<FORM ACTION='/games/BingoServlet/" +
           sessionID + "' Method='POST'>");
          out.println("<INPUT TYPE='submit' VALUE='Bingo'>");
          out.println("</FORM></BODY></HTML>");
    }
}
```

Listing 6.2 shows how the servlet prepares to rewrite the URL. The user's name is acquired and then a unique session ID is generated for that particular user. A preassigned connection is accessed from the `ServletContext` and used to write the session ID and name to a local database. Finally, the page is generated with each button linked to a different URL including the session ID. If the user selects Bingo, they will access the `BingoServlet`. Listing 6.3 displays the code for this class.

Listing 6.3: BingoServlet.java

```
import javax.servlet.*;
import javax.servlet.http.*;
import java.io.*;
```

```
import java.util.*;
import java.sql.*;

public class BingoServlet extends HttpServlet {
   public void doPost(HttpServletRequest req,
                              HttpServletResponse res)
      throws ServletException, IOException {
         String sessionID = req.getPathInfo();
         String userName="";
         if (sessionID == null) {
            // Redirect the user back to the login screen.
            // If a session ID is null, it indicates the
            // user has not logged into the system.
         }

         Connection con = (Connection)
           getServletContext().getAttribute("Connection");
         userName = (String)SessionIDUtility.getSessionValue(
           con, sessionID, "name");

         res.setContentType("text/html");
         PrintWriter out = res.getWriter();
         out.println("<HTML><BODY>");
         out.println("<H1>Your turn: " + userName +
                   "</H1>");
         // generate the bingo game


         out.println("For help, click " +
            "<A HREF='Help/'+ sessionID +
            "?rules=Bingo'>Click here for help</A>");
         out.println("</FORM></BODY></HTML>");
   }
}
```

Listing 6.3 shows how the servlet accesses the session ID from the URL path by using the request method `getPathInfo()`. Remember, this method returns the path information listed after the servlet path and before the query string. A connection to the associated database is acquired, and the session ID is used to extract data associated with the current user. After the `name` value is obtained, it is incorporated into the Bingo page. Finally, a hyperlink is used to provide help; it too contains the session ID value, in case the Help servlet needs the session-related user data.

Using Methods to Encode the URL

Instead of manually generating a session ID and physically adding it to the URL, the API provides methods that manage the task for the developer. The `HttpServletResponse` class offers the following two methods:

- `public String encodeURL(java.lang.String url)`
- `public String encodeRedirectURL(java.lang.String url)`

The `encodeURL(...)` method rewrites the specified URL to include a session ID if needed. If one is not needed, the method returns the original URL. An unchanged URL can result from a server that does not support URL rewriting or from a server that has the feature turned off. As for the semantics of how the URL is encoded, that feature or technique is server-specific. In general, it is good practice to have all URLs emitted by a servlet run through this method to ensure application-wide access to the session ID.

The second method is similar to the first in that it, too, encodes the passed-in URL by adding the session ID. It differs, however, in when it is used. At times there is a need for a servlet to temporarily redirect a response to a different location. This is done by using the `HttpServletResponse`'s method `sendRedirect(`*`String url`*`)`. Before calling this method, the URL should be encoded by using a method specifically designed to handle URL encoding for a redirected response: `encodeRedirectURL(`*`String url`*`)`. The reason for using a different method is that a redirect URL is different from a normal URL. For a *redirect URL*, all non-ASCII values must be converted to their hexadecimal values; this includes ampersands and equal signs. For a normal URL, the ampersands and equal signs do not need to be converted to hexadecimal format. This distinction is critical and necessary for the `sendRedirect(...)` method to work. The following is an example of a rewritten URL:

```
http://localhost:8080/servlet/OverviewServlet;
jsessionid=4347
```

To encode links in your URL, you must make slight modifications to the HTML code. Here is an example of how to rewrite the URL to include an encoded URL in a form:

```
String urlSession = res.encodeURL("servlet/OveriewServlet");
out.println("<FORM ACTION='" + urlSession + "'" +
                  " METHOD='POST'>");
```

```
out.println("<INPUT TYPE='submit' VALUE='Exit'>");
out.println("</FORM></BODY></HTML>");
```

If your intent is to encode a URL for a link, you simply include an encoded String instead of the standard URL:

```
out.println("Click " +
  "<A HREF='"+ res.encodeURL("servlet/OverviewServlet") +
  "'>here</A>");
```

For the container to encode the URL with a session ID, three conditions usually exist:

- The browser supports URL encoding.
- The browser does not support cookies.
- The session tracking feature is turned on.

When using the encodeURL(...) method, the session ID is stored as a path parameter. As such, you must call req.getPathInfo() to retrieve the ID value.

NOTE

You can also access the ID by calling req.getSession() to acquire a handle to the actual session object, assuming one exists. Using the session instance, the ID value can then be accessed by calling session.getId(). This object is covered in more detail in the upcoming "Using the HttpSession Object" section.

The servlet can also use the following HttpServletRequest methods to learn more about the methodology used to generate the ID, as well as its validity:

- public boolean isRequestedSessionIdFromCookie()
- public boolean isRequestedSessionIdFromURL()
- public boolean isRequestedSessionIdValid()

These methods validate the session object and its place of origin. If the session is not valid, the servlet can redirect the user to a new screen to log in again. If the session ID was obtained from the URL, the servlet might opt to perform a different task than if it was obtained from a cookie.

Using Cookies

Another way to perform session tracking is through persistent cookies. Remember, a *cookie* is an object containing small amounts of information sent by a servlet to a web browser, then saved by the browser, and later sent back to the server. Because the cookie's value can uniquely identify a client and maintain client data, using cookies is an optimal way to track sessions.

A cookie is created by using two parameters: a name and a value. The constructor is as follows:

```
public Cookie(String name, String value)
```

Unlike a hidden value, which must exist in all servlet pages, a cookie is added to the servlet's response object, and is propagated to all servlets accessed during the session.

TIP

The servlet specification mandates that the name of the value used to track the session for a cookie must be called `JSESSIONID`.

NOTE

The ID name must be all uppercase when used within a cookie, but lowercase when used in URL rewriting.

A cookie can be added to an `HttpServletResponse` object in the following way:

```
Cookie cookie = new Cookie("JSESSIONID", "567");
res.addCookie(cookie);
```

If another servlet is interested in accessing this information, it can call the `getCookies()` method of the `HttpServletRequest` class:

```
public Cookie[] getCookies()
```

Using the example from the preceding "Rewriting the URL" section, you can create a cookie to add the session ID. Listing 6.4 demonstrates how to use cookies to rewrite the `OverviewServlet`.

Listing 6.4: Using Cookies with the OverviewServlet

```
import javax.servlet.*;
import javax.servlet.http.*;
import java.io.*;
import java.util.*;
```

```
public class OverviewServlet extends HttpServlet {
   public void doPost(HttpServletRequest req,
                      HttpServletResponse res)
     throws ServletException, IOException {
      String name = req.getParameter("name");
      String sessionID =
         SessionIDUtility.generateSessionID();
      Cookie cookie = new Cookie("JSESSIONID",
                                 sessionID);
      res.addCookie(cookie);

      res.setContentType("text/html");
      PrintWriter out = res.getWriter();
      out.println("<HTML><BODY>");
      out.println("<H1>The Game Center</H1>");
      out.println("<P>Press a button to play:</P>");

      out.println("<FORM ACTION='/games/Checkers'" +
                  " Method='POST'>");
      out.println("<INPUT TYPE='submit'" +
                  " VALUE='Checkers'></FORM>");
      out.println("<FORM ACTION='/games/BingoServlet'" +
                  " METHOD='POST'>");
        out.println("<INPUT TYPE='submit' VALUE='BINGO'>");
        out.println("</FORM></BODY></HTML>");
   }
}
```

The `BingoServlet` can then use its request object to get all the cookies associated with the session. The modified code would look similar to Listing 6.5.

Listing 6.5: Using Cookies with the BingoServlet

```
import javax.servlet.*;
import javax.servlet.http.*;
import java.io.*;
import java.util.*;
import java.sql.*;

public class BingoServlet extends HttpServlet {
   public void doPost(HttpServletRequest req,
                      HttpServletResponse res)
```

```
        throws ServletException, IOException {
          String sessionID;
          String userName;
          Cookie[] cookies = req.getCookies();
          if (cookies != null) {
            for (int i=0; i<cookies.length; i++) {
               String id = cookies[i].getName();
               if(id.equals("JSESSIONID")) {
                   sessionID = cookies[i].getValue();
                   break;
               }
            }
          }
          Connection con =
            getServletContext().getAttribute("Connection");
          userName =
            (String) SessionIDUtility.getSessionValue(
               con, sessionID, "name");
          res.setContentType("text/html");
          PrintWriter out = res.getWriter();
          out.println("<HTML><BODY>");
          out.println("<H1>Your turn: " + userName +
                      "</H1>");
          // generate the bingo game

          out.println("For help, click " +
             "<A HREF='Help/?rules=Bingo'>" +
             "Click here for help" +
             "</A>");
          out.println("</FORM></BODY></HTML>");
      }
  }
```

In this example, you get all the cookies associated with the request. You filter through each cookie until you come across the one called `JSESSIONID`. By using the assigned ID, the `doPost(...)` method can then use the `getSessionValue(...)` method within the `SessionIDUtility` class to get the user's name. In this example, you could have just added the user's name to the cookie. Instead, we opted to show you the approach using a session ID value because a session usually contains more than one data element. Notice that the hyperlink to the `Help` servlet no longer contains the ID value within its URL. When the `Help` servlet is invoked, it will receive the existing session cookies within its request object.

The final and most convenient way to handle session data is to pass an `HttpSession` object, which implicitly contains the client's data, back and forth between all session-related servlets.

Using the *HttpSession* Object

Ways to track the session object between client/server requests was discussed earlier, where each example (cookie or URL rewriting) used a database for persistent storage of session data. In this section, the `HttpSession` object replaces the database for persistent storage, and uses one of the methods previously discussed to propagate the session ID.

NOTE

Internally, the container determines the method used to transmit the session ID between the client and server (whether it used cookies or URL rewriting).

The servlet creates an `HttpSession` object to maintain data for the entire duration of a transaction. Assuming the client's browser supports session management, an `HttpSession` object is created when the client first accesses a web application. Data can then be written to or retrieved from this object.

WARNING

It is important to understand that a session exists only within its original context. For example, if a servlet uses the `RequestDispatcher` to forward its request to another application, a new session is created that is different from the calling servlet.

To access a session object, use the `HttpServletRequest` method:

```
public HttpSession getSession()
```

The method returns the `HttpSession` object tied to the client requesting the current servlet. If the object does not exist, the `getSession()` method will automatically create a new `HttpSession` instance.

The other method used to access a session object is as follows:

```
public HttpSession getSession(boolean create)
```

This method differs from the previous version in that it requires a `boolean` value:

- A `true` value creates a new session object if one does not already exist.
- A `false` value prevents a session object from being created if one does not exist.

A `false` value is really what distinguishes this method from its overloaded `getSession()` method. Instead of creating a new session without further validation, the developer might want to redirect the user back to a login page before a session is created. Once created, the session object will continue to accumulate stored data until the session is terminated.

Data is stored to an `HttpSession` object as attributes:

```
public void setAttribute(String name, Object value)
```

The `setAttribute(...)` method binds a Java object to a specified key name. Another servlet can then use the `HttpSession` object and access its data by using the following method:

```
public Object getAttribute(String name)
```

The `getAttribute(...)` method uses the key name to find and return the associated object.

Once again, revisit the `OverviewServlet` in Listing 6.4 to see how this approach changes the code. See Listing 6.6.

Listing 6.6: Using an HttpSession Object with the OverviewServlet

```
import javax.servlet.*;
import javax.servlet.http.*;
import java.io.*;
import java.util.*;

public class OverviewServlet extends HttpServlet {
   public void doPost(HttpServletRequest req,
                      HttpServletResponse res)
      throws ServletException, IOException {
        String name = req.getParameter("name");

        HttpSession session = req.getSession();
        session.setAttribute("name", name);

        res.setContentType("text/html");
        PrintWriter out = res.getWriter();
        out.println("<HTML><BODY>");
        out.println("<H1>The Game Center</H1>");
        out.println("<P>Press a button to play:</P>");
```

```
            out.println("FORM ACTION='/games/Checkers'" +
                        " MethodMETHOD='POST'>");
            out.println("<INPUT TYPE='submit' VALUE='" +
                        "Checkers'></FORM>");
            out.println("<FORM ACTION='/games/BingoServlet'" +
                        " MethodMETHOD='POST'>");
            out.println("<INPUT TYPE='submit' VALUE='Bingo'>");
            out.println("</FORM></BODY></HTML>");
      }
   }
```

Using the session object is both a clean and convenient approach to storing client data. The actual session instance is stored at the web application level, whereby each `ServletContext` maintains its own pool of `HttpSession` objects.

TIP

Remember, each application has one `ServletContext`, and each context has multiple sessions for each client that accesses the application.

Retrieving the attributes is as easy as adding them. Listing 6.7 is the `BingoServlet` modified to use the session object either to redirect the user back to a login screen (if the session object is `null`) or to extract client data.

Listing 6.7: Using an HttpSession Object with the BingoServlet

```
import javax.servlet.*;
import javax.servlet.http.*;
import java.io.*;
import java.util.*;

public class BingoServlet extends HttpServlet {
   public void doPost(HttpServletRequest req,
                      HttpServletResponse res)
                throws ServletException, IOException {

      HttpSession session = req.getSession(false);
      if(session == null) {
         ServletContext sc =
           getServletConfig().getServletContext();
         RequestDispatcher disp =
           sc.getRequestDispatcher("/servlet/LoginServlet");
```

```
            disp.forward(req, res);
            return;
        }

        String userName =
          (String)session.getAttribute("name");

        res.setContentType("text/html");
        PrintWriter out = res.getWriter();
        out.println("<HTML><BODY>");
        out.println("<H1>Your turn: " + userName +
                "</H1>");
        // generate the bingo game
...
        out.println("For help, click " +
          "<A HREF='Help/?rules=Bingo'>" +
          " Click here for help</A>");
        out.println("</FORM></BODY></HTML>");
    }
}
```

The preceding example demonstrates two ideas. The first is how a servlet can redirect a request to a login screen if a session does not exist. The second is how a servlet within the same context automatically receives session data acquired from previous servlets. This is shown by using the `getAttribute(...)` method. The key value name is passed as a parameter to access its associated object. Remember, the name value was set by the `OverviewServlet`.

Adding an attribute is as easy as removing one. To unbind an attribute, call the method:

```
public void removeAttribute(String name)
```

After this method is invoked on an attribute, it is no longer accessible by any servlet within the application.

The final method of interest is the one that enables a servlet to list all the attributes associated with the current session:

```
public Enumeration getAttributeNames()
```

The `getAttributeNames()` method returns an `Enumeration` object of all current attributes. If a session has no attributes, a `null` value is returned.

Sometimes there is a need to respond to changes to a session's attributes. The servlet API provides several session listener classes designed specifically for this purpose.

HttpSessionBindingListener

By implementing the `HttpSessionBindingListener`, your application can be notified when an object is bound or unbound to a session object. The interface has two primary methods that must be defined:

- `valueBound(`*`HttpSessionBindingEvent event`*`)`
- `valueUnbound(`*`HttpSessionBindingEvent event`*`)`

The `valueBound(...)` method is called before the object is made available through the `getAttribute(...)` method. In contrast, the `valueUnbound(...)` method is called after the object is no longer available via the `getAttribute(...)` method of the `HttpSession` interface. The listener is passed an `HttpSessionBindingEvent`, which contains the session object, the name, and the value of the object either bound or unbound to the session.

NOTE

Both methods are `public` and have a `void` return value.

HttpSessionListener

By implementing the `HttpSessionListener`, your application can be notified when a session is created or destroyed. The interface has two primary methods that must be defined:

- `sessionCreated(`*`HttpSessionEvent event`*`)`
- `sessionDestroyed(`*`HttpSessionEvent event`*`)`

As intuition would suggest, the `sessionCreated(...)` method is called after the session is produced. In contrast, the `sessionDestroyed(...)` method is called to notify the application that the session was invalidated. Each method provides a handle to the `HttpSessionEvent` object. This instance provides access to the session object.

NOTE

Both methods are `public` and have a `void` return value.

To register session listeners to the container, you must include the `listener` tag in the `web.xml` document. For example:

```
<listener>
    <listener-class>
        ConnectionPoolHandler
    </listener-class>
</listener>
```

The container determines the type of listener defined and then establishes an abstract link between the session and the listener. When changes occur to the session, the appropriate listener is notified.

So far, this chapter has covered how to create and maintain sessions by using several approaches—as well as how to respond to session changes. It is now time to discuss how sessions are invalidated.

Invalidating Sessions

A session can be invalidated in multiple ways. It can expire automatically, after a specified or default period of inactivity, or a servlet can explicitly invalidate a session through method calls. Before learning about these options, it is important to understand the effects on the application and client when a session is nullified. Basically, all the attribute data is lost. If you want to retain session information after it is invalidated, it should be stored in an external resource such as a database or a long-term cookie. For example, say you have a user who has a login name and password stored in a database. When they log into the system, a session is created and data is added to monitor their activity. After they log off or a session is about to be terminated, the data can be stored to that user's name or account in a database for later retrieval. Brokerage firms are known for using this approach as a means of justifying their user's transactions.

Logically, you would expect a session object to terminate when the client is done with an application. You would expect this to occur when the client leaves the site, terminates the browser, or simply walks away from the application for a period of time. Unfortunately, the application is not notified when such occurrences take place because of the nature of the HTTP protocol.

NOTE

The HTTP protocol is stateless, and by design will close the connection after each request to the server. As a result, an application is not notified after each connection is closed.

Because the server cannot distinguish the intent of the client, the server will keep the session alive during inactive periods for a default period. To change that default time, the `web.xml` document can be modified to identify the number of minutes the server will keep the session alive during inactive periods.

The `session-config` tag holds all configuration tags for the application's session. The `session-time` tag defines the number of inactive minutes a session will exist before the server terminates the object. The following is sample code for the `web.xml` file used to change the default termination period:

```
<web-app>
    ...
    <session-config>
        <session-timeout>
            15
        </session-timeout>
    </session-config>
</web-app>
```

TIP

The servlet specification requires that the timeout value be specified in whole numbers. Some servers allow the use of negative values to indicate that sessions should not be terminated. The server's documentation will provide more details on this capability.

A second approach to modifying the life of a session is to have individual servlets define the inactive time period before a session is destroyed. The `HttpSession` interface provides the following methods:

- `public void setMaxInactiveInterval(`*`int secs`*`)`
- `public int getMaxInactiveInterval()`

These methods allow fine-grained control. Instead of applying a time period to the entire application, you can set the time to specific servlets. The benefit of this approach is that you can customize the timeout period per user or after certain activities have taken place, such as a lengthy database lookup.

WARNING

Notice that the time is measured in seconds rather than minutes.

The `getMaxInactiveInterval()` method returns the value set. If the `set` method is not used and the time is set by using the `session-timeout` tag, the `getMaxInactiveInterval()` method will return the timeout value defined within the `web.xml` file.

The third approach is pretty abrupt. The `HttpSession` interface provides the following method:

```
public void invalidate() throws IllegalStateException
```

After a handle to the session is obtained, the `invalidate()` method can be called to close the session and unbind all associated objects. If the session is already invalidated, an `IllegalStateException` object is thrown.

Now that you've learned how to end a session, it is important for you to understand the best practices associated with a session's timeout period. Given specific scenarios, you should know whether a session object would be invalidated sooner versus later. Table 6.2 breaks down the strategies.

TABLE 6.2: Session Invalidation Strategies

Type	Example	Session Timeout Periods	Explanation
Secure web applications	Online banking	Shorter	Prevent imposters from invading abandoned systems.
Resource-intensive applications	Database connections	Shorter	Enable servers to reclaim or release resources quickly.
Non-resource-intensive applications	No database connections	Longer	Maximize convenience rather than focusing on server scalability.
Shopping cart applications	Stores	Longer	A timeout might cause client to forget original items.
Applications that cache database information	News sites	Depends	Shorter period results in a larger cache. Longer sessions cause the database lookup to process more slowly.

Determining how an application should manage a session is achieved by balancing convenience, user security, and server efficiency. A site that logs off a user too quickly could become incredibly inconvenient for users who need to take short breaks from a transaction to check e-mail or take a phone call. For security purposes, however, you don't want to keep certain sessions open for extended periods of inactivity. Imagine a bank web application that stores the user's login and account information in a session. If the data remains available while the user has stepped away from the application for an extended period of time, there is greater risk of fraud. Finally, efficiency should be considered. A client session might be using resources that are expensive to the system, such as a database connection. The longer this object is maintained, the slower the application and server might run. In such cases, sessions should not have long inactive periods.

DETAILED SESSION MANAGEMENT

Investments, Inc. is interested in providing their customers with online access to their investment accounts. The application must enable users to place orders, purchase stocks, and sell stocks. All clients will need to establish secure login accounts to access their private information. As a consultant, you are asked to design a session strategy that will best meet the company's security needs and provide client convenience.

One of the biggest concerns of the company is to ensure that decisions made by the client can be validated. A partnering company recently had a client claim they did not intend to purchase a particular batch of stocks. Because the company did not maintain every procedure taken by the client, they could not prove the client was responsible for their own error.

To minimize complexity, you have decided to utilize the session object provided by the servlet API. Whenever the user triggers an event, all entered information and trigger options are written to the session. Because security is a huge priority, inactive periods are kept to a minimum. If the user is in the middle of a transaction and has to leave the application, they would prefer to log in again rather than risk the corruption of their account.

CONTINUED →

Finally, you must consider when to store the information to a database. Normally, the session data is removed after the object is removed. To retain it for legal purposes, you want to write the session data to a database before the session is terminated. To ensure that the data is written before the session is invalidated, you create an `HttpSessionListener`. After the session is destroyed due to inactivity or the user logs out, which would cause a call to `session.invalidate()`, the listener is notified and the `sessionDestroyed(`*`HttpSessionEvent e`*`)` method is called. By using the `HttpSessionEvent`, you can retrieve a handle to the session object to extract all the data and write it to a database. The end result is an application that provides security and a legal trail.

What's Next

This chapter covered the various ways to manage a session object. It began by discussing the ways to monitor or handle session data; those processes are as follows:

Method 1: Hidden values

```
out.println("<INPUT TYPE='hidden'" +
                    "NAME='mailingAddress'" +
                    "VALUE='" + address + "'>");
```

Method 2: URL rewriting

```
out.println("<FORM ACTION='BingoServlet/' + sessionID +
                      "' METHOD='POST'>");
```

or

```
String urlSession = res.encodeURL("servlet/MyServlet");
out.println("<FORM ACTION='" + urlSession + "'" +
                      " Method='POST'>");
out.println("</FORM></BODY></HTML>");
```

Method 3: Cookies

```
Cookie cookie = new Cookie("JSESSIONID", "567");
res.addCookie(cookie);
```

Method 4: Sessions

```
HttpSession session = req.getSession();
```

This chapter then addressed ways to invalidate a session and the associated strategies. Here are the three ways to invalidate a session:

- `<session-config><session-timeout>60</session-timeout></session-config>`
- `HttpSession.setMaxInactiveInterval(...)`
- `HttpSession.invalidate()`

Finally, the circumstances in which you should provide long versus short inactive periods for a session were discussed.

Chapter 3, "The Basic JSP API," and Chapter 5, "Introducing JavaBeans," discussed how to move code from the JSP pages into JavaBeans. That is an excellent technique for getting coding out of JSP pages; however, that technique does not allow you to completely separate the HTML from the Java code. Conditional statements and loops wrapped around HTML are particularly problematic to separate. The next chapter will explain custom tags that can be used to solve these problems.

Chapter 7
Using Custom Tags

Chapter 3, "The Basic JSP API," and Chapter 5, "Introducing JavaBeans," succeeded in removing a large amount of the Business Logic from the Presentation layer using JavaBeans; however, this does not completely separate Java code from the HTML. For example, what if you wanted the JSP page to generate a table on-the-fly? This could be done with HTML, but the ability to highlight a row or change the content to another language is limited. Scriptlet or servlet code would be required.

Inevitably, the lack of functionality available in the standard JSP actions results in the developer having to write Java code in two ways: Either embed a plethora of scriptlet code within the page, or create a servlet to handle the functionality. The first option is not optimal because scriptlet code makes a page difficult to read, maintain, and expand. The second option is feasible, but requires the developer to provide an `include` or `forward` action every time a custom behavior is needed. Each attribute name must be known to set its value; in addition, each attribute must

Adapted from *Java™ 2 Web Developer Certification Study Guide*, Second Edition by Natalie Levi

ISBN 0-7821-4202-8 $59.99

be listed in a separate `jsp:param` tag. Again, this approach works, but means that any complex graphical functionality must be handled within a servlet rather than a JSP. Ideally, all presentation-related logic should be handled by the JSP. This chapter discusses how to expand the current JSP library by enabling developers to create custom JSP actions.

The use of *custom tags* (also known as *custom actions* or *tag extensions*) helps provide a clear division of labor between the web page designer and the software developer. Similar to XML, a custom tag takes the place of scriptlets, and sometimes beans, to provide the web designer the functionality to accomplish a particular task. Instead of doing the following:

```
The random number assigned to you is:
   <%= (int)Math.random()*100 %>
```

The designer could use a tag to accomplish the task:

```
The random number assigned to you is: <custTag:randomValue/>
```

Designing the page becomes a matter of plugging in the appropriate tags to achieve the correct design. The developer, on the other hand, creates tag classes to accomplish generic tasks. In fact, custom tags can take the place of servlets to provide an all-JSP presentation tier. Each task can be customized via attributes passed from the calling page at runtime. The tag has access to all objects available to the JSP page, such as `request`, `response`, and `out`. In addition to being nested, custom tags can also communicate with one another. They allow for complex behavior while ultimately simplifying the readability and maintainability of the JSP page.

Featured in this chapter:

- ▶ Development of a custom tag
- ▶ Description of the custom tag API
- ▶ Explanation of TLD Files

A Basic Custom Tag

Four components are required to ensure that a custom tag action performs correctly:

`MyTagName.class` is the custom action class you write to define the tag's functionality.

`taglibName.tld` is an XML file that defines a tag library and is also known as the tag library descriptor (TLD).

web.xml is an XML file that contains tag libraries available to the application.

MyJspPage.jsp is a JSP page that utilizes tags defined in the associated web.xml document.

A custom tag's body or functionality must exist in a special class that ultimately implements the Tag interface. This interface defines the life-cycle methods of the tag, enabling developers to include appropriate logic where necessary.

To simplify implementation, the API also provides a support class called BodyTagSupport. The BodyTagSupport class extends the TagSupport class, which in turn implements the Tag interface. BodyTagSupport also implements the BodyTag interface, which extends the Tag interface. This class reduces the number of methods the developer must define. We will talk about the interfaces and supporting classes in greater detail as the chapter progresses. Listing 7.1 is a code example of a basic tag that generates a random value.

Listing 7.1: A Basic Custom JSP Tag

```
package tagext;

import java.io.*;
import javax.servlet.jsp.*;
import javax.servlet.jsp.tagext.*;

public class RandomValue extends BodyTagSupport {

    public int doStartTag() throws JspException {
        return SKIP_BODY;
    }
    public int doEndTag() throws JspException {
        int value = (int)(Math.random()* 100);
        try {
            pageContext.getOut().write("" + value);
        } catch (IOException e) {
            throw new JspException(e.getMessage());
        }
        return EVAL_PAGE;
    }
}
```

On a simple level, the two methods defined contain the behavior of the tag. The `doStartTag()` is called to process the start, or opening, of the `tag` instance. Depending on the constant returned, the body that lies between the opening and closing tags will be either executed or ignored. Although this method is not necessary in this example because it performs default behavior, it is included to help you understand what is being called. Next, the `doEndTag()` method is invoked. In this example, a random value is generated and written to the tag's output stream. When compiled, the custom JSP class file should be placed within the application context's `/WEB-INF/classes` directory.

The next step is to create a *tag library descriptor (TLD)* file. A TLD is an XML document that describes a tag library. It contains one or many related tag extensions. For this example, the TLD file `tagext.tld` might look like the following:

```
<?xml version="1.0" encoding="ISO-8859-1" ?>
<!DOCTYPE taglib PUBLIC
  "-//Sun Microsystems, Inc.//DTD JSP Tag Library 1.2//EN"
  "http://java.sun.com/dtd/web-jsptaglibrary_1_2.dtd">
<taglib>
  <tlib-version>1.0</tlib-version>
  <jsp-version>1.2</jsp-version>
  <short-name>demo</short-name>
  <description>Simple demo library.</description>

  <tag>
      <name>randomValue</name>
      <tag-class>tagext.RandomValue</tag-class>
      <body-content>empty</body-content>
      <description>First example</description>
  </tag>
  ...
</taglib>
```

Each custom tag is embedded within its own set of `<tag></tag>` elements. Name and content information is included to enable JSPs to identify and use a particular tag. Each tag will be discussed in detail later.

For now, will map your `tagext.tld` file to the application via the `web.xml` document. The following elements must be included within the deployment descriptor to allow all JSPs to utilize the defined custom tags:

```
<?xml version="1.0" encoding="ISO-8859-1" ?>
<!DOCTYPE web-app PUBLIC
  "-//Sun Microsystems, Inc.//DTD Web Application 2.3//EN"
  "http://java.sun.com/dtd/web-app_2_3.dtd">
```

```
<web-app>
<!-- Tag Library Descriptor -->
<taglib>
   <taglib-uri>http://www.acme/tagext</taglib-uri>
   <taglib-location>
      /WEB-INF/tagext.tld
   </taglib-location>
</taglib>
...
</web-app>
```

The `taglib` element encapsulates information for the container to locate the library file. Once accessible, all JSPs within the application, including `MyJspPage.jsp`, can utilize each `taglib` or custom tag in the following fashion:

```
<%@ taglib uri="http://www.acme/tagext" prefix="custTag" %>
<HTML>
  <HEAD><TITLE>Your lucky number</TITLE></HEAD>
      <BODY>The random number assigned to you is:
      ➥<custTag:randomValue />
      </BODY>
</HTML>
```

The JSP defines the `tag` element, which maps to the `web.xml` file, which maps to the `tagext.tld`, which maps to the specialized tag class. Figure 7.1 demonstrates the path taken.

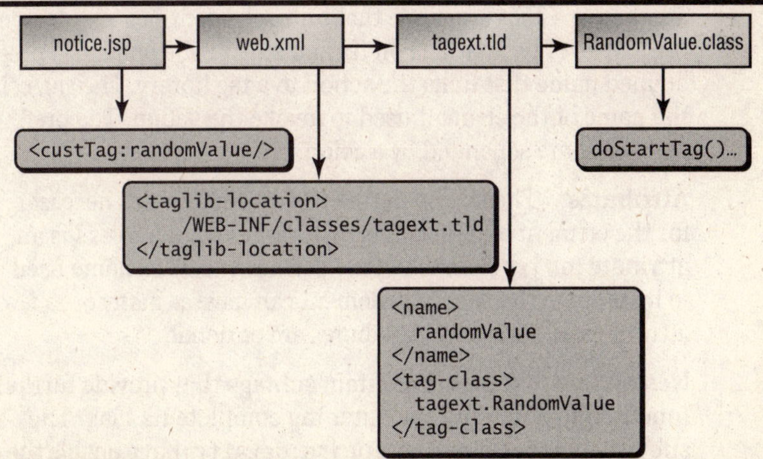

FIGURE 7.1: Custom tag mapping

Each of these files would be located in the following directory structure:

```
MyJspPage.jsp
META-INF/
    MANIFEST.MF
WEB-INF/
    web.xml
    tagext.tld
    classes/
        tagext/
            RandomValue.class
```

Notice that the custom tag `RandomValue` is a `.class` file rather than a `.jsp` file. The remainder of this chapter will focus on the details associated with each of these components. In this section, you will address the nuances used to customize and add additional functionality to a custom tag:

- Defining a tag
- Using the `taglib` element

Defining a Tag

A custom tag, or tag extension, is similar in structure to a standard JSP action tag. It is made up of four parts: a name, attributes, nested tags, and a body:

Tag name This is a name that uniquely identifies the element. It consists of two parts: a prefix and suffix. The *prefix* is a predefined name that links the action to a tag library. The *suffix* is the name of the element used to invoke the action. The prefix and suffix are separated by a colon.

Attributes These help define the characteristics necessary for the element to perform its task. For example, `class` is an attribute for `jsp:useBean` that defines the class name used to instantiate the bean. An element can have as many or as few attributes as necessary. Attributes are optional.

Nested tags A tag can contain subtags that provide further functionality, helping the outer tag complete its task. The subtags `jsp:setAttribute` or `jsp:getAttribute` enable the `jsp:useBean` action to change and access its attribute values. Nested tags are observed and executed at runtime.

Body The content between the opening tag and closing tag, including subtags, is considered the *body content*. A tag extension can control the body content by extracting it from the element's class file and returning a changed value.

Syntactically, a tag extension can look like the following:

```
<prefix:suffix attribute1="value" attribute2="value" >
   <prefix:subSuffix attribute1="value" attribute2="value"  />
   body
</prefix:suffix>
```

Each suffix represents a different JSP tag name associated with a tag class file. A JSP page can call any tag defined within the application's deployment descriptor, as long as the tag has been specified by the JSP `taglib` directive.

Using the *taglib* Element

Before a tag extension can be used within a JSP page, three things must happen:

1. The *JSP page* must include a `taglib` directive to identify which tag libraries to load into memory.
2. The *web.xml* document must use a `taglib` element in conjunction with the `taglib-uri` sub-element to declare, and identify the location of, the TLD file.
3. The *TLD* file must use the `taglib` element in conjunction with the `tag` sub-element to identify each custom tag and its attributes.

The JSP Page

You are required to use the `taglib` directive within the JSP page to identify the use of custom tags. Because the tag contains the necessary information to load the appropriate TLD, it must be defined before any custom tag is used. Once loaded, the TLD, or tag library, provides the current JSP with additional names and attributes of available custom actions.

Locating the correct tag library requires the inclusion of two mandatory attributes along with the `taglib` directive: `uri` and `prefix`. The syntax is as follows:

```
<%@ taglib uri="locationOfTLD" prefix="shortName" %>
```

You can use the uri attribute in two ways. You can map it directly to the URI used within the web.xml's taglib-uri sub-element. When these two values match, the other sub-element within the web.xml file, called taglib-location, will define the absolute location of the file. The second option is for the uri attribute to provide the absolute path to the TLD. At that point, the web.xml file does not need to provide location information. The container will use the information from the JSP page to map to the TLD via the deployment descriptor. Both options are provided to enable the developer to conveniently define the location of the TLD file or to use more abstract measures that grant greater long-term flexibility.

The prefix attribute is also mandatory and defines the prefix name in the tag extension. For example, if prefix="eei", then the tag for an element called calculate would look like <eei:calculate />. The actual value assigned to the prefix attribute is an arbitrary name defined by the HTML designer to enable the JSP container to map the tag to the real tag library. In addition to defining the first portion of a tag extension, the prefix also maps to the shortname element defined within the TLD. When the container encounters the taglib directive, it knows to download the library identified by the uri. When it encounters an element with a defined prefix, it then knows which library to search to efficiently locate the identified tag. This process is known as *prefix mapping*.

The Deployment Descriptor

The web.xml file is the mapping tool used between the JSP page and all other available container resources. The JSP uses the web.xml to locate the TLD. When a JSP attempts to invoke a custom tag, the tag must first be located, and then processed. By modifying the deployment descriptor to include mapping information to the tag library, the JSP can locate the necessary actions to invoke.

A tag library is defined within the web.xml by using the opening <taglib> and closing </taglib> tags. Embedded within, the URI and exact directory location are defined by using both the taglib-uri and taglib-location tags, respectively. The following code snippet demonstrates how to include two libraries within the application's web.xml file:

```
<?xml version="1.0" encoding="ISO-8859-1" ?>
<!DOCTYPE web-app PUBLIC
  "-//Sun Microsystems, Inc.//DTD Web Application 2.3//EN"
  "http://java.sun.com/dtd/web-app_2_3.dtd">

<web-app>
  ...
```

```
<!-- Tag Library Descriptor -->
<taglib>
   <taglib-uri>/taglib1</taglib-uri>
   <taglib-location>
       /WEB-INF/tlds/GeneralTagLib.tld
   </taglib-location>
</taglib>

<taglib>
   <taglib-uri>http://www.eei.com/taglib2</taglib-uri>
   <taglib-location>
       /WEB-INF/tlds/SpecificTagLib.tld
   </taglib-location>
</taglib>
...
</web-app>
```

First, it is important to notice that the web.xml DOCTYPE is web-app. Later, when you are provided with a closer look at the TLD file, you will see that the DOCTYPE is defined as taglib. In addition, the actual DTD file (web-app_2.3.dtd) used to define the web.xml file is different from that used to define TLD files.

The taglib element has two sub-elements. The first sub-element is taglib-uri. It specifies the URI that all JSPs should use to access that tag library. Its path can contain either an absolute path, which includes host and port number, or a relative path using published directories. The mapping between the URI and the actual destination of the TLD is done by using the second sub-element, called taglib-location. This element is used to define the exact location of the TLD file. Unlike the URI, it can contain nonpublished directories such as /WEB-INF and its subdirectories.

When defining paths, it is important to know the difference between the three formats:

Context-relative path If the path starts with a forward slash (/), the path is relative to the application's context path.

Page-relative path If the path does not start with a slash, it is relative to the current JSP page or file. If the include directive is used, which incorporates the response of the identified file attribute, the URI is relative to that defined file. If the include action is used, the URI is relative to the page attribute's value.

Absolute path This is the full path, starting with the protocol and host, necessary to locate the tag library file.

NOTE

There should not be more than one `taglib-uri` entry with the same value in a single `web.xml` file.

Generally, the `taglib-location` element is mapped to a context-relative path, which begins with a forward slash (/), and does not include a protocol or host definition. Specifically, this path is referred to as the *TLD resource path*. The TLD resource path is relative to the root of the web application, and should resolve to a TLD file directly, or to a JAR file that has a TLD file located in the `/WEB-INF` directory.

The following is an example of how the mapping applies.

`web.xml` file:

```
<taglib>
   <taglib-uri>/tagDir</taglib-uri>
   <taglib-location>
      /WEB-INF/tld/taglib.tld
   </taglib-location>
</taglib>
```

Maps to the JSP file `taglib` directive:

```
<%@ taglib uri="/tagDir" prefix="eei" %>
```

Both URIs map to each other, while the location identifies where the `taglib.tld` file resides. After the library is located, the container will load it into memory and examine its contents.

Tag Library Descriptor (TLD)

As you know, the tag library descriptor, or TLD, is an XML document used to identify and describe the list of tag extensions associated with a single tag library. The file contains general information about the library, and available extensions along with their attributes. Listing 7.2 displays a library containing two tags.

Listing 7.2: A Sample TLD

```
<?xml version="1.0" encoding="ISO-8859-1" ?>
<!DOCTYPE taglib PUBLIC
  "-//Sun Microsystems, Inc.//DTD JSP Tag Library 1.2//EN"
  "http://java.sun.com/dtd/web-jsptaglibrary_1_2.dtd">
```

```
<taglib>
   <tlib-version>1.0</tlib-version>
   <jsp-version>1.2</jsp-version>
   <short-name>examples</short-name>

   <description>Simple example library.</description>

   <tag>
      <name>hello</name>
      <tag-class>tagext.HelloTag</tag-class>
      <body-content>JSP</body-content>
      <description>First example</description>
   </tag>
   <tag>
      <name>goodbye</name>
      <tag-class>tagext.GoodByeTag</tag-class>
      <body-content>JSP</body-content>
      <description>Second example</description>
      <attribute>
         <name>age</name>
         <required>true</required>
         <rtexprvalue>true</rtexprvalue>
         <type>java.lang.Integer</type>
      </attribute>
   </tag>
</taglib>
```

The TLD begins with general information about the library. Table 7.1 lists the various tags that can be used to describe the library. The only two required are `jsp-version` and `short-name`.

TABLE 7.1: General TLD Tags

Tag	Explanation
`tlib-version`	The library's version number.
`jsp-version`	The JSP specification version required by the current tag library to function properly. This tag is mandatory.
`short-name`	The `prefix` value of the `taglib` directive. You should not use white space, or start the value off with a digit or underscore. This tag is mandatory.
`description`	A text string describing the library's purpose.

Optional tags for the library are available to provide additional flexibility and functionality. Table 7.2 displays these elements.

TABLE 7.2: Optional TLD Tags

Tag	Explanation
uri	An address that uniquely identifies this taglib.
display-name	The short name for the tag displayed by tools.
small-icon	An optional icon that can be used by tools to identify the tag library.
large-icon	An optional icon that can be used by tools to identify the tag library.
validator	An object used to ensure the conformance of the JSP page to the tag library. It can contain the following sub-elements: validator-class—The class that implements the javax.servlet.jsp.tagext.TagLibraryValidator interface. init-param—The optional initialization parameters. description—The explanation of the validator.
listener	A tag that defines an optional event listener object to instantiate and register automatically. It can contain the following sub-element: Listener-class—The class that must be registered as a web application listener bean.

After the broad library information is defined, custom tags can be declared by using the <tag></tag> elements. Configuration information for the specific action is embedded between these tags. Table 7.3 lists the basic tag options.

TABLE 7.3: Common Custom Tag Options

Tag	Explanation
name	The unique action name. The name defined after the prefix.
tag-class	The fully qualified class name for the custom action that implements the javax.servlet.jsp.tagext.Tag interface.
tei-class	This stands for the TagExtraInfo class. It provides information about the values exported to the corresponding tag class. This class must subclass the javax.servlet.jsp.tagext.TagExtraInfo class. This tag is optional.

TABLE 7.3 continued: Common Custom Tag Options

Tag	Explanation
body-content	Information used by a page composition tool to determine how to manage the tag's body content. The following options are available: JSP—A value that informs the container to evaluate the body of the action during runtime. This is the default. tagdependent—A value notifying the container that it should not evaluate the body of the action. Instead, its contents should be passed to the tag handler for interpretation. empty—A value stating that the body must be empty.

attribute	The tag used to provide information about all available parameters and values exported by the tag. Its sub-elements are as follows:
	name—The name of the attribute. This is required.
	required—A value that indicates whether the attribute is mandatory or optional. This sub-element is optional.
	rtexprvalue—A value that indicates whether the attribute can be dynamically calculated by using an expression. This sub-element is optional. Options include:
	`true | false | yes | no`
	The default is false. If true, the tag might look something like the following:
	`<prefix:action attrib="<%=obj.getValue() %>" />`
	type—The attribute's data type. For literals, the type is always java.lang.String.
	description—The explanation of the attribute.

In addition to the standard tags that define the element, supplementary elements can be included to enhance the use of the extension within a tool or to improve readability. Table 7.4 lists these additional tags.

TABLE 7.4: Additional Custom Tag Elements

Tag	Explanation
display-name	The short name displayed by tools.
small-icon	A file containing a small (16 × 16) icon image. Its path is relative to the TLD. The format must be either JPEG or GIF.
large-icon	A file containing a large (32 × 32) icon image. Its path is relative to the TLD. The format must be either JPEG or GIF.
description	An explanation of the tag.

TABLE 7.4 continued: Additional Custom Tag Elements

Tag	Explanation
`variable`	An element that provides information about the scripting variables. Its sub-elements are as follows: `name-given`—The name as a constant. `name-from-attribute`—The name of the attribute whose value will be given the name of the variable at translation time. `variable-class`—The variable's class name. The default is `java.lang.String`. `declare`—A Boolean representing whether the variable is declared. The default is `true`. Available options are `true` | `false` | `yes` | `no`. `scope`—The scope of the scripting variable. `NESTING` is the default. The other legal values are `AT BEGIN` and `AT END`. `description`—An explanation of the variable.
`example`	A sample of how to use the tag.

A custom tag has a variety of elements to help define the tag's syntax and how it should be used. Some of the elements are basic requirements for the tag, whereas others are optional elements that make the tag more tool-friendly by adding robust features.

After a tag is defined, it can then be configured to perform its task by using the information and attributes provided. Begin by revisiting the second tag in code Listing 7.2:

```
<tag>
    <name>goodbye</name>
    <tag-class>tagext.GoodByeTag</tag-class>
    <body-content>JSP</body-content>
    <description>Second example</description>
    <attribute>
        <name>age</name>
        <required>true</required>
        <rtexprvalue>true</rtexprvalue>
        <type>java.lang.Integer</type>
    </attribute>
</tag>
```

You could invoke this tag within our JSP page in the following fashion:

```
<examples:goodbye age=
  "<%=
        new Integer(application.getInitParameter("age"))
     %>" >
</examples:goodbye>
```

This example provides one attribute called age. It is required and enables the value to be assigned at runtime by using an expression. Because its return type is of the `java.lang.Integer` class, the expression must convert the `String` value to an `Integer` object.

TALKING TO THE WORLD

For several years, WorldTalk Inc. has provided the Internet community a service that translates web sites to the clients' desired language. To ensure that their teams of designers are specialized experts in design and that their teams of developers are experts in programming, the company has begun to separate worker tasks.

Standard JSPs have greatly helped the company move toward this goal, because the JSPs enable designers to focus on HTML and use available tags to take care of basic functionality. The problem with this approach is that designers are forced to create complex HTML code that is not reusable because they are using JSP and have limited default programming functionality.

To solve this problem, management chose to migrate the application toward the use of custom tags. The development team began working on a library of tags that provide translation functionality. For example, designers can now use a tag called `formatDate.jsp` to present the date in the appropriate fashion. Optional attributes include the `locale` of the machine, the `pattern` describing the date style, the `value` being the actual date, and others. By creating a library of tags, the developers have enabled the designers to create pages by utilizing tags that handle all the functionality necessary to create the item or result desired. The developers handle Unicode translations, and the designers focus on layout.

The final piece needed to bring tag extensions together is the actual tag class. The next section will discuss the various types of custom tags and their life cycles.

Tag Handler

As with all Java advanced technologies, creating a component that conforms to a particular API requires the implementation of an interface. Custom tags abide by this rule. When you are creating a custom tag, it is required that the class implement the interface `javax.servlet.jsp.tagext.Tag`. The interface provides several important methods that define the life cycle of the tag. By implementing the methods correctly, the container can manage the tag to deliver an expected and consistent behavior.

The Tag interface is the most basic protocol between the Tag handler and the implementing JSP page. It defines the methods that should be invoked at the starting and ending tag. The interface `javax.servlet.jsp.tagext.IterationTag` is a subinterface and provides additional functionality whereby the tag can loop through its body multiple times. Still one level lower is the `javax.servlet.jsp.tagext.BodyTag` interface, which allows the manipulation of the body content. By implementing any one of these interfaces and a little work, you can create a custom tag that suits your needs.

To minimize the work, the API provides support classes that implement the interfaces for you. They define the most uncommonly changed methods and leave the most frequently modified methods abstract. Figure 7.2 demonstrates the hierarchy between the interfaces and support classes discussed. The solid lines represent `extends`, and the dotted lines signify `implements`.

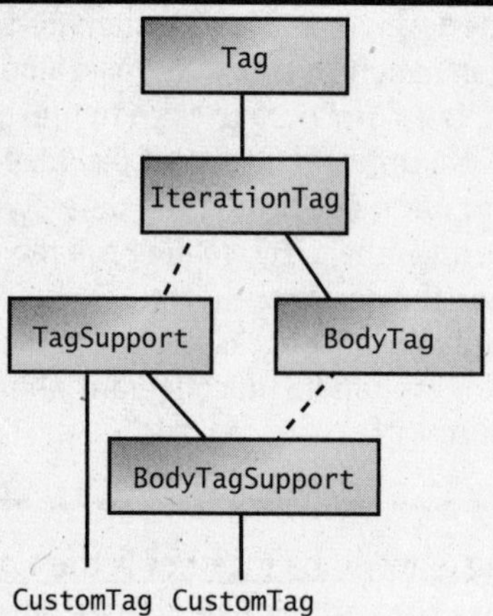

FIGURE 7.2: The tag hierarchy

A custom tag can implement any one of the interfaces or simply extend a support class. This section covers the functionality of each tag interface and abstract class:

- Tag interface
- `IterationTag` interface

- BodyTag interface
- Support classes

Deciding which class or interface to utilize is usually based on the life cycle desired and required methods the developer must define. These features will be discussed in detail.

Tag Interface

As mentioned earlier in this chapter, the `javax.servlet.jsp.tagext.Tag` interface defines the most basic protocol between the tag handler and the JSP page that invokes the instance. If you choose to implement this interface, you must define the following six methods:

- `setPageContext(`*`PageContext pageContext`*`)`
- `setParent(`*`Tag tag`*`)`
- `getParent()`
- `doStartTag()`
- `doEndTag()`
- `release()`

The first method that is invoked by the container sets the `pageContext` object, which provides a handle to all the implicit objects. Its signature is as follows:

```
public void setPageContext (PageContext pageContext)
```

The container passes the context to the tag to enable access to the application's implicit variables. Through the `PageContext` convenience methods, such as `getRequest()`, you can alter or provide more information to your tag handler. This method is usually defined by saving a local instance of the context object.

The second method that is invoked by the container is `setParent(`*`Tag tag`*`)`. Its purpose is to provide a local handle to the closest enclosing tag handler. If a tag is nested within another tag, the handle to the outer tag is made available to the inner tag. Given the existence of the corresponding `getParent()` method, tags can communicate with one another by using the `Tag` handle instance. The signature to these methods is as follows:

```
public void setParent(Tag tag)
public Tag getParent()
```

After the `setPageContext(...)` and `setParent(...)` methods are called, the container can begin to process the beginning tag by first invoking any set property methods to set needed tag attributes. For example, if the tag has a string attribute called `name`, a corresponding `setName(...)` method within the tag handler will automatically be invoked. The container will then continue to initialize the tag by calling `doStartTag()`. In addition to initializing the tag even further, this method is responsible for notifying the container about how to evaluate the body of the tag element. The body represents the logic between the opening and closing tags. The method signature is as follows:

```
public int doStartTag() throws JspException
```

Depending on how you would like the body to be handled, you can return one of the following constants:

`int EVAL_BODY_INCLUDE` This constant indicates that the body should be evaluated. Results generated from executing the body are written to the current `JspWriter` `out` variable.

`int SKIP_BODY` This constant indicates that the body should not be evaluated.

Depending on the return value, the body will be either evaluated or skipped. The `doEndTag()` method is then invoked. It processes the end tag for the element to determine how the remaining JSP page should be evaluated. The signature for the method is as follows:

```
public int doEndTag() throws JspException
```

As you can see, this method returns an `int` value as well. Again, the constant informs the container about how to proceed. The following return values are available:

`int EVAL_PAGE` As the name suggests, this constant indicates that the container should evaluate the rest of the JSP page.

`int SKIP_PAGE` This option indicates that the rest of the page should not be evaluated and that the request is in fact complete. If this request was created by a `forward` or `include` from another page, only the current JSP page is complete.

TIP

The specification states that if the TLD defines the action's `body-content` as `empty`, the `doStartTag()` method must return `SKIP_BODY`.

TIP

If SKIP_BODY is returned and a body is present, it is not evaluated.

Both the doStartTag() and doEndTag() methods throw a JspException in their signatures. If the method actually throws the exception, the container will generate an error page to notify the client of a JSP problem.

The final method that must be defined is used to clean up any loose ends. The signature is as follows:

```
public void release()
```

When the tag is done processing the beginning element, the body, and the ending element, the container invokes this method to release the tag handler's state. Figure 7.3 displays the life cycle for the Tag interface.

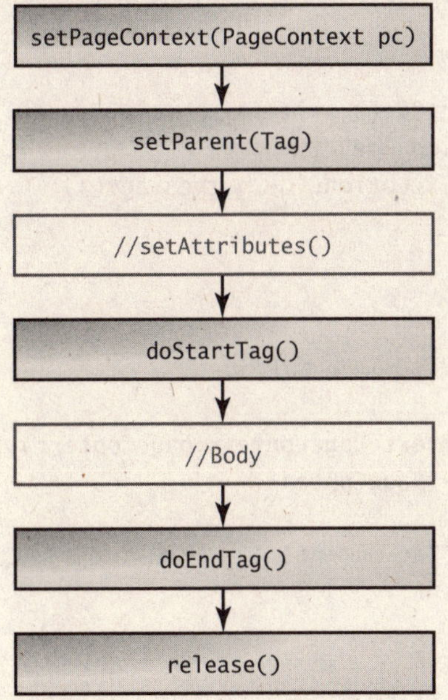

FIGURE 7.3: The Tag interface life cycle

Revisit the custom tag example used to generate a random value. Previously, you saw how to invoke such an action; you will now see the actual code used to generate the action. Listing 7.3 displays the necessary code to implement the Tag interface.

Listing 7.3: Utilizing the Tag Interface

```
package tagext;

import java.io.*;
import javax.servlet.jsp.*;
import javax.servlet.jsp.tagext.*;

public class RandomValue implements Tag {
    private PageContext pageContext;
    private Tag parent;

    public int doStartTag() throws JspException {
        return SKIP_BODY;
    }

    public int doEndTag() throws JspException {
        int value = (int)(Math.random() * 100);

        try {
            pageContext.getOut().write("" + value);
        } catch (IOException ioe) {
            throw new JspException(ioe.getMessage());
        }
        return EVAL_PAGE;
    }

    public void release() {}

    public void setPageContext(PageContext pageContext) {
        this.pageContext = pageContext;
    }
    public void setParent(Tag parent) {
        this.parent = parent;
    }

    public Tag getParent() {
        return this.parent;
    }
}
```

In this example, the `doStartTag()` method notifies the container to skip the body and immediately invoke the `doEndTag()` method. This method generates a random value and writes it to the JspWriter out object. When the method completes, the rest of the JSP page will be evaluated. One thing you should notice is that within a custom action, you do not have direct access to implicit objects. Instead, handles to these variables are accessible from the pageContext object passed as an instance by the container. In the preceding example, the implicit out JspWriter is accessed by calling pageContext.getOut().

TIP

The PageContext class provides the following convenience methods for access to implicit objects: getOut(), getException(), getPage(), getRequest(), getResponse(), getSession(), getServletConfig(), and getServletContext().

IterationTag Interface

The javax.servlet.jsp.tagext.IterationTag interface extends the Tag interface and adds one additional method. As the name suggests, this interface enables the body of the element to be executed multiple times. The functionality is similar to a do/while loop.

In addition to the standard doStartTag() and doEndTag() methods, the IterationTag interface adds the doAfterBody() method. When this method is implemented, the developer can opt to have the body evaluated again. The signature is as follows:

```
public int doAfterBody() throws JspException
```

Depending on how you would like the body to be handled, you can return one of the following constants:

int EVAL_BODY_AGAIN This indicates that the body should be reevaluated. The doAfterBody() method will get called again after evaluating the body.

int SKIP_BODY This notifies the container that the body should not be evaluated. The value of out will be restored, and the doEndTag() method will be invoked.

TIP

If SKIP_BODY is returned, the body is not evaluated and the doEndTag() is then invoked.

As already stated, this interface acts like a do/while loop. It enables the body to be evaluated (that's the do part), and calls doAfterBody() (that's the while part) to determine whether to reevaluate the body. Figure 7.4 displays the life cycle of an IterationTag.

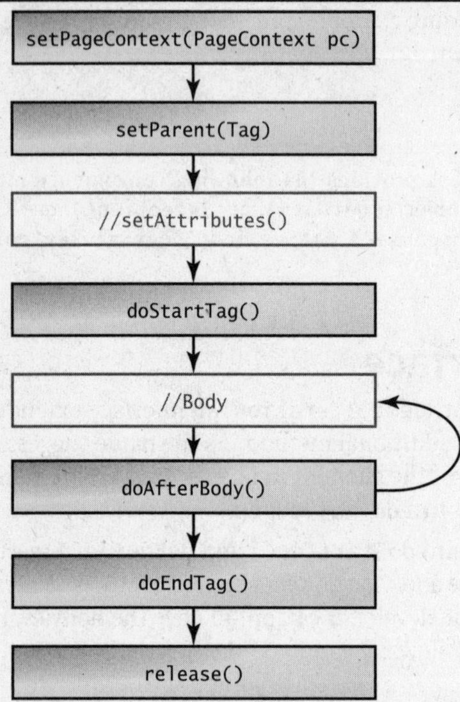

FIGURE 7.4: The IterationTag life cycle

Although this interface is not often used directly, it can be utilized to cycle through an element's body to generate a response. Listing 7.4 takes the previous JSP, which generated a single random value, and now has it generate five random values.

Listing 7.4: Utilizing the IterationTag Interface

```
package tagext;

import java.io.*;
import javax.servlet.jsp.*;
import javax.servlet.jsp.tagext.*;
```

```
public class MoreRandomValues implements IterationTag {
    private PageContext pageContext;
    private Tag parent;
    private int counter;

    public void setPageContext(PageContext pageContext) {
        this.pageContext = pageContext;
    }
    public void setParent(Tag parent) {
        this.parent = parent;
    }

    public int doStartTag() throws JspException {
        return EVAL_BODY_INCLUDE;
    }

    public int doAfterBody() throws JspException {
        int value = (int)(Math.random() * 100);
        counter++;
        if (0 < counter && counter<5) {
            try {
                pageContext.getOut().write(" " + value);
            } catch (IOException ioe) {
                throw new JspException(ioe.getMessage());
            }
            return EVAL_BODY_AGAIN;
        } else {
            return SKIP_BODY;
        }
    }

    public int doEndTag() throws JspException {
        return EVAL_PAGE;
    }

    public void release() {
        counter=0;
    }

    public Tag getParent() {
        return this.parent;
    }
}
```

In this example, the doAfterBody() method generates a new random value if the body has been evaluated fewer than five times. It then takes that value and writes it to the JspWriter object. Because you are simply writing text to the response stream, you access the implicit out variable through the pageContext object and invoke the write(?) method, which takes a String value. The resulting output displays four consecutive random values.

You will not see the IterationTag interface implemented often because its subinterface, javax.servlet.jsp.tagext.BodyTag, offers the ability to iterate and manipulate the body content if necessary. If iterating through the body is not necessary, a support class implements all the necessary methods of this interface and makes coding a tag much easier. That topic will be covered later in this chapter in "Support Classes." For now, take a close look at the BodyTag interface.

BodyTag Interface

The javax.servlet.jsp.tagext.BodyTag interface extends the IterationTag interface and adds the capability to evaluate and alter the body content multiple times. As you know, the body content is the logic between an extension's opening and closing tags. This functionality is made possible with the addition of the following methods:

- public void setBodyContent(*BodyContent bodyContent*)
- public void doInitBody() throws JspException

The setBodyContent(*BodyContent bodyContent*) method is called by the container to provide the tag a handle to the body content. It is invoked after the doStartTag() because the opening tag must first be evaluated to determine whether to execute or skip the body. The BodyContent object is a critical feature for BodyTag handlers. It is important to understand how this object works to be able to get your output to display correctly.

With basic JSPs, output is written to the response stream by using the JspWriter out implicit variable. Until now, you too have written directly to the out variable by using the pageContext method getOut(). This approach works well when you need to write either a String, int, or char value to the stream; however, when the goal is to manipulate a tag's body content and then write its information to the response stream, the standard out object falls short. To accomplish this task, you must first write to the tag's BodyContent object. The class actually extends the JspWriter class, and is therefore a buffered writer. But what distinguishes it from its parent class is that it contains the tag's evaluated body content. From the BodyContent object, you can extract the body and manipulate its content. When you are ready to display your results, the BodyContent object must be written to the implicit out response stream. To understand how the container handles the body content, look at the following JSP code:

```
<syb:grandparent>
    This is the body
</syb:grandparent>
```

When the container reads the syb:grandparent tag, it executes the tag's doStartTag() method. This method creates a new BodyContent writer instance specifically for this tag. The implicit out variable is then redirected to the instance for future use. When the body is evaluated, the contents are transferred to the BodyContent object. After a BodyContent instance is initialized, you can invoke any one of the following methods on it:

- public void clearBody()
- public abstract String getString()
- public abstract Reader getReader()
- public JspWriter getEnclosingWriter()
- public abstract void writeOut(*Writer out*)
- public void flush()

NOTE

The BodyContent has a buffer size that is unbound and cannot be flushed. In fact, the flush() method is overridden to prevent the parent class JspWriter from attempting to flush when this method is called.

As you can see, you can clear the body, read from it, or call getString() to convert the contents to a String and return its value. The last two methods are important, because they are used to alter the content.

When you specifically write to the BodyContent instance, you are not writing to the implicit out located on the bottom of the stack. Instead, you must access the outer-layer stream by calling getEnclosingWriter(). This method returns a JspWriter, which is the implicit out variable if your tag is an outer tag. The term *outer tag* means the custom action is not nested within another action. If it is nested, you write your body content to the enclosing outer tag's body content. The task of sending the current body content to the enclosing writer is handled by the `writeOut(?)` method. This method writes the content of the calling `BodyContent` instance to the `Writer` object parameter. The parameter you pass is usually the result of a call to `getEnclosingWriter()`.

NOTE

The implicit `out` object can be accessed by most JSP actions by using the method `pageContext.getOut()`. The problem with accessing the `out` object directly is that custom tags need to access their body content and manipulate that data before sending it back to the response stream. A basic `JspWriter` does not offer such functionality. In addition, by writing directly to the `pageContext.getOut()`, anything that is currently in the buffer can be potentially overwritten.

The way data is written to the response stream is especially critical and essential for handling tags that are nested. *Nested tags* are tags within another tag. Consider the following JSP example, in which `pc` stands for the `pageContext` object:

```
<syb:grandparent>   <-- pc.pushBody() bodyContent 1 -->
    <syb:parent>    <-- pc.pushBody() bodyContent 2 -->
        <syb:child> <-- pc.pushBody() bodyContent 3 -->

        </syb:child>
    </syb:parent>
</syb:grandparent>
```

The code consists of three nested tags. The `child` tag is within the `parent` tag, and the `parent` tag is within the `grandparent` tag. The problem is that there is only one implicit `out` variable to which all tags must eventually forward their output. To prevent potential overwrites, each tag has its own `BodyContent` object. When the container accesses the opening tag, it calls the action's `doStartTag()` method, which causes the `pageContext` to call its `pushBody()` method. This method creates a new `BodyContent` object for that particular tag. With each tag owning its own `BodyContent` or `JspWriter`, your first instinct might be to have the tag write directly to its own `BodyContent` object. That, however, fails to work. The implicit `out` is located at the bottom of the stack, whereas each additional `BodyContent` writer is stacked one on top of the other. If you opt to `writeOut(?)` to the current `BodyContent`, the output will not be sent to the implicit `out` stream.

Instead, it will be sent to itself. The following code sample demonstrates this concept:

```
JspWriter jspOut = getBodyContent();
bodyContent.writeOut(jspOut);
```

NOTE

The method `getBodyContent()` is available within the `BodyTagSupport` class. It returns the current body content instance. If you are implementing the `BodyTag` interface, a handle to the body content should be saved locally when the `setBodyContent(`*`BodyContent bodyContent`*`)` method is invoked by the container. The support class will be discussed in more detail later in this chapter.

This example writes the contents of the current `BodyContent` into the current `BodyContent` writer `jspOut`. The implicit `out` variable is never accessed, and the stream is left empty. Basically, this example accomplishes nothing because it writes itself to itself.

When you call `getEnclosingWriter()`, you access the enclosing action's `BodyContent` object or `JspWriter`. If tags are nested, each will call `getEnclosingWriter()` and access their outer tag writer, concatenating their information to the previous buffered data. Eventually, you'll reach the outermost layer and write the buffered stream to the response stream. The correct way to write output is as follows:

```
JspWriter bcOut = bodyContent.getEnclosingWriter();
bodyContent.write(" data  ");
bodyContent.writeOut(bcOut);
```

If this code snippet is run as an outer tag, `bcOut` is actually the implicit `JspWriter out` variable. If the tag is executed as a nested tag, the `bcOut` variable is actually the outer tag's `BodyContent`.

Given the earlier nested example, the child tag must call `getEnclosingWriter()` to access the content of the parent; the parent tag will then call `getEnclosingWriter()` to get the grandparent tag's content writer. Finally, the grandparent calls `getEnclosingWriter()` to gain access to the implicit `out` object writer, which transfers information to the response stream. Figure 7.5 shows how nested tags eventually access the response stream in comparison to a single tag.

When a stack of writers exists, the `getEnclosingWriter()` method ensures that you concatenate current data with the parent's data to eventually output all data to the response stream.

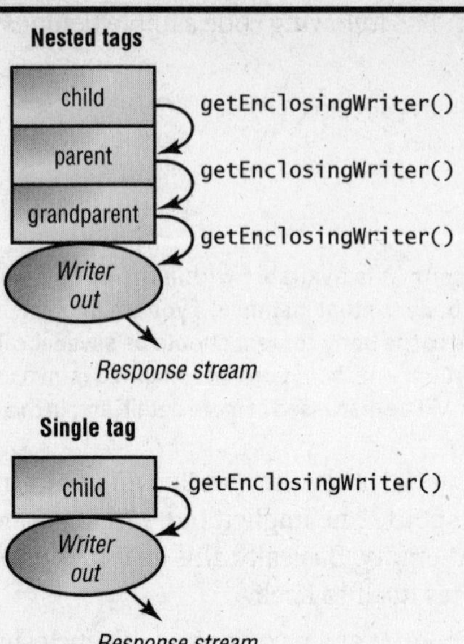

FIGURE 7.5: Accessing the enclosing writer

Now that you have a better understanding of `BodyContent`, you can get back to the life cycle of the `BodyTag` interface. As discussed earlier in this chapter, the `doStartTag()` method is called to determine whether the body should be evaluated. If the answer is yes, a `BodyContent` object is created and associated with the tag by an invocation of the `setBodyContent(...)` method. After the content is set, there is opportunity to initialize any variables prior to reading the body. This is done when the `doInitTag()` method is called. Its purpose is to process code that should be taken care of before the body of the `BodyTag` is evaluated for the first time. The `doAfterBody()` method is called next to determine whether the body should be reevaluated. After there is no longer a need to iterate through the body, the `doEndTag()` method is invoked. Finally, before the `Tag` handler is sent to the garbage collector, the `release()` method is called to release any unnecessary resources. Figure 7.6 demonstrates the life cycle for this interface.

To demonstrate how this interface is used, you are going to create a `LoopTag` handler to print the body content to the client the number of times specified by an attribute.

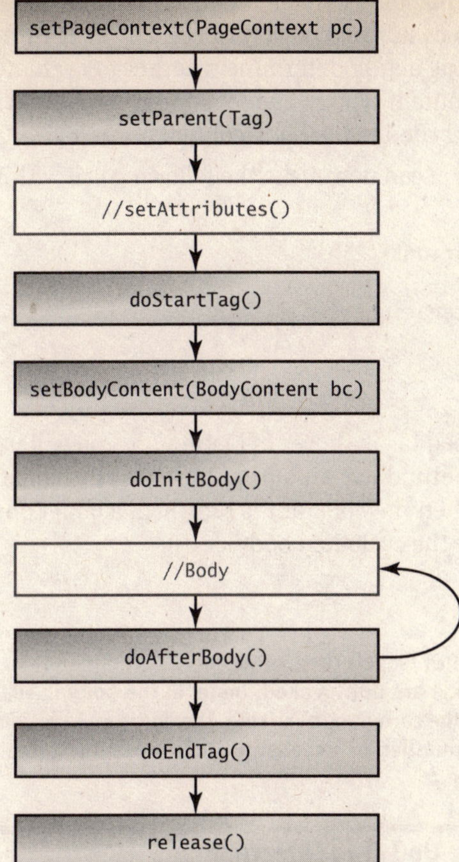

FIGURE 7.6: The BodyTag life cycle

First, you need to define the tag in the tag library descriptor:

```
<tag>
    <name>loop</name>
    <tag-class>tagext.LoopTag</tag-class>
    <body-content>JSP</body-content>
    <attribute>
        <name>iterations</name>
        <required>true</required>
        <rtexprvalue>true</rtexprvalue>
        <type>java.lang.Integer</type>
    </attribute>
</tag>
```

Notice that you define the body-content with the default value JSP. This tells the container to evaluate the body of the action at runtime. If you would rather have the *action* determine whether to evaluate the body, you can define the content type as tagdependent. Finally, to force the body to be empty, simply define the body-content as empty.

With this tag in place, you can now make the following call within our JSP page:

```
<examples:loop iterations="2">
   Test 1 <BR>
   <examples:loop iterations="2">
      Test 2 <BR>
   </examples:loop>
</examples:loop>
```

The code for the described tag is shown in Listing 7.5. You will notice that the doStartTag() method has an option to return the constant EVAL_BODY_BUFFERED. When the constant is returned, a bodyContent object is created to capture the evaluated body.

NOTE

If EVAL_BODY_INCLUDE is returned, the setBodyContent(...) and doInitBody() methods are not invoked. Instead, the body is evaluated and passed through to the current out variable. The doAfterBody() method is then invoked the number of necessary iterations, until finally the doEndTag() is invoked.

Listing 7.5: Utilizing the BodyTag Interface

```
package tagext;

import java.io.*;
import javax.servlet.jsp.*;
import javax.servlet.jsp.tagext.*;

public class LoopTag implements BodyTag {
    private PageContext pageContext;
    private BodyContent bodyContent;
    private Tag parent;
    private int iterations;

    public void setPageContext(PageContext pageContext) {
        this.pageContext = pageContext;
    }
```

```
public void setParent(Tag parent) {
    this.parent = parent;
}

public void setIterations(int iterations) {
    this.iterations = iterations;
}

public int doStartTag() throws JspException {
    if(iterations>0) {
        return EVAL_BODY_BUFFERED;
    } else {
        return SKIP_BODY;
    }
}

public void setBodyContent(BodyContent bodyContent) {
   this.bodyContent = bodyContent;
}

public void doInitBody() throws JspException {}

public int doAfterBody() throws JspException {
   if(iterations > 0) {
      iterations--;
      return EVAL_BODY_AGAIN;
   } else {
      try {
        if(bodyContent != null) {
          JspWriter out=
             bodyContent.getEnclosingWriter();
          bodyContent.writeOut(out);
        }
      } catch (IOException e) {
          throw new JspException();
      }
      return SKIP_BODY;
    }
}

public int doEndTag() throws JspException {
   return EVAL_PAGE;
}
```

```
    public void release() {}

    public Tag getParent() {
        return this.parent;
    }
}
```

The point of this code is to determine whether the tag has a body. If it does, the doAfterTag() method extracts the contents and writes it out to the bodyContent. The iteration counter is decremented and checked to determine whether to repeat the behavior in the doAfterBody() method.

TIP

By the time a tag's doEndTag() method is invoked, the container might have already reused the body content instance. Consequently, you should not use the BodyContent object in the doEndTag() method; instead, it should be handled within the doAfterBody() method.

NOTE

The BodyContent object is flushed when the highest-level parent object (similar to the Object class) clears its buffer. The highest-level parent object would be a tag that is not nested within any other tag. When that object calls writeOut(...), the buffer is flushed.

Ultimately, the code example produces the following output:

```
Test 1
Test 2
Test 2
Test 1
Test 2
Test 2
```

A common use for the IterationTag or BodyTag is to extract data from a java.sql.ResultSet object returned from a database call. With each iteration, the current record is extracted in some standard format, which is defined within the body content.

Depending on the task at hand, you can implement any one of these three interfaces. To simplify matters, however, a few support classes are provided to limit the number of methods you have to define when creating a custom tag.

Support Classes

To reduce the amount of redundant work and provide additional functionality, *support classes* are made available. The API provides a variety of support classes; the three that most closely pertain to the exam objectives will be covered.

Two of the three classes implement the Tag interface and define the methods for the developer. They include the following:

javax.servlet.jsp.tagext.TagSupport is used for basic tags that do not manipulate the tag's body. TagSupport implements IterationTag, which extends the Tag interface.

javax.servlet.jsp.tagext.BodyTagSupport is used for tags that intend to make changes to the tag's body content. Although these classes implement the methods of the interface, the most commonly used methods are written with limited functionality. This encourages the developer to override the intended method to define custom behavior. In addition to making tag extensions easier to write, the class also provides a few supplementary methods to expand the tag's capabilities. BodyTagSupport extends TagSupport. BodyTagSupport also implements the BodyTag interface, which in turn extends IterationTag.

The third support class is used to provide additional information to the tag:

javax.servlet.jsp.tagext.TagExtraInfo is provided by the tag library author to describe additional translation-time information not described in the TLD.

In this section, these three classes will be discussed because they are often used when creating custom tags.

The *TagSupport* Class

The javax.servlet.jsp.tagext.TagSupport class implements the IterationTag interface, granting it the standard Tag life cycle. The class is also able to iterate through the tag body multiple times, without making changes to the body. This utility class is considered the *base class*, which offers basic functionality for new tag handlers. Because all the life-cycle methods are implemented, they have default return values that you should know. Table 7.5 defines those defaults.

TABLE 7.5: Default Return Values for TagSupport Tags

Method	Default Return Value
doStartTag()	SKIP_BODY
doAfterBody()	SKIP_BODY
doEndTag()	EVAL_PAGE

In addition to defining the standard interface methods, the TagSupport class offers two instance variables and some convenience methods for greater functionality. The variables are as follows:

> **protected String id** is a value that can be assigned to the tag for future reference.
>
> **protected PageContext pageContext** provides the tag with access to the JSP page implicit objects, such as the JspWriter object out, or the HttpSession object, known as session.

Because the Tag interface method setPageContext(...) is now defined for you, the pageContext variable must be accessible to the class. The id variable is defined by using a method called setId(...) and indirectly accessible by using the getId() method.

Another feature of the TagSupport class is its capability to maintain a collection of values. A *tag value* is any java.lang.Object with an associated String key. This concept is similar to a java.util.Map. You can set and get the value of a tag by using the following TagSupport methods:

- public Object getValue(*String key*)
- public java.util.Enumeration getValues()
- public void removeValue(*String key*)
- public void setValue(*String key, Object o*)

As with a java.util.Map, you set the value of the tag by passing a unique key and the value itself. Internally, the TagSupport class maintains a Collection (it returns an Enumeration) of values that you can enumerate by using the getValues() method. Because you can add values, you can also remove them by identifying the object you intend to eliminate via its key.

In addition to the previous methods defined, one other convenience method is available to this class. It is static and used to help tags coordinate with one another. Its signature is as follows:

- `public static final Tag findAncestorWithClass(`*`Tag from, java.lang.Class class`*`)`

Sometimes you might need the help of an outer tag to resolve a problem with a current nested tag. You can get the handle to any parental tags from within a tag by using either the `getParent()` method or by calling `findAncestorWithClass(...)`. The method `getParent()` returns only your immediate parent. In contrast, the `findAncestorWithClass(...)` method enables multiple-layer subtags to acquire a handle to any outer ancestral tag class. This method takes two arguments. The first parameter is the `Tag` handle from which you want the container to begin its search for the target class. The second parameter is the target `java.lang.Class` whose `Tag` handle you are requesting.

The `findAncestorWithClass(...)` method is used to return a handle to an ancestor tag class that is nested. For example:

```
<outer-outer>
   <outer>
      <inner (makes ancestor request)>
         Body
      </inner>
   </outer>
</outer-outer>
```

It is related to nesting tags within the JSP page, not a parental hierarchy.

Consider the following code example:

```
public int doStartTag() throws JspException {
    Class className=com.company.TagName.class;
    Tag ancestor = TagSupport.findAncestorWithClass(this,
       className);
    TagSupport ts = (TagSupport)ancestor;
    ServletRequest req = pageContext.getRequest();
    ts.setValue("quantity", req.getParameter("qty"));
  return SKIP_BODY;
}
```

Imagine that the example's `doStartTag()` method exists within a tag that is nested within several other tags. The `com.company.TagName .class` is a great-great-great grandparent class. Given such a scenario, the `findAncestorWithClass(...)` method will return a handle to that relative, allowing the current tag to modify a parameter value. In contrast, the method `getParent()` will return only the immediate enclosing tag class.

NOTE

For the `findAncestorWithClass(...)` method to locate a parental relative, the child tag must be nested within the parent tag in the JSP page. In addition, the parent tag cannot evaluate its body.

The `findAncestorWithClass(...)` method can be called within any tag-handler method. Because the method is static, the handler class does not need to subclass `TagSupport`. A `Tag` instance is returned, so if the ancestral class is of a different data type, you must cast it to access the class's methods or instance variables.

When subsequent tags need to pass information or get information from a parental relative, they can use the `Tag` handle to access its attribute methods.

The *BodyTagSupport* Class

The `javax.servlet.jsp.tagext.BodyTagSupport` class extends the `TagSupport` class and implements the `BodyTag` interface. The design provides the `BodyTagSupport` class the added features of the `TagSupport` class and the capability to modify the body of the extension as defined by the `BodyTag` interface. This support class provides an iteration life cycle with the capability to alter the body content that exists between the opening and closing tags. It also can add and remove tag values.

In addition to the standard methods and variables defined by its inherited class and interfaces, the `BodyTagSupport` class offers a new instance variable and some convenience methods to access the `BodyContent` and the surrounding `JspWriter`. The new variable is as follows:

> **`protected BodyContent bodyContent`** provides a handle to the data that exists between the opening and closing tag elements.

In addition to the new variable, the class also adds the following two methods:

- `public BodyContent getBodyContent()`
- `public JspWriter getPreviousOut()`

Because the support class defines the `setBodyContent(...)` method, accessing the `BodyContent` object can be done either by accessing the instance variable `bodyContent` or by using the accessor method `getBodyContent()`.

The other method, `getPreviousOut()`, saves you the hassle of first accessing the `BodyContent` object to then get the enclosing `JspWriter`. So instead of calling

```
JspWriter out= getBodyContent().getEnclosingWriter();
```

you can simply call

```
JspWriter out = getPreviousOut();
```

Again, this is simply a convenience method that provides access to the enclosing tag's writer. Given the potential for nested tags, this approach ensures that writing done in an inner tag will be concatenated to the outer tag's output.

Because the `BodyTagSupport` class extends the `TagSupport` class and provides implementation for the `BodyTag` interface, it offers the most default custom tag functionality. As a result, it is used most often when creating custom tags that utilize their body content. If you revisit the code for `LoopTag`, you can see how the code is greatly simplified; see Listing 7.6.

Listing 7.6: Utilizing the BodyTagSupport Class

```
package tagext;

import java.io.*;
import javax.servlet.jsp.*;
import javax.servlet.jsp.tagext.*;

public class LoopTag extends BodyTagSupport {
    private int iterations;

    public void setIterations(int value) {
        this.iterations = value;
    }

    public int doAfterBody() throws JspException {
        if(iterations>1){
           iterations-;
           return EVAL_BODY_BUFFERED;
        } else {
           try {
```

```
                if(bodyContent != null) {
                    bodyContent.writeOut(getPreviousOut());
                }
            } catch (IOException e) {
                throw new JspException();
            }
            return SKIP_BODY;
        }
    }
}
```

In this example, you should notice a few things. There is no need to define the standard set methods of the tag and its subclassing interfaces. Also, you use the `bodyContent` variable directly because it is available from the `BodyTagSupport` class. Finally, you call `getPreviousOut()` instead of using the `BodyContent` object to access the enclosing `out` variable.

The *TagExtraInfo* Class

Until now, you have seen one way for a JSP page to access attribute values. When an action tag declares the value for an attribute, the JSP page can utilize the variable directly if a `set`*XXX*`(...)` attribute method is defined. Listings 7.5 and 7.6 use the `iterations` variable, which is passed from the JSP page. After the `setParent(...)` method is invoked, the container calls the `setIterations(...)` method, passing in the attribute value from the JSP page. Although this approach is effective, it requires the tag to individually define each and every attribute in the tag library descriptor. In addition, you are unable to specify the scope of the attribute. Instead, the attribute is available for the life of the action.

Another approach is available that provides more flexibility and manageable code (meaning you can create an action with 100 variables without having a huge TLD). By extending the abstract class `TagExtraInfo` and overriding one or two of its methods, you can provide a list of variables with differing scopes to the JSP page and scriptlets that the action might utilize. To create this list, you must override the first method in the list below. The second method is optional and simply adds greater functionality:

- `public VariableInfo[] getVariableInfo(`*TagData data*`)`
- `public boolean isValid(`*TagData data*`)`

The container invokes the `getVariableInfo()` method when attributes for the action are requested. A `TagData` instance is passed to the method containing translation time attribute/value pair information defined within the JSP page. Consider the following code:

```
<syb:profile name='Chris Cook'>
    Welcome to our site <%= name %><br>
</syb:profile>
```

In this example, the `TagData` object would contain a `String` key called `name` with an associated value `Chris Cook`. It acts like a `java.util.Map` by holding a collection of objects, which are accessible through their `String` key values. When overriding the `getVariableInfo()` method, you can use the `TagData` handle to call the `getAttribute(`*`String name`*`)` method and pass in the name of the attribute to acquire its value. The class `ProfileTagInfo` demonstrates how the method can be overridden.

```
public class ProfileTagInfo extends TagExtraInfo {
   public VariableInfo[] getVariableInfo(TagData data) {
      return new VariableInfo[] {
         new VariableInfo(
             data.getAttributeString("name"),"
             "java.lang.String",  // variable's data type
             true,                // True means variable
                                  // is new
             VariableInfo.NESTED  // scope
         )
      };
   }
}
```

Creating a `VariableInfo` object requires passing in four parameters to its constructor. The first is the name of the variable, which is passed as a String. To prevent runtime errors or unexpected results, the name of each variable should be unique because it is the name of the actual attribute. The second argument is the fully qualifying class name of the variable's data type. The third is a `boolean`. When set to `true`, a new variable is created by the action and declared within the translated servlet. The variable overrides the value of an existing variable if necessary. A `false` declaration means the variable already exists. The last argument is an `int` value. It represents the scope of the variable. Table 7.6 describes your choices.

TABLE 7.6: VariableInfo Scope Options

Scope	Description
VariableInfo.AT_BEGIN	The variable is accessible from the start of the action tag until the end tag is reached.
VariableInfo.AT_END	The variable is not accessible until after the end tag is reached.
VariableInfo.NESTED	The variable is available only within the action's body.

Figure 7.7 shows the scope range for each constant graphically.

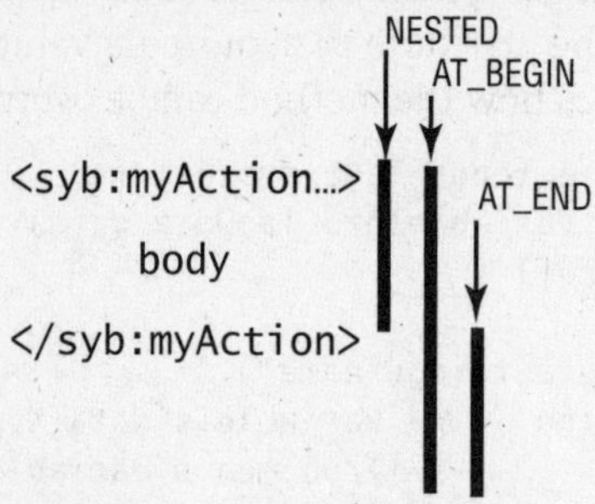

FIGURE 7.7: Scope range

As you can tell, AT_BEGIN has the greatest possible scope, whereas NESTED covers the action's body, and AT_END covers everything thereafter. Some of these arguments can be defined dynamically with the use of the TagData object passed by the container.

The second method that is commonly overridden, but optional, provides elegance to the action's attribute. The isValid() method is used to validate the attributes passed to a tag at translation time. It receives a TagData instance, which can be used to filter out unacceptable values. For example, you might accept only certain object types or numbers within a particular range. The default implementation returns a true for all attributes. If configured to return false, it is still the developer's responsibility to utilize the attribute correctly.

Now that you have seen how to create the list of variables, you will learn how to link the variables to the JSP page. The process begins with the container. When it comes across a variable within a scriptlet, it attempts to locate the value by looking to the tag library descriptor. An instance of the implementing class of TagExtraInfo is available by using the tei-class element to define it. Take a look at an example:

```
<taglib>
   <tag>
         <name>profile </name>
         <tag-class>ProfileTag</tag-class>
         <tei-class>ProfileTagInfo</tei-class>
         <body-content>JSP</body-content>
         <attribute>
            <name>name</name>
            <required>true</required>
            <rtexprvalue>true</rtexprvalue>
        </attribute>
   <tag>
</taglib>
```

The container locates the class and loads it into memory. At that point, all the variables are available by mapping the JSP variable name to the variable's key name.

In this example, you defined the scope of the variable name as NESTED. That works fine when you want to use the variable within scriptlets located inside nested actions. If, however, the scope is defined as AT_END, the variable must be saved to the JSP's PageContext. Remember, the PageContext object is one of the first objects set within the page. It lasts for the life of the page and can hold attributes. Consider the following code:

```
public int doEndTag() throws JspException {
   pageContext.setAttribute("name", "Sasha");
   return EVAL_PAGE;
}
```

In this example, the attribute name is accessible from within a JSP page after the closing tag for this action is read. If the scope for the variable were AT_BEGIN, you would need to associate it to the pageContext before the doStartTag() method. Fundamentally, it is important to know that attribute variables defined within the PageContext are accessible from within the JSP page and embedded scriptlets.

NOTE

The PageContext object is a major resource for storing and accessing variables. It contains handles to implicit objects and page attributes.

Utilizing the TagExtraInfo class provides a clean way to incorporate a significant number of attributes into an action. The attributes can be used from within the custom tag class, the action itself, and scriptlets.

What's Next

This chapter covered the topics needed to understand custom tags. It began by discussing custom tag fundamentals, including the ways to call a custom tag and the elements that are necessary within the JSP and web.xml file to locate the tag library. It also discussed how to create a tag library descriptor file, which maintains all the tags and their attributes. Finally, this left you with the core behind custom tags—the actual action or tag class.

The unique features of each interface and class that utilize the parent Tag interface were addressed. The details associated with each Tag interface are emphasized to ensure a thorough understanding of the Tag, IterationTag, and BodyTag life cycles. Each interface serves a slightly different purpose and should be utilized accordingly.

This chapter also covered the importance and role that the pageContext plays in a custom tag by providing access to the application's implicit variables and TagExtraInfo attributes. Finally, the impact of the BodyContent object and how to effectively write information out to the client was covered.

This chapter concluded the coverage of servlets and JSP pages. The next chapter will discuss the JNDI API, which is used throughout J2EE applications to access naming and directory services.

Part II
Naming Services, Databases, and Security

Chapter 8

Java Naming and Directory Interface (JNDI)

Part II

Naming and directory services provide a fast, simple way to search for data in a common repository. In that respect, these services are similar to databases, but they are optimized to be more appropriate for applications in which the data is accessed more than it is changed. Possibly without knowing it, you probably use naming and directory services on a daily basis. When you access a file on your computer, the file system uses an internal naming service to locate the file. When you log in to a network operating system, that operating system typically uses a directory service to locate and verify your login information. When you type a URL into a browser, a directory service (the Domain Naming Service, or DNS) is used to determine the IP address that is referenced by that URL. When you use your company's employee search tool to query for the phone number or e-mail address of a co-worker, that tool is likely searching through a directory service to find the information.

Written for *Enterprise Java™ 2, J2EE™ 1.3 Complete*
by Victor Peters and Michael Ernest

J2EE applications will frequently use naming and directory services for the following purposes:

- To search a common repository of data that can be quickly accessed from anywhere on the network. Frequently, this data includes user information, security access control lists, and information about network resources.
- To obtain remote stubs of Enterprise JavaBean (EJB) objects.
- To access objects provided by the J2EE server, such as resource factories and transaction control services.

There are many different kinds of naming and directory services available, and they support a variety of different protocols and APIs to access them. To save the Java programmer from the hassle and maintenance headaches of learning, programming, and maintaining code for each different kind of naming and directory service, Sun created the Java Naming and Directory Interface (JNDI). JNDI is not a naming or directory service, but rather it is an API that allows Java programs to easily interact with almost any naming and directory service.

Featured in this chapter:

- An explanation of the purpose and characteristics of naming and directory services.
- An overview of various types of naming and directory services currently available.
- Examples of how to configure and use JNDI to access naming and directory services.
- An introduction to using JNDI with LDAP compliant directory services.
- An introduction to how directory services can be utilized by J2EE applications.

Naming Services

A naming service is a system that binds unique names to values, and provides an easy and fast way to locate those values by providing their associated unique name. Naming services are similar to a white pages phone book that binds names to phone numbers and provides an easy way to locate those phone number values by searching for the associated name.

Naming Service Features

The two fundamental operations that all naming services provide are:

Binding Adding an object to the naming service along with its unique name.

Lookup Retrieving an object from the naming service by searching for the unique name and retrieving the associated object.

Many naming services provide these features:

Easy Accessibility Remote network access and flexible Application Programming Interfaces (API) allow a variety of client applications to access and share the data in one naming service. Some form of security is usually available to restrict which applications and users may access the data.

Fast Lookups Usage of fast algorithms that speed up lookup operations.

Persistence Guaranteed storage of the data in the naming service.

Hierarchical Structure Organization of the entries into contexts and sub-contexts.

Partitioning, Replication, and Federation Distribution of the contents of the naming service between different machines for reliability and efficiency, and the coordination between different naming services to fulfill a lookup request.

To better understand the capabilities of naming services, consider an example in which you might use a naming service: suppose that you are writing an internal employee e-mail directory application. This application tracks the names and e-mail addresses of all employees in the company. When a user enters an employee's name, the program will return the e-mail address of that employee. This application could use a naming service to bind employee names with their e-mail addresses.

Binding

When data is inserted into a naming service, a unique name is always provided along with an associated object value. The operation of adding a new entry into a naming service is called *binding* because we say that the naming service is binding the value to the unique name. In the e-mail application example, as new employees are hired, their e-mail addresses would be bound to their employee names in the naming service. Figure 8.1 shows a small sample of what the naming service would be storing for our company.

NAME	VALUE
"Victor Peters"	"VictorPeters@NextStepEducation.com"
"June Leon"	"JuneLeon@NextStepEducation.com"
"Barbara Frisvold"	"bFrisvold@NextStepEducation.com"
"James Behrends"	"jBehrends@NextStepEducation.com"
"Carol Peters"	cPeters@NextStepEducation.com"

FIGURE 8.1: Sample data in naming service

Readers who are familiar with the `HashMap` or `Hashtable` classes in the `java.util` package may recognize that naming service binding is exactly analogous to the `put` method of `HashMap` or `Hashtable`. These classes have the same basic purpose as a naming service, except without the extra peripheral services such as remote access and security.

Lookup

A lookup is the operation in which you provide a unique name to the naming service which then returns the associated value, assuming that name was previously bound to a value. When a user enters an employee name in the e-mail application, the application will look up that name in the naming service and then retrieve the associated e-mail address value.

Readers who are familiar with the `HashMap` or `Hashtable` classes may recognize that lookups are exactly analogous to the `get` method of `HashMap` or `Hashtable`.

Easy Accessibility

Naming services usually allow remote access from multiple simultaneous clients. Naming services usually also provide an API that makes them accessible from a variety of programming platforms. These two factors mean that a variety of diverse enterprise applications and clients can access the same data in a shared naming service. To see the value of these features, consider a scenario in which the company has several different applications that all need to look up employee e-mail addresses; those applications could include the e-mail directory discussed previously in this chapter, an e-mail client program, and a cafeteria system that sends out e-mails of the monthly cafeteria menu to all employees. The company certainly doesn't want to have separate copies of all the e-mail addresses for each of these applications. That type of redundancy of data would cause unnecessary waste in entering and maintaining duplicate lists. Having one naming service with remote access means that these three systems that might all be running on separate servers can all share the same list. It is possible that our three applications are written using very different technologies, such as servlets/JSPs, EJBs, and C++ classes. But with flexible APIs, it is likely that they can still all share the same data in the single naming service.

Fast Lookups

One of the most important features of almost all naming services is the capability to perform lookup operations quickly, even though there are likely to be a large number of entries. Consider our e-mail application; the average e-mail address entry in our naming service probably only changes once every year or two. In that same period, there might be hundreds, even thousands, of requests for that e-mail address. The magnitude of this ratio of hundreds of lookups per one binding is common for many kinds of enterprise data. Naming services are usually optimized to provide fast lookups, probably at the detriment of binding performance. As a result, naming services are best suited for data that changes relatively infrequently compared to the number of lookup requests.

Persistence

Because naming services often have crucial data in them, it is usually important that they persist the data to permanent storage and provide some level of fault tolerance to reduce the chance of losing the data. Some readers might now be wondering whether there are significant differences between databases and naming services because they provide the following similar features: They both provide a means of storing and retrieving data based on unique identifiers; they both provide easy remote accessibility from diverse types of client software; they both provide relatively fast lookups with large sets of data; and they both provide reliable long term persistence of data. In fact, naming services are similar to databases. The primary differences are that naming services are generally simpler and offer more limited capabilities, and are likely to provide faster lookups. Some naming services actually use full database products as their persistence tool behind the scenes.

Hierarchical Structure

One final characteristic of naming services is that they usually store data in a structure of contexts and sub-contexts. In the e-mail application example, imagine that there are 30,000 employees in the company. It would be more effective to be able to group the name-value pairs into sub-contexts, perhaps by department within the company. Part of our company e-mail directory with this new context organization is shown in Figure 8.2.

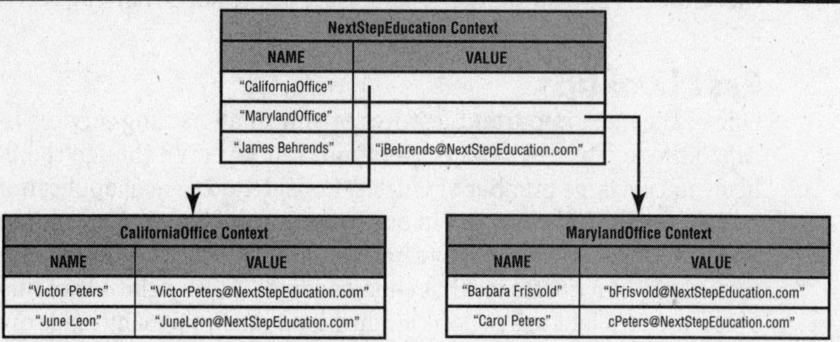

NextStepEducation Context
NAME
VALUE
"CaliforniaOffice"
"MarylandOffice"
"James Behrends"
"jBehrends@NextStepEducation.com"
CaliforniaOffice Context
NAME
VALUE
"Victor Peters"
"VictorPeters@NextStepEducation.com"
"June Leon"
"JuneLeon@NextStepEducation.com"
MarylandOffice Context
NAME
VALUE
"Barbara Frisvold"
"bFrisvold@NextStepEducation.com"
"Carol Peters"
cPeters@NextStepEducation.com"

FIGURE 8.2: Hierarchical structure of a naming service

This structure is exactly the same structure we see when the thousands of files on a computer are grouped into sub-directories. Just as a computer file system is composed of directories that can contain files and sub-directories, a naming service is composed of contexts that have name-value pair entries and sub-contexts. There can be any number of layers of sub-contexts. The reason that file system directory structures and naming service context structures are exactly analogous is because operating systems file systems actually are a naming service where unique filenames are bound to file entries.

Partitioning, Replication, and Federation

Large naming services often allow the data to be partitioned, which allows different contexts to be stored on different machines. In Figure 8.2, it is possible that our "NextStepEducation" context and "California" context might be stored on a server in our California office, and our "Maryland" context might be stored on a server in our Maryland office. This might improve performance by distributing the workload and keeping data closer to its most common clients. Data can also be replicated and stored on multiple servers to allow better fault tolerance and load balancing of lookup requests.

Notice that with partitioning, a lookup operation might involve accessing data from multiple servers. To take this a step further, it is possible that a completely different naming service, possibly operated by a different company and possibly using a different naming service technology, could have a binding containing a context from our naming service. That means that doing a lookup could involve communicating to multiple naming services. This is called a *federated lookup* when a lookup call accesses multiple naming or directory services. In our e-mail example, Figure 8.3 shows a layout that might require a federated lookup. Another company might have a naming service that has a "Vendor" context, which could have a binding of the name training to our "NextStepEducation" context. As a result, somebody doing a lookup in their name service might request a lookup that involves one our contexts. In this case, the two naming services would work together to fulfill the request.

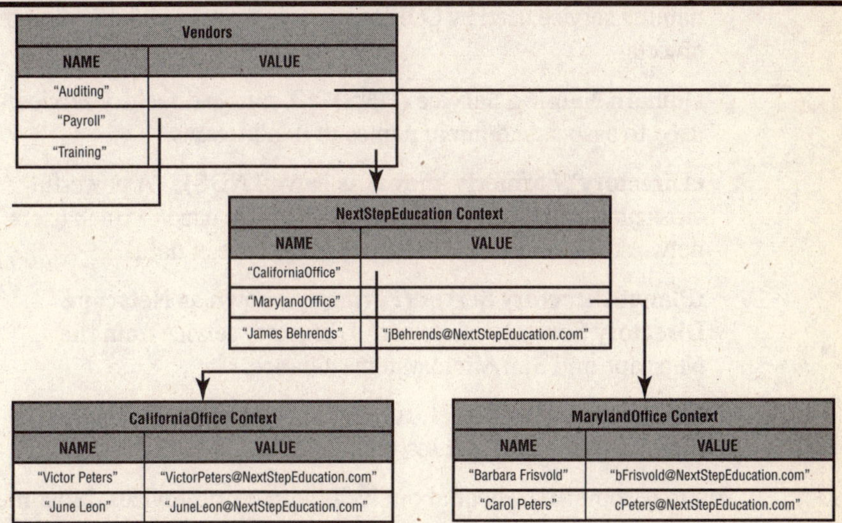

FIGURE 8.3: Federated example

Directory Services

To understand the difference between naming services and directory services, consider some additional functionality you might want to add to the e-mail example application. Imagine you want to be able to store employee's titles and phone numbers in addition to their e-mail addresses. You would like to allow users to make more sophisticated searches. The users should be able to search for employee data by using any combination of first name, last name, phone number, title, and e-mail address as the search criteria. Directory servers have all the features of naming services, but they additionally allow the user to store attributes about an object and to allow searches based on those attributes.

There are a wide variety of naming and directory services on the market for different purposes. Here is a sample list of some of the types or specific naming and directory services available:

File Systems An OS file system is a naming service that associates filenames with handles to file objects.

RMI Registry A simple naming service used by RMI applications to store stubs of remote objects.

CORBA Common Object Service (COS) Naming Service A naming service used by CORBA services to store stubs to remote objects.

Domain Naming Service (DNS) A simple directory service used to associate domain names to IP addresses.

eDirectory (Formerly known as Novell NDS) A powerful cross platform directory service that can be used to track users, network resources, and most any other type of data.

iPlanet Directory Server (Formerly known as Netscape Directory Server) A powerful directory service from the Netscape and Sun Microsystems alliance.

Microsoft Active Directory A directory service integrated with Windows and .net technologies.

You may sometimes hear about X.500 directory services. Most major directory services, including some of the ones listed above, are based on an underlying architecture called X.500. X.500 is a massive set of guidelines for directory services. There is a corresponding X.500 Directory Access

Protocol (DAP) that allows access to X.500 directory services; however, X.500 DAP is a rather heavy and complicated protocol for talking to directory services. The Lightweight Directory Access Protocol (LDAP) was created to provide a simpler protocol for talking to X.500 directory services. LDAP is not a directory service, nor is it an architecture for directory services. It is a specification of a protocol and API for communicating with directory services that comply with it. In addition to X.500 directory services, there are many other directory services that are accessible through LDAP. LDAP accessible directory services include eDirectory, iPlanet Directory Server, Microsoft Active Directory, and, in fact, almost all major directory services.

Java Naming and Directory Interface (JNDI)

There are many naming and directory services available on the market for a wide variety of purposes and from a wide variety of vendors. Over the last decade many directory services have standardized on providing access through common protocols such as the Lightweight Directory Access Protocol (LDAP). There has not been a complete standardization of protocols, however. Without some help from the nice folks at Sun, writing Java programs that use different directory services would require a programmer to learn the various different protocols and APIs that are associated with those different services. This configuration is shown in Figure 8.4. Not having a standard API like JNDI would slow down development, increase the learning curve, and complicate code maintenance.

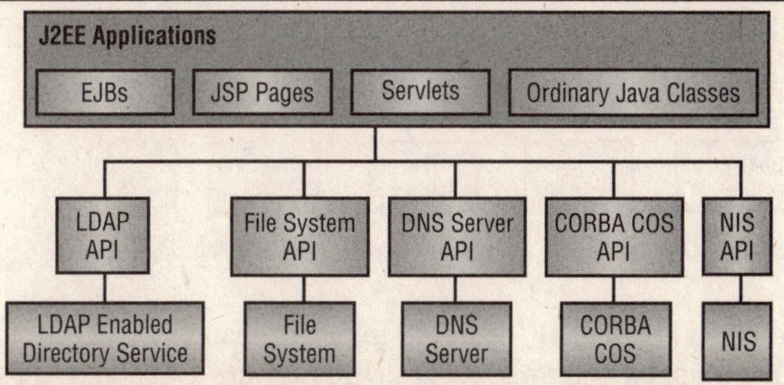

FIGURE 8.4: Coding to proprietary APIs

Fortunately, coding to individual APIs is not necessary because Sun created JNDI. JNDI is not a directory service; it's not even a driver to talk to a directory service. JNDI is merely a standard specification and API that indicates how different naming and directory service drivers should be developed so that they can support the same Java interface. JNDI allows Java programmers to write essentially the same code regardless of what type of directory service they are communicating with. You can freely download or buy a JNDI compliant service provider (driver) for the particular kind of naming or directory service with which you need to communicate. Regardless of which service provider you use and which directory service you access, you can use the same JNDI method calls. This approach is shown in Figure 8.5. As a result of JNDI, the learning curve, development effort, and code maintenance are all simplified. Unfortunately, you still need to know quite a bit about the underlying directory service. One reason for this is that the naming conventions to specify the locations of entries for bind, lookup, and search operations on directory services are not standardized. In contrast, because all major relational databases support standard SQL (although most have their own non-standard additions), the same standard SQL used with JDBC should work on most relational databases. But because directory services don't have a universal naming standard such as SQL, the same is not true for directory services.

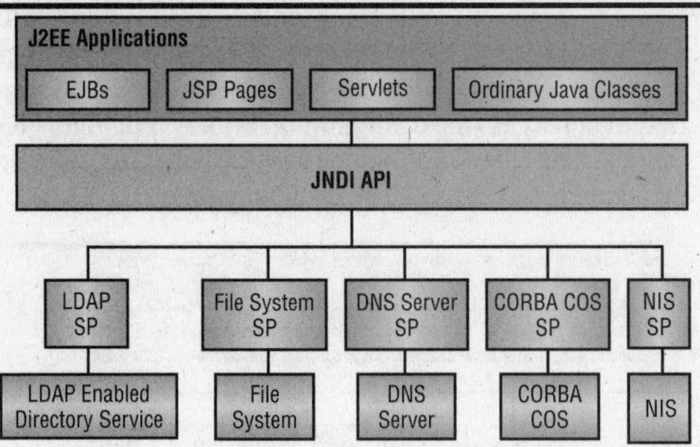

FIGURE 8.5: Using JNDI to access different types of directory services

As you read about JDBC and JMS in future chapters, you will see that they follow a similar pattern to JNDI. JDBC provides a standard API so that you can use different JDBC drivers to connect to different databases. JMS provides a standard API so that you can use different JMS service providers (drivers) to connect to different messaging services. JNDI provides a standard API so that you can use different JNDI service providers to connect to different naming and directory services.

JNDI Package Structure

JNDI is made up of five packages:

- `javax.naming` provides the API for accessing naming services. This package includes the Context interfaces that have lookup and binding operations.
- `javax.naming.directory` extends `javax.naming` to provide the API for accessing directory services. It focuses on capabilities for setting attributes and performing searches based on attributes.
- `javax.naming.event` provides the API for listening to naming and directory services to be notified when contexts or entries are changed.
- `javax.naming.ldap` provides support for LDAPv3 operations. Many applications that communicate with LDAP servers will only need to use the classes in the `javax.naming` and `javax.naming.directory` interfaces. Only applications that want to take advantage of special LDAP features will need this package.
- `javax.naming.spi` is not used by applications; it is used by developers of JNDI service providers (drivers). JNDI is divided into an API and a Service Provider Interface (SPI). The API is used by application developers and is defined by the first four packages. The SPI is used by writers of service providers and is defined by this package.

What You Need To Use JNDI

To use JNDI you need a few elements, which are usually easy to get:

JNDI API The JNDI API is packaged with J2SE 1.3 and above, and J2EE 1.2 and above; therefore, most readers should already have the JNDI API via J2SE or J2EE. If necessary, you can download the newest version of the JNDI API from the download section of `http://java.sun.com/products/jndi`.

Service Provider To communicate with a naming or directory service, you need a service provider (driver) for that specific type of service. J2SE 1.3 includes the service providers to connect to LDAP servers, CORBA COS, and the RMI registry. J2SE 1.4 includes those service providers plus the service provider for DNS. The full list of service providers along with download information is available at `http://java.sun.com/products/jndi/serviceproviders.html`.

A Naming or Directory Service The service provider is only the driver to connect to a naming or directory service, but you still need an actual service to connect to. Naming and directory services include the file system of your operating system, the RMI registry that comes standard with Java, the naming or directory service that comes with your J2EE server, DNS servers, and a variety of other services.

File System Lookup Example

The file system lookup example will use the file system service provider to look up files in the computer's file system. Most readers are less likely to actually use this service provider than some of the other service providers, such as the LDAP service provider, but the advantage of this example is that everyone has a file system, so anyone can run this example without having to worry about installing or configuring a naming or directory service. The beauty of JNDI is that most of the details of using any service provider are the same, so as you learn how to use this service provider, you are learning how to use any JNDI service provider.

Listing 8.1 shows the code for this example. It will take a name provided by the user and look up that name in the file system. If the name is a valid filename, the `File` object is returned from the JNDI service provider, and the application prints the filename and full path of that file. If the name is a valid directory name, the service provider returns the `Context` object and then the program uses that context to print the names of all the files and sub-directories in that directory. If any other type of object is returned, that object is printed. If the name is not a valid name in the file system, the service provider throws a `NameNotFoundException` and the program prints an error message.

Listing 8.1: FileSystemExample.java

```
import javax.naming.Context;
import javax.naming.InitialContext;
```

```
import javax.naming.NamingEnumeration;
import javax.naming.NameClassPair;
import javax.naming.NamingException;
import javax.naming.NameNotFoundException;
import java.util.Hashtable;
import java.io.File;

public class FileSystemExample {
  public static void main(String args[]) {
    if (args.length != 1) {
      System.out.println("Enter the name to lookup.");
    }
    else {
      try {
        Hashtable props = new Hashtable();
        props.put(Context.INITIAL_CONTEXT_FACTORY,
          "com.sun.jndi.fscontext.RefFSContextFactory");
        Context ctx = new InitialContext(props);
        Object obj = ctx.lookup(args[0]);
        if (obj instanceof File) {
          File f = (File) obj;
          System.out.println("This name is bound to" +
            "the file " + f.getName() +
            " with a full path of " + f.getPath());
        }
        else if (obj instanceof Context) {
          System.out.println("This name is bound to " +
            "a directory with the following contents:");
          Context subCtx = (Context) obj;
          NamingEnumeration listing = subCtx.list("");
          while (listing.hasMore()) {
            NameClassPair entry =
              (NameClassPair) listing.next();
            System.out.println(entry.getName() +
              " is of the class " + entry.getClassName());
          }
        }
        else {
          System.out.println("This entry is bound to the " +
            "following object: " + obj);
        }
      }
```

```
        catch (NameNotFoundException e) {
          System.out.println(args[0] + " is not bound in " +
            "this context.");
        }
        catch (NamingException e) {
          System.out.println("Unexpected JNDI error " +
            "occurred.");
        }
      }
    }
  }
```

This example begins with import statements for various classes from the `javax.naming` package. Because this example is using a naming service, it only requires the `javax.naming` package, not any of the other JNDI packages such as `javax.naming.directory`.

After verifying that the user provided one command line argument, the program prepares to create an `InitialContext`. By obtaining the `InitialContext`, the program makes a connection to the naming service, which provides the context for the performance of JNDI operations. For JNDI to provide an `InitialContext`, it needs to know what kind of service implementation you are going to use. In many cases, JNDI will also need to know other properties, such as where the naming or directory service is located and security authentication information for the naming or directory service. In this example, the service provider will default to providing an `InitialContext` based on the root directory on `localhost` and does not require security authentication. To set the initialization property for the service provider that should be used in this case, the program creates a `Hashtable` and assigns `"com.sun.jndi.fscontext.RefFSContextFactory"` (one of the JNDI service provider implementations provided by Sun) to the property `Context.INITIAL_CONTEXT_FACTORY`. This `Hashtable` is passed into the constructor of `InitialContext`. The FSContext service provider is not included with the J2SE or J2EE. To run this example, you will need to download `fscontext.jar` from `java.sun.com/products/jndi` and then put that jar file somewhere in the classpath.

The code then obtains an `InitialContext` object. `InitialContext` is a subclass of `Context`; for generality, it is legal and perhaps preferable to set the new `InitialContext` to a `Context` reference. This context represents the root directory of the computer on which it is running. The program then does a lookup of the name specified by the command line argument `args[0]`. Lookup does not know what kind of object it is returning, so the return value must be typecast or put into an `Object` reference.

If the lookup argument is a filename in the InitialContext, which is the root directory in this case, lookup will return a java.io.File object representing it. The first if statement prints the filename and pathname if a File is returned. For example, running the program on a Windows machine with this command line:

```
java FileSystemExample config.sys
```

produced the output:

```
This is the file config.sys with a full path of C:\config.sys
```

If the lookup argument is a sub-directory of the root directory, the lookup will return a Context object, in which case the program prints the name of the directory and then lists all the entries in that context. The list method of Context returns a NamingEnumeration object. NamingEnumeration is a subinterface of Enumeration. When you call the list method of Context, the NamingEnumeration will contain NameClassPair objects for each entry in that context. NameClassPair represents entries in the context, and has methods to retrieve the name and the class of the entry. For example, running the program on my computer with this command line:

```
java FileSystemExample jdk1.4
```

produced the output:

```
The name you specified is bound to a directory with the
   following contents:
bin is of the class javax.naming.Context
COPYRIGHT is of the class java.io.File
demo is of the class javax.naming.Context
docs is of the class javax.naming.Context
include is of the class javax.naming.Context
jre is of the class javax.naming.Context
lib is of the class javax.naming.Context
LICENSE is of the class java.io.File
readme.html is of the class java.io.File
README.txt is of the class java.io.File
src is of the class javax.naming.Context
src.zip is of the class java.io.File
```

It is possible to bind non-File objects into a JNDI context with the file system provider, in which case the lookup could return that other type of object. This should not happen in this example, but the code provides an else clause for any other objects, just in case.

If the argument to lookup is not a file or directory and is not bound in this context, lookup will throw a NameNotFoundException and the catch block prints an appropriate error message. There is also an exception for the more generic NamingException to catch any other problems that may occur.

javax.naming Package API

The javax.naming package is the only package you will usually use to access a naming service and is one of the primary packages you will use to access directory services. This section lists some of the most important interfaces, classes, and methods in this package. This is not a complete listing of the javax.naming package API. As always, for a full API reference, you should consult the J2SE or J2EE API documentation.

Context

The Context interface represents a context in the naming service. This is the most fundamental of the interfaces in JNDI and provides the basis for lookup and binding operations. Every method in this interface can throw a NamingException. The most commonly used methods include:

public void bind(String name, Object obj) throws NamingException Binds the second parameter into the current context with the first parameter as the name. The name may include the path of a sub-context relative to the current context to bind the object into. If there is already an object bound to that name in that context, the method will throw a NameAlreadyBoundException, which is a subclass of NamingException.

public void rebind(String name, Object obj) throws NamingException This operation does the same thing as the bind operation. The only difference is that if the name is already bound to another object, it will overwrite the previous binding instead of throwing a NameAlreadyBoundException.

public void unbind(String name) throws NamingException This operation will remove the binding for that name in this context or the specified sub-context. If the binding does not exist, it throws a NameNotFoundException, which is a sub-class of NamingException. This method tends to be used more often than the bind method.

public Object lookup(String name) throws NamingException This returns the object that was previously bound to the specified name. If the binding does not exist, it throws a NameNotFoundException.

public NamingEnumeration list(String name) throws NamingException This returns an enumeration of all the names and class types of the objects bound in the sub-context specified by the parameter. If `name` is the empty string, the method will list all names bound in this context. In either case, the `NamingEnumeration` will include both regular objects and sub-contexts bound in that context; however, it will not recursively list the next layer of sub-contexts.

public NamingEnumeration listBindings(String name) throws NamingException This method is similar to the `list` method. While the `list` method only returns the names and class types, the `listBindings` method also returns the actual objects that are bound. As a result, this is a much heavier operation because it is returning all the bound objects. You should use this method if you will need to access all, or most, of the objects bound to this context. If you will probably not need to access the actual values of most of the bindings, you should use the previous method.

public Context createSubcontext(String name) throws NamingException This method creates a new sub-context in the current context. If the name specified is already bound in the current context, the method throws a `NameAlreadyBoundException`.

The `bind`, `rebind`, and `createSubContext` methods are demonstrated in this code snippet. This partial example creates a new sub-context called stubs and attempts to bind a payroll tracking object and vacation tracking object into that new context. The payroll tracking object is only bound if there is not already an object bound in this context called "PayrollTracker," which there shouldn't be because it is a brand new context.

```
try {
  Context ctx = new InitialContext();
  PayrollSystem payroll = //create payroll object
  VacationSystem vacation = //create vacation object
  ctx.createSubcontext("stubs");
  Context stubsCtx = (Context) ctx.lookup("stubs");
  stubsCtx.bind("PayrollTracker", payroll);
  stubsCtx.rebind("VacationTracker", vacation);
}
catch (NamingException e) {
  e.printStackTrace();
}
```

InitialContext

`InitialContext` is a class that implements the `Context` interface. The `InitialContext` provides a way to access a context to use as a starting point from which you can perform lookups. Because `InitialContext` implements `Context`, it supports all the methods in `Context` and can be referred to by a `Context` reference variable. From the application programmer's perspective, the only major difference between `InitialContext` and `Context` is that `InitialContext` has a publicly available constructor used to create the `InitialContext`; all other contexts are usually created behind the scenes when you call methods such as `lookup` that return a sub-context. There are two constructors in `InitialContext`:

`public InitialContext() throws NamingException`

`public InitialContext(Hashtable env) throws NamingException` When an `InitialContext` is created, JNDI needs to know which service provider you intend to use initially and where the naming service is. In addition, it may need to know service provider–specific properties for configuration or security. If you use the second form of the constructor that takes a `Hashtable`, it will search for all these properties in that `Hashtable`. Regardless of which constructor you use, it will also search in the system properties, and it will search in any jndi.properties files located in your CLASSPATH or in the $JAVA_HOME/lib directory. For driver specific properties, it will also search for a `jndiprovider.properties` file included with the service provider.

Your J2EE server may automatically set up the necessary properties to access its naming service from within a J2EE application; otherwise, you may specify these properties in a `jndi.properties` file in the CLASSPATH. Or to specify these values in your code, you may create a `Hashtable`, add the properties to it, and pass that `Hashtable` in the code. This last approach is shown in the earlier example.

Name

All of the methods in the `Context` interface that take a `String` name, such as `bind`, `rebind`, `unbind`, and `lookup`, have an overloaded method that takes a `Name` instance instead of a `String` instance. `Name` is an interface with two implementing classes: `CompositeName` and `CompoundName`.

The String name you may pass into a Context method is equivalent to a CompositeName. A CompositeName may contain parts from different naming services. A CompoundName is a name that may only contain components from one naming service. If you are constructing a JNDI name dynamically based on user input, you may find it easier to do so by creating a CompositeName and then passing that name to a Context method. You probably will not create your own CompoundName, but some methods that return Name references will return a CompoundName method. When you have a Name reference, you can use its get methods or the NameParser interface to retrieve the components that make it up.

NamingException

NamingException is a subclass of Exception that has 25 different direct or indirect subclasses that define different kinds of JNDI exceptions. Because almost every method in JNDI throws a NamingException, you will almost always have to handle NamingException when you do any JNDI programming. In some cases, it may be beneficial to have additional catch blocks that catch subclasses such as NameNotFoundException, NameAlreadyBoundException, InvalidNameException, ServiceUnavailableException, or NamingSecurityException. The only time you need to catch subclass exceptions is if you want to write some separate code when those types of exceptions occur. NamingException has several get methods that may be helpful: getExplanation(), getRemainingName(), getResolvedName(), and getRootCause().

J2EE Reference Implementation Server Naming Service

All J2EE servers are required to provide a CORBA Common Object Service (COS) naming service. This naming service will have bindings for a variety of objects, such as instances of DataSource and UserTransaction, for J2EE applications and clients to look up and use. J2EE servers may also include other naming services and J2EE applications can additionally use third-party naming and directory services. J2EE servers may allow applications and clients to bind objects into the J2EE naming service; however, the J2EE specification does not require that. The specification only requires that J2EE applications and clients be allowed to look up objects that the server bound into that naming service.

Lookup of References to EJB Home Objects

An EJB client uses an EJB home to create or find an EJB instance. The J2EE server will place a reference to the EJB home object into the naming service where any EJB client can look it up. When you deploy the bean, you will specify what JNDI name that bean should be bound to. Simply for organizational purposes, the J2EE server recommends but does not require that you place the EJB home reference in a context named "`ejb`". If you specified a JNDI name of "*`ejb/StockSelector`*", an EJB client that wanted to use that EJB home would use the following code to look it up:

```
Context ctx = new InitialContext();
Object o = ctx.lookup("ejb/StockSelector");
```

Note that the `InitialContext` constructor might likely be passed a `Hashtable` for JNDI properties, but that would depend on how the client was specifying those properties (as discussed in the `InitialContext` section earlier in this chapter.)

If the client to the bean is a J2EE component, such as a servlet or another bean, the lookup may be done slightly differently. When you deploy the J2EE component that is the client to the bean, you can specify an alias JNDI name that this component will use to look up that bean. The lookup will then be done within the context for this J2EE component. Each J2EE component, such as a servlet or a bean, is given its own context in which the J2EE server binds objects that only need to be accessed by that component. A J2EE component can access its context via the JNDI context name "`java:comp/env`", which will be mapped automatically by the J2EE server to the specific context name for that component. In this case, the lookup would look like:

```
Context ctx = new InitialContext();
Object o = ctx.lookup("java:comp/env/ejb/StockSelector");
```

In either case, the home object that is returned should be typecast to the correct data type. Due to restrictions imposed by the CORBA specification, which is used by J2EE servers, the home object must be narrowed before it is typecast. If the home object is of the type `ChimpanzeeHome`, the following code would narrow and typecast the home object that was retrieved in either of the previous lookups:

```
ChimpanzeeHome ch = (ChimpanzeeHome)
 PortableRemoteObject.narrow(o, ChimpanzeeHome.class);
```

NOTE

EJB development and deployment is discussed in Chapters 20, 21, 22, and 23.

Lookup of JDBC *DataSources*

Most J2EE applications communicate with databases using JDBC, which requires creating or acquiring a JDBC connection. Creating a JDBC connection requires providing several pieces of configuration data, such as the name of the JDBC driver that is being used as well as the location of the database. Specifying these details in your code is undesirable because it makes it difficult to change to a different database. Instead, J2EE servers allow you to specify these JDBC configuration settings in your J2EE server configuration. The J2EE server will then use those configuration settings to create an appropriate `DataSource` object, which in turn creates and hands out `Connection` objects. The J2EE server will place this `DataSource` object in the naming service. The result of this approach is that a J2EE application that needs a JDBC `Connection` object can use JNDI to lookup the `DataSource` object and then simply call the `getConnection` method of `DataSource` to acquire a `Connection` object without specifying any JDBC configuration information in the code.

In the J2EE server configuration, you will specify the name that the JDBC `DataSource` should be bound to. Simply for organizational purposes, the J2EE specification recommends, but does not require, that the `DataSource` should be placed in a context called "`jdbc`". The compound name of a `DataSource` binding, therefore, might be *"jdbc/AccountingDB"*.

When you deploy a J2EE component, such as a servlet or EJB, you can specify an alias JNDI name that this component will use to look up a `Datasource` within it's context. You might specify that the *"jdbc/AccountingDB"* `DataSource` should be available in this component's context by the name *"jdbc/AcctDB"*, in which case the following code snippet would allow that component to get a JDBC connection:

```
Context ctx = new InitialContext();
DataSource ds = (DataSource)
   ctx.lookup("java:comp/env/jdbc/AcctDB");
Connection con = ds.getConnection();
```

NOTE

Chapter 9 discusses the details of using a `DataSource` object to retrieve a JDBC `Connection` to access a database.

Part II

Lookup of JMS Destinations

Many J2EE servers may want to communicate via Message Oriented Middleware (MOM) to send asynchronous or guaranteed messages to other components. Java Messaging Service (JMS) is a Java API for accessing MOM, just as JNDI is used to access naming services and JDBC is used to access databases. Just as JNDI and JDBC require configuration settings to create a JNDI `InitialContext` or a JDBC `Connection`, JMS requires configuration settings to create a connection to a JMS `Queue` or `Topic`. To keep the deployment details out of your code, J2EE servers allow you to configure JMS queues and topics and then look them up in JNDI. The J2EE specification recommends, but does not require, that these JMS destinations be placed in a context named "*jms*". The pattern for doing this is essentially identical to configuring and doing a lookup of a JDBC DataSource. A lookup of a JMS destination will usually look similar to:

```
Context ctx = new InitialContext();
Queue orderQ = (Queue)
    ctx.lookup("java:comp/env/jms/OrderQueue");
```

NOTE

JMS is discussed in Chapter 17.

Lookup of JavaMail and URL Connection Factories

Similar to the previously discussed way that JDBC `DataSource` and JMS destinations can be acquired through JNDI, the J2EE server should also allow you to acquire JavaMail connection factories and URL connection factories. The deployer will specify the JavaMail or socket configuration settings in the J2EE server and then the J2EE application can look up these factories. The J2EE specification recommends that JavaMail connection factories be placed in the "*mail*" context, and socket factories be placed in the "*url*" context.

Lookup of *UserTransaction* Object

The `UserTransaction` interface has methods such as `commit` and `rollback` for managing transactions. J2EE servers are required to place a `UserTransaction` object into the naming service by the name "`java:comp/UserTransaction`". This allows J2EE components to use JNDI to look up objects to control their transactions. It should be noted, though, that J2EE servers are not required to let all components look up that object if they feel it is inappropriate for a certain type of component to use this object.

NOTE

Chapter 22 discusses the details of using a `UserTransaction` object to control transactions.

RMI Registry

Remote Method Invocation (RMI) can be used as a mechanism for a Java class on one machine to call a method of a Java class running on a different machine. RMI requires that the client application receive a *stub* object from the server machine. This stub object will be responsible for creating the network message that triggers the RMI call on the server application. The RMI registry is a simple naming service that allows an RMI server to bind a stub object to a unique name and then allows RMI clients to look up that stub by that unique name. This provides an easy way for the distributed RMI clients to get the RMI server stub object. The RMI registry offers a simpler although less robust API for accessing the RMI registry than JNDI. When accessing the RMI registry, you will use the `Naming` class in the `java.rmi` package. Although it is a different API, you will notice great similarities to what you are learning here. Just like a `Context`, the `Naming` class has bind, `rebind`, `list`, and `lookup` methods. Unlike JNDI, these methods are static, and you will not need to explicitly request an `InitialContext`. The following code binds an RMI stub for a remote object into the RMI registry. The RMI remote object in this example is an object of the `DateFinderImpl` class. (The code for this class is not shown because Chapter 18 will have full RMI examples.) This RMI remote object is bound to the RMI registry by the name "`DateF`".

```
//create the RMI remote object
DateFinderImpl dfi = new DateFinderImpl();
//bind it to the naming service
Naming.rebind("DateF", dfi);
```

For the sake of example, if that code was running on a computer with an IP address of 64.27.12.1, an RMI client, usually running on a different machine that wanted to use the `DateFinderImpl`, could use the following code to look up the `DateFinderImpl` stub:

```
DateFinder df = (DateFinder)
  Naming.lookup("rmi://64.27.12.1/DateF");
```

RMI applications are not required to use the RMI registry. Any directory service and service provider that allow binding of Java remote objects can be used to store the stub objects. In that case, the RMI programmer could use the JNDI API instead of the `java.rmi.Naming` class. The JNDI code to bind the remote object would be the same as the previously shown JNDI code:

```
Context ctx = //a previously created context
ctx.bind("DateF", dfi);
```

Note that some directory services, such as LDAP, may require a different format for the name to which the object is bound. The next section will discuss LDAP naming conventions.

The RMI client could then use a standard JNDI lookup to get the remote object:

```
Context ctx = //a previously created context
DateFinder df = (DateFinder) ctx.lookup("DateF");
```

NOTE

Remote Method Invocation (RMI) is discussed in Chapter 18.

LDAP

Most major directory services are LDAP-compliant. LDAP-compliant directory services can be accessed through the standard LDAP protocol, which allows you to access the directory service without programming to a vendor specific naming convention or architecture. J2SE 1.3 and above includes a JNDI service provider for LDAP. Through this service provider, you can use JNDI to access the wide variety of LDAP-compliant directory services. As you've seen, the beauty of JNDI is that as you change to a new service provider, the changes in the code can seem trivial. You're actually gaining two benefits with this approach: you make your access code more generic, hence more portable, and you can install a new or updated provider without disturbing the code that drives it. Here's a code fragment that illustrates the cosmetic changes from the previous listings, using classes from `javax.naming.directory` to access an LDAP server:

```
// create context environment
try {
   Hashtable ctxEnv = new Hashtable();
```

```
    DirContext context;
    ctxEnv.put(Context.INITIAL_CONTEXT_FACTORY,
       "com.sun.jndi.ldap.LdapCtxFactory");
    ctxEnv.put(Context.PROVIDER_URL,
       "ldap://pipeline:389/o=Trainers");
    ctxEnv.put(Context.SECURITY_AUTHENTICATION, "none");
    context = new InitialDirContext(ctxEnv);
    ...
}
```

The LDAP service provider is specified by setting `Context.INITIAL_CONTEXT_FACTORY` to `"com.sun.jndi.ldap.LdapCtxFactory"`. After specifying the service provider, two new elements come into play. The value associated with `Context.PROVIDER_URL` is an LDAP server address in URL syntax. Port 389 is the well-known port for LDAP servers, shown here for clarity. The string `"o=Trainers"` declares the search base for any queries. The value associated with `Context.SECURITY_AUTHENTICATION` means your client will identify itself as "anonymous" to the server.

You also see the `javax.naming.directory.InitialDirContext` class is used in this example. `InitialDirContext` extends `InitialContext` and implements `javax.naming.directory.DirContext`, which in turn declares the behavior relevant to directories: binding, searching, and getting and setting attributes. `DirContext` and `InitialDirContext` are typically used instead of `Context` and `InitialContext` when working with any kind of directory service.

All of the configuration settings could be read from a property file or abstracted by a factory method, which would aid in factoring out as many provider "details" from the source code as possible. Nonetheless, LDAP's underlying model is worth a closer look. An LDAP directory's complex structure, designed to support access to a large, distributed mass of records through a common view, ultimately does change the approach to lookups you've seen in JNDI so far.

LDAP Features

The key features of an LDAP-compliant directory include:

Operations How to connect to an LDAP server, and add, delete, and modify records.

Structure LDAP maintains a domain-aware, hierarchical namespace, so one large database can be broken into subtrees and distributed, promoting scalability.

Naming How records, or entries, are referenced, which has a direct bearing on the JNDI user.

Security LDAP supports authentication and data encryption schemes, detailed later in this chapter.

Replication The capability to copy whole or partial trees to other servers promotes greater availability to clients.

NOTE

It's also possible to combine several LDAP directories, in fact even different kinds of data sources, into one meta directory server. iPlanet's Meta Directory Server is an example of this. See `http://wwws.sun.com/software/products/meta_directory/` **for details.**

Operations LDAP directories support operations expected of any data repository: add, delete, modify, search, bind, and unbind are all specified in LDAP version 2. Version 3 provides support for operations called extensions and controls, which make it possible to augment standard operations without losing compliance.

A full rundown of operations can be found in RFC 1777 (version 2) and RFC 2251 (version 3). Text versions of these documents are available as rfc1777.txt and rfc2251.txt via FTP at `ftp://ftp.isi.edu/in-notes/`.

Structure Correlating a file system to an LDAP directory probably isn't intuitive on first sight, but the concepts are the same. A host name or IP address and port number identify a directory's location in a network; the top-level directory is marked by a root suffix, which is synonymous with a file system's root directory; and each entry's fully qualified, or distinguished name, acts like a path to a file object.

Figure 8.6 shows a simple directory structure. The root suffix at the top of the hierarchy is called a suffix because it is the last element specified when referring to an entry. This form follows the convention used by naming services like DNS, where a top-level domain name, such as .com or .net, is a reserved word that terminates the name to be resolved.

Similar to file systems, directory nodes express locations through a chain of identifiers. Unlike file systems, identifiers are not simple names. They are instead a name-value pair known as a relative distinguished name, or RDN for short. This naming style serves the same purpose as a file system folder, in one sense, but also offers more powerful searching potential than a simple string name.

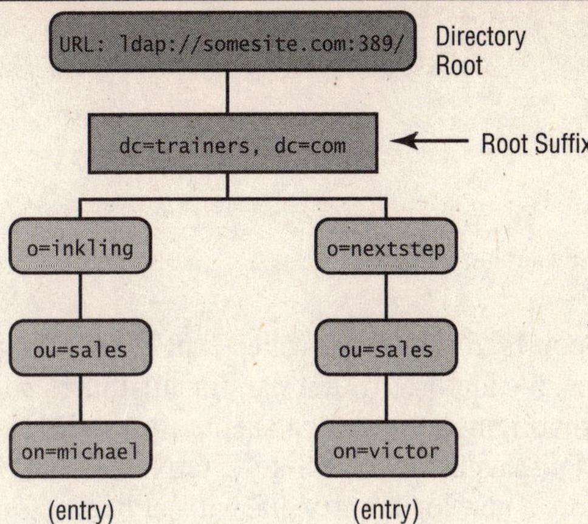


```
dn: cn=victor, ou=sales, o=nextstep, dc=trainers, dc=com
dn: cn=michael, ou=sales, o=inkling, dc=trainers, dc=com
```

FIGURE 8.6: LDAP Structure Example

As Figure 8.6 shows, it's common to use organization units as nodes below the root suffix; `inkling` is unique from `nextstep` simply by naming. Each sub-domain's organization is free to be organized as it prefers, including mirroring another branch's structure. In the example, `inkling` and `nextstep` both have an RDN of ou=Sales without conflicting.

NOTE

In the X.500 specification, country codes are required top-level attributes because it was designed from the start to support global directory navigation.

A distinguished name is thus a concatenated string of all identifiers leading from the leftmost RDN to the root suffix. This is the same as an absolute path to an object in a file system, except that in LDAP syntax it's expressed left-to-right from the bottom up.

Naming Every distinguished name points to an entry, which is a collection of name-value pairs or attributes. For ease of learning, think of these attributes as an entry's state data. Bear in mind, however, that there's more to it than the simple diagram shown in Figure 8.7 suggests.

```
dn:  cn=SamuraiJack, ou=cartoons, o=basiccable

   Attribute Name              Value
   cn                          SamuraiJack
   firstName                   Sam
   lastName                    Jackson
   uid                         4532
   phoneNumber                 x41722
   <other required>
   <any optional>
   ...
```

FIGURE 8.7: LDAP Naming Example

An RDN that points to an entry is called that entry's naming attribute. To avoid collisions, it's important that naming attributes hold values that will render new distinguished names to separate two RDNs under one parent RDN. Imagine using an RDN like "firstName=Joe" instead of "uid=5252" to store a new login entry; life will get harder for subsequent entries much sooner in the first case!

As any Java programmer should be able to appreciate, attribute names aren't arbitrary or loosely-typed variable names, but rather are object classes. Using the diagram in Figure 8.7, notice that each attribute name is really an LDAP entity called an objectClass. These entities all have the following defined traits:

OID a globally unique numeric identifier

superior a parent object class (the root class is Top)

requires attributes that an entry must specify

allows attributes that an entry may specify

All distinguished names have a unique path in a directory, but they also define, by an aggregation of RDNs, all the attributes that are and might be available within the entry. This is a powerful approach to expediting a search. It also explains why modifying an entries can take much longer than a search: Changing an entry could mean changing its distinguished name, which in turn could mean significant effort in relocating it within the directory.

Security Directories can contain a great amount of diversely typed information, some of which may not be intended for the review of any interested client. You may want the phone numbers of everyone to be available to all users, for example; social security numbers, on the other hand, should probably only be available to department heads, human resources, or other responsible parties.

Authentication Because the importance of authentication, authorization, and data encryption over the network may indeed vary with the kind of information requested, it falls upon the LDAP client to define the level of authentication it wants to employ whatever access is available at that level.

anonymous Synonymous with "guest" or "nobody" authority.

simple Clear-text password authentication.

SASL Simple Authentication and Security Layer. First supported in LDAP v3, SASL is a pluggable authentication scheme. It's possible to use any scheme agreeable to both client and server. Commonly supported methods include Kerberos, X.509, and S/Key.

The LDAP server dictates what security tools are available, so it's useful to be able to query it. This list is available via a top-level attribute, supportedSASLMechanisms. Using the object reference that was created in the introductory code fragment:

```
Attributes attrs;
NamingEnumeration enum;
String sasl = new String("supportedSASLMechanisms");
String server = new String("ldap://pipeline:389);
...
//continuation of try code above
attrs = context.getAttributes(server, new String[](sasl));
enum = attrs.getAll();
while (enum.hasMore()) {
   Attribute attr = (Attribute)enum.next();
   System.out.println(attr);
   System.out.println("Attribute id: " + attr.getID());
   System.out.println();
}
...
```

You've taken advantage of a few classes from the `javax.naming.directory` package in this example, which should be explained before going on. The subclass of `Enumeration`, `NamingEnumeration`, may seem unnecessary, but it's provided so that `next()`, `hasMore()`, and `close()` can throw `NamingExceptions` during the enumerating process.

`Attributes` and `Attribute` are interfaces that address the underlying schema of directory-based attributes. The `Attribute` interface has two methods, `getAttributeDefinition()` and `getAttributeSyntax-Definition()`, which return `DirContext` objects that contain attribute schema and syntax definitions, respectively. Note we've left out the exception handling to reduce clutter.

Network Data Encryption JNDI provides the `javax.naming.ldap` package to support Transport Layer Security (TLS), a feature specified in LDAP v3. In short, if the server supports LDAP v3, requests and responses can be protected in a Secure Sockets Layer (SSL) session, using the classes `StartTLSRequest` and `StartTlsResponse`.

```
import javax.net.ssl.SSLSession;
import javax.naming.ldap.*;

...
SSLSession session;
StartTLSResponse response;
StartTLSRequest request = new StartTlsRequest();
LdapContext ldapctx = new InitialLdapContext();
// unprotected LDAP operations start here
response = (StartTlsResponse)
   ldapctx.extendedOperation(request);
session = response.negotiate();
// Protected LDAP operations start here
session.close();
```

The request object is the parameter to an extended operation; the response object initiates an SSL communication through the method `negotiate()`, which if successful provides the transport for session traffic after that.

Replication Though not an issue directly affecting JNDI programmers, it's worth noting that directory services are designed to accommodate both partitioning and merging of directory data structure. Partitioning allows for keeping data close to its most likely subscribers (imagine for example a truly global directory of login data), while merging allows for keeping (or creating) a single repository.

Of course, moving data around takes time away from availability, or at the very least response time, so unless such goals are critical to the enterprise, it often makes more sense to proxy requests from the directory server to another. This is no different in concept from the way DNS servers chain together to retrieve an IP address that hasn't been cached before. Support for forwarding requests in LDAP comes in the form of referrals.

Supporting referrals was the initial motivation for creating an URL-based syntax for LDAP. They were not at first considered in LDAP because the design committee thought the protocol too complex for client-to-server referral communication. URL addressing, described by RFC 2255 for LDAP v3, made the idea much more palatable.

Referrals are treated as exceptions so clients must acknowledge that the initial context has failed and is returning a referral instead of response data. In JNDI, the class `javax.naming.ldap.LdapReferralException`. `LdapReferralException` inherits `getReferralInfo()`, and overrides `getReferralContext()` from `javax.naming.ReferralException`. `ReferralException` is a subclass of `javax.naming.NamingException`.

`getReferralInfo()` retrieves information such as the referral URL; `getReferralContext()` returns the context environment, useful for getting and setting property values before passing the request.

NOTE

Incidentally, you can set the LDAP version you use with the property `java.naming.ldap.version`. The legal values are 2 and 3. Use the same technique for altering the context as you have seen previously in this chapter.

What's Next

Total portability across naming services is, of course, the dream. The reality is that not all service implementations can be made to look completely the same, any more than all databases or operating systems can be made to look the same—at least not without sacrificing the features that separate some tools from their competitors in the first place.

JNDI nonetheless does allow for a great deal of abstraction that reduces much of this variation to property values, which in turn can be relegated to files instead of being embedded in source code. This approach gives the programmer flexibility, if not full portability, in addressing a variety of lookup services through one set of interfaces.

In the case of LDAP, a broadly popular and still changing technology, many feature differences that cannot be suitably contained as property values can be addressed through extensions or controls, which the serious JNDI/LDAP developer can find reference to in any full-scale treatment of the two technologies.

The next chapter will explore JDBC. Just as JNDI provides a standard interface for connecting to naming and directory services, JDBC provides a standard interface for connecting to relational databases. Since most enterprise applications are heavily reliant on a database, JDBC is one of the most essential elements of J2EE.

Chapter 9

Database Connectivity (JDBC)

Part II

Most J2EE applications require the use of a database system for a wide variety of purposes often including tracking corporate data, tracking user profiles, storing user requests, and maintaining application metadata. This chapter will explore how any Java application, including a J2EE application, can access a wide variety of databases using a single and consistent application programming interface: the Java Database Connectivity (JDBC) API.

Featured in this chapter:

- Database client/server methodology
- Java's JDBC API
- JDBC's drivers
- The JDBC-ODBC bridge
- `DataSource` Interface

Updated from *Java™ 2 Developer's Handbook™*
by Philip Heller and Simon Roberts
ISBN 0-7821-2179-9 $59.99

RDBMS Models

In a relational database management system (RDBMS), data is stored as rows of distinct information in tables. A structured language (Structured Query Language, or SQL) is used to query (retrieve), store, and change the data. SQL is an ANSI standard, and all major commercial RDBMS vendors provide mechanisms for issuing SQL commands.

NOTE

The evolution of relational data storage began in 1970 with the work of Dr. E. F. Codd. Codd's rules for relational modeling of data formed the basis for the development of systems to manage data. Today, RDBMSs are the result of Codd's vision.

Single-Tier Database Design

The early RDBMS applications were developed based on an integrated model of user interface code, application code, and database libraries. This single binary model ran only on a local machine, typically a mainframe. Figure 9.1 illustrates the monolithic single-tier database design.

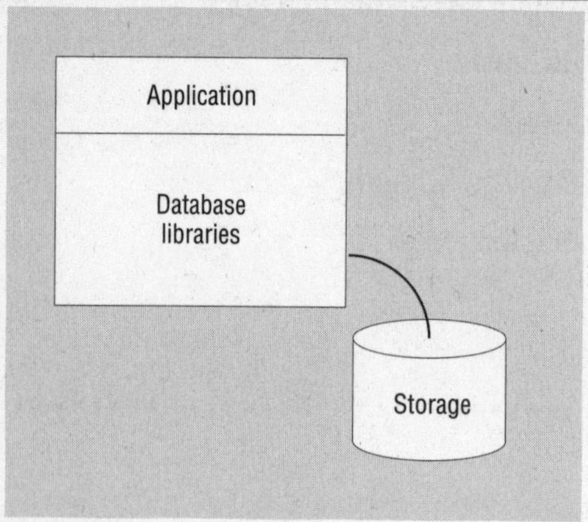

FIGURE 9.1: The monolithic single-tier database design

These applications were simple but inefficient, and they did not work over LANs. The model did not scale, and the application and user interface code were tightly coupled to the database libraries. Furthermore, the monolithic approach did not allow multiple instances of the application to communicate with *each other*, so there was often contention between instances of the application.

NOTE

It is typical for the terms *RDBMS* and *DBMS* (Database Management System) to be used interchangeably because almost all major commercial databases are relational and support some form of SQL to allow the user to query the relations between data tables.

Two-Tier Database Design

Two-tier RDBMS models appeared with the advent of server technology. Communication-protocol development and extensive use of LANs and WANs allowed the database developer to create an application front end that typically accessed data through a connection (*socket*) to the back-end server. Figure 9.2 illustrates a two-tier database design, where the client software is connected to the database through a socket connection.

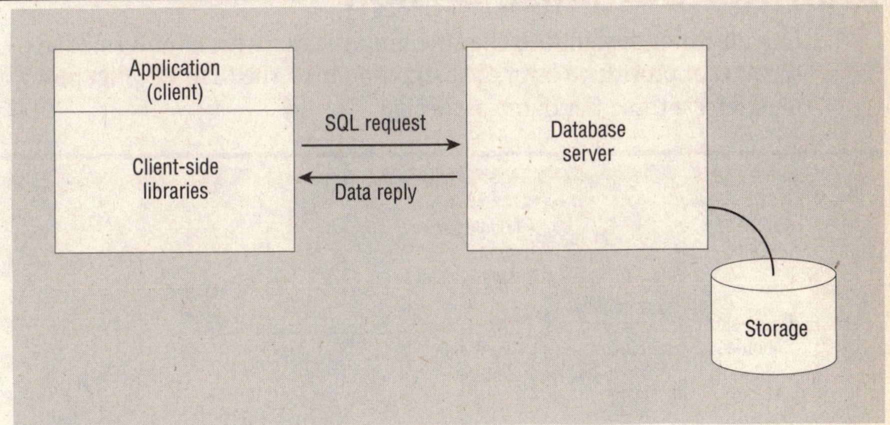

FIGURE 9.2: The two-tier database design

Client programs (applying a user interface) send SQL requests to the database server. The server returns the appropriate results, and the client is responsible for formatting the data. Clients still use a vendor-provided library of functions that manages the communication between client and server. Most of these libraries are written in the C language.

Despite the success of client/server architectures, two-tier database models suffer a number of limitations:

- They are limited by the vendor-provided library. Switching from one database vendor to another requires rewriting a significant amount of the client application's code.
- Version control is an issue. When the vendor updates the client-side libraries, the applications that use the database must be recompiled and redistributed.
- Vendor libraries deal with low-level data manipulation. Typically, the base library deals only with fetches and updates on single rows or columns of data. This can be enhanced on the server side by creating a stored procedure, but the complexity of the system then increases.
- All of the intelligence associated with using and manipulating the data is implemented in the client application, creating large client-side runtimes. This drives up the cost of each client seat.

Multitier Database Design

In a multitier design, the client communicates with an intermediate server that provides a layer of abstraction from the RDBMS. Figure 9.3 illustrates a three-tier database design.

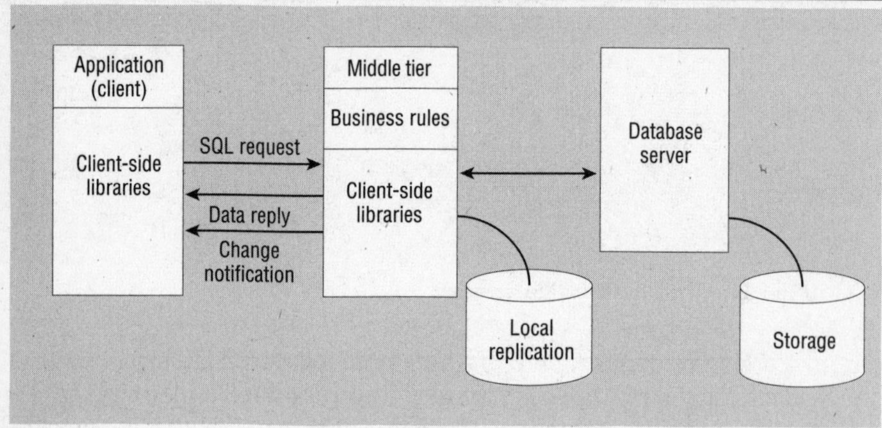

FIGURE 9.3: A three-tier database design

The intermediate layer is designed to handle multiple client requests and manage the connection to one or more database servers. The intermediate-tier design provides several advantages over the two-tier design. The middle tier has the following characteristics:

- It is multithreaded to manage multiple client connections simultaneously.
- This tier can accept connections from clients on a variety of vendor-neutral protocols (from HTTP to TCP/IP). It can then marshal the requests to the appropriate vendor-specific database servers, and return the replies to the appropriate clients.
- Developers can program the middle tier with a set of "business rules" that manage the manipulation of the data. Business rules might include anything from restricting access to certain portions of data to making sure that data is properly formatted before being inserted or updated.
- The tier prevents the client from becoming too heavy by centralizing process-intensive tasks and abstracting data representation to a higher level.
- Having the tier in the middle isolates the client application from the database system and frees a company to switch database systems without needing to rework the business rules.
- The tier can asynchronously provide the client with the status of a current data table or row. For example, suppose that a client application had just completed a query of a particular table. If a subsequent action by another distinct client *changed* that data, the first client could receive notification from an intelligent middle-tier program.
- The tier can provide significant security benefits by handling the real database behind a gateway system.

The JDBC API

Java offers several benefits to the developer creating front-end and middleware applications for a database server. The platform-independent nature as well as the adaptability of Java allows a wide variety of different kinds of clients to connect with the database system. Enterprise JavaBeans can provide a very scalable and robust database access and persistence layer. Servlets and JSP pages provide an ideal way for thin web browser clients or any variety of other HTTP-based clients to access database resources.

The JDBC API is designed to allow developers to create Java code that can access almost any relational database without needing to continually rewrite their code. Despite standards set by the ANSI committee, each database system vendor has a unique way of connecting to its system. Any type of Java code, including Java servlets, JSP pages, Enterprise JavaBeans, and plain Java classes, can use JDBC.

Features of the JDBC API

The JDBC API was first introduced with release 1.1 of the JDK. JDK 1.4 contains JDBC 3.0, which is composed of the java.sql and javax.sql packages. JDBC provides application developers with a single API that is uniform and database independent. The API provides a standard to write to, as well as a standard that takes all of the various application designs into account.

The API's database independence is due to a set of Java interfaces that are implemented by a driver. The driver takes care of translating the standard JDBC calls into the specific calls required by the database it supports. The application is written once and then moved to the various drivers. The application remains the same; the drivers change. Drivers may be used to develop the middle tier of a multitier database design, as illustrated in Figure 9.4.

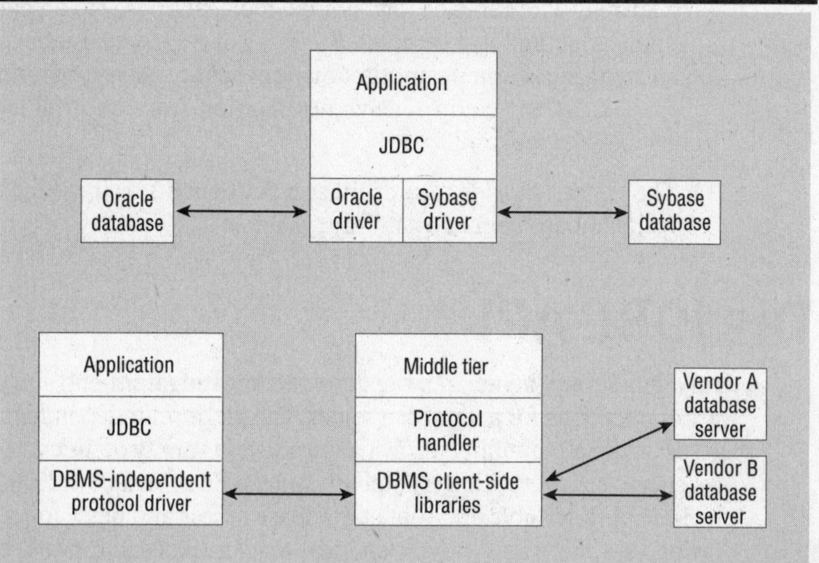

FIGURE 9.4: JDBC database designs

NOTE

There is a subtle difference between the terms *middle-tier software* and *middleware*. Middle-tier software performs some kind of data processing. Middleware simply packages and transports data without doing any processing.

In addition to providing developers with a uniform and database-independent framework, JDBC also provides a means of allowing developers to retain the specific functionality that their database vendor offers. JDBC drivers must support ANSI SQL-2 Entry Level, but JDBC allows developers to pass query strings directly to the connected driver. These strings may or may not be ANSI SQL, or SQL at all. The use of these strings is up to the underlying driver. (Of course, using this feature limits your freedom to change database back ends.)

Every Java client or J2EE application that uses JDBC must have at least one JDBC driver, and each driver is specific to the type of DBMS used. A driver does not, however, need to be directly associated with a database.

JDBC is *not* a derivative of Microsoft's Open Database Connectivity (ODBC) specification. JDBC is written entirely in Java; ODBC is a C interface. Both JDBC and ODBC, however, are based on the X/Open SQL Command Level Interface (CLI). JavaSoft provides a JDBC-ODBC bridge that translates JDBC to ODBC. This implementation, done with native methods, is very small and efficient. The JDBC-ODBC bridge is discussed later in the chapter.

JDBC Interface Levels

There are two JDBC interface levels:

- The Application layer is where the developer uses the API to make calls to the database via SQL and retrieve the results.
- The Driver layer handles all communication with a specific driver implementation.

Figure 9.5 illustrates the Driver and Application layers.

Fortunately, the application developer only needs to use the standard API interfaces to guarantee JDBC compliance. The driver developer is responsible for developing code that interfaces to the database and supports the JDBC application level calls. It is important, however, to understand the Driver layer, and how some of the objects that are used at the Application layer are created by the driver.

There are four main interfaces that every driver layer must implement, and one class that bridges the Application and Driver layers. The four interfaces are `Driver`, `Connection`, `Statement`, and `ResultSet`. The `Driver` interface implementation is where the connection to the database is made. In most applications, the `Driver` is accessed through the `DriverManager` class—providing one more layer of abstraction for the developer.

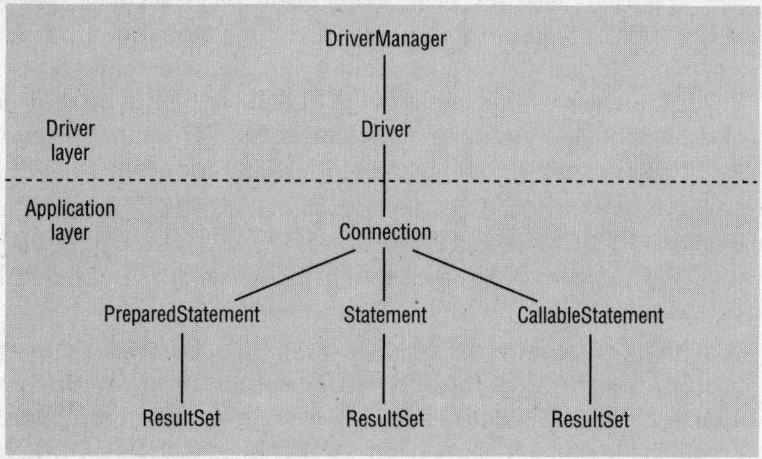

FIGURE 9.5: JDBC API components

The `Connection`, `Statement`, and `ResultSet` interfaces are implemented by the driver vendor, but these interfaces specify the methods that the application developer can use. They allow the developer to create statements and retrieve results without having to think about where the objects are coming from or worry about what specific driver the application will use. The following sections discuss the Driver and Application layers in more detail.

The Driver Layer

`Driver` is an interface. Each vendor supplies a class that implements this interface. The other important class is the `DriverManager` class, which sits above the Driver and Application layers. The `DriverManager` class is responsible for loading and unloading drivers and making connections through drivers. The `DriverManager` class also provides features for logging and database login timeouts.

NOTE

Remember that the driver does not need to connect directly to a database, and can support a new protocol for a multitier database design.

The Driver Interface Every JDBC application must have at least one JDBC driver implementation. The `Driver` interface allows the `DriverManager` and JDBC Application layers to exist independently of the particular database used. A JDBC driver is an implementation of the `Driver` interface class.

Drivers use a string to locate and access databases. The syntax of this string is similar to a URL string and is referred to as a URL. The purpose of a JDBC URL string is to separate the application developer from the driver developer. JavaSoft defines the following goals for driver URLs:

- The name of the driver-access URL should define the type of database being used.
- The user (application developer) should be free from any of the administration of creating the database connection; therefore, any database connection information (host, port, database name, user access, and passwords) should be encoded in the URL.
- A network naming system may be used so that the user does not need to specifically encode the exact hostname and port number of the database.

The URL syntax used by the World Wide Web supports a standard syntax that satisfies these goals. JDBC URLs have the following syntax and structure:

```
jdbc:<subprotocol>:<subname>
```

where `<subprotocol>` defines the type of driver, and `<subname>` provides the network-encoded name, as in:

```
jdbc:oracle:products
```

In this example, the database driver is an Oracle driver, and the subname is a local database called `products`. This driver is designed to know how to use the subname when making the connection to the Oracle database.

The programmer can include the location of the database host and the specific port:

```
jdbc:msql://dbserver.eng:1112/bugreports
```

Part II

In this example, an `msql` database driver type is used to locate a server named `dbserver` in the `eng` domain and attempt to connect to a database server on port 1112 that contains a `bugreports` database, using the default username and password to connect.

NOTE

The Java Software Division of Sun Microsystems acts as an informal registry for JDBC subprotocol names to ensure that they are unique.

The `Driver` interface specifies several methods. From a practical programming point of view, the two most important methods look like this:

`public Connection connect (String url, Properties info) throws SQLException` Checks the subprotocol name of the URL string passed for a match with this driver. If there is a match, the driver should then attempt to make a connection to the database using the information passed in the remainder of the URL. A successful database connection will return an instance of the driver's implementation of a `Connection` interface. The `SQLException` should be thrown only if the driver recognizes the URL subprotocol but cannot make the database connection. A `null` is returned if the URL does not match a URL the driver expected. The username and password are included in an instance of the `Properties` container class.

`public boolean acceptsURL (String url) throws SQLException` Explicitly "asks" the driver if the URL is valid. Note that, typically, the implementation of this method checks only the subprotocol specified in the URL, not whether the connection can be made.

Both of these methods throw `SQLException` if there is trouble with the remote database.

The `Driver connect()` method is the most important method, and is called by `DriverManager` to obtain a `Connection` object. The `Connection` object is the starting point of the JDBC Application layer (see Figure 9.5, shown earlier). The `Connection` object is used to create `Statement` objects that perform queries.

The `Driver connect()` method typically performs the following steps:

- Checks to see if the given URL string is valid
- Opens a TCP connection to the host and port number specified

- Attempts to access the named database table (if any)
- Returns an instance of a Connection

NOTE

Connection is a Java interface, so the object returned is actually an instance of the vendor's implementation of the Connection interface.

The DriverManager Class The DriverManager class is actually a utility class used to manage JDBC drivers. The class provides methods to obtain a connection through a driver, register and deregister drivers, set up logging, and set login timeouts for database access. The important DriverManager methods are listed below. Because they are static, they may be referenced through the interface. SQLException is thrown if there is trouble with the remote database.

public static synchronized Connection getConnection (String url, Properties info) throws SQLException Attempts to return a reference to an object implemented from the Connection interface. The method sweeps through a vector of stored Driver classes, passing the URL string and Properties object info to each in turn. The first Driver class that returns a Connection is used. info is a reference to a Properties container object of tag/value pairs, typically username/password. This method allows several attempts to make an authorized connection for each driver in the vector.

public static synchronized Connection getConnection (String url) throws SQLException Calls getConnection (url, info) with an empty Properties object (info).

public static synchronized Connection getConnection (String url, String user, String password) throws SQLException Creates a Properties object (info), stores the user and password strings into it, and then calls getConnection (url, info).

public static synchronized void registerDriver(java .sql.Driver driver) throws SQLException Stores the instance of the Driver interface implementation into a vector of drivers, along with an instance of securityContext, that identifies where the driver came from.

Part II

public static void setLogWriter(java.io.PrintWriter out)
Sets a private static `java.io.PrintWriter` reference to the `PrintWriter` object passed to the method.

TIP

The driver implementation can make use of two static object references that are stored through set*Type* methods and accessed by the driver through get*Type* methods: an integer that specifies login timeout and a `PrintStream` object used to log driver information.

Drivers are registered with the `DriverManager` class, either at initialization of the `DriverManager` class or when an instance of the driver is created.

When the `DriverManager` class is loaded, a section of static code (in the class) is run, and the class names of drivers listed in a Java property named `jdbc.drivers` are loaded. This property can be used to define a list of colon-separated driver class names, such as:

```
jdbc.drivers=imaginary.sql.Driver:oracle.sql.Driver:weblogic
  .sql.Driver
```

Each driver name is a class name (including the package declaration) that the `DriverManager` will attempt to load through the current `CLASSPATH`. The `DriverManager` uses the following call to locate, load, and link the named class:

```
Class.forName(driver).newInstance();
```

If the `jdbc.drivers` property is empty (unspecified), the application programmer must create an instance of a `Driver` class.

In both cases, the `Driver` class implementation must explicitly register itself with the `DriverManager` by calling:

```
DriverManager.registerDriver (this);
```

Here is a segment of code from the imaginary `Driver` (for the Mini-SQL database). The `Driver` registers itself whenever an instance of the imaginary driver is created:

```
...

public class iMsqlDriver implements java.sql.Driver

{

  static

  {
```

```
    try
    {
      new iMsqlDriver();
    }
    catch (SQLException e)
    {
      e.printStackTrace();
    }
  }
  /**
   * Constructs a new driver and registers it with
   * java.sql.DriverManager.registerDriver()
   * as specified by the JDBC protocol.
   */
  public iMsqlDriver() throws SQLException {
     java.sql.DriverManager.registerDriver(this);
}
...
```

The primary use of DriverManager is to get a Connection object reference through the getConnection() method:

```
Connection conn = null;
conn = DriverManager.getConnection
         ("jdbc:sybase://dbserver:8080/billing", dbuser,
            dbpasswd);
```

This method goes through the list of registered drivers, and passes the URL string and parameters to each driver in turn through the driver's connect() method. If the driver supports the subprotocol and subname information, a Connection object reference is returned.

The DriverManager class is not required to create JDBC applications; it is possible to get a Connection object directly from the driver. For example, if a driver class name is XxxDriver, the code below can be used to get a Connection from the driver:

```
Connection conn;
conn = new XxxDriver().connect
  ("jdbc:sybase://dbserver:8080/billing",props);
```

This means of obtaining a `Connection` is not as clean, however, and leaves the application developer dependent on the `Driver` implementation class to provide security checks. Also, the driver class is now hardcoded into the software, so the advantages of JDBC's vendor independence are lost.

DataSource Interface Although using the `DriverManager` class to retrieve `Connection` objects provides better adaptability than directly creating connections from the `Driver` interface, it is still not ideal. It still requires that the driver class name, URL, and configuration information either be placed in the application code or be read from configuration parameters or property files. J2EE applications will usually use the `DataSource` interface to retrieve connections instead of directly using the `DriverManager` interface.

The `DataSource` interface was introduced in JDBC 2.0 and is in the javax.sql package. A portion of the `DataSource` interface definition follows:

> **`Connection getConnection () throws SQLException`**
> Attempts to establish a connection with the data source that this `DataSource` object represents. This method requires that any necessary username and password be provided by the server configuration.
>
> **`Connection getConnection (String username, String password) throws SQLException`** Attempts to establish a connection with the data source that this `DataSource` object represents.

The J2EE system administrator or application deployer should configure a data source by specifying the JDBC driver name, URL, and configuration in the J2EE server configuration files in a manner that is vendor specific. For details on how to specify the JDBC data source in your J2EE server, consult the server's documentation. The J2EE server will then place the `DataSource` object in JNDI so that J2EE applications can look it up and then use it to get `Connection` objects.

A servlet or JSP deployer can specify that they use this `DataSource` by placing a resource-ref tag inside the web-app tag in the web.xml deployment descriptor. Similarly, an EJB deployer can place the same resource-ref tag inside the bean description in the ejb-jar.xml deployment descriptor. (EJB development and deployment is discussed in Chapters 20, 21, and 22.)

The resource-ref tag in either deployment descriptor appears like the following:

```
<resource-ref>
  <res-ref-name>jdbc/EmployeeAppDB</res-ref-name>
  <res-type>javax.sql.DataSource</res-type>
  <res-auth>Container</res-auth>
  <res-sharing-scope>Shareable</res-sharing-scope>
</resource-ref>
```

When a J2EE developer needs a `Connection`, they will look up the `DataSource` object in JNDI, which is discussed in Chapter 8. The lookup name is "java:comp/env" plus the res-ref-name specified in the deployment descriptor. For example, to look up the above `DataSource` and then obtain a `Connection` from it, the programmer would do the following:

```
Context initCtx = new InitialContext();
javax.sql.DataSource ds = (javax.sql.DataSource)
  initCtx.lookup("java:comp/env/jdbc/EmployeeAppDB");
java.sql.Connection con = ds.getConnection(); [TE - Exception
  handling?]
```

Notice that this mechanism does not require the programmer to specify any JDBC driver specific information in the code! Changing to a new database or new JDBC driver requires only changing the configuration in the J2EE server. By changing the data source configuration in the J2EE server, all of the servlets, JSPs, and EJBs that use that data source will automatically be using the new configuration.

ConnectionPoolDataSource Interface Creating a new connection to a database is a very expensive operation that may take a couple of seconds; thus, it can be exceedingly detrimental to your application performance to create a new connection every time you need to communicate a database. On the other hand, it is also usually not desirable for every servlet, JSP, and EJB to keep their own connection to the database constantly open because this could potentially result in hundreds of `Connection` objects being opened. Having all the servlets, JSP pages, and EJBs share one database connection is also not usually acceptable because this can create a tremendous bottleneck. The ideal solution is to use a connection pool. A connection pool keeps a set of connections, and allows application components to borrow a connection, use it, and return it. All your servlets, JSP, and EJBs can share one reasonably sized pool of database connections.

JDBC 2.0 added a ConnectionPoolDataSource interface for this purpose; however, J2EE application developers should not need to directly use this interface. Instead, the DataSource interface implementation of most JDBC drivers automatically use the ConnectionPoolDataSource internally. You should verify that your JDBC driver does support connection pooling through DataSource; if it does, the ds.getConnection() code returns a logical database connection from the connection pool. When you call the close method on that connection, it will return the logical database connection back to the connection pool. Using the connection pool does not require any special code.

XADataSource Interface Many J2EE servers support distributed transactions that involve multiple databases. For example, you could run a SQL statement on a Connection from one DataSource for an Oracle database, and run a SQL statement on a Connection from a DataSource for a SQL Server database. If your J2EE server supports distributed transactions, you can specify that those two SQL statements are in the same transaction, and must commit or rollback together. Distributed transactions are discussed further in Chapter 22.

JDBC 2.0 added an interface called XADataSource to allow JDBC drivers to support distributed transactions. As with the ConnectionPoolDataSource, you should not need to directly use the XADataSource class. If your JDBC driver and J2EE server support distributed transactions, they should use this interface behind the scenes. You don't have to write any special code for this purpose.

The Application Layer

The Application layer encompasses three interfaces that are implemented at the Driver layer, but are used by the application developer. In Java, the interface provides a means of using a general type to indicate a specific class. The interface defines methods that *must* be implemented by the specific classes. For the application developer, this means that the specific Driver class implementation is irrelevant; simply coding to the standard JDBC APIs will be sufficient. (Of course, this is assuming that the driver is JDBC-compliant, which means that the database is at least ANSI SQL-2 Entry Level.)

The three main interfaces are Connection, Statement, and ResultSet. A Connection object is obtained from the driver implementation through the `DriverManager.getConnection()` method call. After a `Connection` object is returned, the application developer may create a `Statement` object to issue SQL against the database. If the SQL that was submitted was a `SELECT` query, the result set is returned in a `ResultSet` object.

The Connection Interface The `Connection` interface represents a session with the database connection provided by the `Driver`. Typical database connections include the ability to control changes made to the actual data stored through transactions. On creation, JDBC connections are in an *auto-commit* mode—there is no rollback possible. After getting a `Connection` object from the driver, the developer should consider setting auto-commit to `false` with the `setAutoCommit (boolean b)` method. When auto-commit is disabled, the `Connection` will support both `Connection.commit()` and `Connection.rollback()` method calls. The level of support for transaction isolation depends on the underlying support for transactions in the database.

NOTE

A *transaction* is a set of operations that are completed in order. A *commit* action makes the operations store (or change) data in the database. A *rollback* action undoes the previous transaction before it has been committed. Transactions are discussed in more detail in Chapter 22. Enterprise JavaBeans (EJB) should not use the setAutoCommit, commit, and rollback methods in the Connectioninterface. Chapter 22 explains how EJB manages transactions.

A portion of the `Connection` interface definition follows. As usual, `SQLException` is thrown in case of trouble with the remote database.

`Statement createStatement () throws SQLException` The `Connection` object implementation will return an instance of an implementation of a `Statement` object. The `Statement` object is then used to issue queries.

`PreparedStatement prepareStatement (String sql) throws SQLException` The `Connection` object implementation will return an instance of a `PreparedStatement` object that is configured with the `sql` string passed. The driver may then send the statement to the database, if the database (driver) handles precompiled statements; otherwise, the driver may wait until the `PreparedStatement` is executed by an `execute` method.

CallableStatement prepareCall (String sql) throws SQLException The Connection object implementation will return an instance of a CallableStatement. CallableStatements are optimized for handling stored procedures. The driver implementation may send the sql string immediately when prepareCall() is complete or may wait until an execute method occurs.

void setAutoCommit (boolean autoCommit) throws SQLException Sets a flag in the driver implementation that enables commit/rollback (false) or makes all transactions commit immediately (true).

void commit () throws SQLException Makes all changes made since the beginning of the current transaction (either since the opening of the Connection or since the last commit() or rollback()).

void rollback() throws SQLException Drops all changes made since the beginning of the current transaction.

The primary use of the Connection interface is to create a statement:

```
Connection conn;
Statement stmt;
conn = DriverManager.getConnection(url);
stmt = c.createStatement();
```

This statement may be used to send SQL statements that return a single result set in a ResultSet object reference. Statements that need to be called a number of times with slight variations may be executed more efficiently using a PreparedStatement. The Connection interface is also used to create a CallableStatement whose purpose is to execute stored procedures.

Most of the time, the developer knows the database schema beforehand and creates the application based on the schema; however, JDBC provides an interface that may be used to dynamically determine the schema of a database. The Connection interface getMetaData() method will return a DatabaseMetaData object. The instance of the class that implements the interface provides information about the database as a whole, including access information about tables and procedures, column names, data types, and so on. The implementation details of DatabaseMetaData are dependent on the database vendor's ability to return this type of information.

The Statement Interface A *statement* is the vehicle for sending SQL queries to the database and retrieving a set of results. Statements can be SQL updates, inserts, deletes, or queries; statements may also create or drop tables. The `Statement` interface provides a number of methods designed to ease the job of writing queries to the database. The important `Statement` methods are listed below. As usual, `SQLException` is thrown if there is a problem with the remote database.

`ResultSet executeQuery(String sql) throws SQLException` Executes a single SQL query and returns the results in an object of type `ResultSet`.

`int executeUpdate(String sql) throws SQLException` Executes a single SQL query that returns a count of rows affected rather than a set of results.

`boolean execute(String sql) throws SQLException` A general way to execute SQL statements that may return multiple result sets and/or update counts. This method is also used to execute stored procedures that return `out` and `inout` parameters. The `getResultSet()`, `getUpdateCount()`, and `getMoreResults()` methods are used to retrieve the data returned. (This method is less likely to be used than `executeUpdate()` and `executeQuery()`.)

NOTE

The `in` parameters are parameters that are passed into an operation. The `out` parameters are parameters passed by reference; they are expected to return a result of the reference type. The `inout` parameters are `out` parameters that contain an initial value that may change as a result of the operation. JDBC supports all three parameter types.

`ResultSet getResultSet () throws SQLException` Returns the result of a statement execution as a `ResultSet` object. Note that if there are no results to be read, or if the result is an update count, this method returns `null`. Also note that once read, the results are cleared.

Part II

`int getUpdateCount() throws SQLException` Returns the status of an `Update`, an `Insert`, or a `Delete` query; a stored procedure; or a DDL statement. The value returned is the number of rows affected. A `-1` is returned if there is no update count, or if the data returned is a result set. Once read, the update count is cleared.

`boolean getMoreResults() throws SQLException` Moves to the next result in a set of multiple results/update counts. This method returns `true` if the next result is a `ResultSet` object. This method will also close any previous `ResultSet` read.

Statement methods may or may not return a `ResultSet` object, depending on the `Statement` method used. The `executeUpdate()` method, for example, is used to execute SQL statements that do not expect a result (except a row-count status):

```
int rowCount;
rowCount = stmt.executeUpdate
   ("DELETE FROM Customer WHERE CustomerID = 'McG10233'");
```

SQL statements that return a single set of results can use the `executeQuery()` method. This method returns a single `ResultSet` object. The object represents the row information returned as a result of the query:

```
ResultSet results;
results = stmt.executeQuery("SELECT * FROM Stock");
```

SQL statements that execute stored procedures (or trigger a stored procedure) may return more than one set of results. The `execute()` method is a general-purpose method that can return either a single result set or multiple result sets. The method returns a boolean flag that is used to determine whether there are more result sets. Because a result set could contain either data or the count of an operation that returns a row count, the `getResultSet()`, `getMoreResults()`, and `getUpdateCount()` methods are used. Here is an example:

```
// Assume SQLString returns multiple result sets
// returns true if a ResultSet is returned
int count;
ResultSet results;
if (stmt.execute (SQLstring))
```

```
{
  results = stmt.getResultSet();
  // false, an UpdateCount was returned
}
else
{
  count = stmt.getUpdateCount();
}

// Process the first results here ....

// Now loop until there are no more
//results or update counts
do
{
  // Is the next result a ResultSet?
  if (stmt.getMoreResults())
  {
    results = stmt.getResultSet();
  }
  else
  {
    count = stmt.getUpdateCount();
  }

  // Process next results (if any) here ....

}
while ((results != null) && (count != -1));
```

The PreparedStatement Interface The PreparedStatement interface extends the Statement interface. When there is a SQL statement that requires repetition with minor variations, the PreparedStatement provides the mechanism for passing a precompiled SQL statement that uses parameters.

```
public interface PreparedStatement extends Statement
```

`PreparedStatement` parameters are used to pass data into a SQL statement, so they are considered `in` parameters and are filled in by using `set`*`Type`* methods:

```
// Assume priceList is an array of prices that needs
// to be reduced for a 10% off sale, and reducedItems
// is an array of item IDs
int reduction = 10;
PreparedStatement ps = conn.prepareStatement
    ("UPDATE Catalog SET Price = ? WHERE ItemID = ?");
// Do the updates in a loop
for (int i = 0; i < reducedItems.length; i++)
{
  //Note that the setType methods set the value of the
  //parameters noted in the SQL statement with question
  //marks (?). They are indexed, starting from 1 to n.
  ps.setFloat
      (1, (priceList[i]*((float)(100-reduction)/100)));
  ps.setString(2, reducedItems[i]);
  if (ps.executeUpdate() == 0)
  {
    throw new ApplicationSpecificException
        ("No Item ID: " + reducedItems[i]);
  }
}
```

NOTE

The `set`*`Type`* methods fill the value of parameters (marked by question marks) in a `PreparedStatement`. These parameters are indexed from 1 to *n*.

Parameters hold their current values until either a new `set`*`Type`* method is called, or the method `clearParameters()` is called for the `PreparedStatement` object. In addition to the execute methods inherited from `Statement`, `PreparedStatement` declares the `set`*`Type`* methods listed in Table 9.1. Each method takes two arguments: a parameter index, and the primitive or class type, as shown in Table 9.1.

TABLE 9.1: The set*Type* Methods

METHOD SIGNATURE	JAVA TYPE	SQL TYPE FROM THE DATABASE
void setBigDecimal (int index, BigDecimal x)	java.math .BigDecimal	NUMERIC
void setBoolean (int index, boolean b)	Boolean	BIT
void setByte (int index, byte b)	Byte	TINYINT
void setBytes (int index, byte x[])	Byte array	VARBINARY or LONGVAR BINARY
void setDate (int index, Date d)	java.sql.Date	DATE
void setDouble (int index, double d)	Double	DOUBLE
void setFloat (int index, float f)	Float	FLOAT
void setInt (int index, int i)	Int	INTEGER
void setLong (int index, long l)	Long	BIGINT
void setNull (int index, int sqlType)	–	java.sql.Types lists SQL types by number, and null is integer 0 (zero)
void setShort (int index, short x)	Short	SMALLINT
void setString (int index, String s)	java.lang.String	VARCHAR or LONGVAR CHAR
void setTime (int index, Time t)	java.sql.Time	TIME
void setTimestamp (int index, Timestamp ts)	java.sql.Timestamp	TIMESTAMP
void setAsciiStream(int index, InputStream istr, int length)	InputStream	LONGVARCHAR
void setBinaryStream(int index, InputStream istr, int length)	InputStream	LONGVARBINARY
void setUnicodeStream(int index, InputStream istr, int length)	InputStream	LONGVARCHAR

TIP

It is widely recommended that J2EE developers always use the PreparedStatement interface instead of the Statement interface. If you are executing a series of identically formatted SQL statements, a PreparedStatement should certainly provide better performance. In addition, many servers can cache prepared SQL statements between requests. Some JDBC 3.0 drivers have the ability to cache PreparedStatements; thus, even if identical statements are executed by completely different clients or requests, there may be a performance gain from using PreparedStatements. Some also argue that regardless of performance issues, the PreparedStatement interface is more object oriented and maintainable due to the way it takes variable data through parameters.

The CallableStatement Interface The `CallableStatement` interface is used to execute SQL stored procedures. `CallableStatement` inherits from the `PreparedStatement` interface, so all of the `execute` and `set`*`Type`* methods are available. The syntax of stored procedures varies among database vendors, so JDBC defines a standard way to call stored procedures in all RDBMSs.

```
public interface CallableStatement extends PreparedStatement
```

The JDBC uses an escape syntax that allows parameters to be passed as `in` parameters and `out` parameters. The syntax also allows a result to be returned. If this syntax is used, the parameter must be registered as an `out` parameter.

Here is an example of a `CallableStatement` with an `out` parameter:

```
CallableStatement cs = conn.prepareCall("{call
  getQuote(?, ?)}");
cs.setString (1, stockName);
// java.sql.Types defines SQL data types that are returned
// as out parameters
cs.registerOutParameter(2, Types.FLOAT);
cs.executeUpdate();
float quote = cs.getFloat(2);
```

`CallableStatement` defines a set of `get`*`Type`* methods that convert the SQL types returned from the database to Java types. These methods match the `set`*`Type`* methods declared by `PreparedStatement`, and are listed in Table 9.2.

NOTE

The get*Type* methods access data in each column as the result of a query. Each column can be accessed by either its position in the row, numbered from 1 to *n* columns, or by its name, such as `custID`.

TABLE 9.2: The get*Type* Methods

METHOD SIGNATURE	JAVA TYPE	SQL TYPE FROM THE DATABASE
`BigDecimal getBigDecimal (int index, int scale)`	`java.math.BigDecimal`	NUMERIC
`boolean getBoolean(int index)`	`Boolean`	BIT
`byte getByte(int index)`	`Byte`	TINYINT
`byte[] getBytes(int index)`	`byte array`	BINARY or VARBINARY
`Date getDate(int index)`	`java.sql.Date`	DATE
`double getDouble(int index)`	`Double`	DOUBLE
`float getFloat(int index)`	`Float`	FLOAT
`int getInt(int index)`	`Int`	INTEGER
`long getLong(int index)`	`Long`	BIGINT
`short getShort(int index)`	`Short`	SMALLINT
`String getString(int index)`	`String`	CHAR, VAR CHAR or LONGVAR CHAR
`Time getTime(int index)`	`java.sql.Time`	TIME
`Timestamp getTimestamp (int index)`	`java.sql.Timestamp`	TIMESTAMP

NOTE

It is the responsibility of the JDBC driver to convert the data passed from the database as SQL data types into Java values.

The ResultSet Interface The `ResultSet` interface defines methods for accessing tables of data generated as the result of executing a `Statement`. `ResultSet` column values may be accessed in any order—they are indexed and may be selected by either the name or the number (from 1 to *n*) of the column. `ResultSet` maintains the position of the current row, starting with the first row of data returned. The `next()` method moves to the next row of data.

A partial look at the `ResultSet` interface follows. Vendors that implement this interface have the option of caching the results on the remote side, so there is the possibility of a communication problem. For this reason, the following methods listed throw `SQLException`.

`boolean next() throws SQLException` Positions the `ResultSet` to the next row. The `ResultSet` row position is initially just before the first row of the result set.

`ResultSetMetaData getMetaData() throws SQLException` Returns an object that contains a description of the current result set, including the number of columns, the type of each column, and properties of the results.

`void close() throws SQLException` Normally a `ResultSet` is closed when another SQL statement is executed, but it may be desirable to release the resources earlier.

As with the `CallableStatement` interface discussed earlier, the resulting data can be read through `get`*`Type`*`()` methods. Note, however, that values can be accessed either via column names or column numbers; callable statements can use only column numbers. Recall that column numbers begin at 1. Here is an example:

```
// Pass a query to the statement object

ResultSet rs = stmt.executeQuery
    ("SELECT * FROM Stock WHERE quantity = 0");

// Get the results as their Java types
// Note that columns are indexed by
//an integer starting with 1,
// or by the name of column, as in "ItemID"
System.out.println("Stock replenishment list");
while (rs.next())
{
  System.out.println
      ("Item ID: " + rs.getString("ItemID"));
```

```
    System.out.println
        ("Next ship date: " + rs.getDate(2));
    System.out.println ("");
}
```

The ResultSetMetaData Interface Aside from being able to read data from a `ResultSet` object, JDBC provides an interface to allow the developer to determine what type of data was returned. The `ResultSetMetaData` interface is similar to the `DatabaseMetaData` interface in concept, but it is specific to the current `ResultSet`. As with `DatabaseMetaData`, it is unlikely that many developers will use this interface because most applications are written with an understanding of the database schema and column names and values; however, `ResultSetMetaData` is useful in dynamically determining the `MetaData` of a `ResultSet` returned from a stored procedure.

NOTE

SQL LONGVARBINARY and LONGVARCHAR data types can be of arbitrary size. The `getBytes()` and `getString()` methods can read these types up to the limits imposed by the driver. The limits can be read through the `Statement.getMaxFieldSize()` method. For larger blocks of data, the JDBC allows developers to use input streams to return the data in chunks. (Streams must be read immediately following the query execution—they are automatically closed at the next get of a `ResultSet`.) You can also send large blocks of data by using `java.io.OutputStream` as a parameter. When a statement is executed, the JDBC driver makes repeated calls to read and transmit the data in the streams.

Scrollable or Updatable ResultSets By default, when you execute a `Statement` that creates a `ResultSet`, the `ResultSet` is read-only and the rows can only be read in order; however, JDBC 2.0 and above drivers allow you the option of making a `ResultSet` that is updatable or scrollable. To do this, you must supply two additional parameters to the `Connection` interface's `createStatement`, `prepareStatement`, or `prepareCall` methods.

`Statement createStatement (String sql, int resultSetType, int resultSetConcurrency)` throws `SQLException`

PreparedStatement prepareStatement (String sql, int resultSetType, int resultSetConcurrency) throws SQLException

CallableStatement prepareCall (String sql, int resultSetType, int resultSetConcurrency) throws SQLException

The resultSetType parameter can be one of the following three values:

ResultSet.TYPE_FORWARD_ONLY This is the default value; it creates a forward only ResultSet.

ResultSet.TYPE_SCROLL_INSENSITIVE Creates a forward and backward scrollable ResultSet that will not reflect any changes to the database data after the query data is returned.

ResultSet.TYPE_SCROLL_SENSITIVE Creates a forward and backward scrollable ResultSet that will be updated if the database data changes, even after the query data is returned.

The resultSetConcurrency parameter can be one of the following two values:

ResultSet.CONCUR_READ_ONLY This is the default value; creates a read-only ResultSet.

ResultSet.CONCUR_UPDATABLE Creates an updatable ResultSet that allows updates, insertions, and deletions, and will send those changes to the database.

The following code would make a forward and backward scrollable ResultSet:

```
Statement stmt;
stmt = conn.createStatement
  (ResultSet.TYPE_SCROLL_INSENSITIVE,
   ResultSet.CONCUR_READ_ONLY);
ResultSet results;
results = stmt.executeQuery("SELECT * FROM Stock");
```

If the ResultSet is scrollable, in addition to next(), you may use previous(), first(), last(), absolute(int), and relative(int) methods to move around the ResultSet.

The following code would make an updatable ResultSet:

```
Statement stmt;
stmt = conn.createStatement
  (ResultSet.TYPE_FORWARD_ONLY,
   ResultSet.CONCUR_UPDATABLE);
ResultSet results;
results = stmt.executeQuery("SELECT * FROM Stock");
rs.updateInt("quantity", 3);
rs.updateRow();
```

If the ResultSet is updatable, you can update values in the current row by using the updateXXX methods, such as updateInt and updateString methods in the ResultSet interface. After you update the values, the database is not updated until you call the updateRow() method of ResultSet. You can use the deleteRow and insertRow ResultSet methods to delete and insert rows.

A JDBC Database Example

As an example of the concepts presented in this chapter, we'll work with a hypothetical database that stores information related to a large catalog ordering system. This simple database includes a table called Customer, which has the following schema:

CustomerID	VARCHAR
LastName	VARCHAR
FirstName	VARCHAR
Phonenumber	VARCHAR
StreetAddress	VARCHAR
Zipcode	VARCHAR

Here is the definition of a simple `Customer` object with two primary methods, `insertNewCustomer()` and `getCustomer()`:

`public Customer(Connection conn)` The constructor for the class. The `Customer` constructor receives a `Connection` object, which it uses to create `Statement` references. In addition, the constructor creates a `PreparedStatement` and three `CallableStatements`.

public String insertNewCustomer(String lname, String fname, String pnum, String addr, String zip) throws insertFailedException, SQLException Creates a new customer record, including a new ID. The ID is created through a stored procedure that reads the current list of customer IDs and creates a new reference. The method returns the new ID created or throws an exception if the insert failed.

public CustomerInfo getCustomer(String custID) throws selectException, SQLException Returns an object that contains the data in the Customer table. An exception is thrown if the customer ID passed does not exist or is not properly formatted, or if the SQL statement fails.

public static synchronized boolean validateZip(String zip) throws SQLException A utility method used to validate the zip code. A `true` value is returned if the zip code exists in the ZipCode table in the database.

public static synchronized boolean validateID(String id) throws SQLException A utility method to validate a customer ID. If the ID exists, the method returns `true`.

The full code for the Customer class is shown in Listing 9.1.

Listing 9.1: Customer.java

```
// Customer record class
// This class is used to store and access customer data from the
// database
import java.sql.*;

public class Customer
{
  private Connection conn;
  private PreparedStatement insertNewCustomer;
  private CallableStatement getNewID;
  public static CallableStatement checkZip;
  public static CallableStatement checkID;

  // Customer constructor: store a local copy of the
  // Connection object create statements for use later
  public Customer (Connection c)
```

```
{
  conn = c;

  try
  {
    insertNewCustomer = conn.prepareStatement
       ("INSERT INTO Customers VALUES (?, ?, ?, ?, ?, ?)");
    getNewID = conn.prepareCall("{call getNewID (?)}");
    checkID = conn.prepareCall("{call checkID (?,?)}");
    checkZip = conn.prepareCall("{call checkZip (?, ?)}");
  }
  catch (SQLException e)
  {
    System.out.println("Cannot create statements");
  }
}

// Method for creating a new customer record.
// The customerID is generated by a stored procedure
// call on the database
public String insertNewCustomer
    (String lname, String fname, String pnum,
    String addr, String zip)
    throws insertFailedException, SQLException
{
  String newID;

  // Get a new customer ID through the stored procedure
  if ((newID = getNewID ()) == null)
  {
    throw new insertFailedException
        ("could not get new ID");
  }

  // Insert the new customer ID
  insertNewCustomer.setString (1, newID);
  insertNewCustomer.setString (2, lname);
  insertNewCustomer.setString (3, fname);
  insertNewCustomer.setString (4, pnum);
  insertNewCustomer.setString (5, addr);
  insertNewCustomer.setString (6, zip);

  // Execute the statement
  if (insertNewCustomer.executeUpdate() != 1)
```

```
    {
      throw new insertFailedException ("could not insert");
    }
    return (newID);
  }

  // Get a single customer record with this ID
  // Note: this method maps the returned data onto a
  // CustomerInfo container object
  public CustomerInfo getCustomer(String custID)
      throws selectException, SQLException
  {
    // Check the ID first
    if (!validateID (custID))
    {
      throw new selectException
         ("no customer with ID: " + custID);
    }

    // Create the select statement
    Statement stmt = conn.createStatement();

    // Get the results
    ResultSet rs = stmt.executeQuery
        ("SELECT * FROM Customer WHERE CustID = " + custID);
    rs.next();

    // Create a CustomerInfo container object
    CustomerInfo info = new CustomerInfo();

    // Populate the CustomerInfo object
    // Columns are indexed starting with 1
    info.CustomerID = rs.getString(1);
    info.LastName = rs.getString(2);
    info.FirstName = rs.getString(3);
    info.PhoneNumber = rs.getString(4);
    info.StreetAddress = rs.getString(5);
    info.Zip = rs.getString(6);

    return (info);
  }
```

```
  // Method for validation of a customer's zip code
  // This method is public so that it can be called from
  // a user interface
  public static synchronized boolean validateZip(String zip)
     throws SQLException
  {
    // Make call to stored procedure to validate zip code
    checkZip.setString (1, zip);
    checkZip.registerOutParameter (2, Types.BIT);
    checkZip.executeUpdate();
    return (checkZip.getBoolean(2));
  }

  // Method for validating a customer ID
  // This method is public so that it can be called from
  // a user interface
  public static synchronized boolean validateID(String id)
      throws SQLException
  {
    // Make call to stored procedure to validate
    // customer ID
    checkID.setString (1, id);
    checkID.registerOutParameter (2, Types.BIT);
    checkID.executeUpdate();
    return (checkID.getBoolean(2));
  }

  //Method for retrieving a new customer ID from the database
  private String getNewID() throws SQLException
  {
    // Make call to stored procedure to get
    // customer ID from DB
    getNewID.registerOutParameter(1, Types.VARCHAR);
    getNewID.executeUpdate();
    return getNewID.getString(1);
  }
}

// Exceptions

// insertFailedException is a general exception for
// SQL insert problems
class insertFailedException extends SQLException
```

```
{
  public insertFailedException(String reason)
  {
    super (reason);
  }
  public insertFailedException()
  {
    super();
  }
}

// selectException is a general exception for SQL select
     problems
class selectException extends SQLException
{
  public selectException(String reason)
  {
    super (reason);
  }

  public selectException()
  {
    super ();
  }
}
```

TIP

The `CustomerInfo` class is a simple container object. Container classes make it easier to pass a complete customer record to and from any method that manipulates the Customer table in the database. Data can be stored in the container class and then passed as a single object reference, rather than having to pass each element as a single reference. The code for CustomerInfo is shown in Listing 9.2.

Listing 9.2: CustomerInfo.java

```
// A container object for the Customer table
public class CustomerInfo
{
  String CustomerID;
  String LastName;
  String FirstName;
```

```
    String PhoneNumber;
    String StreetAddress;
    String Zip;
  }
```

Finally, to test the simple Customer class, Listing 9.3 shows a simple Java application that illustrates loading a Sybase driver, then making a connection, and passing the Connection object returned to a new instance of a Customer object.

Listing 9.3: Example.java

```
// A simple Java application that illustrates the use of
// DriverManager,
// Driver, Connection, Statement and ResultSet

import java.sql.*;


public class Example
{
  Connection sybaseConn;

  // main
  public static void main(String arg[])
  {
    // Look for the URL, username and password
    if (arg.length < 3)
    {
      System.out.println("Example use:");
      System.out.println
          ("java Example <url> <username> <password>");
      System.exit(1);
    }

    // Create an instance of the class
    Example ex = new Example();

    // Initialize the connection
    ex.initdb(arg[0], arg[1], arg[2]);

    // Test the connection-write a customer and
    // then read it back
    ex.testdb();
  }
```

```
// method to initialize the database connection
// The Connection object reference is kept globally
public void initdb(String url, String user, String passwd)
{
  // Try to open the database and get the connection
  try
  {
    // Note that this example assumes that
    // Java property "jdbc.drivers"
    // that is loading the appropriate driver(s) for
    // the URL passed in the getConnection call.
    // It is possible to explicitly create an
    // instance of a driver as well, for example:
    // new sybase.sql.Driver(); or
    // Class.forName("sybase.sql.Driver");

    // Create a connection
    sybaseConn = DriverManager.getConnection
         (url, user, passwd);

    }
    catch (SQLException e)
    {
      System.out.println("Database connection failed:");
      System.out.println(e.getMessage());
      System.exit(1);
    }
}

// Simple method to test the Customer class methods
public void testdb()
{
  String custID = null;

  // Create the instance of the Customer class
  Customer cust = new Customer (sybaseConn);

  try
  {
    // Now insert a new Customer
    custID = cust.insertNewCustomer
```

```
          ("Jones", "Bill", "555-1234",
           "5 Main Street","01234");
    }
    catch (SQLException e)
    {
      System.out.println("Insert failed:");
      System.out.println(e.getMessage());
      System.exit(1);
    }

    try
    {
      // Read it back from the database
      CustomerInfo info = cust.getCustomer(custID);
    }
    catch (SQLException e)
    {
      System.out.println("Read failed:");
      System.out.println(e.getMessage());
      System.exit(1);
    }
  }
}
```

This example, as shown in Listing 9.1 through Listing 9.3, illustrates the use of the CallableStatements to issue stored procedure calls that validate the zip code, customer ID, and the PreparedStatement to issue an Insert SQL statement with parameters that will change with each insert.

This example also illustrates code that will run with any JDBC driver that will support the stored procedures used in the Customer class. The driver class names are loaded from the jdbc.drivers property so code recompilation is not required.

JDBC Drivers

One of the real attractions of the JDBC API is the ability to develop applications knowing that all of the major database vendors are working in parallel to create drivers. A wide variety of drivers are available both from database vendors and third-party developers. In most cases, it is wise to shop around for the best features, cost, and support.

TIP

JDBC drivers are being released from so many vendors and at such a rapid rate that a definitive list is just not practical, and would be obsolete by the time it was printed. For information on current driver vendors, their product names, and what databases they support, a good source is `http://splash.javasoft.com/jdbc/jdbc.drivers.html`.

Types of Drivers

Drivers come in a variety of flavors according to their construction and the type of database they are intended to support. JavaSoft categorizes database drivers into four types:

Type 1 A JDBC-ODBC bridge driver, shown in Figure 9.6, implemented with ODBC binary code, and in some cases, a client library as well. The bridge driver is made up of three parts: a set of C libraries that connects the JDBC to the ODBC driver manager, the ODBC driver manager, and the ODBC driver. (See the next section for more information about the JDBC-ODBC bridge.)

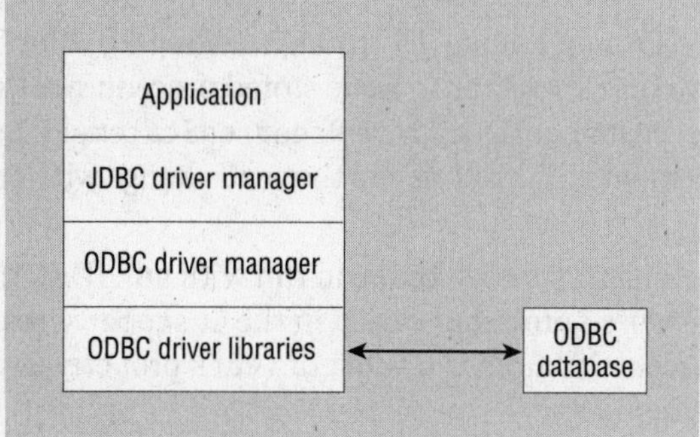

FIGURE 9.6: JDBC-ODBC bridge driver

Type 2 A native library-to-Java implementation, as shown in Figure 9.7. This driver uses native C language library calls to translate JDBC to the native client library. The drivers use C language libraries that provide vendor-specific functionality, and tie these libraries (through native method calls) to the JDBC. These drivers were the first available for Oracle, Sybase, Informix, DB2, and other client-library-based RDBMSs.

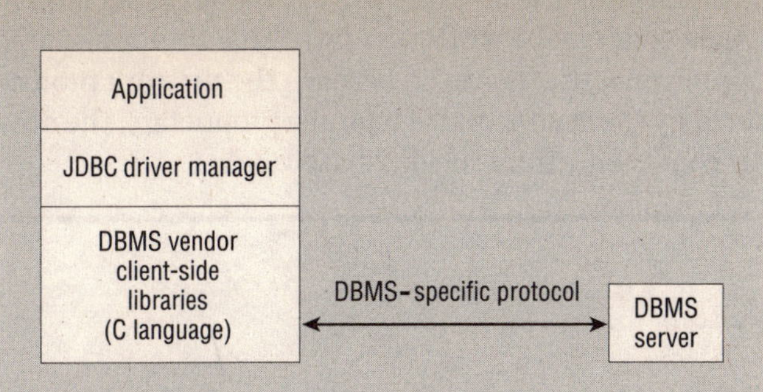

FIGURE 9.7: Native library-to-Java driver

Type 3 A network-protocol Java driver, as shown in Figure 9.8. JDBC calls are translated by this driver into a DBMS-independent protocol and sent to a middle-tier server over a socket. The middle-tier code contacts a variety of databases on behalf of the client. This approach is becoming the most popular, and is by far the most flexible. This approach also deals specifically with issues relating to network security, including passing data through firewalls.

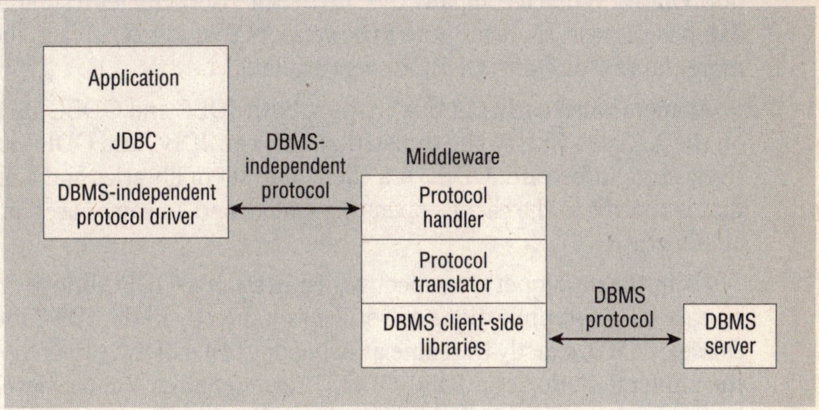

FIGURE 9.8: DBMS-independent network protocol driver

Type 4 A native-protocol Java driver, as shown in Figure 9.9. JDBC calls are converted directly to the network protocol used by the DBMS server. In this driver scenario, the database vendor supports a network socket, and the JDBC driver communicates over a socket connection directly to the database server. The client-side code can be written in Java. This solution is practical for intranet use; however, because the network protocol is defined by the vendor and is typically proprietary, the driver usually comes only from the database vendor.

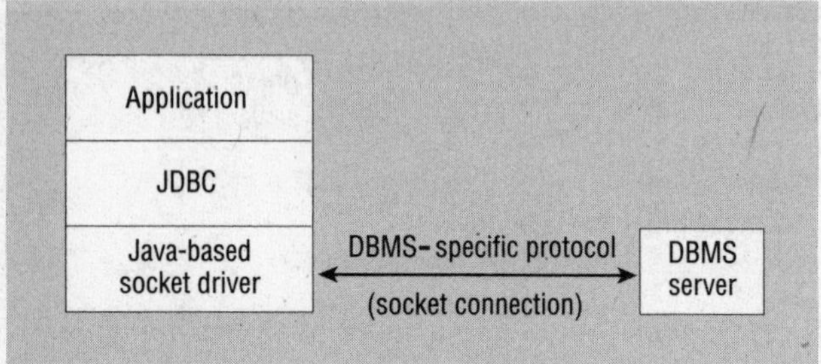

FIGURE 9.9: DBMS-protocol all-Java driver

The JDBC-ODBC Bridge

The JDBC-ODBC bridge is a JDBC driver that provides translation of JDBC calls to ODBC operations. There are a number of DBMSs that support ODBC. When a company the size of Microsoft creates a standard for database access, there are sure to be vendors that follow; in fact, there are more than 50 different ODBC drivers available.

As mentioned earlier in this chapter, both JDBC and ODBC are based on the X/Open CLI, so the translation between JDBC and ODBC is relatively straightforward. ODBC is a client-side set of libraries and a driver that is specific to the client's operating system and, in some cases, machine architecture.

From the developer's perspective, using a JDBC-ODBC bridge driver is an easy choice—applications will still speak directly to the JDBC interface classes, so it is exactly the same as using any other JDBC driver; however, the implementation of a JDBC-ODBC bridge requires that the developer be aware of what is required to run the application. Because ODBC calls are made using binary C calls, the client must have a local copy of the ODBC driver, the ODBC driver manager, and the client-side libraries. The JDBC-ODBC bridge is not the best choice for portability or performance, although it may be an acceptable and simple driver when developing test systems and prototypes.

What's Next

The interest in Java has created a number of new strategies for moving data between the database system and the front-end user. In this chapter, the JDBC API was presented as the primary technique for connecting Java applications to database systems. The JDBC solves the problem of connecting a single application to a multitude of database systems by isolating the interface that the developer uses and the driver that is used to connect to the database. This JDBC code can be used by any Java technology including Java servlets, JSP pages, Enterprise JavaBeans, and plain Java classes.

The next chapter will explore ways to make JDBC code more effective and powerful through the use of the `RowSet` interface and a custom `ResultSet` based class.

Chapter 10

Advanced Database Programming

Virtually all non-trivial JSP applications rely on heavy database use. A lot of power can be leveraged into any application with the support of a good database. Database programming is a subject worthy of several large books. In this chapter, we'll focus on the elements and problems that especially concern JSP developers.

So far, we've covered several programming topics and equipped you with tools and approaches to solve many of the common problems facing JSP developers. This chapter will detail some techniques for making your data access classes more robust, and you'll see how they can be used to accomplish more with less code and with more flexibility. When we're done, you'll be able to factor out data manipulations so that they're removed from the raw JSP code, and you'll be a step closer to having an architecturally pure Presentation layer.

Adapted from *Mastering*™ *JSP*™ by Todd Cook

ISBN 0-7821-2940-4 $49.99

Featured in this chapter:

- Problems with `java.sql.ResultSet`
- The JDBC `RowSet`
- The `DittoResultSet`
- Moving data access away from the Presentation layer

Problems with *java.sql.Connection* and *java.sql.ResultSet*

Database support in Java has made steady progress, but with so many different kinds of databases and interactions possible, database support is still being added and improved. Database access classes are spread over several large packages, namely, `java.sql` and `javax.sql`, as well as the JDBC drivers developed by database companies and third parties, and any extensions they provide.

Until recently, there have been some obstacles with only awkward workarounds for some database manipulations. The `java.sql.ResultSet` class has some annoying features:

- If the database connection is closed, a `ResultSet` object originating from that connection is consigned to garbage collection, even if the `ResultSet` object hasn't gone out of its original scope.
- Passing a `ResultSet` causes the database resource to go out of scope, and the `ResultSet` is consigned to garbage collection.
- Creating a new `ResultSet` on a connection consigns previous `ResultSets` to garbage collection—even if the `ResultSets` objects haven't gone out of scope.

Because Java doesn't immediately destroy objects, these annoying behaviors may not show up until you put a load on the Java environment; however, if you create two `ResultSets`, use one, use the other, and then try to call the first one again, the first `ResultSet` won't be there. This still sounds too abstract, so we have a little demo. Listing 10.1 shows the code for the ResultSetLimitations JSP.

Listing 10.1: ResultSetLimitations.jsp

```
<%@ page import="java.sql.*"%>
<jsp:useBean id="connectMan" class="c10.ConnectionManager"
  scope="session"  />
<jsp:setProperty name="connectMan" property="*" />
<HTML>
<HEAD>
<TITLE>
Result Set Limitations
</TITLE>
</HEAD>
<BODY>
<H1>
Result Set Limitations
</H1>
<%
 connectMan.getConnection();
 %>Fetching accounts into Result Set #1
 <BR>
<%
 ResultSet RS1 = connectMan.executeQuery(
 "SELECT account_id, biz_name, rep_fname, "
  + " rep_lname, rep_phone from accounts");

if ( RS1.next() )
{
  %>Printing out the first business phone number
    to show that <br>  we got some information:
<%= RS1.getString("rep_phone") %>
<%
      RS1.beforeFirst();
      // reset cursor to original position
 }
else
 {
 %>Problem fetching data<%
 }
%>
 <BR>
 Fetching orders into Result Set #2
 <BR>
<%
```

```
ResultSet RS2 = connectMan.executeQuery(
"select o.order_id, a.biz_name, "
+ "o.timeordered, o.timeshipped, o.paid "
+ " from orders o, accounts a "
+ " where o.account_id = a.account_id ");

if ( RS2.next() )
{
 %>Printing out the first order id to show that
 <br>
 we got some information from orders:
<%= RS2.getString("order_id") %>
<%
  RS2.beforeFirst();
  // reset cursor to original position
 }
 else
 {
 %>Problem fetching data<%
 }%>
<BR>
Account information shown in light blue (ResultSet 1)<BR>
 Order information shown in white (ResultSet 2)
<BR>
<%
String[] mArAccountFields = new String [] { "account_id",
 "biz_name", "rep_fname", "rep_lname", "rep_phone" };
String[] mArAccountHeaderNames = new String [] {
 "Account Id", "Business Name",
 "Representative First Name", "Last name", "Phone"};
String[] mArOrderFields = new String [] { "order_id",
 "biz_name", "timeordered", "timeshipped", "paid"};
String[] mArOrderHeaderNames = new String [] {
 "Order Id", "Business Name", "Time ordered",
 "Time shipped", "Paid"};
%>
<table bgcolor="lightblue" border="1">
 <TR>
 <% for( int i=0;
         i < mArAccountHeaderNames.length;
         i++ )
       { %>
        <TD><% out.print(mArAccountHeaderNames[i]); %></TD>
   <% } %></TR><%
```

```
        while ( RS1.next() )
          {
         %><TR><%
              for ( int ii = 0;
                  ii < mArAccountFields.length; ii++ )
            {%><TD><%
           try
             {
              if (RS1.getString(mArAccountFields[ii])
                                      == null)
                out.print ( " " );
              else
                out.print( RS1.getString(
                            mArAccountFields[ii]) );
             }
            catch (Exception ee)
             {
              out.print(" ");
             }
                  %></TD><%
             } %></TR><%
         } %>
    </table>

    <table bgcolor="white" border="1">
     <TR>
     <% for( int i=0;
             i < mArOrderHeaderNames.length;
             i++ )
           { %>
            <TD><% out.print(mArOrderHeaderNames[i]);%></TD>
      <%    } %></TR><%

        while ( RS2.next() )
         {
         %><TR><%
          for ( int ii = 0;
                ii < mArOrderFields.length; ii++)
            {%><TD><%
             try
               {
                if (RS2.getString(mArOrderFields[ii])
                                            == null)
```

Part II

```
                    out.print ( " " );
                else
                    out.print( RS2.getString(
                                  mArOrderFields[ii]));
            }
            catch (Exception ee)
            {
                out.print(" ");
            }
         %></TD><%
        } %></TR><%
     } %>
</table>
</BODY>
</HTML>
```

The JSP connects to the database and tries to get two ResultSets; the code prints out a value from each one to show that it received data for each `ResultSet`. The first `ResultSet` is printed out, the second one throws an Exception that is caught, and blank spaces are printed out, as shown in Figure 10.1. Quite a pitfall.

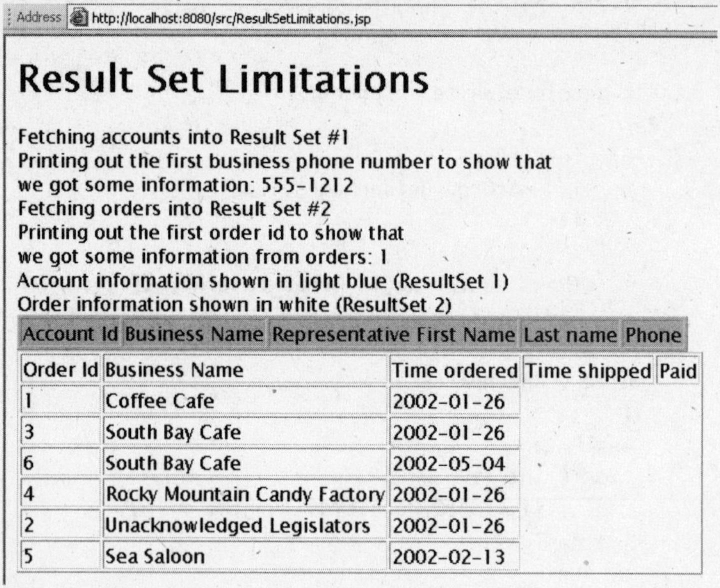

Address http://localhost:8080/src/ResultSetLimitations.jsp

Result Set Limitations

Fetching accounts into Result Set #1
Printing out the first business phone number to show that
we got some information: 555-1212
Fetching orders into Result Set #2
Printing out the first order id to show that
we got some information from orders: 1
Account information shown in light blue (ResultSet 1)
Order information shown in white (ResultSet 2)

Account Id	Business Name	Representative First Name	Last name	Phone

Order Id	Business Name	Time ordered	Time shipped	Paid
1	Coffee Cafe	2002-01-26		
3	South Bay Cafe	2002-01-26		
6	South Bay Cafe	2002-05-04		
4	Rocky Mountain Candy Factory	2002-01-26		
2	Unacknowledged Legislators	2002-01-26		
5	Sea Saloon	2002-02-13		

FIGURE 10.1: The limitations of a ResultSet

You have a few options. Some developers write JSPs with data access code inside the pages (a no-no, and done in this book only to illustrate other concepts expediently). Fortunately, the code in this chapter will eliminate that temptation. Some developers access the data in a properly abstracted object (away from the Presentation layer). Because passing a `ResultSet` causes it to quickly destruct, however, developers often resort to some awkward construction, such as passing it back as one giant string or as a vector. Passing back vectors or special string constructions to JSPs violates the principle that object layers should be insulated from one another.

One solution is to choose a database and a driver that support the new JDBC classes. Unfortunately, this approach restricts the portability of the code, and in effect ties your implementation to a specific database and even perhaps a certain version of the database and the database driver. It's the standard approach, but it clashes with the Java mantra *write once, run anywhere*.

Another solution is to use a custom class that replaces the `ResultSet` object. This approach has the advantage of being platform independent. Best of all, using a custom class during early development doesn't preclude a later migration to the vendor-specific JDBC implementations.

Before we look at the intricate details of properly solving this pesky problem, let's look at proof that the problem can be solved. The `DittoResultSet` used on the SolvingResultSetLimitations JSP, shown in Listing 10.2, is discussed in detail in the next section.

Listing 10.2: SolvingResultSetLimitations.jsp

```
<%@ page import="java.sql.*,c10.DittoResultSet"%>
<jsp:useBean id="connectMan" class="c10.ConnectionManager"
 scope="session"  />
<jsp:setProperty name="connectMan" property="*" />
<HTML>
<HEAD>
<TITLE>
Solving Result Set Limitations
</TITLE>
</HEAD>
<BODY>
<H1>
Solving Result Set Limitations
</H1>
```

```
<%
 connectMan.getConnection();
 %>Fetching accounts into DittoResultSet Set #1
 <BR>
<%
 DittoResultSet RS1 =
   connectMan.executeQueryReturnDittoResultSet(
 "SELECT account_id, biz_name, rep_fname, rep_lname,"
 + " rep_phone from accounts");

if (RS1.next())
{
  %>Printing out the first business phone number
    to show that <br>  we got some information:
  <%= RS1.getString("rep_phone") %>
<%
      RS1.beforeFirst();
      // reset cursor to original position
 }
else
 {
 %>Problem fetching data<%
 }
%>
 <BR>
 Fetching orders into DittoResultSet Set #2
 <BR>
<%
  DittoResultSet RS2 =
   connectMan.executeQueryReturnDittoResultSet(
  "select o.order_id, a.biz_name, o.timeordered, "
  + " o.timeshipped, o.paid "
  + " from orders o, accounts a "
  + " where o.account_id = a.account_id ");

 if ( RS2.next() )
 {
  %>Printing out the first order id to show that
  <br>
  we got some information from orders:
  <%= RS2.getString("order_id") %>
<%
      RS2.beforeFirst();
```

```
        // reset cursor to original position
    }
    else
    {
    %>Problem fetching data<%
    }%>
  <BR>
  Account information shown in light blue (DittoResultSet 1)
  <BR>
   Order information shown in white (DittoResultSet 2)
  <BR>
  <%
  String[] mArAccountFields = new String [] { "account_id",
   "biz_name", "rep_fname", "rep_lname", "rep_phone" };
  String[] mArAccountHeaderNames = new String [] {
   "Account Id", "Business Name",
    "Representative First Name", "Last name", "Phone" };
  String[] mArOrderFields = new String [] { "order_id",
   "biz_name", "timeordered", "timeshipped", "paid" };
  String[] mArOrderHeaderNames = new String [] { "Order Id",
    "Business Name", "Time ordered",
    "Time shipped", "Paid"};
  %>
  <table bgcolor="lightblue" border="1">
  <TR>
   <% for( int i=0; i < mArAccountHeaderNames.length; i++)
        { %>
        <TD><% out.print(mArAccountHeaderNames[i]); %></TD>
     <%     } %></TR><%
      while ( RS1.next() )
        {
         %><TR><%
            for (int ii = 0;
             ii < mArAccountFields.length;
             ii++ )
           {%><TD><%
           try
             {
               if (RS1.getString(mArAccountFields[ii])
                                                   == null)
                out.print ( " " );
                else
```

```
                out.print( RS1.getString(
                           mArAccountFields[ii]) );
              }
            catch (Exception ee)
             {
             out.print(" ");
             }
                 %></TD><%
          } %></TR><%
          } %>
</table>

 <table bgcolor="white" border="1">
 <TR>
 <% for( int i=0;
         i < mArOrderHeaderNames.length;
         i++ )
      { %>
     <TD><% out.print(mArOrderHeaderNames[i]); %></TD>
   <% } %></TR><%

   while ( RS2.next() )
     {
       %><TR><%
          for (int ii = 0;
           ii < mArOrderFields.length; ii++ )
         {%><TD><%
           try
           {
              if (RS2.getString(mArOrderFields[ii])
                                           == null)
               out.print ( " " );
               else
               out.print( RS2.getString(
                            mAr0rderFields[ii]) );
           }
         catch (Exception ee)
           {
            out.print(" ");
           }
       %></TD><%
        } %></TR><%
       } %>
```

```
</table>
</BODY>
</HTML>
```

The resulting page is shown in Figure 10.2.

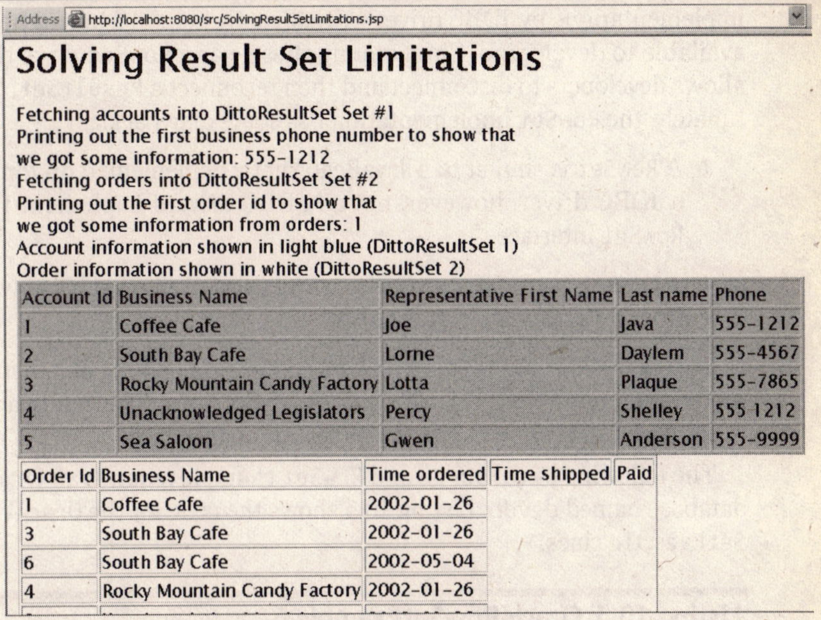

Address http://localhost:8080/src/SolvingResultSetLimitations.jsp

Solving Result Set Limitations

Fetching accounts into DittoResultSet Set #1
Printing out the first business phone number to show that
we got some information: 555-1212
Fetching orders into DittoResultSet Set #2
Printing out the first order id to show that
we got some information from orders: 1
Account information shown in light blue (DittoResultSet 1)
Order information shown in white (DittoResultSet 2)

Account Id	Business Name	Representative First Name	Last name	Phone
1	Coffee Cafe	Joe	Java	555-1212
2	South Bay Cafe	Lorne	Daylem	555-4567
3	Rocky Mountain Candy Factory	Lotta	Plaque	555-7865
4	Unacknowledged Legislators	Percy	Shelley	555 1212
5	Sea Saloon	Gwen	Anderson	555-9999

Order Id	Business Name	Time ordered	Time shipped	Paid
1	Coffee Cafe	2002-01-26		
3	South Bay Cafe	2002-01-26		
6	South Bay Cafe	2002-05-04		
4	Rocky Mountain Candy Factory	2002-01-26		

FIGURE 10.2: The Solving ResultSet Limitations JSP

The `ConnectionManager` class was modified with an extra function:

```
public DittoResultSet executeQueryReturnDittoResultSet
                                        (String sql)
                                   throws SQLException
  {
    getConn();
    return new DittoResultSet(statement.executeQuery(sql));
  }
```

Of course, the class could be modified for additional functionality as necessary.

Besides the custom method illustrated with the `DittoResultSet`, there's an official J2EE solution.

RowSet: The JDBC 2.*x* Solution to ResultSet Problems

With the release of the JDBC 2.*x* API specification, and subsequent implementations by JDBC driver writers, many helpful features became available to developers. Chief among these was a `RowSet` class that allows developers to disconnect and then reconnect a `ResultSet`. Unfortunately, the `RowSet` implementation has some drawbacks:

- A `RowSet` is similar to a JavaBean that's implemented on top of a JDBC driver; however, not all JDBC drivers implement the `RowSet` interface.
- A `RowSet` cannot be created from a `ResultSet`; it must be derived from a `javax.sql.DataSource`.

The `javax.sql.DataSource` offers connection pooling and distributed transaction services. Unfortunately MySql doesn't currently have a JDBC driver that implements the `DataSource` interface.

The following `DataSource` and `RowSet` example requires an Oracle database named devdb. Listing 10.3 shows the code for the `OracleRowSetExample` class.

Listing 10.3: OracleRowSetExample

```
import java.sql.*;
import javax.sql.*;
import oracle.jdbc.driver.*;
import oracle.jdbc.pool.OracleDataSource;

/**
 * Description:  Demostrates RowSet functionality
 *               from the JDBC 2.x API
 * Note:         Requires an Oracle Database
 */

public class OracleRowSetExample
{

  public OracleRowSetExample()
  {
  }
```

```
 public void fetchRow()
  {
  }

public final static void main (String[] args)
 {
  System.out.println( "Note: requires a Oracle Database");
  OracleRowSetExample rse = new OracleRowSetExample();
    rse.TestDataSource();
 }

 private void TestDataSource ()
  {
   try
    {
     // Create a OracleDataSource instance explicitly
     OracleDataSource ods = new OracleDataSource();
     // Set the user name, password,
     // driver type and network protocol
     ods.setUser("scott");
     ods.setPassword("tiger");
     ods.setDriverType(
      "jdbc:oracle:thin:@localhost:1521:devdb");
     ods.setNetworkProtocol("tcp");

     // Retrieve a connection
     Connection conn = ods.getConnection();
     getUserName(conn);
     // Close the connection
     conn.close();
     conn = null;
    }
   catch (Exception e)
    {
     e.printStackTrace();
     System.out.println(e.getMessage() ) ;
    }
  }

  private void getUserName(Connection conn)
       throws SQLException
  {
```

```
        // Create a Statement
        Statement stmt = conn.createStatement ();
        // Select the TNAME column from the tab table
        ResultSet RS = stmt.executeQuery
        ("select TNAME from tab");
        // Iterate through the result
        // and print the table names
        while (RS.next ())
          System.out.println ("Table name is "
                            + RS.getString (1 ));
        // Close the ResultSet
        if ( RS != null)
           RS.close();
        // Close the Statement
        if (stmt != null)
           stmt.close();
      }
    }
```

The JDBC 2.*x* classes are powerful, and offer many features that will ease programming tasks for developers. With the burden of support falling to database driver writers, however, the *write once run anywhere* promise of 100 percent Java behaves more like *your mileage may vary*. Although the JDBC 2.*x* functionality might be ideal for your business and development environment, it's more likely that you'll migrate to that framework. For many small businesses and developers, switching to a database with JDBC 2.*x*+ support or waiting for drivers to be released are simply not viable options. Perhaps an option in the interim is to use custom classes such as the `DittoResultSet`.

DittoResultSet—A Robust, Simple Replacement for *java.sql.ResultSet*

To create a proper architecture, you need to separate the Data Access tier from the Presentation layer. One option is to use the advanced JDBC classes, and a particular database and driver that support those classes. Another option is to have a back-end object access the data, process it for presentation, and send it back to the Presentation layer. This is perhaps the ideal choice, but often requires extensive efforts. For example, if

XML/XSL is used, documents and style sheets must be written first. Another approach is to use custom classes to abstract the data to an intermediary form. Many developers use custom classes to do this abstraction process in which read-only data sets are used, such as with prototypes and reporting applications. Review custom classes carefully, and test them thoroughly before implementing them in your architecture.

The `DittoResultSet` is a custom class for abstracting data for read-only use. The `DittoResultSet` is a class that acts as a one-way wrapper for a `java.sql.ResultSet`. A `DittoResultSet` is constructed by passing in a `ResultSet`. The `ResultSet` is read completely into a private, ordered data structure. The original `ResultSet` (and its invisible connection to the database) disappears, and yet the data stays intact.

Beyond implementing the basic `ResultSet` functions, the `DittoResultSet` can be passed from function to function (moving seamlessly from the Data Access to the Presentation layer). The contents can be read multiple times. The row count of the `ResultSet` is readily available, and it can transform a `ResultSet` into an XML data representation. All these features are potentially helpful for customizing the Presentation layer, but none are available in the standard `java.sql.ResultSet`. Listing 10.4 shows the code for the `DittoResultSet` class.

Listing 10.4: DittoResultSet.java

```
package c10;

import java.sql.*;
import java.text.*;
import java.util.*;

/**
 * Title:       DittoResultSet
 * Description: Simulates a disconnected, non-updateable
 *              ResultSet without the extra overhead and
 *              the often unneeded functionality of
 *               other implementations.
 * Disclaimer:  Test thoroughly for your environment.
 *              No warrantee expressed or implied.
 *              Use at your own risk.
 * Copyleft:    Publically available under the
 *              GNU Lesser GPL (General Public License)
 *              see lesser.txt included with this file
 *              distribution or:
```

```
 *           http://www.gnu.org/copyleft/lesser.txt
 *           Permission granted for publication here.
 * Company:  www.cookconsulting.com
 *           (visit for updated versions)
 * @author  Todd Cook
 * @version 1.3
 */

public class DittoResultSet
 {
    private Vector vHeaderNames;
    private Vector vRows;
    private String strSeparator =
     "DRS"
      + System.currentTimeMillis()
      + "Sep";
    private int iRow = -2;
    private HashMap hmHeaders;
    private String dittoResultSetNullValue
       = "DRSNull"
         + System.currentTimeMillis()
         + "Val";
    private int iRowCount = 0;

  public DittoResultSet ()
   {}

  public String getDittoResultSetNullValue ()
   {
    return dittoResultSetNullValue;
   }

  public void setDittoResultSetNullValue (String
                              NewDittoResultSetNullValue)
   {
    if (NewDittoResultSetNullValue!= null)
    dittoResultSetNullValue =
         NewDittoResultSetNullValue.trim();
   }

  public String getStrSeparator ()
   {
    return strSeparator;
```

```
 }

public void setStrSeparator (String
                           NewStrSeparator)
 {
  if (NewStrSeparator!= null)
  strSeparator = NewStrSeparator.trim();
 }

/**
 * Constructors Section
 */

public DittoResultSet (ResultSet rs)
 {
  try
    {
      ResultSetMetaData rsmd = rs.getMetaData();
      int iCol = rsmd.getColumnCount();
      vHeaderNames = new Vector (iCol);
      hmHeaders = new HashMap (iCol);
      vRows = new Vector();
      for (int ii=1; ii < iCol+1; ii++)
       {
        vHeaderNames.addElement(
                 (Object) rsmd.getColumnName( ii) );
        hmHeaders.put(
          rsmd.getColumnName(ii).toUpperCase(),
                                  new Integer(ii));
       }
        StringBuffer sb;
        Iterator itvHN ;
        // can't make an iterator for a hashmap
        String strVal ="";
          while (rs.next())
            {
             sb = new StringBuffer ();
             itvHN = vHeaderNames.iterator();
            while( itvHN.hasNext())
              {
                String strHeader = (String) itvHN.next();
                // System.out.println (
                //  "strHeader=" + strHeader);
```

```
                    if (rs.getString( strHeader  ) != null)
                        {
                         sb.append( rs.getString(strHeader) );
                        }
                    else
                        {
                         sb.append(dittoResultSetNullValue);
                        }
                     sb.append( strSeparator);
                    }
                   vRows.addElement((Object) sb.toString());
                  }
             iRow = -1;// used in implementation of next()
        }
       catch (SQLException e)
        {
          e.printStackTrace();
        }
     }

     public String RsToXML (ResultSet rs)
      {
       StringBuffer sb = new StringBuffer();
       try
        {
          ResultSetMetaData rsmd = rs.getMetaData();
          int iCol = rsmd.getColumnCount();
          vHeaderNames = new Vector (iCol);
          sb.append( "<DRS>");
          for (int ii=1; ii < iCol+1; ii++)
           {
            vHeaderNames.addElement( (Object)
            rsmd.getColumnName( ii) );
            //sb.append( "<"+ rsmd.getColumnName( ii) + ">");
           }
            Iterator itvHN ;
            String strHeaderName = "";
            int i=1;
          while (rs.next())
            {
              sb.append( "<Row id=\"" + i + "\">");
              itvHN = vHeaderNames.iterator();
              while( itvHN.hasNext() )
```

```
                {
                 strHeaderName = (String) itvHN.next();
                 sb.append("<" + strHeaderName + ">");
                 sb.append(rs.getString( strHeaderName));
                 sb.append("</" + strHeaderName + ">");
                }
              sb.append("</Row>");
              i++;
              sb.append(strSeparator);
             }
           sb.append("</DRS>");
           setNumberOfRows(i);
          }
        catch (SQLException e)
          {
           e.printStackTrace();
          }
        return sb.toString();
      }

    /**
     *  Data Access Methods
     */

    public String getString (String SQLHeaderName)
      {
       String strTmp="";
        try
          {
           String strPackedRow =
                       (String) vRows.elementAt(iRow);
           int iNamePos =  Integer.parseInt(
               (hmHeaders.get(SQLHeaderName.toUpperCase()
                                              )).toString());
             // jeez, how ugly is that!
           int i = 1;
           int posInStr = 0;
           for ( ; i < iNamePos; i++ )
             {
              posInStr =
               strPackedRow.indexOf(strSeparator, posInStr)
                                    + strSeparator.length();
             }
```

```
            int EndofStr =
              strPackedRow.indexOf(strSeparator, posInStr);
            strTmp =  strPackedRow.substring
                           (posInStr, EndofStr);
          }
        catch (Exception e)
          {
           e.printStackTrace();
           System.out.println(e.getMessage());
          }
        strTmp = strTmp.trim();
        if (strTmp.equals(dittoResultSetNullValue))
            return null;
        else
            return strTmp;
      }

   public String getString (int iNamePos)
      {
       String strTmp="";
        try
         {
          String strPackedRow = (String)
                             vRows.elementAt(iRow);
          int i = 1;
          int posInStr = 0;
          for ( ; i < iNamePos; i++ )
            {
             posInStr =
              strPackedRow.indexOf(strSeparator, posInStr)
                                + strSeparator.length();
            }
           int EndofStr =
             strPackedRow.indexOf(strSeparator, posInStr);
           strTmp =  strPackedRow.substring
                               (posInStr, EndofStr);
         }
        catch (Exception e)
         {
           e.printStackTrace();
           System.out.println(e.getMessage());
         }
        strTmp = strTmp.trim();
```

```
    if (strTmp.equals(dittoResultSetNullValue))
        return null;
    else
        return strTmp;
  }

public int getInt (int iNamePos)
 {
  return (java.lang.Integer.parseInt(
                 getString(iNamePos)));
 }

public int getInt (String SQLHeaderName )
 {
      return (java.lang.Integer.parseInt(
                 getString(SQLHeaderName)));
 }

public void close()
 {
  //Should clear out the member values
      vRows.clear();
      iRow = -2;
      hmHeaders.clear();
 }

public boolean next ()
 {
  if (iRow == -2)
      return false;
       // perhaps should throw exception,
       // since it regularly means RS not loaded
  if (iRow+1 == vRows.size())
      return false;
  if (iRow == -1)
     {
      iRow =0;
       // means rs was loaded and
       // it's ready to look at first row
      return true;
     }
  if (iRow == 0)
```

```
        {
         iRow++;
         return true;
        }
     if (iRow == vRows.size())
         return false;
     else
        {
         iRow++;
         return true;
        }
    }

   public void beforeFirst()
    {
     if (getNumberOfRows() > 0)
         iRow = -1;  // move to beginning of DRS
    }

   public int getNumberOfColumns ()
    {
      // like a zero based 'array'
     return hmHeaders.size() + 1;
    }

   public int getNumberOfRows()
    {
     if (iRowCount == 0 && (vRows != null))
        {
         iRowCount = vRows.size();
        }
     return iRowCount;
    }

   private void setNumberOfRows (int RowCount)
    {
     iRowCount = RowCount;
    }

   public String getRow(int i)
    {
      if (i >=  vRows.size())
         return "";
```

```
        else
           return (String)vRows.elementAt(i);
     }

   public String getHeaderName(int i)
     {
        return (String)hmHeaders.get(new Integer(i));
     }

  /**
   *  Testing should be done by an external class
   *  DittoResultSet should never contain any DB info
   *  or implementation specific info
   */

   public final static void main (String[] args)
     {
       System.out.println("Main not implemented."
                 + " Test with an external class.");
     }
  }
```

The DittoResultSet implements many of the commonly used ResultSet methods, namely next(), close(), getString(String), getString(int), getInt(int), and getInt(String). Additionally, a default database null value can be set, and the separator for segregating the internal data representation can also be set, in the unlikely event that a SQL query will have a field that matches exactly to "DRS" + System.currentTimeMillis() + "Sep" or "DRSNull" + System.currentTimeMillis() + "Val".

The DittoResultSet class could be further expanded. It would be nice to implement some of the useful function of the ResultSet class, such as updating fields, and it would be nice to serialize the class so it could be sent across the wire or stored for later use. One benefit of using custom code is that your objects can be lightweight because they include only what you need to use.

Although practical usage and feedback about the DittoResultSet has indicated that it performs excellently, we recommend that you test it thoroughly before incorporating it into your designs.

Testing the DittoResultSet and incorporating it into an architecture is easy. Simply build your ConnectionManager class with a reference to the DittoResultSet, and implement a member function such as the following:

```
DittoResultSet public execDrsSQL (String SQL)
{
 // build a D.R.S. object immediately after getting an RS
  return new DittoResultSet(connectMan.executeQuery(SQL));
}
```

It would be preferable to modify the ConnectionManager class to return a DittoResultSet. JavaBeans and JSPs can then reference the DittoResultSet, and the data can be passed without the fear of exceptions or garbage collection.

WARNING

Of course, you should not abuse classes such as the DittoResultSet by storing excessive queries in them that tax server resources. It's always a good practice to write queries that select only the information you need.

Moving Data Access Away from the Presentation Layer: A Quiz Application Example

The DittoResultSet class shows one, albeit proprietary, approach to abstracting out the Data Access layer from the Presentation layer. Good design can help separate the elements into a clean design.

Here's a quiz application example that helps illustrate another way in which planned design can remove data access code from the Presentation layer. The quiz application is basically a configurable multiple-choice quiz that uses a database table to pull vocabulary words and definitions. The class design supports randomization of the vocabulary lookups, as well as authentication of the scoring. Listing 10.5 shows the code for the WordLookup class.

Listing 10.5: WordLookup.java

```
package c10;
import java.util.*;
```

```
import java.sql.*;
import c13.ConnectionManager;

/**
 * Description: A class for looking up words
 *              from a numbered table.
 */

public class WordLookup
 {
  private int numAdditionalAnswers = 1;
  private String qry =
   "select word, shortdefinition as definition "
   +" from "+ table + " where appearCount =";
  private String table = "";
  private String sQuestionWord="";
  private Vector vAnswers;
  private Random rn;
  private Random rn2;
  private ConnectionManager cm;
  private int randomLimit = 3;
  private String keyword = "";
  private String keywordDefinition = "";
  private int tableCount = 1 ;
  private String response = "";
  private boolean bTableStartsWithZero = false;
  private String lowerPercentage = "";
  private String upperPercentage = "";
  private String displayFont = "";
  private int numberOfTries = 2;
  private int attempts = 0;

  public WordLookup()
   {
    cm = new ConnectionManager ();
    rn = new Random();
    vAnswers = new Vector();
   }

  /**
   * Get/Set Properties
   */
```

```
public int getNumAdditionalAnswers()
 {
   return numAdditionalAnswers;
 }

public void setNumAdditionalAnswers (int
                             NewNumAdditionalAnswers)
 {
   numAdditionalAnswers = NewNumAdditionalAnswers;
 }

public int getNumberOfTries()
 {
   return numberOfTries;
 }

public void setNumberOfTries (int NewNumberOfTries)
 {
   numberOfTries = NewNumberOfTries;
 }

public int getAttempts()
 {
   return attempts;
 }

public void setAttempts (int NewAttempts)
 {
   attempts = NewAttempts;
 }

public void IncrementAttempts()
 {
   attempts++;
 }

public void ClearAttempts()
 {
   attempts = 0;
 }

public Vector getRandomAnswers()
 {
```

```
        return vAnswers;
      }

    public String getQuery()
      {
        return qry ;
      }

    public void setQuery (String newQuery)
      {
        qry = newQuery;
      }

    public String getResponse()
      {
        return response ;
      }

    public void setResponse (String newResponse)
      {
        response = newResponse;
      }

    public String getTable()
      {
        return table ;
      }

    public void setTable (String newTable)
      {
        table = newTable;
      }

    public int getTableCount()
      {
        return tableCount;
      }

    public void setTableCount (int newTableCount)
      {
        tableCount = newTableCount ;
      }
```

```
public int getRandom()
 {
   return rn.nextInt( randomLimit );
 }

public void setRandomUpperLimit (int iLimit)
 {
    randomLimit = iLimit;
 }

public void setLowerPercentage(String NewLowerPercentage)
 {
   if (NewLowerPercentage != null)
       lowerPercentage = NewLowerPercentage.trim();
 }

public String getLowerPercentage ()
 {
   return lowerPercentage;
 }

public void setUpperPercentage(String NewUpperPercentage)
 {
   if (NewUpperPercentage != null)
       upperPercentage = NewUpperPercentage;
 }

public String getUpperPercentage()
 {
   return upperPercentage;
 }

public void setDisplayFont (String NewDisplayFont)
 {
  if (NewDisplayFont != null)
      displayFont = NewDisplayFont;
 }

public String getDisplayFont()
 {
   return displayFont;
 }
```

```
public void setKeyword (String NewKeyword)
 {
  if (NewKeyword != null)
      keyword = NewKeyword;
 }

public String getKeyword ()
 {
   return keyword;
 }

public void setKeywordDefinition (String
                               NewKeywordDefinition)
 {
   if (NewKeywordDefinition != null)
       keywordDefinition = NewKeywordDefinition;
 }

public String getKeywordDefinition ()
 {
  return keywordDefinition;
 }

/**
 *  Processing code
 */

public void useDatabase(String DatabaseName)
 {
  if (DatabaseName != null)
   try
    {
     cm.getConnection();
     cm.executeQuery(" use " + DatabaseName );
    }
  catch (SQLException sqle)
    {
     System.out.println ( sqle.getMessage()
              + " trouble switching to database: "
                          + DatabaseName);
    }
 }
```

Part II

```
public Vector PullRandomAnswers()
 {
    vAnswers.clear();
    for (int ii =0, j = getNumAdditionalAnswers();
             ii < j; ii++)
      {
       // while(not in array of numbers
       //  previously selected)
       String def = "";
       while ( (def = pullDefinition(
                 rn.nextInt(getTableCount() )
                  )).length() < 1 )
                ; // empty execution, to skip empty items
       vAnswers.addElement((String) def);
      }
   vAnswers.insertElementAt(
                (String) getKeywordDefinition(),
                rn.nextInt(getNumAdditionalAnswers()) );
  return vAnswers;
 }

public int getRandomInRange (int ii)
 {
  return rn2.nextInt(ii);
 }

public int PullTableCount ()
 {
  int iCount = 1;
 try
  {
   cm.getConnection();
   ResultSet rs = cm.executeQuery(
             "select count(*) from " + getTable());
   if (rs.next())
   iCount = rs.getInt(1);
  }
 catch (SQLException sqle)
  {
   System.out.println ( sqle.getMessage());
  }
  setTableCount (iCount);
```

```
  setRandomUpperLimit (iCount);
 return iCount;
 }

public String pullDefinition (int iID )
 {
 String sDefinition ="";
 try
  {
   cm.getConnection();
   // System.out.println(getQuery() + iID ) ;
   ResultSet rs = cm.executeQuery( getQuery() + iID );
    if (rs.next())
       sDefinition = rs.getString("definition");
  }
 catch (SQLException sqle)
  {
   System.out.println ( sqle.getMessage()
                      + " Query: "
                      + getQuery()
                      + " def ="
                      + sDefinition );
  }
 return sDefinition;
}

public String pullRandomKeyword ()
 {
  try
   {
    cm.getConnection();
    // System.out.println( getQuery() + getRandom());
    ResultSet rs = cm.executeQuery( getQuery()
                                  + getRandom() );
    rs.next();
    keyword  = rs.getString("word");
    setKeywordDefinition(rs.getString("definition"));
   }
 catch (SQLException sqle)
   {
   System.out.println ( sqle.getMessage());
   System.out.println ( keyword);
```

```
      System.out.println (keywordDefinition);
      }
      // System.out.print("keyword: " + keyword);
      // System.out.print(" definition: "
      //                        + keywordDefinition);
     return keyword;
    }

   public String getDisplayFontTag (String displayWord)
    {
     return "<font face=\"" + getDisplayFont() +"\">"
          + displayWord + "</font>";
    }

   public static void main(String[] args)
    {
     WordLookup wL = new WordLookup();
     wL.useDatabase("greek");
     wL.setTable ("greek.babrius1");
     System.out.println(wL.PullTableCount());
     wL.setRandomUpperLimit( wL.getTableCount() );
     wL.setQuery(
       " select word, shortdefinition as definition "
         + " from babrius1 where appearCount =");
     wL.pullRandomKeyword();
     System.out.println( wL.getKeyword() );
     System.out.println( wL.getKeywordDefinition() );
     wL.setNumAdditionalAnswers(4);
     System.out.println( wL.getRandomAnswers().toString());
    }
}
```

A QuizBean

A simple QuizBean manages the application's score keeping. Listing 10.6 shows the code for the QuizBean class.

Listing 10.6: QuizBean.java

```
package c10;

import java.util.*;
```

```
public class QuizBean
 {
  private int iScore = 0;
  private int questionsCorrect = 0;
  private int questionsWrong = 0;
  private Vector vQuestionsWrong;
  private Vector vQuestionsRight;
  private String sKeywordStartTag = "";
  private String sKeywordEndTag = "";
  private java.util.Random rn ;
  private boolean checkAnswer = false;
  private boolean moveToNextWord = true;

  public QuizBean()
   {
    rn = new java.util.Random();
   }

  public boolean IsMoveToNextWord()
   {
    return moveToNextWord;
   }

  public void setMoveToNextWord (boolean bNewMoveToNextWord)
   {
    moveToNextWord = bNewMoveToNextWord;
   }

  public boolean IsCheckAnswer()
   {
    return checkAnswer;
   }

  public void setCheckAnswer(boolean bCheckAnswer)
   {
    checkAnswer = bCheckAnswer;
   }

  public void setCheckAnswer(String bStringCheckAnswer)
   {
    if (bStringCheckAnswer.equalsIgnoreCase("true"))
       {
        checkAnswer = true;
```

```
            return;
          }
        if (bStringCheckAnswer.equalsIgnoreCase("false"))
          {
            checkAnswer = false;
            return;
          }
        else
          {
            System.err.println("Odd values being passed "
                                  + "to the string to boolean "
                                  + "setCheck Answer: "
                                  + bStringCheckAnswer );
          }
      }

    public int getNextRndInt()
      {
        return rn.nextInt();
      }

    public void IncrementCorrectCount()
      {
       questionsCorrect++;
      }

    public void setQuestionsCorrect(int NewNumberCorrect)
      {
       questionsCorrect = NewNumberCorrect;
      }

    public int getQuestionsCorrect()
      {
       return questionsCorrect;
      }

    public void IncrementIncorrectCount()
      {
       questionsWrong++;
      }

    public void setQuestionsIncorrect(int NewNumberIncorrect)
      {
```

```
      questionsWrong = NewNumberIncorrect;
    }

  public int getQuestionsIncorrect()
    {
      return questionsWrong;
    }

  /**
    * Not implemented
    */

  public final static void main (String[] args)
    {
      System.out.println("Main() not implemented");
    }
}
```

The code is a fairly straightforward class with get/setProperty methods and score-keeping functions that compare and track correct and incorrect answers. You could further refine the QuizBean to keep track of which items were unsuccessful answers, and allow the user to return later to focus on those problem areas.

JSPs Supporting the Quiz Application

Two JSPs support the quiz application. One JSP configures the database, and another JSP actually hosts the quiz application. Listing 10.7 shows the code for the ConfigDB JSP.

Listing 10.7: ConfigDB.jsp

```
<%@ page errorPage="ConfigDBErrorPage.jsp" %>
<jsp:useBean class="c10.WordLookup"
  scope="session" id="WL"/>
<jsp:setProperty name="WL" property="*" />
<HTML>
<HEAD>
<TITLE>
Quiz DB Configuration
</TITLE>
</HEAD>
<BODY>
```

```
<H1>
Quiz DB Configuration
</H1>
<FORM method="post">
Select Topic:
<select name="table">
<option selected
 value="<%=WL.getTable()
           %>"><%=WL.getTable()%></option>
<option value=""></option>
<option value="babrius1">Babrius - versifier of Aesop
  </option>
</select>
<%
// setup code
  WL.setQuery(
   "select word, shortdefinition as definition "
   +" from babrius1 where appearCount =");
   WL.useDatabase("greek");
%>
<BR>
Select Number of Additional Answers:
<select name="numAdditionalAnswers">
<option select
 value="<%=WL.getNumAdditionalAnswers()
           %>"><%=WL.getNumAdditionalAnswers()%></option>
<option value="1">1</option>
<option value="2">2</option>
<option value="3">3</option>
<option value="4">4</option>
<option value="5">5</option>
<option value="6">6</option>
<option value="7">7</option>
<option value="8">8</option>
<option value="9">9</option>
<option value="10">10</option>
<option value="11">11</option>
<option value="12">12</option>
<option value="13">13</option>
<option value="14">14</option>
<option value="15">15</option>
<option value="16">16</option>
```

```
</select>
<BR>
Specify the number of tries before giving the answer
<select name="numberOfTries">
<option select
  value="<%=WL.getNumberOfTries()
        %>"><%=WL.getNumberOfTries()%></option>
<option value="1">1</option>
<option value="2">2</option>
<option value="3">3</option>
<option value="4">4</option>
<option value="5">5</option>
<option value="6">6</option>
<option value="7">7</option>
<option value="8">8</option>
<option value="9">9</option>
<option value="10">10</option>
<option value="11">11</option>
<option value="12">12</option>
<option value="13">13</option>
</select>
<BR>
Choose Font:
<select name="displayFont">
<option value="Sgreek,Sgreek Fixed,Sgreek Medium">
       Sgreek - For Greek Texts</option>
</select>
<BR>
<BR>
<INPUT TYPE="SUBMIT" NAME="Submit" VALUE="Submit">
<INPUT TYPE="RESET" VALUE="Reset">
</FORM>
<BR>
When done, click here to go to the
  <a href="Quiz.jsp">Quiz</a>
</BODY>
</HTML>
```

The Select Number of Additional Answers drop-down list box causes the quiz application to generate more or fewer radio button answers. The Specify the Number of Tries Before Giving the Answer drop-down list box changes the application's mercy limit before it indicates the correct answer.

Figure 10.3 shows the configuration page.

Part II

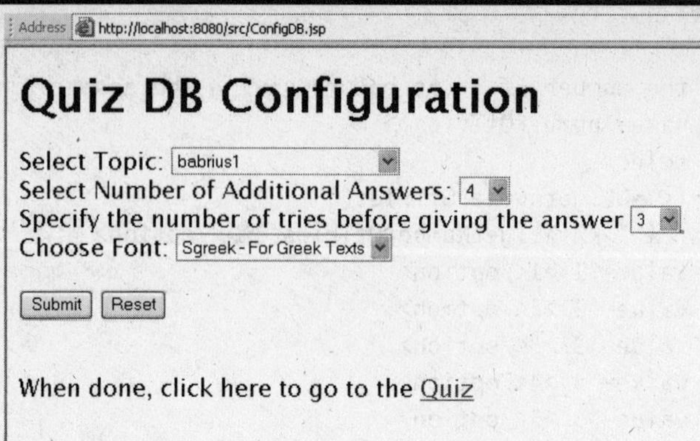

FIGURE 10.3: The Quiz DB Configuration page

Listing 10.8 shows the code for the ConfigDBErrorPage JSP.

Listing 10.8: ConfigDBErrorPage.jsp

```
<%@ page isErrorPage="true" %>
<HTML>
<BODY>
<H1>Error page ConfigDB</H1>
<BR>
<BR>An error occured in the bean.
Error Message is: <%= exception.getMessage() %>
<BR>
Stack Trace is : <PRE><FONT COLOR="RED"><%
 java.io.CharArrayWriter cw =
        new java.io.CharArrayWriter();
 java.io.PrintWriter pw =
        new java.io.PrintWriter(cw,true);
 exception.printStackTrace(pw);
 out.println(cw.toString());
 %>
</FONT>
</PRE>
</BODY>
</HTML>
```

TIP

Of course, if your database is properly set up, you shouldn't see the error page.

The heart of the quiz application is the Quiz JSP, which interacts with the `WordLookup` and `QuizBean` JavaBeans. The Quiz JSP dynamically creates a form that causes the page to reload itself, passing parameters that request the JavaBeans to check a word selection or move on to another word. Examine the JSP code in Listing 10.9, and notice the lack of Data Access methods; everything is done through the JavaBean interfaces.

Listing 10.9: Quiz.jsp

```
<%@page import="java.util.*" %>
<%@ page errorPage="ConfigDBErrorPage.jsp" %>
<jsp:useBean class="c10.WordLookup"
 scope="session" id="WL"/>
<jsp:setProperty name="WL" property="*" />
<jsp:useBean class="c10.QuizBean"
 scope="session" id="Scorekeeper"/>
<jsp:setProperty name="Scorekeeper" property="*" />
<HTML>
<HEAD>
<TITLE>
Quiz
</TITLE>
</HEAD>
<BODY>
<%
 if ( Scorekeeper.getQuestionsCorrect() == 0
      && Scorekeeper.getQuestionsIncorrect() == 0)
  {
  // initialization code
      WL.PullTableCount();
      WL.PullRandomAnswers();
      Scorekeeper.setMoveToNextWord(true);
  }
%>
<%  // scoring
String scoreMessage ="";
   if (WL.getKeywordDefinition().equalsIgnoreCase(
                          request.getParameter("answer")) )
  {
   scoreMessage ="Correctly Answered!    "
   + WL.getDisplayFontTag(WL.getKeyword()) + " : "
   + WL.getKeywordDefinition() ;
```

```
      Scorekeeper.setCheckAnswer(true);
      Scorekeeper.setMoveToNextWord(true);
      Scorekeeper.IncrementCorrectCount();
      WL.ClearAttempts();
     }
     else
     {
     if (request.getParameter("answer") != null)
     {
     WL.IncrementAttempts();
     Scorekeeper.IncrementIncorrectCount();
     Scorekeeper.setCheckAnswer(false);
     Scorekeeper.setMoveToNextWord(false);
       if (WL.getNumberOfTries() == WL.getAttempts())
        {
        scoreMessage = "Sorry, the answer was:"
           + WL.getKeywordDefinition() ;
        Scorekeeper.setMoveToNextWord(true);
        }
        }
     }
%>
Questions Answered Correctly:
 <%= Scorekeeper.getQuestionsCorrect() %>
<br>
Questions Answered Incorrectly:
 <%= Scorekeeper.getQuestionsIncorrect() %>
<H3>
Quiz
</H3>
<a href="ConfigDB.jsp">Configuration</a><BR>
<BR>
<%
  if (Scorekeeper.IsMoveToNextWord())
     WL.pullRandomKeyword();
%>
<%= WL.getDisplayFontTag(WL.getKeyword()) %>
<BR>

<FORM method="post" name="QuizChoices">
<%   Vector vPageAnswers = new Vector();
```

```
        if (Scorekeeper.IsMoveToNextWord())
        {
         vPageAnswers = WL.PullRandomAnswers();
        }
        else
        {
         vPageAnswers = WL.getRandomAnswers();
        }
        for (int ii = 0, j = WL.getNumAdditionalAnswers();
                 ii < j; ii++)
          {
           %><input type="radio"
            onClick="javascript:submit()"
              name="answer" value="<%
           out.print( vPageAnswers.elementAt(ii));
           %>"><%
           out.print( vPageAnswers.elementAt(ii));
            %><BR>
        <%
          }
           %>
      <BR>
      <input type="hidden" name="checkAnswer" value="true">
      <input type="button" value="Next Word"
       onClick="javascript:
        document.all.QuizChoices.checkAnswer.value='false';
         submit();">
      <BR>
      </FORM>
      <%= scoreMessage %>
      </BODY>
      </HTML>
```

Figure 10.4 shows the Quiz application in action.

The quiz application has two key features:

- It doesn't have any Data Access layer function inside the JSP code.
- Much of the business logic of a quiz has been implemented inside JavaBeans so that the JSPs can focus on the Presentation layer.

Part II

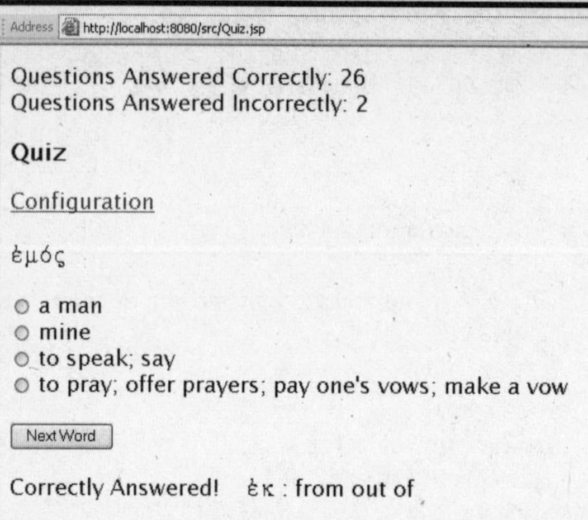

FIGURE 10.4: Quiz.jsp reloads itself, and tracks the user's progress.

WHAT'S NEXT

Advanced database programming is a subject that could easily span several books. Some issues concern JSP developers more than others.

Because JSP is the preferred Presentation layer, it seems natural that more often than not JSP developers are called on to create and deliver quick and dirty prototypes. Developers can make their prototypes less dirty by factoring out the data access functions by using the newer features of the JDBC API, such as the `DataSource` and `RowSet`, or by using a utility class such as the `DittoResultSet`. The JDBC API classes have the disadvantage that they tie Java code to a particular database at compile time. Custom utility class implementations such as the `DittoResultSet` are not tied to a database, and are more portable. Custom classes don't eliminate the need for the JDBC APIs, but they can make it easier to abstract data access methods and ease the difficulty of refactoring code.

It's difficult to find a more important topic than database programming. Nothing would please us more than to have you continue your interest in database design and programming. With the basic tools and concepts covered in this chapter, you can feel free to concentrate on pursuing the finer points of database design and usage.

Web-based applications are especially vulnerable to attacks to their security. The next chapter will explore the issues of web security. In addition it will explain how to make web-based J2EE applications secure.

Chapter 11

Secure Web Applications

As computer technology advances, the number and type of services available over the network increases. Convenience, however, has a price. The transfer of critical information creates business vulnerabilities that many wish to overlook. For numerous companies, the one area that requires the most attention receives the least: security. Security is a crucial aspect of any application that exchanges privileged information. This chapter will address the basic weaknesses a system faces, and identify key elements that should be considered to create a secure system and limit exposure to outside threats. This chapter will focus on the majority of J2EE systems that use servlets and JSP pages as their front-end components.

Featured in this chapter:

- Web security issues
- BASIC declarative security authentication

Part II

Adapted from *Java™ 2 Web Developer Certification Study Guide*, Second Edition by Natalie Levi

ISBN 0-7821-4202-8 $59.99

- FORM declarative security authentication
- Web deployment descriptor security tags

Security Issues

Most people find entertainment in sports, movies, talking, and other benign activities; however, many individuals receive amazing satisfaction and gratification from invading computer systems and either corrupting or capturing vital data. These individuals, known as *hackers* or *attackers*, thrive on system vulnerabilities. Utilizing various hacker tools, they are often able to scan systems to locate holes through which they can enter and attack. For many, it's a game; with others, it's for more personal reasons such as revenge. Regardless of the motives of potential attackers, securing your web application should be a priority to ensure the integrity of your data and application. This process begins by implementing the four basic security principles:

- Authorize
- Authenticate
- Provide data confidentiality
- Monitor access

In addition to these principles, the following security concerns will be addressed:

- Malicious code
- Web site attacks

Authentication and Authorization

The onset of the Internet caused network security to become a huge concern. When Java first hit the market, it was known as the Internet language. It marketed applet development as the product that provided a secure environment for clients accessing unknown sources over the Internet. Restricting applet access to the client system, however, was not a successful solution to security. Instead, other means of protection were needed to enable authorized access without limiting functionality.

The Java language has matured since its creation, and now offers several technologies to authenticate and authorize an outside user for access to a server application. The concern is no longer focused on the applet client, but rather a J2EE client (servlet or JSP) attempting to access an enterprise application.

Figure 11.1 provides a visual representation of these two approaches to security: the client-server approach, in which the aim is to secure the client, and the J2EE approach, in which the aim is to secure the server.

Client-server security

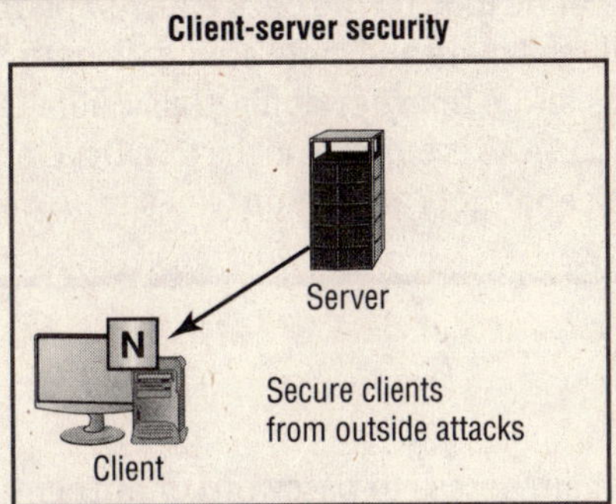

J2EE security

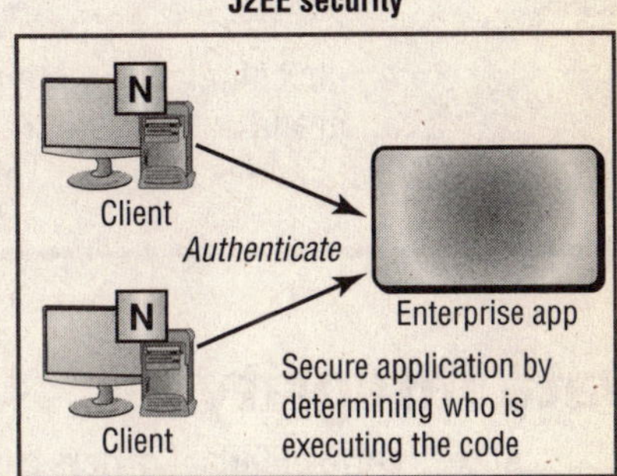

FIGURE 11.1: Security strategies

When a client requests information, the server has no way of determining who is making the request. The client's IP address fails to define the user because that user can attempt to access a server from various computers. In addition, it is easy for a user to falsify their IP address to disguise their identity. Consequently, the server must determine the client via user authentication and authorization, which will be explained in just a moment.

The focus here is on J2EE security and the processes used to protect the web application from false or unwanted clients. *Authentication* is the process whereby the client supplies credentials to prove their identity. Most often proof is provided via a password. Other examples include the swipe of a card or digital certificates, and one day perhaps even retinal scans or fingerprints.

Each user within a secure system is mapped to an identifier, also known as a *principal*. When logging into a system, a principal is usually recognized by their user ID. The `conf/web.xml` file is then used to associate principals with one or more *roles*. Roles are given privileged access to certain parts of the web application (again, through definitions in the `conf/web.xml`). Roles will be discussed in a bit more detail in the "Auditing" section of this chapter. Authorization is the process where a principal is given privileged access due to their role.

JAVA AUTHENTICATION AND AUTHORIZATION SERVICE

With the introduction of the Java Authentication and Authorization Service (JAAS) API, authentication can be handled by utilizing pluggable modules configured to authenticate by using something as simple as a username and password, or something more complex such as a SmartCard reader. JAAS offers an enterprise application a variety of services for authentication on the back end. As vendors standardize this API, you will see more and more applications using complex pluggable modules rather than developing basic authentication and authorization code. JAAS is bundled in the Java Developer Kit 1.4 and is also available separately at the Sun web site.

Data Integrity

Access control fails if others can gain access to password or authentication information as it is transmitted over the network. Encrypting information protects data and provides another level of security. The protocol called Secure Sockets Layer (SSL) was developed to use public key cryptography to encrypt communication between the client and server. A *public key* is an encryption scheme, either generated by software or issued by a third party, used to encode or decode information. Sitting between the HTTP and TCP/IP protocol, SSL encrypts the data to prevent hackers from acquiring confidential information. Anyone attempting to intercept the data transfer will simply encounter indecipherable nonsense.

Two main security concerns are solved when using public key cryptography. The first is confidentiality. Because the data is encrypted, you are guaranteed privacy. The second security concern is integrity. As long as the intended recipient can decode the information properly, you can be fairly sure that the data was not tampered with during transmission.

Auditing

Auditing users is a way of ensuring that users who log in successfully access only those resources that are appropriate to their role. The servlet security model is *role-based*. This means that users are assigned to roles, such as Manager, Employee, or Guest. Each role is assigned certain privileges, and access is granted to roles rather than users. To determine whether to provide a client with access to a given resource, the server:

1. Discovers which roles are available
2. Checks to see which roles are allowed
3. Checks to see whether the user is assigned to any available roles

Notice that security evolves around the role rather than the user. By using a server-specific tool, users are mapped to particular roles. The granularity of permissions can be defined at a finer level. By using the tool or the deployment descriptor, you can specify the method permissions for each role as well.

Access for each role can be denoted in two ways: through declarative security or programmatic security.

Declarative Security

Declarative security uses the deployment descriptor to specify which resources a role can access. The advantage of this approach is that implementing security is independent of source code; when security changes must be made, there is no need to recompile or make changes to the code.

By including the `security-constraint` tag in your `web.xml` file located in the `/WEB-INF` directory, you can define each resource and the roles that have access. Here is an example of how to restrict a particular directory to users that have the role of Administrator.

```
<security-constraint>
    <web-resource-collection>
        <web-resource-name>
            Admin area
        </web-resource-name>
        <url-pattern>
            /admin/*
        </url-pattern>
    </web-resource-collection>
    <auth-constraint>
        <role-name>
            Administrator
        </role-name>
    </auth-constraint>
</security-constraint>
```

The web-resource-name tag defines the human-language name for the resource, and url-pattern identifies the location of the resource. Within the security-constraint tag, you can then define which roles have access to the identified resources by using the auth-constraint tag. Keep in mind that you can list more than one role-name within the authorization group.

Users and roles are usually mapped to an *access list* stored by the server. Sometimes it's a simple file containing each user's login name, password, and role. Other times it's stored as a database with encrypted employee information.

NOTE

When discussing BASIC authentication later in this chapter, we will go into more detail on user mapping and show you how Tomcat manages user role information.

Programmatic Security

There are times when declarative security is not specific enough. You might need to limit access within a particular method based on a user. This kind of granularity requires security to extend itself to the method source code, which is done by using *programmatic security*. Within a method such as doGet(...), you might want to determine who is making the request and then, based on the result, determine whether to execute a particular response.

There are three Java methods within the javax.servlet .HttpServletRequest class that provide information about the user making a request:

String getRemoteUser() returns a String of the username used to log in to the web site.

boolean isUserInRole(String role) indicates whether the user accessing the servlet is assigned to the passed-in role.

Principal getUserPrincipal() returns a java.security .Principal object representing the user who is logged in.

Here is an example of how programmatic security can filter activity based on the user:

```
import javax.servlet.*;
import javax.servlet.http.*;
import java.io.*;
import java.util.*;
```

```
public class AccessServlet extends HttpServlet {
    public void doGet(HttpServletRequest req,
                      HttpServletResponse res)
      throws ServletException, IOException {

        res.setContentType("text/plain");
        PrintWriter out = res.getWriter();

        String username = req.getRemoteUser();
        if (username == null) {
            out.println("You are not logged in.");
        } else if ("Mary".equals(username)) {
            out.println("Hello Mary,
                    glad you can join us");
        } else {
            out.println("Hello " + username);
        }
        out.close();
    }
}
```

Depending on who makes a GET request, the message returned is different. Mary gets the most personal message; general users simply get a basic "Hello." If a user is not logged in, `getRemoteUser()` returns `null`. This example has Mary assigned to the role of GeneralUser. With this said, the deployment descriptor would look similar to the following:

```
<security-constraint>
    <web-resource-collection>
        <web-resource-name>
            AccessServlet
        </web-resource-name>
        <url-pattern>
            /serlvet/AccessServlet
        </url-pattern>
    </web-resource-collection>
    <auth-constraint>
        <role-name>
            GeneralUser
        </role-name>
    </auth-constraint>
</security-constraint>
```

All users assigned to the role of GeneralUser have access to the `AccessServlet`. Within the servlet, you use programmatic security to deliver a different message depending on the user. Each tag will be thoroughly discussed in the BASIC authentication section later in this chapter.

As you can see, declarative and programmatic security can be used together. The downside of defining security measures within code is that changes to security will result in the need to recompile the code.

Malicious Code

In the technical world, the term *malicious code* is synonymous with *virus*. Unfortunately, many people thrive on developing software that locates system vulnerabilities to attack. Sometimes the code is kind enough to simply overflow a particular folder with messages of love; however, at other times viruses have been known to wipe out entire hard drives. There are no flags or method calls that can protect your system against these types of assaults. One solution is the use of antivirus software. Antivirus software is critical in keeping your system safe from potential code attacks. Simply installing the software is not enough. Staying current is most important. Because new viruses are being developed every day, the software must be updated on a regular basis. The goal is to stay one step ahead of the attacker.

Web Site Attacks

When establishing a web site, assume the site will be attacked. Even if the information isn't critical, hackers often use other people's systems for the sole purpose of hiding their trail. By bouncing from machine to machine, they can arrive at a destination with a trail too difficult to trace. One form of protection against hacker activity on your system is the utilization of a firewall.

Firewalls block network traffic by limiting access to most ports and unauthorized users. Once again, the firewall requires the client to provide proper authorization to enter the system. Unfortunately, firewalls are not foolproof because there are ways to bypass security by impersonating an authorized user.

Another tactic to help prevent attacks is the installation of intrusion detection tools. There are a number of tools you can use to detect attackers. Packet sniffers, for example, enable you to view all the traffic on your network. If any activity looks odd, you can use your firewall to block the intruder.

At a minimum, a protected system requires firewalls, intruder detection, and antivirus software. All these preventive techniques can succeed only if user authentication isn't compromised. The next section will discuss the different ways to authenticate a user.

Authentication Types

The web container provides four authentication techniques to determine client validity:

BASIC authentication requires the client to provide a user login name and password in order to access protected data.

FORM authentication adds a bit of elegance to logging in. It enables an application to request authorization by using a customized HTML page.

DIGEST authentication provides a little bit more security in that it encrypts the login name and password to prevent others from acquiring this privileged information while it travels over the network.

CLIENT-CERT authentication stands for client certificate. This approach requires the client to provide a digital certificate containing information about the issuer, signature, serial number, key type, and more. Basically, it is a complex object used to identify the client.

This section will show you how each technique is used to authenticate users who want to gain access to the web application.

BASIC

The simplest form of authentication is known as HTTP basic authentication, or BASIC. As its name indicates, an application utilizing this form of certification asks for basic information, such as the user's login name and password. The data is then transferred to the server by using BASE64 encoding for validation. The good news is that this process is easy to implement; the bad news is that it doesn't offer much security beyond authenticating the client. If intercepted, the username and password could easily be decoded by running a simple BASE64-decode on the data. If a web site provides information that is not critical for an exclusive group, BASIC could be an option.

When a user attempts to access information protected in this fashion, the browser will automatically display a dialog box requesting the user's login name and password. This process is automatic and cannot be customized.

You must identify within the deployment descriptor the code requiring protection, the type of authentication, and who is to gain access. When the client attempts to access this code, a dialog box similar to the image in Figure 11.2 appears.

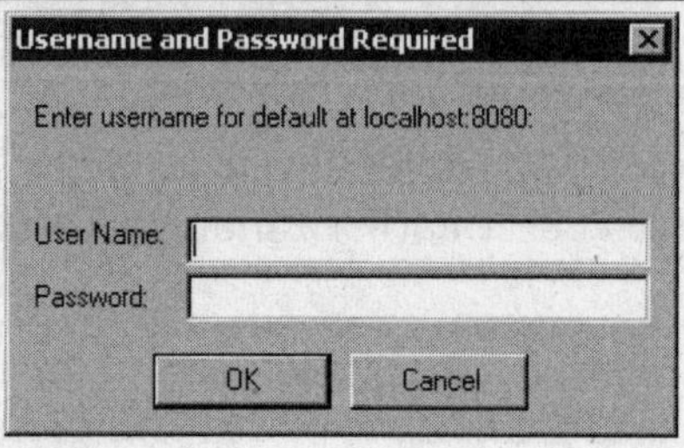

FIGURE 11.2: BASIC authorization dialog box

One of the benefits Java offers is the capability to define security outside the application source. There is no need to recompile Java code when security options are changed. When using servlets, the security permissions are defined within the `web.xml` file. Before examining the needed XML elements, begin by looking at a simple servlet:

```
import javax.servlet.*;
import javax.servlet.http.*;
import java.io.*;
import java.util.*;

public class PrivateServlet extends HttpServlet {
    public void doGet(HttpServletRequest req,
                      HttpServletResponse res)
      throws ServletException, IOException {

        res.setContentType("text/plain");
        PrintWriter out = res.getWriter();

        out.println("You are accessing" +
               "private information");
    }
}
```

This servlet serves no other purpose but to print a message. The goal is to restrict access to this servlet to a small group of privileged users. To accomplish this task, you must modify the `web.xml` file to include our security requirements. There are three groups to include, and their order is critical: `security-constraint`, `login-config`, and `security-role`.

The *security-constraint* Element

The first tag group that must be defined is `<security-constraint> </security-constraint>`. These tags are critical because they define what code is protected. The following sample shows what elements are included within this constraint:

```
<security-constraint>
   <web-resource-collection>
      <web-resource-name>
         SecretProtection           <!-- name for tool-->
      </web-resource-name>
      <url-pattern>
         /servlet/PrivateServlet <!--protected servlet-->
      </url-pattern>
      <url-pattern>
         /servlet/Secret
      </url-pattern>
      <http-method>
         GET                  <!-- protected http method -->
      </http-method>
      <http-method>
         POST
      </http-method>
    </web-resource-collection>
    <auth-constraint>
      <role-name>
         broker                  <!-- role with access -->
      </role-name>
      <role-name>
         administrator
      </role-name>
    </auth-constraint>
</security-constraint>
```

Within the `security-constraint`, there are two sub-elements:

- `web-resource-collection`
- `auth-constraint`

The `web-resource-collection` element defines three important features of the protected code:

> The **`web-resource-name`** is the name used by a tool to reference the servlet. The name must be specified even if a tool is not used.
>
> The **`url-pattern`** indicates the URL pattern to the source code requiring protection. If alias names are used to reference servlets, those too should be included.

The **http-method** indicates all HTTP methods that should have restricted access. If no HTTP method is specified all methods are protected.

TIP

Remember: The methods defined within the `http-method` element apply to all servlets defined by the `url-pattern` element.

The `auth-constraint` element defines any number of roles that can have access to the protected code. Remember, all users belong to roles. For example, a user with a login of Bob14 can belong to the broker and employee roles. This information is usually defined within a server-specific access list or database. Tomcat uses the `conf/tomcat-users.xml` file to characterize each group. The file might look similar to the following:

```
<tomcat-users>
  <user name="Mandy"  password="secret" roles="broker" />
  <user name="Tim21"  password="secret"
                      roles="administrator" />
  <user name="Bob14"  password="secret"
                      roles="broker, employee" />
</tomcat-users>
```

The *login-config* Element

The second tag group is defined within the `<login-config></login-config>` tags. It is here that the type of container authentication is defined. The following sample shows what elements are included within this constraint:

```
<login-config>
   <auth-method>
      BASIC     <!--BASIC, DIGEST, FORM, CLIENT-CERT -->
   </auth-method>
   <realm-name>
      Default          <!-- Optional, used for BASIC -->
   </realm-name>
</login-config>
```

Within the `login-config` tags, there are two sub-elements:

- `auth-method`
- `realm-name`

The `auth-method` element is used to define authentication types of basic, digest, form-based, and client-side certificates. Specifically, the methods must be defined as BASIC, DIGEST, FORM, or CLIENT-CERT. Keep in mind that these method types are case sensitive.

The `realm-name` element is used by the BASIC authentication to identify a specific area of a web site. For example, if there is a member area of the web site, this value might be "Members Area."

The *security-role* Element

The final basic security tag group is defined by the `<security-role>` `</security-role>` tags. Within these elements are defined roles the application might use to limit access. Generally, this listing is beneficial to tools because they provide the application assemblers or deployers a list of roles to select from to assign to methods.

```
<security-role>
    <description>
        Represents all fulltime employed individuals.
    </description>
    <role-name>
        employee
    </role-name>
</security-role>
```

Within the `security-role` tags, there are two sub-elements:

- `role-name`
- `description`

The `role-name` tag is required and defines available roles for the application to utilize. The `description` tag, as the name implies, provides a description of the particular role being listed.

In summary, BASIC authentication requests client authentication when a request for protected data is made. To set up this process, the `web.xml` file must be configured to include `security-constraint` information, which defines what data is protected, and `login-config` data, which defines the type of authentication the container should implement, and it must define the available roles by using the `security-role` tag.

FORM

In an attempt to provide more elegance to the art of validating users, FORM-based authentication is available. Rather than rely on the browser's default pop-up dialog box to request the user's login name and password, the application can provide its own custom form to request this information. The benefit to the FORM approach is aesthetic. Essentially you can guarantee that all users, regardless of which browser they use, will see the same login screen (possibly with the company's logo displayed).

Several requirements are necessary to ensure that the custom form communicates correctly with the server's access list:

- The FORM method must be `POST`.
- The action or URL must be defined as `j_security_check`.
- The attribute for the username must be `j_username`.
- The attribute for the password must be `j_password`.

Utilizing these values enables the server to access the correct attributes given the standardized names. Take a look at a simple custom form, called `Login.html`:

```
<HTML>
   <BODY>
      <FORM ACTION='j_security_check' METHOD='POST'>
      <P>Welcome to my custom login screen!</P>
      <P>Name: <INPUT TYPE='text' NAME='j_username'
                                   SIZE=15></P>
      <P>Password: <INPUT TYPE='password' NAME='j_password'
                                          SIZE=15></P>
      <P><INPUT TYPE='submit' VALUE='OK'></P>
      </FORM>
   </BODY>
</HTML>
```

As you can see, each name is defined by the standard rules and results in a custom form that can be used for login purposes. See Figure 11.3.

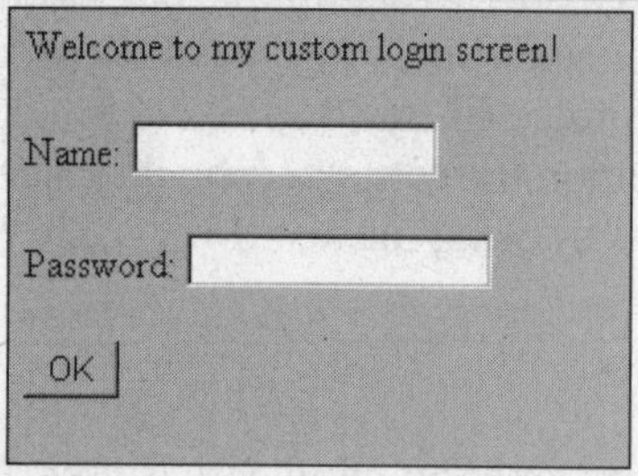

FIGURE 11.3: Custom authentication form

If the user attempts to log in but fails, you can no longer rely on the browser's error dialog box. Consequently, when creating a login form, you must also create an error form. Once again, keep it very simple and define the following `Error.html` page:

```
<HTML>
    <BODY>
      You failed to log in successfully.
      Hit the "Back" button to try again.
    </BODY>
</HTML>
```

On their own, the `Login.html` and `Error.html` pages are not linked—meaning that when the user clicks the OK button, there is no direct connection to the error page. Instead, the two pages "communicate" via an intermediary. Basically, when someone tries to log in, the server verifies authenticity of the client by using `j_username` to get the username and then using `j_password` to get the password. If there is a failure, the server must be able to find the error form to display. The connection between the code and server is made within the `web.xml` file. Once again, you need to make modifications to this document to inform the server of the name and whereabouts of the login and error pages used during FORM authentication.

The one area that changes is within the `login-config` tags. In addition to identifying the type of authentication, you must also define the location for the custom login page and custom error page:

```
<login-config>
    <auth-method>
        FORM
    </auth-method>
    <form-login-config>
        <form-login-page>
            /Login.html
        </form-login-page>
        <form-error-page>
            /Error.html
        </form-error-page>
    </form-login-config>
</login-config>
```

Within the `login-config` tags, you not only define the type of authentication, but if it is of type FORM, you include a sub-element group called `form-login-config`.

The *form-login-config* Element

Fundamentally, this tag is used to help the server locate the forms to display during appropriate times. The two sub-elements are as follows:

- `form-login-page`
- `form-error-page`

As their names indicate, the `form-login-page` tag defines the login page that should be used when a request for protected code is made. This page is displayed instead of the default login dialog box used with BASIC. Similarly, the `form-error-page` defines the error page that will be displayed if authorization is denied.

Customizing your login and error page displays is fairly easy. The trick is to follow the naming conventions within your login pages and modify the deployment descriptor to locate those files.

DIGEST

As stated previously, one of the greatest security limitations of BASIC authentication is that information is transferred over the network in simple BASE64-encoded text. Someone snooping the line can easily capture a client's username and password to gain access to the site. DIGEST adds an extra layer of security when authenticating the user. Instead of transferring the password, the server creates a *nonce*, a random value that is unique. An example of a nonce could be the client's IP address followed by a time stamp and some random data. It might look something like this:

```
127.0.0.1:86433665446:dujehIIJRTGDKdkfj
```

The server sends the nonce to the client; then things get interesting. The client uses a secure encryption algorithm to create, or hash, a digest. A *digest* is a one-directional, encrypted value that represents data. In this case, the digest consists of the nonce, username, and password. Figure 11.4 shows the simple process used to generate a digest.

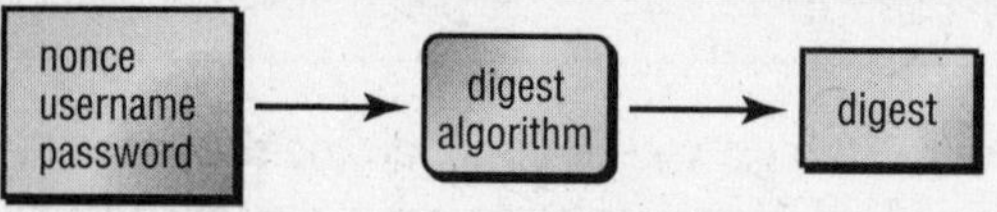

FIGURE 11.4: Creating a digest

After the digest is generated, the client sends the digest back to the server. The server then uses the nonce it sent originally and the username and password on file to generate a digest on its end. The server compares the digest sent by the client to the one generated locally. If they match, the client can access the protected resource. If not, access is denied.

If the client is valid. Figure 11.5 illustrates the process.

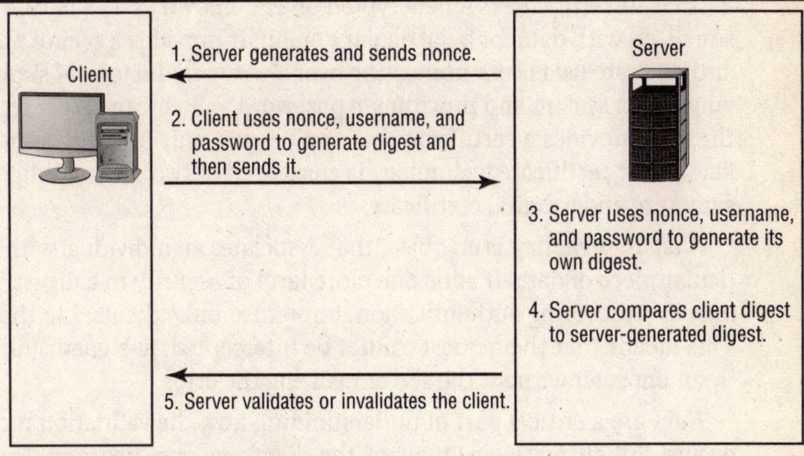
Client
Server
1. Server generates and sends nonce.
2. Client uses nonce, username, and password to generate digest and then sends it.
3. Server uses nonce, username, and password to generate its own digest.
4. Server compares client digest to server-generated digest.
5. Server validates or invalidates the client.

FIGURE 11.5: The DIGEST process

The nonce is critical in that it protects against attackers who intercept the hash value and intend to reuse it at a later date. Because the nonce contains a time stamp and a random value, the request will most likely time out and be removed from the server at a later time, causing the client's request to be invalidated.

Unix administrators are familiar with password encryption. Often passwords are stored in a secure file; however, if someone manages to gain administrative access, they can view this information. Because passwords are considered extremely sensitive and critical data, the OS encrypts them so even the administrator cannot know these values. If an attacker captures the hashed password/digest, they will not have access to the user. Instead, they will need to guess various passwords and generate a digest to see whether there was a match. This is because a digest is considered a one-way transformation of data.

Most browsers implement DIGEST authentication in their own manner, making it difficult to set up and use. If it were easier, HTTP authentication could widely provide useful low-level security.

CLIENT-CERT

HTTPS client authentication, or CLIENT-CERT, is the strongest form of authentication. HTTPS is HTTP over Secure Socket Layer (SSL). Instead of simply providing a username and password, the client must provide that information in addition to a personal certificate for authorization to access the server.

A *client certificate* is an encrypted object, known as a signature, personalized with data for a particular person. It provides a secure way to authenticate users communicating over a network. Instead of simply logging into a system and providing a password, which can be decrypted, the user provides a certificate that can be read only by using a special key. Client certificate technology is composed of two pieces: a digital signature and a digital certificate.

A *digital signature* is an object that associates an individual with a particular piece of data. It adds one more level of security to a digest. Not only is it providing authentication, but it also links the user to the data. This means that the request cannot be intercepted, re-signed, and sent by an imposter without the server realizing the error.

Keys are a critical part of understanding how the validation process occurs. Prior to any login attempts, the client generates two keys. The first is a *private key* that holds the individual's authentication code and is stored in a secure location, on a SmartCard or in a file. It should be known and accessed only by its owner. The second is a *public key* given to all receivers to validate the authenticity of the user attempting to log in. When using servlets, the server stores all public keys of users who can access the system in a database or Lightweight Directory Access Protocol (LDAP) directory server. When a client then tries to access a protected site, they are prompted to provide a username and password. When transmitting this information, a digest is generated along with a digital signature by using the client's private key. The digest is then sent to the server, which uses its public key to unlock the signature. If the public key is a forgery and not part of the key pair used by the private key, the signature will not unlock, and the user is invalidated. Figure 11.6 demonstrates the process.

Digital signatures provide integrity by guaranteeing that the data hasn't changed since it was signed. Basically, it is impossible for an attacker to re-create the signature with a new set of data without access to the user's private key. Any alteration of data invalidates the digital signature. In addition, a digital signature also provides authentication because after someone signs something, they cannot deny having done so.

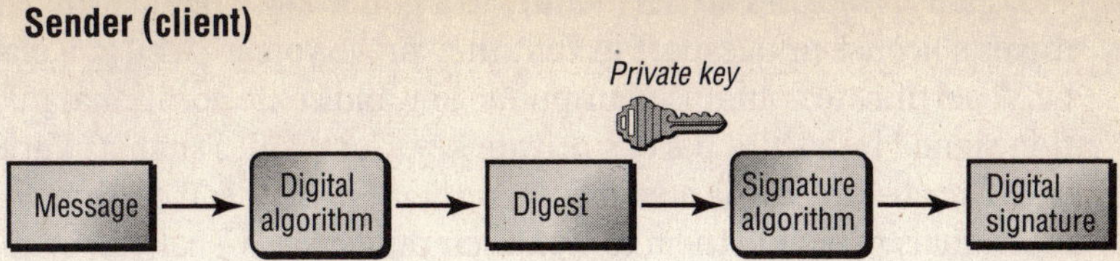

FIGURE 11.6: Digital signatures

Scenarios that were previously threatening pose no or little threat when using certificates. Here are some potential scenarios:

- If the object is retrieved during its commute to its destination by an unauthorized receiver, that person will be unable to extract its information because they lack the key.
- Because the certificate also has a time stamp associated with it, a retrieved certificate is invalidated after a period of lapsed time; thus it cannot be forged during future login attempts.
- Obtaining a stolen public key serves no purpose because although it allows you to verify the person sending the certificate, it does not grant you access to the system they are attempting to access.

Unfortunately, digital signatures are not 100 percent safe. When a public key is delivered to a user, there is a possibility that an attacker will acquire this value. You cannot be certain your public key belongs to the client intended unless the key was transferred in an absolutely secure environment. A common problem is known as man-in-the-middle attacks. Someone places themselves between the client and server, and manages to intercept the authentication and pose as a valid user. If they manage to intercept and alter the public key, they can configure the public key to recognize a false signature. The goal is to prevent them from manipulating the public key maintained at the target site. One solution to protecting a public key during its transfer is to encrypt communication or use direct connections; the other solution is to use digital certificates.

Digital certificates attach identity to a public key. They act similarly to a driver's license or passport in that they prove you are who you claim to be. A certificate contains your public key and some additional information signed by a third party's private key. Companies such as VeriSign and Thawte, known as a *certificate authority (CA)*, sell certificates to individuals to enable them to sign their public key. Usually a certificate contains the information outlined in Table 11.1.

TABLE 11.1: Certificate Information

INFORMATION	DESCRIPTION
Version	Version of the certificate (v1, v2, v3). Each version contains different attributes.
Serial number	Integer value unique to the CA issuing the certificate.
Signature algorithm	Algorithm used to sign the certificate.
Subject	Whom the certificate is issued to. This item can include a common name, organization or organizational unit, the organization's location, state, and country.
Subject public key	Public key of the certificate. This is the most important piece.
Signature	Signature signed by the CA.

NOTE

If a single attribute is changed, the certificate is invalidated. When information needs to be altered, the CA needs to reissue a new certificate.

Instead of sending a public key to intended recipients, you transfer a certificate. If the certificate is intercepted and altered, the certificate and the key within are invalidated. Consequently, the man-in-the-middle technique fails to compromise the client or server. Of course, there is room for certificate corruption. If the certificate authority is not reliable, they can create forged certificates, allowing attackers to act as imposters.

For the most part, client certificates provide the most security but do require the most work. When data transactions are critical and security is essential, a client certificate ensures authentication, authorization, data integrity, and confidentiality. By designing a site where the client must initially provide a certificate and then a digest with each request, you can be almost fully assured that the client is who they say they are and the data they are sending is in its original form.

WHEN SECURITY IS A PRIORITY

You have just been hired to work on securing a web site managed by the government. Fairly confidential information is available on this site for officials to access while off site. Your role is to ensure that only authorized users are granted access and to protect the information from malicious attacks.

Due to the sensitive nature of the information, high security is a priority, which means that BASIC, FORM-based, and DIGEST authentication are not options. Mandating certificates becomes the primary option. Each user's private key can be stored on a SmartCard; however, that limits usage to systems that have readers or this device. For systems without this mechanism, you could provide users a CD-ROM containing their authentication information.

Because most browsers fail to automatically support client authentication, you must develop the code to handle the security measures. As a precautionary measure, this machine should be separate from the main system, and at a minimum a firewall would sit between the two. Multiple firewalls between layers of systems and security clearance will further secure the system against harmful attacks. The systems should also be audited regularly to look for unauthorized activity. By using advanced tracking tools, you can notify appropriate members when security breaches are made. Because of the multiple layers of the system, the intruders likely can be stopped before accessing critical information. Utilization of the above security precautions allows the system to be well defended from unauthorized users yet accessible to its intended audience.

Deployment Descriptor Tags

Now that you've read about each piece separately, a final sample of how security is handled as a whole within the `web.xml` file is provided. See Listing 11.1.

Listing 11.1: Web.xml-Authentication

```
<web-app>
    <servlet>
        <servlet-name>
            secret
        </servlet-name>
        <serlvet-class>
            SalaryServlet
        </servlet-class>
    </servlet>

    <security-constraint>
        <web-resource-collection>
            <web-resource-name>
                SecretProtection
            </web-resouce-name>
            <url-pattern>
                /servlet/SalaryServlet
            </url-pattern>
            <url-pattern>
                /servlet/secret
            </url-pattern>
            <http-method>
                GET
            </http-method>
            <http-method>
                POST
            </http-method>
        </web-resource-collection>
        <auth-constraint>
            <role-name>
                manager
            </role-name>
        </auth-constraint>
    </security-constraint>

    <login-config>
        <auth-method>
            FORM
        </auth-method>
        <form-login-config>
```

```
                <form-login-page>
                    /Login.html
                </form-login-page>
                <form-error-page>
                    /Error.html
                </form-error-page>
            </form-login-config>
        </login-config>
    </web-app>
```

Table 11.2 lists all the tags used for security in the deployment descriptor.

TABLE 11.2: Security Tags

Element	Description
security-constraint	A general element that defines protected resources and roles.
web-resource-collection	A general element that defines the protected resources.
web-resource-name	The human-language name used to reference the protected resource.
url-pattern	The location of the protected resource.
http-method	The methods that the defined roles can access. If no http-method is defined, the default implicitly lists all HTTP methods.
auth-constraint	A general element that defines all roles with access to the protected resources.
role-name	The name of the group with access.
login-config	A general element that defines login configuration information.
auth-method	The type of authentication used by the application.
form-login-config	A general element that defines the configuration information pertaining to forms used in FORM authentication.
form-login-page	The location and file used to display a custom authentication page.
form-error-page	The location and file used to display a custom error page.

WHAT'S NEXT

This chapter covered the key elements a developer should consider to ensure security for their application. Depending on the degree of security needed for the web applications you're running, you should consider the following security principles:

- Authorization
- Authentication
- Data integrity
- Auditing (access control)

You should consider each principle and aim for measures that provide a balance between security, and convenience for you and the users.

Servlet containers offer four types of authentication used to ensure different levels of security:

BASIC The most simple and least secure is HTTP basic authentication. It requests the user's login name and password and transmits the data in a simple encoded format.

FORM To avoid using the browser's authentication dialog, you can use form-based authentication. This process enables you to customize your authentication and error pages to suit your web site.

DIGEST Added security can be achieved through HTTP digest authentication. Instead of transmitting your password over the network, a digest is submitted between client and server.

CLIENT-CERT The last type discussed is HTTPS client authentication. It offers the most security and provides the most guarantees by requiring clients to have a private key and a corresponding certificate in order to be authenticated.

To enable security in the application, modifications to the `web.xml` file are required. Several tags are used to identify the resources that are protected, the location of those resources, the type of authentication used, the methods that can be accessed, and the roles a user must belong to for privileged access.

There is more buzz about XML and web services in the enterprise application development community than almost any other technologies. Currently, most J2EE support of XML and web services is through separate downloadable API packages that can be added to your J2EE environment. Recognizing the importance of these technologies, the addition of XML and web services support directly into J2EE, will be the largest change in J2EE 1.4. The next chapter will be the first of a series of chapters that discuss XML and web services.

Part III
XML, SOAP, and Messaging

Chapter 12

XML for Data Description

As a Java programmer, you've surely heard quite a bit about XML in the last couple of years. This chapter will get you up to speed on the technology and the lingo as quickly as possible so you can start realizing the benefits of XML. After you've started developing applications that use XML, the "XML at a Glance" and "Rules of XML" sections of this chapter will serve as quick XML references.

Featured in this chapter:

- Introduction to XML
- What XML has to do with commerce
- The rules of XML
- When and why you should use XML
- Available APIs for interfacing with XML

Adapted from *Java™ Developer's Guide to E-Commerce with XML and JSP* by Bill Brogden and Chris Minnick

ISBN 0-7821-2827-0 $49.99

What Is XML?

Extensible Markup Language (XML), created in 1996 by the World Wide Web Consortium (W3C), is a subset of the Standard Generalized Markup Language (SGML). XML was designed to be a flexible, yet formal, metalanguage for use on the Internet.

A *metalanguage* is a language for describing languages. For example, you could say that an English dictionary and an English grammar book together make up a metalanguage for English.

In the case of XML, its purpose is to describe markup languages. A *markup language* uses tags to identify structure in data. Hypertext Markup Language (HTML), the most common markup language in use today, was originally written in SGML but can be, and has been, written using XML.

HTML was designed to be used for the specific task of marking up scientific and academic papers. As you are well aware if you have done any web development, HTML is stretched beyond its limits and is busting at the seams from all of the attempts over the years to make it fit the webmaster's every need. Many people have called XML a replacement for HTML. This is not exactly accurate.

Where HTML contains a fixed set of tags, XML does not contain any tags. Instead, XML gives you the ability to create markup languages that actually fit your specific application. In this book, we'll be creating an e-commerce application. The markup language that we use for this application will contain tags (such as `<price>` and `<quantity>`) that are meaningful to e-commerce.

XML applications typically have the following types of data and auxiliary functions:

- The XML data file itself, which follows a rigid structure
- Optionally, a Document Type Definition (DTD), which defines the structure of the XML file
- Optionally, style sheet information, which tells how the data should be formatted for output
- An XML processor and various utilities for manipulating and reformatting the data

XML and E-Commerce

Web developers are used to thinking about what tags do to text. We expect that HTML's bold tag, <b> (`font`), will make text bold. In actuality, though, <b> (`font`) has no inherent meaning at all. How text inside of tags is displayed is entirely up to the program that parses the data. In the case of HTML, this program is usually a web browser. Because HTML documents are usually created to be read by humans using web browsers, many HTML tags specify how data should be formatted rather than identify information. The purpose of XML is to make it possible to separate the data in a document from the code that specifies how the data should be displayed, thus making it easy to extract data programmatically.

For example, imagine that you are a light bulb reseller, and your website features the latest price information from various lighting manufacturers. Rather than check the manufacturers' sites for updated prices, you decide to write a program to read the product information from the various sites, add 10 percent to the manufacturer's price for yourself, and display the product information on your own site. One of your suppliers is ABC Lighting. Listing 12.1 is a part of an HTML product information table from ABC Lighting's website.

Listing 12.1: An HTML Table Containing Product Information

```
<table>

<tr>
  <th>Product Name</th>
  <th>Description</th>
  <th>Price</th>
</tr>

<tr>
  <td><b>Flashlight</b></td>
  <td>Portable light, without fire!</td>
  <td>$9.95</td>
</tr>

<tr>
  <td><b>Neon Light</b></td>
  <td>Nothing says "class" like Neon lighting.</td>
```

Part III

```
    <td>$14.75</td>
  </tr>

  </table>
```

The HTML document specifies only how the text should be formatted. Extracting information from a static HTML page is a tricky business at best. If you want to get the price of the flashlight from the preceding example, you can look for the text in the third column of the row that has `Flashlight` in the first cell, but you're risking that your program will fall apart the next time the site's design is changed or the product's name is changed.

There is a chance that some of the lighting manufacturers are dynamically generating their web pages from a database. In that case, you might be able to work with the webmasters of each site to create an interface to their data, but this can be a time-consuming and confusing process that could be different for each database from which you need to get data. It would be much easier if the document itself contained all of the information needed to extract meaningful information.

Listing 12.2 demonstrates how the same information can be presented in an XML document.

Listing 12.2: An XML Document Containing Product Information

```
<?xml version="1.0" standalone="no"?>
<!DOCTYPE ABC_Lighting:catalog SYSTEM "catalog.dtd">

<ABC_Lighting:catalog xmlns:ABC_Lighting =
   "http://www.abclighting.com">

<ABC_Lighting:product>
<ABC_Lighting:name>Flashlight</ABC_Lighting:name>
<ABC_Lighting:description>Portable light, without fire!
</ABC_Lighting:description>
<ABC_Lighting:price>$9.95</ABC_Lighting:price>
</ABC_Lighting:product>

<ABC_Lighting:product>
<ABC_Lighting:name>Neon Light</ABC_Lighting:name>
<ABC_Lighting:description>Nothing says "class" like Neon
   lighting.
```

```
</ABC_Lighting:description>
<ABC_Lighting:price>$14.75</ABC_Lighting:price>
</ABC_Lighting:product>

</ABC_Lighting:catalog>
```

The first line in this document is the XML declaration, and provides information to XML parsers. The *XML declaration* indicates the type of the document and the version of XML that it is written for. This statement is not required, but it is standard practice to begin XML documents with this line. The `standalone = "no"` attribute indicates that this document has a Document Type Definition (DTD). The next line is the Document Type Declaration. This statement specifies which DTD the document conforms to—in this case, the DTD is called `catalog.dtd`. Note that although they have the same initials, there is a big difference between a Document Type Definition and a Document Type Declaration. A Document Type Declaration is used to indicate to which Document Type Definition an XML document conforms.

The Document Type Declaration also tells what the root element of the document is. The *root element* is the element that encloses everything else in the document. In this case, the root element is `ABC_Lighting:catalog`. The part of the element name before the colon is the tag's namespace. Namespaces are not required, but they can be used to ensure uniqueness of tags. If ABC Lighting were to start selling products manufactured by other companies on its website, namespaces would eliminate the possibility of errors caused by identically named, but differently structured, elements from the outside data.

Here is what `catalog.dtd` might look like:

```
<!ELEMENT ABC_Lighting:catalog (product)*>
<!ELEMENT ABC_Lighting:product (name, description?, price+)>
<!ELEMENT ABC_Lighting:name (#PCDATA)>
<!ELEMENT ABC_Lighting:description (#PCDATA)>
<!ELEMENT ABC_Lighting:price (#PCDATA)>
```

This DTD specifies the elements that can appear in a catalog, the order in which they must appear, and the number of times they can or must appear. Using the XML data and the DTD, programmatically identifying and extracting useful information from an XML document is simple.

XML RESOURCES

Check the following additional resources for the latest developments, insights into future plans for XML, and tools for working with XML:

- World Wide Web Consortium (`www.w3c.org`)
- O'Reilly & Associates, Inc.'s XML.com (`www.xml.com`)—one of the best commercial XML information sites on the Web
- The XML Industry Portal (`www.xml.org`)
- xmlhack (`www.xmlhack.com`)—a news site for XML developers
- Enhydra (`www.enhydra.org`)—home of the Enhydra Java/XML application server
- The Unicode Consortium (`www.unicode.org`)

The Many Uses of XML

XML can be deployed on the client side or on the server side. The following sections explore each approach. Additionally, XML can be used for data storage, which is also discussed following the client and server sections.

XML on the Client

On the client side, XML enables a level of customized data presentation that is very difficult or impossible to achieve using HTML. For example, web-enabled devices, such as Personal Digital Assistants (PDAs) or mobile phones, require that pages be formatted differently than standard web browsers. The typical way to deliver a site to small-screen devices has been to create an entirely different version of the site. By using structured data in XML documents, however, the data is separated from the formatting, and all you need to do to customize the display of your site on different types of devices is to apply a different style sheet to the data.

XML on the Server

XML is having the biggest impact today on the server. One application of XML on the server side is messaging. *Messaging* is the exchange of data between applications or computers. For applications, computers, and businesses to share information, they must decide on a message format.

To understand the potential impact that XML could have in messaging, it's important to know a little about the history of messaging. Deciding on a standard for sending messages has been a problem ever since humans began to communicate, but I'll only go back about 30 years.

Electronic commerce, or e-commerce, as defined by the European Workshop on Open System's Technical Guide on Electronic Commerce (EWOS TGEC 066), covers diverse activities such as marketing, contract exchange, logistics support, settlement, and interaction with administrative bodies (that is, tax and custom data interchange). Electronic Data Interchange (EDI) dates back to the 1970s, when it was introduced by the Transportation Data Coordinating Committee (TDCC). In industries such as finance, which have been networked for over 30 years, EDI has been the standard electronic commerce messaging format. EDI grew out of the need for businesses to be able to exchange commercial data in a standard format. The problem with EDI systems is that they are expensive to set up and maintain, and often require dedicated networks.

In the 1980s, electronic mail for workgroups began to spring up and be implemented in corporations. As vendors attempted to establish their email solutions as the standard, a much larger number of businesses began to rely on electronic messaging. Packages such as Microsoft Mail and Lotus cc:Mail allowed smaller companies to exchange intraoffice messages, but they did not generally scale well and became difficult to manage. Providing connectivity with the world outside of the local area network (LAN) proved to be difficult as well. The bottom line, though, was that, as with the rest of computing, messaging was becoming increasingly decentralized. The movement of electronic messaging away from centralized, tightly controlled, dedicated networks opened up the technology to more users and uses. Decentralization also resulted in compatibility nightmares, duplication of effort, and an inability to leverage organizational shared knowledge.

By the time the Internet emerged, companies were all too familiar with the need for standard, flexible ways for businesses and people to communicate and conduct electronic commerce. A freely available, standardized electronic messaging format would have the power to impact every type of communication, whether commercial or not.

The first step, though, was to agree on a language. This is where XML comes in. The chief reason that XML is perfect for designing messaging formats is its simplicity. XML has no optional features, it's not tied to any one operating system or vendor, and it's compatible with a large base of tools and applications that have been developed over the years for SGML. XML's strict enforcement of its well-formedness rules ensures that any

XML parser will be able to read and comprehend any XML document. In addition, many more people are familiar with using markup languages than are familiar with the message formats required to build EDI systems. Using XML, message formats can be created by anyone who can write a well-formed XML document.

Another use for XML in web documents is to specify metacontent. *Metacontent*, or content about content, can make it possible for search engines to retrieve much better results. For example, if you were looking for news stories that took place in Austin, Texas, you might search for *Austin Texas News.* Because most search engines today simply index all of the content in a site, chances are very good that many of the results returned from this search would not really be what you were looking for. If news articles from Austin were written as structured XML documents, you would be able to perform much less ambiguous searches, such as `City = Austin, State = TX, StoryType = News`.

XML for Data Storage

XML can also be used to create databases. XML stores data in a tree structure. Although XML documents are not (by a long shot) the most efficient way to store data, they do have their advantages. As with messaging, the most important benefit is simplicity. Tree structures are an intuitive and familiar way to organize data. In addition, almost any type of data structure can be represented by an XML data tree–from relational databases to object-oriented databases to hierarchical structures. Another important advantage of using XML for data storage is that XML supports the Unicode character set. As a result, any international character you're ever likely to use is legal in XML documents.

Unicode is the official way to implement the Universal Character Set (UCS) defined by the International Standards Organization (ISO); it is the universal character encoding standard used for representation of text for computer processing. Unicode uses UCS Transformation Formats (UTFs) to change character encodings to actual bits.

The XML Specification requires that XML processors must support two UTFs: UTF-8 and UTF-16. UTF-16 uses two bytes to represent every character. UTF-8 uses the one-byte ASCII character encodings for ASCII characters, and represents non-ASCII characters using variable-length encodings. UTF-8 is useful if you need to maintain compatibility with ASCII. The downside to UTF-8 is that it uses anywhere from 1 to 3 bytes to represent non-ASCII characters. If your text is mostly ASCII, UTF-8 saves space. If you are using non-ASCII characters, UTF-8 wastes space.

The default encoding in XML is UTF-8. The character encoding you want to use for a document is specified in the XML declaration using the encoding attribute, as in the following example:

```
<?xml version="1.0" standalone="no" encoding="UTF-8"?>
```

Rules of XML

Today's HTML browsers generally attempt to display anything, no matter how odd or poorly formed the HTML markup may be. XML processors, on the other hand, are required to generate a fatal error when they come across a markup error. A *fatal error* means that the application will halt processing and display an error message. This strictness is often referred to as *draconian error-handling*. Although this type of all-or-nothing error handling may seem primitive to HTML writers, and possibly even to SGML authors, it is necessary to help ensure that XML documents will be interpreted the same way in every XML processor.

An XML document that follows the rules of XML syntax is said to be *well formed*. XML's authors wrote well-formedness into the specification to prevent XML from becoming a victim of something similar to the browser wars. The end result of the so-called browser wars between Microsoft and Netscape was that HTML writers today have to constantly worry about compatibility. If this type of fragmentation were to happen to XML, it would be worthless.

An *XML processor* is a software module that provides applications with access to data stored in XML documents. XML processors can be either validating or non-validating. A validating processor will check the structure of the document against the rules specified in a DTD, and a non-validating processor will check only to make sure that the document conforms to the rules of XML.

Defining a Well-Formed XML Document

All of the text in an XML document can be divided into two broad categories: character data, and markup. *Markup* is anything that begins with a < and ends with a >, or that begins with a & and ends with a ;. *Character data* is everything that is not markup. Character data can further be divided into two categories: parsed and unparsed character data. *Parsed character data,* or PCDATA, is parsed by an XML processor. *Unparsed character data,* naturally, is not parsed.

Listing 12.3 shows an example of a well-formed XML document.

Listing 12.3: A Well-Formed XML Document

```
<?xml version="1.0" standalone="yes"?>

<beverage>
  <name>Canned Water</name>

  <manufacturer>
    <name>Extra Good Beverages</name>
    <url href = "http://www.extragoodbev.com"/>
  </manufacturer>

  <nutrition_facts serving_size="1 can">

    <calories>
      <amount unit="g">0</amount>
    </calories>

    <fat>
      <amount unit="g">0</amount>
    </fat>

    <sodium>
      <amount unit="mg">0</amount>
    </sodium>

    <carb>
      <amount unit="g">0</amount>
    </carb>

    <protein>
      <amount unit="g">0</amount>
    </protein>

  </nutrition_facts>

</beverage>
```

The first thing you should notice about this document is the `standalone="yes"` attribute in the XML declaration. This indicates that this document does not use a DTD. XML documents are not required to use DTDs. In fact, applications that use XML data will often not use a DTD to increase performance in cases where structure and reusability are not as important.

Following the XML declaration are elements. *Elements* are the most common form of markup; they are delimited by angle brackets, and they describe the data they surround. Elements are made up of a starting tag and an ending tag (`<beverage></beverage>`, for example). The name of an element is called its *generic identifier (GI)*, or its *type*. The text between the start and end tag is called the element's *content*. For example, the following element's type is `book`, and the name of the book is the element's content.

```
<book>Java Developer's Guide to XML</book>
```

An element that has no content is called an *empty element*. You can combine the start tag and end tag of an empty element by putting the slash at the end of the start tag: `<br/>`. XML also allows you to write empty elements using a starting tag and an ending tag, for example: `<br></br>`.

There are actually two types of empty elements: those that are defined as empty and can never have content, and those that just happen to not have content. To distinguish between the two, it is recommended that you use a start-tag/end-tag pair for elements that contain no data, and the empty element tag format for elements that are defined as empty.

For example, HTML's `br` element cannot contain data and should be written as `<br/>`. If, on the other hand, your XML document has an instance of an element that currently has no content but may have content at some point, you should use the standard element syntax, like this:

```
<cupboards></cupboards>
```

Elements can have attributes. *Attributes* are name-value pairs inside of the start tag of an element. In the following example, `src`, `width`, and `height` are attributes of `img`.

```
<img src = "balloons.gif" width="100" height="100"/>
```

TIP

If you want to start writing your HTML code to be compatible with XML, you may notice that the HTML break tag is particularly troublesome. Some browsers won't understand `<br/>` and will interpret `<br></br>` as two line breaks. To overcome this problem, put a space between the `br` and the slash: `<br />`.

Part III

In XML, attribute values must be in either single or double quotes. A list of the well-formedness rules that XML documents must adhere to can be found at the end of this chapter.

DTDs and Validity

A DTD is a means for you to explicitly define the structure of a class of XML documents. For example, a DTD for a catalog of animals might specify that each animal must have a name, an animal type, and a sound. The DTD for this animal catalog would look like this:

```
<!ELEMENT animal-list (animal)*>
<!ELEMENT animal (name,type,sound)>
<!ELEMENT name (#PCDATA)>
<!ELEMENT type (#PCDATA)>
<!ELEMENT sound (#PCDATA)>
```

If this were the standard zoology DTD (it isn't), any zoologist could be sure that their data would be usable by any other zoologist, and that they were working with the same rules for lists of animals. An XML document that conforms to the rules of the DTD for which it was written, as well as to the rules of XML in general, is considered well formed and valid. Here is an example of a well-formed XML document that conforms to the preceding DTD:

```
<?xml version="1.0" standalone="no"?>
<!DOCTYPE animal-list SYSTEM "zoology.dtd">
<animal-list>
  <animal>
    <name>Bessie</name>
    <type>cow</type>
    <sound>moo</sound>
  </animal>
  <animal>
    <name>Rover</name>
    <type>dog</type>
    <sound>woof</sound>
  </animal>
</animal-list>
```

NOTE

The words that are in all-capital letters in the preceding examples are XML keywords. Writing them in all caps is actually not just a stylistic choice. As a result of XML's case-sensitiveness, an XML processor will produce an error if a keyword is not in all caps. As far as XML is concerned, `DOCTYPE` and `Doctype` are no more similar than `DOCTYPE` and `EGGDROP`.

Element Declarations

The most basic type of declaration in a DTD is the `<!ELEMENT>` declaration. The format for an element declaration is `<!ELEMENT elementname rule>`.

Every element that is used in your XML document must be defined in the DTD, if you're using one. There are several rules that you need to follow when naming elements:

- Element names should not contain < or >.
- The name of an element must begin with a letter or an underscore. After the first character, it can contain any number of letters, numbers, hyphens, periods, or underscores.
- Element names cannot start with the string `xml` (in any combination of uppercase or lowercase letters).
- Colons are forbidden, unless you are using namespaces.

Content Specification

In the rule portion of an element declaration, you specify what can appear in the contents of the element. If you want to declare an element that cannot contain any data, you can use the `EMPTY` type (for example, `<!ELEMENT img EMPTY>`).

A good example of an empty element is the HTML `img` element. To make this element valid in an XML document, you write it using the empty element syntax, as in the following example:

```
<img src="mycar.jpg"/>
```

If you only want to allow parsed character data in an element, use the following declaration:

```
<!ELEMENT mymemoirs #PCDATA>
```

You can also specify which element types may appear inside of an element, in what order they must appear, and how many times they can appear, as in the following example:

```
<!ELEMENT mymemoirs (title, author, philosophizing, sad_story,
  funny_story, lesson, conclusion)>
```

In this example, each of the element types listed must appear once (and only once) inside of the `mymemoirs` element, in the order that they are listed in the declaration.

NOTE

The elements that appear inside of the `mymemoirs` element are called its children, and `mymemoirs` can be referred to as their parent. Any element can be a child of any number of other elements in a document. Elements that are more than one level separated from each other are referred to as grandchildren, great-grandchildren, and so forth (or as grandparents, great-grandparents, and so forth in the other direction). You can also just talk about relationships between elements in terms of ancestors and descendants.

You can write more flexible rules by using *occurrence operators.* The following shows the three possibilities.

Symbol	Meaning
?	Must occur zero or one time
+	Must occur one or more times
*	May appear any number of times or not at all

Here is the `mymemoirs` declaration again, rewritten using occurrence operators:

```
<!ELEMENT mymemoirs (title, author, philosophizing+, sad_story*,
    funny_story*, lesson+, conclusion)>
```

You can specify that a choice needs to be made between elements by using the vertical bar (`|`), as in the following example:

```
<!ELEMENT mymemoirs (title, author, philosophizing+, sad_story*,
    funny_story*, lesson+ | conclusion)>
```

In this declaration, `mymemoirs` is allowed to have one or more `lesson` or `conclusion` elements—but not both. Even more complicated rules can be defined by using nested parentheses. Listing 12.4 shows how the complete `mymemoirs.dtd` might look.

Listing 12.4: A Complete Version of *mymemoirs.dtd*

```
<!ELEMENT mymemoirs (title, author, philosophizing+, sad_story*,
   funny_story*, (lesson+ | conclusion)*)>
<!ELEMENT title (#PCDATA)>
<!ELEMENT author (#PCDATA)>
<!ELEMENT philosophizing (paragraph)*>
<!ELEMENT sad_story (paragraph*, letter*,(lesson |
   conclusion)*)>
<!ELEMENT funny_story (paragraph*, letter*,(lesson |
   conclusion)*)>
<!ELEMENT letter (paragraph)*>
<!ELEMENT lesson (paragraph)*>
<!ELEMENT conclusion (paragraph)*>
<!ELEMENT paragraph (#PCDATA)>
```

The least strict rule, of course, is "anything goes." You can use ANY as the rule to specify that parsed character data or elements can appear inside of this element, as in the following example:

```
<!ELEMENT mymemoirs ANY>
```

NOTE

Such a broad rule as the ANY element type really doesn't seem to fit in the rigid structure of XML. Generally, if you write a DTD that uses the ANY keyword, you're probably doing something wrong, and you should see if there's a better way.

Attribute Declarations

Attributes are used to associate name-value pairs with elements. Attributes are defined using attribute declarations. The format for an attribute declaration in a DTD is:

```
<!ATTLIST target_element name type default_value ?>
```

Attributes are used to provide additional information about elements. It is sometimes difficult to decide whether a piece of data should be an attribute or an element.

For example, both of the following pieces of XML could be used to accomplish the same goal:

```
<dog name = "Snuggles"></dog>
```

or

```
<dog>
   <name>Snuggles</name>
</dog>
```

The following are some examples of attribute declarations (their meaning will be explained shortly):

```
<!ATTLIST dog name CDATA #REQUIRED>
<!ATTLIST dog gender (male | female) #IMPLIED>
<!ATTLIST dog species #FIXED "Canis familiaris">
```

There are nine different types of attributes, and they fall within three different categories: string, tokenized, and enumerated. String attributes are defined using the CDATA keyword as the type, as in the following example:

```
<!ATTLIST dog name CDATA>
```

The value of this string can be any valid character string.

There are several tokenized attribute types. The most important of these are ID and IDREF. Attributes with the IDREF type can be used for a simple form of linking. Attributes of type ID can be used to uniquely identify elements. ID attributes must uniquely identify the element in which they are used. For example, the following attribute declaration creates a required product ID tag:

```
<!ATTLIST product id ID #REQUIRED>
```

IDs and IDREFs can be used much like anchors in HTML. The value of an IDREF attribute must be the value of the ID attribute of another element. For example, the following piece of a DTD declares an element with an ID attribute and an element with an IDREF attribute that refers to the first element:

```
<!ELEMENT product (name,description,price)>
<!ATTLIST product id ID #REQUIRED>
<!ELEMENT featured_products (product_reference)*>
<!ELEMENT product_ref (#PCDATA)>
<!ATTLIST product_ref link IDREF #IMPLIED>
```

An XML file that uses this DTD might have a section that looks like this:

```
<product id= "X4343">
  <name>rock</name>
```

```
</product>
<featured_products>
  <product_ref link = "X4343">a rock</product_ref>

</featured_products>
```

Enumerated attribute types list possible values that the attribute can contain. For example, if you wanted to declare an attribute called `angle_type` for an element called `triangle`, you could specify the possible values as follows:

```
<!ATTLIST triangle angle_type (obtuse | acute | right)
  #REQUIRED>
```

Attribute defaults can be used to declare that an element must contain a particular attribute, and even what the value of the attribute must be. The following mini-table shows the three keywords that may be used and what they mean. If you don't specify a default value, `IMPLIED` is implied.

Attribute Default	Definition
`#REQUIRED`	Every occurrence of the named element must have this attribute.
`#IMPLIED`	No default is specified.
`#FIXED`	The element must have this attribute, and the attribute value must be the value specified.

Entity Declarations

Declaring entities allows you use entity references. An *entity reference* is a series of characters that substitute for a different series of characters. A common use is to denote symbols that might otherwise be mistaken for markup. If you've written much HTML, you've probably come across entity references. The most common type of entity is the general entity. *General entities* are entities that can substitute for characters inside of an XML document. The format for general entity declarations is:

```
<!ENTITY name "replacement characters">
```

Entity references take the form `&entityname;`. There are five built-in general entities in XML. You do not need to declare these in your DTD, although the XML specification recommends that you do anyway, for interoperability. The five built-in entities are shown in the following mini-table.

Entity Reference	Replacement Text	Character
&	&	&
<	<	<
>	>	>
'	'	'
"	"	"

You can declare these entities using the following declarations:

```
<!ENTITY lt     "&#38;#60;">
<!ENTITY gt     "&#62;">
<!ENTITY amp    "&#38;#38;">
<!ENTITY apos   "&#39;">
<!ENTITY quot   "&#34;">
```

NOTE

The < and & characters in the declarations of `lt` and `amp` are doubly escaped to meet the requirement that entity replacement be well formed. In other words, the & symbol and the < symbol are the two symbols that signal to an XML processor that the text that follows is a new XML markup statement. If these characters weren't doubly escaped in these entity declarations, the XML processor would interpret them as the beginning of a new piece of markup before the entity declaration ends and would generate an error.

The built-in entity references are essential for creating XML documents in which you want to use any of these characters as character data rather than as part of the markup. General entity references that you define yourself are useful for assigning names to character codes that you need to use frequently. For example, to declare an entity reference to represent the trademark symbol (™), you could use the following declaration:

```
<!ENTITY tm "&#8482">
```

The trademark symbol could then be inserted into any XML document that uses a DTD with this declaration. For example:

```
<product_name>
Super Drink&tm;
</product_name>
```

Although entities may be used in the definitions of other entities, an important rule to keep in mind is that you may not make circular references.

Invalid:

```
<!ENTITY myentity "please see &myotherentity; ">
<!ENTITY myotherentity "please see &myentity; ">
```

Valid:

```
<!ENTITY tm "&#8482">
<!ENTITY myentity "I enjoy Super Drink&tm; ">
```

Declaring Parameter Entities You can also declare entity references that will be replaced by their entity definitions in the DTD. This type of entity is called a parameter entity. *Parameter entity* references begin with a percent sign and may not be used in XML documents—only in the DTD in which they are defined. Here is an example of a use for a parameter entity:

```
<!ENTITY % actors " (Joe, Mary, Todd, Bill, Jane)* ">
<!ELEMENT dialog %actors;>
```

Declaring External Entities *External entities* are a way of including external files in your XML documents. They are declared as follows:

```
<!ENTITY latest_prices SYSTEM
    "http://www.getthepricesofthings.com/today.xml">
```

After declaring an external entity, you can include the XML content specified into your document by using an entity reference— `&latest_prices;` in this case.

Declaring Unparsed Entities *Unparsed entities* can be used to include non-XML data in an XML document. The keyword `NDATA` is used to define an entity as unparsed. For example:

```
<!ENTITY bookcover SYSTEM
    "http://www.sybex.com/books/xml/javadevguide.gif" NDATA gif>
```

Immediately following `NDATA` is the *notation data keyword*. This keyword is declared using a notation declaration. *Notation declarations* (or notations/plural) provide additional information (such as identifying information) or, in this case, format information for unparsed data. Notation keywords are defined using `<!NOTATION>` declarations. For example:

```
<!NOTATION gif SYSTEM
  "-//CompuServe//NOTATION Graphics Interchange Format 89a//EN">
```

Unparsed Character Data: CDATA, Comments, and Processing Instructions

Parsed character data does not contain markup. Therefore, if you want to include the characters < or & in the contents of an element, you need to escape them. One way to escape these characters is to use their numeric character references (`<` and `&`, respectively), or you can use XML's built-in entity references (`t;` and `&#amp;`, respectively). If you don't want to worry about escaping these characters, you can use a *CDATA section* to designate a block of text as unparsed character data—as explained in the following section.

CDATA Sections

CDATA sections start with the string `<![CDATA[` and end with `]]>`. None of the characters in a CDATA section will be parsed, except for the string `]]>`. If you wanted to include an XML example inside of an XML document, rather than escaping every < and & by using `<` and `&`, you could include the entire block that contains these characters inside of a CDATA section. For example:

```
<example>
Here is an example of a well-formed XML document:
<!CDATA[
<?xml version="1.0" standalone="yes"?>
<beverage>
  <name>Super-Drink</name>
  <manufacturer>
    <name>Extra Good Beverages</name>
    <url href = "http://www.extrasuperbev.com"/>
  </manufacturer>
</beverage>
]]>
</example>
```

Using XML Comments

XML *comments* work the same as HTML comments, as the following demonstrates:

```
<!--this text is commented out. -->
```

Comments may appear anywhere inside a document, outside of other markup. They are not part of a document's character data and cannot be used by an XML parser.

In HTML, comments are often used to contain text that is available to programs but is not part of the document. For example, CGI commands and JavaScript are often put inside of comments in HTML documents. XML parsers are allowed to completely ignore comments, so this trick should not be used. Instead, XML features processing instructions for this purpose.

WARNING

In my experience, Internet time is not really faster; it's actually much like daylight saving time. Just as the borrowed hour of daylight always bites you back by throwing off your schedule for a week when "normal time" resumes, neglecting to comment your code in the interest of saving time will result in much bigger problems later on.

Processing Instructions

Processing instructions (PIs) are used to include information in your document that is intended to be used by applications. Like comments, processing instructions are not considered to be part of the character data of a document. Unlike comments, XML parsers must pass processing instructions through to applications.

Processing instructions begin with <? and end with ?>. The first word in a PI is the name of the application the processing instruction is intended for. You may also use a notation name to associate a URI (Universal Resource Identifier) with an application name. Following the identifying information, a PI may contain any type of character data that you like. The following is an example of a PI:

```
<?playsounds sounds.mp3?>
```

This PI might cause an application that knows what to do with it to play the mp3 file that is indicated.

XML Schema

Although DTDs are currently the standard for defining XML document types, they do have several serious limitations. DTDs were inherited from SGML, where they were originally designed for defining markup languages for documents, not for creating database schemas. The biggest limitation of DTDs is that they don't give you enough control over the contents of elements. For example, DTDs provide no way to specify that

```
<todaysdate>09/01/2000</todaysdate>
```

is valid, whereas

```
<todaysdate>Eggs, Toast, Coffee</todaysdate>
```

is not valid. Occasionally, you may also want to specify more exact limits on the number of times elements can occur. This also isn't possible using DTDs.

As a result of the limitations of DTDs and the increasing use of XML for data storage, several alternatives are being considered. The front-runner among these is currently the XML Schema Definition language (XSD).

NOTE

For more information on schemas, see *XML Schemas* by Chelsea Valentine et al. (Sybex 2002).

XML schemas have the same purpose as DTDs: to define classes of XML documents. The main difference is that XML schemas divide elements into two types: complex and simple.

Elements that contain other elements or attributes as well as character data have *complex types,* and elements that only contain character data have *simple types.* Attributes always have simple types. Listing 12.5 shows an XML schema for a product catalog. Listing 12.6 shows an XML document that uses this schema.

Listing 12.5: The Catalog Schema *(catalog.xsd)*

```
<xsd:schema xmlns:xsd="http://www.w3.org/1999/XMLSchema">

<xsd:element name="Catalog" type="CatalogType"/>

<xsd:complexType name="CatalogType">
<xsd:element name="product" type="ProductType"/>
<xsd:attribute name="onSaleDate" type="xsd:date"/>
<xsd:attribute name="partNum" type="Sku"/>
</xsd:complexType>

<xsd:complexType name="ProductType">
```

```
<xsd:element name="productName" type="xsd:string"/>
<xsd:element name="quantity_in_stock">
<xsd:simpleType base="xsd:positiveInteger">
<xsd:maxExclusive value="500"/>
</xsd:simpleType>
</xsd:element>
<xsd:element name="price" type="xsd:decimal"/>
<xsd:element name="description" type="xsd:string"
   minOccurs="0"/>
</xsd:complexType>

<xsd:simpleType name="Sku" base="xsd:string">
<xsd:pattern value="\[A-Z]{3}-[A-Z]{3}d{3}"/>
</xsd:simpleType>

</xsd:schema>
```

Listing 12.6: A Catalog *(mycatalog.xml)*

```
<?xml version="1.0"?>
<catalog>
  <product partNum="ABC-PRO336" onSaleDate="12/12/2004">
    <productName>BigSoft Xtreminator 3.36</productName>
      <quantity_in_stock>20</quantity_in_stock >
      <price>195.99</price>
  <description>Managing your life has never been so
      easy.</description>
   </product>
<product partNum="ABC-PRO343" onSaleDate="12/12/2004">
<productName>E-Dev ProntoWorks</productName>
      <quantity_in_stock>35</quantity_in_stock >
      <price>299.99</price>
<description>The premier integrated rapid e-development suite
   for busy e-professionals.</description>
   </product>
</catalog>
```

Elements that have complex types are defined using the `complexType` (`font`) element. Elements with complex types contain other elements and attributes. The elements and attributes contained within complex elements are defined using the `element` and `attribute` elements, respectively. For example, in Listing 12.5, `item product` is defined as a complex type.

Inside of the definition of the product type are five elements: `productName`, `quantity_in_stock`, `price`, `comment`, and `partNum`.

Elements with simple types have no attributes and do not contain any other elements. XSD contains a set of built-in simple types, which includes such types as `string`, `binary`, `boolean`, `double`, `float`, and so forth. Additional simple types can be derived from the built-in types. For example, the preceding example defines the simple type `Sku`, which is based on the `string` type.

The process used to derive new simple types from existing ones is called *restriction*. Note that the definition of the `Sku` data type uses a regular expression to define a pattern that the contents of any element or attribute that uses this type must follow.

XML Schemas have much more flexible occurrence constraints than DTDs. DTDs only allow you to specify that elements must occur zero, one, one or more, or any number of times. In addition to these constraints, XML Schema allows you to specify a minimum or a maximum number, a value, or a range of values, as well as even more complicated constraints.

Creating Style Sheets with XSL

Extensible Stylesheet Language (XSL) is a language for expressing style sheets. XSL *style sheets* are used to specify the presentation of XML documents that are to be read by people.

For example, a designer may create a style sheet for an XML product catalog. This style sheet could say what fonts, font sizes, borders, and so forth will be applied to the document when it and the style sheet are combined using an XSL style sheet processor.

There are two steps that a style sheet processor goes through to apply a style sheet to XML data. The first is *tree transformation*. You could, for example, write a style sheet that would put the products in your catalog in alphabetical order, or number them before outputting them. Transformation can also move and perform computations on XML data.

The second step involved in the presentation process is *formatting*. Formatting is the actual process of applying style, font sizes, page breaks, and so forth to data.

To allow you to accomplish these two tasks, the XSL Specification consists of three separate languages:

XML Path Language (XPath) A language for referencing parts of an XML document

XSL Transformations (XSLT) The language used to generate a result tree

Extensible Stylesheet Language (XSL) XSLT plus a description of a set of Formatting Objects and Formatting Properties

Suppose that you have information about your music library in an XML document, as shown in Listing 12.7.

Listing 12.7: Sample Music Library *(MyMusic.xml)*

```
<?xml version="1.0"?>
<library>
  <cd>
    <title>Just Singin' Along</title>
    <artist>The Happy Guys</artist>
    <description>A lovely collection of songs that the whole
      family can sing right along with.
    </description>
    <song><title>I'm Really Fine</title></song>
    <song><title>Can't Stop Grinnin'</title></song>
    <song><title>Things Are Swell</title></song>
    <purchase_date>2/23/1954</purchase_date>
  </cd>
  <cd>
    <title>It's Dot Com Enough for Me: Songs From Silicon
       Somewhere</title>
    <artist>The Nettizens</artist>
    <description>A collection of the best folk music from
      Internet companies.</description>
    <song><title>My B2B Is B-R-O-K-E</title></song>
    <song><title>Workin' in a Cubicle</title></song>
    <song><title>Killer Content Strategy</title></song>
    <song><title>She Took the Bricks, I Got the
      Clicks</title></song>
    <purchase_date>7/12/2000</purchase_date>
  </cd>
</library>
```

Say you want to create a printable list of everything in your library. One way to do this would be to apply a style sheet to the document that transforms it into HTML. Listing 12.8 is a style sheet that does just that.

Listing 12.8: A style sheet for HTML output *(CDstyle.xsl)*

```
<?xml version="1.0"?>
<xsl:stylesheet xmlns:xsl="http://www.w3.org/TR/WD-xsl">
<xsl:template match="/">
<TABLE STYLE="border:1px solid black; width:300px">
<TR STYLE="font-size:10pt; font-family:Verdana; font
     weight:bold; text-decoration:underline">
<TD>Title</TD>
<TD>Artist</TD>
</TR>
<xsl:for-each select="library/cd">
<TR STYLE="font-family:Verdana; font-size:12pt; padding:0px
   6px">
<TD><xsl:value-of select="title"/></TD>
<TD><xsl:value-of select="artist"/></TD>
</TR>
</xsl:for-each>
</TABLE>
</xsl:template>
</xsl:stylesheet>
```

You can link to XSL style sheets from XML documents using a processing instruction. For example:

```
<?xml-stylesheet href="CDstyle.xsl" type="text/xsl"?>
```

And you can use Cascading Style Sheets (CSS) to apply format to XML data. In that case, you would link to the style sheet using a processing instruction more like this one:

```
<?xml-stylesheet href="CDstyle.css" type="text/css"?>
```

Listing 12.8 shows a basic example of the template-driven transformation of XML data using XSL. The XSLT finds data that matches a pattern and inserts it into a point in a template. Pattern matching is a very important part of XSL. Take a look at the pattern being applied in the second part of this example:

```
<xsl:for-each select="library/cd">
```

This line will loop through each instance of the `cd` element inside of the `library` element. If you wanted to create a comma-separated list of the songs on each `cd`, you could create another loop inside of this loop, as in the following example:

```
...
<xsl:for-each select="library/cd">
```

```
<TR STYLE="font-family:Verdana; font-size:12pt; padding:0px
   6px">
<TD><xsl:value-of select="title"/></TD>
<TD><xsl:value-of select="artist"/></TD>
<TD>
<xsl:for-each select="song">
    "<xsl:value-of select="title"/>"
<xsl:if test="context()[not(end())]">, </xsl:if>
</xsl:for-each>
</TD>
</TR>
</xsl:for-each>
...
```

When opened in a web browser that supports XSL, the XML document will look like the example shown in Figure 12.1.

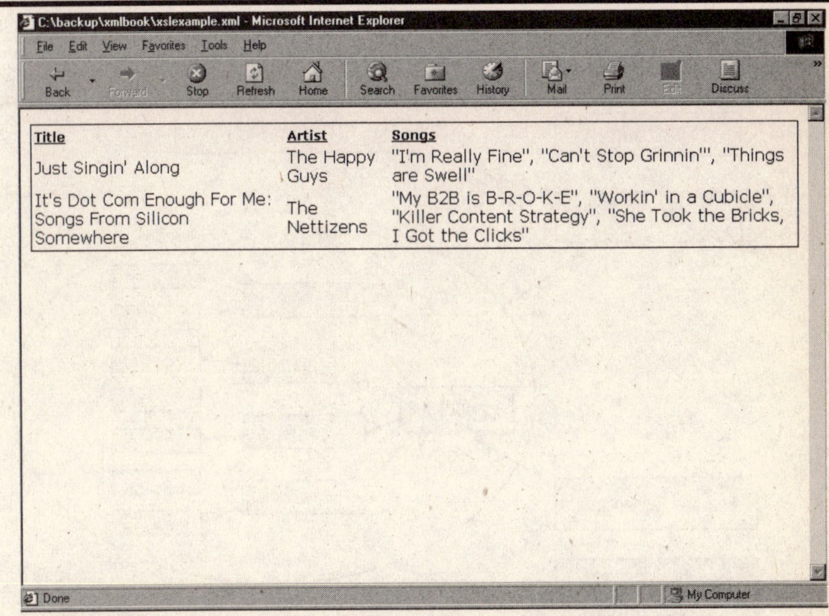

FIGURE 12.1: The result of applying `CDstyle.xsl` to `MyMusic.xml`

For more information on XSLT, see *Mastering XSLT* by Chuck White (Sybex, 2002).

Using XML in Applications

Every major database vendor now provides, or has plans to provide, means for transferring data between a relational database and XML documents, and numerous third-party and other tools are also available. Data can easily be retrieved from any database and converted to XML for use by this application without having to modify the application. This is perhaps the biggest advantage of writing your application to use XML data: The use of a standard into which any type of data can be converted ensures that your application will be easily usable with legacy and future data.

Let's look at the two approaches to writing Java programs that process XML.

The DOM and SAX Programming Models

The orientation of SGML is a complete document, so it is hardly surprising that XML started out thinking in Document Object Model (DOM) terms. All DOM processing assumes that you have read and parsed a complete document into memory so that all parts are equally accessible. This approach is shown symbolically in Figure 12.2.

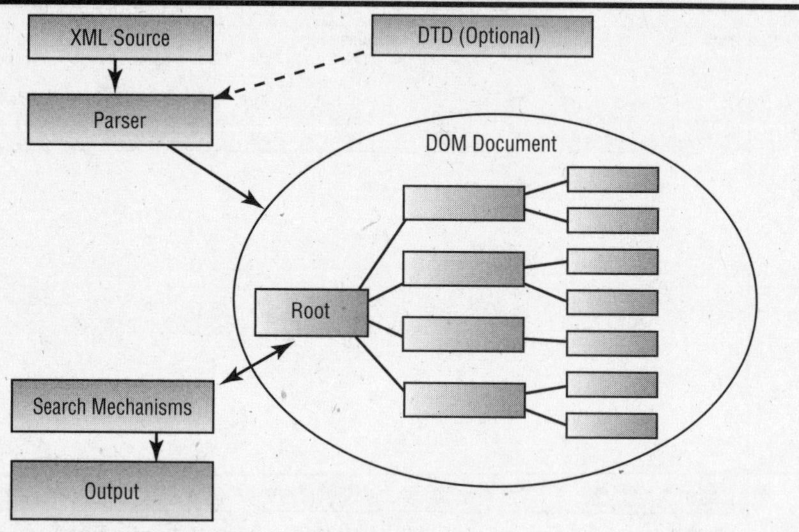

FIGURE 12.2: Document Object Model processing

As people started programming with the DOM, it was found to be pretty clumsy if all you wanted to do was to pick out a few elements. Furthermore, the memory requirements could get restrictive, if not downright impossible. Thus, the Simplified API (application programming interface) for XML (SAX) was born of necessity. Both the DOM and SAX specify application programming interfaces that have been implemented in a number of languages in addition to Java.

As shown in Figure 12.3, a SAX parser makes a single pass through an XML file, reporting what it has parsed by calling various methods in your application code. The SAX documentation uses the term *event* for what happens when the parser decides it has identified an element in the XML document, so these methods are called *event handlers*. When the parser reaches the end of the document, the only data in memory is what your application saved.

As mentioned earlier, and as shown in Figures 12.2 and 12.3, the use of a DTD is optional in XML.

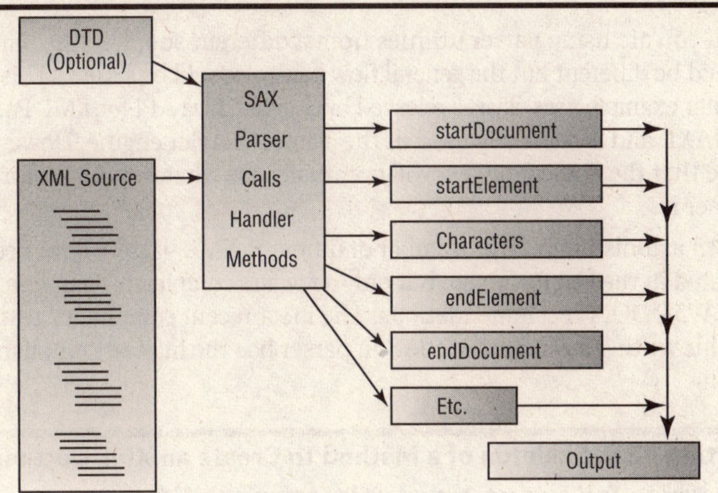

FIGURE 12.3: Simplified API for XML processing

Both models can be useful for servlet and JSP programming, as I demonstrate in upcoming examples. First, let's look at the Java tools for both DOM and SAX. These are tools for the "level 1" DOM and SAX version 1. Just to keep things complicated, SAX version 2 and DOM level 2 are in the works. By the time you read this, parsers implementing these new versions will probably be available.

Programming with the DOM

The definitive API for working with the Document Object Model is provided by the `org.w3c.dom` package, a recommendation of the World Wide Web Consortium. This API consists entirely of interface definitions plus a single exception class. The basic idea is that an XML document is turned into a DOM consisting of Java objects that implement these interfaces. Every part of the document becomes an object, and the connections between the objects reflect the hierarchy of the document.

Parsing XML to Create a DOM From the programmer's standpoint, creating a DOM is simplicity itself because all the work is done by the parser. All the programmer has to do is create an input stream, select a parser, and stand back. Listing 12.9 shows a skeleton of a method to read from a file using utility classes from the `com.sun.xml.parser` package and to return a `com.sun.xml.tree.XmlDocument` object. The `XmlDocument` class implements the `Document` interface as specified in the W3C recommendation.

If you are using parser utilities from a different supplier, the names would be different but the general flow control would be similar. This particular example uses classes released by Sun as "Java API for XML Parsing" or JAXP and is currently used in the Tomcat servlet engine. However, note that the Tomcat project will eventually use whatever Sun's current parser is.

An astonishingly large number of different XML parsers have been created in the last few years, but only a few are completely compliant with the W3C DOM recommendations. The most recent compliance tests as of this writing indicate that the Sun parser has the highest compliance rating.

Listing 12.9: Skeleton of a Method to Create an XML Document

```
public XmlDocument exampleDOM(String src ) {
  File xmlFile = new File( src ) ;
  try {
    InputSource input = Resolver.createInputSource( xmlFile );
    // ... the "false" flag says not to validate
    XmlDocument doc = XmlDocument.createXmlDocument (input,
       false);
   return doc ;
  }catch(SAXParseException spe ){
```

```
      // handle parse exception here
    }catch( SAXException se ){
      // handle other SAX exceptions here
    }catch( IOException ie ){
      // handle IO exceptions here
    }
    return null ;
  }
```

Once you have a DOM in memory, you manipulate it using methods provided in the DOM interface recommendation as embodied in the `org.w3c.dom` package plus additional methods as provided by the available toolkit.

NOTE

JAXP is a new Java API that gives a unified way to process XML documents using SAX, DOM, and XSLT. J2EE 1.4 will include JAXP and several other Java APIs for working with XML. In the meantime, these Java XML APIs are available as a separate free download from Sun called the Java XML Pack. You can get more information and download the Java XML Pack by going to `http://java.sun.com/xml`.

Programming with SAX

The basic steps required to process an XML document with SAX can be summarized as:

- Create one or more custom classes to handle the events that the SAX parser detects
- Create an object to provide an input stream of characters
- Create a parser from one of the toolkits
- Attach the event-handling classes to the parser
- Attach the input stream to the parser, and start parsing
- Handle all of the events in your custom classes to capture the data you are interested in, to detect errors, and so on

As you can see, SAX processing of XML involves a programming philosophy that is completely different than using the DOM. Deciding which approach to use for a particular application is your most important design decision. Table 12.1 summarizes the important considerations.

TABLE 12.1: Comparison of DOM and SAX Programming

Programming Factor	DOM Style	SAX Style
Memory requirements	May be quite large	Only as large as the items retained in memory
Startup time	Slower because every element is parsed	Faster, especially if the elements of interest are easy to locate
Repeated search time	Faster because everything is in memory	Slower because every search involves a new parsing run
Modification capability	Very flexible	Limited to writing a new XML document with every pass

XML at a Glance

This section can be used as a guide to the most common rules of XML. For the complete XML specification, please visit `www.w3c.org`.

Well-Formedness Rules

- Each element must have a start tag and an end tag, except in the case of empty elements, which can use the empty-element syntax.
- The names of start tags and end tags must match. Remember that XML is case sensitive.
    - Incorrect: `<Name></name>`
    - Correct: `<name></name>`
- Elements must be properly nested.
    - Incorrect: `<p><b>some text</p></b>`
    - Correct: `<p><b>some text</b></p>`
- Element names should not contain < or > and must start with a letter or underscore.

- Element names cannot start with the string `xml` (in any combination of upper or lowercase letters).
- Colons are forbidden in element names, unless you are using namespaces.
- No attribute may appear more than once in the same start tag or empty-element tag.
- Attribute values must be enclosed in quotes.
- Attribute values cannot contain direct or indirect entity references to external entities.
- The replacement text of any entity referred to directly or indirectly in an attribute value (other than <) must not contain a <.

Elements

Here we summarize XML elements and the way they are declared. This discussion includes usage and declaration syntax for elements.

Usage

Example elements:

```
<tag/>

<tag attribute="value" />

<tag attribute="value">some text</tag>
```

Element Declarations

Syntax:

```
<!ELEMENT elementname rule>
```

Element Types	Example Declaration
EMPTY	<!ELEMENT url EMPTY>
#PCDATA	<!ELEMENT name #PCDATA>
ANY	<!ELEMENT contacts ANY>
Mixed	<!ELEMENT list (#PCDATA | item)*>
Children	<!ELEMENT co-worker (title, name, address)>

Attributes

Here we summarize the format for attribute declarations. This discussion includes attribute syntax, type, declarations, and defaults.

Syntax:

```
<!ATTLIST target_element name type default_value ?>
```

Attribute	Types	Example Declaration
String	CDATA	<!ATTLIST image url CDATA ?>
Tokenized	ID	
	<!ATTLIST id ID	
	#REQUIRED ?>	
	IDREF	
	IDREFS	
	ENTITY	
	ENTITIES	
	NMTOKEN	
	NMTOKENS	
Enumerated		<!ATTLIST list type (ordered | bullet) "bullet" ?>

Attribute Default	Definition
#REQUIRED	Every occurrence of the named element must have this attribute.
#IMPLIED	No default is specified.
#FIXED	The element must have this attribute, and the attribute value must be the value specified.

Entities

Here we summarize entity usage and declarations. This discussion includes usage examples, declaration information, and syntax.

Usage

Examples:

```
Copyright &copy; 2001 Sybex Inc.
while( a %lt; b ) // to present Java code in HTML
```

Entity Declarations

Syntax:

```
<!ENTITY name "replacement characters">
```

Type of Entity	Example	Description
General	<!ENTITY publisher "Sybex">	Can be used only in XML data
Parameter	<!ENTITY %cdata "#CDATA">	Can be used only in DTD
External	<!ENTITY stockquotes SYSTEM "quotes.xml">	Used for including external XML files
Unparsed	<!ENTITY picture SYSTEM "picture.jpg" NDATA jpg>	Used for including non-XML files

What's Next

This chapter has explored the fundamentals of XML, which are required to do any XML data sharing or web services. The most powerful fundamental feature of XML is the ability to define the structure of a document and validate any document against that structure. A Document Type Definition (DTD) defines the rules that a type of document must follow to be valid. Validating parsers can use a DTD to determine if a document is valid. This is especially useful when sharing documents between different departments or companies in order to ensure that the sender and the receiver are following the same formatting rules.

Simplified API for XML (SAX) and the Document Object Model (DOM) provide two alternative ways to parse an XML document. DOM is usually more appropriate when the intention is to read the entire XML document, and SAX may be more appropriate when the intention is to only read a few specific elements from the document. Both SAX and DOM can be used in Java using classes from w3c or the new standard JAXP Java API from Sun Microsystems. The next chapter will explore ways that XML can be used in JSP page development. In particular, the next chapter will explore XSLT which has been rapidly growing in popularity.

Chapter 13

Presenting XML With JSP

You have seen XML in many environments: JSP tags are XML compliant, Tomcat uses XML extensively in its configuration files, and the JSP specification mandates the use of XML in the WAR (web archive JavaServer configuration). In addition, many projects of the Apache software organization's *Jakarta* developers' group use XML extensively.

XML is extensible in that users can define their own tag elements, unlike other markup languages such as HTML. Also where HTML often produces documents that are essentially standalone and isolated from one another, XML is often used to define relationships between documents, as well as to order the data inside the document.

Because XML was designed from the start to be flexible, it has myriad of uses. From a web designer's perspective, in simplistic terms, XML can be thought of as HTML that lets you

Adapted from *Mastering*™ *JSP*™ by Todd Cook

ISBN 0-7821-2940-4 $49.99

define your own tags. A database programmer might see XML as wrapping the data with the data definitions, allowing the data to identify itself, its organization, and significance even when far from its original source. To a quality assurance engineer, XML is a standard whereby the format can be validated when parsed by itself and validated against a document definition. All these users feel comfortable with XML because XML is designed to be human and machine readable.

XML has the potential to assist a well-rounded JSP developer looking for a way to lessen their troubles. And indeed, XML is changing the way enterprise applications interact, and XML support is growing strong. The future of JSP is bound to be intertwined with the flexibility and power that XML delivers.

Featured in this chapter:

- Using XML
- Writing XSL templates
- Generating HTML from XML
- Migrating data with XML/XSL

Do I Really Have to Learn XML to Write JSPs?

By writing JSPs thus far in the book, you have already been exposed to some XML. But to go far, XML is the key because many JSP extensions and accessories rely on XML-based implementations, such as Tomcat, Ant, and JMeter.

Still, you might fairly question: "I've heard a lot of hype about XML, but at a glance it seems quite complicated. Are there practical uses that I can incorporate into my JSP development to ease my learning curve as well as immediately add some worthwhile functionality?" Yes, we'll show you some practical uses of XML, and we'll cover the building blocks with a gradient approach so that you can quickly harness the power of XML. Because management most often appreciates innovations that add immediate value, we'll center our approach on practical uses.

This chapter will not make you a master of XML, but it will cover two or three fairly easy to understand ways of applying XML to JSP projects. Although XML can do many things, we'll examine features of XML that provide a flexible Presentation layer because JSP is the Presentation layer of choice for Enterprise Java Applications.

How Does XML Relate to HTML?

The next version of HTML will be XHTML. The World Wide Web Consortium (W3C; `www.w3.org`) put together a draft of XHTML by reformulating HTML version 4.01 into XML. The primary advantages are the following:

- XHTML pages are cleaner.
- XHTML can be validated against the rules for properly formed XML and a document template.
- XHTML binds the data more closely to its underlying organization—preserving hierarchies and relations—rather than just laying out the document's presentation.

You can convert HTML to XHTML by hand or by using tools. HTML Tidy is an open-source program that was started with support from the W3C, and it is now being supported by a group of developers at the Source Forge open-source software development site at `http://tidy.sourceforge.net`.

Although XML files look similar to HTML files in design and layout, there are some important differences.

Displaying XML

Listing 13.1 is the DTD that we'll be using in this chapter.

Listing 13.1: Poem.dtd

```
<?xml version="1.0" encoding="ISO-8859-1"?>
<!ELEMENT Poem (Language, Author, Title, AkaTitle,
 Meter, Name, Pattern+, Scansion+, Stanza+, Line+,
  Translation+, Language, Description+, Text+,
   Para+, Translator+)>
<!ELEMENT Language (#PCDATA)>
<!ELEMENT Author (#PCDATA)>
<!ELEMENT Title (#PCDATA)>
<!ELEMENT AkaTitle (#PCDATA)>
<!ELEMENT Meter (#PCDATA)>
```

```
<!ELEMENT Name (#PCDATA)>
<!ELEMENT Pattern (#PCDATA)>
<!ELEMENT Scansion (#PCDATA)>
<!ELEMENT Stanza (#PCDATA)>
<!ELEMENT Line (#PCDATA)>
<!ELEMENT Translation (#PCDATA)>
<!ELEMENT Language (#PCDATA)>
<!ELEMENT Description (#PCDATA)>
<!ELEMENT Text (#PCDATA)>
<!ELEMENT Para (#PCDATA)>
<!ELEMENT Translator (#PCDATA)>
```

The DTD starts out with the XML declaration, followed by a series of element tags. The document type `Poem` is treated as an element that is defined by other elements, demarcated by parentheses. The order of the elements in the parentheses dictates the expected order in the corresponding XML document.

As you can see in Listing 13.1, an author isn't really an optional attribute of a poem because every poem must have an author even if the poem is attributed to anonymous. In fact, although unlikely, a poem could have more than one author, and this possibility for plurality is represented in the DTD by the plus sign after the item in the document definition: `<!ELEMENT Poem (Language, Author+`. This document definition assumes that a poem be written in only one type of language.

Each element is specified as `#PCDATA`, which stands for Parsed Character Data. A DTD can specify only text and groupings of text; to specify datatypes, such as number, date, or money, you must use an XML schema. Listing 13.2 shows an XML document that conforms to the Poem.dtd.

Listing 13.2: Horace1.5.xml

```
<?xml version="1.0" encoding="utf-8"?>
<!DOCTYPE Poem SYSTEM "Poem.dtd">
<!-- Simple comment -->
<Poem>
<Language>Latin</Language>
<Author>Horace</Author>
<Translator></Translator>
<Title>Ode 1.5</Title>
<AkaTitle>To a Flirt</AkaTitle>
<Meter>
```

```
<Name>Fourth Asclepiadean</Name>
<Pattern>
<Scansion>---uu-//-uu-uX</Scansion>
<Scansion>---uu-//-uu-uX</Scansion>
<Scansion>---uu-X</Scansion>
<Scansion>---uu-uX</Scansion>
</Pattern>
</Meter>
<Stanza>
<Line>Quis multa gracilis te puer in rosa</Line>
<Line>perfusus liquidis urget odoribus</Line>
<Line>grato, Pyrrha, sub antro?</Line>
<Line>cui flavam religas comam</Line>
</Stanza>
<Stanza>
<Line>simplex munditiis? heu quotiens fidem</Line>
<Line>mutatosque deos flebit et aspera</Line>
<Line>nigris aequora ventis</Line>
<Line>emirabitur insolens</Line>
</Stanza>
<Stanza>
<Line>qui nunc te fruitur credulus aurea,</Line>
<Line>qui semper vacuam, semper amabilem</Line>
<Line>sperat, nescius aurae</Line>
<Line>fallacis. miseri, quibus</Line>
</Stanza>
<Stanza>
<Line>intemptata nites. me tabula sacer</Line>
<Line>votiva paries indicat uvida</Line>
<Line>suspendisse potenti</Line>
<Line>vestimenta maris deo.</Line>
</Stanza>
<Translation>
<Description>Literal Translation</Description>
<Text>
<Para>Who's the slender youth, saturated with rose
 perfume, O Pyrrha, pressing you in the pleasant grotto?
For whom do you tie back your golden hair
 with simple elegance?
</Para>
<Para>
Alas, how often he will cry over changing gods and
```

Part III

```
your fidelity; and he will be astonished,
 unaccustomed to the dark winds and the bitter seas,
</Para>
<Para>he who now enjoys you, thinks everything is golden,
 and hopes you will be always lovely, always free
 of passion for another, is gullible and ignorant
 of your deceptive breezes.</Para>
<Para>Misery to those men you shine as
 naive and unattempted!
 For me, a votive plaque on a sacred temple wall
 shows that I have survived
 and hung up my wet clothes
 to the powerful god of the ocean.
</Para>
</Text>
<Translator>Todd Cook</Translator>
</Translation>
</Poem>
```

The raw display of Horace1.5.xml in Internet Explorer is shown in Figure 13.1.

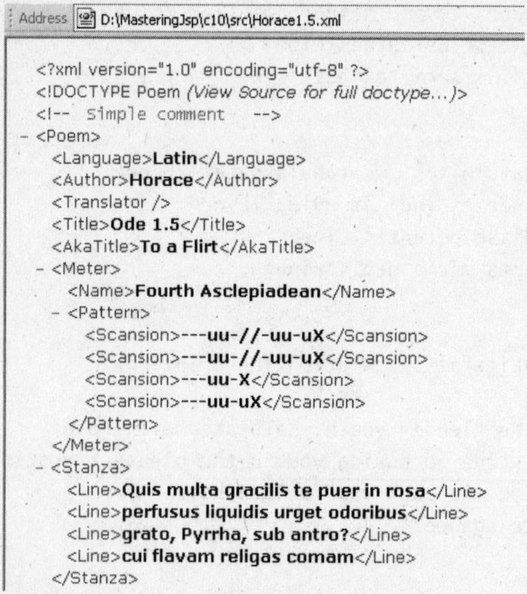

```
Address  D:\MasteringJsp\c10\src\Horace1.5.xml

  <?xml version="1.0" encoding="utf-8" ?>
  <!DOCTYPE Poem (View Source for full doctype...)>
  <!-- Simple comment  -->
- <Poem>
    <Language>Latin</Language>
    <Author>Horace</Author>
    <Translator />
    <Title>Ode 1.5</Title>
    <AkaTitle>To a Flirt</AkaTitle>
  - <Meter>
      <Name>Fourth Asclepiadean</Name>
    - <Pattern>
        <Scansion>---uu-//-uu-uX</Scansion>
        <Scansion>---uu-//-uu-uX</Scansion>
        <Scansion>---uu-X</Scansion>
        <Scansion>---uu-uX</Scansion>
      </Pattern>
    </Meter>
  - <Stanza>
      <Line>Quis multa gracilis te puer in rosa</Line>
      <Line>perfusus liquidis urget odoribus</Line>
      <Line>grato, Pyrrha, sub antro?</Line>
      <Line>cui flavam religas comam</Line>
    </Stanza>
```

FIGURE 13.1: Raw XML display in a browser

Everything displays because the document is validated against the DTD. Figure 13.2 shows what happens when a tag is not accounted for. An extra tag element has been added to the file Horace1.5withDTDerror.xml.

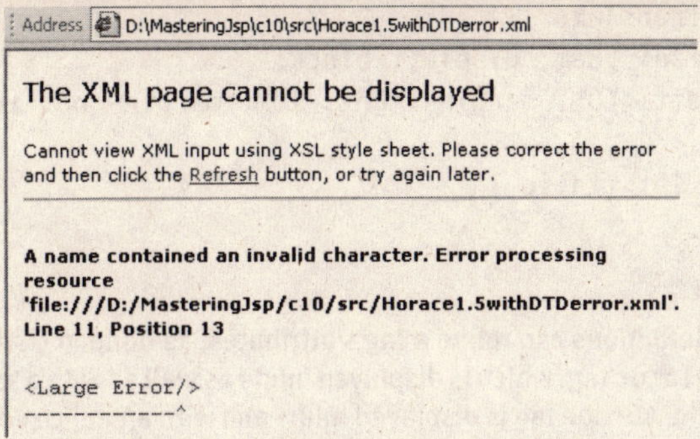

Address D:\MasteringJsp\c10\src\Horace1.5withDTDerror.xml
The XML page cannot be displayed
Cannot view XML input using XSL style sheet. Please correct the error and then click the Refresh button, or try again later.
A name contained an invalid character. Error processing resource 'file:///D:/MasteringJsp/c10/src/Horace1.5withDTDerror.xml'. Line 11, Position 13
<Large Error/>
------------^

FIGURE 13.2: An XML file that does not agree with its specified DTD throws an error, preventing display of the document.

The raw XML display is quite ugly, and now we'll look at how we can improve that display using a Cascading Style Sheet (CSS) on the client side.

Using XML by Itself on the Client Side

Before we show you the advantages of XML and JSP, let's look at how you can harness some XML formatting features of the current browsers. Although full XML\XSL formatting is not available, you can use CSS custom definitions for formatting purposes. Listings 13.3 and 13.4 are CSS definitions for the poem Horace1.5.xml, mentioned earlier.

Listing 13.3: StudentsLatin.css

```
Author, Translator, Title
    { display: inline }
Language, AkaTitle, Meter, Scansion, Stanza,
 Line, Para, Description
    { display: block }
Author, Translator, AkaTitle
    { font-style: italic }
Title
    { font-size: 1.3em }
```

Part III

```
Stanza
    { margin-left: 10%; margin-right: 10%; margin-top: 2em }
Description, Para
    { margin-left: 10%; margin-right: 10%; margin-top: 2em }
Translation, Translator
    {  font-size: .8em; display: block;
     margin-left: 10%; margin-right: 10%; margin-top: 1em }
Translator
    { font-style: italic }
```

NOTE

Multiple CSS definitions can refine a tag's attributes, as done in Listing 13.3 with the `Translator` tag, which is displayed inline as well as with a specified font, whereas the `Author` tag is displayed inline and with an italicized font.

Listing 13.4: TeachersLatin.css

```
Author, Title
    { display: inline }
AkaTitle, Stanza, Line
    { display: block }
Author, Translator, AkaTitle
    { font-style: italic }
Title
    { font-size: 1.3em }
Stanza
    { margin-left: 10%; margin-right: 10%; margin-top: 2em }
Language, Name, Pattern, Translation
    { display: none }
```

NOTE

You can hide custom tags from view using CSS definitions, for example, `display: none`.

To apply the CSS definitions to the XML document, you must mention them in the header, such as this:

```
<?xml version="1.0" ?>
<?XML:stylesheet type="text/css" href="StudentsLatin.css"?>
<!DOCTYPE Poem SYSTEM "Poem.dtd">
<Poem>...
```

This produces the display shown in Figure 13.3.

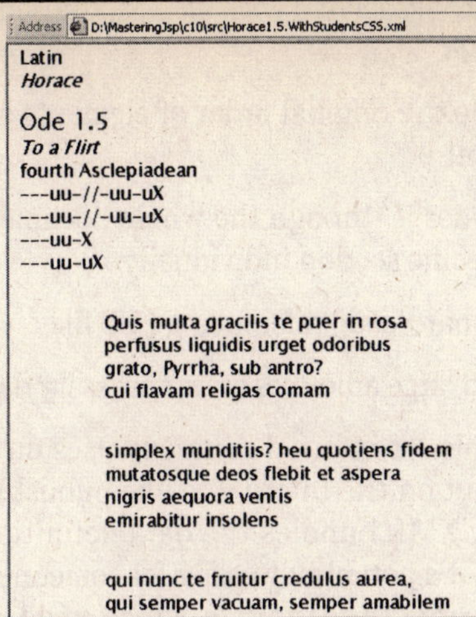

FIGURE 13.3: An XML file displayed using Student View CSS

And the teacher style sheet is referenced similarly:

```
<?xml version="1.0"?>
<?XML:stylesheet type="text/css" href="TeachersLatin.css"?>
<!DOCTYPE Poem SYSTEM "Poem.dtd">
<Poem>...
```

This listing produces results according to the CSS definitions, as shown in Figure 13.4.

Address D:\MasteringJsp\c10\src\Horace1.5.WithTeachersCSS.xml

Horace Ode 1.5
To a Flirt

Quis multa gracilis te puer in rosa
perfusus liquidis urget odoribus
grato, Pyrrha, sub antro?
cui flavam religas comam

simplex munditiis? heu quotiens fidem
mutatosque deos flebit et aspera
nigris aequora ventis
emirabitur insolens

qui nunc te fruitur credulus aurea,
qui semper vacuam, semper amabilem
sperat, nescius aurae
fallacis. miseri, quibus

intemptata nites. me tabula sacer
votiva paries indicat uvida
suspendisse potenti
vestimenta maris deo.

FIGURE 13.4: An XML file displayed using Teacher View CSS

The following disadvantages are associated with an XML presentation that uses CSS:

- CSS can only modify or hide the original order of elements and tags in the original document.
- Specifying a behavior cascades it through the whole document; there's no way to treat a specific section individually.
- You must hand-generate or hard-code referencing CSS files.
- Files can potentially contain large amounts of unnecessary data.
- The file may only be suitable for internal company uses on an intranet. Sending the file out on the Internet is like publishing part of a database because XML bundles the data definitions along with the data. Hence, it's potentially easier for someone to examine how internal applications use the data, which could create a security risk or possibly aid competitors.
- Currently only a few browsers support native XML/CSS display.

Internet Explorer has done a good job in championing the method of data presentation. We'd like to give a standing ovation to Microsoft for their efforts with XML. Unfortunately, Microsoft Word 2000 generates XML that mangles even the smallest, simplest document into something that strains the XML tenet of human readability. Consequently, we won't cover Microsoft's proprietary approach to XML.

To change the display order of the XML document, to provide individual processing to a specific section, or to screen out unnecessary data, you need to use an XSL (Extensible Stylesheet Language) stylesheet.

WRITING XSL TEMPLATES

XSL templates (XSLTs) are a new technology that has been added to the larger picture of XML. XSL does for XML files what CSS does for HTML files, and in addition it allows powerful object-oriented programming to take advantage of an XML file's enforced object hierarchy. In simple terms, these abilities let you change the display of a paragraph on a page without necessarily having those presentation changes cascade and affect other paragraphs farther down in the document unless explicitly desired. Additionally, an XSL template can instruct the display to change the order of the elements of a document, such as placing the author before the title or at the top or bottom of the page.

XSL templates are often used to configure a transformation, often referred to as an XSLT. An XML transformer loads and parses an XML document and an XSL document and executes the XSL formatting and transformation instructions on the XML document to create a new document. The resulting transformed document need not necessarily be in XML format.

NOTE

For more information about XSLT, see *Mastering XSLT* by Chuck White (Sybex, 2002).

XSL Basics

After the XML declaration tag, the XSL declares itself as a stylesheet, and it references a namespace, which defines some conventions:

```
<xsl:stylesheet
  xmlns:xsl="http://www.w3.org/1999/XSL/Transform"
    version="1.0">
```

The stylesheet then declares the output that the transformer will generate, such as this:

```
<xsl:output method="html" indent="yes"/>
```

The template section is next. The template is the container for the body of the document:

```
<xsl:template match="Poem">
```

In this example, the template is matched against the main XML definition of `poem`; however, this is only the beginning. XSL lets you specify templates to be matched against any XML element. This behavior allows XSL to process repeated sections in an object-oriented manner.

Object-Oriented Design in a Template

Let's look at a subset of the processing to see how templates can be used to handle different quantities of XML tags within a document.

Meter is a quantity that can vary from poem to poem. There are two types of meter: accentual and quantitative. *Accentual meter* is determined by the spoken stress accents of the words. English and the Germanic languages are spoken with stress accents, and their poetry uses accentual meters (think of Shakespeare's iambic pentameter). *Quantitative meter* is determined by the long or short vowel quantities of each syllable. Latin and the Romance languages de-emphasize stress accents and focus on the length of time it takes to pronounce the syllables. Latin and Romance language poetry typically use quantitative or syllabic meters.

The metrical pattern of some poems can be defined in one line; other poems have metrical patterns than need to be defined by multiple lines. Such is the case with our two example poems. The following snippet from the XSL file uses a hierarchy of templates to accommodate situations in which a metrical pattern is defined by multiple lines of scansion. The `Meter` template pulls the meter's name value, prints it, and then calls the `Pattern` template for each pattern section. The `Pattern` template calls the `Scansion` template for each line of scansion, and the line of scansion is printed out. Although this template hierarchy is a little tricky to visualize, the flexibility it affords should be clear when viewing the transformation of the poems in this chapter's sample application (Horace's ode 1.5 has four lines of scansion, while his ode 1.11 has only one line of scansion).

```
      <xsl:apply-templates select="Meter"/>
. . .
<xsl:template match="Meter">
      Meter: <xsl:value-of select="Name"/>
      <br/>
      <xsl:apply-templates select="Pattern"/>
</xsl:template>

<xsl:template match="Pattern">
      <xsl:apply-templates select="Scansion"/>
</xsl:template>

<xsl:template match="Scansion">
      <xsl:value-of select="."/>
      <br/>
</xsl:template>
```

This seems like a lot of work, but it's required to accommodate the flexibility of the possible XML meter representations. For example, a whole meter can be defined by two stanzas (verse paragraphs) with different scansions.

Value Selection in a Template

You select value in a template by referencing the desired element's tag designation, for example:

```
<xsl:value-of select="Name"/>
```

Or you can pull one or more values using the dot operator:

```
<xsl:value-of select="."/>
```

Listing 13.5 is a template that manipulates the two poems.

Listing 13.5: LatinStudent.xsl

```
<?xml version="1.0"?>
<xsl:stylesheet
 xmlns:xsl="http://www.w3.org/1999/XSL/Transform"
  version="1.0">
<xsl:output method="html" indent="yes"/>
<xsl:template match="Poem">
<HTML>
  <HEAD>
    <TITLE>Latin Student Viewing -
     <xsl:value-of select="AkaTitle"/></TITLE>
  </HEAD>
  <BODY>
   <xsl:value-of select="Author"/>
   <xsl:value-of select="Title"/> Also known as:
   <xsl:value-of select="AkaTitle"/>
   <br />
   <table cellspacing="0" width="600">
    <tr>
     <td>
      <xsl:apply-templates select="Meter"/>
     </td>
    </tr>
   </table>
   <table width="600">
    <xsl:apply-templates select="Stanza"/>
    <xsl:apply-templates select="Translation"/>
   </table>
  </BODY>
</HTML>
</xsl:template>
```

```
<xsl:template match="Meter">
   Meter: <xsl:value-of select="Name"/>
   <br/>
   <xsl:apply-templates select="Pattern"/>
</xsl:template>

<xsl:template match="Pattern">
   <xsl:apply-templates select="Scansion"/>
</xsl:template>

<xsl:template match="Scansion">
  <xsl:value-of select="."/>
   <br/>
</xsl:template>

<xsl:template match="Stanza">
  <tr>
   <td>
   </td>
  </tr>
    <xsl:apply-templates select="Line"/>
  <tr>
   <td>
   </td>
  </tr>
</xsl:template>

<xsl:template match="Line">
  <tr>
    <td>
      <xsl:value-of select="."/>
    </td>
  </tr>
</xsl:template>

<xsl:template match="Translation">
  <tr>
   <td>
    <hr/>
   </td>
  </tr>
  <tr>
   <td>
```

```
        <xsl:value-of select="Description"/><br />
       </td>
      </tr>
      <tr>
       <td>
        by <i><xsl:value-of select="Translator"/></i>
       </td>
      </tr>
      <xsl:apply-templates select="Text"/>
    </xsl:template>

    <xsl:template match="Text">
       <xsl:apply-templates  select="Para"/><br />
    </xsl:template>

    <xsl:template match="Para">
      <tr>
        <td>
          <xsl:value-of  select="."/>
        </td>
      </tr>
    </xsl:template>

    </xsl:stylesheet>
```

Notice that the title bar and the heading line values are constructed from the document, moving them around from their original positioning.

The LatinTeacher stylesheet, shown in Listing 13.6, is quite plain, but it will serve well later in showing that parts of an XML document can be excluded from the output of the transformation, namely here, the translation.

Listing 13.6: LatinTeacher.xsl

```
<?xml version="1.0"?>
<xsl:stylesheet
 xmlns:xsl="http://www.w3.org/1999/XSL/Transform"
 version="1.0">
<xsl:output method="html" indent="yes"/>

<xsl:template match="Poem">
<HTML>
  <HEAD>
```

```
        <TITLE>Latin Teacher Viewing</TITLE>
      </HEAD>
      <BODY>
      <table cellspacing="0" width="600">
       <tr>
        <td>
         <xsl:value-of select="Author"/>,
          <xsl:value-of select="Title"/>
        </td>
       </tr>
       <tr>
        <td>
         (Also know as: <xsl:value-of select="AkaTitle"/> )
        </td>
       </tr>
        <xsl:apply-templates select="Meter"/>
       </table>

       <table width="600">
         <xsl:apply-templates select="Stanza"/>
       </table>
      </BODY>
    </HTML>
    </xsl:template>

    <xsl:template match="Meter">
       <tr>
        <td>
         Meter: <xsl:value-of select="Name"/>
        </td>
       </tr>
       <xsl:apply-templates select="Pattern"/>
    </xsl:template>

    <xsl:template match="Pattern">
       <tr>
        <td>
        </td>
       </tr>
       <xsl:apply-templates select="Scansion"/>
       <tr>
        <td>
        </td>
```

```
    </tr>
  </xsl:template>

  <xsl:template match="Scansion">
    <tr>
     <td>
      <xsl:value-of select="."/>
     </td>
    </tr>
  </xsl:template>

  <xsl:template match="Stanza">
    <tr>
     <td>
     </td>
    </tr>
    <xsl:apply-templates select="Line"/>
    <tr>
     <td>
     </td>
    </tr>
  </xsl:template>

  <xsl:template match="Line">
    <tr>
     <td>
      <xsl:value-of select="."/>
     </td>
    </tr>
  </xsl:template>

  </xsl:stylesheet>
```

The main difference between the two XSL stylesheets is that the teacher stylesheet does not show any translations, and the presentation is a little bit cleaner.

Before looking at the transformations, let's look at the other poem we'll be using in our template examples (see Listing 13.7).

Listing 13.7: Horace1.11.xml

```
<?xml version="1.0" encoding="utf-8"?>
<!DOCTYPE Poem SYSTEM "Poem.dtd">
```

```
<Poem>
<Language>Latin</Language>
<Author>Horace</Author>
<Translator></Translator>
<Title>Ode 1.11</Title>
<AkaTitle>Seize the Day</AkaTitle>
<Meter>
<Name>Fifth or Greater Asclepiadean</Name>
<Pattern>
<Scansion>---uu-//-uu-//-uu-uX</Scansion>
</Pattern>
</Meter>
<Stanza>
<Line>
Tu ne quaesieris--scire nefas--quem mihi, quem tibi
</Line>
<Line>
finem di dederint, Leuconoe, nec Babylonios
</Line>
<Line>
temptaris numeros. ut melius, quidquid erit, pati.
</Line>
<Line>
seu pluris hiemes seu tribuit Iuppiter ultimam,
</Line>
<Line>
quae nunc oppositis debilitat pumicibus mare
</Line>
<Line>
Tyrrhenum: sapias, vina liques et spatio brevi
</Line>
<Line>
spem longam reseces. dum loquimur, fugerit invida
</Line>
<Line>
aetas: carpe diem quam minimum credula postero.
</Line>
</Stanza>
<Translation>
<Language>English</Language>
<Description>Literal Translation</Description>
```

```
<Text>
<Para>
You shouldn't desire--it's forbidden to know--the
 ends that the gods have determined for me and you,
 Leuconoe.  Don't let Babylonian astrology tempt you;
 whatever your future will be, it's better to endure
 it with patience.  Whether or not Jupiter allots only
 one more winter, or sends many more to wear
 down the Tuscan cliffs to ocean sand, be wise,
 drink the best of your wine, and prune back hopes
 for a long life to the brief span we have.  While
 we've been chatting, jealous time will have already
 fled: seize the day, trust as little as possible to
 tomorrow.
</Para>
</Text>
<Translator>Todd Cook</Translator>
</Translation>
</Poem>
```

Now let's look the XSL in action. On the one hand, you can write a Java program that will use an XML transformer to generate the output. On the other, you can use a browser that performs the XSL transformation. Unfortunately, viewing the transformation in a browser does not screen out the unnecessary information, but fortunately it can be a convenient way to debug the writing an XSL.

Displaying XML/XSL Templates

XML referencing an XSL stylesheet can be displayed in a browser that supports XML (currently Internet Explorer versions 5 and 6, and Netscape 6). You reference the stylesheet as you would reference a scripting element. The files we have been working with were changed so that the XML file includes a reference to an XSL stylesheet, as shown in Listing 13.8. Figure 13.5 shows the display that results.

Listing 13.8: Horace1.11withXSLStudentReference.xml

```
<?xml version="1.0"?>
<?xml-stylesheet type="text/xsl" href="LatinStudent.xsl"?>
<Poem>
. . . [etc]
```

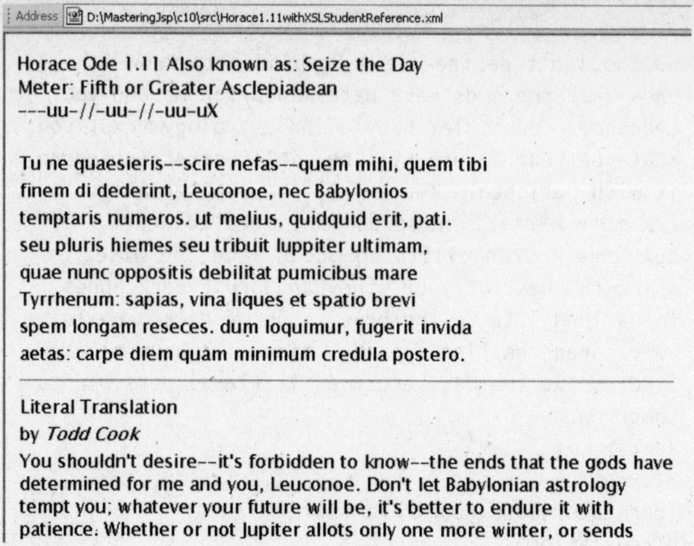

Address D:\MasteringJsp\c10\src\Horace1.11withXSLStudentReference.xml

Horace Ode 1.11 Also known as: Seize the Day
Meter: Fifth or Greater Asclepiadean
---uu-//-uu-//-uu-uX

Tu ne quaesieris--scire nefas--quem mihi, quem tibi
finem di dederint, Leuconoe, nec Babylonios
temptaris numeros. ut melius, quidquid erit, pati.
seu pluris hiemes seu tribuit Iuppiter ultimam,
quae nunc oppositis debilitat pumicibus mare
Tyrrhenum: sapias, vina liques et spatio brevi
spem longam reseces. dum loquimur, fugerit invida
aetas: carpe diem quam minimum credula postero.

Literal Translation
by *Todd Cook*
You shouldn't desire--it's forbidden to know--the ends that the gods have determined for me and you, Leuconoe. Don't let Babylonian astrology tempt you; whatever your future will be, it's better to endure it with patience. Whether or not Jupiter allots only one more winter, or sends

FIGURE 13.5: An XML file displaying data using an XSL stylesheet transformed by an XML/XSL compliant browser

Listing 13.9 shows the same file heading but with a reference to the LatinTeacher stylesheet. Figure 13.6 shows the display that results.

Listing 13.9: Horace1.11withXSLTeacherReference.xml

```
<?xml version="1.0"?>
<?xml-stylesheet type="text/xsl" href="LatinTeacher.xsl"?>
. . . [etc]
```

Referencing a stylesheet such as this seems great, but there are some serious drawbacks to using hard-coded XSL references:

- Only certain, recent browsers support XSL references.
- All the XML file's original data format is transmitted, even if the viewer only wanted to view a small subset of the data. This causes increased traffic on the network, and also means you can't restrict portions of the code with XSL references.
- Stylesheet references can't be easily written out dynamically; web servers display a `.jsp` file differently even if XML is inside.

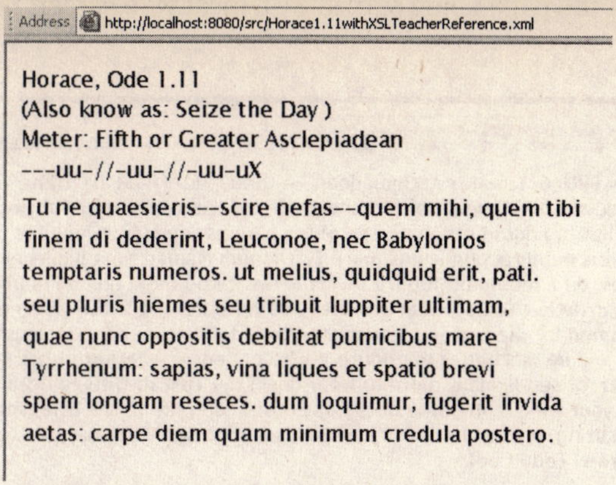

Address http://localhost:8080/src/Horace1.11withXSLTeacherReference.xml

Horace, Ode 1.11
(Also know as: Seize the Day)
Meter: Fifth or Greater Asclepiadean
---uu-//-uu-//-uu-uX

Tu ne quaesieris--scire nefas--quem mihi, quem tibi
finem di dederint, Leuconoe, nec Babylonios
temptaris numeros. ut melius, quidquid erit, pati.
seu pluris hiemes seu tribuit Iuppiter ultimam,
quae nunc oppositis debilitat pumicibus mare
Tyrrhenum: sapias, vina liques et spatio brevi
spem longam reseces. dum loquimur, fugerit invida
aetas: carpe diem quam minimum credula postero.

FIGURE 13.6: An XML file displaying data using an XSL stylesheet transformed by an XML/XSL compliant browser

To see the difference between how a browser handles a raw XML/XSL file locally and how it handles the same file sent from a web server, examine the project file `JspHorace1.11withXSLStudentReference.xml.jsp`. When double-clicked in a file browser, the file appears as shown in Figure 13.7. Notice that the URL shows that the page resides on the local hard drive.

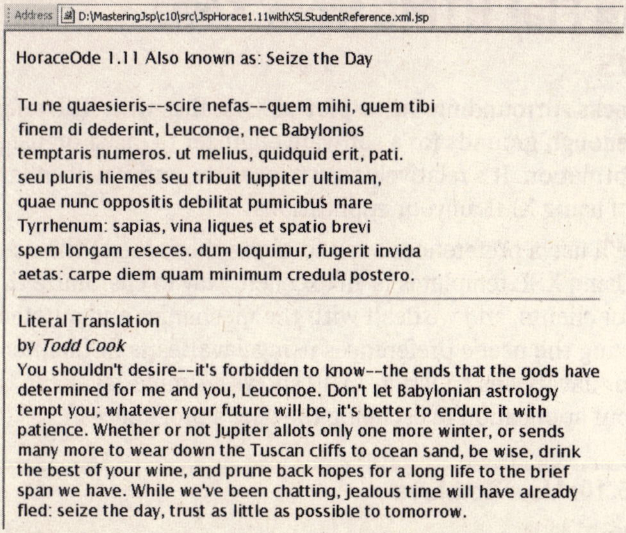

Address D:\MasteringJsp\c10\src\JspHorace1.11withXSLStudentReference.xml.jsp

HoraceOde 1.11 Also known as: Seize the Day

Tu ne quaesieris--scire nefas--quem mihi, quem tibi
finem di dederint, Leuconoe, nec Babylonios
temptaris numeros. ut melius, quidquid erit, pati.
seu pluris hiemes seu tribuit Iuppiter ultimam,
quae nunc oppositis debilitat pumicibus mare
Tyrrhenum: sapias, vina liques et spatio brevi
spem longam reseces. dum loquimur, fugerit invida
aetas: carpe diem quam minimum credula postero.

Literal Translation
by *Todd Cook*
You shouldn't desire--it's forbidden to know--the ends that the gods have determined for me and you, Leuconoe. Don't let Babylonian astrology tempt you; whatever your future will be, it's better to endure it with patience. Whether or not Jupiter allots only one more winter, or sends many more to wear down the Tuscan cliffs to ocean sand, be wise, drink the best of your wine, and prune back hopes for a long life to the brief span we have. While we've been chatting, jealous time will have already fled: seize the day, trust as little as possible to tomorrow.

FIGURE 13.7: When you double-click an `.xml` file that has a `.jsp` extension or drag it into a browser, you see this display.

Figure 13.8 shows the page being served by a local web server; notice the URL.

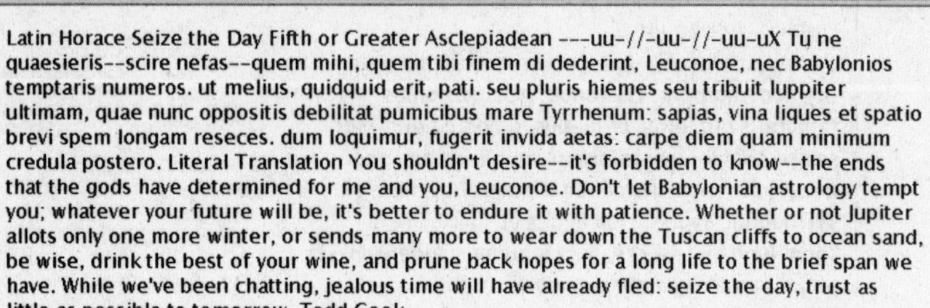
Address http://localhost:8080/src/JspHorace1.11withXSLStudentReference.xml.jsp
Go
Latin Horace Seize the Day Fifth or Greater Asclepiadean ---uu-//-uu-//-uu-uX Tu ne quaesieris--scire nefas--quem mihi, quem tibi finem di dederint, Leuconoe, nec Babylonios temptaris numeros. ut melius, quidquid erit, pati. seu pluris hiemes seu tribuit Iuppiter ultimam, quae nunc oppositis debilitat pumicibus mare Tyrrhenum: sapias, vina liques et spatio brevi spem longam reseces. dum loquimur, fugerit invida aetas: carpe diem quam minimum credula postero. Literal Translation You shouldn't desire--it's forbidden to know--the ends that the gods have determined for me and you, Leuconoe. Don't let Babylonian astrology tempt you; whatever your future will be, it's better to endure it with patience. Whether or not Jupiter allots only one more winter, or sends many more to wear down the Tuscan cliffs to ocean sand, be wise, drink the best of your wine, and prune back hopes for a long life to the brief span we have. While we've been chatting, jealous time will have already fled: seize the day, trust as little as possible to tomorrow. Todd Cook

FIGURE 13.8: When a `.jsp` file display is served by a JavaServer Engine, you see this display.

But what if you want to save bandwidth by sending out only the necessary parts of the document? What if your application needs to prevent some data from being seen by some users? What if end users don't have browsers that support the XSL transformation? You then need to write a Java application that does the transformation.

Generating Flat HTML from XML Documents

The drawbacks surrounding the display of XML files with XSL references should be enough grounds for a software engineer to insist on using an XSL transformation. It's relatively easy to execute, and it will enhance the flexibility of using XML in your applications.

First, we'll use a preferences bean to cache the value of the user's template. Using XSL templates is an excellent way to customize the presentation for clients, and we dealt with the mechanics and automation of customizing the user's preferences using JavaBeans in Chapter 5, "Introducing JavaBeans." Listing 13.10 shows a simple JavaBean that will assist our application in cacheing the user's preferences.

Listing 13.10: UserXml.java

```
package c13;

public class UserXml
{
```

```
    private String textFormat = "";

    public UserXml()
     {
     }

    public void validate()
     {}

    public String getTextFormat()
     {
      return textFormat;
     }

    public void setTextFormat(String NewTextFormat)
     {
      if (NewTextFormat != null)
         textFormat = NewTextFormat.trim();
     }

    public boolean IsPrefsSet()
     {
      if (textFormat.length() > 0)
          return true;
      else
          return false;
     }
  }
```

Next we have a class that performs all the work of the transformation using classes from the Java API for XML Processing 1.1. The class, shown in Listing 13.11, has a `main()` function implemented for self-testing.

Listing 13.11: XMLXSLConverter.java

```
package c13;
// Imported TraX classes
// Works fine with Jaxp 1.1.3 or greater
import javax.xml.transform.TransformerFactory;
import javax.xml.transform.Transformer;
import javax.xml.transform.Source;
import javax.xml.transform.stream.StreamSource;
import javax.xml.transform.stream.StreamResult;
import javax.xml.transform.TransformerException;
```

```
import
 javax.xml.transform.TransformerConfigurationException;
import org.xml.sax.SAXException;
// Imported java.io classes
import java.io.FileOutputStream;
import java.io.IOException;
import java.io.ByteArrayOutputStream;

public class XMLXSLConverter
{
   private String inputFile ="";
   private String outputFile ="";
   private String media = null;
   // These params can all be null
   private String title = null;
   private String charset = null;
   private String xslToUse = "";
   private String directoryPath = "./src/";
   // Whole files, or their assignments
   // could be stored in a DB

 public void setInputFile (String NewInputFile)
  {
   if (NewInputFile != null)
     inputFile= NewInputFile.trim();
  }

 public String getInputFile ()
  {
   return inputFile;
  }

 public void setOutputFile (String NewOutputFile)
  {
   if (NewOutputFile != null)
     outputFile= NewOutputFile.trim();
  }

 public String getOutputFile ()
  {
   return outputFile;
  }

 public void setXslToUse (String NewXslToUse)
  {
```

```
    if (NewXslToUse != null)
      xslToUse = NewXslToUse.trim();
  }

  public String getXslToUse()
  {
    return xslToUse;
  }

  public void setDirectoryPath (String NewDirectoryPath)
  {
    if (NewDirectoryPath != null)
      directoryPath = NewDirectoryPath.trim();
  }

  public String getDirectoryPath()
  {
    return directoryPath;
  }

  public boolean PullXslFromXml()
  {
    try {
              TransformerFactory tFactory =
                       TransformerFactory.newInstance();
          Source stylesheet =
            tFactory.getAssociatedStylesheet(
               new StreamSource( inputFile ), media,
                                        title, charset);
          xslToUse = stylesheet.toString();
          // Source stylesheet = new StreamSource(
          //"D:\\MasteringJsp\\c13\\src\\HoraceTest.xsl");
        }
        catch (Exception e)
       {
          System.out.println("Error Message: "
                                   + e.getMessage());
             e.printStackTrace();
             return false;
       }
     return true;
  }
```

Part III

```
public String ConvertToHTML() throws
      TransformerException,
      TransformerConfigurationException, SAXException,
      IOException
  {
   System.out.println("Xml file: "
                    + directoryPath +inputFile);
   java.io.ByteArrayOutputStream BaosHtml =
                  new java.io.ByteArrayOutputStream();
     try
      {
       Source stylesheet;
        TransformerFactory tFactory =
               TransformerFactory.newInstance();
       if ( xslToUse.length() < 1)
        // try to pull it since it wasn't initialized
       {
       stylesheet = tFactory.getAssociatedStylesheet
        (new StreamSource( directoryPath + inputFile ),
                               media, title, charset);
       }
       else
       {
        stylesheet = new StreamSource
                        (directoryPath + xslToUse);
        System.out.println("Full path to xsl: "
                           + directoryPath + xslToUse);
       }  //could be improved

     Transformer transformer =
                tFactory.newTransformer(stylesheet);
     transformer.transform(new StreamSource(
         new java.io.File( directoryPath + inputFile )),
                        new StreamResult ( BaosHtml ));
     System.out.println("HTML: \n"
                      + BaosHtml.toString());
     }
    catch (TransformerException se)
     {
     System.out.println("Error Message: "
                        + se.getMessage());
     se.printStackTrace();
```

```
    System.out.println(se.getLocationAsString() );
    //  System.out.println(spe.getLineNumber());
        return BaosHtml.toString();
    }
  catch (Exception e)
    {
     System.out.println("Error Message: "
                               + e.getMessage());
     e.printStackTrace();
       return BaosHtml.toString();
    }
  return BaosHtml.toString();
}

public void WriteHtmlFileToDisk()
      throws TransformerException,
       TransformerConfigurationException, SAXException,
        IOException
 {
  try
    {
    TransformerFactory tFactory =
                 TransformerFactory.newInstance();
    Source stylesheet =
             tFactory.getAssociatedStylesheet
               (new StreamSource( inputFile ),
                         media, title, charset);
    // Commented out entries below illustrate
    // retrieving the HTML as one large "String"
    // java.io.ByteArrayOutputStream strOut =
          //        new java.io.ByteArrayOutputStream();
    Transformer transformer =
       tFactory.newTransformer(stylesheet);
        transformer.transform(new StreamSource(
         new java.io.File ( inputFile )),
          new StreamResult(
           new java.io.FileOutputStream(outputFile )));
     // new StreamResult ( strOut ));
    System.out.println("The result is a new file:"
                                 + outputFile );
     // System.out.println("The result is a new file:"
                 /// + strOut.toString());
    }
```

```
      catch (Exception e)
        {
         System.out.println("Error Message: "
                                  + e.getMessage());
         e.printStackTrace();
        }
    }

    public XMLXSLConverter()
     {
     }

    public static void main(String[] args)
        throws TransformerException,
                  TransformerConfigurationException,
                  SAXException, IOException
    {
     String strFileSep =
               System.getProperty("file.separator");
      try
       {
        XMLXSLConverter xmlslConv = new XMLXSLConverter();
        xmlslConv.setInputFile(
         System.getProperty("user.dir") + strFileSep
                + "src" + strFileSep + "HoraceTest.xml" );
        xmlslConv.setOutputFile(
         System.getProperty("user.dir") + strFileSep
                 + "src" + strFileSep + "HoraceTest.text");
        TransformerFactory tFactory =
                TransformerFactory.newInstance();
       // Nifty feature: the Transformer factory
       // pulls the StyleSheet from the XML file
       //      Source stylesheet =
       //          tFactory.getAssociatedStylesheet
       //                (new StreamSource( inputFile ),
       //                     media, title, charset);
       // However you may want to specify
       //  your own stylesheet
       Source stylesheet = new StreamSource(
           System.getProperty("user.dir") + strFileSep
                 + "src" + strFileSep + "HoraceTest.xsl");
        java.io.ByteArrayOutputStream strOut =
                  new java.io.ByteArrayOutputStream();
```

```
            Transformer transformer =
                      tFactory.newTransformer(stylesheet);
           transformer.transform( new StreamSource(
               new java.io.File ( xmlslConv.getInputFile() )),
            // Commented out entries below illustrate
            //  producing the XML as a text file
            // new StreamResult(new java.io.FileOutputStream(
            // xmlslConv.getOutputFile() )));
                new StreamResult ( strOut ));
          // System.out.println("The result is a new file: "
          //  + xmlslConv.getOutputFile() );
          System.out.println("The result is a new file: "
                                        + strOut.toString());
          }
        catch (Exception e)
          {
           System.out.println("Error Message: "
                                  + e.getMessage());
           e.printStackTrace();
          }
      }
    }
```

The XMLXSLConverter first requires the input and output files to be specified. A TransformerFactory is then created, which does the bulk of the work. If an XSL stylesheet isn't specified, the TransformerFactory examines the XML file for a hard-coded XSL file reference. A stream source is passed to the TransformerFactory, and then XML/XSL transformation occurs. The XMLXSLConverter class wraps the input-output filenames and functionality so that you can concentrate on the Presentation layer.

To test the XMLXSLConverter class successfully, you may need to change the absolute paths specified in the `main()` function, depending on where you installed the files. The SelectView JSP, shown in Listing 13.12, sets up the transformation. Again depending on where you installed the files, you may need to change the path set in the page's scriptlet tag. Ideally, the paths should be retrieved from a database.

Listing 13.12: SelectView.jsp

```
<jsp:useBean scope="session" class="c13.UserXml"
 id="XUserPrefs"/>
<jsp:setProperty name="XUserPrefs" property="*"/>
<jsp:useBean scope="session" class="c13.XMLXSLConverter"
```

Part III

```
 id="XMSLDocConverter" />
<jsp:setProperty name="XMSLDocConverter" property="*"/>
<HTML>
<HEAD>
<TITLE>
Select View
</TITLE>
</HEAD>
<BODY>
<H1>
Select a view and a text
</H1>
<FORM method="post">
Select Text Viewing format
<select name="xslToUse">
<option selected
 value="<%= XMSLDocConverter.getXslToUse()
  %>"><%= XMSLDocConverter.getXslToUse()%></option>
<jsp:include page="XslFiles.html"  flush="true"/>
</select>
<BR>
<BR>
Select Text
<select name="inputFile">
<option selected
 value="<%= XMSLDocConverter.getInputFile()
  %>"><%= XMSLDocConverter.getInputFile()%></option>
<jsp:include page="XmlFiles.html"  flush="true"/>
</select>
<BR>
<BR>
<INPUT TYPE="SUBMIT" NAME="Submit" VALUE="Submit">
<INPUT TYPE="RESET" VALUE="Reset">
</FORM>
<%
if (request.getParameter("xslToUse") != null)
 XUserPrefs.setTextFormat(XMSLDocConverter.getXslToUse());
 if (XUserPrefs.IsPrefsSet())
  {
  XMSLDocConverter.setDirectoryPath(
   "D:\\MasteringJsp\\c13\\src\\" );
 // xml user bean could perform authorizations,
```

```
 // score keeping, progress tracking, etc
 %>
<form action="TransformedText.jsp" method="POST">
<input type="button" onClick="javascript:submit()"
 value="See the text">
</form>
<%}%>
</BODY>
</HTML>
```

The page is configured with two dynamically included HTML files, one listing the available XSL templates (see Listing 13.13) and another showing available XML files (see Listing 13.14). The HTML files are dynamically included so as to make the application easy to configure during development.

Listing 13.13: XmlFiles.html

```
<option value="Horace1.5.xml">
Horace Book 1, Fifth Ode
</option>
<option value="Horace1.11.xml">
Horace Book 1, Eleventh Ode
</option>
```

Listing 13.14: XslFiles.html

```
<option value="LatinStudent.xsl">Student View</option>
<option value="LatinTeacher.xsl">Teacher View</option>
```

After the user has made selections, a button appears. Clicking this button sends the user to the TransformedText JSP, shown in Listing 13.15, where the transformation is called and the results are displayed.

Listing 13.15: TransformedText.jsp

```
<jsp:useBean scope="session" class="c13.XMLXSLConverter"
 id="XMSLDocConverter"/>
<% response.setContentType("text/html");%>
<%= XMSLDocConverter.ConvertToHTML()%>
```

We deliberately kept the TransformedText JSP simple, but its awkward construction of simply displaying the HTML returned should suggest to you how easily it could be extended. You can build a JSP from several transformations, and you can write custom elements as well.

From applying the LatinTeacher.xsl template to the Horace.1.5.xml file we get the display shown in Figure 13.9.

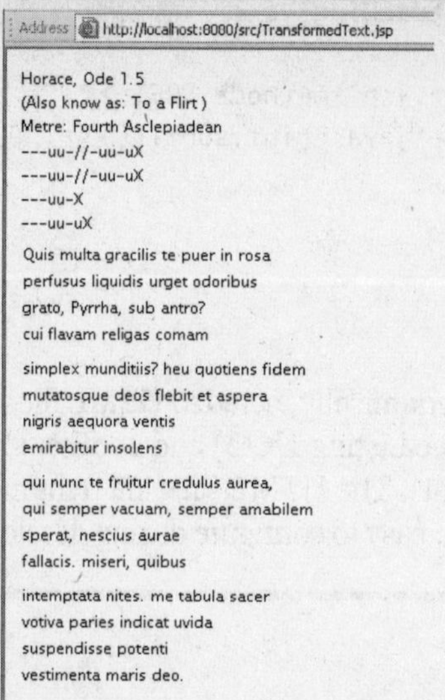

FIGURE 13.9: Horace1.5.xml filtered through the LatinTeacher XSL stylesheet

From applying the LatinStudent.xsl template to the Horace.1.5.xml file, we get the display shown in Figure 13.10.

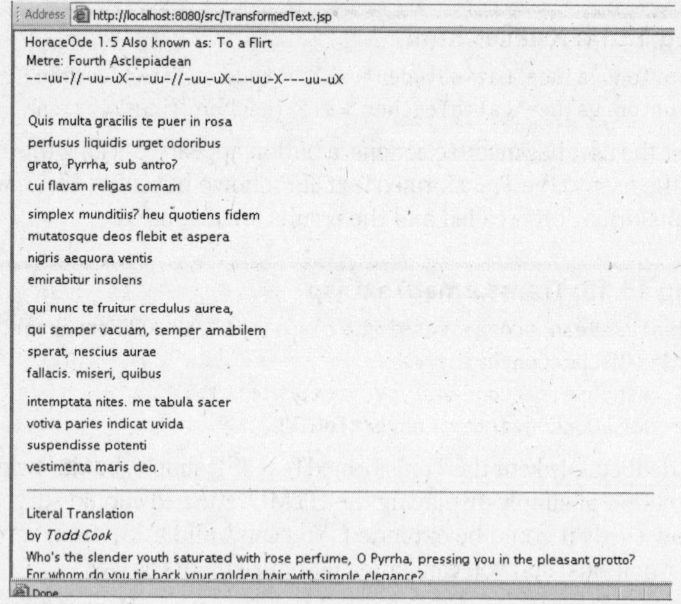

Address http://localhost:8080/src/TransformedText.jsp
HoraceOde 1.5 Also known as: To a Flirt
Metre: Fourth Asclepiadean
---uu-//-uu-uX---uu-//-uu-uX---uu-X---uu-uX
Quis multa gracilis te puer in rosa
perfusus liquidis urget odoribus
grato, Pyrrha, sub antro?
cui flavam religas comam
simplex munditiis? heu quotiens fidem
mutatosque deos flebit et aspera
nigris aequora ventis
emirabitur insolens
qui nunc te fruitur credulus aurea,
qui semper vacuam, semper amabilem
sperat, nescius aurae
fallacis. miseri, quibus
intemptata nites. me tabula sacer
votiva paries indicat uvida
suspendisse potenti
vestimenta maris deo.
Literal Translation
by Todd Cook
Who's the slender youth saturated with rose perfume, O Pyrrha, pressing you in the pleasant grotto?
For whom do you tie back your golden hair with simple elegance?
Done

FIGURE 13.10: Horace1.5.xml filtered through the LatinStudent XSL stylesheet

The client-side source contains only the elements specified, which saves networking bandwidth, hides sections, and prevents the outside world from knowing the internal details of the XML file's data layout.

If you examine the generated web page's source, shown in Listing 13.16, you will find that the XHTML tags for a line break <br/> have been reformatted to fit the old HTML tag, simply <br>.

Listing 13.16: Client-Side Source Generated by LatinStudent.xls and Horace.1.11.xml

```
<HTML>
<HEAD>
<META http-equiv="Content-Type"
 content="text/html; charset=UTF-8">
<TITLE>Latin Student Viewing -
     Seize the Day</TITLE>
</HEAD>
<BODY>HoraceOde 1.11 Also known as:
   Seize the Day<br>
<table width="600" cellspacing="0">
<tr>
<td>
   Meter: Fifth or Greater Asclepiadean
   <br>---uu-//-uu-//-uu-uX<br>
</td>
</tr>
</table>
<table width="600">
<tr>
<td></td>
</tr>
<tr>
<td>
Tu ne quaesieris--scire nefas--quem mihi, quem tibi
</td>
</tr>
<tr>
<td>
finem di dederint, Leuconoe, nec Babylonios
</td>
</tr>
<tr>
```

```
<td>
temptaris numeros. ut melius, quidquid erit, pati.
</td>
</tr>
<tr>
<td>
seu pluris hiemes seu tribuit Iuppiter ultimam,
</td>
</tr>
<tr>
<td>
quae nunc oppositis debilitat pumicibus mare
</td>
</tr>
<tr>
<td>
Tyrrhenum: sapias, vina liques et spatio brevi
</td>
</tr>
<tr>
<td>
spem longam reseces. dum loquimur, fugerit invida
</td>
</tr>
<tr>
<td>
aetas: carpe diem quam minimum credula postero.
</td>
</tr>
<tr>
<td></td>
</tr>
<tr>
<td>
<hr>
</td>
</tr>
<tr>
<td>Literal Translation<br>
</td>
```

```
</tr>
<tr>
<td>
   by <i>Todd Cook</i></td>
</tr>
<tr>
<td>
You shouldn't desire--it's forbidden to know--the
 ends that the gods have determined for me and you,
 Leuconoe.  Don't let Babylonian astrology tempt you;
 whatever your future will be, it's better to endure
 it with patience.  Whether or not Jupiter allots only
 one more winter, or sends many more to wear
 down the Tuscan cliffs to ocean sand, be wise,
 drink the best of your wine, and prune back hopes
 for a long life to the brief span we have.  While
 we've been chatting, jealous time will have already
 fled: seize the day, trust as little as possible to
 tomorrow.
</td>
</tr>
<br>
</table>
</BODY>
</HTML>
```

The effect is completely transparent: Neither the end user nor the browser can tell that the resulting file was generated from an XML file.

Improving the XSL-XML Transformation Application

This chapter's application shows a skeletal implementation of the XSL-XML transformation and highlights a design that you can customize just by adding more XML and XSL files, and by changing the dynamically included combo box HTML files, namely `XmlFiles.html` and `XslFiles.html`. The current design might be inefficient for a large-scale implementation, unless some sort of cacheing mechanism were added.

OPTIMAL CACHEING: A QUESTION OF ALGORITHMS

Cacheing is often touted as an excellent way to improve scalability. Cacheing can make a big difference, but it's not a panacea. You can improve your chances for success by answering the following questions:

- How much memory do you have?
- How often are the objects needed?
- How much time is saved by the cacheing?

You can determine the available memory with a system call, but to properly scope things out, you must know what other demands applications and the system can periodically make; otherwise, you'll have to make occasional system calls to ensure that the cacheing function isn't becoming a resource hog.

How often the objects are needed is tied to the question of how much time it takes to generate the required object. Although it's tempting to save every object in memory, don't forget that operating system will often page swap memory to disk, even if the system just temporarily needs more memory to function. Remember, disk access is usually about ten times slower than memory access. Obviously, if it takes almost as much time to generate the object as it takes to retrieve it from disk, there is little merit in implementing and maintaining the cacheing mechanism.

If the objects can be updated and changed, and further requests need to reflect the new object state, it's probably better to use a database to control the cacheing, transaction, and update mechanisms.

Extending the XML-XSL Application

You can extend and improve this application in several ways. You can store the XML files as character data in a database, or you can break them up according to their tags so that the files are cross-searchable. You can then modify the files and reflect the changes. You can easily write a set of supporting pages that do the following:

- Allow students to submit and revise their translations.
- Allow teachers to view progress and compare.
- Allow students to vote on the best translation.
- Display a photo of the winner of the contest.

All these pages can be represented as essentially different views of the document and its data.

Data Migration Using XML/XSL

Because JSP and database application development are often closely allied, you can expect many exciting changes in database programming because of the flexibility of XML. Database designers and programmers have a great need to keep track of data types to maintain integrity and seamless functioning. Their needs were instrumental in adding XML schemas to the XML specification.

You can use XML schemas to specify data types and validation rules for XML elements, and you can write XSL templates that transform the data in XML files. A carefully architected system will reuse common templates, and use templates as insulating buffers in handling the data between applications.

What's Next

The Web has been described as the greatest library in the world, with all the books dumped on the floor. A large part of the problem was that HTML documents were organized and distributed without any foresight as to how to order and structure the data in the documents. Not only was the hierarchy flattened, but the identifications were smeared away into just visual labels. No wonder search engines had such difficulties, and still today they must churn constantly through web pages in an effort to uncover the invisible hierarchy of the web and the content of its pages.

XML has the potential to bring order to the chaos of the web by bundling the data definitions with the presentation of the data, which allows for easy transformations. For document authors and businesses, XML can save countless hours by enabling the smooth transformation of information from one format to another.

You can use XSL to script the transformation of XML to HTML. You should see this as just the beginning of the possibilities, for XSL can be used to transform XML into different XML documents. Your data can remain pliable, and you can work on adapting the data to many applications.

The next three chapters will explore how to use XML for messaging between enterprise applications. The next chapter will explore various existing XML messaging solutions. The following two chapters will focus on the SOAP protocol.

Chapter 14

Understanding XML Messaging

To understand why people are so excited about XML-based messaging, you must first consider the general state of messaging mechanisms in the network-connected world of distributed computing. After a review of various communication architectures, this chapter takes a look at the early history of messaging developments leading up to SOAP (Simple Object Access Protocol). Keeping track of all of the different players in this game is difficult, so the most significant initiatives will be discussed.

Featured in this chapter:

- Messaging essentials
- Message-oriented Java APIs
- Java and XML
- The XML predecessors of SOAP

Adapted from *SOAP Programming with Java™*
by Bill Brogden

ISBN 0-7821-2928-5 $49.99

MESSAGING ARCHITECTURES

The major distinctions you have to draw on when discussing the exchange of messages between communicating entities have to do with addressing and immediacy. With a point-to-point design, the creator of a message addresses it to exactly one recipient. With a publish/subscribe design, the creator sends the message to a third-party server. The recipients, who are subscribers to this particular kind of message, copy it from the server; therefore, the recipients in a publish/subscribe architecture are identified by their interest in a particular topic, not by their address. Figure 14.1 illustrates these different architectures.

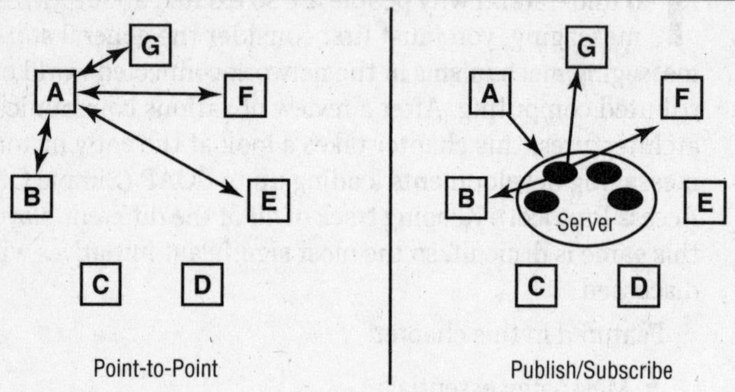

FIGURE 14.1: Point-to-point versus publish/subscribe

Immediacy has to do with the time relationship between sender and recipient. If the sender waits for an immediate response, it is a synchronous relationship. For example, in TCP/IP, the base protocol of the Internet, every message is acknowledged so that sender and recipient are synchronized. In a synchronous relationship, if the sender is waiting for an acknowledgement and none is sent, the communication has failed.

In contrast, in an asynchronous relationship, the sender transmits the message without expecting an immediate response. This provides much greater flexibility because the receiving agent can pick up the message when processing power is available. Furthermore, the system does not fail if the receiving agent is temporarily off the network. The drawback is that now the entire system depends on the server.

The Mental Shift

For many programmers, changing from an architecture in which you can expect an immediate response to calling a function to an asynchronous system requires a major mental shift. This shift is comparable to that required on going from a strictly procedural and single-threaded program to the event-oriented and multithreaded programs found on modern desktop systems and web servers.

Sometimes it just doesn't seem right that a collection of processes exchanging asynchronous messages whenever they feel like it can be as fast and as powerful as a system built around immediate response to requests. The contrast is as strong as that between "free market" and "command" economies.

You can expect to encounter this brand of computing more and more as you work with distributed objects. Many software architects feel that this is the only way to build resilient and failsafe systems. For a mind-bending example, consider the Jini and JavaSpaces technology for distributed systems that Sun is promoting:

```
http://java.sun.com/products/javaspaces/
```

The Spectrum of Complexity

Messaging has a spectrum of complexity ranging from simple message passing to creating and operating on remote objects. At the simple end of the spectrum, the treatment of the message is defined by the protocol in use. For example, with e-mail, the Multipurpose Internet Mail Extensions (MIME) protocol defines the treatment of the message content.

At the complex end of the spectrum, the protocol simply ensures delivery of the message. The receiving party must interpret the message content in terms of objects, methods, resources, and sequence of operations. It is at this complex end of the messaging spectrum that SOAP operates.

The Pioneer: EDI

Until relatively recently, the great bulk of electronic messages didn't go through the Internet at all, but rather through private networks. In spite of the fact that the format for this Electronic Data Interchange (EDI) of messages is highly industry-specific and not particularly flexible, it is still the primary means of business-to-business (B2B) data exchange. Before the rise of the Internet, communication took place on expensive leased lines or private networks. Now it is much cheaper to create a virtual private network (VPN) by sending encrypted data over the Internet, but the underlying messages still use EDI coding.

There are many industries that have an extensive investment in EDI and are going to be slow to change to Internet-based web services. Examples include hospitals, banks, and insurance companies; however, the advantages to be gained in terms of greater flexibility and lower communication costs appear to make it inevitable that even these industries will have to replace existing EDI applications.

Messaging Systems as Applications

Recent years have seen the rise of major applications for the enterprise that can be called Message-Oriented Middleware (MOM) applications. The Lotus company was one of the first to recognize that unifying the data communications for an enterprise could yield significant benefits and command a premium price. The success of the Lotus Notes application verified that corporations realized the benefits that could stem from this unification.

As the communication channels used by enterprises have expanded to include e-mail, websites, fax, voice mail, the short message service on cellular phones, personal digital assistants, and the wireless Internet, the scope of messaging systems has expanded to keep up. Lotus now talks in terms of *Unified Messaging* to encompass all of these channels.

The way in which the information resources of an organization are viewed has shifted from emphasis on the giant mainframe database to emphasis on information flow within the organization, with customers, with suppliers, and with the public. It is widely anticipated that the value of B2B transactions on the Internet will continue to exceed the value of consumer transactions.

Java Message Service

Just as JDBC (Java Database Connectivity) has become the standard interface for communication between Java programs and SQL databases, Sun hopes to make Java Message Service (JMS) the standard interface between Java programs and commercial messaging systems. The JMS package provides abstractions for message creation and delivery systems and encoding for simple data types.

Although JMS defines several types of message, an XML type is not currently one of these types; therefore, vendors of JMS-compliant messaging systems have to provide XML as a proprietary type. In view of the rapid rise in importance of SOAP it seems a safe bet that an XML type will be in the JMS package soon. See Chapter 17 for more information on JMS.

Directory Systems

An essential part of messaging systems are directories that let a potential client program locate the correct way to address a service. Getting these directory services right is not a trivial task.

The Java Naming and Directory Interface (JNDI) is a standard Java language extension that provides a standard interface for addressing a variety of different directory and naming systems, such as Novell NetWare NDS, CORBA Naming Service, and JMS services. See Chapter 8 for more information on JNDI.

As the number of web services increases rapidly, just finding the kind of service you need requires more and more effort. A number of initiatives to create these super directory services have been undertaken. For example, IBM, Microsoft, and Sun are involved with establishing the Universal Description, Discovery, and Integration (UDDI) standard.

The objective of UDDI (see `www.uddi.org`) is to create a sort of web-based, universal, Yellow Pages-type directory for companies, which publishes the existence of web services in a single registry to promote business networking. UDDI represents one of the earliest uses of SOAP protocols.

After you have located a service, you have to determine how that service wants to see requests formatted and how it will return results. It appears that the standard for accomplishing this will be Web Services Description Language (WSDL). Using XML formatting, a WSDL document provides all of the information needed to send a message to a SOAP-based web service and interpret the reply.

Communicating Objects

The most important of the non-XML based schemes for message passing and remote procedure calls are CORBA and DCOM. Before looking at these schemes, some important terms need to be defined:

Interface Definition Language (IDL) The language used to specify the interface an object uses to communicate with the outside world.

Marshalling The process of turning the structure of a program object into a stream of bytes is called marshalling.

Serializing Another term for marshalling.

Unmarshalling The process of turning a stream of bytes back into the original object structure.

Deserializing Another term for unmarshalling.

Encoding Turning data items into a form that can be transmitted by a particular protocol. For example, to include the binary data that makes up an image in an XML message, the bytes must be encoded as characters compatible with XML tags.

Another Pioneer: CORBA

A pioneering effort to get reliable communication of objects between disparate systems was the Common Object Request Broker Architecture (CORBA). The Object Management Group (OMG; see `www.omg.org`) was set up to create a protocol capable of providing communication between objects on completely different operating systems and written in different languages. An Object Request Broker (ORB) provides the interface needed for a client program to talk to a remote object.

Because the initial CORBA specification was released in 1992, it has had quite a long time for refinement compared to other technologies. Many software vendors produce CORBA-compliant products. In spite of–or perhaps because of–its maturity, CORBA is considered a difficult programming technology to master.

The OMG created a standard Interface Definition Language (IDL) that permits definition of an object's interface in a language-independent fashion. OMG also created a protocol–Internet Inter-ORB Protocol (IIOP)–for message communication over the Internet. The OMG is currently working on creating a SOAP-CORBA interface standard. See Chapter 19 for more information on CORBA.

The Component Object Model

The Component Object Model (COM) is a Microsoft specification for integrating components within an application. This communication is low-level, but can allow components written in different languages to interact. Distributed COM (DCOM) is a more recent development that allows components to interact over a network. The form of interaction is essentially a remote procedure call similar to Remote Method Invocation (RMI) in Java.

COM and DCOM are considered mature technologies because COM has been around since 1995. The specifications for COM and DCOM have been turned over to the Open Group for standardization efforts. Although Microsoft Windows systems are the primary users of DCOM, there is no reason it could not be extended to use on other operating systems.

Remote Method Invocation

In Java, the RMI provides the simplest approach to communication between objects in distributed systems. Added to the standard Java library in JDK 1.1, and subsequently enhanced, RMI is the core technology for Java object to Java object communication.

The RMI classes allow programmers to treat a remote object as if it resides within the local application. All a programmer has to do is determine the public interface to be exposed by the remote object. The `rmic` utility program examines the interface and creates classes called the *stub* and *skeleton* classes.

The resulting architecture is shown in Figure 14.2. On the server side, the server application registers the interface with the `rmiregistry` and waits for a connection. A client application uses the `rmiregistry`, that lives on the network at a standard port, to obtain an instance of the stub class that implements the desired interface. Calls made to the stub class instance behave as if the remote object is in the local JVM address space.

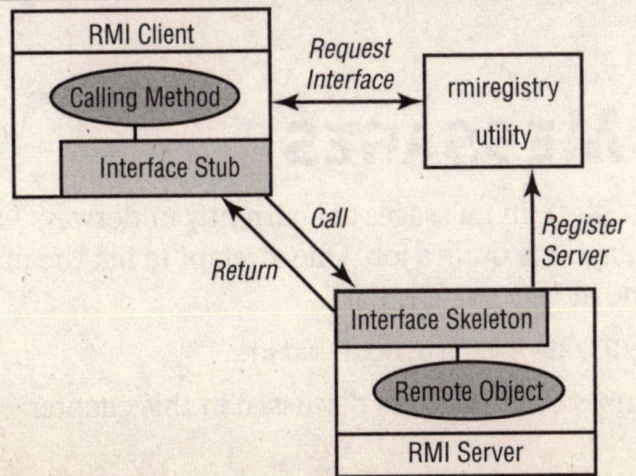

FIGURE 14.2: Architecture of Java Remote Method Invocation

The details of serializing objects, deserializing objects, and socket communication between systems are handled by the stub and skeleton classes. These classes use standard Java serialization techniques. Errors on the server side are signaled to the client by `RemoteException` objects that behave just like an exception thrown on the local system.

Advantages and Disadvantages of RMI

The most obvious advantages of Java RMI are ease of use and complete compatibility of data types. For programmers, all details of serialization and communication are taken care of by the RMI classes. As long as an object is serializable, it can be used in a call to a remote object method. For these reasons, RMI is the essential technology for all-Java distributed applications.

RMI has some disadvantages as well. Naturally, it can be used only between a Java client and a Java server. Furthermore, both sides of the communication link must have access to matching class files. Another disadvantage is that the ports used are likely to be blocked by firewalls and proxy servers. For these reasons, RMI is most successful within intranets. See Chapter 18 for more information on RMI.

RMI and IIOP

For the Java 2 Platform, Sun created tools capable of bridging the gap between Java RMI objects and CORBA-compliant objects written in other languages. If you have to communicate with remote objects in legacy systems, this standard extension may be your best choice. The RMI-IIOP package comes standard with the JDK 1.3 and subsequent versions of Java.

XML-Based Messages

Many initiatives to use XML in messages are currently underway. Just keeping track of the players is quite a job. One attempt to list the major initiatives can be found at:

`www.w3.org/2000/03/29-XML-protocol-matrix`

Table 14.1 summarizes the initiatives discussed in this chapter.

TABLE 14.1: Summary of XML Messaging and Related Technology Initiatives

Acronym	Organization	Status	Comments
XML-RPC	UserLand	In use with many languages	XML Remote Procedure Call is a system for transmission of messages and remote procedure calls with HTTP and XML. This is the direct ancestor of SOAP.
JAXM	Sun	In early release	Java API for XML Messaging, based on the ebXML project.
SOAP	Microsoft, IBM, UserLand, DevelopMentor	Version 1.1	Simple Object Access Protocol is a system for transmission of messages and remote procedure calls and a more complex extension of XML-RPC.
WDDX	Allaire	In use since 1998	Web Distributed Data Exchange is a lightweight, XML-based data exchange technology.
RSS	O'Reilly	In active use	Rich Site Summary is a system for syndication of site content.
EbXML	OASIS, Sun, UN/CEFACT	Standard is available	Electronic Business XML is a complex set of specifications designed to enable a global electronic marketplace with XML. SOAP will be used as the messaging protocol. Due to backing by OASIS and UN/CEFACT, this is likely to become a widely used standard in competition with BizTalk.
BizTalk	Microsoft	Available	A set of XML schema standards for business-to-business communication that is simpler than ebXML.
XAML	Bowstreet, HP, IBM, Oracle, and Sun	Proposed	Transaction Authority Markup Language is a system to define business transactions.
WSDL	IBM, Microsoft	Available	Web Services Description Language is a system for describing the interface and protocols used by a web service.

TABLE 14.1 continued: Summary of XML Messaging and Related Technology Initiatives

Acronym	Organization	Status	Comments
UDDI	IBM, Microsoft, Sun	Available	A web-based, universal, Yellow Pages–type directory for companies that enter their web services in a single directory.
XML encoding for SMS	W3C initiative	In draft	XML for Short Message Services is a message service used in mobile phone networks.

The Forerunner to SOAP: XML-RPC

The XML-RPC protocol was invented by Dave Winer at UserLand in 1998, and first implemented in the Frontier web server. It sends a remote procedure call using an HTTP POST request with XML 1 encoding. Using the widely supported HTTP protocol makes it possible to add XML-RPC processing to any web server that supports CGI (Common Gateway Interface) programming. Furthermore, using this standard protocol allows penetration of typical firewalls, making it easy to install an XML-RPC server without compromising security.

XML-RPC hits a happy balance between power and complexity, using a simple solution that is easy to program yet can transmit many kinds of data. The original SOAP proposal was based largely on XML-RPC.

Although SOAP has extended XML-RPC, this simpler approach is easier to implement and is still generating a lot of activity. It is by no means certain that XML-RPC will be replaced by SOAP. The home page at the `www.xmlrpc.com` website lists pointers to many implementations of the protocol in many languages. An example usage is retrieval of RSS (Rich Site Summary) data.

XML-RPC messages are sent with an HTML POST header and a content type of `text/xml`. XML encoding follows version 1 and does not use a DTD or namespaces. Listing 14.1 shows a request to a hypothetical lookup service.

Listing 14.1: An Example XML-RPC Request

```
POST /RPC2 HTTP/1.0
User-Agent: Frontier/5.1.2 (WinNT)
```

```
Host: someserver.com
Content-Type: text/xml
Content-length: 181

<?xml version="1.0"?>
<methodCall>
  <methodName>lookup.getStateFromAreaCode</methodName>
   <params>
      <param> <value><int>512</int></value>
      </param>
   </params>
</methodCall>
```

The data contained in the <methodName> tag is quite flexible; it could name a Java class and method, a Perl script file to be executed, or any other resource. The order of the <param> tags inside the <params> must be consistent with the method being called.

The response format is also simple, as shown in Listing 14.2. Only a single <param> is returned if the call succeeds, but because this can be a collection of values, this limitation is not serious. If an error resulted from the attempt, the <methodResponse> will contain a <fault> tag giving both an error code and a text representation of the problem.

Listing 14.2: An Example of a Response to the Request

```
HTTP/1.1 200 OK
Connection: close
Content-Length: 158
Content-Type: text/xml
Date: Fri, 17 Jan 2001 11:50:13 GMT
Server: UserLand Frontier/5.1.2-WinNT
<?xml version="1.0"?>
<methodResponse>
   <params>
      <param> <value><string>Texas</string></value>
   </param> </params>
</methodResponse>
```

Data types supported by XML-RPC are quite compatible with Java. The <int> data type is a 32-bit (4-byte) signed integer exactly corresponding to Java `int` values. Table 14.2 summarizes the allowed data types.

TABLE 14.2: XML-RPC Data Types

XML-RPC Data Tag	Corresponding Java Data Type
<int> or <i4>	`Int`
<boolean>	`boolean`
<string>	`java.lang.String`
<double>	`Double`
<dateTime.iso8601>	`java.util.Date`
<struct>	`java.util.Hashtable`
<array>	`java.util.Vector`
<base64>	`byte array`
<nil/>	`Null`

The `<struct>` and `<array>` types can be nested so you can build complex structures. Because the request and response message must be parsed by XML parsers that have obvious restrictions on characters, arbitrary binary data must be encoded in a base64 character stream.

The Major Players

As you have seen, there is a lot of activity in the area of XML messages and network communication. Here is a summary of the organizations that will most likely play the most significant part in the ongoing revolution:

Apache A nonprofit organization devoted to the development of open-source software. Apache has a number of projects related to Java, XML, and SOAP. Several of these projects use code contributed by IBM and Sun. Due to the very widespread use of the Apache web server, this organization has credibility in spite of a loose organization.

Microsoft Codevelopers of UDDI, WSDL, and SOAP. Creators of the BizTalk messaging standard and .NET Web services based on XML and SOAP. Microsoft has committed to extensive use of XML in future products. Microsoft provides many XML- and SOAP-related tools, but these are not written in Java due to Microsoft's long-running lawsuits with Sun.

Sun Developer and custodian of the Java language, active participant in XML, ebXML, and promoting web services. Intends to use the Apache version of SOAP as a lightweight messaging system in web services.

IBM Committed to the use of Java and XML, developing many XML applications, contributed the SOAP4J code to the Apache organization to serve as the basis for Apache SOAP.

Oracle The major supplier of database systems for Internet applications, Oracle provides extensive facilities for using XML in connection with database operations, including support for SOAP.

OASIS The Organization for the Advancement of Structured Information Standards is a nonprofit international organization dedicated to creation of public standards, heavily involved with ebXML.

UN/CEFACT The United Nations Centre for Trade Facilitation and Electronic Business is heavily involved with coordinating the acceptance of business communication standards all over the world.

W3C The World Wide Web Consortium creates recommendations for standards such as XML, XSL, SOAP, and many other protocols. Widely accepted as the authority in spite of not having governmental status.

WHAT'S NEXT?

This chapter has explored the different technologies and approaches for remote messaging and how XML could be useful in this arena. The next chapter will build on this background of XML based messaging, to discuss the current state of one of the most hyped technologies in recent memory, SOAP. Because final standards for SOAP are likely to be defined by the XML Protocol working group of the W3C, the approach this group is taking is emphasized.

Chapter 15

A Survey of SOAP

With the background of XML-based messaging in Java established in Chapter 14, "Understanding XML Messaging," we move on to the current state of the SOAP standard. What you'll find is that although the basic *documentation* of SOAP version 1.1 is widely accepted, it does not constitute a standard. The first task of this chapter is to survey the status of SOAP as it evolves into a potential standard. From there, it examines the basic components of SOAP messages and some important SOAP-related developments.

Featured in this chapter:

- How SOAP got started
- Who determines the standard
- What's in a SOAP message?
- How SOAP handles attachments
- Where WSDL and UDDI fit in

Adapted from *SOAP Programming with Java*™
by Bill Brogden

ISBN 0-7821-2928-5 $49.99

The Status of SOAP

As of this writing, the nearest thing to a standard is the W3C Note dated May 8, 2000, entitled "Simple Object Access Protocol (SOAP) 1.1." This document was created by a group of authors from organizations involved in the Internet. The authors and their sponsoring organizations are as follows (in alphabetical order):

- Don Box, DevelopMentor
- David Ehnebuske, IBM
- Gopal Kakivaya, Microsoft
- Andrew Layman, Microsoft
- Noah Mendelsohn, Lotus Development Corp.
- Henrik Frystyk Nielsen, Microsoft
- Satish Thatte, Microsoft
- Dave Winer, UserLand Software, Inc.

The full text of the original note can be found on the Web at:

```
http://www.w3.org/TR/2000/NOTE-SOAP-20000508
```

A proposed extension to the original note, called "SOAP Messages with Attachments," was submitted to the W3C in December 2000. This proposal provides a way for a SOAP 1.1 message to be carried inside a MIME (Multipurpose Internet Mail Extensions) multipart message. The purpose of this proposal was to provide a way to transmit a SOAP message with a variety of additional data as attachments. The full text of this note can be found at:

```
http://www.w3.org/SOAP
```

As notes, these documents have no real force. They are intended to serve as a basis for the formation of a working group in the area of XML-based protocols. The Apache, IBM, and Microsoft groups working on SOAP implementations, however, appear to be sticking to the frameworks outlined in the notes. Any more widely recognized standard will probably have to come from the activities of the W3C XML Protocol Working Group.

XML Protocol Working Group

In recognition of the widespread interest in using XML for messaging and remote procedure calls over the World Wide Web, the W3C created an XP working group in September 2000. This group includes members from all the major organizations interested in using the Web for this purpose, as well as many smaller organizations. The original plan was that a recommendation would be released in September 2001, and the working group would be terminated in April 2002; however, many questions have arisen, and as of this writing, the group is still working on drafts. The XML Protocol working group home page can be found at:

```
http://www.w3.org/2000/xp/Group/
```

The approach that the XP working group is taking is to create a *requirements document* and then evaluate the SOAP 1.1 design versus these requirements. Where SOAP is found deficient, improved solutions will be recommended. The current draft of the requirements document can be found at the working group home page.

Scope of the XP Working Group

In establishing the charter of the XP working group, the W3C recognized that a very large number of other XML- and HTTP-related standardization efforts are ongoing. The working group is expected to confine itself to the design of the following components of an XML-based messaging protocol:

Envelope The protocol must provide a structure that can enclose all other components for transport. The method chosen must allow for interoperation between system and extensibility. It must also allow for transfer of the message between intermediaries (that is, store and forward, and so on).

Data encoding The protocol must define a mechanism to represent a variety of data types, including complex objects. This mechanism must be based on the XML Schema recommendations.

RPC convention The protocol must provide a convention for representation of a remote procedure call (RPC) in the body of the message.

HTTP transport The working group will develop a mechanism for transport of XP messages using HTTP.

In addition to designing these components, the working group is expected to give the following requirements a high priority:

Simplicity To keep the protocol easy to understand, easy to implement, and easy to evolve, the working group is expected to strive for simplicity.

Evolvability and extensibility The protocol must provide a design that permits extensions that do not interfere with each other.

This is rather a tall order. In recognition of this fact, the working group charter also lists areas that XP groups should not address or should consider a low priority. These are areas that are being tackled by other industry groups or are considered too complex to tackle in the time available:

Binary data Although XML provides a handy representation of many languages that can be expressed in text, exactly how to support binary data is better addressed by other groups.

Compact encoding and compression It is one of the design principles of XML that terseness is of minor importance. An XML representation is frequently many times larger than the basic data it marks up. Unfortunately, many potential areas of application for XP, such as wireless devices, are bandwidth sensitive. To keep things simple, compression techniques are outside the scope of the working group.

Additional transport mechanisms The XP working group is expected to focus on HTTP as a transport mechanism and only consider others if time is available.

Metadata descriptions of services It is envisioned that web services using XP will be advertising their availability with some sort of metadata description. It is recognized that other groups are creating these services, such as WSDL (Web Services Description Language).

Relation of XP to Other Standards

Because there are so many activities related to XML going on in the W3C and other organizations, the XP working group specifically recognizes that other developing standards may impact the final recommendations.

In particular, the XML Schema and XML Linking working groups are clearly important. Fortunately, these specifications are closer to a final recommendation than the XP specifications. The XML Schema standard is particularly important because it is the basis for the standard methods of encoding various data types in SOAP messages.

There is a good deal of cross-fertilization between the XP working group and other groups working on various XML and messaging APIs, such as ebXML and Sun's JAXM project.

Other Standards Organizations

The Internet Engineering Task Force (IETF) has activities related to message transport and XML digital signatures that are expected to be relevant to SOAP. IETF activities are summarized at `www.ietf.org`.

The Components of SOAP 1.1

This discussion will closely follow the approach used to define SOAP in the original note. The basic features of the SOAP specification can be divided into three areas:

Envelope The protocol provides a structure (envelope) that defines what is in a message, directs the message to a specific recipient, and defines whether it is optional or mandatory.

Data encoding The protocol defines a serialization mechanism to represent a variety of application data types.

RPC convention The protocol defines a convention for representation of remote procedure calls and responses.

The intent of this three-part specification is to allow for maximum flexibility in implementation of each part with minimum interference with other parts. For example, the way an envelope is implemented should have no impact on the data encoding convention.

In addition to the three points just described (which define a message), a messaging system needs a *transmission method*. Although the initial examples of SOAP followed the XML-RPC path and used HTTP transmission, alternate methods of message transmission are not ruled out by the specification. The main alternatives that developers have been exploring are SMTP and Java Message Service (JMS).

Implementing SOAP in Java

The Apache implementation of SOAP in Java is organized along the same lines as the organization of a SOAP message; therefore, there is an `org. apache.soap.Envelope` class that implements the methods needed to define an envelope. The major elements possible inside an envelope are the Header, Body, and Fault—each element is represented by a class in the `org.apache.soap` package.

Sun's Java API for XML Messaging (JAXM) also follows the same general approach, with classes in the `javax.xml.soap` package for Header and Body. It is pretty clear, however, that it won't be possible to mix and match classes between the implementations. Changing an application from one implementation to another will be a serious undertaking.

Things Left Out of SOAP

As discussed in Chapter 14, messaging systems can get pretty complicated. The XML-RPC protocol, which served as the starting point for SOAP, is one of the simplest messaging technologies around. Although SOAP adds complexity, the designers intentionally left out some features that appear in other object-oriented messaging systems.

SOAP does not attempt to provide for distributed control of object creation, object activation, or garbage collection. SOAP also does not attempt to provide for bidirectional communication. The original SOAP 1.1 proposal does not attempt to provide for flexible attachments to SOAP messages, but this has been addressed in the "SOAP Messages with Attachments" note.

The original proposal also considers a single SOAP message at a time. Any protocol for transmission of collections of messages would have to be provided by modification of the 1.1 version of the standard.

SOAP and Namespaces

Let's look at the actual messages created in an example remote procedure call. Listing 15.1 and Listing 15.2 show the messages transmitted between client and server in the address book example provided in the 2 Apache SOAP distribution of August 2000. The server is Tomcat version 3.2, and the client is the `GetAddress` in the `samples.addressbook` package.

Listing 15.1: Transmission of an RPC Message by HTTP

```
POST /xml-soap/servlet/rpcrouter HTTP/1.0
Host: localhost:9000
Content-Type: text/xml
Content-Length: 450
SOAPAction: ""

<SOAP-ENV:Envelope
   xmlns:SOAP-ENV="http://schemas.xmlsoap.org/soap/envelope/"
   xmlns:xsi="http://www.w3.org/1999/XMLSchema-instance"
   xmlns:xsd="http://www.w3.org/1999/XMLSchema">
<SOAP-ENV:Body>
<ns1:getAddressFromName xmlns:ns1="urn:AddressFetcher"
   SOAP-ENV:encodingStyle=
   ➥"http://schemas.xmlsoap.org/soap/encoding/">
<nameToLookup xsi:type="xsd:string">John B. Good
➥</nameToLookup>
</ns1:getAddressFromName>
</SOAP-ENV:Body>
</SOAP-ENV:Envelope>
```

The first five lines are HTTP request headers that are followed by a blank line. The meaning of these lines is discussed later in this chapter in the section "Transmission with HTTP." The `<SOAP:Envelope>` tag pair encloses the entire remaining message. The opening tag establishes three namespaces, `SOAP-ENV`, `xsi` and `xsd`:

SOAP-ENV The namespace for SOAP envelope elements

xsd The namespace for data types defined in the XML Schema standard

xsi The namespace for data types as used in a particular instance

The namespace specific to the `AddressFetcher` class is established by the first tag inside the `<SOAP-ENV:Body>` as `ns1`. Namespaces are essential to SOAP because they prevent possible confusion with respect to different applications by providing unique identifiers. Namespace declarations appear as attributes in an element, and are in force only between the opening and closing tags of that element. In Listing 15.1, the `nameToLookup` is defined to be an `xsd:string` type variable.

Part III

Unfortunately, a complete and final standardization of XML Schema has not yet been achieved as of this writing. The evolving standard is not a single document, but rather a group of interrelated documents, and there are many potential points of conflict between SOAP implementations using slightly different schema. As an example, a recent note in the Apache SOAP users mailing list described a situation in which a Microsoft server was expecting the first namespace declaration, but the Apache code expected the second:

```
xmlns:xsi="http://www.w3.org/2000/08/XMLSchema-instance"
```

```
xmlns:xsi="http://www.w3.org/1999/XMLSchema-instance"
```

Now let's look at the response from the sample application, as shown in Listing 15.2. The response headers are discussed in the "Transmission with HTTP" section. Note that the remainder of the response is entirely contained with `<SOAP-ENV:Envelope>` tags just as the request was. In the body, the tag pair named for the method called, `ns1:getAddressFromNameResponse`, completely encloses another tag pair named `return`. The `return` tag establishes a new namespace `urn:xml-soap-address-demo` and encloses the payload of returned data, each item of which is characterized by a data type such as `xsd:int` or `xsd:string`.

Listing 15.2: Response from the *getAddressFromName* Method Call

```
HTTP/1.0 200 OK
Content-Type: text/xml; charset=UTF-8
Content-Length: 902
Set-Cookie2: JSESSIONID=o51hzvqx51;Version=1;
➥Discard;Path="/xml-soap"
Set-Cookie: JSESSIONID=o51hzvqx51;Path=/xml-soap
Servlet-Engine: Tomcat Web Server/3.2.1 (JSP 1.1; Servlet 2.2;
   Java 1.2.2; Windows NT 4.0 x86; java.vendor=
   ➥Sun Microsystems Inc.)

<SOAP-ENV:Envelope
   xmlns:SOAP-ENV="http://schemas.xmlsoap.org/soap/envelope/"
   xmlns:xsi="http://www.w3.org/1999/XMLSchema-instance"
   xmlns:xsd="http://www.w3.org/1999/XMLSchema">
<SOAP-ENV:Body>
<ns1:getAddressFromNameResponse xmlns:ns1="urn:AddressFetcher"
```

```
    SOAP-ENV:encodingStyle=
    ➥"http://schemas.xmlsoap.org/soap/encoding/">
<return xmlns:ns2="urn:xml-soap-address-demo" xsi:type=
➥"ns2:address">
<phoneNumber xsi:type="ns2:phone">
<exchange xsi:type="xsd:string">456</exchange>
<areaCode xsi:type="xsd:int">123</areaCode>
<number xsi:type="xsd:string">7890</number>
</phoneNumber>
<zip xsi:type="xsd:int">12345</zip>
<streetNum xsi:type="xsd:int">123</streetNum>
<streetName xsi:type="xsd:string">Main Street</streetName>
<state xsi:type="xsd:string">NY</state>
<city xsi:type="xsd:string">Anytown</city>
</return>
</ns1:getAddressFromNameResponse>
</SOAP-ENV:Body>
</SOAP-ENV:Envelope>
```

More About Namespaces

A Uniform Resource Identifier (URI) is used to uniquely define a namespace in XML in lines such as the following from Listing 15.2:

```
<SOAP-ENV:Envelope
   xmlns:SOAP-ENV="http://schemas.xmlsoap.org/soap/envelope/"
```

This line establishes a namespace prefix of SOAP-ENV, and identifies it with the URI of `"http://schemas.xmlsoap.org/soap/envelope/"`. Note that the element is named using the prefix that is established in the attribute. This namespace prefix is in force only up to the matching closing element.

You have already noticed the similarity between namespace declarations and addresses used to locate resources on the Web; however, don't assume that there is a real addressable document at that address. There are three terms in use here:

URI (Uniform Resource Identifier) This is the most general term; the other two are subsets of URI.

URL (Uniform Resource Locator) This form is used to locate a particular resource on the Web.

URN (Uniform Resource Name) This form is used as a unique descriptor of a resource that will always be available.

The SOAP Envelope

The XML grammar rules for a SOAP Envelope are laid down in the note as follows:

- The element name is "Envelope."
- The element must be present in a SOAP message.
- The element may contain namespace declarations as well as additional attributes. If present, such additional attributes must be namespace-qualified. Similarly, the element may contain additional subelements. If present, these elements must be namespace-qualified and must follow the SOAP Body element.

The namespace for elements and attributes in the envelope is required to be like the following:

```
http://schemas.xmlsoap.org/soap/envelope/
```

Any other namespace should cause an error return. There is no provision for versioning of the envelope syntax.

The SOAP Header

The Header portion of a SOAP message is intended for use as a flexible area for extending message content. The designers envision that the Header area might be used for message routing, authentication, transaction management, or payment information. The XML grammar rules for a SOAP Header are laid down in the note as follows:

- The element name is Header.
- The element may be present in a SOAP message. If present, the element must be the first immediate child element of a SOAP Envelope element.
- The element may contain a set of header entries, each being an immediate child element of the SOAP Header element. All immediate child elements of the SOAP Header element must be namespace-qualified.

When a SOAP message passes through intermediaries on its way to the final recipient, the intermediaries may use information in the Header to control further processing of the message. If an intermediary recognizes and processes a Header element, it must strip that element out of the Header when the message is retransmitted, as shown in Figure 15.1. Elements inside the Header can have two attributes that have special importance—the `actor` and the `mustUnderstand` attributes.

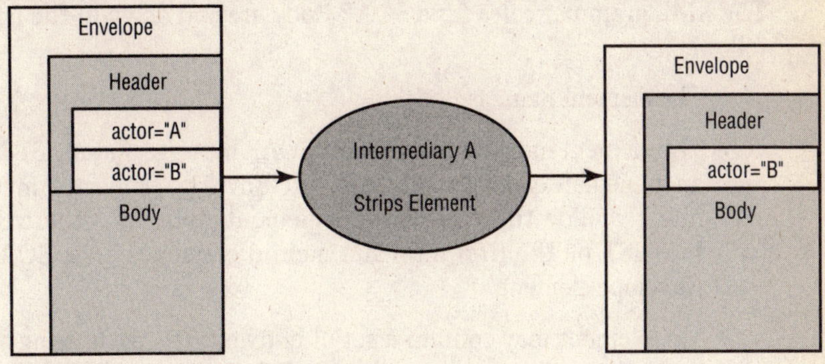

FIGURE 15.1: Processing of a message by an actor

The *actor* Attribute

The `actor` attribute designates the recipient of a particular header element. This actor processes the header element and removes it from the total SOAP header. Figure 15.1, shown earlier, suggests how intermediary actor processes perform an operation and forward the remaining headers and SOAP body.

The SOAP *mustUnderstand* Attribute

An element inside the Header may have an attribute named `mustUnderstand` that indicates whether the recipient of the message must process the element correctly or can safely ignore the element. The `mustUnderstand` attribute has numeric values of either 1, meaning true, or 0, meaning false.

If the process by an actor with a `mustUnderstand` attribute of 1 fails, a SOAP fault element must be generated as part of the return message body. The specification calls for four elements inside the fault element:

A fault code An initial set of codes is provided in the note, but it is expected that this will be expanded.

A fault string A human readable explanation.

A fault actor This designates the entity that found the fault.

A detail element This is generated only if the fault was in the body of the SOAP message.

The SOAP Body

The XML grammar rules for a SOAP Body are laid down in the note as follows:

- The element name is Body.
- The element must be present in a SOAP message and MUST be an immediate child element of a SOAP Envelope element. It must directly follow the SOAP Header element if present; otherwise it MUST be the first immediate child element of the SOAP Envelope element.
- The element may contain a set of body entries, each being an immediate child element of the SOAP Body element. Immediate child elements of the SOAP Body element may be namespace-qualified. SOAP defines the SOAP Fault element, which is used to indicate error messages.

Transmission with HTTP

Let's look again at the HTTP request headers from Listing 15.1. The first line defines this as POST type request directed to the `rpcrouter` servlet in the `xml-soap` application of the server, and using HTTP 1. The second line gives the host and port number. In this case, port 9000 is used to send the request through the `UtilSnoop` application to trap the content of both request and response. `UtilSnoop` retransmitted the request to Tomcat.

```
POST /xml-soap/servlet/rpcrouter HTTP/1.0
Host: localhost:9000
Content-Type: text/xml
Content-Length: 450
SOAPAction: ""
```

The declaration of the content type as `"text/xml"` is required for HTTP messages containing a SOAP Envelope. The `SOAPAction:` Header is required in a SOAP request message. It can be used to indicate the intent of the request, or, as in this case, an empty string indicates that the request URI indicates the intent. The SOAPAction: line can also be empty, but it must appear. The purpose of the SOAPAction: Header is to enable servers to filter and direct SOAP messages.

SOAP HTTP Responses

Let's look again at the headers in the response from Listing 15.2. The first line is the usual HTTP status code, which in this case indicates that the message was received and processed. If an error occurs while processing the request, a 500 code indicating an internal server error would appear. As with the request, the content type of "text/xml" is required.

```
HTTP/1.0 200 OK
Content-Type: text/xml; charset=UTF-8
Content-Length: 902
Set-Cookie2: JSESSIONID=o51hzvqx51;Version=1;Discard;
➥Path="/xml-soap"
Set-Cookie: JSESSIONID=o51hzvqx51;Path=/xml-soap
Servlet-Engine: Tomcat Web Server/3.2.1 (JSP 1.1; Servlet 2.2;
➥Java 1.2.2; Windows NT 4.0 x86; java.vendor=
➥Sun Microsystems Inc.)
```

The Set-Cookie lines give the session id generated for the transaction in both "original" Netscape cookie style and the RFC 2109 style (Set-Cookie2:). In an application requiring an exchange of multiple messages, this session id could serve as a unique identifier.

SOAP Messages with Attachments

The SOAP messages with attachments proposal has been published as a W3C Note at http://www.w3.org/TR/SOAP-attachments. In this scheme, the MIME multipart message format is used to bundle a complete standard SOAP message with additional data in a "SOAP message package." The SOAP message, occupying the first position in the package, can incorporate references to the other parts of the message using a naming convention described in the note. SOAP message packages can be transmitted by HTTP, SMTP, or any other message protocol.

The example given in the W3C Note will serve to demonstrate the kind of situation for which a SOAP message package could be used. This example is the submission of an insurance claim to a SOAP-enabled processing application. The basic SOAP remote procedure call message is accompanied by a TIFF format image of a signed insurance claim form. The SOAP message gives processing instructions and includes a reference to the claim form image.

WSDL, UDDI, and SOAP

Web Services Description Language (WSDL) is an XML-based markup language for describing web services such as SOAP. This system is currently under development by IBM, Microsoft, and other industry leaders. The basic idea is that a WSDL description can give enough detail to enable automated or semi-automated creation of programs to access web services such as SOAP servers.

WSDL is considered an essential part of the industry initiative called Universal Description, Discovery, and Integration (UDDI). The purpose of UDDI is to provide a way for businesses to create descriptions of available online services. If this all works out, a person trying to locate a web service to fill a particular need would be able to perform the following steps:

1. Look up potential services in a UDDI directory.
2. Use WSDL to uncover the interfaces needed to access the service.
3. Use the interface description to create SOAP messages that access the service and return the desired results.

Sun Microsystems and SOAP

As interest in SOAP as a universal XML-based messaging and remote procedure call mechanism grew during 2000, I could not help but notice that Sun Microsystems was not saying anything about it. This seemed odd because Java developers at Sun have been in the forefront of XML applications.

As discussed in Chapter 14, the main XML business messaging–related project at Sun, ebXML (electronic business XML), has received widespread acceptance. The UN/CEFACT and OASIS organizations released a finished standard for ebXML in June 2001. The main objection to the use of SOAP in this standard had been a requirement for arbitrary attachments to ebXML messages, a capability that was not present in SOAP 1.1.

The publication of the "SOAP Messages with Attachments" note by the W3C has removed this objection. As a result, OASIS and UN/CEFACT have announced that these organizations are committed to the use of SOAP as the basic standard for XML messaging in ebXML. Due to the involvement of the UN, it appears that ebXML will have international acceptance as a framework for business-to-business communication.

Java API for XML Messaging

Sun's official Java API for XML Messaging (JAXM) v1.0 supports SOAP 1.1 and the proposed SOAP with attachments standard. The current status of this project should be found at:

```
http://java.sun.com/xml/jaxm/index.html
```

The API goes beyond support for SOAP protocol messaging as used in ebXML, by defining "Messaging Profiles." SOAP 1.1 would be defined in one of these profiles, but other profiles for other messaging standards can be defined; therefore, JAXM is intended to be a generalized API capable of being used with a variety of standards for required header information. This design is similar to the way the Java API for XML Parsers (JAXP) is intended for use as a generalized approach to working with various XML parsers. The "factory" design pattern is heavily used in both APIs.

An unusual feature distinguishing JAXM from other SOAP implementations is that the JAXM is intended to work in the environment of Java 2.3 and higher servlet, or J2EE 1.3 and higher containers, not as a free-standing application. Because these use the most recent servlet APIs, JAXM will mainly be used by developers on the cutting edge of Java technology.

J2EE 1.4

Sun Microsystems's focus in moving from J2EE 1.3 to J2EE 1.4, which is due to be released in the first half of 2003, is centered around adding support for web services. J2EE 1.4 will provide the infrastructure for components that use JAX-RPC and JAXM for web services communication. The JAX-RPC v1.0 API and JAXM v1.0 API will be included as a standard part of J2EE, and will allow J2EE developers to easily use and provide web services. JAXR v1.0 API, which is analogous to JNDI for web services, will be included as a standard API in J2EE v1.4 to allow XML registries. JAXP, which standardizes Java access to SAX, DOM, and XSLT parsing, will be updated to JAXP v1.2. All of these new APIs are being integrated into the J2EE component models to allow proper integration of the J2EE technologies.

Tracking the Status of SOAP

As with many Internet-related technologies, many books on SOAP are out of date the minute they are printed. It's suggested that you check the following web resources to keep up with the changes:

```
http://soap.weblogs.com/
http://msdn.microsoft.com/soap/
http://www.w3.org/2000/xp/
http://www.w3.org/TR/
```

What's Next?

Now that the reader has been introduced to the quickly evolving development of SOAP, the next chapter will cover how to setup a SOAP application. This chapter will discuss the Apache SOAP project examples using the Tomcat server.

Chapter 16

A SOAP Server Example

To give you a feel for what goes on in a typical SOAP application, this chapter follows the installation of the Apache SOAP 2.2 package on a Tomcat server. This approach uses a servlet to process a SOAP request and generate a response. If you don't already have SOAP running on a web server, just follow along and you'll have one up and running by the end of this chapter.

Featured in this chapter:

- Setting up a SOAP server
- SOAP in a Tomcat server environment
- Additional tools you need
- Deploying your first SOAPservice
- How a SOAPservice works
- Things that may go wrong

Part III

Adapted from *SOAP Programming with Java*™
by Bill Brogden

ISBN 0-7821-2928-5 $49.99

NOTE

Because the Apache SOAP project is still evolving, some details may change between when this chapter is written and when you read this. The basics should remain the same, however, because they depend on the SOAP standard.

Using Tomcat Server

The SOAP example in this chapter uses the Tomcat v4.0 server freely available from the Apache organization. Appendix A explains how to download, install, set up, configure, and run Tomcat. Before attempting the SOAP examples, you should verify that your Tomcat installation is working correctly by running a couple of the servlet and JSP examples that come with Tomcat.

Installing a SOAP Web Application

At a minimum, the SOAP package you download from the Apache organization website at `xml.apache.org` contains some documentation, example SOAP client programs, and the `soap.war` file. If your Tomcat installation contains an earlier version of Apache SOAP, including the `soap` directory itself, you must remove all traces of that installation before proceeding.

With your Tomcat server not running, copy the `soap.war` file to the Tomcat `webapps` directory where Tomcat finds and expands it on startup. Also, modify the `server.xml` file in the `conf` directory by adding the following context information for the soap application context following the "Tomcat Root Context" entry:

```
<Context path="/soap" docBase="soap" debug="1"
➥reloadable="true">
</Context>
```

This tag establishes the web application context as follows:

path The physical directory relative to the `webapps` directory root.

docBase The relative URL the web server uses for this application.

debug Establishes a level of debugging output, with 0 being the minimum.

reloadable When true, the servlet engine checks for a new version of the servlet class file before responding to a request. If the new version exists, the old servlet is destroyed and a new object created with the new code.

Consult the Tomcat documentation files for more details on other possible parameters in a web application `Context`.

What the WAR File Installs

Now start Tomcat. When Tomcat finds that there is a WAR file that does not have a corresponding application directory, it creates a SOAP application directory and all of the required subdirectories with their resources. You should find that subdirectories named `admin`, `META-INF`, and `WEB-INF` have been created. Following the Java Servlet API requirements, all of the class files required to run the examples, and the `web.xml` file that controls the use of them, are in the WEB-INF directory.

Take a look at the `web.xml` file for the `soap` application. There are servlet name entries for `rpcrouter` and `messagerouter`. At this point, it may not be ready to run because SOAP requires other Java packages that are not normally included in the SDK distribution. What are now called "optional packages" used to be known as "standard extensions." Whatever they are called, Java has a formal Java Extension Mechanism for naming these packages and locating them where the JVM can find them.

If, for some reason, Tomcat does not automatically expand the WAR file, you can use any zip-compatible utility to expand it in the `webapps` directory. Be sure to use the option that preserves directory structure.

Additional Libraries Needed

To make full use of Apache SOAP, you must get the mail and activation library jar files:

```
http://java.sun.com/products/javamail/

http://java.sun.com/products/beans/glasgow/jaf.html
```

Because these are standard extensions, you can place `mail.jar` and `activation.jar` in the `JAVA_HOME\jre\lib\ext` directory, and they will be found automatically when you start Tomcat.

The `mail.jar` extensions implement the Java Mail API and are used when processing SOAP messages with attachments. The `activation.jar` file provides the API for the JavaBeans Activation Framework. This standard extension API provides convenient methods for dealing with arbitrary data objects.

An XML Parser Library

Naturally, you must have an XML parser library installed on your system. Until recently, conflicts between different XML parser packages have caused a lot of trouble for programmers experimenting with SOAP. SOAP requires the namespace support in DOM 2 and SAX level 2; you can get some very strange error messages if your system has an earlier parser on the classpath.

Fortunately, this type of problem has been largely alleviated by the arrival of Sun's JAXP 1.1 package, which is a standard API in JDK1.4. You can read more about the design philosophy behind it at:

```
http://java.sun.com/xml/
```

The Apache organization's Xerces parser is also compatible with the JAXP package. Consult the `xml.apache.org` website for the latest versions.

Testing the Installation

With all of these support libraries installed, it is time to test the main server classes that Apache SOAP installs. Assuming you installed Tomcat on port 8080, point your browser to:

```
http://localhost:8080/soap/servlet/rpcrouter
```

The response should be similar to the following message, indicating that the `rpcrouter` servlet is correctly installed:

```
SOAP RPC Router
Sorry, I don't speak via HTTP GET- you have to use HTTP POST
   to talk to me.
```

Likewise, if you point your browser to the following address:

```
http://localhost:8080/soap/servlet/messagerouter
```

The browser display should be similar to the following message, indicating that the `messagerouter` servlet is correctly installed:

```
SOAP Message Router
Sorry, I don't speak via HTTP GET- you have to use HTTP POST
  to talk to me.
```

The `rpcrouter` servlet is used to demonstrate remote procedure calls (RPCs), in which the output of a Java method is returned. The `messagerouter` servlet is used to demonstrate a more general approach to XML messaging.

You should also verify that the Apache SOAP administration utilities are running correctly by pointing your browser to the following address:

```
http://localhost:8080/soap/admin/index.html
```

A page giving several administration choices on the left side should be shown. These choices are as follows:

List This lists all deployed services. Clicking any item displays the properties of the service.

Deploy This displays a form called the Service Deployment Descriptor Template that you can fill in to deploy a new service.

Undeploy This displays a list of deployed services. Selecting one removes it from the system.

Deploying a Server Application

Your installation of Apache SOAP includes a `samples` directory with examples that act as clients to services dispatched by the `rpcrouter` and `messagerouter` servlets. These sample applications are run from the command line. Because the sample applications all use classes in the Apache SOAP library, you must modify your classpath to include the `soap.jar` file. Here is a command used to set the classpath for running the sample clients from the sample directories:

```
SET CLASSPATH=.;../..;path_to_soap_lib\soap.jar
```

There are two ways to deploy an Apache SOAP service: by filling in a form through the Apache administration page as just discussed, or by executing the `ServiceManagerClient` utility with the **`deploy`** command

and the name of an XML-formatted file containing the deployment information. Each of the sample directories contains .cmd (for Windows) and .sh (for Unix) files that execute the utility and deploy the sample service. Here is an example command line:

```
java org.apache.soap.server.ServiceManagerClient
   http://localhost:8080/soap/servlet/rpcrouter deploy
   DeploymentDescriptor.xml
```

The mysteries of the deployment descriptor are covered later in this chapter. For now, the AddressBook example needs to be deployed so you can actually see SOAP in action.

Deploying the *AddressBook* Service

In the soap\samples\addressbook directory is a testit.cmd file that contains a sequence of commands that deploys the AddressBook service, tests retrieval of built-in data, adds more data, tests that, and finally undeploys the service. This file is shown in Listing 16.1. Note that for presentation here, the longer lines have been wrapped.

If your server is at a different URL, be sure to change the references in the file. While logged in to the soap\samples\addressbook directory, execute the testit file from a command line and observe the results.

Listing 16.1: The *testit.cmd* File

```
@echo off
echo This test assumes a server URL of
   http://localhost:8080/soap/servlet/rpcrouter
echo Deploying the addressbook service...
java org.apache.soap.server.ServiceManagerClient
   http://localhost:8080/soap/servlet/rpcrouter deploy
   DeploymentDescriptor.xml
echo .
echo Verify that it's there
java org.apache.soap.server.ServiceManagerClient
   http://localhost:8080/soap/servlet/rpcrouter list
echo .
echo Getting info for "Mr Good"
java samples.addressbook.GetAddress
   http://localhost:8080/soap/servlet/rpcrouter "John B. Good"
```

```
echo .
echo Adding "John Doe"
java samples.addressbook.PutAddress
   http://localhost:8080/soap/servlet/rpcrouter "John Doe" 123
   "Main Street" AnyTown SS 12345 800 555 1212
echo .
echo Query "Mr Doe" to make sure it was added
java samples.addressbook.GetAddress
   http://localhost:8080/soap/servlet/rpcrouter "John Doe"
echo .
echo Adding an XML file of listings
java samples.addressbook.PutListings
   http://localhost:8080/soap/servlet/rpcrouter
   ➥sample_listings.xml
echo .
echo Get everyone!
java samples.addressbook.GetAllListings
   http://localhost:8080/soap/servlet/rpcrouter
echo .
echo Undeploy it now
java org.apache.soap.server.ServiceManagerClient
   http://localhost:8080/soap/servlet/rpcrouter undeploy
   urn:AddressFetcher
echo .
echo Verify that it's gone
java org.apache.soap.server.ServiceManagerClient
   http://localhost:8080/soap/servlet/rpcrouter list
```

If this file of commands does not run all the way through, consult the "Troubleshooting Server-Side SOAP" section later in this chapter for possible causes.

To deploy the service and leave it deployed, save a revised version of `testit.cmd` with the `undeploy` command line edited out. If you call this file `deploy.cmd` and execute it, the service will be deployed and stay resident.

Now send your browser to the administration page at:

```
http://localhost:8080/soap/admin/index.html
```

Select the list option, and you should see an entry for `urn:AddressFetcher`. Click this item to display the characteristics of this service. Figure 16.1 shows the display. Due to the length of some of the entries, you must scroll around the page.

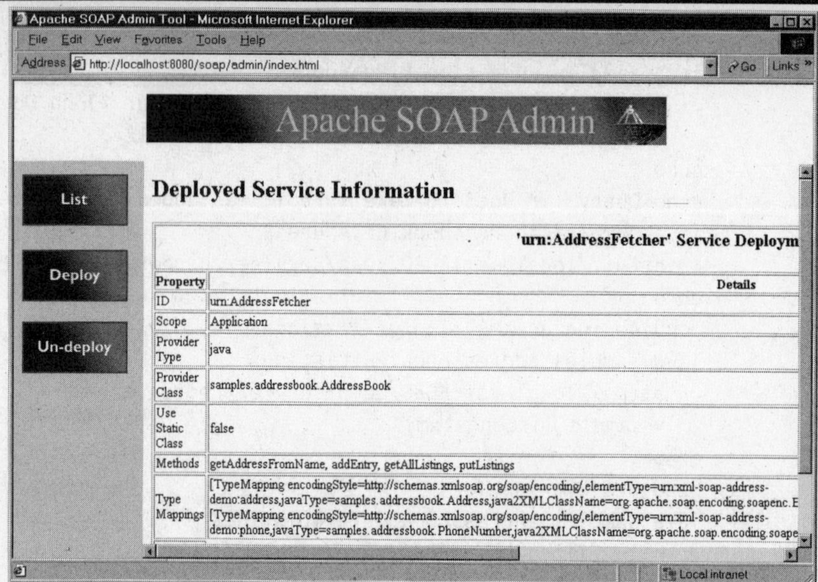

FIGURE 16.1: The Apache SOAP Admin display for the *AddressBook* service

What Deployment Created

Somewhere in the server's SOAP web application directory structure is a file that contains information on SOAP services the system is now aware of. In version 2.2 of Apache SOAP, this file is named `DeployedServices.ds`, and it contains a serialized Java `Hashtable` representing all of the current services. This mechanism may change in later versions.

The `AddressBook` service installation did not create any database of addresses; therefore, if you restart Tomcat, only the example addresses built into the code will be there. In general, SOAP has nothing to say about how services maintain their data.

Running the Address Client

Now try running one of the client classes that uses the `AddressBook` service. This assumes that you have run the revised version of `testit.cmd` with the `undeploy` command line edited out, so that the service is deployed. With Tomcat running and the CLASSPATH set as just discussed, execute the following command from the command line (the command has been word-wrapped to fit on the page, but it should all be on one line):

```
java samples.addressbook.GetAddress
   http://localhost:8080/soap/servlet/rpcrouter "John B. Good"
```

Note that because John B. Good contains spaces, the phrase must be enclosed in quotes. You should get back the example address as translated by `GetAddress`:

```
123 Main Street
Anytown, NY 12345
(123) 456-7890
```

If `GetAddress` does not execute, check your CLASSPATH setting. If you get an error message from the server, go to the "Troubleshooting Server-Side SOAP" section. If you refer to Listing 16.2, which contains the full text of the response, you can see that the `GetAddress` class had to deal with a complex SOAP message to abstract and format that address. The typical client operations are discussed in later chapters.

Now try the same query with a name that is not in the example data:

```
F:\ApacheXML\SOAP\soap-2_2\samples\addressbook>java
   samples.addressbook.GetAddress
   http://localhost:8080/soap/servlet/rpcrouter "John Doe"
```

You should receive the message:

```
I don't know.
```


How Deployment Works

Apache SOAP can get the information to deploy a service in two ways: from the online Apache SOAP Admin manager, which processes form data entered by a user, or with the `deploy` function of the `rpcrouter` servlet, which processes data sent by the `ServiceManagerClient` application. This application uses information from a deployment descriptor file such as that shown in Listing 16.2.

Listing 16.2: The Deployment Descriptor for the *AddressFetcher* Service

```
<isd:service xmlns:isd="http://xml.apache.org/xml-soap/
➥deployment"
     id="urn:AddressFetcher">
<isd:provider type="java"
```

```
    scope="Application"
    methods="getAddressFromName addEntry getAllListings
    ➥putListings">
    <isd:java class="samples.addressbook.AddressBook"
    ➥static="false"/>
  </isd:provider>
  <isd:faultListener>org.apache.soap.server.DOMFaultListener
  </isd:faultListener>

  <isd:mappings>
    <isd:map encodingStyle=
       "http://schemas.xmlsoap.org/soap/encoding/"
       xmlns:x="urn:xml-soap-address-demo" qname="x:address"
       javaType="samples.addressbook.Address"
       java2XMLClassName=
         "org.apache.soap.encoding.soapenc.BeanSerializer"
       xml2JavaClassName=
         "org.apache.soap.encoding.soapenc.BeanSerializer"/>
    <isd:map encodingStyle=
    ➥"http://schemas.xmlsoap.org/soap/encoding/"
       xmlns:x="urn:xml-soap-address-demo" qname="x:phone"
       javaType="samples.addressbook.PhoneNumber"
       java2XMLClassName=
         "org.apache.soap.encoding.soapenc.BeanSerializer"
       xml2JavaClassName=
         "org.apache.soap.encoding.soapenc.BeanSerializer"/>
  </isd:mappings>
  </isd:service>
```

Take a look in detail at the information in the deployment descriptor file, on a tag-by-tag basis. A more expanded form of this discussion can be found in the Apache SOAP user's guide documentation.

isd:service This tag defines the `isd` namespace and gives the name of the service as `"urn:AddressFetcher"` in the `id` attribute. The `isd` namespace is in force until the closing `isd:service` tag. Optional attributes in this tag (not illustrated in the example) are

***type* attribute** If the service is message-oriented instead of being a RPC, use `type="message"`.

***checkMustUnderstands* attribute** This attribute may have the value true or false. If true, the server must be able to throw a fault if the SOAP message has headers marked as `MustUnderstand`.

***isd:provider scope* attribute** The `scope` attribute corresponds to the `scope` term used in Java servlets and JSP for various objects. In particular, it corresponds to the usage of scope in JSP `useBean` tags. In the SOAP server case, it refers to the object that the server creates to respond to requests directed to the `urn:AddressFetcher` service. Selecting the `scope` has important consequences for service design. The possible values for `scope` are:

Application Once created, the object is available to all requests until the server is stopped. Because the `urn:AddressFetcher` service has application scope, each request can add data to the object and subsequent requests will see the changed data.

Session A new copy of the object is created for each session. This means that if a session maintaining mechanism is in place, subsequent requests from the same client will see the same object. The SOAP 1.1 standard does not require session maintaining capability, but subsequent standards may change this.

Request The object lives only for the duration of the request. Note that although page scope has meaning for JSP pages, it is meaningless for SOAP.

***isd:provider methods* attribute** This is a list of names of methods that the service implements separated by spaces.

***isd:provider type* attribute** This designates the language to be used. Apache SOAP can execute various scripting languages, a capability not discussed at this time. Because the type is `"java"`, the `isd:provider` tag has a child tag named `isd:java`. This tag carries two attributes:

***isd:java class* attribute** The fully qualified name of the Java class that implements the service.

***isd:java static* attribute** This attribute can be either false or true, but all of the Apache SOAP samples use false.

isd:faultlistener This designates the Java class that processes `SOAPFaultEvent` events. When an exception or other error occurs in a SOAP service, an attempt is made to return a valid SOAP message containing information about the cause of the problem. A fault listener is responsible for composing extra information about the cause of the problem.

isd:mappings This optional tag encloses one or more `isd:map` tags that define how to serialize specific Java types not included in the set of basic type serializers provided with Apache SOAP. An optional attribute named `defaultMappingRegistry` can be named in this tag if you want to override the normal default Registry.

isd:map Each map tag contains attributes describing how a Java type is converted from Java to XML and back.

Mapping and the SOAP Mapping Registry

Each type of variable that is transmitted to a server by a SOAP message must be translated from XML to a Java primitive or reference variable and, in turn, variables returned by the RPC must be encoded from Java into XML. Selecting the right method to accomplish a conversion is accomplished by "type mapping" data. This data lives in a registry, which is an object of the type `org.apache.soap.encoding.SOAPMappingRegistry` by default.

The `SOAPMappingRegistry` class has a large set of predefined type mappings, so for many cases you won't have to define special conversions. As of Apache SOAP 2.2, these predefined type mappings include:

- Java primitive types, such as `int`, `float`, `boolean`, `byte`, and so on, and their corresponding wrapper classes
- Java arrays
- `java.lang.String`
- `java.util.Date`
- `java.util.GregorianCalendar`
- `java.util.Vector`
- `java.util.Hashtable`
- `java.util.Map` (requires SDK 1.2 or later)

- `java.math.BigDecimal`
- `javax.mail.internet.MimeBodyPart`
- `java.io.InputStream`
- `javax.activation.DataSource`
- `javax.activation.DataHandler`
- `org.apache.soap.util.xml.QName`
- `org.apache.soap.rpc.Parameter`
- `java.lang.Object` (a deserializer for null objects only)

As you can see, this is a pretty impressive list, so why does the address server define extra map tags such as the following?

```
<isd:map encodingStyle=
➥"http://schemas.xmlsoap.org/soap/encoding/"
    xmlns:x="urn:xml-soap-address-demo" qname="x:phone"
    javaType="samples.addressbook.PhoneNumber"
    java2XMLClassName=
      "org.apache.soap.encoding.soapenc.BeanSerializer"
    xml2JavaClassName=
      "org.apache.soap.encoding.soapenc.BeanSerializer"/>
```

This mapping illustrates one of the serializers that Apache SOAP provides but which is not built into the `SOAPMappingRegistry` class. The `BeanSerializer` class uses introspection to provide serialization for Java classes that implement the JavaBean convention of get and set methods for all variables that must be serialized.

The preceding example map declaration says that the Java object that appears in a SOAP message to the `AddressFetcher` server with the name phone can be handled by the standard `BeanSerializer` class for conversion both from XML to Java and from Java to XML. The bean serializer creates an object of the `samples.addressbook.PhoneNumber` type using the no-arguments constructor and then sets the object variables using the matching set methods.

The Actual Deploy Request

Recall that the command to deploy the service looks like this:

```
java org.apache.soap.server.ServiceManagerClient
```

```
http://localhost:8080/soap/servlet/rpcrouter deploy
DeploymentDescriptor.xml
```

`ServiceManagerClient` is a class in the `org.apache.soap.server` package that turns a deployment descriptor into a message directed to the `deploy` method of the service manager.

The `UtilSnoop` program was used to capture the SOAP message sent to the `rcprouter` servlet when the command just shown is executed. The complete message is shown in Listing 16.3 with long lines wrapped to fit the page and some additional indenting supplied to aid readability. What a monster! Aren't you glad that Apache SOAP supplies the `ServiceManagerClient` to handle this?

Listing 16.3: The SOAP Message That Deploys the Address Service

```
<?xml version='1.0' encoding='UTF-8'?>
<SOAP-ENV:Envelope
   xmlns:SOAP-ENV="http://schemas.xmlsoap.org/soap/envelope/"
   xmlns:xsi="http://www.w3.org/1999/ XMLSchema-instance"
   xmlns:xsd="http://www.w3.org/1999/XMLSchema">
<SOAP-ENV:Body>
<ns1:deploy xmlns:ns1="urn:xml-soap-service-management-service"
 SOAP-ENV:encodingStyle=
 ➥"http://schemas.xmlsoap.org/soap/encoding/">
<descriptor xmlns:ns2="http://xml.apache.org/xml-soap"
   xsi:type="ns2:DeploymentDescriptor">
<faultListener xmlns:ns3=
➥"http://schemas.xmlsoap.org/soap/encoding/"
   xsi:type="ns3:Array" ns3:arrayType="xsd:string[1]">
   <item xsi:type="xsd:string"
   >org.apache.soap.server.DOMFaultListener</item>
</faultListener>
<providerClass xsi:type="xsd:string"
   >samples.addressbook.AddressBook</providerClass>
<serviceType xsi:type="xsd:int">0</serviceType>
<serviceClass xsi:type="xsd:string" xsi:null="true"/>
<methods xmlns:ns4="http://schemas.xmlsoap.org/soap/encoding/"
   xsi:type="ns4:Array" ns4:arrayType="xsd:string[4]">
<item xsi:type="xsd:string">getAddressFromName</item>
<item xsi:type="xsd:string">addEntry</item>
<item xsi:type="xsd:string">getAllListings</item>
```

```
<item xsi:type="xsd:string">putListings</item>
</methods>
<providerType xsi:type="xsd:byte">0</providerType>
<scriptLanguage xsi:type="xsd:string" xsi:null="true"/>
<mappings xmlns:ns5="http://schemas.xmlsoap.org/soap/encoding/"
  xsi:type="ns5:Array" ns5:arrayType="ns2:TypeMapping[2]">
<item xsi:type="ns2:TypeMapping">
  <encodingStyle xsi:type="xsd:string"
    >http://schemas.xmlsoap.org/soap/encoding/</encodingStyle>
  <elementType-ns xsi:type="xsd:string"
    >urn:xml-soap-address-demo</elementType-ns>
  <elementType-lp xsi:type="xsd:string"
    >address</elementType-lp>
  <javaType xsi:type="xsd:string"
    >samples.addressbook.Address</javaType>
  <xml2JavaClassName xsi:type="xsd:string"
    >org.apache.soap.encoding.soapenc.BeanSerializer
  </xml2JavaClassName>
  <java2XMLClassName xsi:type="xsd:string"
    >org.apache.soap.encoding.soapenc.BeanSerializer
  </java2XMLClassName>
</item>
<item xsi:type="ns2:TypeMapping">
  <encodingStyle xsi:type="xsd:string"
    >http://schemas.xmlsoap.org/soap/encoding/</encodingStyle>
  <elementType-ns xsi:type="xsd:string"
    >urn:xml-soap-address-demo</elementType-ns>
  <elementType-lp xsi:type="xsd:string"
    >phone</elementType-lp>
  <javaType xsi:type="xsd:string"
    >samples.addressbook.PhoneNumber</javaType>
  <xml2JavaClassName xsi:type="xsd:string"
    >org.apache.soap.encoding.soapenc.BeanSerializer
  </xml2JavaClassName>
  <java2XMLClassName xsi:type="xsd:string"
    >org.apache.soap.encoding.soapenc.BeanSerializer
  </java2XMLClassName>
</item>
</mappings>
<checkMustUnderstands xsi:type="xsd:boolean"
  >false</checkMustUnderstands>
```

```
<defaultSMRClass xsi:type="xsd:string" xsi:null="true"/>
<ID xsi:type="xsd:string">urn:AddressFetcher</ID>
<props xsi:type="ns2:Map" xsi:null="true"/>
<isStatic xsi:type="xsd:boolean">false</isStatic>
<scriptFilenameOrString xsi:type="xsd:string" xsi:null="true"/>
<scope xsi:type="xsd:int">2</scope>
</descriptor>
</ns1:deploy>
</SOAP-ENV:Body>
</SOAP-ENV:Envelope>
```

The `deploy` service turns the message into a `DeploymentDescriptor` object containing all of the information describing a deployed service. It is this object that is used to locate the correct class to perform a service and translate the input to it. In the present version of Apache SOAP, this object is written out as a serialized `Hashtable` to the `DeploymentDescriptor.ds` file.

How *AddressBook* Works

Follow the steps that the `rpcrouter` servlet takes to handle a message directed to the service that was just installed. Here is how the `GetAddress` client is used to send the query message. Note that, as usual, this single-line command has been word-wrapped to fit this page:

```
java samples.addressbook.GetAddress
    http://localhost:9000/soap/servlet/rpcrouter "John B. Good"
```

The actual HTTP transmission to the `rpcrouter` servlet is shown in Listing 16.4. Recall that the message type `getAddressFromName` was defined in the deployment descriptor `isd:provider` tag as shown in Listing 16.2.

Listing 16.4: The Complete Transmission to the *AddressFetcher* Service

```
POST /soap/servlet/rpcrouter HTTP/1.0
Host: localhost
Content-Type: text/xml; charset=utf-8
Content-Length: 492
SOAPAction: ""
```

```
<?xml version='1.0' encoding='UTF-8'?>
<SOAP-ENV:Envelope
   xmlns:SOAP-ENV="http://schemas.xmlsoap.org/soap/envelope/"
   xmlns:xsi="http://www.w3.org/1999/XMLSchema-instance"
   xmlns:xsd="http://www.w3.org/1999/XMLSchema">
<SOAP-ENV:Body>
<ns1:getAddressFromName xmlns:ns1="urn:AddressFetcher"
 SOAP-ENV:encodingStyle=
 ➥"http://schemas.xmlsoap.org/soap/encoding/">
   <nameToLookup xsi:type="xsd:string">John B.
   ➥Good</nameToLookup>
</ns1:getAddressFromName>
</SOAP-ENV:Body>
</SOAP-ENV:Envelope>
```

Because the HTTP transmission is a POST, it is the `doPost` method in the `rpcrouter` servlet that gets the request. Just like any other servlet derived from `javax.servlet.http.HttpServlet`, the entire information from the client request comes in with a `HttpServletRequest` object, and the entire response goes through a `HttpServletResponse` object.

As you may recall from the `web.xml` declarations, the class handling `rpcrouter` is `RPCRouterServlet` in the `org.apache.soap.server.http` package. The detail of the handling of the request is not covered here because implementation details may change. Instead, follow the general processing steps in terms of the functionality of objects involved:

1. The first step is to parse out the entire SOAP envelope. The `doPost` method creates an XML parser and uses several utility classes to create a `Call` object from the `HttpServlet-Request` input.

   A `Call` object is the general object used to represent a RPC in both server and client processing. The `Call` class is in the `org.apache.soap.rpc` package.

2. The next step is to use the `targetID` string from the `Call` object to locate the corresponding `DeploymentDescriptor`. In this case, this string has the value `"getAddressFrom-Name"` so the `DeploymentDescriptor` is the one that was established by deploying the address server. If the target service is not known, an exception is thrown resulting in an error message being returned to the client.

Part III

3. Using more utility classes, an object of the required class is located. Depending on the scope declared in the `DeploymentDescriptor`, the utilities may provide a new object or one that was created earlier. In this example, the service has application scope and the implementing object of the `samples.addressbook.AddressBook` class may have been created earlier.
4. Actual deserializing of parameters and execution of the target method is carried out by the `RPCRouter` utility class using reflection. It is important to note that the order of parameters in the SOAP request message must match the order in the actual method, although in this case the method takes only a single name, `String`.
5. The value returned by the method is encoded into a `Response` object. The class used is `Response` in the `org.apache.soap.rpc` package. Although Java methods can return only a single value, that value can be an array, custom object, `Hashtable`, or other collection, so there really is no limit on the returned data. In the case of the `AddressBook` server, the `getAddressFromName` is declared as returning an object of the `Address` class from the `samples.addressbook` package.
6. The Response is used to build a SOAP envelope that is finally transmitted back to the client.

Listing 16.5 shows the complete response text, with some lines reformatted for readability and to fit the page. Note that the content of the SOAP body is a tag named `getAddressFromNameResponse`, a name created by concatenation of the method called with `Response`.

Listing 16.5: The Complete Response

```
HTTP/1.0 200 OK
Content-Type: text/xml; charset=utf-8
Content-Length: 946
Date: Thu, 05 Jul 2001 16:50:38 GMT
Server: Apache Tomcat/4.0-b5 (HTTP/1.1 Connector)
Set-Cookie: JSESSIONID=
➥E2A72237428486B3A28127C5E72992C6;Path=/soap

<?xml version='1.0' encoding='UTF-8'?>
<SOAP-ENV:Envelope
```

```
    xmlns:SOAP-ENV="http://schemas.xmlsoap.org/soap/envelope/"
    xmlns:xsi="http://www.w3.org/1999/ XMLSchema-instance"
    xmlns:xsd="http://www.w3.org/1999/XMLSchema">
<SOAP-ENV:Body>
<ns1:getAddressFromNameResponse
    xmlns:ns1="urn:AddressFetcher" SOAP-ENV:encodingStyle=
      "http://schemas.xmlsoap.org/soap/encoding/">
<return xmlns:ns2="urn:xml-soap-address-demo"
    xsi:type="ns2:address">
<phoneNumber xsi:type="ns2:phone">
<exchange xsi:type="xsd:string">456</exchange>
<areaCode xsi:type="xsd:int">123</areaCode>
<number xsi:type="xsd:string">7890</number>
</phoneNumber>
<zip xsi:type="xsd:int">12345</zip>
<streetNum xsi:type="xsd:int">123</streetNum>
<streetName xsi:type="xsd:string">Main Street</streetName>
<state xsi:type="xsd:string">NY</state>
<city xsi:type="xsd:string">Anytown</city>
</return>
</ns1:getAddressFromNameResponse>

</SOAP-ENV:Body>
</SOAP-ENV:Envelope>
```


Troubleshooting Server-Side SOAP

The old saying "you can always tell the pioneers—they are the ones with the arrows in their backs" is certainly true for programmers trying to get SOAP running. This section attempts to explain how you can save countless hours of debugging by relating some of the problems that others have experienced. The main Apache SOAP list of Frequently Asked Questions (FAQ) is maintained at:

```
http://xml.apache.org//soap/faq/index.html
```

Classpath Problems

A large fraction of the problems that Java programmers experience when trying to get a Java SOAP application running seems to be related to the CLASSPATH used by the Java Virtual Machine (JVM) to locate class code. To see why this is, look at Java's conventions for the use of the CLASSPATH environment variable.

Classpath Conventions

Historically speaking, the Java CLASSPATH has been a source of endless confusion, frustration, and wasted time to Java programmers. Sun has attempted to reduce the confusion by making some aspects of class location automatic. As detailed in the `tooldocs` section of the Java SDK documentation, the Java Virtual Machine attempts to load classes in *this order*:

1. **Bootstrap classes:** These are the standard library classes, such as those in the `java.lang` package, that are typically found in the files `rt.jar` and `i18n.jar`. The convention is that these files are in the `\jre\lib` directory of the Java SDK installation. The JVM finds this directory by navigating from the JAVA_HOME directory where the `java.exe` program is found.
2. **Extension classes:** Also known as standard extensions, these classes are in packages beginning with `javax`. An example would be the e-mail related classes in the `mail.jar` file or the XML parser classes in `jaxp.jar` and `crimson.jar`. By convention, these are found in the `\jre\lib\ext` directory of the Java SDK installation.
3. **User application classes:** These are the specific classes required to run an application such as Tomcat itself or your custom servlet. The `-classpath` command line option or the CLASSPATH environment variable is used to locate user application classes.

With this order in mind, you can see how certain types of problem arise. If you have an older XML parser in your standard extensions directory, it does not matter that your CLASSPATH lists a new version of the parser; it will never be found, and you will get strange error messages. I would hate to tell you how many days I wasted tracking this one down.

You also have to consider the web application conventions as described in the Java Servlet API. A servlet such as `rpcrouter` automatically has access to classes and JAR files under the `WEB-INF` directory belonging to the SOAP web application.

However, any other web application will not have access to class and jar files in the SOAP WEB-INF directory, nor will SOAP services have access to class and jar files in other web applications. This absolute separation is designed into the servlet API so that a web application can be moved to any server without dependence on other applications. Sometimes this means you will have multiple copies of jar files.

Setting CLASSPATH

Unfortunately, setting the classpath used by a servlet container is not the subject of standardization. The installation documentation that comes with Apache SOAP describes how to handle some of the common servers. If you examine the batch files used to start Tomcat, you will find that extensive manipulation of classpath and related environment variables occurs. If necessary, you can insert specific paths that you want Tomcat to have available in these batch files.

XML Parser Problems

XML parser incompatibility is the most frequent cause of difficulty in getting a SOAP server running. SOAP requires a parser compatible with DOM level 2 and SAX 2 because namespaces are heavily used. When Apache SOAP 2.2 was first released, a large number of people had problems because they were using the Xerces version 1.3.1 XML parser package. This parser version failed to handle namespaces correctly, and caused mysterious errors.

Many people have had problems due to earlier parser versions that may have been installed by other programs. Versions of Sun's web server development kit from before development was turned over to the Apache organization have caused lots of trouble. Your best bet is to clear old parsers out of your system and stick to the latest Sun JAXP package.

Mystery Errors

This section discusses error messages that appear to make no sense, or sound completely impossible. You might see these when trying to run one of the SOAP samples or one of your own clients.

Unsupported response content type Your SOAP client may show this due to errors that prevent the server from generating an XML-formatted response. The server error message has a content type of text/html but the SOAP client is expecting text/xml. The real cause of the error has nothing to do with this error report from the client; you must examine the actual message content with one of the snoop utilities (see the "snooping on messages" section later in this chapter).

Connection refused You can get this if something is wrong with the URL specified for the server or if the server is not actually running. Using the wrong port number is a possible cause, particularly if you have been debugging with one of the snoop utilities.

Unable to resolve target Normally this means that the service class cannot be found. Possible causes include a misspelled method in a request, or an error in constructing the service class object. You should use the SOAP administration utility service listing to verify that the service is deployed and that the names that the service uses correspond with your client usage.

Debugging Tools

Because the Tomcat server is entirely written in Java, you can start the entire server through a debugger. This is pretty tricky because you must supply the command-line parameters that are normally set up by the batch files. Look at the startup batch files for clues on how to do this and for the name of the class that actually has the normal Java `main` method. In the current copy of Tomcat, this is:

```
org.apache.catalina.startup.Bootstrap
```

Certain Java Integrated Development Environments (IDEs) provide built-in support for running Tomcat in the debugger.

Snooping on Messages

A surprising number of SOAP problems can be solved by looking at the text of the messages sent between client and server. The SOAP distribution provides a utility named `TcpTunnelGui` in the `org.apache.soap.util.net` package for capturing these messages, and I have written the `UtilSnoop` utility that performs a similar function.

The basic idea of these utilities is to interpose the utility between the client and server. Instead of having the client connect directly with the SOAP server, the client connects with the utility on a different port. The utility relays the request data stream to the server on the normal port while keeping a copy of every character sent. The returned response data is treated the same way.

The `UtilSnoop` utility is available on the *SOAP Programming with Java* book website at

```
http://www.lanw.com/books/javasoap/
```

WHAT'S NEXT

The last few chapters have explored the quickly evolving web services technologies for XML based messaging. For those who want a more proven and stable mechanism for robust messaging the next chapter may be a good answer. More and more enterprise applications are utilizing Message Oriented Middleware (MOM) servers in order to send asynchronous and reliable message between different parts of the application. The next chapter introduces you to how these messaging servers can be utilized and how they can be accessed using the Java Messaging Service (JMS) API.

Chapter 17

Java Messaging Service (JMS)

The Java Messaging Service (JMS) specification introduced in 1998 defines the interfaces and standard behavior for asynchronous messaging. This model includes a middleman that takes responsibility for delivering the message for the sender, allowing the sender to continue executing Java statements without waiting for receipt or processing of the message.

Featured in this chapter:

- Client/Server Messaging
- Message-Oriented Middleware (MOM)
- Point-to-Point Messaging
- Publish and Subscribe Messaging
- JMS Queues
- JMS Topics

Written for *Enterprise Java™ 2, J2EE™ 1.3 Complete*
by Vince E. Marco

- JMS Messages
- Message Filtering
- Message Prioritizing
- Transacted Sessions
- Architecture and Design with JMS

Client/Server Messaging

The communication between applications or components is referred to as *messaging*. Messaging is often categorized into synchronous and asynchronous behavior. Synchronous messages indicate a single thread of execution in which the sender waits until the message is fully processed by the receiver before continuing to execute more statements. Another name for this model of messaging is the *Request/Reply* model, which has many examples such HTTP, RMI, CORBA, and so on. Figure 17.1 shows an example of synchronous messaging. Notice the client waits until all the synchronous calls have completed before continuing on executing.

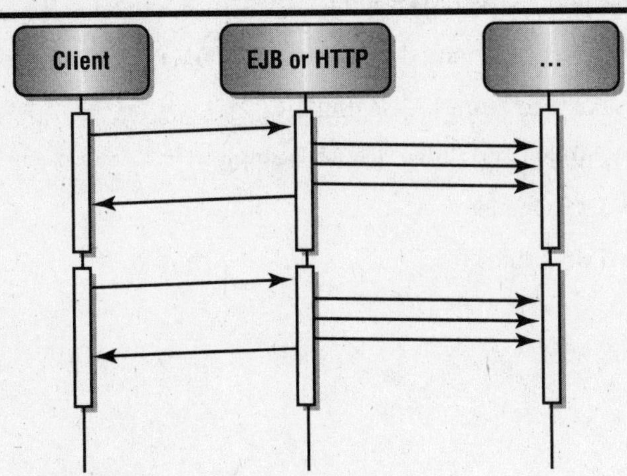

FIGURE 17.1: Synchronous messaging

Asynchronous Messaging

Asynchronous messaging uses a delivery system to take responsibility for delivering messages to interested receivers. So why would you be interested in asynchronous messaging? The answer in most cases is performance. If a client does not need to wait for a response, the most effective messaging will be asynchronous. In Figure 17.2, the JMS destination takes responsibility for delivering the message, and the client can go on executing Java statements.

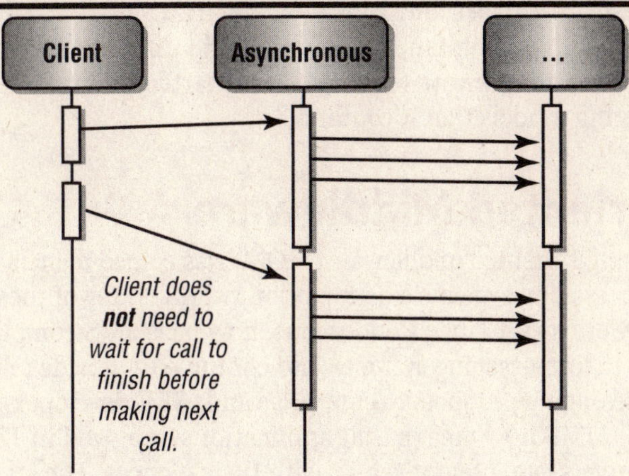

FIGURE 17.2: Asynchronous messaging

This type of messaging is extremely useful when no reply is needed by the client. This eliminates situations where clients are waiting on processes to finish their task, and improves the overall performance of the entire system. Another clear advantage of JMS messaging is that it produces a loosely coupled messaging system.

JMS is a client/server technology. An application server providing JMS is the server. Application components connecting to JMS are JMS clients. Application components that send JMS messages are often referred to as "producers." Application components that receive JMS messages are referred to as "receivers."

Producers send messages to JMS destinations rather than to an explicit receiver, thereby eliminating a dependency on the receiver. This means that messages can be sent even if a receiver is busy or inactive, and the message will be received when the receiver is ready for the message. A JMS producer isn't aware of the receiver class, or even how many different receivers are consuming messages from their target destination. This "loose coupling" produces a system that is much less fragile and more scalable.

JMS Destinations

JMS operates as a delivery middleman. Senders send messages to explicit JMS destinations that hold messages until receivers request a message from the destination. For a sender to get a message to a receiver, they must both obtain a connection to the same destination. JMS destinations consist of Queues and Topics. These are discussed in detail, but in order to fully understand them we should understand where message-oriented middleware (such as JMS) started and take a look at the messaging models that it contains.

Message-Oriented Middleware

The term message-oriented middleware (MOM) was coined to include the proprietary messaging systems existing prior to JMS. Many of these, such as IBM's MQSeries and Tibco Rendezvous, now have JMS-compliant interfaces for their messaging systems, and continue to provide reliable and robust messaging products to enterprise and J2EE developers. For these systems, JMS now means that applications deployed in J2EE application servers can integrate easily with their services. The standard has also produced new vendors for JMS services. These services are either stand-alone messaging services that can interface into existing J2EE application servers, or they are JMS implementations by the applications servers themselves. Figure 17.3 shows a MOM server and the connected clients, senders and receivers of messages. These clients can be standalone applications, servers, or J2EE components.

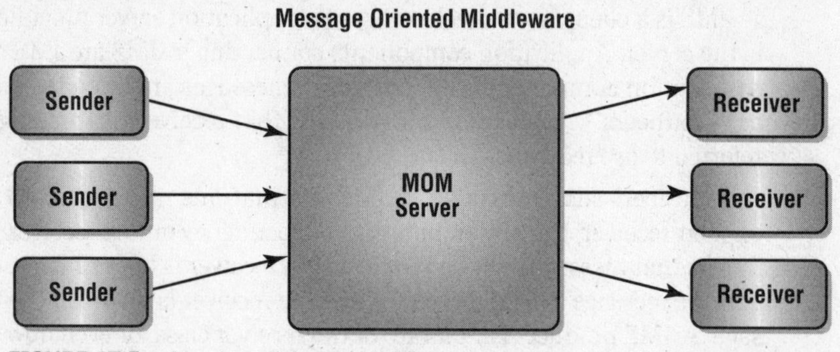

FIGURE 17.3: Message-Oriented Middleware

The systems that comprise the MOM category of networking services generally provide three types of messaging: point-to-point, publish/subscribe, and request/reply. The request/reply message type is a synchronous messaging type, provided by Enterprise JavaBeans (EJBs). JMS includes both point-to-point and publish/subscribe messaging types. Take a look at each one of these in more detail.

Point-to-Point Messaging

Point-to-point messaging is defined by a clear and distinct rule: Each message has only one receiver. Point-to-point messaging is not the same as JMS, but rather, is a model of messaging. It is one of the messaging models supported by JMS.

The primary constructs for point-to-point messaging are deques (pronounced "decks") and queues. The best way to understand a deque is to think of playing cards. As cards are placed on a deck of cards, they are placed on top of the pile. As cards are "received" from the deque they are taken off the top of the pile. This model is often referred to as Last-In-First-Out (LIFO) processing.

A queue is a First-In-First-Out processing strategy. This is generally the desired behavior for point-to-point messaging systems. A concrete example of a queue is a line at the grocery store. Customers are processed in the order they enter the line.

In JMS, point-to-point messaging is provided by queues. These queues are JMS destinations, and do support multiple senders and multiple receivers. Think of a queue as a deck of cards with multiple players around the table, each putting a card on the deck. Each message is represented by a card, and has only one sender, but multiple senders place messages (cards) on the queue. The same is true for receivers. Each receiver pulls messages (cards) from the deck, and each message (card) has only one receiver that pulls it off the queue. To avoid confusion with deques as in our first card example, our cards are removed from the bottom of the pile in a First-In-First-Out (FIFO) manner. In Figure 17.4, we see an example of a JMS Queue. Notice the progression of messages in a FIFO manner through the queue.

Point-to-point messaging is useful when processing tasks. Receivers, such as the message-driven EJBs that are discussed later in this chapter, can be added during high-traffic periods to scale up processing, and dropped off during inactive periods to avoid taking up resources for unused receivers waiting for a message. Because each message, which represents a unit of work, is processed by only one receiver, there is no duplication of effort.

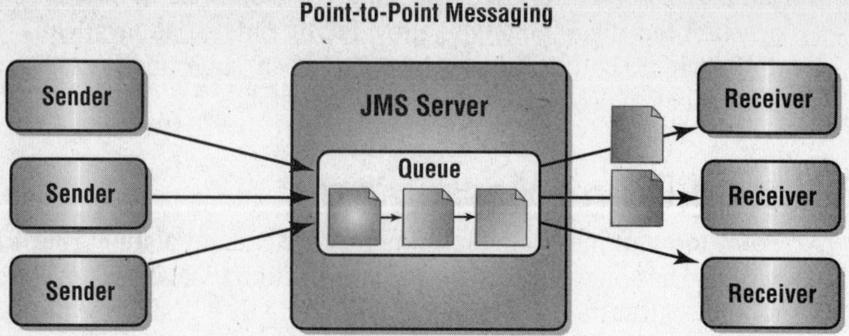

FIGURE 17.4: Point-to-Point JMS Messaging

Publish and Subscribe Messaging

The model for publish and subscribe messaging also involves a single sender for each message; however, each message can have multiple receivers. This model is more like a copier than a card deck. Every message can be received by all receivers (or subscribers) on that JMS destination. Our example here is that of an email list service. The creator of the e-mail sends it to the list service address. The list service then duplicates the e-mail and sends it to all of the subscribers of the list service. Figure 17.5 shows an example of the publish and subscribe model, using JMS Topics.

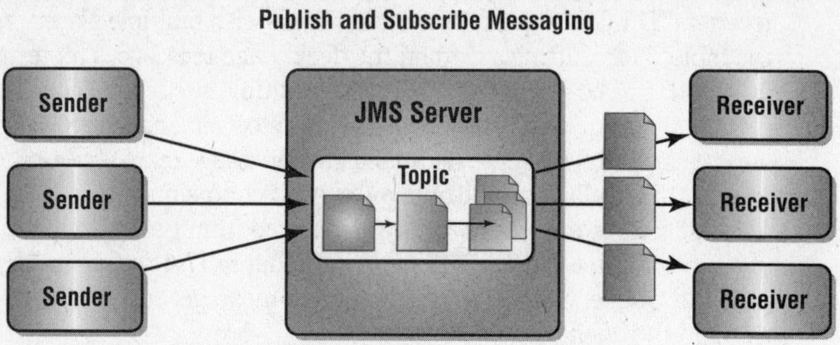

FIGURE 17.5: Publish and Subscribe messaging with JMS Topics

The JMS destination type that provides publish and subscribe services are called topics. JMS clients actually use the same methods to send and receive messages for both queues and topics; however, there are some slight differences in establishing connections to the destination, which will be covered in the next section.

Sending to a JMS Destination

To send a message to a JMS destination (topic or queue), a Java application needs to establish a session with JMS. This process may be different, depending upon your application server or JMS provider, but usually begins by looking up the ConnectionFactory in JNDI. This is a class for creating a connection to JMS. The connection is created by calling the `createQueueConnection()` or `createTopicConnection()` methods. A connection can be used for additional JMS destinations of the same type as the connection. In the following code example, notice that the Java Naming and Directory Interface (JNDI) is used to obtain the connection factory and the Queue. It is not necessary to use JNDI, but it is a convenient and appropriate use of JNDI since these objects are lightweight. A session is then created from the connection. The next step is to create a sender from the session. Several senders can be created from the session. The session is responsible for adding unique identifiers for each message and putting the messages in a FIFO order. The final step is to start the connection. Here is an example of client code to initialize a queue connection for a JMS sender:

```
// Get a JNDI initial context
Context jndi = new InitialContext();
// Get a connection factory for creating the connection to JMS
QueueConnectionFactory factory = (QueueConnectionFactory)
    jndi.lookup("javax.jms.QueueConnectionFactory");
// Get the JMS destination (Queue in this case)
Queue queue = (Queue)jndi.lookup("javax.jms.exampleQueue");
// Create a JMS connection
QueueConnection conn = factory.createQueueConnection();
// Create a QueueSession (non-transacted, auto-acknowledged)
QueueSession session = conn.createQueueSession(false,
    Session.AUTO_ACKNOWLEDGE);
// Create a sender on the JMS destination
QueueSender sender = session.createSender(queue);
// Start the connection
conn.start();
```

The session is now used to create messages, and the sender is used to send those messages. After a connection, session, and sender are established, they can be repeatedly used to create and send many messages. The code following is an example of the Java statements needed to send

JMS messages once the connection, session, and sender are set up:

```
// Create and send a JMS message
TextMessage msg = session.createTextMessage("<message>This is
   a text message</message>");
sender.send(msg);
```

NOTE

The example message is an XML message that is also a text message. TextMessages do not need to be XML, but they are a good vehicle for sending XML messages asynchronously.

Creating a publisher to a topic is much the same, except you are dealing with a TopicConnectionFactory on down. Notice `createPublisher()` is called instead of `createSender()`. The following is example code to set up a JMS Topic and publish a JMS message:

```
// Get a JNDI initial context
Context jndi = new InitialContext();
// Get a connection factory for creating the connection to JMS
TopicConnectionFactory factory = (TopicConnectionFactory)
    jndi.lookup("javax.jms.TopicConnectionFactory");
// Get the JMS destination (Topic in this case)
Topic topic = (Topic)jndi.lookup("javax.jms.exampleTopic");
// Create a JMS connection
TopicConnection conn = factory.createTopicConnection();
// Create a TopicSession (non-transacted, auto-acknowledged)
TopicSession session = conn.createTopicSession(false,
     Session.AUTO_ACKNOWLEDGE);
// Create a publisher (sender) on the JMS destination
TopicPublisher publisher = session.createPublisher(topic);
// Start the connection
conn.start();
// Create and publish (send) a JMS message
TextMessage msg = session.createTextMessage(
     "<message>This is a text message</message>");
publisher.publish(msg);
```

Receiving from a JMS Destination

A session with JMS is also needed to receive a message from a JMS destination (topic or queue). A single session may be used to create both senders and receivers, although this is not necessary. Frequently JMS clients are focused upon sending or receiving. Notice that the process is the same up through the point at which you create the session.

```
// Get a JNDI initial context
Context jndi = new InitialContext();
// Get a connection factory for creating the connection to JMS
QueueConnectionFactory factory = (QueueConnectionFactory)
     jndi.lookup("javax.jms.QueueConnectionFactory");
// Get the JMS destination (Queue in this case)
Queue queue = (Queue)jndi.lookup("javax.jms.exampleQueue");
// Create a JMS connection
QueueConnection conn = factory.createQueueConnection();
// Create a QueueSession (non-transacted, auto-acknowledged)
QueueSession session = conn.createQueueSession(false,
     Session.AUTO_ACKNOWLEDGE);
// Create a receiver on the JMS destination
QueueReceiver receiver = session.createReceiver(queue);
// Start the connection
conn.start();
```

At this point, you have some options for receiving messages. The first decision is whether to receive messages synchronously in the client thread. If you choose this route, you can choose from the following three blocking calls:

```
Receiver.receive();                // wait until a message
                                   //   is received
Receiver.receive(long timeout);    // wait until a message is
                                   //   received or the
                                   //   timeout expires
Receiver.receiveNoWait();          // return a message if one
                                   //   is waiting, otherwise
                                   //   return null immediately
```

Part III

Asynchronous receiving allows the JMS client to receive messages while doing other tasks. This model involves creating a callback class, which will be invoked by the session when a message is delivered. Figure 17.6 shows a JMS Queue with an asynchronous message receiver. The session on the receiving side calls the MessageListener whenever a message is received.

If asynchronous receiving is desired, such as not in the receiving clients thread, you must provide a callback class. This is done by calling the `set-MessageListener(new MyListener())` method on the receiver. You also must implement the `MessageListener` interface in our `MyListener` class. This interface has one method that must be implemented called `onMessage()`.

```
Class MyListener implements MessageListener
{
    void onMessage(Message msg)
    {
        // … do whatever processing we want to do …
    }
}
```

Asynchronous Receiving

JMS Server
Queue
Sender
session
Receiver
session
MessageListener

FIGURE 17.6: Asynchronous JMS Receiving

The code for receiving from JMS topics is the same as for queues, except all calls use topic instead of queue to distinguish the destination type in the method names.

JMS Messages

Messages in JMS consist of three distinct parts: the header, the properties, and the body. The header consists of a standard set of fields used primarily by the system in performing several functions such as prioritizing or expiring messages. Figure 17.7 shows a JMS message with its three parts:

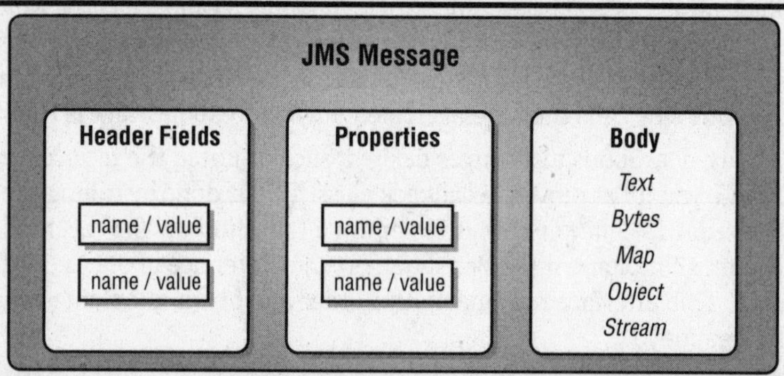

FIGURE 17.7: JMS Message structure

These fields are described in the following table:

Field	Description	Defined By
JMSCorrelationID	This field is used to associate one message with another message to produce an asynchronous request/response.	Application
JMSDeliveryMode	Designates message as PERSISTENT or NON-PERSISTENT. A persistent message is stored by the JMS server until delivery is acknowledged from the receiver. If the server crashes, it will recover messages in the persistent store automatically.	send() method
JMSDeliveryTime	Specifies the earliest time that a message may be delivered to a consumer. Useful for delaying delivery as well as sorting and filtering messages by a receiver.	send() method
JMSDestination	This is the destination (queue or topic) to which the message is sent.	send() method
JMSExpiration	Designates the number of seconds the message is allowed to live. Many systems automatically factor in the current Greenwich Mean Time to produce an absolute expiration time. If set to zero, the message will never expire. After a message expires, it is removed from the system and cannot be delivered.	send() method
JMSMessageID	A string that uniquely identifies each JMS message.	send() method
JMSPriority	Specifies a priority level. JMS defines 10 priorities (0-9), with 9 given the highest priority. Destinations can be sorted by priority by configuring a destination key.	Message Consumer
JMSRedelivered	A boolean flag set to true when a message is redelivered due to no acknowledgment.	JMS server

Field	Description	Defined By
JMSReplyTo	Indicates a JMS destination (queue or topic) to which reply messages should be sent.	Application
JMSTimeStamp	The time the JMS server accepts a message for delivery. The value is in Java milliseconds.	JMS server
JMSType	This indicates the type of message being sent. The JMS specification allows some flexibility for providers to indicate custom types; for example, indicating that a TextMessage is of type XML.	Application

The header fields are followed by the message property fields. These fields are application-specific name/value pairs added to a message by the sender, and retrievable by the receiver. These are set using type-specific accessor methods on the JMS message object. The name is a java.lang.String, and the value may be one of boolean, byte, double, float, int, long, short, and String.

The body is the actual payload of the message. There are several different body types from which to choose, including `BytesMessage`, `MapMessage`, `ObjectMessage`, `StreamMessage`, and `TextMessage`. The `BytesMessage` payload is an uninterpreted stream of bytes, and provides stream-oriented accessors. The `MapMessage` is a set of name/value pairs in which the names are strings and the values are Java primitive types. The `ObjectMessage` payload is a serializable Java object, with accessors of `setObject()` and `getObject()`. The `ObjectMessage` class automatically handles serializing the object on a send and marshalling that object on a receive. The `StreamMessage` class is similar to the `BytesMessage`, except that only Java primitive types are written to or read from the stream. And lastly, a `TextMessage` has a payload of a `java.lang.String`. This is useful for sending text messages such as XML between JMS clients.

Notice that messages are created by the Session via `createBytesMessage()`, `createMapMessage()`, `createObjectMessage()`, `createStreamMessage()`, `createTextMessage()`, and so on. This is done to serialize the message creation IDs by the Session. The `QueueSender` and `TopicPublisher` objects are responsible for sending a message to the JMS server. These client-side objects can be configured with default settings for JMSDeliveryMode, JMSPriority, and JMSExpirationTime. Each message also can override these settings using their own accessors for each field.

Message Acknowledgment

There are various options for message acknowledgment. An acknowledgment is a receiver's way of telling the server that it has successfully received a message. The available types of acknowledgment are:

AUTO_ACKNOWLEDGE	The session will automatically acknowledge the receipt of a message after the consumer JMS client returns from the call to receive or exists the onMessage() handler method.
DUPS_OK_ACKNOWLEDGE	The session will lazily acknowledge the delivery of messages when idle time permits. This setting can result in duplicate message delivery.
CLIENT_ACKNOWLEDGE	Client will acknowledge receipt of message by calling the acknowledge() method on the message. All consumed messages are acknowledged, not just the message invoked.

JMSDeliveryMode

The delivery mode of a message can be set to DeliveryMode.PERSISTENT or DeliveryMode.NON_PERSISTENT. If a message is persistent, messages will be put into a perisistent store on the server until the message receipt is acknowledged. If the JMS server were to crash or be recycled, persistent messages will be recovered while non-persistent messages will be lost. Non-persistent messages are much faster and less resource intensive, and can be effectively used for event-based information that is not critical in nature.

Prioritized Messages

Messages in JMS are prioritized. When a subscriber or receiver requests a message or is delivered a message asynchronously, the order of messages is determined by the JMSPriority field. This field is an integer value between 0 and 9, where 9 is the highest priority. The default setting is 5, and can be overridden in the QueueSender, TopicPublisher, or on any individual message prior to sending. Within each priority level the messages will be delivered in a first in, first out (FIFO) order.

Message Filtering

JMS provides a server-side filtering mechanism for any client receiving JMS messages. This filter can be specified by the client when creating a receiver or subscriber from the Session object. The filter is a simple SQL-like statement that addresses the header and property fields on each message. The benefit of message filtering is that it is performed at the server, and thereby can reduce the amount of message traffic significantly for a client only interested in receiving specific messages. Some examples of message selectors are:

- `amount > 50 and product_category in (book, music)`
- `(last_name such as Johnson or first_name such as Bob) and age > 30`
- `end_year is not NULL and start_year between 1990 and 1995`
- `end_year - start_year >= 5`

JMS Sessions

The session object is responsible for much of the JMS contract with the client. This session provides an interface for creating queue senders, receivers, and browsers. A browser is much like a receiver, except it doesn't remove messages from the queue. Instead, it allows a client to view messages without actually receiving them. The session also provides an interface for creating topic publishers and subscribers. When creating a subscriber, a boolean value called noLocal may be specified to avoid receiving messages published on the same connection. This might be the case if a single client is both a publisher and subscriber to a given topic. If noLocal is true, they will not receive their own published messages; otherwise, they will receive all messages published to the topic.

Also, a `TopicSession` has a method called `createTemporaryTopic()` that will return a temporary topic that can be used for the duration of the connection to send messages to this client. This is rarely used, but can be effective when passed to receivers via the JMSReplyTo header field.

Transacted Sessions

A session can be transacted by specifying true for the transacted parameter when creating the session. A transacted session takes on specific behavior to support the JMS session participating in a local or distributed transaction.

On the sender side, messages do not actually get sent to the server until a `commit()` is called. Instead the messages get collected in the session and can be forgotten with a `rollback()` method call on the session. On the receiver side, messages do not get acknowledged on the server until a `commit()`. If a rollback occurs, all non-committed receives are effectively undone and will be received on subsequent receive calls or `onMessage()` invocations. Figure 17.8 shows an example transacted JMS session, and how messages are effected in both sender and receiver sessions. Notice that only the sending and receiving actions are transacted. JMS messages themselves are not effected by transactions.

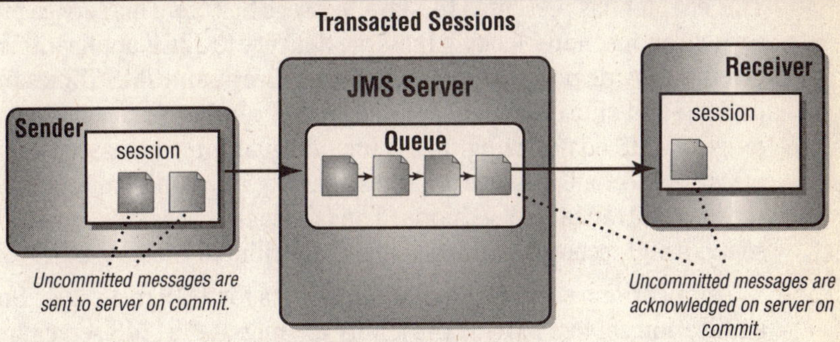

FIGURE 17.8: Transacted JMS sessions

Durable Subscribers

When creating a subscriber on the session, the client can choose to create a durable subscriber. A durable subscriber is a subscriber that needs to receive all messages sent to a topic whether the client is active or inactive. JMS will store all messages that are to be delivered to a durable subscriber in the persistent store, and will ensure delivery when the subscriber becomes active. If the message expires while in the persistent state, it will not be delivered to the durable subscriber. For durable subscriptions to work, the JMS client must also set the client identifier on the connection.

Designing with JMS

Applications can use JMS to provide robust asynchronous messaging. This messaging can provide for effective processing of messages, as well as provide a system that is loosely coupled. These are aspects of enterprise applications that become more important as the application grows in size.

Another common approach to JMS usage in enterprise applications involves designing a set of application events, and using JMS as the circulatory or central nervous system of the application. This approach to large-scale applications enables the deployment of new subsystems without the redeployment of existing subsystems within the application, largely because new subsystems merely subscribe to the architected events of the system.

What's Next

This chapter has presented the Java Message Service. This service provides asynchronous, non-blocking message delivery to J2EE applications. JMS Queues provide point-to-point message delivery, and JMS Topics provide publish-and-subscribe message delivery. Several options enable a wide range of JMS customizing. These include guaranteed message delivery, message selectors, message priorities, message properties, multiple message types, and transacted sessions. The transacted sessions enable JMS senders and receivers to participate in distributed transactions.

Applications servers provide the targets for JMS messages. Some application servers provide the ability to "migrate" a JMS server around a cluster of J2EE servers. Other vendor support for JMS includes interfacing with existing messaging services such as MQSeries, or Tibco's Rendezvous. Chapter 20, "EJB Architecture and Clients," also discusses how message-driven enterprise beans are used to bridge the gap between JMS and Enterprise JavaBeans (EJBs).

Part IV

Remote Communications and Enterprise JavaBeans

Chapter 18

Persistence and Remote Method Invocation

The ability to call code running on another computer is a critical functionality for enterprise applications. J2EE offers several alternatives for executing remote code, including servlets, Java IDL with CORBA, JAX-RPC, JAXM, and RMI. While each of these alternatives is explained in this book, this chapter will focus on one of the most effective of these mechanisms: RMI. Remote Method Invocation (RMI) is an ideal solution when you have a Java object that needs to call a method on a Java object running on a different computer. RMI code can be written directly in J2EE applications. In addition, Enterprise JavaBeans (EJB), discussed in Chapters 20, 21, and 22, use RMI as the underlying communication mechanism between beans and their clients.

Updated from *Java™ 2 Developer's Handbook™*
by Philip Heller and Simon Roberts

ISBN 0-7821-2179-9 $59.99

Featured in this chapter:

- Object persistence and serialization
- RMI basics
- Callbacks in RMI
- Dynamic class loading in RMI
- Remote object activation

Object Persistence

A Java object ordinarily lasts no longer than the program that created it. An object may cease to exist during runtime if it is reaped by the garbage collector. If it avoids that fate, it still goes away when the Java Virtual Machine (JVM) is shut down.

In this context, *persistence* is the ability of an object to record its state so that it can be reproduced in the future, perhaps in another environment. For example, a persistent object might store its state in a file. The file can be used to restore the object in a different runtime environment. It is not really the object itself that persists, but rather the information necessary to construct a replica of the object. When an object is *serialized*, all of the object's data, but not its methods or class definition, are written to a stream.

Serialization

An object records itself by writing out the values that describe its state. This process is known as *serialization* because the object is represented by an ordered series of bytes. Java provides classes that write objects to streams and restore objects from streams.

The main task of serialization is to write out the values of an object's instance variables. If a variable is a reference to another object, the referenced object must also be serialized. Serialization may involve serializing a complex tree structure that consists of the original object, the object's objects, the object's object's objects, and so on. An object's ownership hierarchy is known as its *graph*.

Not all classes are capable of being serialized. Only objects that implement the `Serializable` or `Externalizable` interfaces may successfully be serialized. Both interfaces are in the `java.io` package. A serializable object can be serialized by another object, which in practice is a type of output stream. An externalizable object must be capable of writing its own state, rather than letting the work be done by another object.

The Serializable Interface

The `Serializable` interface does not have any methods. When a class declares that it implements `Serializable`, it is declaring that it participates in the serialization protocol. When an object is serializable, and the object's state is written to a stream, the stream must contain enough information to restore the object. This must hold true even if the class being restored has been updated to a more recent (but compatible) version.

You can serialize any class as long as the class meets the following criteria:

- The class, or one of its superclasses, must implement the `java.io.Serializable` interface.
- The class can implement the `writeObject()` method to control data that is being saved and append new data to existing saved data.
- The class can implement the `readObject()` method to read the data that was written by the corresponding `writeObject()` method.

If a serializable class has variables that should not be serialized, those variables must be marked with the `transient` keyword. The serialization process will ignore any variables marked as `transient`. Many things—such as static data, open file handles, socket connections, and threads—will not be serializable because they represent items that are JVM-specific.

The Externalizable Interface

The `Externalizable` interface identifies objects that can be saved to a stream, but are responsible for their own states. When an externalizable object is written to a stream, the stream is responsible for storing the name of the object's class; the object must write its own data. The `Externalizable` interface is defined as:

```
public interface Externalizable extends Serializable {

    public void writeExternal (ObjectOutput out)
        throws IOException;
```

```
    public void readExternal (ObjectInput in)
        throws IOException, ClassNotFoundException;
}
```

An externalizable class must adhere to this interface by providing a `writeExternal()` method for storing its state during serialization and a `readExternal()` method for restoring its state during deserialization.

Object Output Streams

Objects that can serialize other objects implement the `ObjectOutput` interface from the `java.io` package. This interface is intended to be implemented by output stream classes. The interface's definition is:

```
public interface ObjectOutput extends DataOutput {
    public void writeObject(Object obj)
        throws IOException;
    public void write (int b) throws IOException;
    public void write(byte b[]) throws IOException;
    public void write(byte b[], int off, int len)
        throws IOException;
    public void flush() throws IOException;
    public void close() throws IOException;
}
```

The essential method of the interface is `writeObject(Object obj)`, which writes `obj` to a stream. Static and transient data of `obj` are ignored; all other variables, including private ones, are written.

Exceptions can occur while accessing the object or its fields, or when attempting to write to the storage stream. If an exception occurs, the stream that the interface is built on will be left in an unknown and unusable state, and the external representation of the object will be corrupted.

The `ObjectOutput` interface extends the `DataOutput` interface. `DataOutput` methods support writing of primitive data types. For example, the `writeDouble()` method writes data of type double, and `writeBoolean()` writes data of type boolean. These primitive-type writing methods are used for writing out an object's primitive instance variables. The primary class that implements the `ObjectOutput` interface is `ObjectOutputStream`. Serializable objects are represented as streams of bytes rather than as characters; therefore, they are handled by streams rather than by character-oriented writers.

When an object is to be serialized to a file, the first step is to create an output stream that talks to the file:

```
FileOutputStream fos = new FileOutputStream("obj.file");
```

The next step is to create an object output stream and chain it to the file output stream:

```
ObjectOutput objout = new ObjectOutputStream(fos);
```

The object output stream automatically writes a header into the stream; the header contains a magic number and a version. This data is written automatically with the `writeStreamHeader()` method when the object output stream is created. Later in this chapter, we will demonstrate how an object input stream reads this header and verifies the object before returning its state.

After writing the header, the object output stream can write the bit representation of an object to the output stream using the `writeObject()` method. For example, the following code constructs an instance of the `Point` class and serializes it:

```
objout.writeObject(new Point(15, 20));
objout.flush();
```

This example shows that serializing an object to a stream is not very different from writing primitive data to a stream. The example writes objects to a file, but the output stream can just as easily be chained to a network connection stream.

NOTE

Without calling the `reset()` method of `java.io.ObjectOutputStream`, you cannot use the same stream to write the same object reference twice.

Deserialization

The `ObjectInputStream` class reads serialized object data. By using the methods of this class, a program can restore a serialized object, along with the entire tree of objects referred to by the primary object, from the stream. Primitive data types may also be read from an object input stream.

Part IV

Object Input Streams

There is only one class constructor in the `ObjectInputStream` class:

```
public ObjectInputStream(InputStream in) throws IOException,
    StreamCorruptedException
```

The constructor calls the class's `readStreamHeader()` method to verify the header and the version that were written into the stream by the corresponding object output stream. If a problem is detected with the header or the version, a `StreamCorruptedException` is thrown.

The primary method of the `ObjectInputStream` class is `readObject()`, which deserializes an object from the data source stream. The deserialized object is returned as an `Object`; the caller is responsible for casting it to the correct type.

The Known Objects Table

During deserialization, a list is maintained of objects that have been restored from the stream. This list is called the *known objects table.*

If the data being written is of a primitive type, it is simply treated as a sequence of bytes and restored from the input stream. If the data being restored is a string, it is read using the string's UTF encoding; the string will be added to the known objects table.

If the object being restored is an array, the type and length of the array are determined. Next, memory for the array is allocated, and each of the elements contained in the array is read using the appropriate read method. After the array is reconstructed, it is added to the known objects table. If it is an array of objects (as opposed to primitives), each object is deserialized and added to the known objects table.

When an object is restored, it is added to the known objects table. The objects to which the original object refers are then restored recursively, and added to the known objects table.

Object Validation

After an object has been retrieved from a stream, it must be validated so it can become a full-fledged object and be used by the program that deserialized it. The `validateObject()` method is called when a complete graph of objects has been retrieved from a stream. If the primary object cannot be made valid, the validation process will stop, and an exception will be thrown.

Security for Serialized Objects

Serialization can involve storing an object's data on a disk file or transmitting the data across a network. In both cases, there is a potential security problem because the data is located outside the Java runtime environment—beyond the reach of Java's security mechanisms.

The `writeExternal()` method is public, so any object can make an externalizable or serializable object write itself to a stream. You should be careful when deciding whether or not `writeExternal()` should serialize sensitive private data. When an object is restored via an ordinary `readExternal()` call, its sensitive values are restored into private variables, and no harm is done; however, while the serialized data is outside the system, an attacker could access the data, decode its format, and obtain the sensitive values. A similar form of attack would involve modifying data values–for example, replacing a password or incrementing a bank balance. A less precise attack would simply corrupt the serialized data.

When an object is serialized, all the reachable objects of its ownership graph are potentially exposed. For example, a serialized object might have a reference to a reference to a reference to an instance of the `FileDescriptor` class. An attacker could reserialize the file descriptor, and gain access to the file system of the machine where the serialized object originated.

The best protection for an object that has fields that should not be stored is to label those fields with the `transient` keyword. Transient fields, like static fields, are not serialized, and therefore are not exposed.

If a class cannot be serialized in a manner that upholds the integrity of the system containing it, it should avoid implementing the `Serializable` interface. Moreover, it should not be referred to by any class that will be serialized, unless its reference is marked `transient`.

Externalizable objects (that is, ones that take care of writing their own data) often use the technique of including invariant data among their instance variables. These invariants serve no useful purpose during normal operation of the class. They are inspected after deserialization; an unexpected value indicates that the external serialized representation has been corrupted.

Serialization Exceptions

There are six types of exceptions that can be thrown during serialization or deserialization of an object:

`InvalidClassException` Typically thrown when the class type cannot be determined by the reserializing stream, or when the class that is being returned cannot be represented on the system retrieving the object. This exception is also thrown if the deserialized class is not declared public, or if it does not have a public default (no-argument) constructor.

NotSerializableException Typically thrown by externalizable objects (which are responsible for their own reserialization) on detection of a corrupted input stream. The corruption is generally indicated by an unexpected invariant value, or simply when you try to serialize a nonserializable object.

StreamCorruptedException Thrown when a stored object's header or control data is invalid.

OptionalDataException Thrown when a stream is supposed to contain an object, but it actually contains only primitive data.

ClassNotFoundException Thrown when the class of the deserialized object cannot be found on the read-side of the stream.

IOException Thrown when there is an error related to the stream from which the object is being written to or read.

Object Stream Processes

Writing an object to a stream is a simple process, similar to the process of writing any other kind of high-level structure. You must create a low-level output stream to provide access to the external medium (generally a file or network). Next, a high-level stream is chained to the low-level stream; for serialization, the high-level stream is an object output stream.

The following code fragment constructs an instance of `Point`, and writes it to a file called `Point.ser` on the local file system. (Note that the .ser extension is the conventional extension for serialized objects.)

```
Point p = new Point(13, 10);
FileOutputStream f = new FileOutputStream("Point.ser");
ObjectOutputStream s = new ObjectOutputStream (f);
try
{
    s.writeObject (p);
    s.flush ();
} catch (IOException e) { }
```

Restoring the object involves opening a file input stream on the file and chaining an object input stream to the file input stream. The `Point` object is read by calling `readObject()` from the object input stream; the return value is of type `Object` and must be cast by the caller. The following code fragment shows how this is done:

```
Point p = null;
FileInputStream f = new FileInputStream("Point.ser");
ObjectInputStream s = new ObjectInputStream (f);
try
{
    p = (Point)s.readObject ();
}
catch (IOException e) {}
```

In the next section, we will develop a simple example that saves and restores an object.

An Introduction to Remote Method Invocation

Java's RMI feature enables a program in one JVM to make method calls on an object located in a different JVM, which could be running on a remote machine. The RMI feature gives Java programmers the ability to distribute computing across a networked environment. Object-oriented design requires that every task be executed by the object most appropriate to that task. RMI takes this concept one step further by allowing a task to be performed on the *machine* most appropriate to the task.

RMI defines a remote interface that can be used to create remote objects. A client can invoke the methods of a remote object with the same syntax that it uses to invoke methods on a local object. The RMI API provides classes and methods that handle all of the underlying communication and parameter referencing requirements of accessing remote methods. RMI also handles the serialization of objects that are passed as arguments to methods of remote objects.

The `java.rmi` and the `java.rmi.server` packages contain the interfaces and classes that define building blocks for creating server-side objects and client-side object stubs. A *stub* is a local representation of a remote object. The client makes calls to the stub, which automatically communicates with the server.

Object Persistence and RMI

When a Java program uses RMI, method parameters must be transmitted to the server and a return value must be sent back to the client. Primitive values can be simply sent byte by byte; however, passing objects, either as parameters or return values, requires a more sophisticated solution.

The remote object instance needs access to the entire graph of objects referenced by a parameter passed to its method. The remote method might construct and return a complicated object that holds references to other objects. If this is the case, the entire graph must be returned, so any object passed to or returned from a remote method must implement either the `Serializable` or the `Externalizable` interface.

NOTE

RMI is similar to the Remote Procedure Call (RPC) feature that Sun introduced in 1985. RPC also required a way to serialize parameter and return value data, although the situation was simpler because of the absence of objects. Sun developed a system called External Data Representation (XDR) to support data serialization. One significant difference between RPC and RMI is that RPC uses the fast but not very reliable UDP protocol; by default, RMI uses the slower but more reliable TCP/IP protocol. By implementing your own subclass of `java.rmi.server.RMISocketFactory`, however, you can choose to run RMI over other socket protocols.

The RMI Architecture

The RMI architecture consists of three layers: the stubs/skeleton layer, the remote reference layer, and the transport layer. The relationships among these layers are shown in Figure 18.1.

When a client invokes a remote method, the request starts at the top with the stub on the client side. The client references the stub as a proxy for the object on the remote machine; all the underlying functionality shown in Figure 18.1 is invisible to the client. The stub code is generated with the `rmic` compiler and uses the remote reference layer (RRL) to pass method invocation requests to the server object.

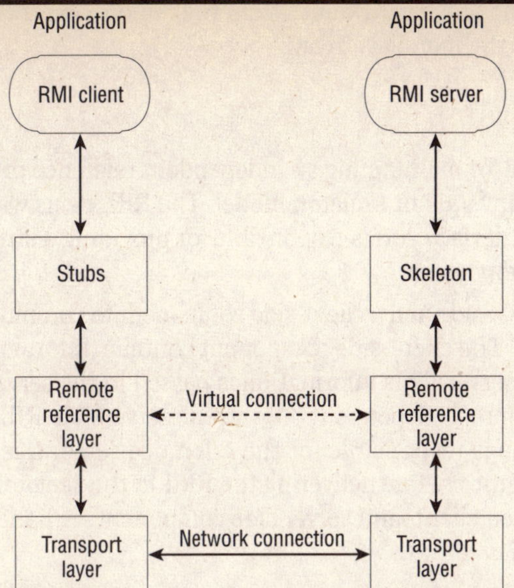

FIGURE 18.1: An overview of the RMI architecture

Stubs

The stub is the client-side proxy representing the remote object. Stubs define all of the interfaces that the remote object implementation supports. The stub is referenced like any other local object by a program running on the client machine. It is a local object on the client side; it also maintains a connection to the server-side object.

The RRL on the client side returns a *marshal stream* to the stub. The marshal stream is used by the RRL to communicate to the RRL on the server side. The stub serializes parameter data, passing the serialized data into the marshal stream.

After the remote method has been executed, the RRL passes any serialized return values back to the stub, which is responsible for deserializing.

The Skeleton

The skeleton is the server-side construct that interfaces with the server-side RRL. The skeleton receives method invocation requests from the client-side RRL. The server-side RRL must unmarshal any arguments that are sent to a remote method. The skeleton then makes a call to the actual object implementation on the server side. The skeleton is also responsible for receiving any return values from the remote object and marshaling them onto the marshal stream.

The RRL

The RRL is responsible for maintaining an independent reference protocol that is not specific to any stub or skeleton model. The RRL deals with the lower-level transport interface and is responsible for providing a stream to the stubs and skeleton layers.

The RRL uses a server-side and a client-side component to communicate via the transport layer. The client-side component contains information specific to the remote server. This information is passed to the server-side component and, therefore, is dependent only on the server-side RRL. The RRL on the server side is responsible for the reference semantics and deals with those semantics before delivering the RMI to the skeleton. The communication between client- and server-side components is handled by the transport layer.

The Transport Layer

The transport layer is responsible for creating and maintaining connections between the client and server. The transport layer consists of four abstractions:

- An *endpoint* is used to reference the address space that contains a JVM. An endpoint is a reference to a specific transport instance.
- A *channel* is the pathway between two address spaces. This channel is responsible for managing any connections from the client to the server and vice versa.
- A *connection* is an abstraction for transferring data (arguments and return values) between client and server.
- The *transport* abstraction is responsible for setting up a channel between a local address space and a remote endpoint. The transport abstraction is also responsible for accepting incoming connections to the address space containing the abstraction.

The transport layer sets up connections, manages existing connections, and handles remote objects residing in its address space.

When the transport layer receives a request from the client-side RRL, it establishes a socket connection to the server. The transport layer then passes the established connection to the client-side RRL, and adds a reference to the remote object to an internal table. At this point, the client is connected to the server.

The transport layer monitors the "liveness" of the connection. If a significant amount of time passes with no activity on the connection, the transport layer is responsible for shutting down the connection. The timeout period is 10 minutes.

An RMI Example

Creating an application that is accessible to remote clients involves a number of steps:

1. Define interfaces for the remote classes.
2. Create and compile implementation classes for the remote classes.
3. Create stub and skeleton classes using the `rmic` command.
4. Create and compile a server application.
5. Start the `rmiregistry` and the server application.
6. Create and compile a client program to access the remote objects.
7. Test the client.

As an example of an RMI application, we will develop a simple credit card system. The server will support creating a new account, as well as performing transactions against an existing account. Because the intention of the example is to show you how to use RMI, there will not be a client-side user interface; the client will simply make a few hardcoded invocations.

The source code for this example, which is shown in the following sections, includes the following files:

- `CreditCard.java`
- `CreditManager.java`
- `CreditCardImpl.java`
- `CreditManagerImpl.java`
- `CardBank.java`
- `Shopper.java`

Defining Interfaces for Remote Classes

The program will use two remote classes. The `CreditCardImpl` class will maintain the username, balance, available credit, and personal ID signature number for a single credit card account. The `CreditManagerImpl` class will maintain a list of `Account` objects, and create new ones when necessary. The server-side application will construct a single instance of `CreditManagerImpl`, and make it available to remote clients.

Each of these classes must be described by an interface: `CreditCard` and `CreditManager`. The client-side stubs will implement these interfaces. The stub classes will be created in a later step by the `rmic` utility. Note that `rmic` imposes several requirements: The interfaces must be public and extend the `Remote` interface; each method must throw `RemoteException`; and the stub and implementation code must reside in a package. Listings 18.1 and 18.2 show `CreditCard` and `CreditManager`.

Listing 18.1: CreditCard.java

```
package credit;

import credit.*;
import java.rmi.*;

public interface CreditCard extends java.rmi.Remote {

    /** This method returns a credit card's credit line. */
    public float getCreditLine() throws
        java.rmi.RemoteException;

    /** This method allows a card holder to pay all or some
        of a balance. Throws InvalidMoneyException if the
        money param is invalid. */
    public void payTowardsBalance(float money) throws
        java.rmi.RemoteException, InvalidMoneyException;

    /** This method allows the card holder to make purchases
        against the line of credit. Throws
        CreditLineExceededException
        if the purchase exceeds available credit. */
    public void makePurchase(float amount, int signature)
        throws java.rmi.RemoteException,
        InvalidSignatureException,
        CreditLineExceededException;
```

```
    /** This method sets the card's personal ID signature. */
    public void setSignature(int pin)
        throws java.rmi.RemoteException;
}
```

Listing 18.2: CreditManager.java

```
package credit;

import credit.*;
import java.rmi.*;
import java.rmi.RemoteException;

public interface CreditManager extends java.rmi.Remote {

    /** This method finds an existing credit card for a given
        customer name. If the customer does not have an
        account, a new card will be "issued" with a
        random personal ID signature and a $5000 starting
        credit line. */
    public CreditCard findCreditAccount(String Customer)
        throws DuplicateAccountException,
        java.rmi.RemoteException;


    /** This method creates a new credit account with a
        random personal ID signature and a $5000 starting
        credit line. */
    public CreditCard newCreditAccount(String newCustomer)
        throws java.rmi.RemoteException;
}
```

Creating and Compiling Implementation Classes

The implementation classes are server-side classes that implement the `CreditCard` and `CreditManager` interfaces.

The `CreditCard` interface is implemented by the `CreditCardImpl` class. This class must implement all of the methods in the `CreditCard` interface, and it extends `UnicastRemoteObject`. To date, there is no support for multicast objects.

The interfaces and classes declare that they belong to the `credit` package. Each of the source files should be compiled with the `-d` <*directoryname*> option to specify a destination directory for the resulting

`.class` files. Within the destination directory, the compiler will automatically create a subdirectory called `credit` (if one does not already exist); then, the class files will be created in the `credit` subdirectory. The destination directory supplied to the `-d` option should be in the class path. An easy way to compile the interfaces and classes is to create a "credit" directory; change directories to the credit directory, and compile the source, as follows:

```
cd credit
javac -d ..\. CreditCard.java
javac -d ..\. CreditCardImpl.java
javac -d ..\. CreditManager.java
javac -d ..\. CreditManagerImpl.java
```

The `CreditManagerImpl` class is responsible for creating and storing new accounts (as `CreditImpl` objects). This class uses a hashtable to store the account objects, keyed by owner name. The source code for the `CreditCardImpl` and `CreditManagerImpl` classes are shown in Listings 18.3 and 18.4.

Listing 18.3: CreditCardImpl.java

```
package credit;

import java.rmi.*;
import java.rmi.server.*;
import java.io.Serializable;

/** This class is the remote object that will referenced by
    the skeleton on the server side and the stub on the
    client side. */

public class CreditCardImpl
    extends UnicastRemoteObject
    implements CreditCard
 {
    private float currentBalance = 0;
    private float creditLine = 5000f;
    private int signature = 0;          // Like a PIN number
    private String accountName;         // Name of owner

    /** Class constructor generates an initial PIN.*/
    public CreditCardImpl(String customer) throws
    java.rmi.RemoteException, DuplicateAccountException {
        accountName = customer;
```

```
        signature = (int)(Math.random() * 10000);
    }

    /** Returns credit line. */
    public float getCreditLine() throws
    java.rmi.RemoteException {
        return creditLine;
    }

    /** Pays off some debt. */
    public void payTowardsBalance(float money) throws
    java.rmi.RemoteException, credit.InvalidMoneyException {
        if (money <= 0) {
            throw new InvalidMoneyException ();
        } else {
            currentBalance -= money;
        }
    }

    /** Changes signature. */
    public void setSignature(int pin) throws
    java.rmi.RemoteException {
        signature = pin;
    }

    /** Makes a purchase. Makes sure enough credit is
        available, then increments balance and decrements
        available credit. */
    public void makePurchase(float amount, int signature)
    throws java.rmi.RemoteException,
    credit.InvalidSignatureException,
    credit.CreditLineExceededException {
        if (signature != this.signature) {
            throw new InvalidSignatureException();
        }
        if (currentBalance+amount > creditLine) {
            throw new CreditLineExceededException();
        } else {
            currentBalance += amount;
            creditLine -= amount;
        }
    }
}
```

Listing 18.4: CreditManagerImpl.java

```
package credit;

import java.rmi.*;
import java.rmi.server.*;
import java.util.Hashtable;

public class CreditManagerImpl extends UnicastRemoteObject
implements CreditManager {
    private static transient Hashtable accounts =
        new Hashtable();

    /** This is the default class constructor that does
        nothing but implicitly calls super() which throws
        a RemoteException. */
public CreditManagerImpl() throws RemoteException { }

    /** Creates a new account. Puts the customer name and
        the customer's credit card in the hashtable. */
    public CreditCard newCreditAccount(String customerName)
    throws java.rmi.RemoteException {
        CreditCardImpl newCard = null;
        try {
            newCard = new CreditCardImpl(customerName);
        } catch (DuplicateAccountException e) {
            return null;
        }
        accounts.put(customerName, newCard);
        return newCard;
    }

    /** Searches the hashtable for an existing account. If no
        account for customer name, one is created and added
        to hashtable.  Returns the account. */
    public CreditCard findCreditAccount(String customer)
    throws DuplicateAccountException, RemoteException {
        CreditCardImpl account =
          (CreditCardImpl)accounts.get(customer);
        if (account != null) {
            return account;
        }
```

```
            // Creates new account. Adds credit card to hashtable
            account = new CreditCardImpl(customer);
            accounts.put(customer, account);
            return account;
        }
    }
```

Creating Stub and Skeleton Classes

After the implementation classes are compiled, the next step is to create the stub and skeleton class files that are used to access the implementation classes. The stub classes are used by the client code to communicate with the server skeleton code.

The `rmic` command automatically creates stub and skeleton code from the interface and implementation class definitions. The syntax of the command is:

```
rmic [options] package.interfaceImpl ...
```

For our example, the following command creates the stubs and skeletons for the `CreditCard` and `CreditManager` remote classes:

```
rmic -d . credit.CreditCardImpl credit.CreditManagerImpl
```

Note that the command requires specification of the package in which the class files reside. This is why all the source modules for the implementation classes declare that they belong to the `credit` package.

The `rmic` command creates four class files in the `credit` package directory:

- `CreditCardImpl_Skel.class`
- `CreditCardImpl_Stub.class`
- `CreditManagerImpl_Skel.class`
- `CreditManagerImpl_Stub.class`

Creating and Compiling the Server Application

Now that the stubs and skeletons have been created, the next step is to create a server-side application that makes these classes available to clients for remote invocation.

The server-side application will be an application class called `CardBank`, whose main job is to construct an instance of `CreditManager`. Except for the line that calls the CreditManager constructor, all of the CardBank code, in Listing 18.5, involves making the CreditManager object available to remote clients. The details of this process are explained after Listing 18.5.

Listing 18.5: CardBank.java

```
import java.util.*;
import java.rmi.*;
import java.rmi.RMISecurityManager;
import credit.*;

public class CardBank {

    public static void main (String args[]) {
        //  Create and install a security manager.
        System.setSecurityManager(new RMISecurityManager());

        try {
            // Create an instance of our Credit Manager.
            System.out.println
               ("CreditManagerImpl: create a CreditManager");
            CreditManagerImpl cmi = new CreditManagerImpl();

            // Bind the object instance to the remote
            // registry. Use the static rebind() method
            // to avoid conflicts.
            System.out.println
               ("CreditManagerImpl: bind it to a name");
            Naming.rebind("cardManager", cmi);

            System.out.println("CreditManager is now ready");

        } catch (Exception e) {
            System.out.println("An error occured");
            e.printStackTrace();
            System.out.println(e.getMessage());
        }
    }
}
```

Applications, by default, run without security managers. In the main method of CardBank, the setSecurityManager() call installs an RMI security manager.

The server "publishes" an object instance by binding a specified name to the instance and registering that name with the RMI registry. There are two methods that allow an instance to be bound and registered:

```
public static void bind(String name, Remote obj)
   throwsAlreadyBoundException, MalformedUrlException,
   UnknownHostException, RemoteException

public static void rebind(String name, Remote obj) throws
MalformedUrlException, UnknownHostException, RemoteException
```

Notice that both methods are static, and ask for a name to reference the object, as well as the remote object instance that is bound to the name. In our example, the object name is `cardManager`. Any machine on the network can refer to this object by specifying the host machine and the object name.

The name argument required by both `bind()` and `rebind()` is a URL-like string. This string can be in this format:

`protocol://host:port/bindingName`

Here *`protocol`* is `rmi`, *`host`* is the name of the RMI server, *`port`* is the port number on which the server should listen for requests, and *`bindingName`* is the exact name that should be used by a client when requesting access to the object. If just a name is given in the string, default values are used. The defaults are `rmi` for the protocol, `localhost` for the server name, and 1099 for the port number.

WARNING

An attempt to bind to any host other than the localhost will result in a `SecurityException`.

Both `bind()` and `rebind()` associate a name with an object. They differ in their behavior when the name being bound has already been bound to an object. In this case, `bind()` will throw `AlreadyBoundException`, and `rebind()` will discard the old binding and use the new one.

Starting the Registry and Server Application

The `rmiregistry` is an application that provides a simple naming lookup service. When the `CardBank` calls `rebind()`, it is the registry that maintains the binding. The registry can be run as an independent program, or it can be created by calling the `java.rmi.registry.LocateRegistry.createRegistry` method and it must be running before the server-side application is invoked. The program resides in the `jdk/bin` directory.

The following two command lines invoke the registry and start up the card bank server:

start rmiregistry

java CardBank

The card bank application prints several status lines as it starts up the service. If there are no errors, you should scc thc following output:

```
CreditManagerImpl: create a CreditManager
CreditManagerImpl: bind it to a name
CreditManager is now ready
```

After an object has been passed to the registry, a client may request that the registry provide a reference to the remote object. The next section shows how this is done.

Naming services such as the rmiregistry are discussed in more detail in Chapter 8, "Java Naming and Directory Interface (JNDI)."

Creating and Compiling the Client Program

The `Shopper` application needs to find a `CreditManager` object on the remote server. The program assumes that the server name has been passed in as the first command-line argument. This name is used to create a URL-like string of this format:

```
rmi://<hostname>/cardManager
```

The string is passed to the static `lookup()` method of the `Naming` class. The `lookup()` call communicates with the `rmiregistry` and returns a handle to the remote object that was constructed and registered. More accurately, what is returned is a handle to a stub that communicates with the remote object.

The return type from `lookup()` is `Remote`, which is the parent of all stub interfaces. When the return value is cast to type `CreditManager`, the methods of `CreditManager` can be invoked on it. Listing 18.6, titled `Shopper.java`, shows how this is done.

Listing 18.6: Shopper.java

```
import java.rmi.*;
import java.rmi.RMISecurityManager;
import credit.*;
```

```
public class Shopper {

    public static void main(String args[]) {

        CreditManager cm = null;
        CreditCard account = null;

        // Check the command line.
        if (args.length < 2) {
            System.err.println("Usage:");
            System.err.println
              ("java Shopper <server> <account name>");
            System.exit (1);
        }

        // Create and install a security manager.
        System.setSecurityManager(new RMISecurityManager());

        // Obtain reference to card manager.
        try {
            String url =
               new String ("//" + args[0] + "/cardManager");
            System.out.println
               ("Shopper: lookup cardManager, url = "+ url);
            cm = (CreditManager)Naming.lookup(url);
        } catch (Exception e) {
            System.out.println
               ("Error in getting card manager" + e);
            System.exit (1);
}

        // Get user's account.
        try {
            account = cm.findCreditAccount(args[1]);
            System.out.println
               ("Found account for " + args[1]);
        } catch (Exception e) {
            System.out.println
               ("Error in getting account for " + args[1]);
            System.exit (1);
}
```

```
            // Do some transactions.
            try {
                System.out.println("Available credit is: "
                                  + account.getCreditLine());
                System.out.println
                    ("Changing pin number for account");
                account.setSignature(1234);
                System.out.println
                    ("Buying a new watch for $100");
                account.makePurchase(100.00f, 1234);
                System.out.println("Available credit is now: " +
                                    account.getCreditLine());
                System.out.println
                    ("Buying a new pair of shoes for $160");
                account.makePurchase(160.00f, 1234);
                System.out.println
                    ("CardHolder: Paying off $136 of balance");
                account.payTowardsBalance(136.00f);
                System.out.println("Available credit is now: "+
                                    account.getCreditLine());
            } catch (Exception e) {
                System.out.println
                   ("Transaction error for " + args[1]);
            }

           System.exit(0);
        }
    }
```

The client expects two command-line arguments. The first argument specifies the server. (For testing on a single machine, specify localhost for the server name.) The second argument is a string that provides an account name. The client program asks the server-side credit manager object for a handle to the credit card object that represents this customer's account. (If the customer has no account yet, one will be created.) The initial random PIN number is modified to something a user will find easier to remember. The client program then makes several purchases and one payment, reporting the available credit after each transaction.

Testing the Client

The final step is to execute the client code. It can be run from any computer that has access to the server and to the supporting classes. Here is a sample session output on a Unix machine, with the remote service running on a host named sunbert (the first line is the invocation; the rest is output):

```
% java Shopper sunbert pogo
Shopper: lookup cardManager, url = //sunbert/cardManager
Found account for pogo
Available credit is: 5000.0
Changing pin number for account
Buying a new watch for $100
Available credit is now: 4900.0
Buying a new pair of shoes for $160
CardHolder: Paying off $136 of balance
Available credit is now: 4740.0
```

After the client program has finished running, the remote objects are still alive. The previous execution created a new account for the customer. A second invocation of the client will work with that account; the available credit numbers in the listing below reflect the current state of the account:

```
% java Shopper sunbert pogo
Shopper: lookup cardManager, url = //sunbert/cardManager
Found account for pogo
Available credit is: 4740.0
Changing pin number for account
Buying a new watch for $100
Available credit is now: 4640.0
Buying a new pair of shoes for $160
CardHolder: Paying off $136 of balance
Available credit is now: 4480.0
```

Advanced RMI

Here are some of the additional features in RMI, which we will explore in the following sections:

- The ability to perform callbacks
- Dynamic class loading
- Object activation, which allows a client to request a reference to a remote object that is not currently active in a JVM

TIP

RMI allows you to define and use a custom socket protocol. By subclassing the `RMISocketFactory` class, you can create your own network protocols, change the network protocol on a per-object basis, or make use of secure network protocols such as Secure Socket Layer (SSL).

Callback Operations

The simple credit card system we developed in the previous section demonstrates a typical client/server application. The `CardBank` server creates an instance of a `CardManager` object, and serves the instance of the object to the `Shopper` client using RMI. That example illustrates some of the underlying communications that RMI handles on the developer's behalf, such as the creation and use of network sockets.

What that example does not show is that RMI is capable of providing two-way communications between objects. For an object's reference to be sent from one place to another, the object's class only needs to implement a `Remote` interface and be exported to receive remote method calls (by extending `UnicastRemoteObject`, an object is automatically exported).

After these two requirements have been met, it is possible to send a remote object from a client to a server in such a way that the server is actually calling the remote methods of the client object. This is the nature of truly distributed applications: There is no distinction between "client" and "server"—each application provides or uses the services of another.

To demonstrate this concept with a practical example, we will extend the `Credit` application. In that example, the customer receives a credit line by simply passing their name to the `CreditManager`. In this example, the customer will fill out `CreditApplication` and then send that application to the `CreditManager`. The `CreditManager` instance will use methods provided by a `CreditApplication` to fill in data that the customer can then validate for the final credit application.

In this example, the client creates a local instance of a `CreditApplication` object and passes a reference to that instance to the server through the `CreditManager`, obtained through the registry. The server executes methods on the `CreditApplication` reference using the same mechanism the client uses—the server holds a reference to a stub instance that forwards requests to the client's local object.

Creating the CreditApplication Object

The CreditApplication object is created in the same way as any other RMI remote object. The object's remote methods are defined in an interface class that extends java.rmi.Remote as shown in Listing 18.7.

Listing 18.7: CreditApplication.java

```
package credit;

import java.rmi.*;

public interface CreditApplication extends Remote {

    public String getCustName ()
    throws RemoteException;

    public void setCreditLine (float amount)
    throws RemoteException;

    public void setCreditCardNumber (String cardNumber)
    throws RemoteException;

}
```

Implementing CreditApplication

The CreditApplicationImpl class, shown in Listing 18.8, is an implementation of CreditApplication, and provides bodies for each of the methods defined in the interface. In addition, CreditApplicationImpl defines the data that a credit application is expected to store. This class extends UnicastRemoteObject so that it is automatically exported upon creation, and it implements a remote interface, CreditApplication, so that it may be passed *by reference* to the server. For cases where a class cannot extend UnicastRemoteObject, the developer can explicitly export an object through the static method, UnicastRemoteObject.exportObject.

Listing 18.8: CreditApplicationImpl.java

```
package credit;

import java.rmi.*;
import java.rmi.server.*;
```

```
public class CreditApplicationImpl
extends UnicastRemoteObject
implements CreditApplication {

    private float creditLine;
    private float creditRate;
    private String creditCardNumber;
    private String custName;
    private String ssn;

    public CreditApplicationImpl (String name, String soc)
    throws RemoteException {
        custName = name;
        ssn = soc;
    }

    public String getCustName () {
        return custName;
    }

    public void setCreditLine (float amount) {
        creditLine = amount;
    }

    public float getCreditLine () {
        return creditLine;
    }

    public void setCreditCardNumber (String cardNumber) {
        creditCardNumber = new String (cardNumber);
    }

    public String getCreditCardNumber () {
        return creditCardNumber;
    }
}
```

Modifying CreditManager

The `CreditManager` interface, shown in Listing 18.9, is modified so that the `CreditApplication` object can be sent to the credit manager. If the customer's application is accepted, the customer will then be issued a valid `CreditCard`.

Listing 18.9: CreditManager.java

```
package credit;

import java.rmi.*;


public interface CreditManager extends java.rmi.Remote {

    /** This method finds an existing credit card for a
        given customer credit number. If the customer
        does not have an account, an InvalidAccountException
        is thrown. */
    public CreditCard findCreditAccount(String customer)
        throws InvalidAccountException, RemoteException;


    /** This method receives an CreditApplication object from
        the customer. On the customer's behalf the server
        will fill in the missing account number, initial
        credit line and rate. */
    public void applyForCard (CreditApplication app)
        throws DuplicateAccountException,
               AccountRejectedException, RemoteException;
}
```

Implementing CreditManager

The implementation of a CreditManager object is changed to reflect the new design. The CreditManagerImpl, shown in Listing 18.10, now uses a private method to create a credit account, which is called only if the customer's credit application is approved.

Listing 18.10: CreditManagerImpl.java

```
package credit;

import java.rmi.*;
import java.rmi.server.*;
import java.util.Hashtable;

public class CreditManagerImpl extends UnicastRemoteObject
implements CreditManager {
    private static transient Hashtable accounts =
    new Hashtable();
```

```
/** This is the default class constructor that does
    nothing but implicitly call super(). */
public CreditManagerImpl() throws RemoteException { }

/** Creates a new account. Puts the customer name and the
    customer's credit card in the hashtable. */
private void newCreditAccount(String name,
    String cardNumber, float creditLine)
    throws DuplicateAccountException,
    RemoteException {
    CreditCardImpl newCard =
        new CreditCardImpl(name, cardNumber, creditLine);
    accounts.put(cardNumber, newCard);
}

/** Searches the hashtable for an existing account. If
    no account for customer name, an
    InvalidAccountException is thrown. */
public CreditCard findCreditAccount(String cardNumber)
throws InvalidAccountException, RemoteException {
    CreditCardImpl account =
        (CreditCardImpl)accounts.get(cardNumber);
    if (account != null) {
        return account;
    } else {
        throw new InvalidAccountException ();
    }
}

/** The Account Manager will determine (based on the
    customer name and social security number) the
    credit line and credit rate. */

public void applyForCard (CreditApplication app)
    throws DuplicateAccountException,
           AccountRejectedException, RemoteException {

    // Here, some other process would determine the
    // customer's credit rating...
    // For now, we'll hardcode that number to 5000.
    app.setCreditLine (5000.0f);

    // Generate a credit card number the user can use.
```

```
            String cardNumber = app.getCustName() +
                (int)(Math.random() * 10000);
            app.setCreditCardNumber (cardNumber);

            // Generate the customer credit card.
            newCreditAccount (app.getCustName(), cardNumber,
            5000.0f);
        }
    }
```

Modifying the Client

The client application, shown in Listing 18.11, is modified only slightly to include the step of applying for credit through a `CreditApplication` object.

Listing 18.11: Customer.java

```
import credit.*;
import java.rmi.*;

public class Customer {

    public static void main(String args[]) {

        CreditManager cm = null;
        CreditApplicationImpl cardApp = null;
        CreditCard account = null;

        // Check the command line.
        if (args.length < 3) {
            System.err.println("Usage:");
            System.err.println("java Customer <server>"+
            "<account name> <social security number>");
            System.exit (1);
        }

        // Create and install a security manager.
        System.setSecurityManager(new RMISecurityManager());

        // Obtain reference to card manager.
        try {
            String url = new String ("//" + args[0] +
            "/cardManager");
```

```
            System.out.println
              ("Shopper: lookup cardManager, url = " + url);
            cm = (CreditManager)Naming.lookup(url);
        } catch (Exception e) {
            System.out.println
              ("Error in getting card manager" + e);
            System.exit(1);
        }

        // Apply for a credit card.

        // Create an instance of a credit card application.

        // Send the credit application to the Credit Manager.
        try {
            cardApp =
               new CreditApplicationImpl(args[1],args[2]);
            cm.applyForCard (cardApp);
        } catch (DuplicateAccountException e) {
            System.out.println
               ("Duplicate Exception applying for credit");
            System.exit (1);
        } catch (AccountRejectedException e) {
            System.out.println
               ("Reject Exception applying for credit");
            System.exit (1);
        } catch (RemoteException e) {
            System.out.println
               ("Remote Exception applying for credit " + e);
            System.exit (1);
        }

        // The application was accepted, let's use the card!
        try {

            System.out.println ("New card number is: " +
               cardApp.getCreditCardNumber() +
               " with a credit line of: " +
               cardApp.getCreditLine());
            account =
               cm.findCreditAccount
                 (cardApp.getCreditCardNumber());
```

```
        System.out.println ("Found account: " +
            cardApp.getCreditCardNumber());
    } catch (Exception e) {
        System.out.println
          ("Error in getting account for " + args[1]);

        System.exit(1);
    }

    // Do some transactions.
    try {
        System.out.println("Available credit is: "
                           + account.getCreditLine());
        System.out.println
           ("Changing pin number for account");
        account.setSignature(1234);
        System.out.println
           ("Buying a new watch for $100");
        account.makePurchase(100.00f, 1234);
        System.out.println("Available credit is now: " +
                           account.getCreditLine());
        System.out.println
           ("Buying a new pair of shoes for $160");
        account.makePurchase(160.00f, 1234);
        System.out.println
           ("CardHolder: Paying off $136 of balance");
        account.payTowardsBalance(136.00f);
        System.out.println("Available credit is now: "+
                           account.getCreditLine());
    } catch (Exception e) {
        System.out.println("Transaction error for " +
        args[1]);
    }

   System.exit(0);
  }
}
```

All that remains is to run `rmic` on the client-side `CreditApplicationImpl` class. The `rmic` utility creates a set of stub classes that the server will use as proxies to the implementation class.

Part IV

Dynamic Class Loading

One of the primary features of RMI is that it has been designed from the ground up as a Java-to-Java distributed object system. RMI is distinct from other systems such as CORBA (discussed in the next chapter) in that it is possible to send a complete object from one remote address space to another. This feature makes it possible to not only pass data over the network, but also to pass behavior–complete class definitions can be passed using the magic of the `RMIClassLoader` and serialization. RMI makes it easy to send a full object graph by passing an object as the argument to a method call. The only requirement for passing an object is that the object be serializable.

How is this useful? Passing an object to another address space makes it possible to use the resources of that address space–CPU cycles, files, database access, and so on. If the type of computation required by the object is complex, sending it from a slower machine to a faster machine is worth the overhead of transferring the object over the network.

NOTE

Traditional RMI communicates between remote address spaces using a custom protocol (the Java Remote Method Protocol) over a standard TCP/IP protocol. RMI now has an alternative underlying protocol called Internet-Inter ORB Protocol (IIOP). RMI-IIOP facilitates communicating with CORBA.

As an example of dynamic class loading, we will continue the bank paradigm of the previous examples and apply RMI to the process of obtaining a loan. Although this example is by no means computation-intensive and could be easily executed locally, the example demonstrates the mechanics of sending an object from one address space to another.

In the example, the client and server both share the definition of an abstract class called `LoanType`. The `LoanType` class defines the `calculatePayment()` method, which returns a `LoanType` object. On the client side, a subclass of `LoanType` defines what the `calculate-Payment` method should do.

The client application requests a reference to a `LoanOfficer` class and then sends an instance of a `LoanType` object to the `LoanOfficer.processLoan` method. This method executes the `calculatePayment` method of the object passed and returns an instance of a `LoanType` object.

NOTE

The `LoanOfficer` doesn't know in advance what code it is going to run. It depends on the subtype of `LoanType` it receives.

Although this looks a little like the callback presented in the previous section, in this example, the server application must recreate (through class loading and serialization) an instance of the object passed as a `LoanType` object before executing the method. The server is working on a copy of the client's `LoanType`.

NOTE

Both the callback mechanism and the dynamic class loading mechanism are triggered by passing objects as arguments to remote methods. The key difference between passing a remote reference (which contains a stub instance) used in a callback versus the serialized instance of an object is whether or not the object being passed implements the `java.rmi.Remote` interface. If an object implements a remote interface, its stub is serialized; otherwise, the object instance is serialized.

Defining the LoanType Class

The `LoanType` class, shown in Listing 18.12, is abstract (as opposed to the interfaces used so far) because many different types of loans could have similar data and methods, differing only in how the interest and monthly payment are calculated (for example, an adjustable rate mortgage or a balloon payment).

Listing 18.12: LoanType.java

```
package bank.loan;
import java.io.Serializable;

public abstract class LoanType implements Serializable {

    private float monthlyPayment,interestRate;
    private int loanAmount, loanDuration;

    // This method is executed by the server on behalf of
    // the client.
    public abstract void calculatePayment();
```

```
        public LoanType(int amount, float rate, int term)
        {
            loanAmount=amount;
            interestRate=rate;
            loanDuration=term;
        }

        public void setMonthlyPayment(float payment)
        {
            monthlyPayment = payment;
        }

        public float getMonthlyPayment()
        {
            return monthlyPayment;
        }

        public int getLoanAmount()
        {
            return loanAmount;
        }

        public float getInterestRate()
        {
            return interestRate;
        }

        public int getLoanDuration()
        {
            return loanDuration;
        }

    }
```

Defining the ConventionalLoan Class

The client defines an instance of a `LoanType` object by extending the abstract class, and providing a method body for `calculatePayment`. This class, `ConventionalLoan`, shown in Listing 18.13, calculates the monthly payment for conventional mortgages.

Listing 18.13: ConventionalLoan.java

```
package bank.loan;

public class ConventionalLoan extends LoanType {

    public ConventionalLoan(int amount, float rate, int term)
    {
        super(amount, rate, term);
    }

    public void calculatePayment()
    {
        // convert the interest rate to decimal percentage
        float interestRate = getInterestRate()/100;

        // calculate the monthly interest rate
        float monthlyInterestRate = interestRate/12;

        // convert the duration of the loan from years in to
        // months
        int numberOfMonths = getLoanDuration() * 12;

        float pmt = (float)(getLoanAmount()*
            (monthlyInterestRate/ (1 - Math.pow((1 +
             monthlyInterestRate), -numberOfMonths))));

        setMonthlyPayment(pmt);
    }


}
```

Creating the LoanOfficer Interface

The client requests a reference to a `LoanOfficer` instance from the server application. The `LoanOfficer` interface, shown in Listing 18.14, defines the `processLoan` method, which takes a single `LoanType` argument and then returns a `LoanType` object, from which the client may extract the monthly payment amount.

Listing 18.14: LoanOfficer.java

```
package bank.loan;

import java.rmi.Remote;
import java.rmi.RemoteException;

public interface LoanOfficer extends Remote
{
    public LoanType processLoan(LoanType loan)
        throws RemoteException;
}
```

Implementing LoanOffice

The implementation of the `LoanOfficer` interface, shown in Listing 18.15, provides a method body for `processLoan`, which executes the `calculatePayment` method of the object passed.

Listing 18.15: LoanOfficerImpl.java

```
package bank.loan;

import java.rmi.Remote;
import java.rmi.RemoteException;
import java.rmi.server.UnicastRemoteObject;

public class LoanOfficerImpl extends UnicastRemoteObject
    implements LoanOfficer {

    public LoanOfficerImpl() throws RemoteException
    {
    }

    public LoanType processLoan(LoanType loan)
        throws RemoteException
    {
        loan.calculatePayment();
        return loan;
    }

}
```

Setting Up the Server

Finally, the server application, shown in Listing 18.16, creates an instance of a `LoanOfficerImpl` object, and registers the implementation with the `rmiregistry`.

Listing 18.16: Lender.java

```
import java.rmi.Naming;
import java.rmi.RemoteException;
import java.rmi.RMISecurityManager;
import bank.loan.*;

public class Lender {

    public static void main (String args[]) {
        //  Create and install a security manager.
        System.setSecurityManager(new RMISecurityManager());

        try {
            // Create an instance of our loan officer.
            System.out.println
               ("Lender: create a LoanOfficer");
            LoanOfficerImpl loi = new LoanOfficerImpl();

            // Bind the object instance to the remote
            // registry.  Use the static rebind() method
            // to avoid conflicts.
            System.out.println
               ("Lender: bind the LoanOfficer to a name");
            Naming.rebind("loanOfficer", loi);

            System.out.println
               ("The LoanOfficer is ready"+
                " to process requests");

        } catch (Exception e) {
            e.printStackTrace();
            System.out.println(e.getMessage());
        }
    }
}
```

Setting Up the Client

The client application, shown in Listing 18.17, creates an instance of `ConventionalLoan`, obtains a remote reference to a `LoanOfficer` object, and passes the instance of the `ConventionalLoan` to `LoanOfficer` through the `processLoan` method. First, the `LoanOfficerImpl` will look in its CLASSPATH for the class file. When the class is not found, it will use the URL supplied in the object's serialized form. This URL would have been set from the client's command line, via the `java.rmi.server.codebase` property. If the server cannot load the `ConventionalLoan` class from the client-supplied URL, it will fail with a `ClassNotFoundException`.

The client application takes four arguments: the hostname of the server, the amount of the loan, the annual percentage rate (as a float), and the number of years for the life of the loan.

Listing 18.17: ConventionalLoanClient.java

```
import java.rmi.Naming;
import java.rmi.RemoteException;
import java.rmi.RMISecurityManager;
import bank.loan.*;

public class ConventionalLoanClient {

   public static void main(String [] args) throws Exception {

        LoanOfficer officer;
        ConventionalLoan conv;

        // Check the command line.
        if (args.length < 4) {
            System.err.println("Usage:");
            System.err.println
               ("java ConventionalLoanClient <server> " +
               "<mortgage amount> <interest rate> " +
               "<number of years>");
            System.exit (1);
        }
    int amount = Integer.parseInt(args[1]);
    float rate = (new Float(args[2])).floatValue();
    int length = Integer.parseInt(args[3]);
```

```
    // Create a new loan instance.
    conv = new ConventionalLoan(amount, rate, length);

        // Create and install a security manager.
        System.setSecurityManager(new RMISecurityManager());

        // Obtain reference to loan officer.
        try {
            String url =
               new String ("//" + args[0] + "/loanOfficer");
            System.out.println
               ("Conventional Client: lookup loanOfficer, "+
                "url = " + url);
            officer = (LoanOfficer)Naming.lookup(url);
        } catch (Exception e) {
            System.err.println
               ("Error in getting loan officer " + e);
        throw e;
            System.exit(1);
}

    // Get the monthly payment.
        try {
        // Use the existing reference to get back
        // the changed instance information.
        conv = (ConventionalLoan)officer.processLoan(conv);
        System.out.println("Your monthly payment will be " +
                conv.getMonthlyPayment());
    } catch (Exception e1) {
            System.err.println
               ("Error in processing loan " + e1);
        throw e1;
        }

    }
}
```

Running the Loan-Processing Application

So far, the examples illustrated in this chapter have made use of two (or three, if you count the rmiregistry) JVMs running on the same host with the same CLASSPATH variable set. For this example, to illustrate that the classes are actually loaded over the network, the rmiregistry, server, and client will be isolated from each other through three steps:

- The server classes (including the stub classes created by rmic) will not be physically located in the same directory as the client application.
- The client class to be uploaded to the server (ConventionalLoan) will not be in the same directory as the server.
- The registry will be completely isolated from both the client and the server.

To load classes dynamically, the client and server applications must create and install an instance of an RMISecurityManager because the RMIClassLoader requires that a security manager be installed. Furthermore, the client and server must declare the URL path to the classes that they are "serving" for applications running in other JVMs to find these classes. The server will be "serving" the stub class for the LoanOfficerImpl, and the client will be "serving" the ConventionalLoan class definition.

To prove that the client's ConventionalLoan class and the server's stub classes are actually transferred between JVMs, do not set the CLASSPATH variable and start the rmiregistry in a directory isolated from the client and server.

WARNING

If the rmiregistry can find the class definitions locally, it will ignore the java.rmi.server.codebase property set from the command line. This is a problem because other JVMs will not be able to download the class definitions.

From the command line, enter:

C:\> **start rmiregistry**

Start the server application from the server directory—again, without setting the CLASSPATH variable. The server must let the registry and the client know where to load classes that are being made available by the server, so set the java.rmi.server.codebase property. From the command line, type:

C:\RMI\agent\server> **java -Djava.rmi.server.codebase=file: /RMI/agent/server/bank.loan.Lender**

NOTE

The `java.rmi.server.codebase` property requires forward slashes to separate the directory names (of the path), and there must be a trailing slash on the last directory.

The output from the server looks like this:

```
Lender: create a LoanOfficer
Lender: bind the LoanOfficer to a name
The LoanOfficer is ready to process requests
```

Start the client application from the client directory—again, do not set the `CLASSPATH` variable. The client must let the server know where the `ConventionalLoan` class is located, so the client application also sets its `codebase` property:

C:\RMI\agent\client> **java -Djava.rmi.server.codebase=file: /RMI/agent/client/bank.loan.ConventionalLoanClient gus 250000 7.25 30**

This example shows a $250,000 mortgage at an annual percentage rate of 7¼ for 30 years, on a server named "gus."

Object Activation

In previous versions of RMI, to obtain a reference to a remote object, the server that generated the instance of the object had to be running (live) in a JVM. This simple mechanism is sufficient for most applications; however, for large systems that create a number of objects that are not used at the same time (or some objects that are not used at all), it is useful to have a mechanism to suspend those objects until they are needed.

The activation mechanism provides this facility. Activation allows a Java object to be bound (named by the registry) and then "activated" at some later date simply by referencing the object through the registry. One of the primary benefits to this approach is that the application that creates the instance of the remote object can terminate or exit normally before the object is ever used. The ability to activate remote objects on request allows RMI system designers much greater flexibility in designing smaller "servers." To make activation work, the RMI team created another daemon process, the Java RMI Activation System Daemon (`rmid`).

The process of finding an object reference is illustrated in Figure 18.2.

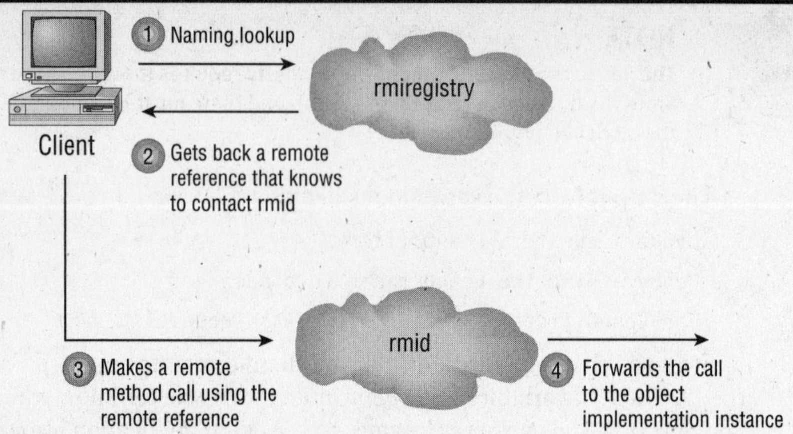
1 Naming.lookup
rmiregistry
Client
2 Gets back a remote reference that knows to contact rmid
rmid
3 Makes a remote method call using the remote reference
4 Forwards the call to the object implementation instance

FIGURE 18.2: Object activation in RMI

The `rmid` process must be run first, through the command line:

C:\> **start rmid**

By default, `rmid` will start on port number 1098 (`rmiregistry` is on port 1099), but you can specify an alternate port:

C:\> **start rmid -port 2001**

To demonstrate the object activation feature, we will extend the loan-processing example presented in the previous section by activating `LoanOfficer` to approve the mortgage loan application.

The client side of this example is just like any other RMI client class because the client requests a remote reference and has no idea that the object is activatable or running as a standard `UnicastRemoteObject`. The "server" side, however, is very different because the server must register the activatable object with the activation system before it terminates.

NOTE

Because the server is not run again when the object is activated, the term "server" does not really apply, and thus the RMI team came up with the term *setup*. This better defines what the activation application does before it exits.

Modifying LoanOfficer

To simplify the example and focus on the elements that make an object activatable, the `LoanOfficer` interface, shown in Listing 18.18, now defines a single method—isApproved—which takes a single argument—a LoanApplication object—and returns a boolean result.

Listing 18.18: LoanOfficer.java

```
package bank.loan;

import java.rmi.Remote;
import java.rmi.RemoteException;

public interface LoanOfficer extends Remote
{
      public boolean isApproved(LoanApplication app)
         throws RemoteException;
}
```

Implementing LoanOfficer and Extending Activatable

The LoanOfficerImpl class implements the LoanOfficer interface and extends the Activatable class instead of UnicastRemoteObject. Note that there is an additional constructor that could be defined for an Activatable class, but this one constructor is all that is necessary for this example.

Similar to the UnicastRemoteObject examples seen earlier in this chapter, an Activatable class needs only to implement a remote interface and to be exported to accept incoming method requests. By extending java.rmi.activation.Activatable, the LoanOfficerImpl, shown in Listing 18.19, class is exported automatically upon construction, but any class (except those that extend UnicastRemoteObject or Activatable) may be exported by using the static method, Activatable.exportObject, as long as it directly or indirectly implements java.rmi.Remote.

Listing 18.19: LoanOfficerImpl.java

```
package bank.loan;

import java.rmi.activation.Activatable;
import java.rmi.activation.ActivationID;
import java.rmi.MarshalledObject;
import java.rmi.Remote;
import java.rmi.RemoteException;
```

```
public class LoanOfficerImpl extends Activatable
    implements LoanOfficer {

    public LoanOfficerImpl
        (ActivationID id, MarshalledObject data)
        throws RemoteException {

        // Register the LoanOfficerImpl with the activation
        // daemon and "export" it on an anonymous port.
        super(id, 0);
    }

    public boolean isApproved(LoanApplication app)
        throws RemoteException
    {
        // Here, some other process would determine whether
        // the customer was approved for the loan.
        // For now, we'll let everyone be approved!
        return true;
    }
}
```

Creating the Activation Setup Class

The setup class, a rewritten `Lender` class, is a bit more complex than the server class for a `UnicastRemoteObject`; however, it is likely that this mechanism will be simplified in future releases.

The `Lender` creates an instance of a URL object that represents the location of the activatable class, `LoanOfficerImpl`. An `ActivationGroupID` is passed to the `ActivationDesc` object, which is registered with `rmid`. Each new JVM that is started by `rmid` will activate objects for only a single `ActivationGroupID`. If a JVM is already running that is associated with this class's `ActivationGroupID`, this object will be created in that JVM rather than starting a new JVM. The `ActivationGroupID` gives greater control over which JVM the activated object runs in.

Next, the static method `Activatable.register` passes the `ActivationDesc` up to `rmid`. The activation group descriptor is all the information that `rmid` will need to create an instance of the `Activatable` class. The `Activatable.register` method returns a remote reference that is then used to register the `Activatable` class with the `rmiregistry`. The setup class, `Lender`, shown in Listing 18.20, then explicitly exits with `System.exit`.

Listing 18.20: Lender.java

```
import java.net.URL;
import java.rmi.activation.Activatable;
import java.rmi.activation.ActivationDesc;
import java.rmi.activation.ActivationGroup;
import java.rmi.activation.ActivationGroupDesc;
import java.rmi.activation.ActivationGroupID;
import java.rmi.MarshalledObject;
import java.rmi.Naming;
import java.rmi.RemoteException;
import java.rmi.RMISecurityManager;
import java.security.CodeSource;
import java.security.PublicKey;
import java.util.Properties;
import bank.loan.*;

public class Lender {

    public static void main (String args[]) {
        if (args.length < 1) {
            System.out.println ("Usage: "+
                "java bank.loan.Lender "+
                "<absolute path to class files>");
            System.exit (0);
        }
        //  Create and install a security manager.
        System.setSecurityManager(new RMISecurityManager());

        try {
            // Create an instance of our loan officer.
            System.out.println
                ("Lender: create a LoanOfficer");

            URL whereTheClassFileIs = new
                URL("file:"+args[0]+"/");

          // These are required for Java 2 Beta 3
            PublicKey [] mySecurity = null;
            CodeSource directions =
                new CodeSource
                (whereTheClassFileIs, mySecurity);
            Properties env =
               (Properties)System.getProperties().clone();
```

Part IV

```
            ActivationGroupID groupID =
                ActivationGroup.getSystem().registerGroup(
                new ActivationGroupDesc(env));

          // Marshalled object is typically used to tell
          // the activated object where to find its
          // persistent data.  Right here it is unused,
          // but required for the ActivationDesc
            MarshalledObject commandLineInfo = null;
            ActivationDesc ad =
                new ActivationDesc
                (groupID, "bank.loan. LoanOfficerImpl",
                    directions, commandLineInfo);

            // Register the activatable class with rmid.
            LoanOfficer lo =
             (LoanOfficer)Activatable.register(ad);
            System.out.println("Registered with rmid");

            // Bind the object instance to the remote
            // registry. Use the static rebind() method
            //to avoid conflicts.
            System.out.println
               ("Lender: bind the LoanOfficer to a name");
            Naming.rebind("loanOfficer", lo);

            System.out.println("The LoanOfficer is "+
              + "ready to process requests");

        } catch (Exception e) {
            e.printStackTrace();
            System.out.println(e.getMessage());
        }

        // The work is done, now exit the program.
        System.exit(0);
    }
}
```

On the client, the `LoanApplication` object is passed to the `LoanOfficer` object. The `LoanApplication`, shown in Listing 18.21, is a simple class that is constructed with the customer's social security number and the loan amount.

Listing 18.21: LoanApplication.java

```
package bank.loan;

public class LoanApplication implements java.io.Serializable{

    private String ssn;
    private int loanAmount;

    public LoanApplication(String loanInfo, int amount) {

    ssn = loanInfo;
    loanAmount = amount;
    }

    public String getApplicant() {
    return ssn;
    }

    public int getRequestedAmount() {
    return loanAmount;
    }
}
```

The client, shown in Listing 18.22, creates an instance of a `LoanApplication`, and requests a `LoanOfficer` reference from the registry.

Listing 18.22: LoanClient.java

```
import java.rmi.Naming;
import java.rmi.RemoteException;
import java.rmi.RMISecurityManager;
import bank.loan.*;

public class LoanClient {

    public static void main(String [] args) throws Exception{

       LoanOfficer officer;
       LoanApplication app;

       // Check the command line.
       if (args.length < 3) {
           System.err.println("Usage:");
```

```
            System.err.println("java LoanClient <server> " +
                    "<social security number> "+
                     "<mortgage amount>");
            System.exit (1);
        }
        String applicant = args[1];
        int loanAmount = Integer.parseInt(args[2]);

        // Create the LoanApplication instance.
        app = new LoanApplication(applicant, loanAmount);

         // Create and install a security manager.
         System.setSecurityManager(new RMISecurityManager());

         // Obtain reference to loan officer.
         try {
            String url = new String ("rmi://" + args[0] + "
/loanOfficer");
            System.out.println
                ("LoanClient: lookup loanOfficer, " +
                "url = " + url);
            officer = (LoanOfficer)Naming.lookup(url);
          } catch (Exception e) {
            System.err.println
                ("Error in getting loan officer " + e);
           throw e;
          }

         // Get the loan approval.
          try {
           boolean approved = officer.isApproved(app);
           System.out.print
              ("Your request for " + loanAmount + " was ");
           if (!approved) {
              System.out.print("not ");
           }
           System.out.println("approved!");

         } catch (Exception e1) {
            System.err.println
               ("Error in processing loan " + e1);
           throw e1;
```

```
        }

        System.exit(0);
    }
}
```

The registry looks up the LoanOfficer object that was registered by the setup application, and returns to the client a remote reference that contacts rmid to create an instance of the class.

WHAT'S NEXT

Java's persistent object support provides a very useful facility for storing and reconstituting objects. This feature is valuable in its own right; moreover, it plays an essential role in remote object invocation by providing a Java-standard protocol for reading and writing object data to and from I/O streams. While successful RMI programming involves a number of steps, the individual steps are not difficult. The examples presented in this chapter provide a template for your own development efforts.

While RMI is constantly compared to CORBA as a distributed object technology, it is important to bear in mind that RMI is capable of sending a full object data graph from one remote JVM to another. This is a feature that is not available in standard CORBA implementations. Furthermore, RMI systems are becoming more widely integrated as customers find that RMI is easier to develop and understand than CORBA. With the addition of activation and the IIOP protocol, RMI is well positioned to continue as an inexpensive and powerful tool for creating object frameworks.

The next chapter discusses CORBA, IIOP, and Java IDL in detail.

Chapter 19

Java IDL and CORBA Connectivity

Many J2EE applications need to communicate with a variety of systems in other environments; therefore, J2EE needs a powerful mechanism for communicating in heterogeneous environments. Java IDL and CORBA provide a solution to this requirement.

Java IDL was introduced with release 1.2 of the JDK, and provides an implementation of the CORBA 2.0 (Common Object Request Broker Architecture) specification. CORBA is a distributed framework designed to support heterogeneous architectures. With CORBA, it is possible to connect two systems that may be running on different machines, and also may be running on different operating systems and written in different programming languages.

Updated from *Java™ 2 Developer's Handbook™*
by Philip Heller and Simon Roberts
ISBN 0-7821-2179-9 $59.99

Part IV

This chapter begins with a discussion of the problem that CORBA was designed to solve. The chapter then covers the CORBA components and IDL, and examines how to develop CORBA services. After the examples, some of the details of IDL-to Java language mapping will be examined. Finally, this chapter will describe how legacy code wrapping works.

Featured in this chapter:

- Heterogeneous environment problems
- An introduction to CORBA
- An introduction to IDL
- CORBA service development
- Mapping language from IDL to Java
- Legacy code wrapping

The Compatibility Problem

CORBA was created to solve a common problem for most large companies; that problem being different computer systems at work within the same company. For example, the graphics department may have Macintoshes running MacOS, the engineering department may have Sun workstations running Solaris, and management may have PCs running Windows. In addition to these systems, a large mainframe may run a proprietary operating system that is central to the operation of the company.

Traditionally, computer manufacturers have attempted to solve the compatibility problem of a heterogeneous environment by creating a line of products that reaches into all areas of a company's business. For example, a single vendor may offer a low-end system, a graphics system, and a high-end server system. This can sometimes solve the problem of compatibility, but it also is costly and leads to vendor dependence; the company must commit to spending more money on a single vendor's solution.

A Heterogeneous Environment Case Study

To understand why companies frequently have heterogeneous environments, consider the case of a fictional book publishing company, Sullivan Publishing.

Since the early 1900s, Sullivan Publishing has printed and bound books, all by hand. The initial "plant" was little more than a small warehouse with several bulky manual printing presses and a leather-cutting table for the book covers.

The business grew over the next 70 years, so Sullivan Publishing moved into larger quarters and bought automatic printing presses and binding machines. As the company grew, so did the quantity of data associated with book inventories and production and marketing costs. To remain competitive, the company needed an information system that would support its manufacturing and inventory goals.

The Mainframe's Role

During the 1970s and 1980s, the company purchased a large mainframe computer, and hired a group of programmers to write and maintain programs to translate the publisher's business process into computer applications.

- Management used programs to produce reports that could be used to evaluate the information compiled by the computer and to make decisions based on that information.
- The production group used programs to track the costs of raw goods and to decide when to buy quality products from paper and ink dealers, so inventory did not sit idle on shelves for too long.
- The marketing group used programs to analyze readership trends and ensure that specific target markets were not missed.
- The graphics department created programs that helped the designers standardize logos and product branding, and used other programs to produce the books' cover artwork.

It is important to note that the *purpose* of the mainframe computer was to provide the decision-makers in the company with tools to maintain and expand the business. The computer, the operating system, and the programming language(s) used to develop the programs were irrelevant to the real purpose of the system, which was to make more money for Sullivan Publishing.

The Evolution of the PC and the Network

As time went on, two events in the evolution of computer technology brought changes to Sullivan Publishing's computer system. The first event was the evolution of the PC as an inexpensive business computer. The PC made it possible for a single department within the company to make relatively small purchases (compared to the mainframe) of computer equipment that would have no impact on the mainframe environment. The local PC resources provided an attractive alternative to the terminals attached to the mainframe—more programs, better performance, local storage, and better games!

The second evolution was the network, which allowed companies to tie their different computer resources together and to share files and data. The network was technically capable of connecting disparate systems because the protocols for the network were designed as standards, independent of a computer's hardware or operating system. This is important because without the network, there is no concept of a distributed software architecture. Figure 19.1 illustrates Sullivan Publishing's network.

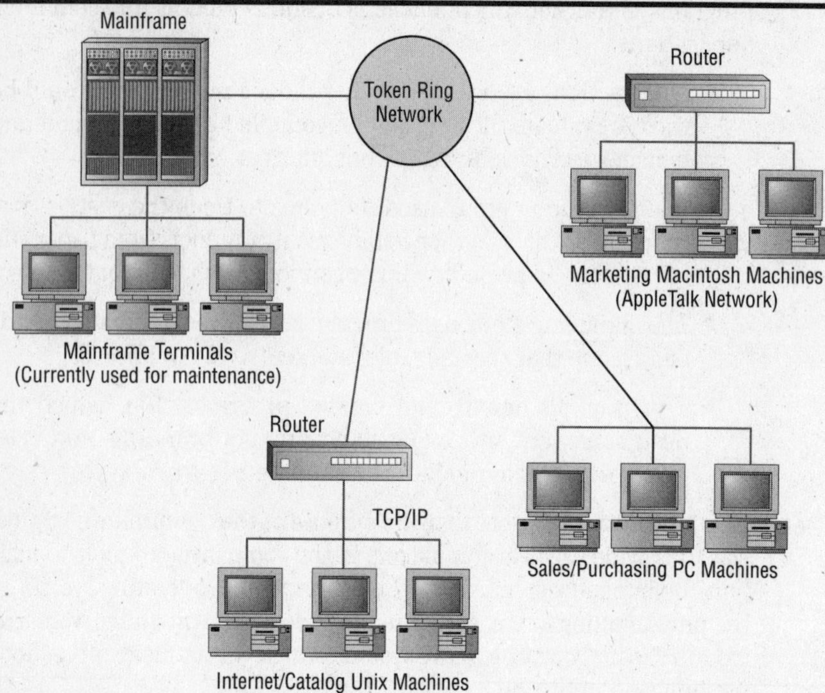

FIGURE 19.1: The network of Sullivan Publishing company (our hypothetical example)

Unfortunately, the dream of sharing information between different systems proved difficult and expensive to implement. Programs could share data only if the data was properly formatted to the computing environment that used it. Computer companies were not interested in the data needs of a printing company, and they developed standards for data formats suited for their own hardware and operating systems; therefore, data and files from the mainframe word processor were incompatible with the word processing programs on the PCs.

Modern Challenges

So now we come to the challenges of the late 1990s. The company's managers would like all of their computers to seamlessly be able to share information. Also, they would like to offer an online buying service.

Sullivan Publishing has evaluated several alternative proposals from a variety of computer vendors. Each vendor promises to integrate the company's business onto a single platform that would make the computers work together as a system again. Each vendor's proposal, however, involves significant rewriting of the existing code base in addition to the purchase of new hardware.

Migration to the Network-Centric Model

The dilemma of the hypothetical publishing company is common in many real companies, although perhaps not as severe. The short-term costs of a migration to a desktop-centric computing model are lower than the initial mainframe costs, but such a solution leads to incompatibilities between systems because they are heterogeneous in nature.

What companies with heterogeneous systems would really like to do is invest in a new software framework that allows them to leave the existing hardware intact and migrate existing software toward a network-centric model, where each computer system is part of the overall business system. Companies want to move applications and systems toward a central model that emphasizes a common look at the business application, regardless of the operating system and programming language the application requires.

Furthermore, companies would like to be able to use the current "legacy" code in its current state until all of the code can be understood, documented, and rewritten for more modern hardware.

An Overview of CORBA

Several years ago, a group of engineers decided to form a consortium of their respective companies and design a reusable "system" that would enable multiple programming and operating system environments to work together. These engineers formed the Object Management Group (OMG). Working together, the OMG members have developed several hundred pages of specifications that define a framework of reusable components. The specification covers the architectural elements that are required to allow one hardware and software system to communicate with another. The OMG is now a consortium of more than 800 companies, and CORBA is the framework that is the result of their work.

A *framework* is a reusable collection of code that is almost "ready-to-use," which means that with some customization, it can be applied to specific implementations. The CORBA framework is designed to make communication between remote address spaces easier to implement. The primary goal of CORBA is to provide software developers with a means for developing systems that do not rely on a single operating system, programming language, or even hardware architecture.

CORBA by itself is not a product that you can buy from a store. The CORBA standard defines how companies can create implementations of the standard. You can purchase implementations from companies such as Iona Technologies and Visigenic (now part of Borland).

A CORBA implementation is composed of several pieces, depending on the vendor's individual application of each standard. A typical CORBA vendor will supply the following components:

- An Object Request Broker (ORB) implementation
- An Interface Definition Language (IDL) compiler
- One or more implementations of Common Object Services (COS), also known as CORBAServices
- Common Frameworks, also known as CORBAFacilities

The Object Request Broker (ORB)

The primary mechanism for connecting objects in different address spaces is a function of the ORB. You can consider the ORB to be an object bus or object pathway. When two CORBA systems wish to communicate between different address spaces, the ORB takes care of making sure that regardless of the hardware, operating system, and software development language used, the remote object invocations will succeed. Figure 19.2 illustrates how an ORB connects objects between a client and a server.

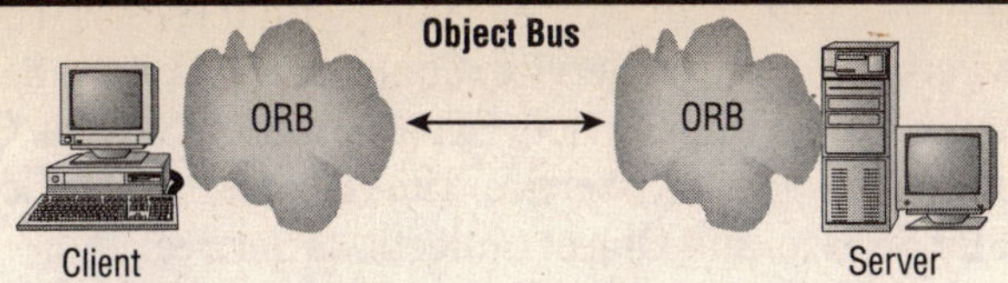

FIGURE 19.2: ORB communication

Typically, an ORB is implemented in one of two ways:

- As a "library" of objects that form an extension of the CORBA runtime
- As a daemon process

In either case, the ORB is responsible for establishing communications with the remote system, marshaling parameters to make remote calls, and managing concurrency of simultaneous requests from multiple clients.

Common Object Services (COS) and Common Frameworks

The ORB does not make up the entire CORBA implementation. Common Object Services are specified to assist the ORB. These services include:

Naming Service Provides a way for CORBA clients to find objects on the network. An implementation server registers an object with a Naming Service using a hierarchical representation similar to a path used by a filename. Clients can request a reference to the object by name, using the Naming Service.

Event Service Allows a client or server to send a message in the form of an event object to one or more receivers. Objects can request to listen to a specific event channel, and the Event Service will notify them of an event on that channel. The Event Service will store events before delivering them, so that clients and servers do not need to be connected.

Security Service Provides a means to authenticate messages, authorize access to objects, and provide secure communications.

Transaction Service Defines a means to control an action against a database or other subsystem. The Transaction Service allows clients and servers to commit or roll back a transaction, even when the transaction affects multiple databases.

Currently, there are a total of 16 services. Along with those listed above, the services are Persistent Object Service, Concurrency Control Service, Life Cycle Service, Relationship Service, Externalization Service, Query Service, Licensing Service, Property Service, Time Service, Notification Service, Object Trader Service, and Object Collections Service.

In addition to the Common Object Services, there are CORBA Facilities and OMG Domains. CORBA Facilities provide higher-level frameworks, such as Internationalization and Time, or Mobile Agents. The OMG Domains define application-level services, typically for vertical markets such as Oil and Gas, Transportation, and Document Preparation; however, few vendors have developed services that support portions of these other specifications.

An Overview of IDL and IIOP

The ORB, Common Object Services, and other CORBA specifications would be difficult for any one vendor to implement if there were not some standard way to define the interfaces that each of these elements require. The definitions of the interfaces in CORBA are created through a set of programming-language independent constructs that are specified by the CORBA Interface Definition Language (IDL).

The original CORBA specifications describe interactions between ORBs in terms of a generic communications protocol they call GIOP. Additionally, the CORBA 2.0 specification introduced the Internet Inter-ORB Protocol (IIOP) standard, a mapping of GIOP that specifies how ORBs communicate over TCP/IP-based networks.

IDL Definitions

IDL provides a programming-language neutral way to define how a service is implemented. The constructs that make up IDL are syntactically similar to C and C++ (and even Java), but they cannot be compiled into a binary program directly. Instead, IDL is intended to be an intermediary language that defines the interfaces that a client will use and a server will implement. IDL is best thought of as a "contract" between the system that makes use of an object and a system that implements an object.

A developer creating a CORBA system models a system using IDL to define the interface that the system will support. This model is an abstract representation of the actual system. For example, the following is a simple IDL file:

```
module Calculator {
   interface Functions {
      float square_root ( in float number );
      float power (in float base, in float exponent );
   };
};
```

This IDL file describes two function keys on a calculator: a square root function and a power function (a number raised to a power). The definition of these functions is abstract–there is no code describing the implementation of these functions, nor is there any definition of the language to be used to implement the functions.

This IDL specification is "compiled" using a tool that creates code for the specific operating system and programming language that the developer needs. Currently, CORBA supports C, C++, Java, SmallTalk, LISP, Python, COBOL, PL/1, and Ada. We'll cover the Java mapping of the most useful IDL constructs later in this chapter.

NOTE

IDL files are "compiled," but this is really a misnomer and illustrates the limited nature of computer terms. An IDL file is actually *translated* from the general constructs that make up IDL to specific programming language constructs (like C, C++ or Java). The files generated by the translation process are not complete, however; they require the implementation details, which the developer must fill in.

IIOP Communications

The IIOP is a TCP/IP implementation of the General Inter-ORB Protocol (GIOP). The GIOP specification defines how ORBs communicate, including how messages are sent, how byte ordering is done for integers and floating-point numbers, and how parameters are marshaled for remote object invocations.

NOTE

IIOP compatibility is required of CORBA vendors who want to advertise that they are 2.0-compliant. The IIOP specification has probably done more to further the cause of CORBA than any other specification. Without IIOP, CORBA vendors are free to implement their own ORB communication protocols, effectively creating a vendor lock—any additional service would need to be purchased from the single vendor.

With CORBA, it is possible to build a client application using one vendor's ORB and IDL compiler, build a server or object implementation with a second vendor's ORB and IDL compiler, and create a set of common services for both client and server with yet a third vendor's ORB and IDL compiler. The IIOP allows each of the three different vendors' products to communicate with each other using a standard set of protocol semantics. (And when you consider that all three of these ORBs could be using a different programming language and running on a different hardware and operating system platform, you get the idea that CORBA is pretty cool!)

A Working CORBA System

Now that you've been introduced to the CORBA components and specifications, let's see how each of these is used to develop a working CORBA system.

Java IDL is now part of the Java 2 Standard Edition. The current release includes a 100% Pure Java ORB, a set of APIs, and a Naming Service (`tnameserv`) that follows the COS Naming Service specification. An IDL compiler (`idlj`) is available as part of Java since JDK1.3, or separately (`idltojava`) for JDK1.2. Java IDL is mostly CORBA 2.3-compliant, and it communicates with any other IIOP (version 1.0)-based ORB. The description here applies in particular to Java IDL, but the process will be similar in most other CORBA implementations.

The process of creating a CORBA system starts with the development of a design, or the outline of what functionality the system is to provide. From there, the design is translated into objects that provide the functionality required by the design. These objects are expressed in terms of IDL interfaces and collected into related modules. The IDL file(s) is then compiled to generate programming language-specific stub and skeleton code, in our case in Java. Stubs implement the interfaces that client applications will use, and skeletons provide CORBA support to object implementations that servers will provide.

After the IDL file is compiled, object implementations are created from the files that are generated, and a server application is created to provide a means for publishing the object references by name through the Naming Service or through their Interoperable Object Reference (IOR). The client application requests a reference to an object through the Naming Service by name and is returned a reference to a generic CORBA object. This object reference is narrowed (like Java casting) to a reference that is actually the stub representation of the remote CORBA object.

The IDL File

CORBA objects are first described by their interface in an IDL file. A CORBA object is also known as a *service*. CORBA services provide operations that may or may not return result(s).

NOTE

Actually, you could develop a CORBA application without using IDL. In fact, there are CORBA products that allow the developer to create Java and C++ code from a visual development tool, skipping over the creation of IDL files; however, an IDL file provides a road map for the development of a sound CORBA system, forcing the developer to think through the problem before generating any executable code. The IDL file also provides written documentation of the creation process and preserves the software design investment. An IDL file from 1998 will continue to provide insight into the design of a system long after CORBA is transformed into a new software paradigm.

There is no concept of data in an IDL definition because IDL interface definitions of services are true object-oriented descriptions. The data is not shown because it is always private and accessed only by an operation, which is public.

For example, consider our sample IDL file:

```
module Calculator {
   interface Functions {
      float square_root ( in float number );
      float power ( in float base, in float exponent );
   };
};
```

`Functions` is a CORBA service (encapsulated in a package or library called `Calculator`) that describes two operations, `square_root` and `power`. An IDL compiler will generate language-specific files, depending on the purpose of the compiler. For example, the IDL compiler for Java IDL will generate Java files.

Stubs and Skeletons

The names of the files generated by the IDL compiler depend on the contents of the IDL file and the IDL compiler used. When using `idltojava`, our sample IDL file (shown in the previous section) will result in the creation of a package directory called `Calculator`, and a Java interface file named `Functions.java` in the `Calculator` directory. `Functions.java` contains an interface declaration for the two operations. When using `idlj`, the actual operations implemented by the server entity will be placed in an interface called FunctionsOperations (placed in a file called FunctionsOperations.java) and the interface Functions will be inherited from FunctionsOperations (and will also be placed in a file called Functions.java).

Other generated files include stub and skeleton files, a Helper class, and a Holder class. Stub files are used by client code to communicate with remote CORBA objects. Skeleton files are used by the ORB to make up-calls to server object implementations. Both Helper and Holder classes provide implementation support to the application. Both client and server applications utilize the Naming Service (provided by an application called `tnameserv`, supplied with the JDK to provide information about the remote object that is requested and served, respectively). Figure 19.3 illustrates how stubs and skeletons are used in a CORBA application.

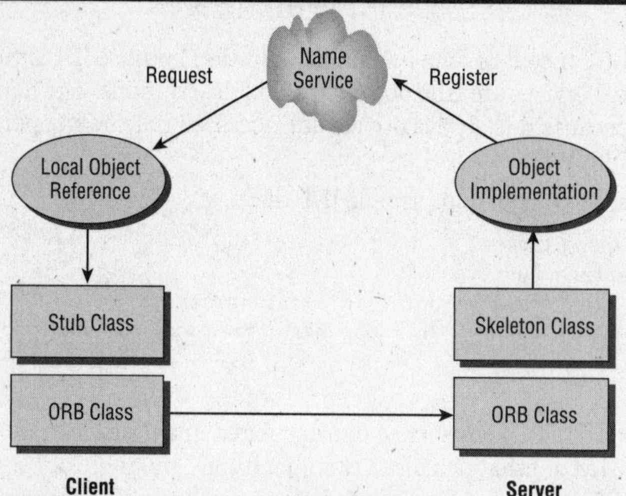

FIGURE 19.3: Using stubs and skeletons in a CORBA application

When the server is started, it creates or is passed an object that is to be referenced. This object implements the operations defined in the IDL file; in our example, it provides method bodies for the `square_root` and `power` methods. The Java class that provides the implementation of the operations defined in the IDL interface `Functions` also extends a generated class that defines skeleton methods. The server registers the reference to this object with the Naming Service.

The client requests a reference to a remote object through the Naming Service. The reference that is returned is used to create a stub object, via the narrow() function present in the Helper class created by the IDL compiler. The client then invokes methods through that stub reference as if the remote server object were local to the client. The stub, in turn, passes requests to the skeleton for processing over on the server side.

CORBA Servers

The Naming Service provides a reference to a CORBA object provided by a server. There are two types of CORBA objects: transient and persistent. Transient objects have the same lifetime as the server that created them—as long as the server is running, the object is available. Persistent objects do not require a running server. If a request is made of an object that is not available because the server that created the object is not running, an ORB daemon will start the appropriate server to activate an object and return its reference. Java IDL has provided support for transient servers since its introduction, support for persistent servers was added in the Java IDL implementation for JDK1.4.

Subclassed Skeleton Classes versus Ties

With Java IDL, you can connect the skeleton support with the actual object implementation in two ways. One way is to inherit skeleton methods directly, by subclassing the skeleton class generated by the IDL compiler. This approach is straightforward—each IDL interface method has a direct correlation to a skeleton method. This first approach is the default for the IDL compilers supplied with Java IDL.

However, for some applications, you may want to reserve the superclass slot for another class, particularly in instances when the classes that are being wrapped by the CORBA skeleton classes already exist. In this case, another implementation may be used that makes the skeleton class delegate the method calls to the appropriate implementation class. These delegation-based skeletons are referred to as *Ties*. Java IDL provides a mechanism for creating a Tie implementation by simply specifying the `-ftie` flag to the `idltojava` or `idlj` applications on the command line.

CORBA Clients

A client application invokes methods on CORBA objects. To invoke a method on a CORBA object, the client must know what methods are available and what arguments each method takes. A client can be written with static or dynamic method invocations.

Static method invocations are the easiest to write because they are generated and type-checked at compile time. A static invocation uses the methods declared by the Java interfaces generated from IDL interface definitions.

Dynamic method invocations are more flexible. They allow the client to discover the object definitions at runtime; however, dynamic method invocations do not type-check arguments, so it is the responsibility of the client to make sure that arguments are valid. Dynamic invocation also requires that the server supports an Interface Repository. The Interface Repository is used to provide the client with method names, types, and argument lists. As of this writing, Java IDL does not provide an Interface Repository, although Java IDL clients can access the Interface Repository provided by another ORB. The method `org.omg.CORBA.Object .get_interface` will throw an exception if the server side is implemented in Java IDL, but it will return a valid reference if the server is another ORB.

The Object Adapter

Some CORBA implementations support the concept of an Object Adapter. The Object Adapter is responsible for creating server objects and returning the object reference (object ID). The Object Adapter is only used on the server side. CORBA specifies that at least one Basic Object Adapter (BOA) be supported; however, the current specification for the BOA is quite vague, so there are different semantics for the implementation of the BOA from vendor to vendor. These differences have made it difficult to port server-side code from one vendor's implementation to another.

The OMG recently released a new specification, deprecating the BOA and replacing it with the Portable Object Adapter (POA). This new specification carefully defines the requirements for a POA, making it possible to move server-side code from one vendor's implementation to another. Java IDL supports a Portable Object Adaptor, starting with JDK 1.4.

A Simple CORBA Service

As described earlier, CORBA services are expressed in terms of IDL interfaces. For example, the CORBA Naming Service is actually defined by an IDL file that describes the interfaces required to provide this "service." To introduce how Java IDL is used, we'll develop a simple CORBA service.

There are ten basic steps to developing the CORBA service:

1. Create an IDL file that represents the interfaces desired.
2. Compile the IDL file using `idl` or `idltojava`.
3. Compile the generated classes using `javac`.
4. Create an implementation class.
5. Create the implementation server.
6. Create the client application (or applet).
7. Compile the implementation, server, and client code.
8. Start the Naming Service application, `tnameserv`.
9. Start the server (which registers with the Naming Service).
10. Start the client.

WARNING

The most important of these steps is the first, but many developers spend too little time in design. One of the drawbacks to a flexible framework is that the design of the framework is what drives the implementation. Changes that are made to the implementation are not reflected in the IDL file automatically. Furthermore, tools for converting an implementation back to IDL are not provided by most CORBA vendors.

The steps and the code for the CORBA service example are described in the following sections.

Creating the IDL File

For this example, you'll use the same sample IDL file presented in earlier sections:

```
module Calculator {
   interface Functions {
      float square_root ( in float number );
      float power (in float base, in float exponent );
   };
};
```

In this IDL file, an IDL interface named `Functions` is enclosed in the naming scope of a module named `Calculator`. The IDL interface `Functions` describes a single service that contains two operations: `square_root` and `power`. The `square_root` operation takes a single floating-point argument, passed by value to the operation, and returns a single float result. The operation `power` takes two float arguments passed by value, and returns a single float result. (The semantics of Java IDL will be discussed in the "IDL to Java Language Mapping" section later in the chapter.)

Compiling the IDL File

For this example, assume that your sample IDL file is in a file named `calc.idl`. To compile the IDL file, use either of the IDL compilers, `idltojava` or `idlj`.

```
idlj -fall calc.idl
idltojava -fno-cpp calc.idl
```

The –fall option (or one of its variants) are expected, to specify to the `idlj` compiler what kind of support the users wants to generate (client vs. server, or implemented using inheritance vs. ties). Run `idlj` without arguments to obtain a description of all options available. The `-fno-cpp` option is used to turn off C/C++ preprocessing when using `idltojava`. This option is useful only if you plan to add preprocessing commands to your IDL files. Other options are described in the document `jidlCompiler.html`, which is shipped with the `idltojava` compiler.

The IDL compiler uses the constructs specified in the IDL file to generate specific Java files and directories. The `module` construct is used as a package specification, and the `interface` construct is used as a Java interface definition. In the sample IDL file, the package name is `Calculator`, and the Java interface file generated is named `Functions.java`. The Java IDL compiler generates the following files for this example:

`Calculator`	The directory/package created by the module declaration.
`Functions`	A Java interface that declares all operations and methods for the remote object.
`FunctionsOperations`	A Java interface that declares only the operations and methods described in the IDL specification (only generated by `idlj`).

`_FunctionsImplBase`	A class that implements the `Functions` interface and provides a single class that the implementation class can extend.
`_FunctionsStub`	Another class that implements the `Functions` interface. This class is used by the client to invoke the methods declared in `Functions` on a remote object.
`FunctionsHolder`	A utility class provided to allow client applications to pass a `Functions` object "by reference" to the server. It is not needed in this example.
`FunctionsHelper`	Another utility class that the client uses to classify object references received from the server as `Functions` objects.

Compiling the Generated Classes

The `idltojava` IDL compiler generates only Java source code, so the generated classes must be compiled. The nice thing about this step is that none of the generated classes will throw compilation exceptions! To compile the generated classes, use the following compiler command:

```
javac Calculator\*.java
```

Creating the Implementation Class

The next step is to provide a Java class that implements the Java interface generated by the IDL compiler. It is recommended that the physical location of the classes that you create remain separate from the generated classes. The generated classes are in the `Calculator` directory already, so the created classes can be created one directory level above them.

Java IDL provides a file that makes this step easy. The `_Functions-ImplBase.java` file is an abstract class file that implements the interface defined in `Functions.java`. Extending this class provides the appropriate skeleton methods that are required to perform the up-calls from the ORB to the implementation methods.

The implementation class must provide method bodies for the interface methods described by the `Functions` interface (generated from the IDL file `calc.idl`). Listings 19.1 through 19.3 show the interfaces produced by `idltojava` and `idlj`.

Listing 19.1: Functions.java (produced by `idltojava`)

```
package Calculator;
public interface Functions
    extends org.omg.CORBA.Object {
    float square_root(float number);
    float power(float base, float exponent);
}
```

Listing 19.2: FunctionsOperations.java (produced by `idlj`)

```
package Calculator;
public interface FunctionsOperations
{
  float square_root (float number);
  float power (float base, float exponent);
} // interface FunctionsOperations
```

Listing 19.3: Functions.java (produced by `idlj`)

```
package Calculator;
public interface Functions extends FunctionsOperations,
   org.omg.CORBA.Object, org.omg.CORBA.portable.IDLEntity
{
} // interface Functions
```

NOTE

As of JDK 1.1, all methods defined in an interface are implicitly public.

The implementation class must therefore provide methods for the `square_root` and `power` methods. By convention, the implementation class adds an `Impl` suffix to the interface name. The implementation class created is shown in Listing 19.4.

Listing 19.4: FunctionsImpl.java

```
// Implementation file for the Functions interface

package Calculator;
```

```
// First, extend the Implementation Base class
public class FunctionsImpl extends _FunctionsImplBase {

        // A constructor is not required, but is recommended
        public FunctionsImpl () {
        }

        // Implement the two special methods
        public float square_root (float number) {
                return (float)Math.sqrt ((double)number);
        }

        public float power (float base, float exponent) {
                return (float)Math.pow ((double)base,
                   (double)exponent);
        }
}
```

This simple implementation returns a square root using the `sqrt()` method and the `pow()` method of the `java.lang.Math` class. Note that these methods take double type arguments, and return a double as a result, so the arguments and the results of the methods should be cast to a float.

Creating the Implementation Server

The next step is to create a server class that will create the implementation object and register it with the ORB and Naming. Similar to the implementation class, this Java class is not generated by the IDL compiler. The server class for this example is shown in Listing 19.5.

Listing 19.5: CalculatorServer.java

```
// The Calculator Server class

import Calculator.FunctionsImpl;

import org.omg.CosNaming.*;
import org.omg.CosNaming.NamingContextPackage.*;
import org.omg.CORBA.*;

public class CalculatorServer {
```

```
    public static void main(String args[])
    {
      try{
        // Create and initialize an instance of an ORB
        ORB orb = ORB.init(args, null);

        // Create implementation and register with ORB
        FunctionsImpl fRef = new FunctionsImpl();
        orb.connect(fRef);

        // Get a handle to the name server
        org.omg.CORBA.Object objRef =
            orb.resolve_initial_references("NameService");
        NamingContext ncRef =
            NamingContextHelper.narrow(objRef);

        // Bind the Object Reference in Naming
        NameComponent nc = new NameComponent("Calc", "");
        NameComponent path[] = {nc};
        ncRef.rebind(path, fRef);

        // Wait for invocations from clients
        java.lang.Object sync = new java.lang.Object();
        synchronized (sync) {
              sync.wait();
        }

      } catch (Exception e) {
         System.err.println("ERROR: " + e);
         e.printStackTrace(System.out);
      }
    }
  }
```

The server code creates and initializes an ORB object and then creates an instance of the object implementation `FunctionsImpl`. The server must publish a reference to this object to the Naming Service for the object to be located. The name of the object reference is arbitrary and formed by creating a naming scope, similar to a filename and path. In the example, the `FunctionsImpl` reference is named `"Calc"` and is a top-level name. Finally, the server waits (indefinitely) for an object request (through the newly created ORB reference). This server is an example of a transient object server; the server application must remain running, for the object to remain available.

Creating the Client Application

The client application will locate a reference to the `Functions` object using the Naming Service. The object reference returned is a CORBA object reference that must be cast or narrowed to the appropriate reference type. The server published the name of the reference as `"Calc"`, so this is the object reference that the client will request of the Naming Service. The client code is shown in Listing 19.6.

Listing 19.6: CalculatorClient.java

```
// Calculator Client

import Calculator.Functions;
import Calculator.FunctionsHelper;
import org.omg.CosNaming.*;
import org.omg.CORBA.*;

public class CalculatorClient
{
    public static void main(String args[])
    {
    try{
        // Create and initialize an instance of an ORB
        ORB orb = ORB.init(args, null);

        // Get a handle to the name server
        org.omg.CORBA.Object objRef =
            orb.resolve_initial_references("NameService");
        NamingContext ncRef =
            NamingContextHelper.narrow(objRef);

        // Look up the object bound to the name "Calc"
        NameComponent nc = new NameComponent("Calc", "");
        NameComponent path[] = {nc};

        // Use the Helper class to "cast" the generic CORBA
        // object reference to a Functions implementation.
```

```
            // The object returned by the narrow method is
            // actually a _FunctionsStub object that implements
            // the methods in the Functions interface
            Functions fRef =
              FunctionsHelper.narrow(ncRef.resolve(path));

            // Use the reference to execute the interface methods
            float sqrt = fRef.square_root (10f);
            float pow = fRef.power (2f, 8f);

            System.out.println
                ("The square root of 10 is: " + sqrt);
            System.out.println
                ("2 to the 8th power is: " + pow);

        } catch (Exception e) {
            System.out.println("ERROR : " + e) ;
            e.printStackTrace(System.out);
        }
        }
    }
```

The client program also creates an instance of an ORB; then requests a reference to an object that matches the naming scope created through the `NamingContext` reference. The object reference that the Naming Service returns is a general CORBA reference, and must be cast, or narrowed, before the object methods can be called. In addition, the object reference will be represented by a stub, on which the client application will invoke methods. The Helper class, generated by the IDL compiler (`idlj` or `idltojava`), makes this easy by providing a method called `narrow()`, which returns a reference to a `FunctionsStub`. With this reference, the `square_root` and `power` methods can be called.

Compiling the Implementation, Client, and Server Code

The newly created implementation, server, and client Java class files are compiled next with the following command line:

```
javac -d . FunctionsImpl.java CalculatorServer.java
   CalculatorClient.java
```

Starting the Naming Service Application

A Naming Service application, `tnameserv`, is provided with Java 2. The Naming Service will listen on a port–number 900 by default–for name resolution and binding requests. You can change the default port number by specifying an argument to `tnameserv`. For example, here the default port number is changed to 1050:

```
tnameserv -ORBInitialPort 1050
```

The Naming Service application responds with something similar to the following output:

```
Initial Naming Context:
IOR:000000000000002849444c3a6f6d672e6f72672f436f734e616d
696e672f4e616d696e67436f6e746578743a312e30000000000010000
0000000000340001000000000000864656661756c740000403000000000
001cafabcafe0000000234ba207b000000000000000080000
000000000000
TransientNameServer: setting port for initial object
references to: 1050
```

The output lists the Naming Service's Interoperable Object Reference (IOR) and the current port number that the Naming Service is listing on. The IOR string is another mechanism for locating a CORBA object reference. The IOR contains information about the location of the object, including the hostname, IP address, and what services the object provides. The IOR is most useful for passing an object reference between two ORB implementations without the need for a Naming Service to locate an object reference.

This works as follows: The server publishes a "stringified" object reference (the string representation of the CORBA object reference) by converting the object reference to a string. For example, the `CalculatorServer` class definition shown earlier in Listing 19.5 includes:

```
try{
   // Create and initialize the ORB
   ORB orb = ORB.init(args, null);

   // Create implementation object and
   // register it with the ORB
   FunctionsImpl fRef = new FunctionsImpl();
   orb.connect(fRef);
   System.out.println (orb.object_to_string (fRef));
}
```

The server will then report the IOR for the `FunctionsImpl` object. The `CalculatorClient` is passed the entire string output as an argument on the command line, and it converts the IOR string to an object reference:

```
try{
   // Create and initialize the ORB
   ORB orb = ORB.init(args, null);

   // Get a reference to an object from third argument
   // on the command line
   org.omg.CORBA.Object objRef =
        orb.string_to_object (args[2]);

   // Use the interface Functions to resolve the actual
   // object reference
   Functions fRef = FunctionsHelper.narrow(objRef);
}
```

Starting the Server

Next, the server is started to register the implementation object with the Naming Service. The server must locate the Naming Service by using the same port number or by using the IOR that the Naming Service published on startup. In this example, the port number is used.

```
java CalculatorServer -ORBInitialPort 1050
```

The server will run until it is killed.

Starting the Client

Now you can run the client application. The client must also be able to locate the Naming Service to contact the appropriate server for a reference to the implementation object:

```
java CalculatorClient -ORBInitialPort 1050
```

The client application produces the following output, indicating that it was successful in locating the server, receiving a reference to the `FunctionsImpl` object, and executing a `square_root` and power operation:

```
The square root of 10 is: 3.1622777
2 to the 8th power is: 256.0
```

IDL-to-Java Language Mapping

Programming conventions for Java and IDL differ slightly. IDL conventions do not require capitalization for the names of modules, interfaces, or operations. In addition, IDL convention uses underscores instead of mixed case for long names. Some of the IDL conventions are the result of the OMG's adoption of a definition language that crosses several programming languages and the attempt to create a standard that satisfies the capabilities of all of these languages.

Here are some general guidelines to follow when developing IDL files:

- An IDL file is composed of several elements that together create a naming scope.
- IDL does not support the overloading and overriding of operations, although inheritance (single and multiple) is supported.

The following sections present an overview of the IDL-to-Java language mapping, focusing on the most commonly used constructs.

TIP

For the complete IDL-to-Java language mapping, refer to `http://www.omg.org/technology/documents/formal/omg_idl_to_java_language_mapping.htm`**. Also, Chapters 5 through 8 of the Java mapping specification are provided as part of the Java IDL documentation (shipped with Java 2). These chapters are available through the file** `/JDK document installation directory/docs/guide/idl/mapping/jidlMapping.html`**.**

IDL Constructs

As examples of how to use some common IDL constructs, take a look at sample IDL files that might be used by Sullivan Publishing, the fictional book publishing company described at the beginning of this chapter.

IDL Modules

The IDL `module` construct is used to define the enclosing scope of a group of IDL interfaces. A `module` can contain one or more interfaces, and can nest other `module` constructs. Each `module` construct compiles to a Java package name. Here is an example of a nested `module` construct:

```
//IDL
module SullivanBooks {
    module BookStore {
        interface Account {
            ...
        };
    };
};
```

The Java code generated by `idltojava` would include the following package declaration:

```
// Java code
package SullivanBooks.BookStore;
...
```

IDL Interfaces

The IDL `interface` construct maps to a Java `interface` class. The IDL compiler generates several Java files from a single IDL `interface` construct:

- A Java `interface` class with the same name as the interface identifier
- A Java interface class with a name build by appending "Operations" to the name of the IDL interface (only when using `idlj`)
- A generated implementation class that contains the skeleton code required for the server-side application
- A stub class
- A Helper class that is used to narrow the object reference returned from a Naming Service to the stub object required by the client
- A Holder class that is used to contain a reference to the IDL type if the interface is passed as an argument in an operation

Given the IDL `module` definition shown in the previous section, the following files are generated (under the `SullivanBooks.BookStore` package directory) using `idltojava`:

- `Account.java`
- `AccountHolder.java`

- `_AccountStub.java`
- `AccountHelper.java`
- `_AccountImplBase.java`

`idlj` will also generate:

`AccountOperations.java`

IDL interfaces can contain attributes, exceptions, and operations.

IDL Attributes An attribute defines a CORBA variable type that may be accessed by predefined methods. CORBA types can either be standard IDL types (listed in Table 19.1) or another IDL interface.

TABLE 19.1: IDL-to-Java Type Mappings

IDL	Java
Float	Float
Double	Double
long, unsigned long	Int
long long, unsigned long long	Long
short, unsigned short	Short
char, wchar	Char
Boolean	Boolean
Octet	Byte
string, wstring	java.lang.String
enum, struct, union	Class

An attribute will generate an accessor and mutator method for the type declared. For example:

```
//IDL
attribute float price;
```

will generate the following Java methods:

```
// Generated Java methods
    float price();
    void price(float arg);
```

The attribute may also be declared read-only, in which case only an accessor method is declared. Note that the IDL compiler does not generate a `price` variable, just the methods to access the variable.

IDL Operations IDL operations are compiled to Java methods. Each operation must declare a return type, and may have zero or more arguments. Arguments to operations declare the call semantics of the argument. These may be `in`, `out`, or `inout`.

An `in` parameter is call-by-value and is mapped directly to the corresponding Java type (see Table 19.1). An `out` parameter uses call-by-reference semantics. Java does not use call-by-reference, so `out` parameters are mapped onto a Java `Holder` class. This class encapsulates a data variable that contains the parameter, and the value of the class reference is passed. Finally, the `inout` parameter semantics are call-by-value/result. This too is mapped onto a Java `Holder` class.

Operations That Raise Exceptions Operations can declare that they raise an exception using the construct `raises (exception)`. Exceptions in the `raises` clause must be declared before they can be used. Here is an example:

```
// IDL
// ... code above not shown
interface account {
  void orderBooks(in BookList books, out string orderID)
    raises (StockException);
};
```

The above operation, `orderBooks`, declares an `in` parameter named `books` of type `BookList` and an `out` parameter that is a string, and raises an exception `StockException`.

An IDL File to Define Three Services

To continue the discussion of IDL constructs, look at a more complete example. Here is the IDL file that Sullivan Publishing will use for its online bookstore:

```
// Sample IDL
module BookStore {

    exception StockException {
        string reason;
    };
```

```
    exception AccountException {
        string reason;
        float creditLine;
    };

    struct Book {
        string title;
        string author;
        string isbn_number;
        float price;
    };

    typedef sequence <Book> BookList;

    interface BookOrder {
        readonly attribute BookList theOrder;
        void addBook (in Book theBook)
          raises (StockException);
        void removeBook (in Book theBook);
        void searchBook (in Book theBook,
          out Book result) raises (StockException);
    };

    interface BookOrderManager {
        BookOrder generateOrder ();
    };

    interface Account {
        readonly attribute string accountID;
        BookOrder getBookOrder ();
        void orderBooks ( in BookOrder order ) raises
          (AccountException);
        void checkStatus ( in BookOrder order,
           out string status );
    };

    struct PayType {
        string cardType;
        string cardNumber;
        string expirationDate;
    };

    interface AccountManager {
        Account getAccount ( in string name,
           in PayType payment );
    };
};
```

This IDL file defines four services:

AccountManager service Generates an `Account` for the customer and allow the customer to generate a book order

Account service Is used to generate a book order, order books, and check the status of a book order

BookOrder service Is used to add or remove books from an order

BookOrderManager service Generates a new order that the `Account` object uses to order books

Customers will open an account, generate a book order with one or more books they add to the order, and place the order.

If a book is not in stock, a `StockException` is raised to let the customer know that the book is out of stock. An `AccountException` is raised if the credit card used to open the account is overdrawn or invalid at the time of ordering.

Object Factories

The factory concept is important in the development of CORBA services. It is sometimes desirable to be able to create new objects on the fly at runtime. This capability is important when the number of objects to be created is not known in advance.

The IDL file shown in the previous section uses object factories. The number of accounts that Sullivan Publishing will have over the life of the company cannot be predetermined. It might be possible to create a number of objects in advance that can then be doled out, but how many is enough? Should you create 10 or 100?

Rather than describe each object as a discrete service that exists on the server, an object factory allows the server to create an instance of an `Account` object for each new customer request. The `AccountManager` service is responsible for receiving a request for a new account and then creating a new `Account` object for that request. Subsequent requests will always return the same object reference given that the account name is the same. Granted, using a single string to create a unique object is probably not enough, but the idea is that some given set of parameters defines what object reference to return. Figure 19.4 illustrates this use of an object factory.

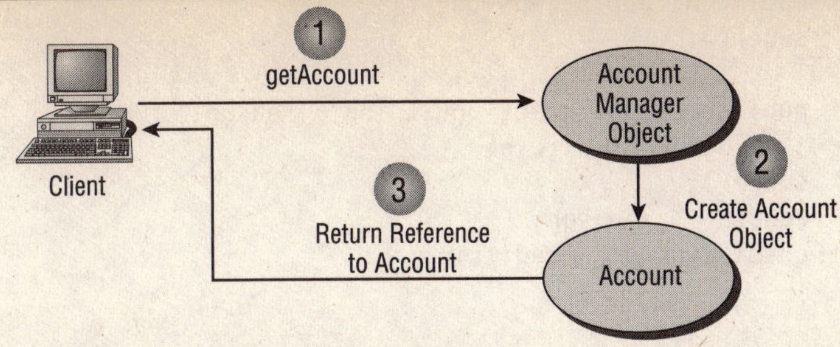

FIGURE 19.4: Using an object factory

Likewise, each `Account` may have one or more `BookOrder` objects. Again, a factory is used to generate new `BookOrder` objects from the `BookOrderManager` object on request.

IDL Exceptions

IDL exceptions are passed as object references, as in Java, but they do not map directly onto the Java Exception API. IDL exceptions extend the `org.omg.CORBA.UserException` class. Exceptions may contain data that is accessed as public members of the named class and may be passed in the construction of the exception. For example, this `exception` construct:

```
// IDL
    exception StockException {
        string reason;
    };
```

is compiled into a Java class (`AccountException.java`):

```
/*
 * File: ./BookStore/AccountException.java
 * From: bookstore2.idl
 * Date: Tue Jan  6 14:13:36 1998
 *   By: idltojava Java IDL 1.2 Nov 12 1997 12:23:47
 */

package BookStore;
public final class AccountException
    extends org.omg.CORBA.UserException {
    //    instance variables
    public String reason;
    public float creditLine;
    //    constructors
```

```
        public AccountException() {
        super();
        }
        public AccountException(String __reason,
           float __creditLine) {
        super();
        reason = __reason;
        creditLine = __creditLine;
        }
    }
```

IDL Structures

The IDL `struct` is a container class that may be used to pass a collection of data as a single object. An IDL `struct` maps to a Java class with public data members. For example, this `struct` construct:

```
    // IDL
        struct Book {
            string title;
            string author;
            string isbn_number;
            float price;
        };
```

maps to a Java `final` class:

```
    /*
     * File: ./BookStore/Book.java
     * From: bookstore2.idl
     * Date: Tue Jan  6 14:13:36 1998
     *   By: idltojava Java IDL 1.2 Nov 12 1997 12:23:47
     */

    package BookStore;
    public final class Book {
        //    instance variables
        public String title;
        public String author;
        public String isbn_number;
        public float price;
        //    constructors
        public Book() { }
        public Book(String __title, String __author,
            String __isbn_number, float __price) {
        title = __title;
        author = __author;
```

```
        isbn_number = __isbn_number;
        price = __price;
        }
    }
```

IDL Type Definitions

IDL provides a construct for naming new IDL types from existing types. The `typedef` construct does not directly map to Java, so the IDL compiler will substitute and replace any instance of the `typedef` name for the actual type in the IDL before compiling it. The `typedef` construct makes it easier to write IDL files, particularly when sequences are required. Here are some examples of `typedef` constructs:

```
// IDL
typedef string CustomerName;
typedef long CustomerSalary;
typedef sequence <long> CustomerOrderID;
```

IDL Sequences

IDL sequences are single-dimension arrays that may be bounded or unbounded. A bounded sequence defines its maximum size in the declaration of the `sequence`. For example, in this `sequence` construct:

```
// IDL
typedef sequence <long, 10> openOrders;
```

A bounded sequence of up to ten IDL long numbers is defined as the type `openOrders`.

The bounds of a bounded sequence are checked as the argument is marshaled and sent. If the bounds of a bounded sequence are exceeded, a `MARSHAL` system exception is raised. Both bounded and unbounded sequences generate a Java Helper and Holder class for each sequence.

IDL Arrays

The IDL `array` construct is used to create a single-dimension fixed-size bounded array of any IDL type. The `array` construct is mapped to Java the same way as the bounded sequence, but uses different semantics. Here is an example:

```
// IDL
const long length = 20;
typedef string custName[length];
```

IDL Enumerations

The IDL enum construct is used to represent an enumerated list. Variables of the enum type can only hold as their values one of the constants listed in the definition for the type. For example:

```
enum City {Boston, NewYork, Chicago, Baltimore};
```

The enum construct maps to a Java final class with the same name:

```
package BookStore;
public final class City {
  public static final int _Boston = 0;
  public static final Calculator.City Boston =
     new Calculator.City(_Boston);
  public static final int _NewYork = 1;
  public static final Calculator.City NewYork =
     new Calculator.City(_NewYork);
  public static final int _Chicago = 2;
  public static final Calculator.City Chicago =
     new Calculator.City(_Chicago);
       // code deleted
}
```

Legacy Applications and CORBA

A business application may include code that is not current or state-of-the-art, but works perfectly well. That code may have been written by engineers who left the company long ago. This type of code is referred to as *legacy* code. One of the drawbacks to legacy code is that it is often deployed on a legacy hardware system as well. The company needs to access this code on its existing hardware platform and be able to use it across its network.

One of CORBA's primary benefits is that it allows developers to wrap legacy code within a CORBA object model. An IDL description of the legacy interfaces is used to produce a set of CORBA objects. These objects can then make calls into the legacy code and expose the legacy system to a network. Figure 19.5 illustrates this approach.

Wrapping legacy code does require some understanding of the way that the code works. The low-level implementation details are not important, but an understanding of the way that the code is called or interfaced with other code modules is necessary. The interfaces and access methods become the foundation of an IDL interface, which is then used to create a CORBA system.

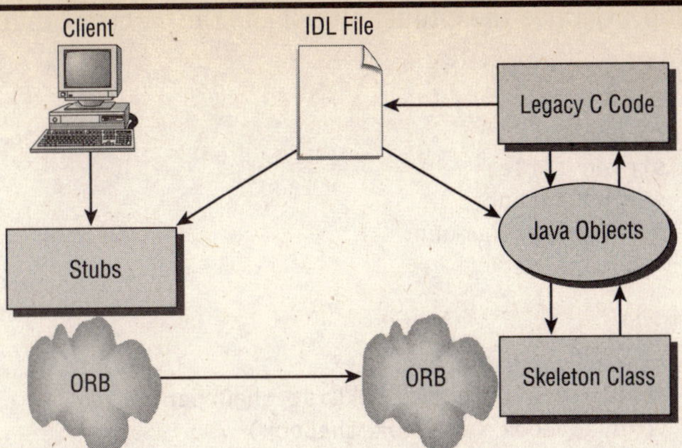

FIGURE 19.5: Legacy COBOL code wrapping

As an example, suppose that Sullivan Publishing (the fictional book publishing company discussed at the beginning of this chapter), in one of its expansions, has purchased a book catalog service. Part of this purchase involved the acquisition of some C code used to search for book records in a database. The current book catalog service is a phone-only service. Sullivan Publishing would like to use the Internet to enable customers to order books, but still preserve the current code that exists for searching the book database. This is an excellent application for CORBA. The legacy C code can be used as is, but will be wrapped by an implementation that will expose the C code to the network.

In this example, Sullivan Publishing purchased inventory-tracking software that was designed to run on a Windows NT computer. The original code was not designed to run on a network, and the original source code is not available, so it is not practical to port the code directly to Java, however, the interface to the code is fairly straightforward—the C code is compiled into a library. For example, calls to the search routines are made as follows:

```
void search (Book *toFind, Book *result);
```

where the parameters are passed as a pointer to a `struct`:

```
struct Book {
    char title [100];
    char author [100];
    char isbn[25];
    float price;
};
```

The developer defined the C function call and the C `struct` in IDL as follows:

```
// IDL
    struct Book {
        string title;
        string author;
        string isbn_number;
        float price;
    };

    interface BookOrder {
        readonly attribute BookList theOrder;
        void addBook (in Book theBook)
           raises (StockException);
        void removeBook (in Book theBook);
        void searchBook (in Book theBook, out Book result)
raises (StockException);
    };
```

Because Sullivan Publishing would like to preserve the legacy C code for the search routine, the `BookOrder` object must be implemented on the Windows NT computer. There are a couple ways to do this.

- Use a CORBA vendor that supports a C language mapping and a Windows NT ORB. Implement the `BookOrder` object in C, directly integrating the library call to the search function.
- Write the implementation class for `BookOrder` in Java on the Windows NT machine, and use a native method to call into the `search` function.

This is a book about Java, so the latter approach will be demonstrated:

```
// Implementation file for the BookOrder interface

import BookStore.*;
import java.util.Vector;

// First, extend the Implementation Base class
public class BookOrderImpl extends _BookOrderImplBase {

    // Keep a vector of books to be ordered
    private final Vector bookList = new Vector();

    // Constructor
    public BookOrderImpl () {
    }
```

```
    //Implement method to return the list of books
    public Book[] theOrder() {
        Book [] bookOrder;
        // Turn the vector into an array
        bookOrder = new Book [bookList.size()];
        bookList.copyInto(bookOrder);
    }
        return bookOrder;
    }

    public void removeBook(Book theBook) {
        // Remove an element from the bookList
        bookList.removeElement (theBook);
    }

    public void searchBook(Book theBook,
      BookHolder result) throws BookStore.StockException {
        // Call the native search function
        search (theBook, result);
        if (result == null) {
         throw new StockException
           ("No book found with ISBN number: "
            + theBook.isbn_number);
    }
}

    // The native method for search
    private native void search
       (Book theBook, BookHolder result);

    // Load the native method from the specified library
    static {
        System.loadLibrary ("orderlib");
    }
}
```

Notice that the search function declared in the native declaration above will actually result in a call to a function called BookOrderImpl_search, which will act as a "bridge" to the existing C search function.

Note also that the server application for the AccountManager object can reside on another machine, such as a Sun workstation. The client application will request a reference to an AccountManager. Using this object reference, the client application will request an instance of an Account (by calling the getAccount method). With this object reference, the client can generate a new `BookOrder` object by calling the `getBookOrder` method. This method gets a reference to the `BookOrderManager` on the Windows NT machine and then returns a `BookOrder` object. To the client application, this all happens through local stub invocations!

WHAT'S NEXT

CORBA makes it possible to develop systems that are independent of a programming language and operating system. The introduction of Java to the programming world and the development of protocol standards have propelled CORBA into the current mainstream of computing.

CORBA provides an intermediary solution to the problem of rewriting code. CORBA makes it possible to preserve a company's current investment in COBOL, C, C++, and Ada applications while making the transition to Java in the long-term. CORBA's standards-based approach also frees decision-makers from making a single vendor choice. Systems that are developed using the CORBA framework and standards are easily adapted to other vendors' products with a minimum of code rewriting.

The future of distributed object programming will undoubtedly include CORBA. It is likely that in a few years, systems will be developed with visually driven tools, eliminating the need to develop IDL files altogether. Furthermore, it is becoming increasingly apparent that software vendors have embraced the standards set forth by the OMG, and the future will include more interoperability across both software and hardware domains.

The following chapters will examine Enterprise JavaBeans (EJB), which are one of the most powerful features of J2EE. Enterprise JavaBeans provide a robust and effective way to build business logic components that are scalable and reliable. EJBs work hand in hand with all of the technologies presented in this book to empower you to make excellent enterprise applications in Java.

Chapter 20
EJB Architecture and Clients

Java initially started as a client-side environment for cross-platform applications and applets. But the same benefits of Java on the client are being applied to server environments. EJBs are a key technology within J2EE, because they provide a server-side component environment for building business frameworks. Our objectives will be to cover:

- What are EJBs?
- EJB Roles and Responsibilities
- J2EE and Container Services
- EJB Scalability
- The EJB Component Marketplace
- How do Clients use EJBs?

Written for *Enterprise Java™ 2, J2EE™ 1.3 Complete* by Vince E. Marco

What Are EJBs?

Enterprise JavaBeans (EJBs) are a business component model for building distributed business objects for deployment in J2EE application servers. EJBs are defined within the J2EE specification. The EJB 1.1 specification has become widely popular with the introduction of persistent components called *entity beans*. Currently, the EJB 2.0 specification has extended these entity beans and added message-driven beans for handling asynchronous messages. These beans will be defined further in the section "Business Components" later in the chapter. Figure 20.1 illustrates how the various versions of Java2 Enterprise Edition and the EJB specification match up, and indicates which version of the J2EE specification includes each various EJB specification.

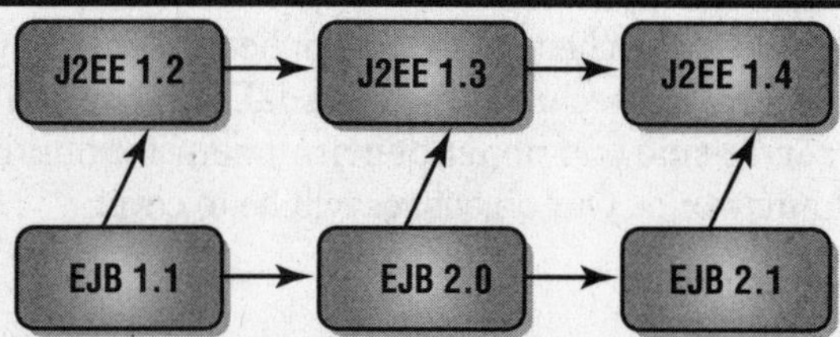

FIGURE 20.1: J2EE and EJB version dependencies

To fully understand the EJB architecture, you will look at EJBs from several different perspectives. You will first view Enterprise JavaBeans as a model and environment for business components. You will also examine EJBs as server-bound components as well as EJBs as distributed objects and the impact this has on business components. You will then compare EJBs to other component architectures. You will look at EJB specialization and the intended roles involved with EJB development and maintenance, and discover how EJBs can foster a marketplace of reusable components. Finally, you will get down to business with EJB containers, services, and scalability.

Business Components

One of the primary objectives of EJBs is to provide a component model for business objects. *Business objects* are defined as objects that effectively organize the information-processing behavior of the business running the software system. To accomplish this effectively, business objects strive to separate technology from the business rules that govern the management of information. Some of these business rules are common to many businesses and components that target these types of rules can be reused and sold as frameworks to many companies. But many business rules are specific to a given business, and therefore require the building and management of custom EJBs. Enterprise JavaBeans provide various types of building blocks for enterprise applications.

There are four types of EJBs, each providing a different behavior to their clients:

- Stateless session beans
- Stateful session beans
- Entity beans
- Message driven beans

Stateless Session Beans (SLSBs)

Session EJBs are *memory-based* components on the application server that are accessed by clients both remotely and locally. These objects do not survive server crashes or shutdowns, but are supported by all the J2EE and container services discussed later in this chapter. Figure 20.2 shows that stateless session beans are pooled as identical components. Subsequent accesses from a client can access different beans in the pool.

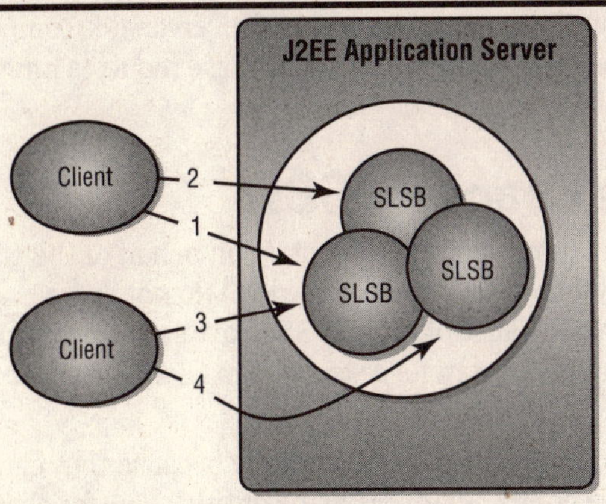

FIGURE 20.2: Pooled stateless session EJB

SLSBs do not maintain state on behalf of the client, and are generally pooled for efficient access. Subsequent invocations from a client may, in fact, access different EJB instances in the pool. This can occur because each invocation of a SLSB method can receive client information via method parameters. Some common uses for stateless session EJBs include business lookups or calculations. Looking up a stock ticker symbol, or calculating sales tax are prime examples.

But stateless session beans have become far more useful than an occasional utility mechanism. Stateless session beans are ideal for handling access from web applications. Because the HyperText Transfer Protocol (HTTP) is used by web applications and is stateless, SLSBs have become popular for handling these requests. Stateless session beans have become a frequent component types for high-level session facades, which Web and web service clients rely on to perform business functions.

As an example, consider a BankTeller stateless session bean that has methods for withdrawing and depositing. Many of these functions are common to all accounts and are well suited for the stateless session bean; however, because the BankTeller is stateless, it cannot be asked to remember aspects of the client's account and must be passed in the account (or AccountID) with each request. This frees the teller to service a new account with each request. This approach reduces the number of method calls needed to accomplish each function, but does require the passing of more information on each request. This works out well, especially with web applications, because the web application is managing HTTP requests in a similar manner.

Even rich client applications running outside the browser benefit from this approach. These applications are accessing the server-side component using a network connection, so optimization of these requests provides a big performance boost.

Stateful Session Beans (SFSBs)

SFSBs are components that maintain their state on behalf of the client. These are also *memory-based* session beans, which do not survive server crashes and shutdowns. Because of this, SFSBs have seen limited use. Figure 20.3 shows a couple of stateful session bean clients, each accessing their own SFSB.

SFSBs do not perform as well as SLSBs, largely because they cannot be pooled, and they are not as reliable as using entity beans for client state. Every SFSB client establishes a new bean instance on the server, largely because this bean will maintain state for that client. This means that if there are 1000 customers on a web site, and each client uses a stateful session bean, the server will have 1000 SFSBs running. Nonetheless, SFSBs do not carry the overhead of entity beans, and are useful in some circumstances.

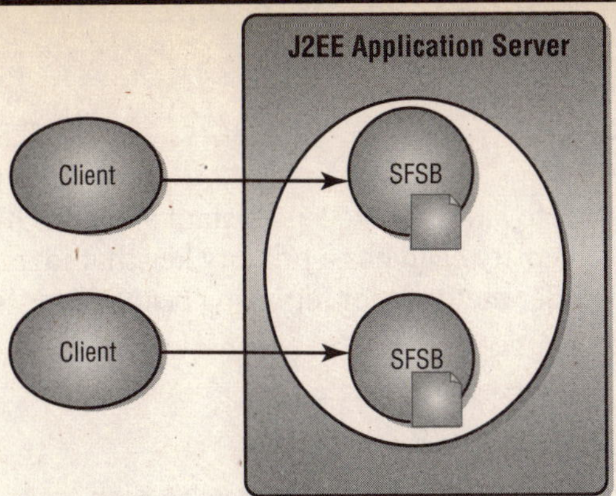

FIGURE 20.3: Stateful session EJB

An example might be a ShoppingCart EJB. The main purpose for this component is to accumulate purchased items during a shopping spree for only one web client. This EJB might have methods such as `addItem()`, `removeItem()`, or `getItems()`, which require a conversational or stateful component. As long as the ShoppingCart didn't need to save purchased items even through a server crash, a stateful session bean might be the component type to use.

NOTE

It is possible—and in many cases, very useful—to use stateless session beans for ShoppingCart behavior by passing an ArrayList that gets stored in the HttpSession. Many situational considerations affect the choice of EJBs.

As an example, if we were to implement a shopping cart as a stateless session bean, our SLSB is unable to save the shopping cart items between client invocations. It would need to retrieve and update these shopping cart items on every call, perhaps using an entity bean. This is a useful approach if our shopping cart needs to persist between sessions and server crashes. If an entity bean is going to be used to save the shopping cart state, then our session bean doesn't need to, and its performance can be optimized by using a stateless session bean.

The stateful session bean approach enables us to cache the shopping cart items right in the stateful session bean, without requiring an entity bean or alternative persistence to store the items. The drawback is that my shopping cart will not survive between user sessions or server crashes, and I will have a stateful bean taking up server resources for every active client using my application.

Entity Beans (EBs)

Entity beans are designed to save state to a persistent store, such as a *relational database*. Each entity bean has a primary key that identifies the bean instance and finder methods for retrieving beans from the persistent store.

NOTE

A persistent store refers to a method for saving state between server crashes or reboots. This store can be a flat file, relational database, object database, or external system. The most common persistent store is a relational database, which manages each entry as one or more row in one or more tables.

Figure 20.4 shows two clients, each accessing an entity bean. These beans are in-memory representations of entries in a database. As state changes in each entity bean, the database (persistent store) is updated to reflect the changes.

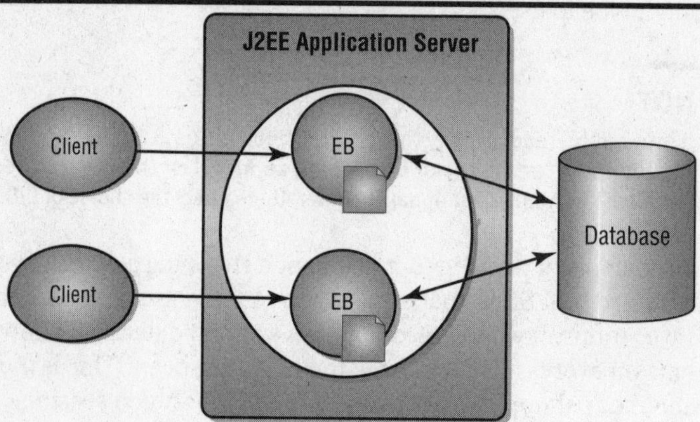

FIGURE 20.4: Entity beans

Entity beans are not limited to relational databases, but relational databases are the most popular persistence store for entity beans. One recurring question among enterprise developers is, "What is the difference between using JDBC in session beans and using entity beans?" The answer is that with session beans, you must explicitly tell the bean to access the database; with entity beans, the server manages when your bean accesses the server.

For instance, if you create a session bean called `Customer`, it will not update the database when you call `setName()` to change the name. You must have an explicit `save()` or `store()` method to tell the session bean to save changes to the database. If this Customer component is an entity bean, however, the server will manage calling the `ejbStore()` method to save changes. The `setName()` call will indicate a needed store to the database, which the server will call. No explicit `store()` or `save()` method is called by the client to ensure the changes are saved. Instead, the server configuration and the active transaction will determine the actual saving of state to the database.

Message Driven Beans (MDBs)

MDBs are the newest type of EJB that were added in the EJB 2.0 specification. MDBs receive asynchronous messages via the Java Messaging Service (JMS). In essence, they respond to messages on configured JMS topics and queues to perform their work. They do not save client state, and do not survive server crashes or shutdowns. They may call services and also invoke session and entity beans. To a large extent you think of MDBs as components that listen for and handle JMS messages.

For example, imagine you have a message-driven bean for processing feedback requests from your web site. The client enters their message, and doesn't expect any specific reply other than acknowledgment that their feedback will be read by someone at the company who can take the appropriate action needed. This is a perfect asynchronous opportunity. Because JMS can guarantee the delivery of the message, the client goes on their merry way without needing to wait for receipt of their feedback message. The FeedBackManager MDB can remain busy processing these feedback requests without even knowing or ever directly connecting with the sender of the message. MDBs are excellent at receiving these asynchronous requests, and can be pooled to handle multiple requests simultaneously.

Figure 20.5 shows clients sending messages to the JMS, and MDBs receiving these messages.

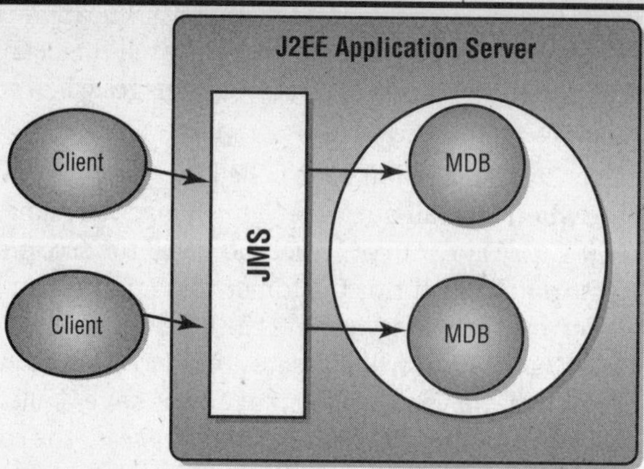

FIGURE 20.5: Message driven beans

MDBs are the only EJB type that can receive asynchronous messages via JMS; however, all EJB types can send messages to JMS. Prior to MDBs, integrating synchronous and asynchronous messaging via EJB and JMS had been only one way, unless a developer created an external Java client to receive asynchronous messages and call EJBs. Now with MDBs, components can be built inside the application server that provide the bridge from asynchronous messaging to synchronous EJBs.

NOTE

EJBs are prevented from managing threads and using sockets for network communication. This prevents them from receiving JMS messages. While MDBs are also not allowed to manage threads or use sockets, they are allowed to receive JMS messages. Since they do not need to serve external clients they can devote their attention to receiving and processing JMS messages.

In many cases, designers want both a synchronous and asynchronous API for a given component. As an example, consider an OrderManager component that processes incoming orders in a synchronous (request/reply) manner. This works well when the client wants to wait around for the processing of the order; however, the manufacturer wants to allow bulk orders with certain high-volume customers without the customer needing to wait for each order to be processed. A BulkOrderManager message driven bean is created that accepts orders via JMS and then turns around and calls the OrderManager to process each order. You get both synchronous and asynchronous order processing without duplicating the code in another bean.

Rich Set of Services

EJBs may be accessed by a variety of clients. These may be Java applets or applications running on a remote client or server machine. These clients might also be servlets, JSPs, or other EJBs running on the application server. Client access can be defined by relative client location and what type of messaging is desired. Client location may be local, or within the same Java Virtual Machine (JVM). Location may also be remote or accessible via a network. EJB 2.0 accommodates both of these locations by providing local and remote references to the server-side EJB component.

EJBs are supported by a rich set of services. These services fall into two categories: implicit and explicit. In Figure 20.6, you see the explicit and implicit services provided by the application server. The explicit services are usable by external applications and components running in the server by explicitly invoking them in the code. The implicit services are provided to internal components via the container, and require no code by the developer.

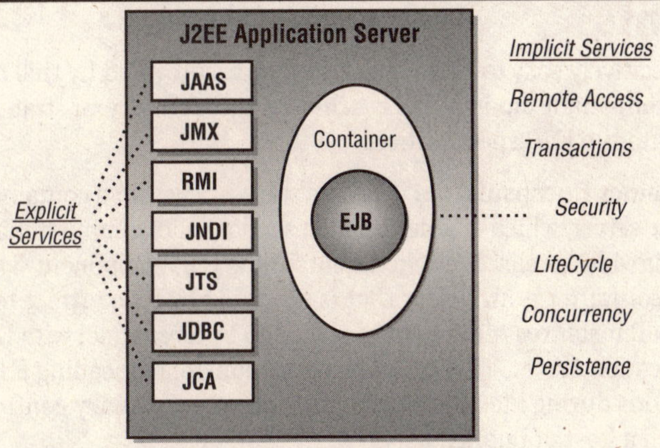

FIGURE 20.6: Explicit and implicit services

EJBs are the business components within the J2EE family of technologies. They provide a robust component model for J2EE-based applications, and focus on enabling the separation of business logic from the services that support them. EJBs are intended to provide a vehicle for platform and application server independence and portability.

Separate Business Logic from Technology

EJBs provide for a separation of business logic from technology. Experience has shown that the business requirements that drive what you build are entirely separate from the software technology that determines how you build your enterprise software. Not only are these separate, but they also change within different cycles. In other words, the reasons you change your business process are different from the reason you adopt new technologies, even though these get mixed up sometimes in the form of your enterprise projects. EJBs help separate project efforts in the implicit and explicit categories, enabling business components that can depend upon a separate set of technology-oriented services.

The results are enterprise software that can adopt new technologies without breaking business rules and logic, and business rules that can change without affecting existing usage of technology.

Making It Easier to Build Business Components

EJBs are relatively easy to build, given the values provided by this robust business component model. This is achieved through several strategies designed into the EJB specification:

Container Encapsulation EJBs always run within a container on the server, which enables implicit services and administration, and provides a reliable environment for the EJB component. The EJB container is an object that is specified by its contract to the EJB instances running inside of it and by its contract with the application server. This container is responsible for calling EJB methods during lifecycle events, providing concurrency control as well a host of implicit services.

Implicit Services Implicit services are provided by the container on every client access, and are configurable within a deployment descriptor, formatted using XML. These services require no code to be developed by the developer, thus simplifying development of the component. These services get applied before and after EJB method calls as well as events sent to the container. Implicit services include remote access, concurrency, lifecycle, persistence, transactions, security, and administration.

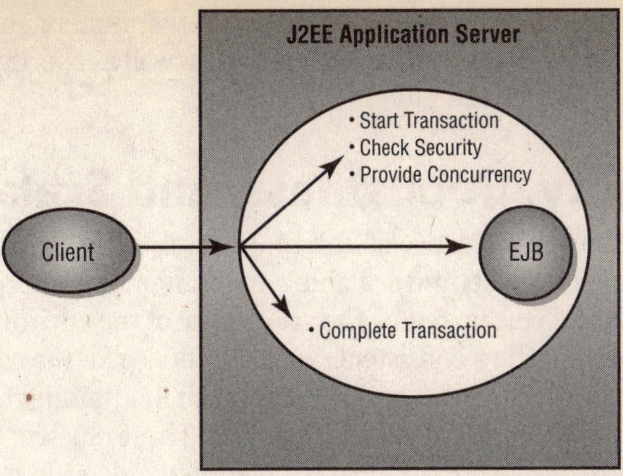

These services include concurrency, transaction management, and security. The container provides these services on each EJB method call by intercepting the method call and then performing needed service calls before and after the method call on the bean instance.

Explicit Services Explicit services are available to the EJB developer for explicit use within the EJB code. Standard services, such as naming, security, database access, and so on, are provided to the developer through easy-to-use interfaces. The Java Connection Framework (JCF) also provides a standard method for defining external custom services for explicit use to EJB developers. Explicit services include naming, database access, security, transactions, and a connector framework for access to custom services (see "J2EE and Container Services" later in this chapter for more information on implicit and explicit services).

Distributed Access After EJBs are developed and deployed, they become distributed objects accessible across a network, increasing client availability and access with a minimal amount of developer effort.

Configurable Environment EJBs provide a deployment descriptor for *configurable* parameters, allowing configurations to occur at deployment time without recompiling code. The deployment descriptors use XML, and are organized to separate vendor dependant settings from generic configurations. These descriptors allow EJB application developers and deployers to configure transactions, security, environment entries, resource and EJB references, persistence, as well as specifying the classes to use for the EJBs.

Reliability, Robustness, and Scalability

An important objective of Enterprise JavaBeans (and of J2EE) is to provide a reliable, robust, and scalable environment for enterprise applications. *Reliability* is measured by the availability of the environment and its capability to provide a consistent quality of service for the components running in the environment. The J2EE approach in attaining reliability and scalability is through clustering of servers. These clusters consist of multiple application servers running in a tight network, each capable of servicing incoming requests for deployed applications.

Load balancing is achieved through a proxy server. This server distributes requests around to different machines in the cluster instead of letting requests hit one server. Many different strategies of load-balancing are usually supported, such as round-robin, random, weighted, and so on. Failover is another aspect of a clustered environment. Failover allows failed requests into one server to execute on a secondary or backup server.

Reliability is achieved via a controlled environment, as well as through load balancing and failover within a clustered environment. In a nutshell, a cluster is a group of servers configured to handle requests, and a proxy that distributes these requests around to the various servers in the cluster. Load balancing refers to the distributing of these requests to various machines in the cluster. Failover, while related to load-balancing, refers to the ability for a request to be sent to a second server in the cluster if the first server requested is unavailable. *Robustness* is provided through a set of implicit and explicit services that handle everything from transactions and security to naming and persistence. *Scalability* is achieved through a clustered environment, and a sound architecture enabling both small and large servers to serve up these components. Both load-balancing and failover are provided by many application servers for EJBs, enabling enterprise development to occur on small, inexpensive machines, and deployment to large clusters capable of supporting the global Internet marketplace.

Server-Side Components

Enterprise JavaBeans are components that live within a server. An EJB server is ideal for efficient and effective access to multiple resources. For instance, an EJB running on a server can be on a high-speed network along with several database servers or legacy systems. It would be impractical to access every service from a dial-up or broadband Internet connection. This server environment is also controlled, unlike most client workstations that run a huge variety of software applications.

Instead, a server environment strives to be unchanging, predictable, and reliable. It targets the running of components and applications that are shared by many clients who access common information and resources. Containing these EJB objects in the robust and reliable environment provided by J2EE application servers is essential to building scalable enterprise applications. This application server environment controls threading, memory-usage, and access to resources, which is difficult to do on the client. This accounts for the vast usage of web- and web service–based solutions in enterprise software solutions.

Another advantage for server-side components is the vast array of services provided by a J2EE application server. These services consist of standard J2EE services, container services, and custom services supported by the Java Connector Architecture (JCA). Custom JCA services are discussed in Chapter 24, "J2EE Connector Architecture."

Every EJB has a home object that is a managerial object providing access to the EJB, and controlling its lifecycle. The home object is itself a distributed object that is obtained via the JNDI naming service, and called to create(), find(), or remove() EJB components.

Distributed Objects

Distributed objects provide a method for accessing objects running on a remote server via an object reference or "stub" that resides on the client computer. Enterprise JavaBeans are distributed objects, and use Remote Method Invocation (RMI) for distributed access. An analogy for RMI might be a remote control and a television. The remote control allows you to control the TV even though you are not within reach of the TV controls. In RMI, the TV is an object running on the server and the remote is any application on the network accessing the object through its remote interface.

Figure 20.7 shows an EJB client that interacts with a remote stub. The client is only aware of the remote interface implemented by the stub. The stub, in turn, communicates with a skeleton on the server that acts as a surrogate for the client by calling methods on the EJB object via the container.

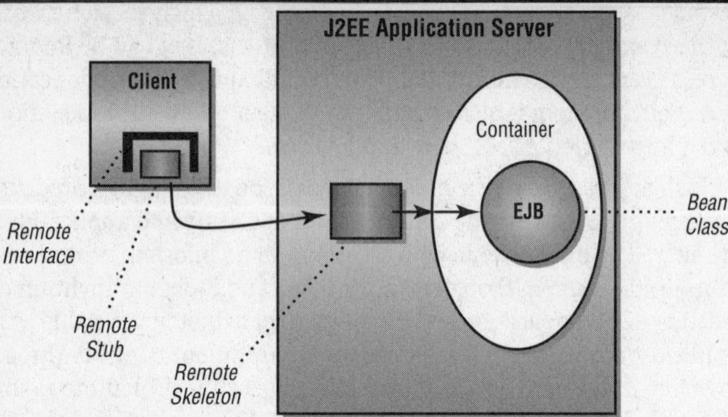

FIGURE 20.7: EJB remote method invocation

Remote EJB clients (not running on the same server) access EJBs via a remote reference. This reference is composed of a remote interface that defines the business methods for the EJB, and a remote stub object that sends the request over the network to the server. This stub implements the remote interface, and works behind the scenes without being explicitly referenced by the client.

EJBs have local references (as of the EJB 2.0 specification) for efficient access to EJB components from clients residing in the same application as the EJB itself.

Figure 20.8 shows the sequence of a client accessing a distributed EJB; you can see that this distributed access is provided largely by RMI. The first step to using an EJB is to get the home RMI stub. The EJB home reference is an RMI object that interacts contains methods for creating (and finding for entity beans) and deleting a server instance of the EJB. We get the home stub from JNDI. Calling a create() method on the home stub causes the container to create an EJB instance on the server and return its RMI stub to the client. The client accesses the RMI stub, which serializes parameters and sends the method request over the network to a skeleton class running on the remote server. This skeleton then marshals the parameters and calls the actual remote object class. Return values are handled the same way as the parameters, except in reverse with the skeleton sending the return object to the stub. See Chapter 18, "Persistence and Remote Method Invocation," for more details on RMI.

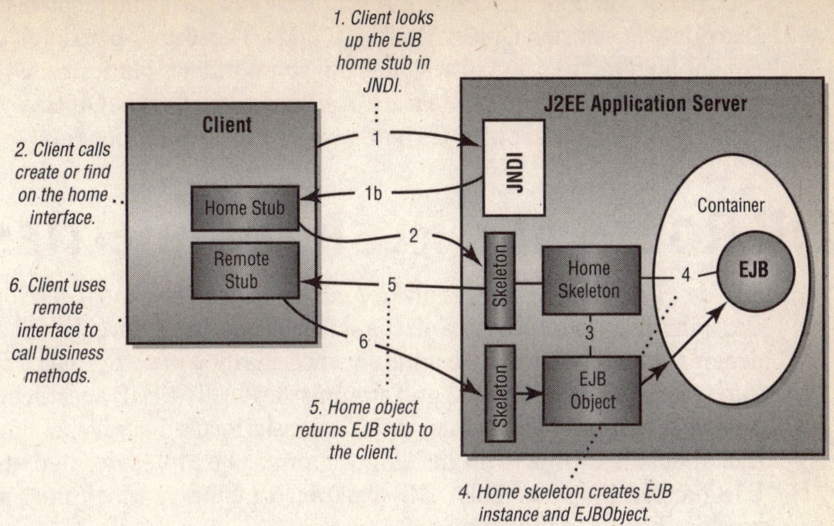

FIGURE 20.8: EJB remote method invocation sequence

The actual RMI objects and the process for creating them are generally assumed by the EJB tools provided by the application server environment. Within RMI this is handled by the RMI compiler (RMIC), which provides a command-line facility for generating the stub and skeleton classes. EJB development, as you will see in Chapter 21, "Session, Entity, and Message Driven Beans," hides or wraps this RMIC process.

Other Component Models

Enterprise JavaBeans are not the first or only component architecture. The Common Object Request Broker Architecture (CORBA) came before EJBs. CORBA's objective is to provide a distributed-object component architecture that is both platform and language independent. Similar to EJBs, CORBA is defined in a specification that identifies several services to support the components; however, CORBA does not require these services as the EJB specification does, and these services are not implicitly provided by the component container. (See Chapter 19, "JavaIDL and CORBA Connectivity," for more information.) The J2EE specification includes both the EJB component model and CORBA component model. CORBA components are accessible via Java IDL (interface definition language), and via the RMI/IIOP protocol.

Another component architecture is Microsoft's .NET and its predecesor Distributed Common Object Model (DCOM). These are Microsoft's component architecture, and is available only on Windows platforms. Other proprietary component models are available, such as WebObjects, but most have faded or adopted current standard component models.

EJB Roles and Responsibilities

EJB developer involvement is divided into specific roles to help developers and administrators specialize on the skills needed to effectively build and deploy these components. Historically, specialization in software has fallen into two areas: development and administration. The EJB specification further divides these roles into additional tasks focused upon enabling further specialization within developer groups. The roles defined are EJB provider, EJB assembler, EJB deployer, container provider, and server provider, as shown in Figure 20.9.

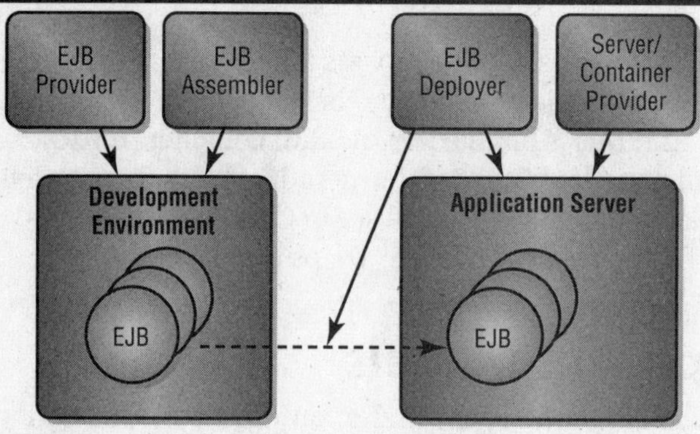

FIGURE 20.9: EJB roles and specialization

These roles help define and guide EJB design and reuse. EJB components are intended for reuse, and because they target large-scale, server-side business behavior, and may target multiple applications within and across enterprise systems.

EJB Provider This role is defined by a developer who focuses on building EJBs. These EJBs are generally grouped as frameworks. They are intended for reuse within organizations and also sold as frameworks targeting specific areas of enterprise development. These frameworks can be described as horizontal, providing generic business functionality, or vertical, providing business behavior specific to one aspect of the business. A developer focuses on designing, coding, and testing EJBs when wearing a provider hat.

EJB Assembler This role is defined by a developer who uses existing EJBs within their applications. Software development benefits from reuse, and EJBs are defined with the intention of assembling EJB components within applications. The focus of assembling EJBs is on client access. This is a good place for new EJB developers to start because they can gain productive EJB experience without having to be an expert on the inner workings or development process of EJBs. This role of assembling EJBs scales up to complex applications that may be accessing several internal, cross-departmental, and purchased frameworks of EJBs.

EJB Deployer This role is defined by a developer or administrator when configuring and deploying EJBs to an application server, and can be categorized into development deployment and production deployment, each with their own sets of issues and objectives. This role exists largely because it is the objective of EJB components to provide components that are configurable without recompiling code. This configuration is accomplished in the XML deployment descriptors, which then get bundled with the code in the ejb jar file. Deployment of EJBs into a production environment is not necessarily different than in development, but more attention is given to pool and cache settings. Another distinct advantage of having a separate deployment role is that often it is effective within a team environment to have one developer specialize in deployment, letting other developers focus upon creating EJB code.

Server and Container Providers The two final roles target the vendors providing EJB environments. These are the developers and companies that provide J2EE application servers and the EJB containers within them that support EJBs. The EJB specification defines EJB containers and the contract they have with application servers to foster a market for functionality at the EJB container level. In this way, customers can select an application server based upon a separate set of criteria from those for the EJB container, allowing flexibility in configuring the J2EE environment to various situations. This approach also enables container providers to bring specific functionality to market faster than the application servers can be updated, as well as providing common container functionality across multiple application-server vendors. So far, containers have not extended past generic J2EE functionality, and cross-application server functionality has not been experienced; for the most part, the server and container provider role is combined into the same provider. But this separation of providers opens up extension possibilities in the future for J2EE platforms.

J2EE and Container Services

Enterprise JavaBeans are supported by a variety of services. These services provide a reliable and robust environment for server-side components. They also enable EJBs to focus more on the business logic of enterprise applications, and spend less time and code on the technical aspects of developing large-scale enterprise applications. Two types of services exist based upon how they are invoked: explicit and implicit.

Explicit Services

Explicit services are requested by EJBs explicitly in the bean code. These services are defined by the J2EE specification, and are generally available to any client (not just EJBs) requesting them. These services include Remote Method Invocation (RMI), Java Database Connectivity (JDBC), Java Naming and Directory Interface (JNDI), Java Transaction Service/JTA (JTS), Java Authentication and Authorization Service (JAAS), the Java Connector Architecture (JCA) and JavaMail/JMS/CORBA.

Remote Method Invocation (RMI) RMI provides distributed object access to the EJBs. (Chapter 18 covers the details of how RMI works and how to use it.) While remote access is considered to be an implicit service, RMI is a service included in J2EE and is available to any explicit client desiring to use it. As you will see in Chapter 18, the primary reason for creating the remote interface for an EJB is to provide RMI access.

Java Database Connectivity (JDBC) JDBC is included in the J2EE suite of services. Of primary importance within the J2EE application server environment is the reliance on DataSources for getting the JDBC connection to the database. JDBC provides an API for submitting SQL-92 statements to many different database products.

J2EE application servers provide JDBC access to relational databases through datasources. These are classes utilize type 3 JDBC drivers, which provide access to database connection pools managed by the application server. Figure 20.10 shows the DataSource access.

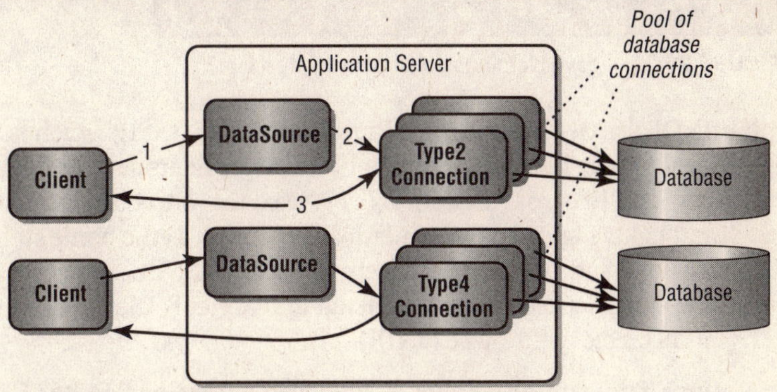

FIGURE 20.10: JDBC DataSource and Type 3 driver

In this manner, clients reuse connections from a pool. They obtain a connection from a DataSource reducing client knowledge or dependence on the pool or on the specific database driver used to connect to the database. This increases portability between application servers and databases. See Chapter 9, "Database Connectivity (JDBC)," for more details on JDBC.

Java Naming and Directory Services (JNDI) JNDI is a service that provides named access to Java objects throughout a J2EE application server environment. JNDI is an API or set of interfaces defined by the J2EE specification for accessing a naming service. As shown in Figure 20.11, each application server provides a naming service that implements the JNDI API for clients to access.

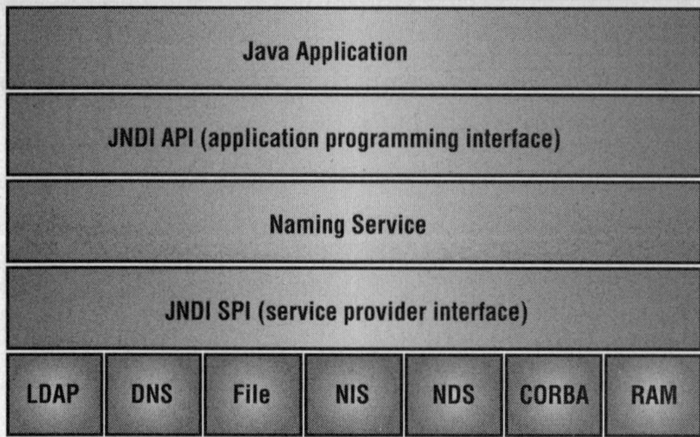

FIGURE 20.11: Java Naming and Directory Interface

JNDI also defines a Service Provider Interface (SPI), which is used to plug into various naming service providers such as LDAP, DNS, CORBA, or RDBMS. JNDI is used to store configuration and lightweight serializable Java objects, such as the home stubs for EJBs and DataSource objects for getting a JDBC connection. JNDI is discussed in further detail in Chapter 8, "Java Naming and Directory Interface (JNDI)."

Java Transaction Service The Java Transaction Service (JTS) is an implementation of the Java Transaction API (JTA). The JTA extends the Object Transaction API (OTA) defined by CORBA and therefore allows CORBA objects and EJBs to participate in the same transactions. Figure 20.12 shows a distributed transaction. Notice the transaction manager is separate from the resource managers, enabling a single transaction manager to interact with multiple resource managers. So what are transactions?

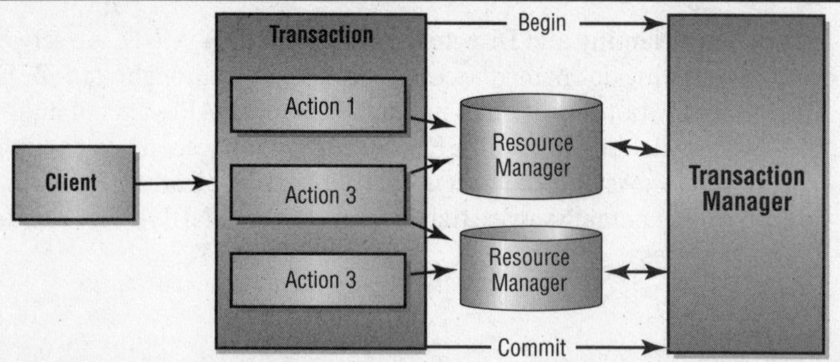

FIGURE 20.12: Distributed transaction

Transactions define a group of one or more actions that can be considered a single atomic action. This sounds simple, but it is not that easy. After actions that are part of a transaction are completed, they may end up getting rolled back if a following action cannot complete. These actions must be undoable, and only be commited if all of the actions in the transaction complete. Transactions are discussed in more detail in Chapter 22, "EJB Transactions and Security."

Java Connector Architecture The Java Connector Architecture (JCA) is a framework for building connectors to custom services. This enables the development of customer services that can participate within transactions managed by a J2EE server, and provides tremendous extendibility to any J2EE application server environment. Chapter 24 discusses the Java Connector Architecture in detail.

EJB Container Services

In addition to the explicit services available to EJBs in the J2EE application server, the specification defines several implicit services to be provided by the EJB container. This container is a construct defined by its contract (interaction) with the application server, and by these services that are provided to EJBs implicitly.

The container provides services on each EJB method call, as well as lifecycle events such as creation and destruction of the component. These implicit services do not require code to be written by the developer. Instead, these services are configurable within the deployment descriptors for the EJB(s). They include Remote Access, Lifecycle, Concurrency, Transactions (via JTS), Security, and Persistence.

Remote Access Remote access refers to the capability of an EJB to be accessed from a client across a network. This is largely handled by RMI as mentioned in the explicit services. Because the application server tools perform all the RMI generation, however, it is considered to be at least a semi-implicit service.

Lifecycle The container also provides lifecycle events for our component. When each major event occurs in the lifecycle of the bean, the container calls a specific method in our bean so that the programmer can write code that will be run whenever that event occurs. These events include creation, removal, context assignment, activation, and passivation. For entity beans, the component also gets called for load, store, find, and post-creation events.

Passivation is the process by which an application server can reclaim resources that have been idle. The server decides when passivation occurs, and can passivate idle EJBs. For example, suppose a client has a shopping cart bean, but they haven't interacted with their shopping cart for 10 minutes. It might be premature to destroy their shopping cart, but the EJB container could passivate the state data in their shopping cart bean to secondary memory storage and then destroy or reuse the bean instance. Activation occurs when a passivated EJB is accessed. It involves the restoring of any EJB state or resource connections followed by the business method call that caused activation. In the shopping cart example, if the client tried to interact with their shopping cart after it had been passivated, the EJB container would activate their shopping cart by creating a new shopping cart bean and then populating it with the data that had been saved to secondary memory. In this way, the user would probably never realize that their shopping cart was not in memory all the time, but the server can be more efficiently utilize its resources. Figure 20.13 shows the EJB container, which provides the implicit services and manages access to the EJB instance.

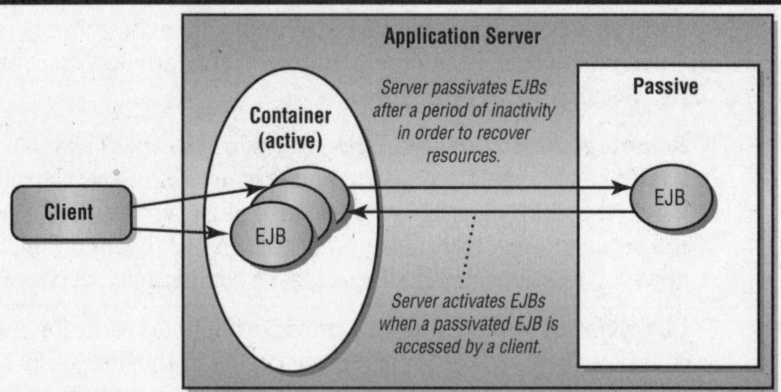

FIGURE 20.13: EJB Passivation and activation

Concurrency Concurrency limits client access within any given EJB instance to a single client and a single thread at a time. This synchronization of the EJB simplifies EJB development, bypassing the problems often associated with multi-threaded development. This is done to help produce a reliable application server environment as well as simplify EJB development. The main purpose of the application server is to provide a reliable environment within which the EJBs can execute. Concurrency control, although limiting, does aid in this endeavor. Alternative methods, such as EJB pooling and cacheing, help to offset the limitations of the single-threaded EJB environment.

Transactions Transactions can be managed either explicitly by the bean (called Bean Managed Transactions, or BMT) or implicitly by the container (called Container Managed Transactions, or CMT). When using CMT, the transaction attribute is configured in the EJBs deployment descriptor, and it determines the containers action before and after the method call. These attributes can be configured per method or any group of methods in the EJB.

NOTE

The container provides implicit demarcation (control) of JTS transactions.

Security Security is also a service that can be configured within the container, as well as accessed through an API within EJB code. EJB security is managed via roles, which are defined in the deployment descriptor and assigned to users and groups defined within a security realm. The realm is determined as a repository of security information, such as an LDAP server or a relational database. Chapter 22 covers security in more detail.

Persistence Entity Beans are provided a framework for persistence of their data to a permanent data store such as a relational database. Two types of persistence exist for entity beans: bean managed persistence (BMP) or container managed persistence (CMP). Bean managed persistence is an explicit method of persistence in which all the SQL or other code to persist the entity bean is located in the EJBs methods. Container managed persistence defines a persistence manager that is invoked by the container to perform all database access. The CMP approach moves the persistence task to the deployment role where EJB fields and relationships are mapped to database table columns.

EJB Scalability

The first technique used to scale an EJB environment is pooling. Pooling enables EJBs to be created and run in pools that serve client requests as needed. Cacheing is another mechanism used, specifically for stateful session beans. This is discussed in more detail in Chapter 23, "EJB Environment, Client, and Design Issues." Figure 20.14 shows a cluster of J2EE servers.

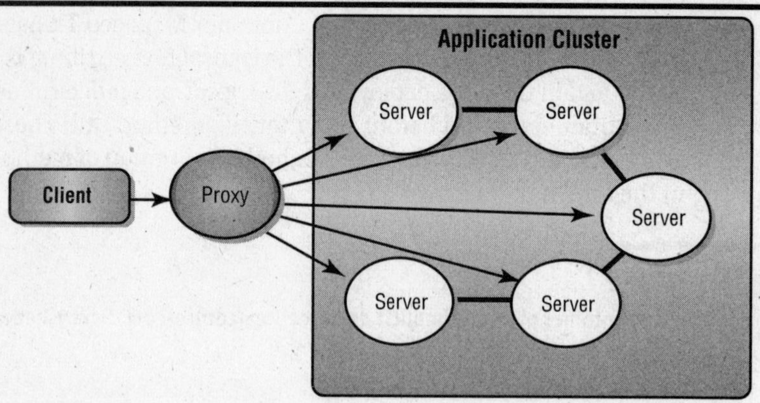

FIGURE 20.14: Application server cluster

For J2EE servers to effectively scale from a small development configuration to a large production environment capable of handling millions of clients, clustering behavior must be defined for the EJB components in a server. A *cluster* is defined as a group of servers providing identical services that provide for *load balancing* and *failover*. EJBs primarily focus upon failover by providing a backup server to access the EJB instance from in the case that the primary server fails.

Stateless session beans are not affected by clustering because their clients should receive the same expected result regardless of which machine in the cluster they access. Stateful session beans are impacted by clustering; after a stateful session bean is created, the client is pinned to that EJB instance on the specific server in the cluster. The application server usually accommodates failover by providing a stateful session EJB instance on a backup server that is synchronized with the primary EJB instance. The remote reference (stub) knows how to failover to the backup EJB instance when the EJB instance on a primary server is unavailable. Entity beans utilize the database to effectively share state across the cluster.

EJB Component Marketplace

All of the services and container functionality means that our EJBs can focus upon performing business logic. Enterprise JavaBeans define a component environment that fosters the reuse of business-oriented components. The EJB visionaries foresee a marketplace of components both between departments in large organizations, as well as frameworks of EJBs sold commercially to boost reuse. Businesses building EJB applications will undoubtably always have custom behavior to develop, but now there is an environment in which robust, reliable custom components can co-exist with off-the-shelf components to rapidly build large-scale systems, as seen in Figure 20.15.

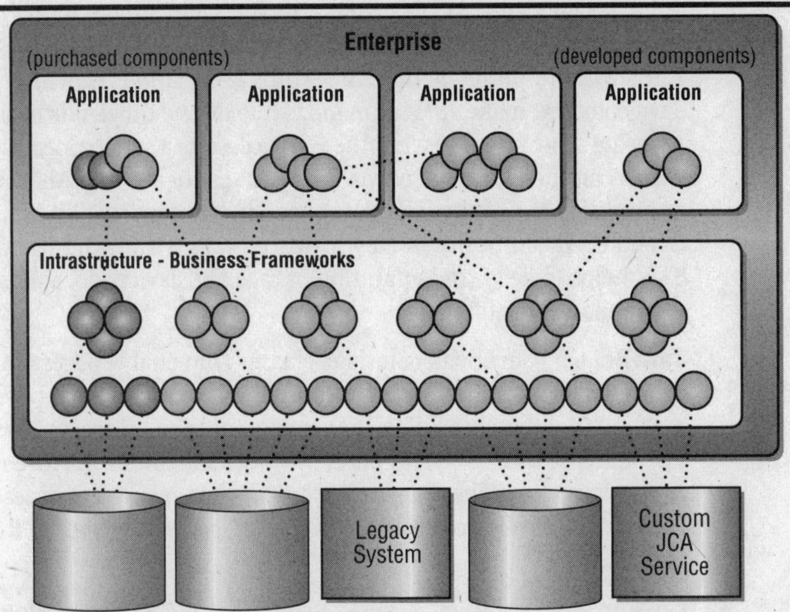

FIGURE 20.15: EJB enterprise architecture

So how do EJBs co-exist with web services? Actually, very effectively. The proliferation of web services increases the need for scalable, robust business components by providing web access to business functions. Web services define a way to expose and access business services via the Web. EJBs can provide a reliable, robust, cross-platform environment for building those services.

Writing EJB Clients

EJB clients are generally written in Java, but also be CORBA clients. Java clients need to have access to JNDI to obtain the EJB home stub to begin access to the EJB.

Common clients are servlets, JSPs, JavaBeans, custom taglibs, Java applications, other EJBs, and, most recently, web services. The following examines each of these.

Servlets Servlets (covered in Chapter 4, "Servlet Web Applications") are common EJB clients. They are Java classes, and therefore have access to JNDI and EJBs. One concern in servlet EJB clients is mixing web UI code with business logic.

Java Server Pages (JSPs) Java Server Pages are tag-based pages that can embed Java code via scriptlets. JSPs can access EJBs without problem, but embedding large amounts of any Java code can make JSPs unmanageable. Many times it is easier to create a Java class to wrap the EJB access as a service locator, which can then be accessed via the `<jsp:usebean>` tag. Another approach is to put the EJB client code in a custom-tag library, which then can be accessed via custom tags within the JSP. This helps to keep the separation of tags and Java code, and is much more maintainable.

JavaBeans JavaBeans are Java classes that enable access to properties via `get` and `set` methods. This provides an effective method for accessing EJBs. Properties can then be accessed via `get` and `set` methods, and business methods can be mirrored in the Java class. These Java classes can then be used to access the EJB effectively from other Java classes, EJBs, servlets, taglibs, and JSPs.

Custom Tag Libraries These are libraries of Java classes along with a descriptor that produce custom tags for JSPs. These are effective EJB clients, effectively producing a tag-based API for accessing EJBs and producing dynamic web content (both HTML and XML).

Java Applications These are GUI or command line-based applications written in Java. These can be used to test or access EJBs. The main consideration for Java applications is that they have access to JNDI on the application server. If a firewall blocks JNDI accesses and is between the Java application and the application server, problems can arise.

Other EJBs Perhaps the most common EJB client is another EJB. The main consideration for accessing EJBs from an EJB is avoiding tight-coupling of the EJBs. This occurs when an explicit JNDI string is used inside of an EJB when accessing another EJB. This situation may cause the breaking of the client EJB when both EJBs are moved to a different application server. The use of EJB references is detailed in Chapter 23.

The newest client on the block is web services. Web services provide access to defined services, which may consist of access to one or more EJBs. Within J2EE application servers, SOAP requests for web services are usually received by a servlet. This servlet generally delegates requests either to specific Java classes, or maps the requests directly to stateless session beans (for RPC/synchronous requests) or JMS for asynchronous requests. Message driven beans can be used to handle the asynchronous JMS requests.

Calling Message Driven Beans (MDBs) Message driven beans do not have a remote interface, or a home interface, and cannot be called directly by a client. To call an MDB, the client must send a JMS message to the proper configured JMS destination. Sending a message to JMS is covered in detail in Chapter 17, "Java Messaging Service (JMS)."

Preparing an EJB Client

In preparation for client EJB access, you need to ensure your client has access to the required classes. If the client is accessing the EJB remotely, it will need access to a client jar file containing the remote interface and the remote stub. A remote client will also need to access JNDI classes to get the home stub. The application vendor usually provides a jar file with the necessary classes needed by a client, as well as instructions for setting the JNDI factory. If the client is within the application server, deploying the EJB jar file will provide the application server access to the necessary client classes. Figure 20.16 shows the packaging and usage of EJB jar files.

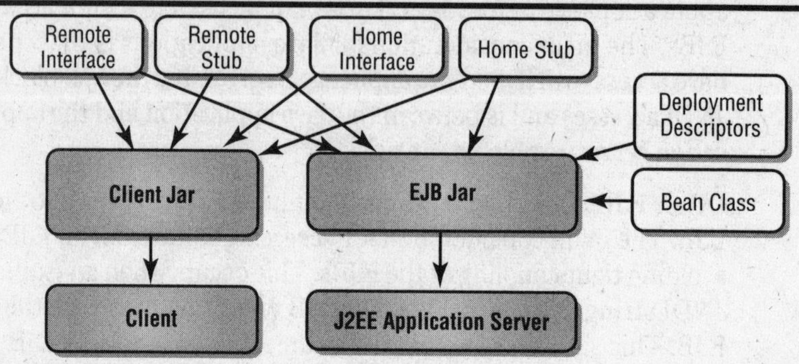

FIGURE 20.16: Client and EJB jar composition

Accessing Remote EJBs

Remote clients are clients that are not running in the same JVM as the application server where the EJBs reside. These clients will be accessing the EJB over a network connection via Remote Method Invocation. The following process works for accessing both session and entity beans but not for message driven beans.

There are four basic steps to accessing EJBs:

1. Get an InitialContext from JNDI.
2. Get the Home stub from JNDI.
3. Use the Home stub to create an EJB reference.
4. Use the EJB reference to call business methods.

As an example, you will create a service locator JavaBean for an Catalog EJB. A service locator class is one that hides the complexity associated with creating, finding, and accessing the desired EJB. This is a good target for this example because its sole purpose is to look up your EJB and serve as its proxy.

Your remote interface for your EJB looks like this:

```
public interface Catalog extends javax.ejb.EJBObject
{  String getName() throws RemoteException;
  void setName(String ) throws RemoteException;
```

```
    Iterator getProducts() throws RemoteException;
    void addProduct(Product product) throws RemoteException;
    void removeProduct(Product product) throws RemoteException;
  }
```

Here is a simple Java application which accesses the EJB. The application is TestCatalog.java and is as follows:

```
import catalog.*;
import javax.naming.*;
import javax.rmi.*;

public class TestCatalog
  {
  public static void main(String[] args)
    {
    private Catalog    catalog = null;

    try
      {
      //
      // First we get the JNDI initial context
      //
      InitialContext jndi = new InitialContext();
      //
      // Second we lookup the Catalog home stub
      //
      Object robj = jndi.lookup("CatalogEJB");
      CatalogHome home = (CatalogHome)
         PortableRemoteObject.narrow(robj,
            CatalogHome.class);
      //
      // Finally we get create the EJB instance
      //
      catalog = home.create();
      //
      // Now we are ready to use the catalog methods
      //
      }
    catch (Exception e)
      {
      e.printStacktrace();
      }
    }
  }
```

Notice a couple of differences between access a standard Java class versus the EJB. First, you must use JNDI to lookup the home stub, and use it to create the EJB reference. Second, you will access the EJB inside of a try-catch block to capture any exceptions. One reason for this is that even though the catalog reference looks like a standard Java object (once created), it can be accessing a server-side object across the network, so there are more points of failure that should be considered.

We called the `narrow()` method on the `PortableRemoteObject` class passing in our home stub, and returning the same stub. This method is used to ensure proper casting even on non-Java remote objects accessed using the RMI/IIOP protocol. We must use this method any time we are casting from a general remote object reference (such as Object) to a more specific remote object reference.

NOTE

IIOP is the Internet inter orb protocol, and is used to bridge one CORBA object request broker to another. It also bridges EJBs to CORBA objects.

Once constructed, however, our calls to the EJB's methods will pretty much be standard Java. The ServiceLocator pattern may be used to simplify client access to an EJB. This pattern consists of a standard Java class which wraps the JNDI lookup to our EJB. It also generally includes a subclass of Exception that represents all logical exceptions thrown from our component.

Following is a service locator class called CatalogJB (for catalog JavaBean). This is a standard Java class that can be used to buffer clients from dependence on EJBs, as well as simplify access to them. It also implements the Serializable interface and may be used as a value object for the Catalog EJB.

NOTE

The Catalog EJB doesn't currently have any state, so no member variables are shown in the CatalogJB class. Normally you would have these member variables if you use this type of class as a value object.

```
   package catalog;

import catalog.ejb.*;
import javax.naming.*;
```

```
import javax.rmi.*;
import java.util.*;

/**
 * JavaBean ServiceLocator for Catalog EJB
 */
public class CatalogJB implements java.io.Serializable
  {
  private transient Catalog   catalog = null;

  /**
   * getEJB() - Returns a Catalog remote interface for
   *            internal (to this class) use.
   */
  protected Catalog getEjb() throws Exception
    {
    if (catalog == null)
      {
      Context jndi = new InitialContext();
      Object robj = jndi.lookup("CatalogEJB");
      CatalogHome home = (CatalogHome)
        PortableRemoteObject.narrow(robj, CatalogHome.class);
      catalog = home.create();
      }
    return catalog;
    }

  /**
   * getName() - Represents a method to access
   *             an EJB method of the same name.
   */
  public String getName() throws CatalogException
    {
    String result = null;
    try
      {
      result = this.getEjb().getName();
      }
    catch (Exception e)
      {
      throw new CatalogException(e);
      }
    return result;
    }
```

```
/**
 * getProducts() - Represents a method used to access
 *              an EJB method of the same name.
 */
public Iterator getProducts() throws Exception
  {
  Iterator result = null;
  try
    {
    result = this.getEjb().getProducts().iterator();
    }
  catch (Exception e)
    {
    throw new CatalogException(e);
    }
  return result;
  }
}
```

Now take a look at a client JSP that uses the service locator class. The advantage we gain from the service locator is that we can dramatically reduce the amount of Java code and utilize the `<jsp:usebean>` action tag.

```
<jsp:usebean id="catalog" class="catalog.Catalog"/>
 ...
 Catalog Name: <jsp:getProperty id="catalog"
    property="name"/>
 <hr/>
 Products:
 <table>
   <jsp:scriptlet>Iterator iter = catalog.getProducts()
      </jsp:scriptlet>
   <jsp:scriptlet>while (iter.hasNext())</jsp:scriptlet>
     <jsp:scriptlet>{</jsp:scriptlet>

<tr><td><jsp:expression>(String)iter.next()</jsp:expression>
   <jsp:scriptlet>}</jsp:scriptlet>
 </table>
 ...
```

The first `<jsp:usebean>` tag creates an instance of the CatalogJB class and puts it into the catalog variable. Subsequent accesses to catalog can occur through either the `<jsp:getProperty>` tag, or within a scriptlet or expression. By using a JavaBean for accessing the EJB and using the 2.3 XML-compliant JSP tags, your jsp is completely tag-based, allowing our content developer access to more HTML tools. Your developer then gets to manage Java code in separate files. This approach simplifies all client access to the Catalog EJB. Another method of using a pure tag-based approach for access to EJBs is by creating custom tags. Some application server products include tools for automatically creating these custom tag libraries based upon your EJB remote interfaces.

Accessing Local EJBs

Clients may access a local interface of an EJB if the client is running in the same JVM (Java Virtual Machine) as the EJB. This is often the case when the client is a JSP, servlet, or web service, and the application server is not clustered.

There are four basic steps to accessing EJBs locally (similar to the remote clients):

1. Get an InitialContext from JNDI.
2. Get the LocalHome stub from JNDI.
3. Use the LocalHome stub to create a Local EJB reference.
4. Use the EJB reference to call business methods.

In the example, you will create a service locator JavaBean for a Catalog EJB. Our remote interface looks similar to this:

```
public interface CatalogLocal extends EJBLocalObject
  {
  String getName() throws EJBException;
  void setName(String ) throws EJBException;
  Iterator getProducts() throws EJBException;
  void addProduct(Product product) throws EJBException;
   void removeProduct(Product product) throws EJBException;
   }
```

Following is our simple Java application that accesses the local EJB. Our application is TestLocalCatalog.java and is as follows:

```
import catalog.*;
import javax.naming.*;
import javax.rmi.*;

public class TestLocalCatalog
  {
  public static void main(String[] args)
    {
```

```
    private Catalog    catalog = null;

    try
      {
      //
      // First we get the JNDI initial context
      //
      Context jndi = new InitialContext();
      //
      // Second we lookup the Catalog local home stub
      //
      Object robj = jndi.lookup("CatalogLocalEJB");
      CatalogLocalHome home = (CatalogLocalHome)
         PortableRemoteObject.narrow(robj,
            CatalogHome.class);
      //
      // Finally we get create the local EJB instance
      //
      catalog = home.create();
      //
      // Now we are ready to use the catalog methods
      //
      }
    catch (Exception e)
      {
      e.printStacktrace();
      }
    }
  }
```

The sequence is pretty much the same as accessing the remote interface. You use the HomeLocal instead of Home, and the CatalogLocal instead of Catalog (or CatalogRemote). Notice that methods in the local interface throw EJBExceptions instead of RemoteExceptions. For a client to use an EJBs local reference, the EJB must have explicitly included a LocalInterface in its deployment jar and deployment descriptor.

The main difference and reason for local interfaces is to optimize access of EJBs, when the EJB and client are in the same JVM. EJB method parameter values are passed by reference, thus avoiding copying (via serialization) these values and increasing speed and efficiency. Notice also that you do not have to use PortableRemoteObject, because you know you are not dealing with a remote object reference.

Architecting EJB Applications

Experts have described architecture as an external view of a system. It also is described as information leading to the effective design and development of a reliable and flexible software system. This chapter has attempted to paint a picture of what Enterprise JavaBeans are, and the environment of the J2EE application server within which they live. This chapter has also focused on defining the services that support EJBs, and focused them on the business logic and functionality they are intended to implement.

One important aspect of EJB design and usage is how applications can best use EJBs. Several patterns have emerged for providing various benefit to EJB designs; enough, in fact, to fill another book (or two). Yet one pattern does emerge to consistently identify effective EJB design and that is the session façade. The façade pattern, shown in Figure 20.17, is simply creating a layer above a set of objects (in this case EJBs) that consolidate and simplify their access.

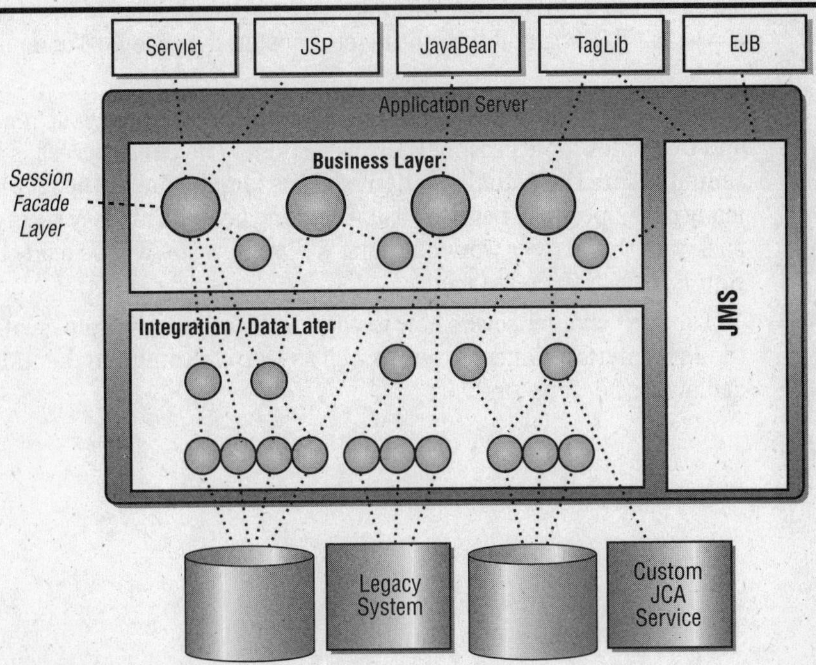

FIGURE 20.17: EJB Session façade pattern

The session façade pattern is focused on client access, hiding much of the complexity of the EJBs and service connectors implemented *underneath the covers*. This pattern forces the separation of client access from data components, and is a good target or facilitator for business logic and rules. This gives you a taste of EJB design patterns, and how you can start to organize EJB applications.

This chapter also examined how applications can access these business components. You are now ready to take a detailed walk through the various types of EJBs in the next chapter.

What's Next

This chapter presented the basic technical aspects of EJBs. It started with what an EJB is, and described the container environment. The types of EJBs were described as stateless session bean, stateful session bean, entity bean, and message driven bean. The explicit and implicit services available to EJBs were covered. EJB roles and responsibilities were presented, as well as EJB scalability and the reuse fostered by the EJB component marketplace.

Finally the chapter presented and finished with some instructions and examples for accessing EJBs as a client. The client access is presented before the actual creation of EJBs largely due to the fact that many developers will begin by using existing beans. This may seem a bit backward, but it does work out quite well as now you will be ready to test your EJBs as you create them.

The next chapter covers how to write EJBs as you dive into creating the Java interfaces and classes, as well as learn to configure the XML deployment descriptors.

Chapter 21

Session, Entity, and Message Driven EJBs

As mentioned in the last chapter, there are four types of EJBs that specifically target various components used in building business frameworks and applications. The first distinguishing factor identifies two different types of messaging: synchronous and asynchronous. Session and entity beans provide synchronous messaging, meaning the client must wait while the EJB is busy processing each method request. This enables the EJB to return a value from the server-side EJB to a local or remote client. Message driven beans (MDB) support asynchronous messages via JMS. As you saw in Chapter 17, "Java Messaging Service (JMS)," asynchronous messaging is a fire-and-forget approach that does not provide for a return response.

The second factor that distinguishes bean types is persistence. Entity beans are the only persistent EJB type. Session beans and MDBs are in-memory components that do not support persistence directly. Entity beans can support a wide variety of persistent stores, but relational database management systems (RDBMSs) are the most common and best supported.

Written for *Enterprise Java™ 2, J2EE™ 1.3 Complete*
by Vince E. Marco

NOTE

Calls to persistent stores, such as through JDBC, can be made from session and message-driven beans; however, these calls are invoked by the client directly. The server automatically calls entity beans persistence methods.

The last distinguishing factor applies only to session beans, and determines whether the component manages state on behalf of the client at all. Stateless session beans (SLSBs) do not manage state on behalf of the client, while stateful session beans (SFSBs) do maintain client state. Although entity beans do manage state on behalf of the client, they are only dedicated to one client when assigned to a primary key, and are considerably different than session beans.

Each type of EJB is well suited to specific tasks, and together they provide component building blocks for enterprise applications.

Featured in this chapter:

- EJB Composition
- Session Beans
- Entity Beans
- Message Driven Beans
- ENC and EJBContexts
- Modeling with EJBs

EJB Composition

EJBs are deployed as jar files. A jar file is created with the jar Java utility that is a Java-based zip file archive and compression utility. The .jar file extension indicates that this archive file contains Java classes and can be used as Java class libraries, not just for EJBs. Take a look at what is needed to put into this jar file to create an EJB. Here we see a the file structure within a deployable jar file containing an EJB. The META-INF folder (which must be at the root of the jar file) contains the deployment descriptor XML files. The other folders in the jar file represent the package structure of the Java class files.

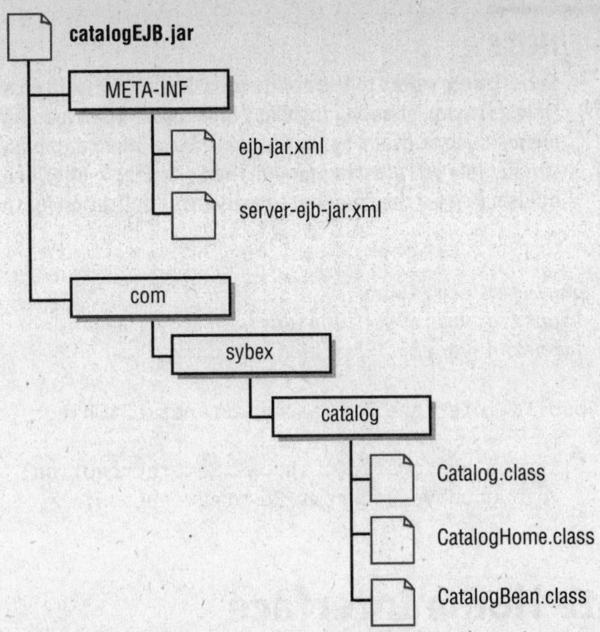

The elements for the EJB jar file include the remote interface, the remote home interface, the local interface, local home interface, the bean class, and the deployment descriptors. You would also include any Java classes used by the EJBs, such as value objects, data access objects, application exception classes, and so on.

Remote Interface

A *remote interface* is a Java interface, so methods will not be implemented here—only declared. In fact, the implementation of this interface is the RMI remote stub that enables remote clients to use your EJB and will be generated for us by the application server or tools provided by the application server vendor. This interface defines the business methods that the client can call on the EJB through the stub. This interface, along with the generated stub class, should be put into a client.jar file for remote access as well as the ejb.jar deployment file. This remote interface must extend javax.ejb.EJBObject, and follow RMI rules, which include all methods throwing RemoteException, and all parameters and return values being serializable.

NOTE

Serializable refers to the ability for a class to be written and restored from an ObjectStream, enabling the class to be moved between Java2 runtime environments (such as over a network or saved to a file or database). To make an object serializable you must implement the Serializable interface, which has no flags, but is a flag for the compiler to activate serialization for the class.

```
package  com.sybex;
import javax.ejb.EJBObject;
import java.rmi.RemoteException;

public interface MyExample extends EJBObject
  {
  String helloWorld() throws RemoteException;
  void goodbye() throws RemoteException;
  }
```

Remote Home Interface

The *remote home interface* is the home interface for remote access to the EJB. This specifies the create methods for how a client can create an EJB. Home interfaces for entity beans also declare find methods for finding an existing entity bean. Similar to the remote interface, you declare but do not implement the methods. These methods will be implemented in a home stub class, which is generated by application server tools. Prior to EJB 2.0, this interface was called the home interface. This interface must extend `javax.ejb.EJBHome`, and also must follow RMI rules.

```
package  com.sybex;
import javax.ejb.EJBHome;
import javax.ejb.CreateException;
import java.rmi.RemoteException;

public interface MyExampleHome extends EJBHome
  {
  MyExample create() throws CreateException, RemoteException;
  }
```

Local Interface

The *local interface* is much like the remote interface, except it is for use by local clients. Local clients are Java instances residing in the same Java

Virtual Machine (JVM) as the EJB instance. This is useful for clients that run inside the same application server instance as the EJB, and optimizes parameter serialization. The local interface is a Java interface that declares local access to EJB business methods. This interface extends `javax.ejb.EJBLocalObject`. It is often useful to add a throws EJBException to force clients to handle system errors that can occur. This is not necessary, however, because `javax.ejb.EJBException` is a runtime exception, and doesn't require a throws clause.

```
package  com.sybex;
import javax.ejb.EJBLocalObject;

public interface MyExampleLocal extends EJBLocalObject
  {
  String helloWorld();
  void goodbye();
  }
```

NOTE

Most remote stub implementations avoid network calls when the client is local; however, all parameters and return values on remote interfaces are copied via serialization. Local interfaces pass non-primitive parameters and then return values by reference, which is faster than passing by value.

Local Home Interface

This is the local version of the home interface. Local clients will obtain the LocalHome to `create()`, `find()`, and `remove()` EJB instances. The local home interface is a Java interface, and also has a stub class that is generated by the application server tools. The local home interface must extend `javax.ejb.EJBLocalHome`.

```
package  com.sybex;
import javax.ejb.EJBLocalHome;
import javax.ejb.EJBException;
import java.rmi.RemoteException;

public interface MyExampleLocalHome extends EJBLocalHome
  {
  MyExampleLocal create() throws CreateException,
     EJBException;
  }
```

Bean Class

The *bean class* is what implements the EJB, and is a Java class. This class implements one of three interfaces in the javax.ejb package: SessionBean, EntityBean, or MessageDrivenBean. These interfaces contain methods that must be implemented in your bean class, and include ejbRemove() for all bean types, and ejbActivate(), ejbPassivate() for session and entity beans. All the bean types must implement a setSessionContext(), setEntityContext(), or setMessageDrivenContext() method depending on which EJB type they are implementing.

The bean class must implement one ejbCreate<XXXX>() method to match each create<XXXX>() method in the home or local home interface. As an example, the method create(int id, String name) must have an ejbCreate(int id, String name) method in the bean class. createFromXML(String xml) must have an ejbCreateFromXML(String xml) in the bean class, as well.

Entity beans must also implement ejbLoad(), ejbStore(), unsetEntityContext(), and ejbFindByPrimaryKey(). Message driven beans must implement an onMessage() method as well, defined in the javax.jms.MessageListener interface. These methods are in addition to any desired business methods, and represent the lifecycle events that the server will call on the EJB, allowing the bean to respond to these standard lifecycle events. Here is an example session bean class:

```
package  com.sybex;
import javax.ejb.SessionBean;
import javax.ejb.EJBException;
import javax.ejb.CreateException;
import javax.ejb.SessionContext;

public class MyExampleBean implements SessionBean
  {
  SessionContext context;

    public void setSessionContext(SessionContext ctx)
     {
       context = ctx;
     }

  public void ejbActivate() throws EJBException {}
  public void ejbPassivate() throws EJBException {}
  public void ejbRemove() throws EJBException {}
```

```
public void ejbCreate() throws CreateException,
  EJBException
  {}

//
// Now the business methods
//
public String helloWorld()
  {
  return "Hello, World!";
  }

public void goodbye() {}
}
```

EJB Deployment Descriptor

The EJB deployment descriptor is named ejb-jar.xml. This contains all the EJB configurations that span across application server products. The intent of the designers of enterprise beans was to push as much into this descriptor as possible, allowing EJB porting to be a minimal configuration effort. This can be achieved if features specific to a vendor's application server are avoided. The following code shows a basic EJB descriptor that defines a session bean with an ejb-name, specifies the classes for the standard EJB elements, and specifies the type to be stateless. These are the minimal settings for a stateless session bean. You'll see other examples of each kind of bean later in the chapter.

```
<ejb-jar>
 <enterprise-beans>
  <session>
   <ejb-name>MyExampleEJB</ejb-name>
   <home>com.sybex.MyExampleHome</home>
   <remote>com.sybex.MyExample</remote>
   <local-home>
    com.sybex.MyExampleLocalHome
   </local-home>
   <local>com.sybex.MyExampleLocal</local>
   <ejb-class>com.sybex.MyExampleBean</ejb-class>
   <session-type>Stateless</session-type>
   <transaction-type>Container</transaction-type>
  </session>
 </enterprise-beans>
</ejb-jar>
```

Server Deployment Descriptor

The *server deployment descriptor* can have various names, and is determined by the application server vendor. Some examples are weblogic-ejb-jar .xml, ias-ejb-jar.xml, jboss.xml, and so on. This descriptor contains configurations for server specific features or bindings. Minimally for your stateless session bean, you need to specify a JNDI name with which to bind the remote home interface. This is the lookup key for your remote clients. Each application server vendor has their own descriptor and format, so consult your application server documentation for the correct set of tags.

Exceptions

Exceptions are divided into two basic types: system and application. System exceptions include either `java.rmi.RemoteException` or `java.lang.RuntimeException`, or any subclass of these classes. Generally, any custom system exceptions you create should extend `javax.ejb.EJBException` (which extends `java.lang.RuntimeException`), but this is not required. These exceptions generally represent an error situation caused by something outside the application. An example might be that a datasource has an error, or the application cannot access JNDI, and so on.

Application exceptions are application classes that extend Exception and represent an error situation that is caused within the application, such as an overdrawn balance, or a declined credit card authorization. Application classes must also be included in the EJB jar file, if the EJB references the application exception. If these applications are also referenced on the remote interface and a client jar is prepared, the application exception classes should be included there as well.

Support Classes

Any classes referenced by the bean class or remote or local interfaces need to be included in the ejb jar file. These may include JavaBean classes (not to be confused with EJBs), Java classes, exception classes, and so on.

SESSION BEANS

This section begins with *session beans*. These components are in-memory objects that live and run within the application server JVM. These beans are ideal for managing business logic and rules because they are faster and more efficient than entity EJBs. They are also a bit easier to code and configure than entity beans, so they provide a great place to start drilling into the EJB types; however, session beans do not come close to protecting and preserving your application's component state as entity beans do.

Stateless Session EJBs

Stateless session EJBs are session beans that do not manage client state. This means that any state must be passed in via method parameters. These beans, along with message driven beans, are the most efficient EJB available, but are also limited in their functionality. These components are well suited clients which can effectively take responsibility for session state, such as servlet and JSP clients that can store client state in the HttpSession, allowing them to access stateless session beans to perform business functionality.

Managing Client State

The first issue is state. What is client state? *Client state* is any information that is different between each client, and is usually maintained in Java attributes. For instance, when you purchase a product from a web site. As you are browsing their web-based catalog, you can place products into your shopping cart. This shopping cart is a manager of the products you wish to purchase until you end the session by either emptying the cart or purchasing the products. Stateless session beans must not maintain any state on behalf of a client. Each and every call to a stateless session bean should be independent of all previous calls. In fact, when stateless session beans are pooled (which is most of the time), subsequent calls from the same client will usually not invoke the same bean instance.

SLSB Lifecycle

The *lifecycle* for a stateless session bean includes several states that an EJB can be in at any given time. Specific events, such as create, remove, and so on, will move beans into various states. Figure 21.1 shows the various lifecycle states for a stateless session bean.

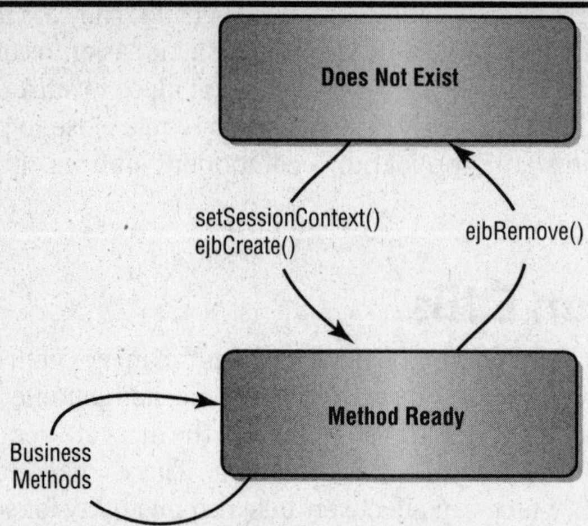

FIGURE 21.1: Stateless session bean lifecycle

Creating a Stateless Session EJB

For this example you will create a Catalog session bean. You will define several methods for getting products and product names. This stateless session bean will have a remote interface, and will not have a local interface.

The first step is to create the remote interface. You will extend `javax.ejb.EJBObject` and follow RMI rules, making your parameters and return values serializable, and throwing RemoteException from your methods.

NOTE

RMI rules indicate that method parameters and return values be serializable Java objects. This is a recursive requirement in that any object instances within these objects must also be serializable, and so on. Too, all methods must throw `java.rmi.RemoteException`, which is what occurs if the network is down (as an example).

```
package com.sybex.catalog;

import java.rmi.RemoteException;
import javax.ejb.EJBObject;
import java.util.Collection;

public interface Catalog extends EJBObject
```

```
  {
  String getName() throws RemoteException;
  Collection getProducts() throws RemoteException;
  }
```

The next step is to create the remote home interface. You will extend EJBHome and again follow RMI rules, just as in the remote interface. Notice that you must also throw CreateException from the `create()` method.

```
package com.sybex.catalog;

import java.rmi.RemoteException;
import javax.ejb.EJBHome;
import javax.ejb.CreateException;

public interface CatalogHome extends EJBHome
  {
  Catalog create() throws RemoteException, CreateException;
  }
```

The local interfaces will not be implemented because your Catalog session bean should be accessible throughout a server cluster (and therefore remotely), so your final code step is to create the bean class. This class implements the SessionBean interface, and provides implementations for methods in that interface. These methods are not required to do anything, but they must be implemented.

```
package com.sybex.catalog;

import java.rmi.RemoteException;
import javax.ejb.SessionBean;
import javax.ejb.EJBException;
import javax.ejb.SessionContext;
import java.util.Collection;
import java.util.Iterator;
import javax.naming.InitialContext;
import javax.rmi.PortableRemoteObject;

public class CatalogBean implements SessionBean
  {
  private SessionContext context;

  public void setSessionContext(SessionContext
     sessionContext) throws EJBException,
   RemoteException
```

```
        {
        context = sessionContext;
        }

      public void ejbActivate()
         throws EJBException, RemoteException
        {}

      public void ejbPassivate()
      throws EJBException, RemoteException
        {}
      public void ejbRemove()
         throws EJBException, RemoteException
        {    }

        public String getName()
          {
           return "My Catalog";
          }

        public Collection getProducts()
          {
            InitialContext jndi = new InitialContext();
        Object robj = jndi.lookup("ProductEJB");
        ProductLocalHome home = (ProductLocalHome)
        PortableRemoteObject.narrow(robj,
             ProductLocalHome.class);
        // Instead of exposing the entity bean to our client,
        // we'll back a collection of value objects.
        Collection products = new ArrayList();
        Collection ebeans = home.findAll();
        Iterator iter = ebeans.iterator();
        while (iter.hasNext())
          {
          Product p = (Product)iter.next();
          products.add(p.getProductInfo());
          }
        return products;
          }
  }
```

Now take a look at each method.

setSessionContext(SessionContext ctx) This method is called by the server when the session bean is created with the context object. Usually the session bean will save a reference to use the context API during the life of the EJB.

ejbActivate() This method gets called by the server upon activation. The method is called after the state of the bean is restored via serialization from the passivated store. This is often used to reestablish resource connections. Stateless session beans do not need to be passivated to reclaim resources. Because these beans are pooled by the server, if the server needs to reclaim an SLSB's resources, it merely destroys the bean. This method needs to be implemented, but may never be called.

ejbPassivate() This method is called by the server during passivation. The method is called before the state of the bean is stored (via serialization) to the passivated store. It is useful to close down resource connections within this method. Just as with the `ejbActivate()` method, this method needs to be implemented but will go unused by stateless session beans.

ejbRemove() This method is called just before the EJB is removed from service. This can occur from `remove()` being called from the remote or local interface, home interface, or if idle timeout exceeds the configured amount. Note that with stateless session beans, the `ejbRemove()` will only be called if the container decides to decrease the size of the pool. On many application servers, this can coincide with an explicit `remove()` or timeout, or at the discretion of the application server.

ejbCreate() This method is called by the container following the `home.create()` method by the EJB client. After the EJB is instantiated, the container calls the `ejbCreate()` method on the instance. This gives the bean instance a chance to control its initialization. Stateless session beans must have a `home .create()` and `ejbCreate()` method with no arguments because the bean instance doesn't retain state on behalf of the client. Resource connections can be established in this method.

getProducts() This is a business method for the Catalog bean, and returns a collection of product value objects. Value objects are serializable, lightweight containers for entity attributes.

Configuring a Stateless Session EJB

You start by adding a `<session>` tag to your ejb-jar.xml descriptor. You then add the ejb-name, classes, and type within your session tag, just like in the previous descriptor example:

```
<ejb-jar>
 <enterprise-beans>
  <session>
   <ejb-name>CatalogEJB</ejb-name>
   <home>com.sybex.catalog.ejbs.CatalogHome</home>
   <remote>com.sybex.catalog.ejbs.Catalog</remote>
   <ejb-class>
    com.sybex.catalog.ejbs.CatalogBean
   </ejb-class>
   <session-type>Stateless</session-type>
   <transaction-type>Container</transaction-type>
  </session>
 </enterprise-beans>
</ejb-jar>
```

The server-specific EJB descriptor must map the `<ejb-name>` to a JNDI name for accessing the EJB's home interface. The following example is for the Weblogic application server located in the file META-INF/weblogic-ejb-jar.xml:

```
<weblogic-ejb-jar>
 <weblogic-enterprise-bean>
  <ejb-name>CatalogEJB</ejb-name>
  <jndi-name>CatalogEJB</jndi-name>
 </weblogic-enterprise-bean>
</weblogic-ejb-jar>
```

Pooling Stateless Session EJBs

An attractive aspects of stateless session EJBs is the ability to pool them. SLSB pools provide an effective support to scalable JSP/servlet-based web applications. The following code shows the weblogic-ejb-jar.xml descriptor with tags adding the configuration of a pool starting out with five bean instances and a maximum of 10 bean instances:

```
<weblogic-ejb-jar>
 <weblogic-enterprise-bean>
  <ejb-name>CatalogEJB</ejb-name>
  <stateless-session-descriptor>
   <pool>
    <max-beans-in-free-pool>5</max-beans-in-free-pool>
    <initial-beans-in-free-pool>
     5
    </initial-beans-in-free-pool>
   </pool>
  </stateless-session-descriptor>
```

```
    <jndi-name>CatalogEJB</jndi-name>
  </weblogic-enterprise-bean>
</weblogic-ejb-jar>
```

Deploying the Stateless Session Bean

At this point you are ready to deploy your Catalog stateless session bean. Start by compiling all the Java files into classes, and bundling these files along with your descriptor XML files into a jar file.

This is where the deployment process varies with each application server. Each server supports a method of verifying the EJB and/or generating the stubs, skeletons, and descriptor instances needed for a complete EJB jar. Most, if not all, application servers provide Java-based command line tools for verifying or compiling the EJB jar file. Many application servers also provide graphical tools for deploying the EJB jar file to the application server.

Deployment

Many application servers support auto or hot deploying, which involves copying the user-bundled jar file into a watched folder. The application server monitors this folder, detects new EJB jar files or modified EJB jar files, and deploys the new or modified EJB jar into the application server automatically. This is useful during development, and provides for rapid deployment and redeployment. Hot deployment is almost always turned off in production mode to save resources as well as prevent unwanted changes from getting pushed into production too soon.

Stateful Session EJBs

Now that you've been through the entire development and deployment cycle with a stateless session bean, it is time to look at stateful session beans. Stateful session beans are memory-based components that manage client state. Each stateful session bean is created by one client, and can maintain state on behalf of that client. Because of this, these EJBs cannot be pooled, and are not as efficient as stateless session beans, especially when scaling up to a large number of requests. It is suggested that a careful and limited use of stateful session beans be considered when designing, developing, and deploying your EJB applications.

The lifecycle of a stateful session bean is similar to that of a stateless session beans. After all, it is a session bean. The main difference between the two types of session beans is in pooling, which stateful session beans do *not* support. Figure 21.2 shows the lifecycle of a stateful session bean. This lifecycle includes three basic states: doesn't exist, method ready, and passive. As an EJB moves between these states, the container calls methods on the EJB bean class to allow user actions to occur.

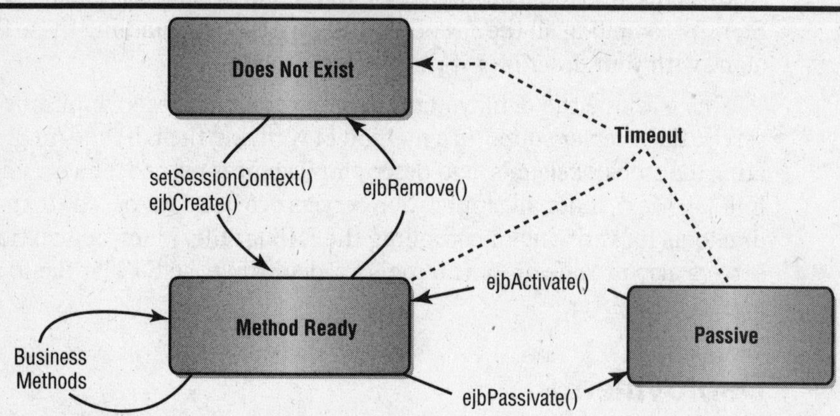

FIGURE 21.2: Stateful session bean lifecycle

`EjbCreate` This event occurs when one of the `home.create()` methods is called to create a stateful session bean. Unlike the stateless session bean, it cannot be called on server startup because stateful session beans are never pooled.

`EjbPassivate` This is called when the server has determined this bean should be passivated, usually due to an idle period. This behaves the same as stateless session beans, and is the place to close down resource connections.

`EjbActivate` This is called when the bean is passivated, and a business method is called. The bean must be activated prior to accessing the business method. This is the place to restore any needed resource connections.

`EjbRemove` This is called when a stateful session bean is removed. An EJB instance is removed either by the client invoking the `remove()` method on the home reference (stub) or following an idle timeout based upon the configuration in the deployment descriptor. For convenience, a remove method is also provided on the remote or local reference.

Creating a Stateful Session EJB

You will now create a ShoppingCart bean. Keep in mind that if a user leaves without checking out, the stateful session bean will probably not be around when the customer comes back. Start with the remote interface:

```
package com.sybex.catalog;
import java.util.Collection;
import javax.ejb.EJBObject;

public interface ShoppingCart extends EJBObject
  {
  void addProduct(ProductInfo pinfo);
  void removeProduct(ProductInfo pinfo);
  Collection getProducts();
  }
```

Now create the home interface:

```
package com.sybex.catalog;
import javax.ejb.CreateException;
import java.rmi.RemoteException;
import javax.ejb.EJBHome;

public interface ShoppingCartHome extends EJBHome
  {
  ShoppingCart create()
          throws RemoteException, CreateException;
  }
```

And lastly, create the bean class:

```
package com.sybex.catalog;
import java.util.Collection;
import javax.ejb.SessionBean;

public class ShoppingCartBean implements SessionBean
  {
  protected SessionContext context = null;
  private List products = new ArrayList();

  public ShoppingCartBean(){}

  public void ejbActivate()
  throws EJBException, RemoteException
    {}
```

```
    public void ejbPassivate()
    throws EJBException, RemoteException
      {}

    public void ejbRemove()
    throws EJBException, RemoteException
      {}

    public void setSessionContext(SessionContext ctx)
    throws EJBException, RemoteException
      {
      context = ctx;
      }

    void ejbCreate() {}

    void addProduct(ProductInfo pinfo)
      {
      products.add(pinfo);
      }

    void removeProduct(ProductInfo pinfo)
      {
      products.remove(pinfo);
      }

    Collection getProducts()
      {
      return products;
      }
    }
```

Configuring a Stateful Session EJB

Configuring a stateful session bean is similar to the stateless session bean you've already done. The primary difference is the <session-type> tag value in the deployment descriptor. There are variations in the server descriptor because you will not have a pool of bean instances to configure.

```
<ejb-jar>
 <enterprise-beans>
  <session>
   <ejb-name>ShoppingCartEJB</ejb-name>
   <home>com.sybex.catalog.ShoppingCartHome</home>
   <remote>com.sybex.catalog.ShoppingCart</remote>
   <ejb-class>
    com.sybex.catalog.ShoppingCartBean
```

```
      </ejb-class>
      <session-type>Stateful</session-type>
      <transaction-type>Container</transaction-type>
    </session>
  </enterprise-beans>
</ejb-jar>
```

Sharing a Stateful Session EJB

It is possible to have two clients share a stateful session bean. This is done by getting a handle from the remote stub. By calling `cart.getHandle()`, you can obtain a serializable object that, when restored via `handle.getReference()`, will return a working remote stub. Because the handle is serializable and can be restored as a separate reference, it may be sent over the network, or stored in JNDI or a database for exchange. This is heavily discouraged, though, because the container still enforces concurrency and will only allow one client access to the bean at a time.

Entity EJBs

Entity beans are components for modeling persistent business data. These enterprise beans maintain both a memory instance of the stateful component and a persistent store entry. This makes entity beans a reliable and effective component for important enterprise data.

A primary key identifies an entity bean. This primary key is used to find any given entity bean instance, and is used to obtain both remote and local references to the entity bean. The primary key must be serializable, and is either one of the primitive wrapper classes in Java, or a custom class.

Two management types for persistence are supported: bean managed persistence (BMP), and container managed persistence (CMP). *Bean managed persistence* allows the user to decide how the bean is persisted. *Container managed persistence* attempts to eliminate persistence coding by allowing the developer to configure persistence mappings and settings in the deployment descriptor, and by restricting the persistence functionality. The tradeoff becomes flexibility (BMP) versus speed and simplicity (CMP). In both BMP and CMP entity beans, it is the server that decides when the entity bean is saved to or retrieved from the persistent store. This is the primary difference between using entity beans and managing your own persistence (perhaps through data access objects) from a session bean. Figure 21.3 shows both BMP and CMP bean instances in the server and the relative location of persistence methods.

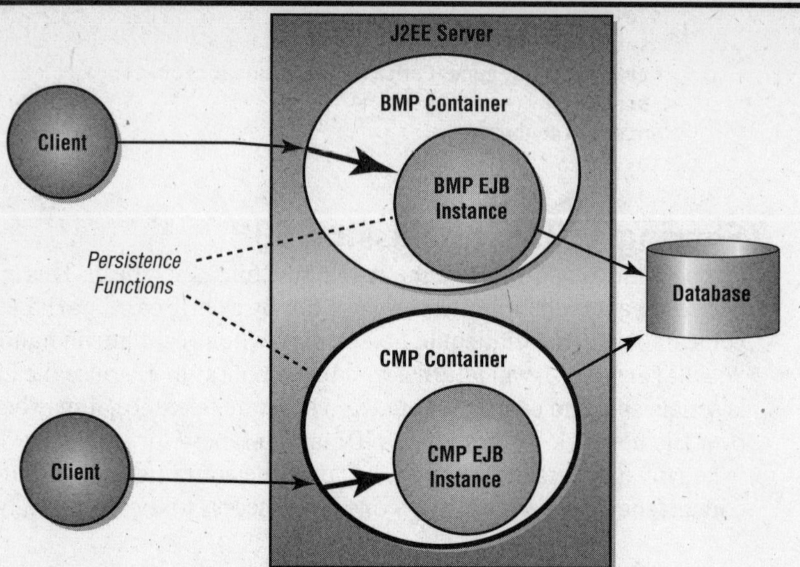

FIGURE 21.3: BMP versus CMP entity beans

Primary Keys

Entity beans define an object called the *primary key*. Its sole purpose is to identify uniquely each entity bean within the system. The primary key is a serializable Java object, and may be any of the primitive wrapper objects such as `java.lang.Integer`, `java.lang.Double`, `java.lang.Float`, `java.lang.Long`, `java.sql.Date`, or `java.lang.String`. Using an existing Java class is an effective way to minimize efforts on the primary key.

But entity beans also support custom primary keys. EJB developers may create their own class to identify an entity bean. This can be especially useful in compound primary keys, where more than one persistent field is used to identify the entity bean. The following is an example of a compound primary key:

```
package com.sybex.catalog;

public class ProductPK implements java.io.Serializable
  {
  public String  productId;
  public String  manufacturerId;

  public ProductPK()
      {}
```

```
public ProductPK(String pid, String mid)
  {
  productId = pid;
  manufacturerId = mid;
  }

public String getProductId()
  {
  return productId;
  }

public String getManufacturerId()
  {
  return manufacturerId;
  }

public boolean equals(Object obj)
  {
  boolean result = false;
  if ((obj != null) && (obj instanceof ProductPK))
    {
    ProductPK other = (ProductPK)obj;
    if (productId.equals(other.getProductId()) &&
        (manufacturerId.equals(other.getManufacturerId()))
      result = true;
    }
  return result;
  }

public int hashcode()
  {
  return (getProductId().hashcode()
    ^ getManufacturerId().hashcode());
  }
}
```

Undefined primary keys were introduced as part of EJB 1.1, and allow a developer to defer declaring the primary key to the deployer. This is useful for making entity beans that are more easily ported to various database products. This is also useful for mapping entity beans to object databases or Enterprise Resource Planning (ERP) systems. With undefined primary keys, the `ejbCreate()` methods return `java.lang.Object`, and the class is configured in the `<prim-key-class>` tag in the ejb-jar.xml descriptor at deployment time.

Bean Managed Persistence (BMP)

BMP beans have persistence code in specific methods that are called by the application server. These methods place the actual persistence logic into the bean code itself. This persistence logic is separated from any business methods not at the class level, but rather at the method level. The following methods must be implemented in the bean class:

`setEntityContext()` This method is used to pass the context into the bean instance. Normal implementations save the context in a local attribute.

`unsetEntityContext()` This method gets called prior to destruction, and should set any local references to the context to null. Because entity bean instances may be pooled and not destroyed, this frees the instance from being associated with the given context.

`ejbActivate()` This method is called after activation, and may be used to restore resource connections.

`ejbPassivate()` This method is called prior to passivation, and may be used to close resource connections.

`ejbRemove()` This method is called upon an explicit remove, and should contain the code to remove the instance from the persistent store.

`ejbLoad()` This method is called when the container would like to load values from the database to the bean instance. For entity beans using JDBC, this method usually contains a select statement to return all the columns for a given row.

`ejbStore()` This method is called when the container would like to update the persistent store. When using JDBC, this usually contains an update statement or statements.

`ejbCreate()` This method is called when a `create()` method on the home interface is called. It usually executes an INSERT database statement(s), and returns the value of the primary key. One `ejbCreate()` method must exist for every `create()` statement in the home interface with matching parameter signature. Figure 21.4 shows the sequence diagram for the creation of and usage of a BMP entity bean.

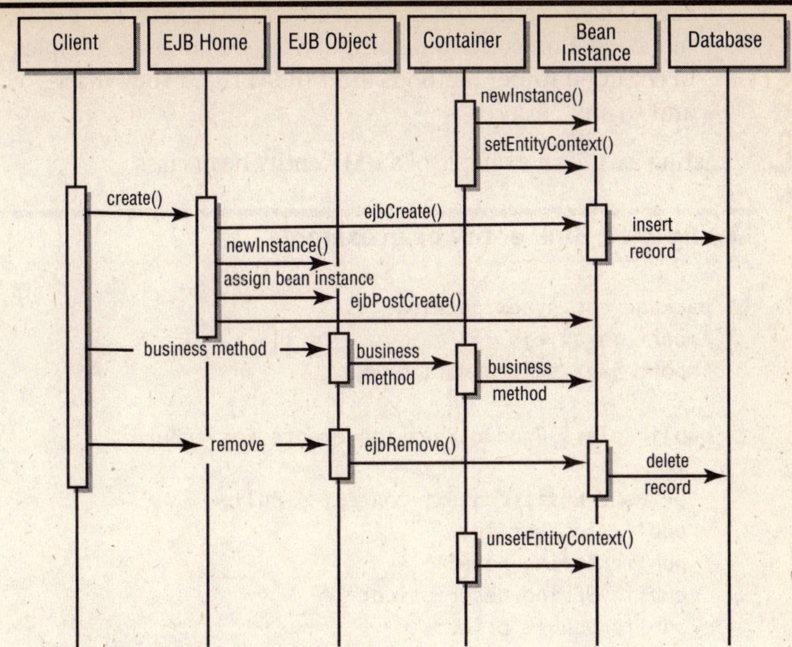

FIGURE 21.4: BMP sequence diagram

`ejbPostCreate()` This method is called *after* the `ejbCreate()` is called. It is for any logic that should be executed *after* the database INSERT statement is executed. One `ejbPostCreate()` must exist for each `ejbCreate()` with the same parameter signature.

`ejbFindByPrimaryKey()` This method is used for finding a specific entity bean instance. It returns the primary key of the found entity bean, or throws an ObjectNotFoundException if the primary key doesn't exist. Note that this doesn't load the values of the bean, but just confirms that the primary key exists in the persistent store.

`ejbFind<SUFFIX>()` These finder methods are similar to ejbFindByPrimaryKey, although they enable finding one or more entity beans based upon user-designed criteria. These methods must match the finder methods declared in the home or local interface. A `home.findByName(String name)` method will require an `ejbFindByName(String)` method in the bean class. These methods may return either the primary key instance, or a collection containing primary key instances. Examples of common finder methods are `findAll()`, `findByName()`, and so on.

Listing 21.1 is an example of a BMP entity bean class.

Listing 21.1: BMP entity bean example

```
package com.sybex.catalog;
import javax.ejb.*;
import java.sql.Connection;

public class ProductBean implements EntityBean
  {
  private EntityContext context = null;
  public Integer id;
  public String name;
  public String description;
  public Double price;

  protected Connection getConnection() /* implemented below */

  public void setEntityContext(EntityContext ctx)
    {
    context = ctx;
  }

  public void unsetEntityContext()
  {
    context = null;
  }

  public void ejbActivate() {}
  public void ejbPassivate() {}
  public void ejbRemove()/* implemented below */
  public void ejbLoad() /* implemented below */
  public void ejbStore() /* implemented below */
  public Integer ejbFindByPrimaryKey(Integer primaryKey)
  public Collection ejbFindByName(String searchstr)
  public Integer ejbCreate(...) /* implemented below */
  public void ejbPostCreate(...) /* implemented below */
```

```
public Integer getId()              /* implemented below */
public void setId(Integer id)       /* implemented below */
public String getName()             /* implemented below */
public void setName(String name) /* implemented below */
public String getDescription()      /* implemented below */
public void setDescription(String s) /* implemented below */
public Double getPrice()            /* implemented below */
public void setPrice(Double p)      /* implemented below */
}
```

As you implement the `ejbRemove()` method, you are focused upon actually removing this beans entries in the database. You are using a convenience method for getting the database connection, which will be discussed later. The prepared statement executes the SQL-92 DELETE statement to remove this beans row from the PRODUCT table. All of the database access is within a try-catch statement, and configured to catch any java.sql.SQLException. Notice that an SQLException is an application exception, and is converted into a system exception. Listing 21.2 is an example of a BMP entity bean `ejbRemove()` method.

NOTE

If you use a connection from a connection pool, you must close the connection at the end of each method. This does not actually close the connection to the database, but rather places the connection back in the pool so others can use it.

Listing 21.2: BMP entity bean class ejbRemove() method

```
public void ejbRemove()
  {
  Connection conn = null;
  PreparedStatement ps = null;
  try
    {
    conn = this.getConnection();
    ps = conn.prepareStatement(
        "DELETE FROM PRODUCT WHERE ID = ?");
    ps.setInt(1, _id.intValue());
    if (ps.executeUpdate() != 1)
      throw (new EJBException(
          "Error removing Product in DB"));
    }
```

```
    catch (SQLException e)
      {
      throw (new EJBException(e));
      }
    finally
      {
      try
        {
        if (ps != null)
          ps.close();
        if (conn != null)
          conn.close();
        }
      catch (SQLException e) {}
      }
    }
```

WARNING

You might desire more robust handling of the close. In the example it is possible for an exception to prevent proper closing of the connection.

The `ejbLoad()` method is called to refresh the entity bean's values with the values in the database reflecting this bean's primary key value. You obtain the primary key from the EntityContext, and execute your SQL SELECT statement to get the row for a given primary key. You then use the field accessors to set the beans fields based upon ResultSet returned by JDBC. Listing 21.3 is an example of a BMP entity bean `ejbLoad()` method.

Listing 21.3: BMP entity bean class ejbLoad() method

```
public void ejbLoad()
  {
  Integer primkey = (Integer)_context.getPrimaryKey();
  Connection conn = null;
  PreparedStatement ps = null;
  ResultSet rset = null;
  try
    {
    conn = this.getConnection();
    ps = conn.prepareStatement("SELECT name, description, " +
      "price FROM product WHERE id = ?");
```

```
      ps.setInt(1, primkey.intValue());
      rset = ps.executeQuery();
      if (rset.next())
        {
        id = primkey;
        name = rset.getString("name");
        description = rset.getString("description");
        price = rset.getDouble("price");
        }
      else
        throw (new EJBException("Error loading Product in DB"));
      }
    catch (SQLException e)
      {
      throw (new EJBException(e));
      }
    finally
      {
      try
        {

        if (ps != null)
          ps.close();
        }
      catch (SQLException e) {}
      try
        {
        if (conn != null)
          conn.close();
        }
      catch (SQLException e) {}
      }
    return _id;
    }
```

The `ejbStore()` method is called by the application server to update the values for an entity bean instance in the data store. Your example method uses JDBC to execute an SQL-92 UPDATE statement to update the row in the table representing your bean. Because developers control the implementation of this method, you may choose to persist an entity bean into multiple tables, or into an object database or flat file if needed. Listing 21.4 is an example of a BMP entity bean `ejbStore()` method.

Listing 21.4: BMP entity bean class ejbStore() method

```
public void ejbStore()
  {
  Connection conn = null;
  PreparedStatement ps = null;
  try
    {
    conn = this.getConnection();
    ps = conn.prepareStatement("UPDATE PRODUCT " +
      "SET name = ?, description = ?, price = ? " +
      "WHERE id = ?");
    ps.setString(1, name);
    ps.setString(2, description);
    ps.setDouble(3, price);
    ps.setInt(4, id.intValue());
    if (ps.executeUpdate() != 1)
      throw (new CreateException(
            "Error updating Product in DB"));
    }
  catch (SQLException e)
    {
    throw (new EJBException(e));
    }
  finally
    {

    try
      {
      if (ps != null)
        ps.close();
      }
    catch (SQLException e) {}
    try
      {
      if (conn != null)
        conn.close();
      }
    catch (SQLException e) {}
    }
  }
```

The ejbFindByPrimaryKey() method is required on all BMP entity beans for finding a given primary key value in the data store. You do not need or want to return the entire data entry; just the primary key. This method simply assures the entity bean that the primary key does exist, and can be loaded within the `ejbLoad()`. Listing 21.5 is an example of a BMP entity bean `ejbFindByPrimaryKey()` method.

Listing 21.5: BMP entity bean class ejbFindByPrimaryKey() method

```
public Integer ejbFindByPrimaryKey(Integer primaryKey)
  throws FinderException
    {
    Connection conn = null;
    PreparedStatement ps = null;
    ResultSet rset = null;
    try
      {
      conn = this.getConnection();
      ps = conn.prepareStatement("SELECT id " +
        "FROM product WHERE id = ?");
      ps.setInt(1, primarykey.intValue());
      rset = ps.executeQuery();
      if (!rset.next())
        throw (new ObjectNotFoundException(
              "Product not found: " + id));
      }
    catch (SQLException e)
      {
      throw (new EJBException(e));
      }
    finally
      {

      try
        {
        if (ps != null)
          ps.close();
        }
      catch (SQLException e) {}
      try
        {
        if (conn != null)
          conn.close();
        }
```

```
        catch (SQLException e) {}
        }
      return primaryKey;
      }
```

The `ejbFindByName()` method is an example of a custom finder method. These methods provide a way to find one or many instances of beans (each represented by a primary key value) within the data store. This method's objective is to return a primary key instance, or a collection of primary key instances matching the implemented criteria. In this example method, you match all Products with a name matching the method parameter String. The `javax.ejb.ObjectNotFoundException` is not needed in this case because you are returning a collection, and are not searching for a specific object. Instead you throw a javax.ejb.FinderException in the case of nothing matching our criteria, and have chosen to throw a system exception if you receive an `java.sql.SQLException` during the execution of the SELECT. Listing 21.6 shows the `ejbFindByName()` method, which is an example of a BMP entity bean custom finder method.

Listing 21.6: BMP entity bean class custom finder method

```
public Collection ejbFindByName(String searchstr)
throws FinderException
  {
  Connection conn = null;
  PreparedStatement ps = null;
  ResultSet rset = null;
  Collection result = new ArrayList();
  try
    {
    conn = this.getConnection();
    ps = conn.prepareStatement("SELECT id " +
      "FROM product WHERE name = ?");
    ps.setString(1, searchstr);
    rset = ps.executeQuery();
    while (rset.next())
      result.add(rset.getObject("id"));
    if (result.size() == 0)
      throw (new FinderException("No Products Found"));
    }
```

```
catch (SQLException e)
  {
  throw (new EJBException(e));
  }
finally
  {
  try
    {
    if (ps != null)
      ps.close();
    }
  catch (SQLException e) {}
  try
    {
    if (conn != null)
      conn.close();
    }
  catch (SQLException e) {}
  }
return primaryKey;
}
```

The `ejbCreate()` methods are focused on creating a new bean instance representation in the data store. In the case of this JDBC example, you need to prepare and execute an SQL INSERT statement. The `ejbCreate()` is responsible for setting up the beans persistent fields as well as performing the insert statement. The `ejbCreate()` method must return an instance of the primary key, which the container associates with the EJBContext for the bean. Any relationships should be handled in the `ejbPostCreate()` because the EJBObject and remote or local stub get created between invocation of the `ejbCreate()` and `ejbPostCreate()`, and will be needed to establish any relationship. In this example, there are no relationships so the `ejbPostCreate()` is empty. Listing 21.7 shows an `ejbCreate()` method with parameters. This method must have a `create()` method on the home interface with the same parameter signature.

Listing 21.7: BMP entity bean class ejbCreate method

```
public Integer ejbCreate(Integer aid,
    String aname, String adesc, Double aprice)
    throws CreateException
  {
  if ((id.intValue() < 1) || (name == null))
    throw (new CreateException("Invalid Parameters"));
```

```
    id = aid;
    name = aname;
    description = adesc;
    price = aprice;
    Connection conn = null;
    PreparedStatement ps = null;
    try
      {
      conn = this.getConnection();
      ps = conn.prepareStatement("INSERT INTO PRODUCT " +
        "(id, name, description, price) " +
        "values (?,?,?,?)");
      ps.setInt(1, id.intValue());
      ps.setString(2, name);
      ps.setString(3, description);
      ps.setDouble(4, price);
      if (ps.executeUpdate() != 1)
        throw (new CreateException(
              "Error creating Product in DB"));
      }
    catch (SQLException e)
      {
      throw (new EJBException(e));
      }
    finally
      {
      try
        {
        if (ps != null)
          ps.close();
        }
      catch (SQLException e) {}
      try
        {
        if (conn != null)
          conn.close();
        }
      catch (SQLException e) {}
      }
    return id;
    }

  public void ejbPostCreate(Integer aid) {}
```

The business methods for a BMP entity bean are the field accessors. These can be exposed in the remote or local interface, but are not needed. Your entity bean can have any business method implemented in it, but many projects have found that separating business logic from data behavior provides the optimal design. Both individual field accessors are implemented, as well as a value object accessor that passes a serializable Java object containing all the fields in the bean. Listing 21.8 shows a BMP entity bean business methods. These are quite frequently `setter` and `getter` methods, because it is an entity bean's primary objective to persist state.

Listing 21.8: BMP entity bean class business methods

```
// Business methods - field accessors
public Integer getId()
  {
  return id;
  }

public void setId(Integer theId)
  {
  id = theId;
  }

public Integer getName()
  {
  return name;
  }

public void setName(String theName)
  {
  name = theName;
  }

public String getDescription()
  {
  return description;
  }

public void setDescription(String theDesc)
  {
  description = theDesc;
  }
```

```
public Double getPrice()
  {
  return price;
  }

public void setPrice(Double thePrice)
  {
  price = thePrice;
  }

// Published method for value object
public ProductInfo getProductInfo()
  {
  ProductInfo vo = new ProductInfo();
  vo.setId(getId());
  vo.setName(getName());
  vo.setDescription(getDescription());
  vo.setPrice(getPrice());
  return vo;
  }
```

Getting a Resource Connection

A method called `getConnection()` was used in the previous code to obtain a JDBC connection. This is a private method, and shows how to access a resource using the JNDI ENC (discussed later in this chapter) from an EJB (see Listing 21.9). This method obtains a DataSource object from JNDI, and uses it to get a JDBC connection. This connection may already be established and in a connection pool. Connection pools are much more efficient than creating a connection every time you need one.

Listing 21.9: Example of a utility getConnection() method

```
private Connection getConnection() throws SQLException
  {
  Connection conn = null;
  try
    {
    Context jndi = new InitialContext();
    DataSource ds = (DataSource)
      jndi.lookup("java:comp/env/jdbc/catalogDB");
    conn = ds.getConnection();
    }
```

```
catch (NamingException e)
  {
  throw (new EJBException(e));
  }
return conn;
}
```

Container Managed Persistence (CMP)

Data access and object persistence can be tedious and repetitious code to write and maintain. To address this problem, Container Managed Persistence (CMP) is provided. The design of CMP moves the persistence code into the container, and out of the bean, which means that the EJB provider doesn't have to code persistence routines if their persistence demands fit within the container provider's CMP features. Figure 21.5 shows a CMP entity bean sequence diagram. Notice the database insert is controlled by the container.

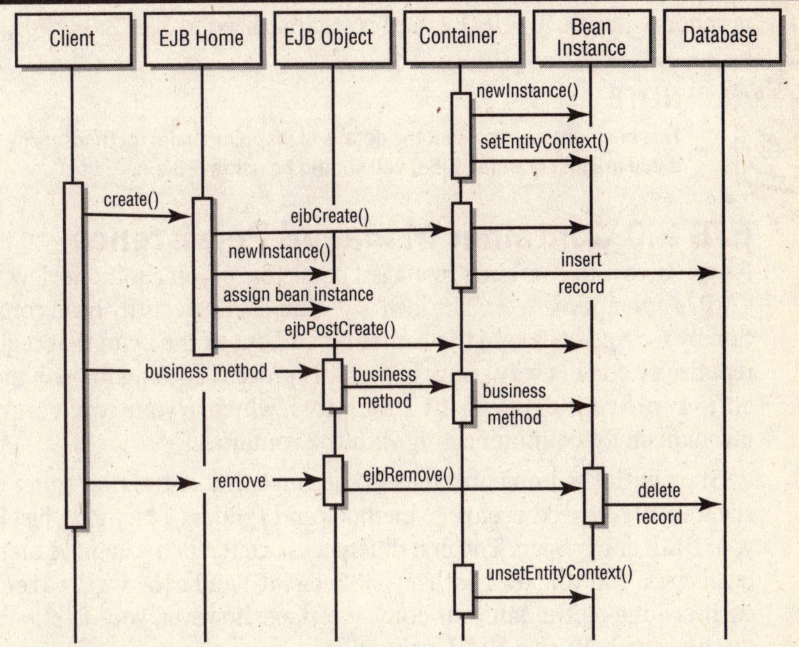

FIGURE 21.5: CMP sequence diagram

To perform the persistence "magic" in the container for a wide variety of entity beans, the developer needs to configure the container in the deployment descriptors. Start in the ejb-jar.xml with `<cmp-fields>`, which declare the persistent fields in the entity bean. These fields then get mapped to specific persistent entities in the server descriptor(s). In the case of relational access, this will be to tables and columns. CMP is generally easier than coding the persistence routines every time, but there are restrictions to the extent of the mapping supported by container providers. Another consideration is that various CMP containers may differ in their implementations, so care needs to be taken to understand porting issues surrounding CMP usage.

EJB 1.1 CMP versus EJB 2.0 CMP

Container managed persistence has changed dramatically between the EJB 1.1 specification and the EJB 2.0 specification; however, container providers are required to support both for backward compatibility reasons. It is recommended that you avoid using EJB 1.1 if at all possible due to the limitations of these entity beans. They will not have access to local interfaces, cannot support `<METHOD-NAME>` suffixes on home `create` methods, and no entity relationships are supported (discussed later in this chapter). Also, mapping `finder` methods to their implementations is vendor-specific in EJB 1.1, and is standardized in EJB 2.0.

NOTE

This book does not present the details of mapping finder methods using EJB 1.1. If you are just learning EJBs, you should be using EJB 2.0.

EJB 2.0 Container Managed Persistence

As you dive into container managed persistence, you should review what CMP is attempting to do. The idea is to simplify CMP entity bean construction by moving code into the container and out of the bean that requires repetitive code in every entity bean. This process is going to push more entries into your deployment descriptors, which is your configuration mechanism for communicating with the container.

Start with the home interface(s) because that is the first thing your clients see. You need `create()` methods and `finder()` methods, just like in your BMP entity bean. The first differences occur when you move on to the bean class. You still need both an `ejbCreate()` and `ejbPostCreate()` for each `create` method in your home interface; however, your `ejbCreate()` methods will return a NULL value:

```
public Integer ejbCreate(Integer id)
  {
  setId(id);
  return null;
  }
```

This is because the primary key will be obtained in the container. The `ejbCreate()` gets called prior to the database insert, so you can set values in persistent fields, but in CMP entity beans you always return NULL from your `ejbCreate()` methods.

Unlike your BMP entity beans, you do not need `ejbFind<SUFFIX>` methods in the bean class. The finder methods are implemented in the container, but you need some way of configuring a SELECT statement within the container. You do this using the EJB Query Language (EJBQL). This enables you to configure your select query that will be executed for you in the container. Start by including a `<abstract-schema-name>` tag for all referenced entity beans in your ejb-jar.xml descriptor. This enables you to include these entity beans in your EJBQL query statements by using the schema name. Now add your <query> elements into the ejb-jar.xml descriptor, which maps your query statement to finder methods. If you have the same finder methods in both local and remote home interfaces, the query will apply to both, unless you specify specifically using the `<result-type-mapping>` tag.

```
<ejb-jar>
  <enterprise-beans>
   <entity>
    <ejb-name>Product</ejb-name>
     ...
    <abstract-schema-name>
     Product
    </abstract-schema-name>
    ...
    <query>
     <query-method>
      <method-name>
       findByManufacturerName
      </method-name>
      <method-params>
       <method-param>
        java.lang.String
       </method-param>
      </method-params>
     </query-method>
     <ejb-ql>
      SELECT OBJECT(p) FROM Product p
      WHERE p.name = ?1
     </ejb-ql>
    </query>
    ...
```

Your bean class must be declared as abstract. This is new in EJB 2.0, and it is because the container will implement `set<FIELD>` and `get<FIELD>` methods in a sub-class of your bean class for accessing persistent fields and relationships. You need to declare these methods (not implement them) in your bean class, just as you would in a Java interface. Figure 21.6 shows an example CMP class diagram. The actual name and implementation of the `Persistence_ProductBean` class may vary with each CMP vendor.

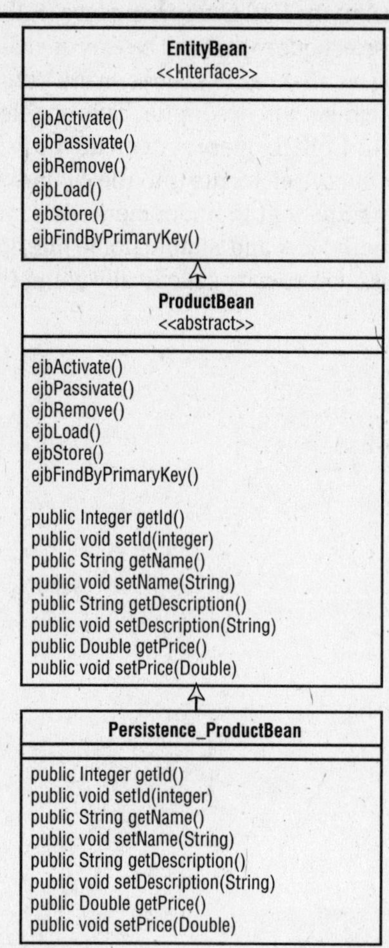

FIGURE 21.6: Example CMP class diagram

Your bean class is reduced in size (compared to the BMP bean class) because the persistence code has moved to the container. You must still implement the EntityBean methods `ejbCreate()`, `ejbPostCreate()`, `ejbActivate()`, `ejbPassivate()`, `ejbRemove()`, `ejbLoad()`, and `ejbStore()`, but you are not required to have any code in these.

Entity Bean Lifecycle

Entity beans have a clearly defined lifecycle. Callback methods get called on the bean class as the bean moves from state to state within the lifecycle. The entity bean lifecycle consists of three basic states, as shown in Figure 21.7. Figure 21.7 shows the CMP entity bean lifecycle, which includes three bean states: does not exist, pooled, and method ready.

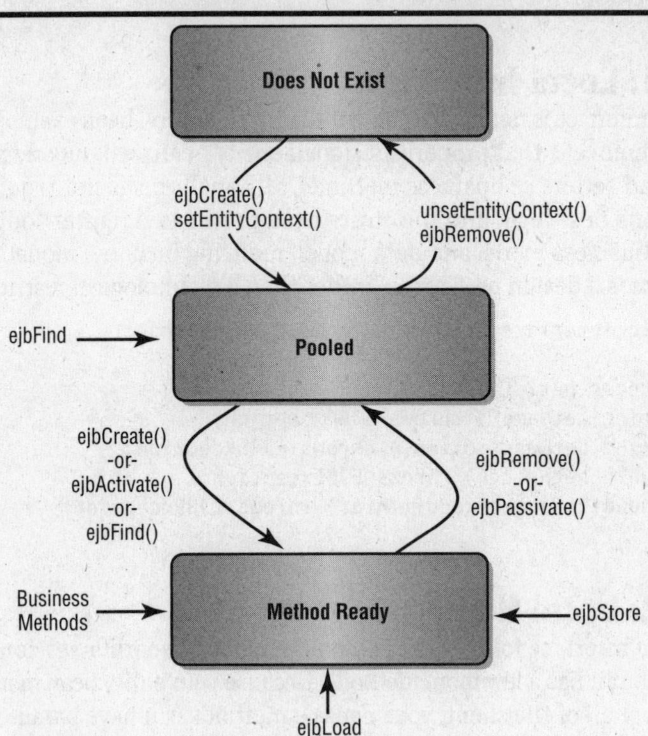

FIGURE 21.7: CMP entity bean lifecycle

Entity beans do maintain client state and, therefore, cannot be pooled as active components (i.e., stateless session beans). Because entity beans have more overhead than session beans, however, it does make sense to pool available entity beans. As you saw in lifecycle, entity beans are available when they are not assigned a primary key to represent. These available entity beans are pooled until a `find` method or `create` method assigns them a primary key and they become active.

Creating an Entity EJB

As an example of creating an entity EJB, you will create a Product entity bean for access by your Catalog session bean. You will be developing and defining only a local interface for this entity bean. You have designed the system to always access the Product through the Catalog, which defines a remote interface and effectively scales throughout your possible cluster. It is possible to have one or both local and remote interfaces on an entity bean. As you will see, the process for these interfaces are not much different than they are on session beans, so to keep this example simple, you will skip the remote interface.

Step 1: Local Interface

The local interface is not much different than your session bean example. The main difference is that properly designed entity beans will mostly have getters and setters as business methods, although this is not required. Putting business logic into the entity bean produces a tighter coupling between business model and data model, reducing business model flexibility. This is a design preference, rather than a technological restriction.

```
public interface Product extends EJBLocalObject
  {
  Integer getId() throws EJBException;
  String getName() throws EJBException;
  String getDescription() throws EJBException;
  Double getPrice() throws EJBException;
  ProductInfo getProductInfo() throws EJBException;
  }
```

Step 2: Local Home

The home interface follows the same pattern as the earlier session bean example, but it has a few more methods. Because your entity bean maintains state on behalf of the client, your `create` methods can have parameters. This allows efficient use of database INSERT statements, avoiding a second UPDATE if values are known at creation time.

```
public interface ProductLocalHome
      extends EJBLocalHome
  {
  Product create(Integer id, String name,
        String desc, Double price)
        throws CreateException, EJBException;
  Product findByPrimaryKey(Integer pk)
```

```
        throws FinderException, EJBException;
  Collection findByName(String name)
        throws FinderException, EJBException;
  }
```

Notice the finder methods declared here in the local home interface. For BMP entity beans, each finder method requires a matching `ejbFindXXX()` method in the BMP bean class. CMP entity beans require that a `<finder-method>` tag exist to configure the finder in the ejb-jar.xml descriptor.

As of EJB 2.0, both BMP and CMP entity beans may also have `ejbHome` methods. These methods also are required to have matching `ejbHome<METHOD>` methods in the bean class. These methods are just utility methods global to all instances of entity bean class.

Step 3: Bean Class

The bean class implements the javax.ejb.EntityBean interface. This interface defines several methods that must be implemented. Listing 21.10 shows the CMP bean class using EJB 1.1, just to show some of the differences. Listing 21.11 shows the CMP bean class as it should be done using EJB 2.0.

Listing 21.10: CMP 1.1 entity bean example

```
public class ProductBean implements EntityBean
  {
  protected EntityContext context = null;

  // Notice these fields are public and must be configured
  // as persistent fields in the deployment descriptors.
  public Integer id;
  public String name;
  public String description;

  public void setEntityContext(EntityContext ctx)
    {
    context = ctx;
    }

  public void unsetEntityContext()
    {
    context = null;
    }
```

```
public void ejbActivate() {}
public void ejbPassivate() {}
public void ejbRemove() {}
public void ejbLoad() {}
public void ejbStore() {}

public Integer ejbCreate(Integer theId)
  {
  id = theId;

  return null;
  }

public void ejbPostCreate(Integer theId)
  {
  }


// Published method for value object
public ProductInfo getProductInfo()
  {
  ProductInfo vo = new ProductInfo();
  vo.setId(id);
  vo.setName(name);
  vo.setDescription(description);
  return vo;
  }
}
```

Listing 21.11: As a CMP 2.0 entity bean

```
public abstract class ProductBean implements javax.ejb
   .EntityBean
  {
  protected EntityContext context = null;

  public void setEntityContext(EntityContext ctx)
    {
    context = ctx;
    }
```

```
public void unsetEntityContext()
  {
  context = null;
  }

public void ejbActivate() {}
public void ejbPassivate() {}
public void ejbRemove() {}
public void ejbLoad() {}
public void ejbStore() {}

public Integer ejbCreate(Integer id)
  {
  setId(id);
  return null;
  }

public void ejbPostCreate(Integer id)
  {
  }

// abstract accessors (new with EJB 2.0)
public abstract Integer getId();
public abstract void setId(Integer id);
public abstract Integer getName();
public abstract void setName(String name);
public abstract String getDescription();
public abstract void setDescription(String desc);

// Published method for value object
public ProductInfo getProductInfo()
{
  ProductInfo vo = new ProductInfo();
  vo.setId(getId());
  vo.setName(getName());
  vo.setDescription(getDescription());
  return vo;
}
}
```

Configuring an Entity EJB

Entity beans are configured in the same manner as session bean—in the ejb-jar.xml and server XML descriptor files. In some cases, a third descriptor representing database field mappings is used based solely upon the application server configuration mechanism for CMP beans. The following is an example of the ejb-jar.xml file tags for your Catalog-Item entity bean using BMP:

```
<ejb-jar>
  <enterprise-beans>
   <entity>
    <ejb-name>ProductEJB</ejb-name>
    <local-home>com.sybex.catalog.ejbs.ProductLocalHome
       </local-home>
    <local>com.sybex.catalog.ejbs.ProductLocal</local>
    <ejb-class>com.sybex.catalog.ejbs.ProductBean</ejb-class>
    <persistence-type>Bean</persistence-type >
    <primary-key-class>java.lang.Integer</primary-key-class>
    <reentrant>False</reentrant>
   </entity>
  </enterprise-beans>
 </ejb-jar>
```

See Listing 21.12–21.14 for examples of the Product configuration for CMP.

Listing 21.12: File ejb-jar.xml descriptor

```
<ejb-jar>
  <enterprise-beans>
   <entity>
    <ejb-name>ProductEJB</ejb-name>
    <local-home>com.sybex.catalog.ejbs.ProductLocalHome
       </local-home>
    <local>com.sybex.catalog.ejbs.ProductLocal</local>
    <ejb-class>com.sybex.catalog.ejbs.ProductBean</ejb-class>
    <persistence-type>Bean</persistence-type >
    <primary-key-class>java.lang.Integer</primary-key-class>
    <reentrant>False</reentrant>
    <cmp-field><field-name>id</field-name></cmp-field>
    <cmp-field><field-name>name</field-name></cmp-field>
    <cmp-field><field-name>description</field-name>
       </cmp-field>
```

```
      <cmp-field><field-name>price</field-name></cmp-field>
    </entity>
  </enterprise-beans>
</ejb-jar>
```

Listing 21.13: File weblogic-ejb-jar.xml descriptor

```
<weblogic-ejb-jar>
 <weblogic-enterprise-bean>
  <ejb-name>ProductEJB</ejb-name>
  <entity-descriptor>
   <entity-cache>
    <max-beans-in-cache>150</max-beans-in-cache>
   </entity-cache>
   <persistence>
    <persistence-type>
     <type-identifier>WebLogic_CMP_RDBMS</type-identifier>
     <type-version>6.0</type-version>
     <type-storage>META-INF/weblogic-cmp-rdbms-jar.xml
        </type-storage>
    </persistence-type>
    <persistence-use>
     <type-identifier>WebLogic_CMP_RDBMS</type-identifier>
     <type-version>6.0</type-version>
    </persistence-use>
   </persistence>
  </entity-descriptor>
  <jndi-name>ProductEJB</jndi-name>
    </weblogic-enterprise-bean>
</weblogic-ejb-jar>
```

Listing 21.14: File weblogic-cmp-rdbms-jar.xml

```
<weblogic-rdbms-jar>
 <weblogic-rdbms-bean>
  <ejb-name>ProductEJB</ejb-name>
  <data-source-name>CatalogDS</data-source-name>
  <table-name>PRODUCT</table-name>
  <field-map>
   <cmp-field>id</cmp-field>
   <dbms-column>ID</dbms-column>
  </field-map>
  <field-map>
```

```
      <cmp-field>name</cmp-field>
      <dbms-column>NAME</dbms-column>
    </field-map>
    <field-map>
      <cmp-field>description</cmp-field>
      <dbms-column>DESCRIPTION</dbms-column>
    </field-map>
    <field-map>
      <cmp-field>price</cmp-field>
      <dbms-column>PRICE</dbms-column>
    </field-map>
  </weblogic-rdbms-bean>
</weblogic-rdbms-jar>
```

CMP Relationships

EJB 2.0 introduces Container Managed Relationships to CMP entity beans. These relationships allow one entity bean to be associated or related to other entity beans. These relationships model relationships in the underlying persistent store. For example, in a relational database, one table can have a foreign key whose values are primary key values in another table, thus creating a relationship between the two tables. In this same manner CMR fields can be configured between two entity beans.

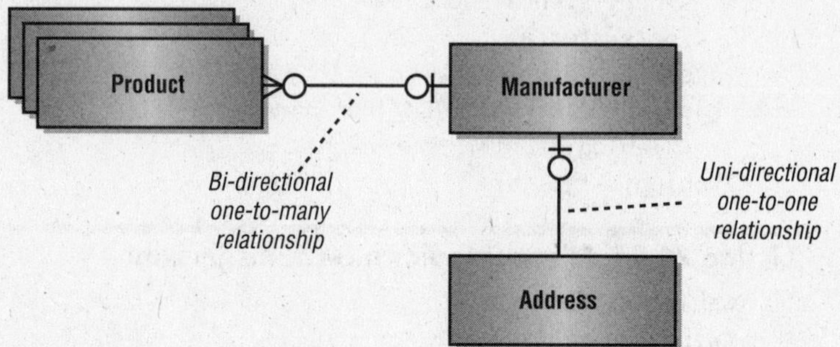

These relationships are defined in terms of visibility and cardinality. Visibility determines whether accessor methods will exist on each of the entity beans defined in the relationship. For example, if your Product entity bean has a relationship with a OrderEntry entity bean, it may not have visibility to the OrderEntry even though the OrderEntry has access to the Product. This would be the case of a uni-directional relationship. A bi-directional relationship has visibility to both of the entity beans from the other. Cardinality determines the number of objects at both ends of the relationship. A one-to-one relationship has just one entity bean on each end of the relationship. A one-to-many or a many-to-one relationship has one entity bean on one side, and many entity beans on the other side of the relationship. A many-to-many relationship has multiple entity beans on both sides of the relationship, and requires the use of a join table in mapping the relationship.

The following shows another entity bean in your catalog framework. Manufacturer has a unidirectional, one-to-one relationship with Address, and a bi-directional, one-to-many relationship with Product. The abstract methods needed in the bean class of the CMP entity bean is shown, as well as the `<cmr-field>` tags in the ejb-jar.xml descriptor:

```
public class ManufacturerBean implements javax.ejb.EntityBean
  {
  ...
  // One-to-one <cmr-field> relationship
  public abstract void setAddress(AddressLocal address);
  public abstract AddressLocal getAddress();
  // One-to-many <cmr-field> relationship
  public abstract void setProducts(Collection products);
  public abstract Collection getProducts();
  }
```

And now the ejb-jar.xml deployment descriptor. Notice that each `<ejb-relation>` contains two `<ejb-relation-role>` tags to define each direction. These are necessary even for uni-directional relationships, because the multiplicity must be specified on each end:

```
// XML ejb-jar.xml deployment descriptor
<ejb-jar>
 <enterprise-beans>
  <entity>
   ...
   <cmr-field>address</cmr-field>
   <cmr-field>products</cmr-field>
  </entity>
 </enterprise-beans>
 <relationships>
  <ejb-relation>
   <ejb-relation-name>Manufacturer-Address</ejb-relation-name>
   <ejb-relationship-role>
    <ejb-relationship-role-name>Manufacturer-has-an-Address
    </ejb-relationship-role-name>
    <multiplicity>One</multiplicity>
```

```
        <relationship-role-source>
          <ejb-name>ManufacturerEJB</ejb-name>
        </relationship-role-source>
        <cmr-field>
          <cmr-field-name>address</cmr-field-name>
        </cmr-field>
      </ejb-relationship-role>
    </ejb-relation>
    <ejb-relation>
      <ejb-relation-name>Manufacturer-Product</ejb-relation-name>
      <ejb-relationship-role>
        <ejb-relationship-role-name>
          Manufacturer-has-many-Products
        </ejb-relationship-role-name>
        <multiplicity>Many</multiplicity>
        <relationship-role-source>
          <ejb-name>ManufacturerEJB</ejb-name>
        </relationship-role-source>
        <cmr-field>
          <cmr-field-name>products</cmr-field-name>
        </cmr-field>
      </ejb-relationship-role>
      <ejb-relationship-role>
        <ejb-relationship-role-name>
          Product-has-a-Manufacturer
        </ejb-relationship-role-name>
        <multiplicity>One</multiplicity>
        <relationship-role-source>
          <ejb-name>ProductEJB</ejb-name>
        </relationship-role-source>
        <cmr-field>
          <cmr-field-name>manufacturer</cmr-field-name>
        </cmr-field>
      </ejb-relationship-role>
    </ejb-relation>
  </relationships>
</ejb-jar>
```

Each relationship must have two relationship roles. These roles determine the visibility. A uni-directional relationship will have a `<cmr-field>` only for visible roles. The multiplicity determines the cardinality. In the database, you will need a foreign key in PRODUCT that holds the primary key of the MANUFACTURER row. The MANUFACTURER table will also need a foreign key pointing to the ADDRESS row representing that entity bean.

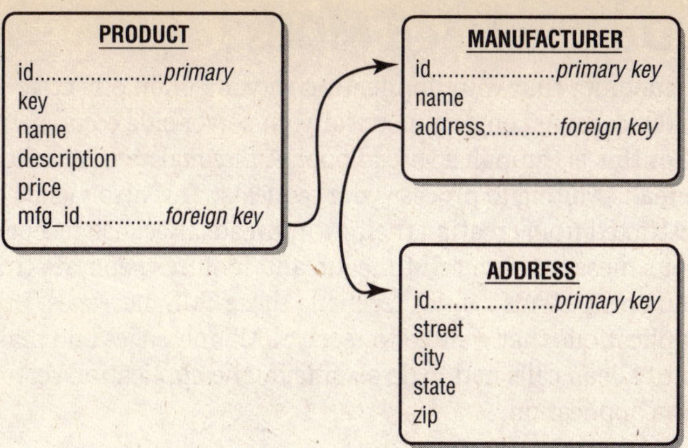

NOTE

Note that BMP entity beans are not affected by relationships because the persistence code is right in the bean; the BMP entity beans are free to implement their own relationships.

Message Driven Beans

Message driven beans are the most recently added bean type, coming in the EJB 2.0 specification. They provide a needed integration between synchronous EJB components and asynchronous JMS messaging. Of the four types of beans, Message Driven Beans are perhaps the easiest to build because they require no remote, local, or home interfaces.

Asynchronous Messaging

Session and entity beans are based upon a request/reply model. This model provides synchronous messaging where the client makes a request and waits for the component to complete its processing and then return a response before resuming its next statement. Asynchronous messaging is more of a fire-and-forget model; the messaging system can guarantee delivery of the message, so that the client can continue on processing other statements. It is akin to the postal system that takes responsibility for delivering the mail so that you do not need to stand by the mailbox until the recipient of your letter receives and responds.

Why Do You Need MDBs?

Remember that your application server's main objective is to provide a reliable, robust environment for your server-side components. One way it does this is through a thread pool. A *thread pool* is a limited number of threads waiting to process your requests. This also means that EJBs are restricted from creating their own threads. Because receiving asynchronous messages is a full-time job and requires separate thread, session and entity beans cannot receiving these JMS messages. Prior to EJB 2.0, applications that wanted to receive JMS messages and make session and entity bean calls had to do so outside the application server in a separate Java application.

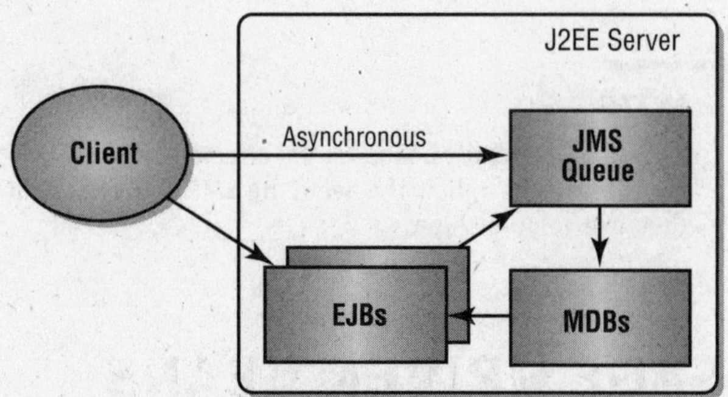

Message driven beans were created for precisely this reason. They do not have any client interfaces. They are comprised of a bean class and a descriptor, and they do one thing and do it well: receive asynchronous messages from JMS. Session and entity beans are capable JMS message senders, and now message driven beans complete the JMS integration as JMS receivers—inside the application server.

MDB LifeCycle

Message driven beans, similar to session and entity beans, have a well-defined lifecycle. The MDBs lifecycle, however, is much simpler containing only two states: Does Not Exist and Method Ready, as shown in Figure 21.8.

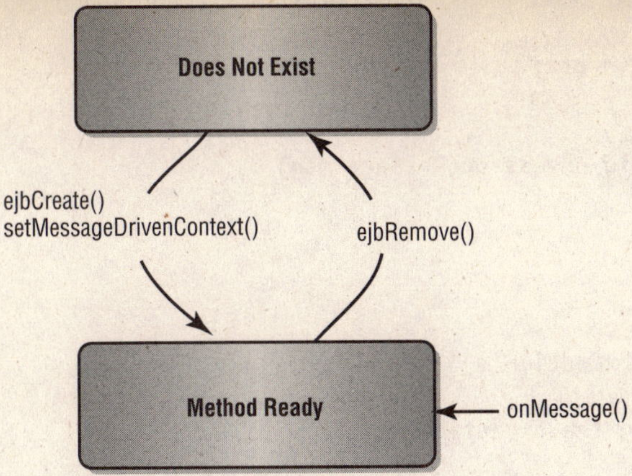

FIGURE 21.8: MDB lifecycle

When the server starts or as MDBs are needed (based on configuration in the descriptor), message driven beans are created. Their `setMessageDrivenContext()` method gets called to give the bean a chance to save a reference to the context. A no-argument `ejbCreate()` method then gets called, after which the bean is in the Method Ready state. It is now waiting and ready to process incoming JMS messages.

Creating a Message Driven EJB

The first step to creating a message driven bean is to create the bean class. You can skip the interfaces because your bean will not need them. Clients can still send messages to message driven beans, but they do so through JMS, not through local or remote stubs. Your message driven bean starts by implementing the `javax.ejb.MessageDrivenBean` interface. This interface has two methods that must be implemented: `setMessageDrivenContext()` and `ejbRemove()`. Your bean class also needs to implement `javax.jms.MessageListener` interface. This interface has one method you must implement called `onMessage()`, which is where your work is done.

```
public class CatalogFeedbackProcessor implements
  MessageDrivenBean
 {
 private MessageDrivenContext context = null;

 public void ejbRemove() {}
```

```
public void setMessageDrivenContext(MessageDrivenContext ctx)
  {
  context = ctx;
  }

public void onMessage(Message msg)
  {
  try
    {
    ...
    }
  catch (Exception e)
    {
    // log the exception
    }
  }
}
```

You can do many things inside of the onMessage() method, such as calling session or entity beans, sending JMS messages, accessing a database, connector service, network socket, or web service via a URL. Because there is no client to throw exceptions to, you should catch and log all exceptions. You don't want problems to go unreported, and you don't want them to interrupt your MDB.

Configuring a Message Driven EJB

The ejb-jar.xml deployment descriptor for a MDB is much the same as session beans, except that there are no <home>, <remote>, <local-home>, or <local> tags.

```
<ejb-jar>
 <enterprise-beans>
  <message-driven>
   <ejb-name>CatalogFeedbackProcessor</ejb-name>
   <ejb-class>com.sybex.catalog.ejbs.CatalogFeedbackProcessor
      </ejb-class>
   <transaction-type>Container</transaction-type>
   <message-driven-destination>
    <destination-type>javax.jms.Topic</destination-type>
    <subscription-durability>Durable</subscription-durability>
  </message-driven>
 </enterprise-beans>
</ejb-jar>
```

The <subscription-durability> indicates that this MDB is a durable subscriber (see Chapter 17 for durable subscribers), which only applies to JMS topics. The actual destination name is configured in the server-specific deployment descriptor.

```
<weblogic-ejb-jar>
  <weblogic-enterprise-bean>
    <ejb-name>CatalogFeedbackProcessor</ejb-name>
    <message-driven-descriptor>
      <pool>
        <max-beans-in-free-pool>100</max-beans-in-free-pool>
        <initial-beans-in-free-pool>5
          </initial-beans-in-free-pool>
      </pool>
      <destination-jndi-name>CatalogFeedback
        </destination-jndi-name>
    </message-driven-descriptor>
    <jndi-name>CatalogFeedbackEJB</jndi-name>
  </weblogic-enterprise-bean>
</weblogic-ejb-jar>
```

Pooling Message Driven Beans

It is possible to pool MDBs in some J2EE application servers. This is useful, especially when you desire the processing of multiple asynchronous messages simultaneously. This is effective, especially when using a JMS queue, where each MDB grabs a message from the queue and processes it, allowing the pool to scale effectively in high-volume situations. Be careful, though; not every application server implements MDB pooling, and some may instantiate MDBs with every JMS message processed by the MDB. Figure 21.9 shows a pool of MDBs configured to received messages from a JMS Queue.

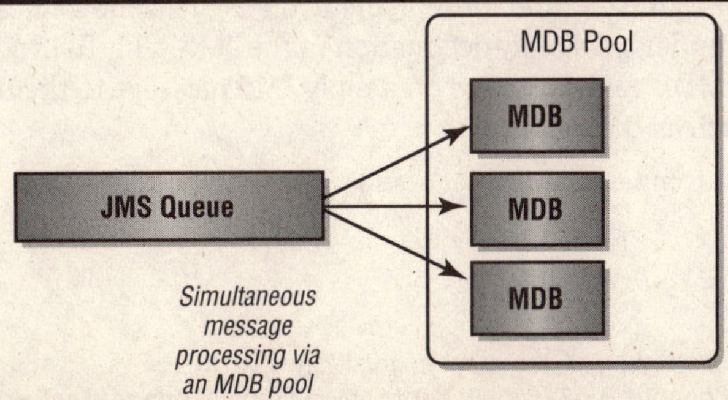

FIGURE 21.9: Pooling MDBs on a JMS Queue

Message Selectors

As you saw in Chapter 17, JMS receivers and subscribers have the capability to selectively receive messages from their destination based upon a message query language. The <message-selector> tag in the ejb-jar.xml descriptor allows you to specify such a query statement, enabling your MDB to selectively receive messages from its configured destination. The following is an example of a message selector in the MDB deployment descriptor:

```
<ejb-jar>
 <enterprise-beans>
  <message-driven>
   <ejb-name>CatalogFeedbackProcessor</ejb-name>
   <ejb-class>com.sybex.catalog.ejbs.CatalogFeedbackProcessor
      </ejb-class>
   <transaction-type>Container</transaction-type>
   <message-selector>MessageType = 'Feedback'
      </message-selector>
   ...
  </message-driven>
 </enterprise-beans>
</ejb-jar>
```

If no <message-selector> is specified, no selector is applied allowing the next available message to be received. Note that it is often necessary to put the message selector into a CDATA section because selector statements are not always valid XML parsed data (such as including "<" or ">").

MDB Asynchronous Replies

Message driven beans are asynchronous, but they can be JMS senders as well as receivers. One method for replying to an asynchronous message is to have the sender set a reply destination in the JMSReplyTo header attribute. The MDB can then send off a reply JMS message to the reply destination, such as the following:

```
public void onMessage(Message msg)
  {
  try
    {
    ...
    Queue replyq = (Queue)msg.getJMSReplyTo();
    QueueConnectionFactory factory = (QueueConnectionFactory)
      jndiContext.lookup("java:comp/env/jms/QueueFactory");
    QueueConnection connect = factory.createQueueConnection();
```

```
      QueueSession session = connect.createQueueSession(true, 0);
      QueueSender sender = session.createSender(replyq);
      TextMessage replymsg = session.createTextMessage();
      replymsg.setText("Message Received");
      sender.send(replymsg);
      connect.close();
      ...
      }
    catch (Exception e)
      {
      // log the error
      }
    }
```

Keep in mind that when using asynchronous replies, it is usually less efficient to poll for reply than use a synchronous call. If the sender of the original message handled by the MDB is a session or entity bean, the effectiveness of using asynchronous replies may be limited.

Acknowledge Modes

As you saw in Chapter 16, "A SOAP Server Example," JMS has the concept of message acknowledgment. Your MDB may decide how to acknowledge message receipt from the JMS destination based upon the `<acknowledge-mode>` tag in the ejb-jar.xml deployment descriptor.

```
<ejb-jar>
 <enterprise-beans>
  <message-driven>
   <ejb-name>CatalogFeedbackProcessor</ejb-name>
   <ejb-class>com.sybex.catalog.ejbs.CatalogFeedbackProcessor
      </ejb-class>
   <transaction-type>Container</transaction-type>
   <acknowledge-mode>Auto-acknowledge</acknowledge-mode>
   ...
  </message-driven>
 </enterprise-beans>
</ejb-jar>
```

Possible configurations are:

`Auto-acknowledge` The container sends an acknowledgment immediately following receipt of the message.

`Dups-ok-acknowledge` The container may delay the acknowledgment to the destination.

Part IV

The main issue is the overhead of acknowledgment. Most MDBs use auto-acknowledge as the overhead is not extreme, and this avoids processing the same message twice.

ENC and EJBContexts

Prior to EJB 1.1, enterprise beans accessed all their environment settings from the EJBContext. This is the context object passed into the bean in the `set<TYPE>Context()` methods. This method defines several methods for accessing the transaction, security, home and local home instances, and environment settings. EntityContext also has a method to get the primary key object for the bean. Here is the EJBContext interface:

```
public interface javax.ejb.EJBContext
{
  // EJB home methods
  public EJBHome getEJBHome();
  public EJBLocalHome getEJBLocalHome();

  // security methods
  public java.security.Principal getCallerPrincipal();
  public boolean isCallerInRole(java.lang.String roleName);

  // transaction methods
  public javax.transaction.UserTransaction getUserTransaction()
    throws java.lang.IllegalStateException;
  public boolean getRollbackOnly()
    throws java.lang.IllegalStateException;
  public void setRollbackOnly()
    throws java.lang.IllegalStateException;

  // deprecated methods
  public java.security.Identity getCallerIdentity();
  public boolean isCallerInRole(java.security.Identity role);
  public java.util.Properties getEnvironment();
}
```

The deprecated methods are based upon EJB 1.0, and are optional for EJB 1.1+ containers. If they are not implemented, a java.lang .RuntimeException will be thrown during access. Starting with EJB 1.1, a special JNDI name space was created, referred to as the Environment Naming Context (or ENC). The ENC was added to allow any enterprise bean to access environment entries, other beans, and resources through entries in the ENC. The ENC is available to all beans, and can be used to access environment entries, resource references, and EJB references. The ENC environment entries, resource references, and EJB references are discussed in Chapter 22, "EJB Transactions and Security."

Modeling with EJBs

Now that you've seen how the various types of EJBs work, as well as how to build and configure these EJB types, one question remains: When and where should you use them? Each type of EJB is oriented toward efficiently and effectively doing a type of task:

Session Beans Modeling business tasks and behavior

Entity Beans Modeling business data

Message Driven Beans Handling business events

It is often useful to use session beans within a Session Facade pattern, providing the public synchronous access to your business functions. These are your business objects, and focus not only on modeling your business behavior, but also upon providing an easy-to-use API to customers of the business model. This can be web applications, rich applications, and, in a growing number of projects, web services.

Session beans in the business model will access a variety of resources including entity beans, data access objects, service connectors to legacy systems, other session beans, and web services. This allows your data integration layer to focus upon accessing database servers and external systems/services.

Message driven beans are designed for creating a loose-coupled, event-oriented handling model that is useful for keeping systems flexible. These beans, unlike their session and entity counterparts, do not require explicit referencing from their clients, and therefore foster loose coupling of messages. They are also effective at processing messages that do not require a response, largely because clients do not need to wait while they do their work.

Enterprise JavaBeans provide these types to complement each other. Designs using EJBs are often faced with the question of whether an EJB should be an entity, session, or MDB. There is no one right or wrong answer, as this will depend upon what requirements your EJB is attempting to fullfill. Keep in mind the following tips:

- Entity beans persist data.
- Session beans perform business logic.
- MDBs process asynchronous messages.
- Use common design patterns.
- Avoid EJBs that try to do too much.

WHAT'S NEXT

In this chapter you looked at each of the various EJB types: stateless session beans, stateful session beans, entity beans, and message driven beans. The focus was to explain how these beans work, what they are suited for, and how to build and configure them.

These components are the J2EE building blocks for designing and constructing robust, scalable enterprise applications. They are the tools for modeling your business information needs and workflow. The next chapter discusses two aspects that thread throughout all EJBs: transactions and security.

Chapter 22

EJB Transactions and Security

This chapter presents the transaction and security services available to all EJB, as specified in the EJB 2.1 specification. One of the many advantages for EJBs are the simplicity they bring to enterprise application development. A good understanding of transactions is essential for the J2EE developer. Security is also a rapidly growing requirement for most enterprise applications.

Featured in this chapter:

- What are transactions?
- Local and distributed transactions
- The two-phase commit
- Transaction attributes
- Transaction isolation
- Transaction management
- Security configuration

Written for *Enterprise Java™ 2, J2EE™ 1.3 Complete*
by Vince E. Marco

WHAT ARE TRANSACTIONS?

Transactions have become a major aspect of enterprise development. A transaction is simply a group of actions that behave as a single action; however, implementing transactions can get complex, as you will see. As an example, consider an automated teller machine (ATM). You have $1000 in your bank account, and you go to the ATM to withdraw $200. This withdrawal behaves as one single action, yet requires several actions behind the scenes:

- The ATM must connect to a server with the account balance for approval.
- The balance is decremented by the amount of the withdrawal.
- An instruction is returned to the ATM to dispense the cash to the user.

Consider for a moment what would happen if the balance were decremented and then instruction to dispense the cash failed, perhaps due to a network problem. The user wouldn't get any cash, yet their account balance is now missing the $200, as shown in Figure 22.1.

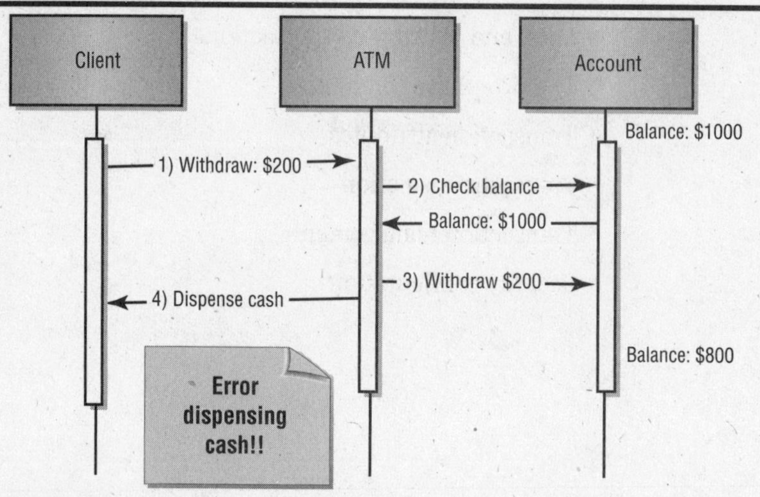

FIGURE 22.1: Example without transaction

What needs to happen now is that a rollback action should occur, adding back the withdrawal amount to leave the account balance in the same condition as when the transaction started. Either all of the transaction succeeds, or none of it succeeds, as seen in Figure 22.2.

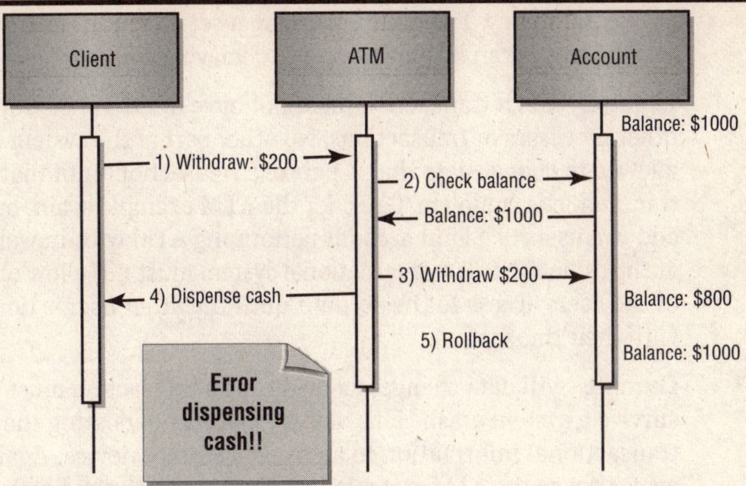

FIGURE 22.2: Example with transaction

The ACID Principles

Transactions are defined by four principles; Transactions must be atomic, consistent, isolated, and durable (ACID):

Atomic This defines the principle demonstrated in the ATM example. A transaction must execute completely, or not at all. This is managed by *commit* and *rollback*. If all the tasks within a transaction succeed, the transaction is committed. If any of the tasks within the transaction fail, any tasks that have already completed must be rolled back. This means that the transaction can result in only two possible outcomes: the state of the system resulting from successful execution of all steps in the transaction, or the state of the system before the transaction began.

Consistent At the end of a transaction, the system data must be consistent with all the business rules of the data model. This consistency is enforced by the developer by ensuring a complete data model and business logic. For example in the ATM scenario, every debit must have an equal credit in the system. If this is not the case, it will not matter if steps get rolled back; even with one transaction, the system will be out of balance. The responsibility falls upon complete design and implementation of the system. Transactions provide the other three principles—the developer provides this one. The atomic principle does go hand-in-hand with consistency. The ability to group a set of actions as one action provides an invaluable tool to achieving consistency.

Isolated Each transaction must not have interference from other processes or transactions. No other part of the system is allowed to change data that is part of a transaction until that transaction is complete. Consider the ATM example again, but add two users of a joint account performing ATM withdrawals at the same time. The transactional system must not allow one of the users access to the account until the other user is done with their transaction.

Durable All data changes made during a transaction must survive a system crash. This usually involves persisting the transactional information to a physical storage device. Again, going back to the ATM example, you must deal with the situation that the server crashes immediately after sending the instruction to dispense the cash. The withdrawal must retain the information from the transaction, or the bank could eventually go out of business from lost withdrawal information.

NOTE

The EJB architecture does not support child (or nested) transactions. The model is a flat transaction model, meaning that if an EJB tries to start a new transaction while currently running in a transaction, the existing transaction must be suspended while the new transaction is active. The suspended transaction resumes when the current transaction completes.

Local and Distributed Transactions

Management of transactions is handled by transaction managers and resource managers. A transaction manager is the supreme authority overseeing the transaction. There can be only one transaction manager per transaction. Resource managers are participants in a transaction, governing a resource's view and participation in the transaction. An example of a resource manager is a JDBC database driver, which manages a connection's participation in a transaction.

Transactions can be categorized as local and distributed. Local transactions have only one resource manager. In a local transaction, the transaction manager and resource manager are often indistinguishable, such as a standard JDBC connection to database through a DataSource. Figure 22.3 shows some local transactions. The transactions are local to the resource managers rather than encompassing multiple resource managers.

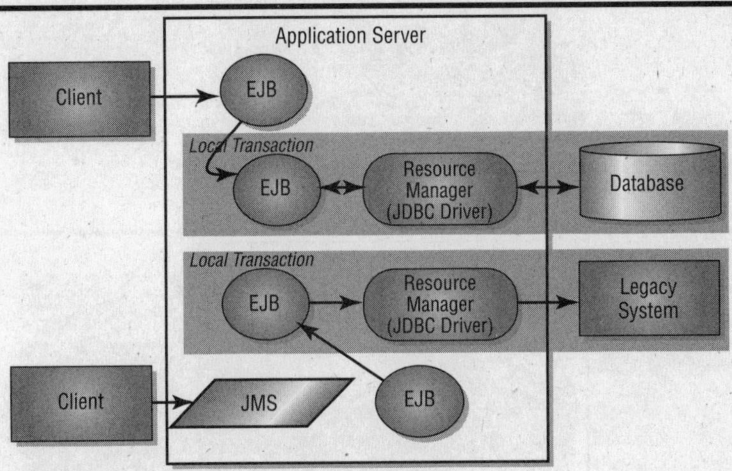

FIGURE 22.3: EJBs using local transactions

A DataSource in J2EE is a serialized reference for obtaining a database connection. This reference abstracts the client use of the database connection from dependence upon whether the connection is obtained from a pool of connections or a single connection. Figure 22.4 shows a DataSource and connection pool of JDBC drivers. Each JDBC driver is a resource manager.

Distributed transactions can span multiple resources, enabling multiple resources to participate in the same transaction. Not only can distributed transactions support multiple resource managers, such as database connections, but also different types of resource managers such as transacted JMS sessions, transactional connectors to legacy systems, and so on, all within the same transaction. Figure 22.5 contains a couple of distributed transactions. Each transaction can have multiple resource managers participating.

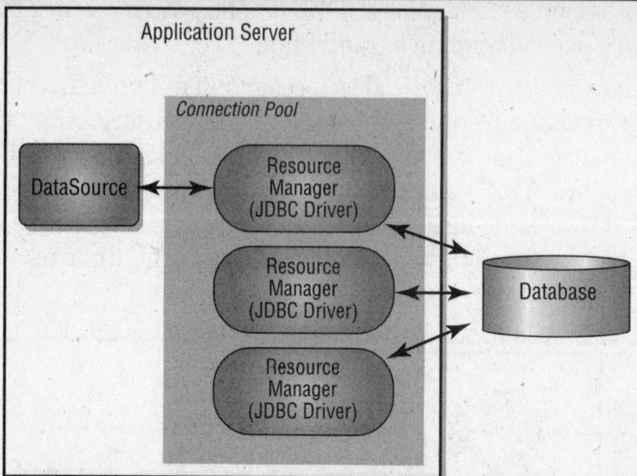

FIGURE 22.4: JDBC connections are resource managers

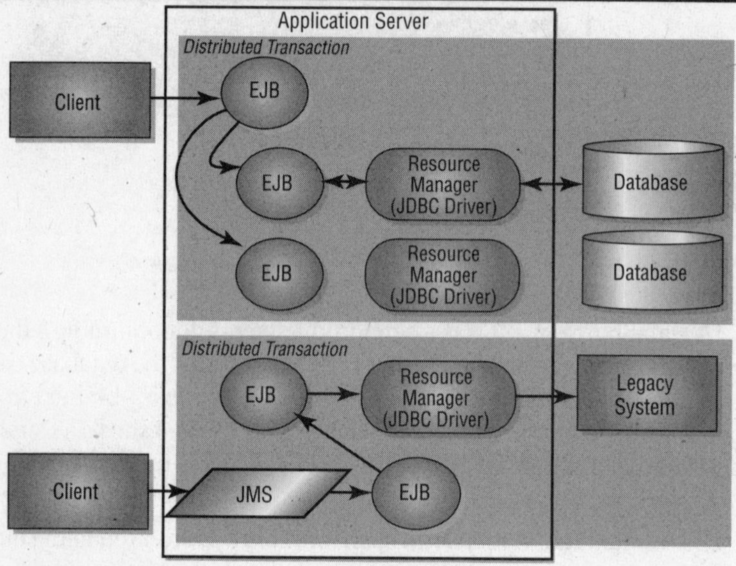

FIGURE 22.5: EJBs using distributed transactions

For database participation in distributed transactions, the transactional DataSource (or TXDataSource) is needed in CMP or BMP entity beans, or session beans using JDBC access. The TXDataSource is used similar to the DataSource, but supports distributed transactions via the XA/AX protocol.

```
DataSource supporting local transaction:
  Context jndi = new InitialContext();
  DataSource ds =(DataSource)
jndi.lookup("java:comp/env/jdbc/MyDataSource");
  Connection conn = ds.getConnection();
```

Here is an example of TXDataSource supporting distributed transaction:

```
  Context jndi = new InitialContext();
  TXDataSource ds = (TXDataSource)
jndi.lookup("java:comp/env/jdbc/MyTxDataSource");
  Connection conn = ds.getConnection();
```

The Two-Phase Commit

To support a distributed transaction, the transaction and resource managers communicate using the XA protocol. This protocol supports a two-phase commit, which will be described. First, look at the need for this two-phase commit process. Consider that you have an application server as your transaction manager, and connections to three databases that are your resource managers (via JDBC drivers). The transaction manager gets the command to commit (either from a client, bean, or container), and asks each resource manager (such as Database) to commit. The first one commits its data; the second one commits its data; but the third indicates that the user is not authorized to commit the data, and rolls back. The first two resource managers will not be able to rollback their changes because the data has already been committed. The transaction is therefore not an atomic transaction, and this is the problem. Figure 22.6 shows why local transactions have a problem with multiple resource managers.

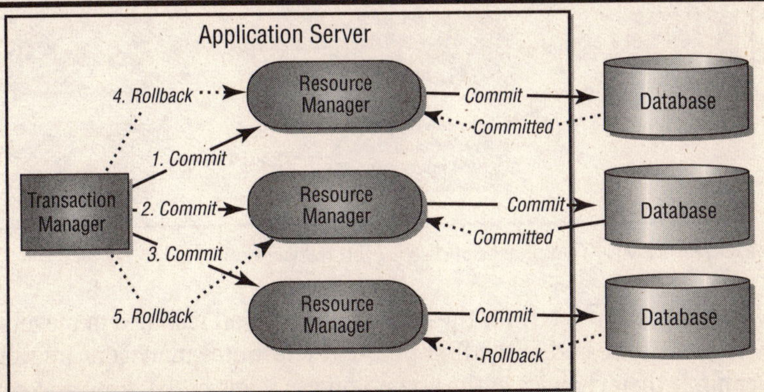

FIGURE 22.6: Problem with local transactions

To solve this problem, the transaction manager implements a two-phase commit via the XA protocol. The transaction model is divided into two distinct phases, which encompass transaction completion. The first phase is the preparation phase, and begins when commit is called on the UserTransaction. Phase one consists of prepare calls to all the resource managers. The resource managers must determine if they can commit their changes without actually committing the changes. If they can successfully commit changes, they return a ready status. If they cannot commit, they indicate a ready-to-rollback status. Figure 22.7 shows the two-phase commit. The transaction manager prepares each resource manager to commit before entering the commit phase.

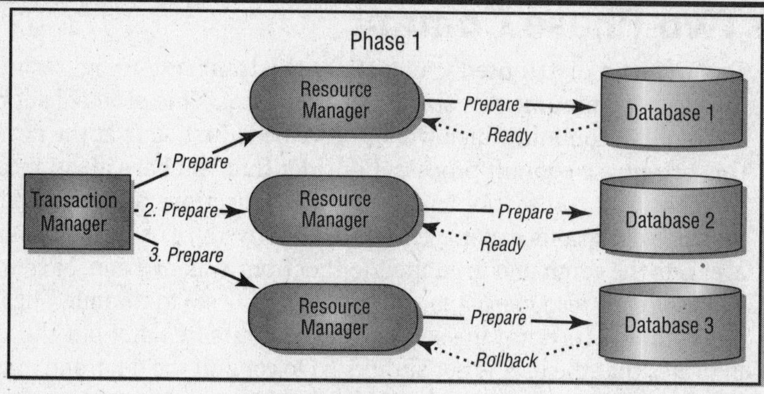

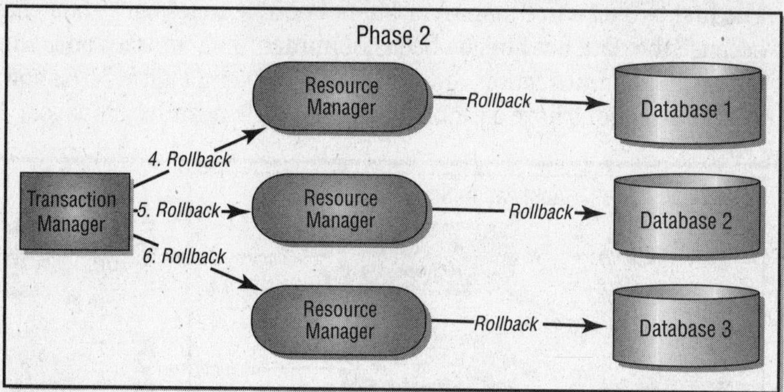

FIGURE 22.7: Two phases of distributed transaction

You are now ready for the second phase. If all resource managers are "ready" at the end of the first phase, the resource managers are called to commit their changes in the second phase. If any of the resource managers need to rollback, all resource managers are instructed to rollback changes in the second phase. Figure 22.8 shows the second or commit phase of a distributed transaction. Notice that the client really doesn't see the separation of phases going on behind the scenes.

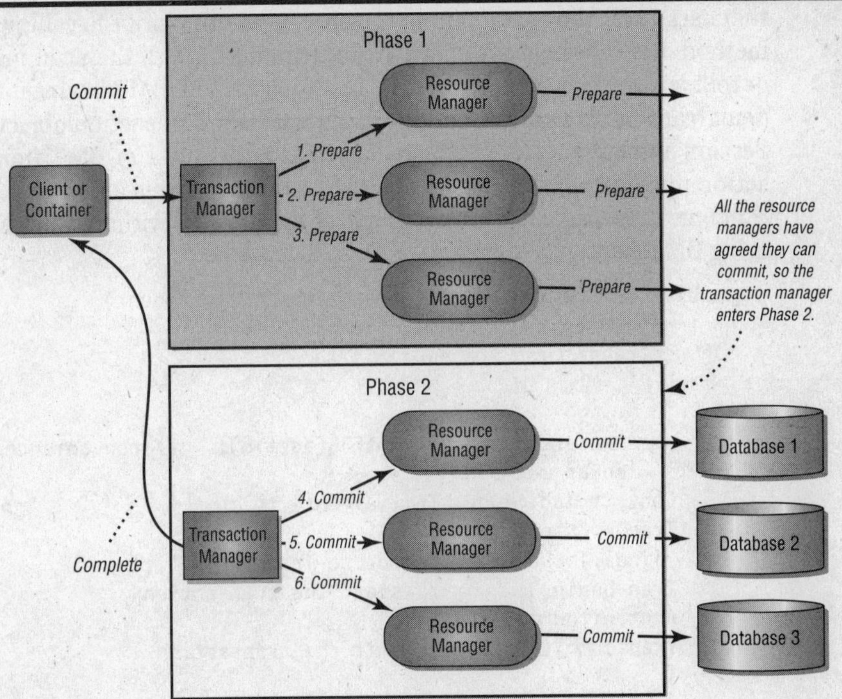

FIGURE 22.8: Phase two of distributed transaction

This two-phase commit process almost always eliminates atomicity problems in distributed transactions; however, it doesn't prevent problems from creeping up in some cases. Heuristic decisions are situations that occur when a resource manager decides to commit or rollback changes without authorization from the transaction manager. Heuristic exceptions occur to indicate problem situations in which heuristic decisions were made that impact atomicity of the transaction.

Transaction Management: CMT versus BMT

Enterprise JavaBeans (EJBs) support two types of transaction management: container managed transactions (CMT), and bean managed transactions (BMT). Container managed transactions are demarcated by the container. This eliminates the need to demarcate transactions in EJB client or bean code. Transaction management is instead configured via attributes that are assigned to EJB methods. When a method is called that uses CMT, the container may begin a transaction prior to calling the method depending on the configured attribute, and will then commit or rollback the transaction after the method is called. BMT beans must demarcate their own transactions using the User Transaction object. Session and message driven beans may use either CMT or BMT transaction management; however, entity bean transactions are always container managed. Here is an example of the AtmEJB withdraw method using BMT:

```
public void withdraw(String acctid, Double amount)
  {
  UserTransaction tran=null;
  try
    {
    Account acct = getAccountEJB(acctid);   // convenience
       lookup method
    Context jndi = new InitialContext();
    Tran = (UserTransaction)
      jndi.lookup("java:comp/UserTransaction");
    Tran.begin();      // start the transaction
    Acct.withdraw(amount);
    Tran.commit();   // commit the transaction
    }
  catch (AccountException e)
// this is the application exception
    {
    if (tran != null)
      {
    // rollback the transaction
      tran.rollback();
      }
    }
  }
```

To declare the transaction management type (CMT or BMT), use a tag in the ejb-jar.xml deployment descriptor. The `<transaction-type>` tag is available inside of `<session>` and `<message-driven>` bean tags in the descriptor. The possible values for this tag are Container for CMT, and

Bean for BMT. Here is an example of our AtmEJB session bean descriptor:

```
<ejb-jar>
  <enterprise-beans>
    ...
    <session>
      <ejb-name>AtmEJB</ejb-name>
      <remote>com.sybex.examples.Atm</remote>
      <home>com.sybex.examples.Atm</home>
      <ejb-class>com.sybex.examples.Atm</ejb-class>
      <transaction-type>Container</transaction-type>
      ...
    </session>
  </enterprise-beans>
</ejb-jar>
```

CMT Transaction Attributes

Container managed transactions are controlled by transaction attributes. This attribute is configured in the deployment descriptor, and associated with one or more EJB methods. The attribute then controls how the container will manage the user transaction for the configured methods. This enables different transaction configurations for each method or any group of methods on the EJB.

Each method can be marked with any of the following transaction attributes:

`NotSupported` The container suspends an existing user transaction, if one is active, for the duration of the called method. The user transaction remains suspended until the method completes and returns, at which point it is resumed. If no transaction is active, nothing is done and the method is executed outside of a transaction.

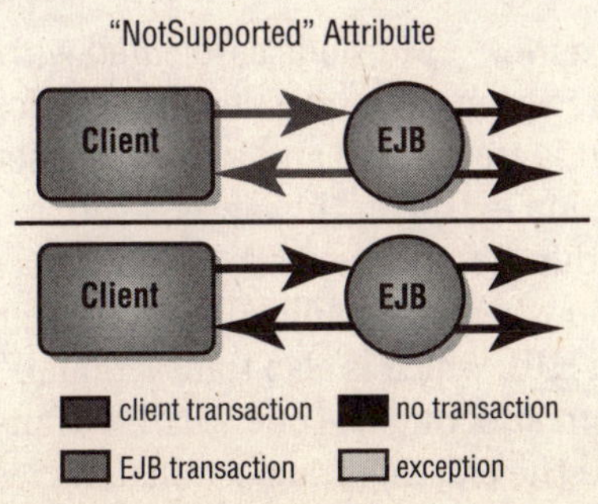

`Supports` Any methods configured with the `Supports` attribute do participate in an active transaction, if one exists; however, a method with this attribute does not require a transaction, and operates fine if no transaction is active.

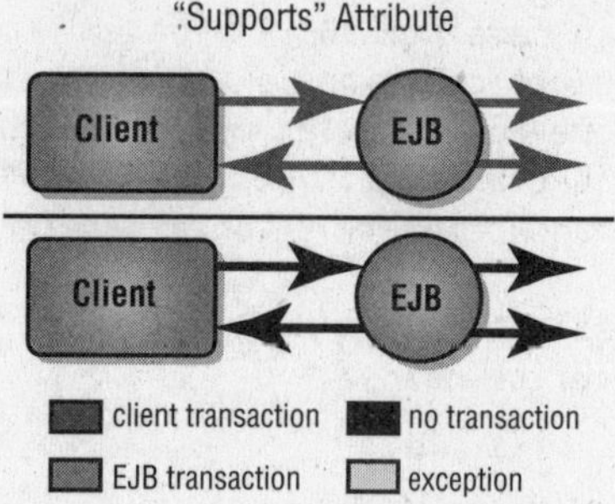

`Required` The `Required` attribute implicitly causes associated methods to be executed within a transaction. If the method is called with an active transaction, the method will be included in that transaction's scope. If, however, no transaction is active, the container starts a transaction for the duration of the method.

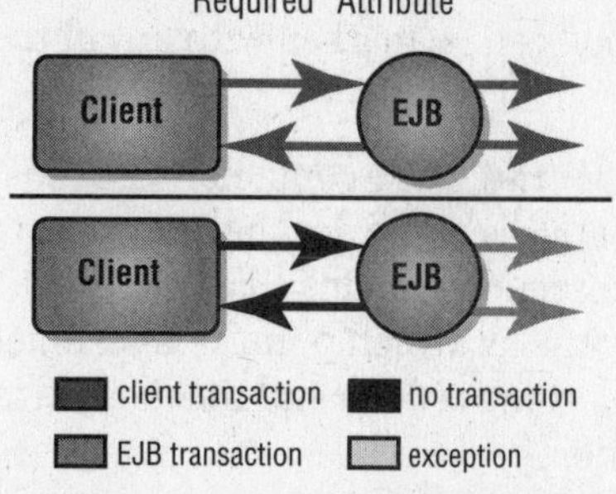

`RequiresNew` Methods associated with the `RequiresNew` attribute always require a new transaction. If a transaction is active, it is suspended and a new transaction is started. If no transaction exists on the method call, a transaction is started for the duration of the method call. This might be useful in a situation where a logging EJB, which is transactional, is called from an EJB, which is also transactional. To prevent the logging EJB from affecting the client EJB's transaction, you want to suspend the existing transaction and create a new transaction for the logging EJB by using the `RequiresNew` attribute.

"RequiresNew" Attribute

Client EJB

Client EJB

client transaction no transaction

EJB transaction exception

Mandatory The `Mandatory` attribute requires that associated methods must be called from an EJB client with an active transaction. The invoked method does participate in the active transaction. If no transaction is active, a javax.transaction .TransactionRequired-Exception is thrown to the client.

"Mandatory" Attribute

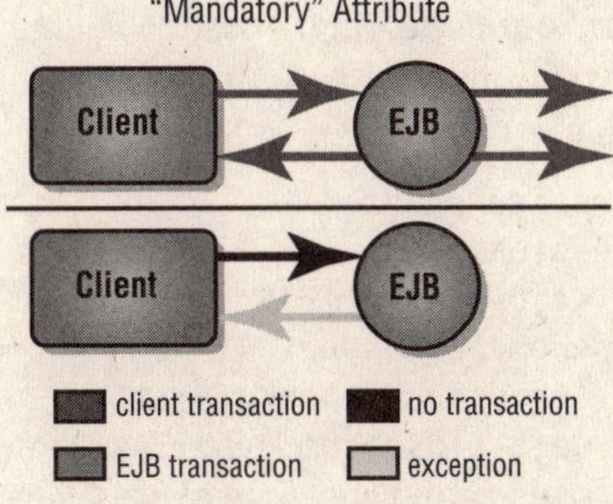

Never The `Never` attribute indicates that the associated method(s) must never be called from an EJB client with an active transaction. If the EJB client has an active transaction, an exception is thrown to them by the container. If no transaction is active, the method performs as expected.

"Never" Attribute

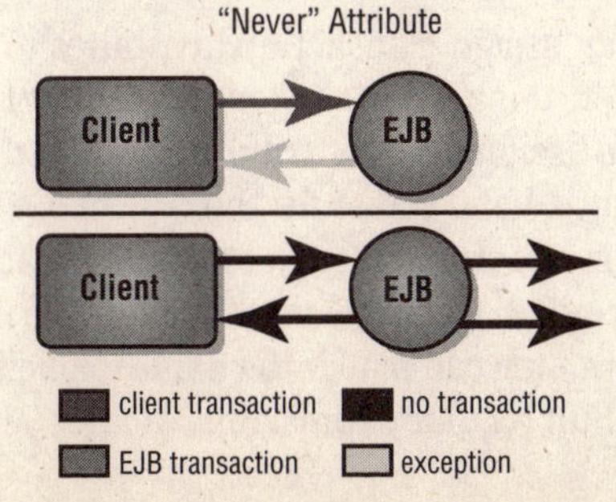

Transaction Attribute Suggestions

The EJB 2.0 specification suggests that entity beans use only the `Required`, `RequiresNew`, and `Mandatory` attributes. This is largely to ensure that all database access occurs inside a transaction. In fact, the `Never`, `Supports`, and `NotSupported` are optional for CMP entity bean support in application servers. Consult your vendor's documentation for more details on which attributes are supported.

Message driven beans may also declare only `NotSupported` or `Required` transaction attributes. Other attributes apply to client initiated transactions, and do not make sense for MDBs.

Configuring CMT EJB Transactions

Now that transaction attributes have been discussed, this section will cover some examples of how to configure these attributes in the deployment descriptor. The transaction type is specified in the bean entity with the `<transaction-type>` tag. Possible values are Container for container managed transactions, or Bean for bean managed transactions.

```
<ejb-jar>
   <enterprise-beans>
      <session>
         <ejb-name>AtmEJB</ejb-name>
         <home>com.sybex.AtmHome</home>
         <remote>com.Atm</remote>
         <ejb-class>com.sybex.AtmBean</ejb-class>
         <session-type>Stateless</session-type>
         <transaction-type>Container</transaction-type>
      </session>
   </enterprise-beans>
   <assembly-descriptor>
      ...
   </assembly-descriptor>
</ejb-jar>
```

Now we can assign transaction attributes to methods by using the `<container-transaction>` tag in the `<assembly-descriptor>` element. This example assigned the attribute `Required` to all the methods in the remote interface. Valid values for the `<method-intf>` tag are Remote, Local, and Home for selecting by each of the interfaces. If the `<method-intf>` tag is not included, methods match on all the interfaces for the EJB. The `<method-name>` tag can match the name explicitly or use basic wildcarding using the *. Full regular expressions are not yet supported.

```
<ejb-jar>
   <enterprise-beans>
      <session>
         <ejb-name>AtmEJB</ejb-name>
         ...
         <transaction-type>Container</transaction-type>
      </session>
   </enterprise-beans>
   <assembly-descriptor>
      <container-transaction>
         <method>
            <ejb-name>AtmEJB</ejb-name>
            <method-intf>Remote</method-intf>
            <method-name>*</method-name>
         </method>
         <trans-attribute>Required</trans-attribute>
      </container-transaction>
   </assembly-descriptor>
</ejb-jar>
```

Application vs. System Exceptions

Exceptions thrown during the method will determine whether the container does a commit or rollback when using CMT. A commit is done by the container if no exceptions are thrown. A system exception is defined as an exception that extends java.lang.RuntimeException or java.rmi .RemoteException. If a system exception is thrown, the container will rollback the transaction automatically at the end of the method. This is done because a system exception indicates that an unrecoverable error occurred during execution.

An application exception is defined as an exception that does not extend java.lang.RuntimeException or java.rmi.RemoteException. If an application exception is thrown, the container will commit the transaction upon completion of the EJB method. It is the responsibility of the EJB developer to cause a rollback if they desire on any application exceptions. This may be done by catching the desired application exception. If you are using BMT, you can call the `setRollbackOnly()` on the `UserTransaction` as shown (AtmBean.java):

```
public void withdraw(String acctid, Double amount)
  {
  try
    {
```

```
    // convenience lookup method
    Account acct = getAccountEJB(acctid);
    }
  catch (AccountException e)
    {
    // this is the application exception
    // container will now rollback transaction
    context.setRollBackOnly(true);
    }
  }
```

If you are using CMT, you can call the setRollbackOnly() on the SessionContext, EntityContext, or MessageDrivenContext depending on your type of EJB.

User Transaction API

Within the EJB model, each client has a specific user transaction instance. Because no transaction nesting is supported, each EJB client will have only one `UserTransaction` object. This can be obtained via a JNDI lookup.

```
    Context jndi = new InitialContext();
    UserTransaction tran = (UserTransaction)
  jndi.lookup("java:comp/UserTransaction");
```

Explicit developer interaction is accomplished via the `javax.transaction.UserTransaction` interface. This interface contains the following methods:

`void begin() throws IllegalStateException, SystemException` Begins the transaction. The thread executing this method is associated with the current transaction, and must complete the transaction before a new transaction is started. An `IllegalStateException` is thrown if this thread is already associated with a transaction. A `SystemException` is thrown if the transaction manager encounters an error.

`void commit throws IllegalStateException, SystemException` Completes the transaction associated with the current thread. The current thread is then no longer associated with a transaction. The same exceptions apply as with the `begin()` method. Also, a `TransactionRolledBackException` can be thrown to indicate that the transaction manager was unable to commit the transaction and instead has rolled it back. A `HeuristicRollbackException` indicates that heuristic decisions were made by one or more resources to roll back the transactions. A `HeuristicMixedException` indicates that heuristic decisions were made by resources to both rollback and commit the transaction, and atomicity has been compromised.

`int getStatus()` This method returns an integer that can be compared with the javax.transaction.Status interface to determine the current state of the user transaction. These values are:

- STATUS_ACTIVE - is active
- STATUS_COMMITED - has been committed
- STATUS_COMMITING - is in process of being committed
- STATUS_MARKED_ROLLBACK - has been marked for rollback (such as Using setRollbackOnly())
- STATUS_NO_TRANSACTION - no active transaction is associated with user
- STATUS_PREPARED - transaction has been prepared (done with phase one)
- STATUS_PREPARING - currently in phase one of a two-phase commit
- STATUS_ROLLEDBACK - outcome has been decided as a rollback
- STATUS_ROLLING_BACK - in process of rolling back
- STATUS_UNKNOWN - status cannot be determined (subsequent calls will likely return actual status)

`void rollback() throws IllegalStateException, SecurityException, SystemException` This method rolls back the transaction. All changes during the transaction are rolled back.

`void setRollbackOnly() throws IllegalStateException, SystemException` This method marks the transaction for rollback, but does not immediately roll back the transaction. This is useful in CMT transactions where a bean needs to indicate a rollback, but needs to let the container actually rollback the transaction. BMT beans should not use this method.

`void setTransactionTimeout(int seconds) throws SystemException` This method sets the life span of a transaction. The transaction must complete before the indicated seconds, or the transaction is automatically rolled back. If not called, the default timeout of the transaction manager is used. Consult your application server vendor documentation to determine actual default.

Transaction Isolation Level

The transaction isolation level restricts access to resource manager changes in one transaction from another transaction. As an example, imagine an ATM has a resource manager to an Oracle database containing account balance information. If a customer withdraws $100 from their account at the same time their spouse withdraws $100 from the joint account, two transactions occur simultaneously. The first transaction will read the account balance, subtract 100, and write the account balance. You need to avoid the situation where the spouse's transaction reads the account balance after the customer's transaction reads the balance but before it writes the new balance, or if the spouse's transaction reads changes from the first transaction before the first transaction rolls back its changes. If this is allowed to happen, the customer's withdrawal will be lost even though they did get their cash, or it will be recorded even though they didn't get their cash.

The EJB specification does not define an API for managing isolation level. This is left up to the resource managers. It is then possible to have a different isolation level for each resource manager involved in a transaction. Isolation is defined in terms of conditions that describe what can happen when two transactions access the same data. The possible values are dirty reads, repeatable reads, and phantom reads.

Dirty Reads A dirty read occurs when the second transaction reads uncommitted changes made by the first transaction. In the ATM example, if the second transaction reads the balance written by the first transaction, only to have the first transaction rollback changes, it is left with data that is "dirty." This data was never actually written to the database and is invalid. The second transaction will not adjust for this rollback and, therefore, the balance will be in error. By allowing "dirty reads" you allow one transaction to read data from another transaction before it is committed. This reduces transaction isolation in order to gain performance.

Repeatable Reads A repeatable read occurs when data read within a transaction is guaranteed to not change if read again in the same transaction. In other words, a second transaction cannot change the value of a subsequent read within the first transaction. This is generally accomplished by locking read data against changes, or creating a snapshot of read data to ensure a repeatable read.

Phantom Reads A phantom read occurs when the first transaction can detect new records added by a second transaction. For example, if the first transaction queries for all products in a catalog, a second transaction inserts a new product. The first transaction re-submits the query, and the phantom product appears.

Serializable This is the most restrictive isolation level, which causes all read and update accesses to be exclusive. A second transaction can neither read nor update data that is being accessed by the first transaction until the first transaction completes.

These various levels of isolation are useful in balancing consistency with performance. JDBC has a method on the java.sql.Connection that allows setting the isolation level. The method is `setTransactionIsolation(int)`.

```
DataSource ds = (javax.sql.DataSource)
jndi.lookup("java:comp/env/jdbc/catalogDS");
Connection conn = ds.getConnection();
Conn.setTransactionIsolation(
Connection.TRANSACTION_SERIALIZABLE);
```

Transaction Scope

The scope of a transaction includes all EJB invocations that participate in the transaction. Because several transaction attributes support the existing user transaction, it is common to architect transactions to model user requests. It is often appropriate to start the transaction as early in the user request as possible. This improves transaction granularity, and effectively models transactional user requests. Web applications are a good fit to this model because the HTTP protocol (and therefore their requests) are stateless. It is useful to create a session bean façade that effectively starts one transaction per request. Lower-level EJBs can then support the existing transaction using the `Supports`, `Requires`, or `Mandatory` attributes to effectively accept or reject each request at the HTTP request granularity. Designing transactions to span HTTP requests is heavily discouraged because the user's continued dialog is not predictable, nor reliable.

Session Synchronization Interface

Because entity beans are intended to model data and their functionality is largely implemented using database drivers, which are resource managers, they naturally participate in our distributed transactions. Stateful session beans may also participate in distributed transactions, but their state is not encompassed by the transaction; therefore, a rollback will not revert to a stateful session bean's state. To accomplish this, you must implement the javax.ejb.SessionSynchronization interface.

This interface contains methods that you must implement. These are hooks that get called automatically on the EJB instance to provide the ability for you to manage state appropriately. They include:

`void afterBegin()` The container calls this method immediately after the start of a new transaction. This is a good place to store attribute values that may need to be reverted if the transaction is rolled back.

`void beforeCompletion()` This method is called by the container immediately before the completion of the transaction. Any resources accessed in this method will participate in the transaction. This can be a good place to perform any state checks that may cause a rollback. This method can call the `rollback()` method by obtaining the `UserTransaction` object as mentioned earlier in this chapter. This is also a good place to perform any updates to the database if there are any so that they will be included with the transaction commit.

`void afterCompletion(boolean committed)` This method is called by the container after the completion of the transaction. The committed argument is true if the transaction was committed, and false if the transaction was rolled back. This is the place to revert any attributes that may need rolled back.

The only transaction attributes that are valid when using the SessionSynchronization interface are `Requires`, `RequiresNew`, and `Mandatory`.

EJB Security

The EJB security model supports both implicit and explicit means for access control. This security model is focused upon making component security easy to build as well as configurable by an application assembler or deployer. The model also is determined to allow EJBs to operate across multiple EJB application servers that use different security mechanisms.

Security is often divided into authentication, authorization, and encryption. The EJB security model currently addresses authentication and authorization. *Authentication* involves identifying who the caller of the EJB is. This involves checking the caller identity against a security realm. The security realm is the mechanism for managing security principals. These principals are individuals or groups that may be identified by user ID and password. Many types of security realms are often supported, such as file-based, database, LDAP, NT, Unix, or custom realms. The calling EJB principal is identified by the user and password on the JNDI lookup. Encryption involves the scrambling of data sent to and from distributed objects, such as EJBs. EJBs do support encryption via the IIOP protocol using the Secure Socket Layer (SSL), largely since IIOP supports transport over SSL.

Security roles may be defined to help simplify and define security assignment groupings. A security role is simply a semantic grouping of permissions that are used by a type of user of the application. Method permissions can then be assigned to each defined security role. These method permissions can apply to home, remote, or local interface methods, and are configured in the ejb-jar.xml deployment descriptor. Figure 22.9 shows how EJB applications enable application-specific roles that assist in mapping EJB methods to users and groups in security realms.

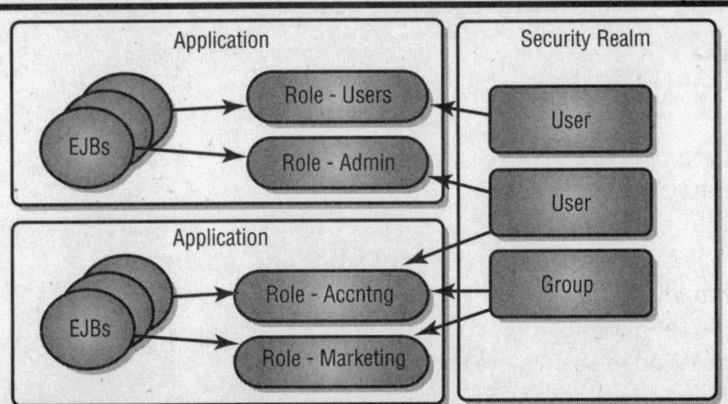

FIGURE 22.9: Role-based EJB security

Container Managed Security (CMS)

It is suggested that developers use container managed security whenever possible. Similar to other container managed services, container managed security is configured in the deployment descriptors and then applied by the container automatically at runtime. To use container managed security, you must:

1) declare security role names

2) associate bean methods to roles

3) map roles to principals

The first step is to declare security role names in our ejb-jar.xml deployment descriptor:

```
<ejb-jar>
  <enterprise-beans>
    ...
  </enterprise-beans>
  <assembly-descriptor>
    <security-role>
      <description> An ATM user</description>
      <role-name>user</role-name>
    </security-role>
    <!-- more security role definitions go here →
  </assembly-descriptor>
</ejb-jar>
```

Next, associate bean methods to roles. The first method permission shown in the following code grants access to all home and remote interface methods to the `user` role. The second method permission shows how to grant access only to the home interface `create` method with an int parameter, to the "`admin` role. This is done with the `<method-permission>` tag:

```
<ejb-jar>
  <enterprise-beans>
    ...
  </enterprise-beans>
  <assembly-descriptor>
    ...
    <!-- more security role definitions go here →
    <method-permission>
      <role-name>user</role-name>
      <method-name>*</method-name>
    </method-permission>
```

```
    <method-permission>
      <role-name>admin</role-name>
      <method-intf>Home</method-intf>
      <method-name>create</method-name>
      <method-params>
        <method-param>int</method-param>
      </method-params>
    </method-permission>
  </assembly-descriptor>
</ejb-jar>
```

The final step is to map security realm principals to the security role(s). This is done in the application server specific deployment descriptor, and is vendor specific. Consult your application server documentation for the XML tag syntax for mapping principals to security roles.

Bean Managed Security

Similar to the other services, bean managed security allows the bean to include security code inside the bean class. This is less portable and requires more work, but provides for more granularity in security checks, such as on a section of code within a method. You will use a combination of deployment descriptor configuration and bean code to do this. Two methods are provided for checking bean managed security in the EJB. These methods are on the `EJBContext` instance that is passed into your EJB via `setSessionContext()`, `setEntityContext()`, or `setMessageDrivenContext()`. If you are going to use bean managed security, you are going to have to save a reference to the context in those methods. Your `EJBContext` methods provide both a role-based method and direct principal access. Here are the methods:

`java.security.Principal getCallerPrincipal()` This gives direct access to the principal for the calling thread obtained from the security realm. You might use this if you decide not to use security roles at all.

`boolean isCallerInRole(String rolename)` This is a convenience method that performs the security check against a role, rather than the principal directly. This is useful for using bean managed security, or a hybrid approach that leverages security roles (defined in the deployment descriptor) with security checks in the bean code.

Notice that the management type for security was not specified. This enables you to use both container and bean managed security in your application. Container security checks are activated by the `<method-permissions>` tag. You can still access the `isCallerInRole()` method even if the container applied a security check before invoking the EJB method.

What's Next

Enterprise applications are transactional by nature, and EJB transactions provide an effective means of supporting robust distributed transactions. The result is that EJB applications may be highly transactional without much additional developer effort. Transaction design, however, can determine the performance of your enterprise application, so care should be taken when designing transactions.

Enterprise applications require security to prevent improper access and hampering of information. EJBs do enable the configuration of security down to the component level. By having a good grasp of how to configure security on your components, much value can be achieved with little effort. J2EE provides the mechanism to separate how security works from how you access and use it. A good balance of configuration and sparse use of security code can provide a portable and highly effective application, or framework of components.

The configurable container transaction and security services are not the only functions provided by EJB containers. The next chapter presents the EJB environment, also configured within the deployment descriptors and very useful to EJB components. Several client and design issues are also covered.

Chapter 23

EJB Environment, Client, and Design Issues

A better understanding of the EJB component environment will lead to better J2EE applications. This chapter takes a look at some of the EJB environment facilities, types of deployments, and some design patterns used in J2EE applications.

Featured in this chapter:

- Enterprise JavaBeans Environment
- EJB Deployment
- Client Issues
- EJB Application Design

Written for *Enterprise Java™ 2, J2EE™ 1.3 Complete* by Vince E. Marco

Enterprise JavaBeans Environment

Enterprise JavaBeans have an environment that is configurable within the deployment descriptors, and accessible to the component at runtime. These facilities are important and necessary for creating configurable, flexible, and loose-coupled EJB applications. Prior to EJB 1.1, an EJB component relied mostly upon the EJBContext object for accessing its environment. With EJB 1.1 and later, the component environment was expanded beyond the EJBContext and into the environmcnt naming context or ENC. This ENC is a space in JNDI that is created for each component, and explicitly accessed with a relative JNDI lookup. This provides access to resource references, EJB references (both local and remote), and environment entries. Next take a look at what these resource references, EJB references, and environment entries are, and what they can do for you.

Resource References

Most enterprise applications require the accessing of resources, such as databases or legacy systems. The designers of Enterprise JavaBeans wanted these components to be able to avoid the configuration of resources inside of component code. They wanted to provide a mechanism for moving resource binding out to the deployment descriptors so that resource configuration could be redirected within the deployment descriptors instead of requiring code to be recompiled and tested.

For example, if an EJB requires a connection to a database, it could be hard coded with the JDBC driver, URL, and other configuration settings for that connection. This approach is undesirable because changing the database location or type now involves modifying the code. You can instead place the JDBC driver details in the configuration of a JDBC DataSource in the server configuration files. When you configure the DataSource, you assign a JNDI name to it. The EJB can then look up that DataSource by the JNDI name, and call the getConnection method on the DataSource without specifying any JDBC driver specific settings. Changing the database driver-specific settings now requires only changing a setting in the server configuration, not in any number of EJBs; however, if you need to switch to a completely different DataSource with a different JNDI name, you would have to change the JNDI name in all the EJBs that look up that DataSource. It would seem, therefore, that an alias JNDI name for the real DataSource JNDI name might be helpful. Figure 23.1

shows an EJB using "hard-wired" DataSource accesses. Any changes to the DataSource name or location requires a recompile of the EJB.

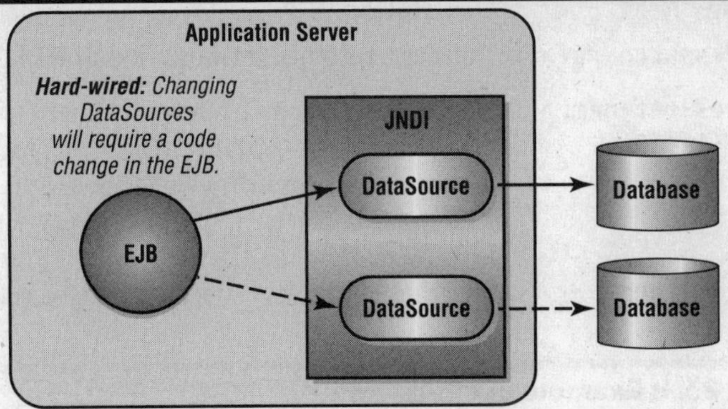

FIGURE 23.1: Using DataSources directly

To resolve the problems arising from direct lookup of DataSource objects (and other resources) from within EJBs, resource references are provided. *Resource references* are entries into each component's environment within the deployment descriptors. The application code accesses the DataSource by using the resource reference, which redirects JNDI to point to the actual DataSource bound within JNDI. This allows an application deployer to change the location of a resource for a single component within the deployment descriptor. Figure 23.2 shows a DataSource access using a resource reference. This is especially useful in eliminating recompiles when deploying to application servers from different vendors.

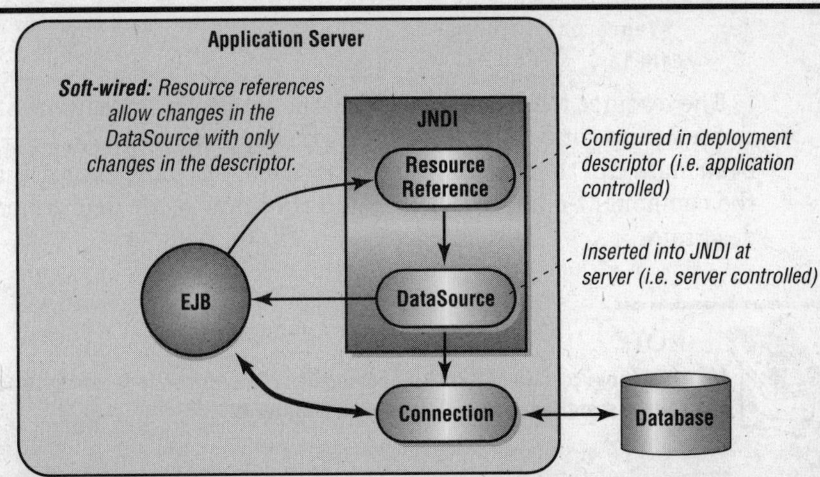

FIGURE 23.2: Using DataSource via resource reference

Part IV

The following tags are used in the ejb-jar.xml deployment descriptor to define resource references. See Listing 23.1 for an example.

Tag	Description
`<resource-ref>`	Defines a resource reference for an EJB
`<res-ref-name>`	Name of the resource reference (client uses: "`java:comp/env/jdbc/CatalogDS`" in JNDI lookup of DataSource)
`<res-type>`	Fully qualified class name of resource
`<res-auth>`	Specifies container- or bean-managed security

Listing 23.1: Example of ejb-jar.xml

```
<ejb-jar>
  <enterprise-beans>
     <session>
        <ejb-name>CatalogItem</ejb-name>
           ...
           <resource-ref>
              <description>The Catalog DataSource
                 </description>
              <res-ref-name>jdbc/CatalogDS</res-ref-name>
              <res-type>x.sql.DataSource</res-type>
              <res-auth>Container</res-auth>
           </resource-ref>
     </session>
  </enterprise-beans>
</ejb-jar>
```

The resource reference is bound to the actual JNDI location within the server-specific XML descriptor. The implementation in the EJB bean class can then access the DataSource normally, except using the component-relative JNDI lookup specified in the deployment descriptor.

NOTE

JNDI lookup code of DataSource and other resources, references, and environment entries is also discussed in Chapter 8.

EJB References

Because EJBs were used within larger and larger enterprise projects, it became common for an EJB to access other EJBs as a client. And just as with resources, EJBs needed a way to avoid tight-coupling of the components to enable frameworks of EJBs to be implemented on multiple application servers, and for multiple customers or projects. This is exactly what EJB references are designed to do.

EJB references are also defined in the deployment descriptors, and allow the JNDI lookups within the bean class implementation to look up an EJB by reference rather than absolute JNDI location. This provides some loose coupling between EJBs that is especially useful in supporting multiple application servers as well as providing the capability to redirect access from an EJB to another without recompiling. Figure 23.3 shows an example of EJB references. These references can point to EJBs inside the same application or those deployed in separate EJB applications.

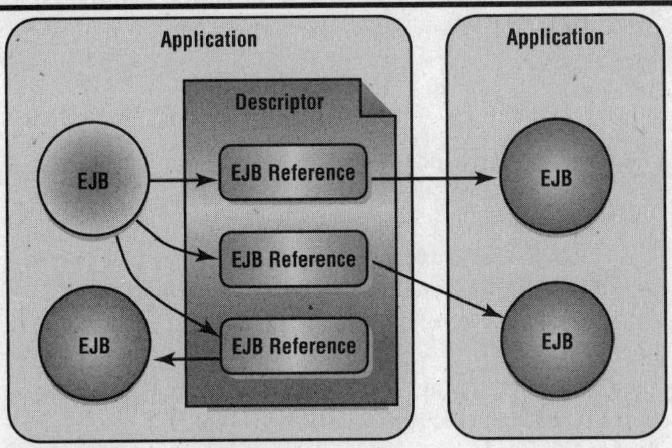

FIGURE 23.3: EJB References

The EJB references are defined in the ejb-jar.xml deployment descriptor using the following tags. See Listing 23.2 for an example.

Tag	Description
`<ejb-ref>`	Defines a remote ejb reference
`<ejb-local-ref>`	Defines a local ejb reference
`<ejb-ref-name>`	Name of the reference (used by client as `java:comp/env/ejb/CatalogItemLocal`)

Tag	Description
<ejb-ref-type>	EJB type (Session or Entity)
<home>	Class of remote home (used only within <ejb-ref>)
<local-home>	Class of local home (used only within <ejb-local-ref>)
<remote>	Class of remote interface (used only within <ejb-ref>)
<local>	Class of local interface (used only within <ejb-local-ref>)
<ejb-link>	<ejb-name> of bean in same JAR used when referenced EJB is in same JAR file

Listing 23.2: EJB reference example (ejb-jar.xml deployment descriptor)

```
<ejb-jar>
  <enterprise-beans>
    <session>
      <ejb-name>Catalog</ejb-name>
         ...
         <ejb-ref>
           <ejb-ref-name>ejb/CatalogItemLocal</ejb-ref-name>
           <ejb-ref-type>Entity</ejb-ref-type>
 <local-home>com.sybex.catalog.CatalogItemLocalHome
      </local-home>
   <local>com.sybex.catalog.CatalogItemLocal</local>
      <ejb-link>CatalogItemLocal</ejb-link>
    </resource-ref>
    </session>
  </enterprise-beans>
</ejb-jar>
```

Environment Entries

Along with access to resources and EJBs, the architects of J2EE also wanted to support the building of EJB components that were configurable. This is done via the use of *environment entries*. These entries are values bound at deployment time and accessed within the bean class implementation. Each component can access their environment with a relative JNDI lookup, which starts with java:comp/env. The java: indicates that you are looking up Java objects. The comp stands for component, and the env is the JNDI context that holds each component's environment entries. Resource and EJB references are environment entries, as well.

The environment supports the following types of entries: String, Integer, Long, Float, Double, Boolean, Byte, and Short. Each entry is defined within the beans `<session>`, `<entity>`, or `<message-driven>` element in the ejb-jar.xml descriptor. Each `<env-entry>` element contains three elements and one optional `<description>` element, as seen in Listing 23.3.

Listing 23.3: Environment entry example (ejb-jar.xml deployment descriptor)

```
<ejb-jar>
   <enterprise-beans>
      <session>
         <ejb-name>Catalog</ejb-name>
          ...
          <env-entry>
                <description>Maximum products per request
                   </description>
               <env-name>MaxProducts</env-name>
               <env-type>java.lang.Integer</env-type>
               <env-value>Container</env-value>
          </env-entry>
      </session>
   </enterprise-beans>
</ejb-jar>
```

The bean class methods may access the environment entries by obtaining them from JNDI.

```
Context  jndi = new InitialContext();
Integer  maxProducts =
   (Integer)jndi.lookup("java:comp/env/MaxProducts");
```

Any constant value in an EJB is a possible `<env-entry>`. It is good practice to use environment entries because it gives the deployer of your beans more flexibility and adaptability without requiring code to be recompiled and retested.

EJB Deployment

After EJB interfaces, classes, and deployment descriptors are written and compiled, the EJB application must be deployed into an application server. This deployment can take many forms, and triggers the loading and execution of the EJB business components. Several deployment types are supported by most application servers to accommodate the needs of specific development and production server environments. Figure 23.4 shows the EJB jar file deployment. When the jar file is deployed into the application server, the EJB home stub, resource and EJB references, and environment entries are placed in JNDI.

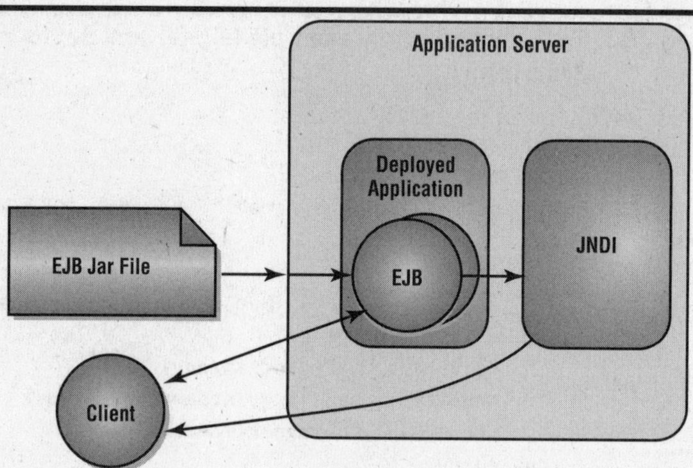

FIGURE 23.4: EJB jar file deployment

The vehicle for all EJB deployments is a Java archive (jar) file. This file is a standard zip archive that is created with the jar command. This jar file must contain a folder entry named META-INF at the root of the file containing the deployment descriptor XML files. This file also contains the class files nested within folders matching their fully qualified package declarations.

The EJB development needs to support easy and rapid deployment of EJB applications as developers code, configure, deploy, fix, and re-deploy their applications until they are ready to support users in a production server environment. This development environment has different and contrasting needs from the target production environment awaiting all EJB applications. This development environment operates most effectively using auto and hot deployment facilities. The production environment, however, is focused on channeling server resources to the application–instead of deployment–and supporting a static environment supporting infrequent and predictable application deployments. The following sections look at the various application deployment types supported by current J2EE application server products.

Auto Deployment

Auto deployment involves the monitoring of a folder or file system path by the application server. When new applications are put into the folder, the application server automatically deploys those applications and makes them available for use. Figure 23.5 shows an example of "auto" deployment supported by most J2EE application servers.

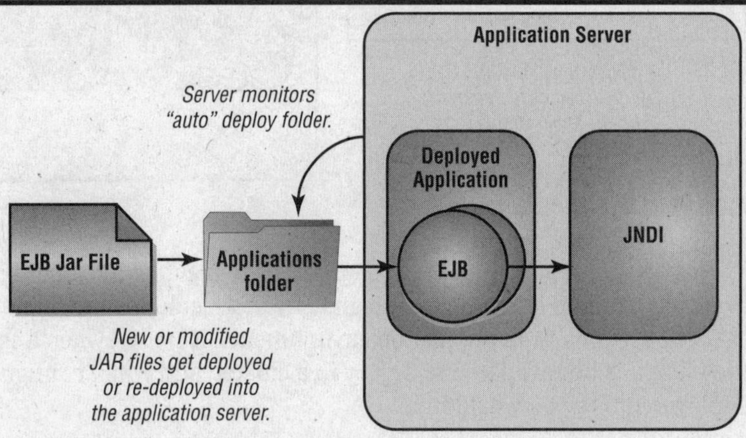

FIGURE 23.5: Automatic deployment

This type of deployment is widely supported by many of the application servers, and is most useful during the development stages of a project. This supports rapid redeployment with little developer involvement, and can be included into developer ANT- or IDE-based builds. The down side is that monitoring a folder takes server resources, and can propagate changes before they are intended. These are usually issues that make auto deployment a poor choice in a production server environment.

Hot Deployment

Hot deployment consists of the capability to deploy or re-deploy EJB applications without restarting the application server. Most servers do provide a Java-based command for hot-deploying applications to specific servers. This is useful in both development and production environments for controlling the deployment of applications, especially to a cluster of servers. Figure 23.6 shows an example of hot deployment. This usually requires a command be issued by the deployer.

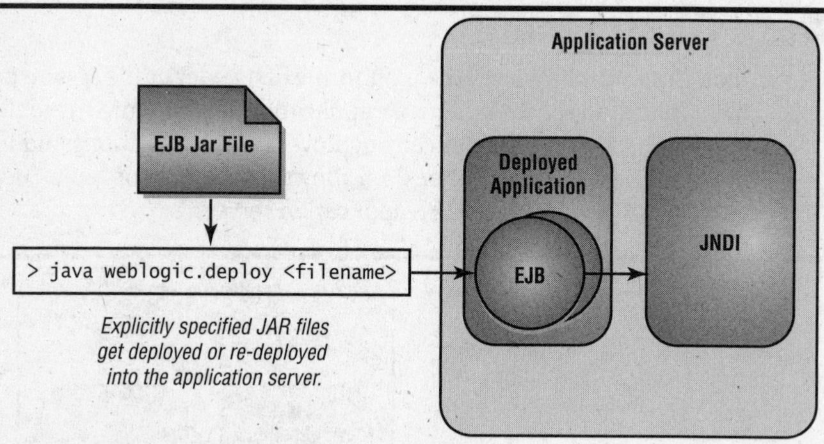

FIGURE 23.6: Hot deployment

Hot deployment is used in development when auto deployment is not available, or when it is easier to integrate the hot-deploy command into the build configuration. In production environments, it is used when a shared file system is not available to deploy in a cluster, and when configured deployment is not available.

Configured Deployment

Configured deployment separates deployment into registration and the actual deployment. Application configuration is usually done via an administration console or properties file. Some servers also require a restart for configuration changes to take effect, although this is usually found on older versions of application servers. One advantage of configured deployment is that the application can usually be configured to run from any absolute file path, and doesn't require copying a folder or deployment archive file to a specific place.

Deployment Features

Many application servers offer various features during deployment. These features target various aspects that ease deployment or development tasks. JBoss, an open source application serve, supports the automatic assignment of the `<jndi-name>` element in the server XML deployment descriptor. During development this is often the only entry needed in the server-specific deployment descriptor, and this feature allows the developer to often defer creation of the server-specific deployment descriptor until later in development. JBoss's use of dynamic proxy RMI stub generation eliminates the need for an ejbc compile step.

NOTE

The "ejbc" command is a step that generates the classes needed for remote RMI access to the EJB. It also checks the validity of the deployment descriptors and Java classes.

Weblogic, a product by BEA Systems, supports auto creation of the generated RMI stubs and skeletons needed for deployment of the EJB. Weblogic will also compile .java files if needed, reducing the development cycle turnaround time.

These are only a couple of examples of application server features that ease the development and deployment of EJBs. Consult your application server documentation for the specific types of deployments and deployment features supported.

Enterprise Archive Files

EJBs are always deployed in JAR (Java archive) files, as specified in Chapter 20. Enterprise archive (EAR) files were added to the J2EE 1.2 specification, however, and provide an application bundle that can contain web and EJB applications. The direct contents of an enterprise archive are JAR files (EJB applications) and WAR files (web applications).

This enables the deployment of an enterprise application, which combines web applications with EJB applications to produce complete component frameworks with working web-user interfaces.

Client Issues

There are several issues to consider when designing and building EJB clients. The first is perhaps what kind of client to build. While it is clear that the web browser has become a popular vehicle for delivering enterprise applications, there are many situations where a rich application client is desired, especially with technologies such as Java WebStart enabling automatic distribution and launching of these clients. The following sections look at each type of application and considerations for using EJBs.

Web Applications

Web applications are the most common EJB client application type. This generally involves server-side client code accessing EJBs from Java Server Pages (JSPs) and servlets. Three concerns immediately come to light when building web applications: optimizing performance, planning for scalability, and managing servlet and JSP complexity.

Optimizing Performance

Because the web can present an application to an incredibly wide audience, and also because Java is an interpreted language, you need to consider performance on every application you build. Of course you need to do the standard web application tasks, such as minimizing the number of web requests, but you can also optimize your EJB designs. You first want to use stateless session beans and message driven beans/JMS whenever you can. These are your best performing components, and MDBs can help to smooth out the peaks for requests that exceed your capacity during heavy bursts of application usage. You also want to keep transactions as coarse-grained as possible. Because users make requests via HTTP (which is a stateless protocol), it is often useful to call into a stateless session bean to effectively begin a container-managed transaction that largely mirrors each logical HTTP request. Effective use of local interfaces for components can also optimize their performance, but this needs to be balanced with the next issue.

Planning for Scalability

To foster reuse of our application, you want to be able to scale this application to a broad audience. The web certainly provides access for this broad audience, but you must be ready to scale your server deployment.

This means you must design and build your applications to enable running in a clustered environment. The first step in planning for clustering is to architect applications using the J2EE Blueprint. This Blueprint focuses on identifying the dependent layers of a J2EE application. After your layers are visible, make sure that all business components called by the user interface layer use remote interfaces. Components that are not exposed to the user interface layer (such as called from other EJBs in the business layer) should generally use local interfaces. Figure 23.7 shows the multiple tiers of J2EE enterprise applications as specified in the J2EE Blueprint.

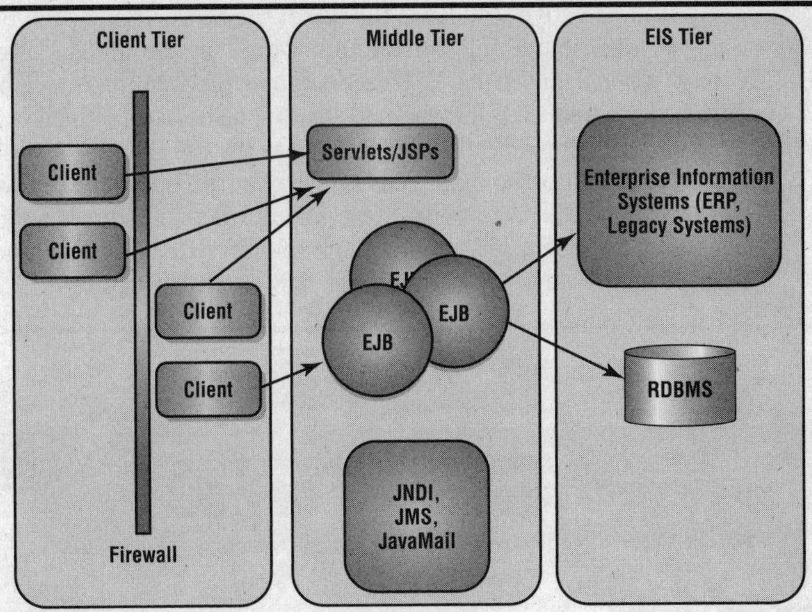

FIGURE 23.7: J2EE Blueprint application tiers

NOTE

The J2EE Blueprints are available at `http://java.sun.com/blueprints/`.

Managing Servlet and JSP Complexity

A key factor in designing and building effective EJB applications is to minimize client complexity. The easier it is to call your business components, the more reuse you will see between projects. One common pitfall in J2EE web applications is to embed growing amounts of Java code into JSPs. Strategies for minimizing this complexity and reducing the amount of Java code involve the use of a Service Locator Pattern, effectively hiding the EJB access code from the JSP. This can be done in basic JavaBean classes, or in custom tag libraries (see Chapters 4 and 7).

NOTE

The Service Locator Pattern is one of the Sun Java Center Patterns available at `http://developer.java.sun.com/developer/technicalArticles/J2EE/patterns`.

Another effective strategy is the use of the Struts framework. Struts is a frcc, open source JSP/servlet framework managed by The Apache Group. When using struts, EJB access can be put into the Action and Form classes, reducing JSP views to struts specific tags (defined in a tag library). This approach effectively combines the use of Java classes and tag libraries while also taking advantage of a free, open-source framework. Perhaps the biggest advantage, though, is that Struts is rapidly becoming a widely used and known framework by J2EE developers. Figure 23.8 shows a web MVC (model-view-controller) pattern.

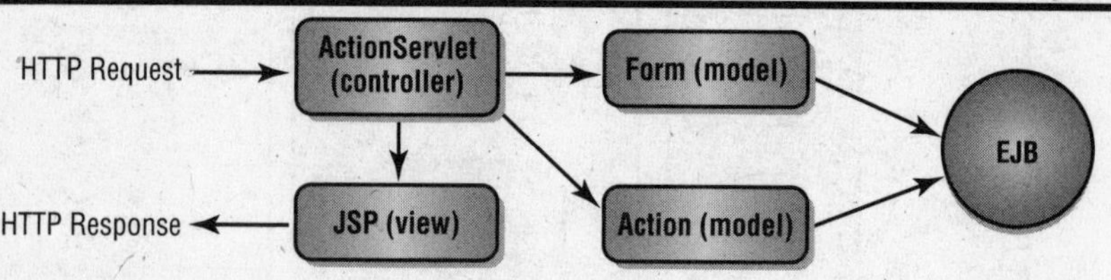

FIGURE 23.8: Model-View-Controller pattern in J2EE

NOTE

The Struts project can be found at `http://jakarta.apache.org/struts/`.

Applets are another consideration for EJB web interfaces. Initially, applets promised the capability for applications to extend the browser through both visual and non-visual Java components served up to the browser along with the application's HTML and images. While applet usage has been limited, it is starting to show up in many situations within a hybrid approach. This often employs a tree navigation applet serving up HTML pages in a multi-framed web application. Your EJB access from the applet can be direct via RMI, or can be via HTTP/XML via a web service, running on the application server. The latter approach provides the advantage of XML messages and working across firewalls, if this is a requirement of the application.

Rich Client Applications

The resurgence of rich client enterprise applications stems from the limitations of the web browser user interface, and distribution technology such as Java WebStart and web services. Many enterprise applications require a more complex interaction with the user that doesn't lend itself to the stateless, hypertext-based interface of a web browser. Client-side validation and interactive user interfaces often require the use of JavaScript and/or applets that can make web applications more complex than a rich client application, while also sacrificing a robust user interface.

The main consideration for EJB access in a rich client application is determining access protocol. Because EJBs are distributed, a rich client can access the EJBs via RMI. Another approach that is rapidly gaining support is the wrapping of component access in a web service. The rich client then accesses a set of web services instead of directly accessing the EJBs, and all messages are then parsed and created using standard XML libraries within the application. The advantage of this approach is the decoupling of the application from the specific component lookup and Java interface/class dependence. The application uses UDDI instead for lookup of the web service, and parses XML messages instead of relying on specific EJB interfaces and parameter classes.

EJB Application Design

This chapter has mentioned several client issues associated with EJB applications, so it might be helpful to also identify several design patterns commonly used within EJB applications to address these and other situations. Design patterns are recurring relationships of the components that can consistently be applied to recurring design issues. Some of these patterns have been mentioned earlier in this chapter, and the following sections focus on a concise description and diagram of these patterns.

Session Façade

The *session façade* is perhaps the most popular pattern in EJB development. It can be applied to effectively address a number of issues in EJB applications. The session façade involves a layering of EJBs in which all external access is made explicitly through a set of stateless session beans. The session façade, shown in Figure 23.9, provides many values including:

- simplifying client access into the business model
- supporting separation of business logic from data access
- providing an explicit set of remote interface targeted EJBs
- enabling course-grained container managed transactions

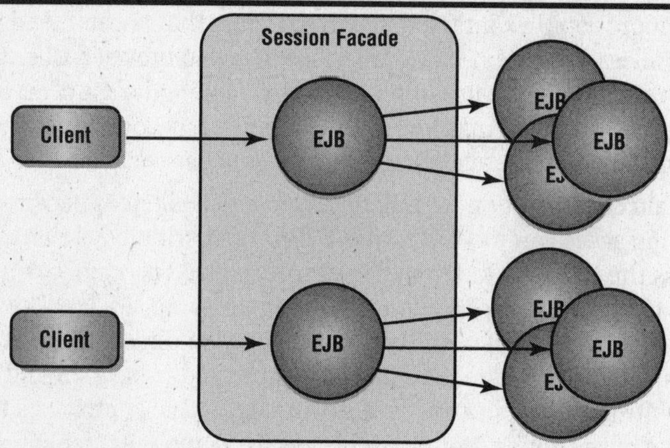

FIGURE 23.9: Session Façade pattern

Value Objects

The *Value Object* pattern can be used effectively with the Session Façade to transport object state between EJBs as well as the user interface. Value Objects are generally Java classes that are sent as parameters and return values between session beans, entity beans, Java classes, and user interface components. These Value Object classes can contain client-side validations, effective mostly when used with applets and rich clients. They may also be aggregated within Session Facades to account for granularity differences between the Session Façade and a finer-grained entity beans.

Service Locator

The *Service Locator* pattern is aimed at hiding the complexity of accessing EJBs. This involves the creation of a Java class that hides the JNDI lookup and home interface access from the client, and effectively hides the EJB access in a proxy class. This Service Locator class, which can be easily accessed from all clients, helps to reduce the clutter that often comes with EJB applications. The drawback is the management of another class associated with each EJB.

Business Delegate

The *Business Delegate* is much like the Session Façade, except that it is largely driven by the client's specific needs instead of the EJB framework. In other words, the Session Façade is a pattern that impacts all clients of a framework, but a Business Delegate can be implemented to simplify framework access specific to the needs of a client. These Business Delegate classes can be used jointly to effectively manage complex business framework access. The Business Delegate is usually a Java class that a client uses to manage access to an EJB framework. Figure 23.10 shows the Business Delegate class pattern.

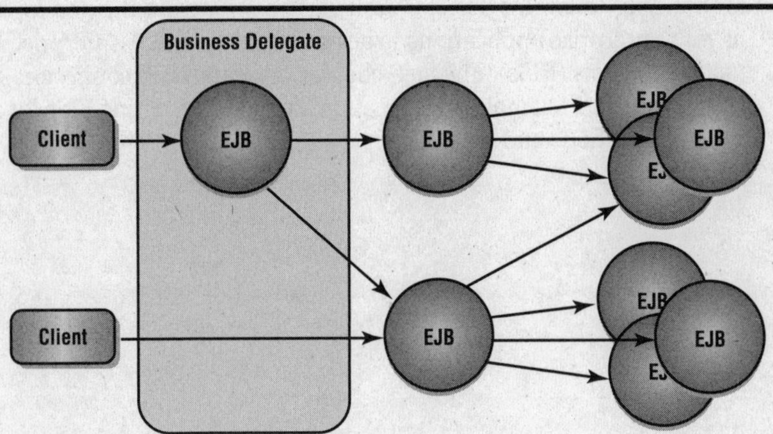

FIGURE 23.10: Business Delegate pattern

Data Access Object

A *data access object* is a pattern used to hide the implementation of access to a database. Entity beans can be considered data access objects as long as business logic is not mixed with the entity bean. The data access object, however, can also be applied to a set of Java classes that wrap entity beans or other persistence mechanisms to effectively buffer the business model from the data access implementation.

The patterns just mentioned are prevalent in EJB applications. This barely scratches the surface because entire books have been written on J2EE patterns. This list gives you a picture of some of the patterns used to address some of the most common EJB design issues.

NOTE

These and other patterns can be accessed online at `http://developer.java.sun.com/developer/technicalArticles/J2EE/patterns`.

WHAT'S NEXT

This chapter has presented EJB environment and deployment. It has also presented some EJB client issues and design patterns to aid in understanding the common ways of organizing EJBs.

To recap, these EJBs strive to provide an ideal component technology for building "business objects." You may desire within the development of your enterprise applications to access existing legacy Enterprise Information Systems (EISs). The next chapter presents J2EE connectors, which provide an ideal technology for creating adapters to existing EISs for access from applications and your EJBs.

Chapter 24

J2EE Connector Architecture

The J2EE Connector Architecture (JCA) defines a set of contracts focused on integrating Enterprise Information Systems (EIS) applications with application servers. The adoption of Enterprise JavaBean (EJB) development with enterprise software projects has emphasized the need for a method of connecting existing information systems into new J2EE-based applications, which we call Enterprise Application Integration (EAI). The objective of producing web browser–based applications that consolidate information access throughout an enterprise has also fueled the demand EAI.

As the information age advances, it is not unusual to find that information outlives the applications that collected it, and even survives the business organizations that created it. This occurs as businesses sell their information repositories, and as businesses merge and split. In many cases, the information systems get connected to new applications in new environments. This chapter takes a look at Enterprise Application Integration and Enterprise Information Systems as well as examines what the JCA provides to facilitate this integration process.

Written for *Enterprise Java™ 2, J2EE™ 1.3 Complete*
by Vince E. Marco

Featured in this chapter:

- Enterprise Application Integration (EAI)
- Enterprise Information Systems (EIS)
- J2EE Connector Architecture
- The Common Client Interface (CCI)
- CCI Client Example
- JCA Messaging

Enterprise Application Integration (EAI)

EAI is defined by the need to integrate multiple information systems, usually within an enterprise application. An enterprise application is a scalable software deployment that manages information for an enterprise or organization. Integration becomes a serious enterprise problem as companies strive to provide uniform access to information within their organizations. One common situation is when a company wants to provide intranet (or Internet) access to information existing within one or more legacy systems. Ideally, many of these efforts also strive to move business logic towards EJBs In these cases, the JCA can be a valuable migration tool by allowing an application to be deployed largely as EJBs, while still relying on legacy systems for information flow. The distinction between what is considered part of the EJB application and what is considered "legacy" is often blurred. However, we do still need tools for managing each type of information. Figure 24.1 shows an enterprise application using EAI. The resource adapters provide integration support for the EJBs.

Another situation involves companies that have merged with or purchased other companies. This causes the need to consolidate existing information systems. Also, it may be that new Enterprise Resource Planning (ERP) software is available commercially, and corporate budgets can be trimmed by purchasing software to replace an existing custom-built system. Either way, these systems must be brought together to produce an enterprise information solution. Figure 24.2 shows an enterprise with multiple EISs and enterprise applications. Users must use each EIS separately because EISs and enterprise applications have not been integrated.

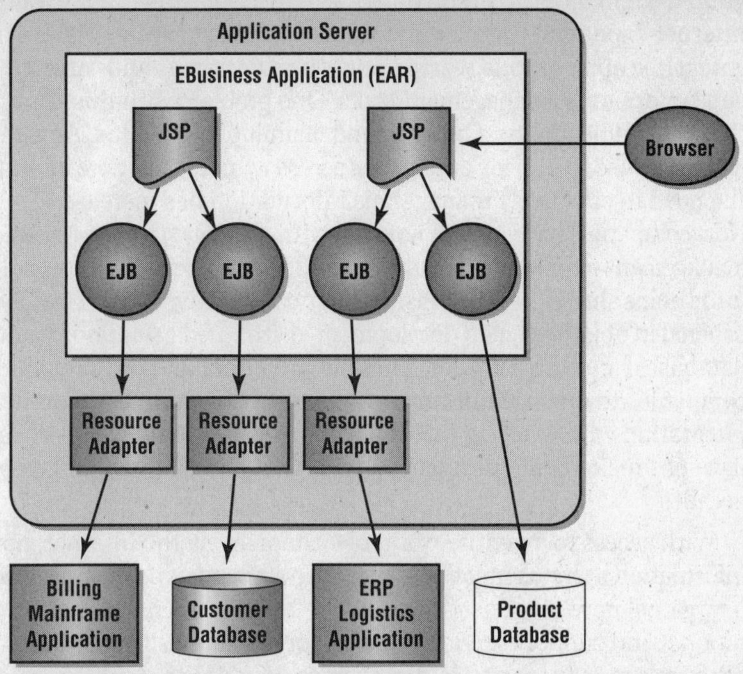

FIGURE 24.1: Enterprise application using EAI

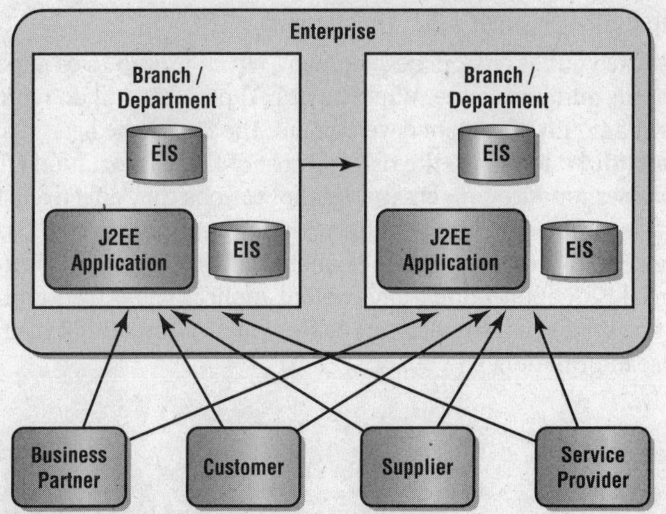

FIGURE 24.2: Non-integrated scenario

EAI is not a new problem domain, but the demand for EAI has been limited when enterprise software was entirely custom and before the Internet expanded the access to enterprise information. Many early enterprise applications existed only on mainframes and targeted only large information management tasks. One problem with this approach is the cost and flexibility of building and maintaining the EISs. As technology has continued to provide enterprises access to more and more information, the need to effectively manage this information has increased as well. Now companies have to deal not only with rapidly changing information management requirements, but also to effectively merge new technologies into their solutions or risk losing their competitive edge. The 1990s ushered in object-oriented development, distributed computing, relational databases, and the Internet. These new technologies have enabled companies to manage information more effectively and efficiently, but integration with existing EIS applications is needed. Many companies have not rushed out to update systems that have worked for years or decades.

With access to an entire world of customers via the Internet, however, information systems must be scalable and must support access via this new global network. Customers clamor for web-based Internet access to product and support services. Internal organizations need intranet applications to manage day-to-day business workflows. And businesses are defining informational exchanges between other related businesses within network-based marketplaces and business-to-business channels. Figure 24.3 shows how users are provided a uniform and integrated access to multiple EISs through J2EE applications.

EAI started out as custom development, which proved to be expensive, problematic, and unreliable. While most EAI projects still do require a significant amount of custom development, the tools have been refined and standardized to reduce the risk and cost of these integration efforts. As businesses produce new enterprise applications they effectively take on the task of replacing or integrating existing applications or EISs. EISs can be relational databases, non-relational databases, legacy applications, commercial ERP applications, and custom applications. An enterprise information system is a standalone deployment of software that manages enterprise information.

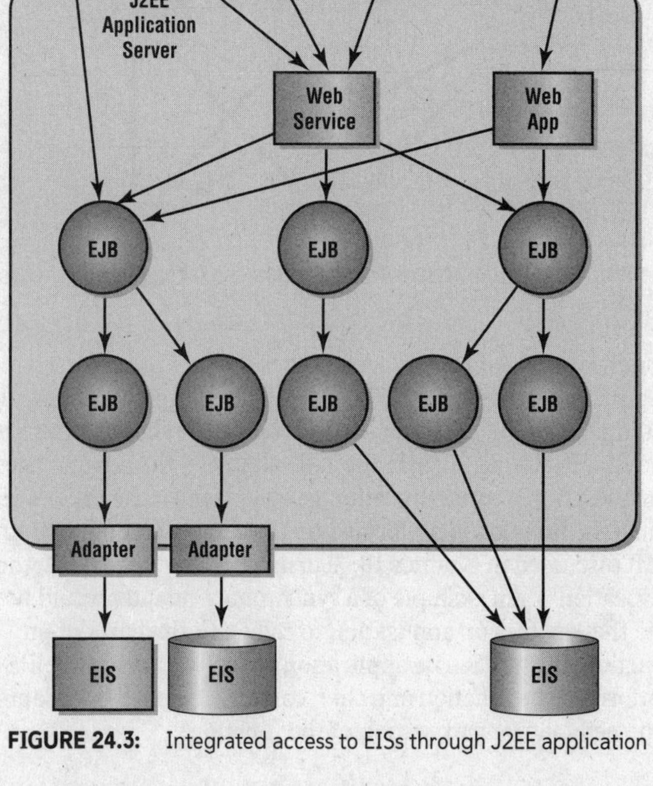

FIGURE 24.3: Integrated access to EISs through J2EE application

Many approaches can be taken in EAI. The four most common approaches are:

Two-Tier Client Server This involves the building of rich client applications which access server applications or a database server. These are not web browser–based solutions, and would generally locate application logic on the client application, on the server (probably in the form of database stored procedures), or both.

These applications would access EIS through exposed interfaces and connect with server-based applications and/or databases usually via low-level or proprietary communications interfaces.

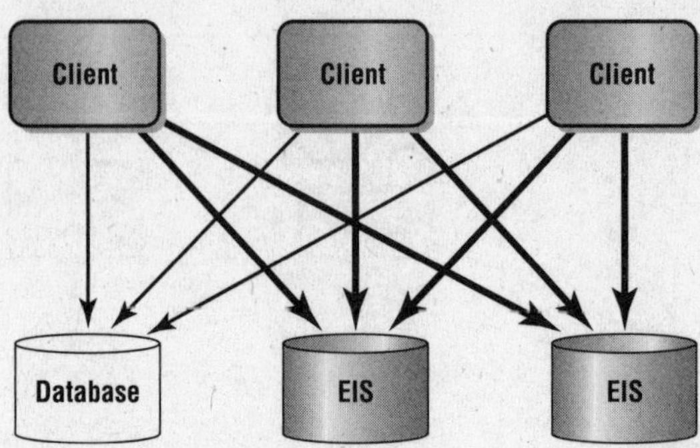

Synchronous Adapters A resource adapter may be used to allow client applications to be written in multiple languages, for multiple operating systems, or to simplify the client's access to the EIS. In the case of synchronous adapters, the adapter uses a request/reply communication model in which the caller waits while the function is performed on the remote end (similar to RMI discussed in Chapter 18, "Persistence and Remote Method Invocation"). An example of a synchronous adapter would be one that enables an application to call an GetInventoryItem function on an EIS. The application would wait while the EIS performed the function and then continue on after the adapter returned following execution of the function.

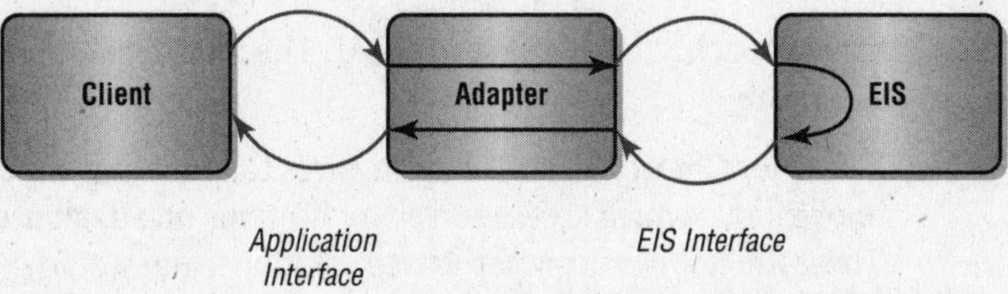

While it is most common for synchronous adapters to allow calls only from the application into the EIS, there is a form of the synchronous adapter to enable bi-directional communication, allowing the EIS to initiate calls into the application as well.

Asynchronous Adapters Asynchronous adapters use a different approach to client/EIS interaction. These adapters work much like JMS (Chapter 17, "Java Messaging Service [JMS]"), allowing calling applications to continue performing tasks before the EIS has completed the request. An example of this would be an adapter that enables an application to call an AddInventoryItem function on an EIS. Instead of making the application wait for a response, the application can continue before the EIS system processes the message. This is useful when there are limited connections to the EIS, or when the application does not need the EIS response to continue processing. As with the bi-directional synchronous adapters it is possible to design and implement bi-directional asynchronous communications.

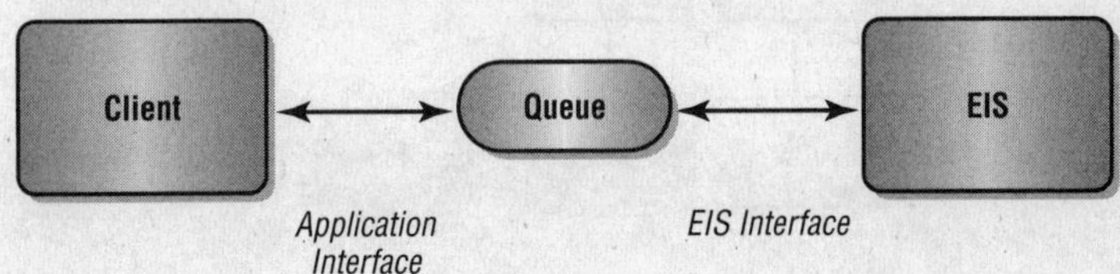

Application Servers Application servers have become a common and natural environment for EAI, largely because they provide all of the necessary aspects for development, deployment, and operation of transactional and secure distributed systems. Since J2EE application servers have a transaction manager for supporting distributed transactions, they provide an environment in which transactions can span EJBs, JMS, database connections, and EIS which support the XA protocol through the JCA. This level of transactional and security integration is many times more difficult (sometimes impossible) within a client application, web browser, or database server.

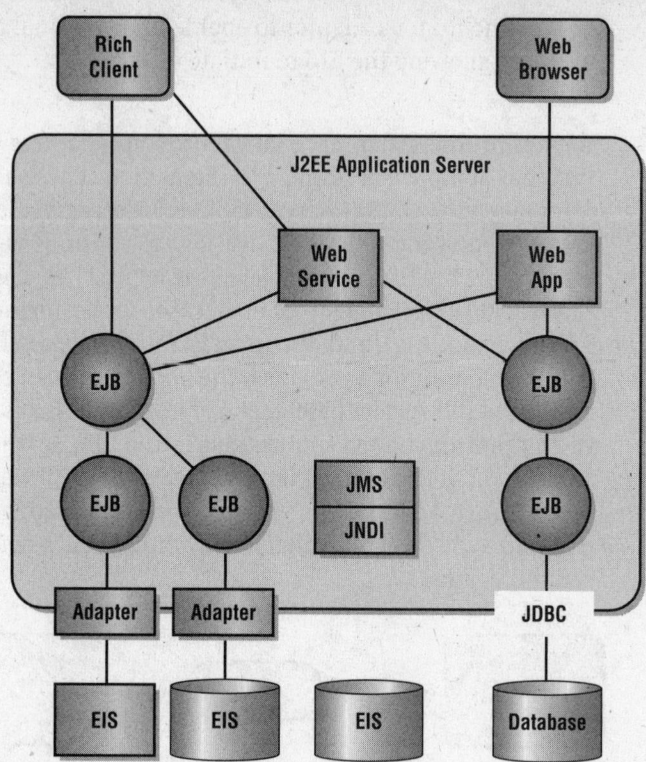

Enterprise Information Systems

This chapter has discussed EAI, but the question still remains—exactly what is an Enterprise Information System? An EIS can be defined as a standalone deployed application or system that manages information for an enterprise. An EIS provides a set of services to an enterprise for the accessing, manipulation, and management of information. A simple example could be a relational database. Accessing the information requires a driver compatible with the client application and database, and the use of SQL for database operations. Generally, databases thought of as EISs also contain business procedures that perform the business functions associated with the management of the information in the EIS. Without these procedures the effort to integrate to the database do not warrant categorizing these as separate EISs, although you get the final say on what is or is not an EIS in your system. On the other end of the complexity and proprietary scale, custom applications perhaps written in COBOL, C, or C++; and run on mainframes, unix servers, AS/400 servers, and so on can be found.

Enterprise Information Systems can contain multiple applications, which perhaps are considered EISs as well. These EISs provide services at several levels of abstraction: system, data, function, and business object (or process) level. These systems are increasingly dependent on an environment that supports distributed transactions and security, largely because of the constant integration of multiple applications.

The various types of EIS applications fall into a few categories:

Custom/Legacy Applications Companies build these to solve a specific set of informational management requirements, and over time become legacy applications. Legacy applications are active applications that a company is moving away from for the management of enterprise information. These generally run on multiple hardware and operating systems, and are often written in different programming languages or environments.

Transaction Processing Systems These are applications that are designed to run in a large-scale mainframe transaction processing system, such as CICS. These applications are generally written in COBOL or assembler and are generally good at processing large amounts of transactional requests. They share aspects of the legacy application category, but due to their focus on processing large amounts of transactional client requests, it is worthwhile to distinguish them.

Legacy Databases These are databases that manage information useful to the business processes of the enterprise. They include many types of databases and schemas that the company is migrating away from, but not yet ready to replace.

Commercial ERP Applications These solutions are generally applications providing Enterprise Resource Planning functionality, and are provided by companies such as SAP, PeopleSoft, IBM, and Oracle. ERP functions cover common enterprise tasks such as management of inventory, people, accounting, time, and projects.

Replacing Enterprise Information Systems

So why not just replace the EIS instead of trying to integrate multiple EISs into a new solution? Enterprise information is, by its very nature, difficult to replace. After the data models are created, the services are defined, and an organization starts managing information in the system, it is difficult at best to change the system. Employees are trained to use existing systems to perform their jobs, and administrators learn the support skills needed to operate and solve day-to-day information management problems. Perhaps the largest reason to support integration with exsisting EISs is that it is difficult for an enterprise to replace an existing system that has been working for years, without impacting their daily business process.

Modern J2EE Enterprise Information Systems

Eventually, changes in the business and technology do force companies to replace their existing EISs. A common approach to this change is to build an application above current EIS systems and then access these current EISs through adapters. This allows an organization to organize their logical business rules in a layer above the legacy EIS systems they would like to replace. This provides for better management of business logic, and offers a more flexible EIS model in which custom and purchased software components can work together to produce a more scalable and robust EIS.

Advantages of this approach include the separation of technologies and the separation of the business model. Consider the example of an existing mainframe application that captures airline reservations. Call centers are populated with terminals connected to the mainframe. Now the company wants to also take reservations from a web site. An application gets built to serve up the web site, but it must call into the EIS either through emulation or a programming interface. Also this separation of technologies applies to the database. By enabling the user interface to rely on a business object framework of EJBs, and these business objects to depend upon the database, you free all three layers to iterate at their own natural rate. It is then possible to adopt new database or user interface technology without breaking your business rules, and visa versa. Figure 24.4 shows this type of application architecture.

EJBs do a good job of fitting into this model because they are business components that support distributed transactional and security models.

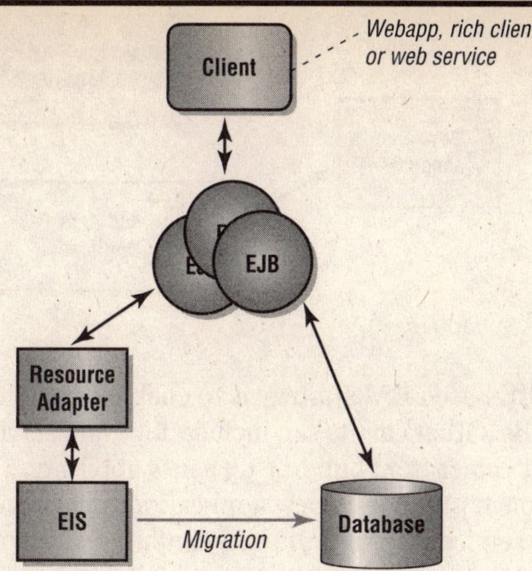

FIGURE 24.4: J2EE application to EIS

J2EE Connector Architecture

There are many ways to address Enterprise Application Integration (EAI) projects. Most of these approaches use proprietary technologies to integrate applications, and quite often involve accessing the Enterprise Information Systems directly. Figure 24.5 shows a proprietary approach to EAI.

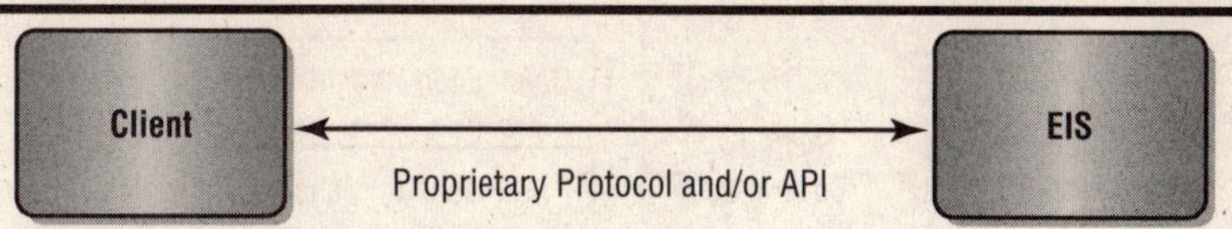

FIGURE 24.5: Proprietary approach to EAI

The J2EE Connector Architecture (JCA) defines a set of standard interfaces and contracts that provide a standardized framework for EAI solutions. This approach involves building resource adapters responsible for interacting with both the client application and the backend EIS. This adapter approach removes the applications dependency on the EIS's API, and provides an ideal target for simplifying the interface to an existing EIS. Figure 24.6 shows the resource adapter approach to EAI defined by the JCA.

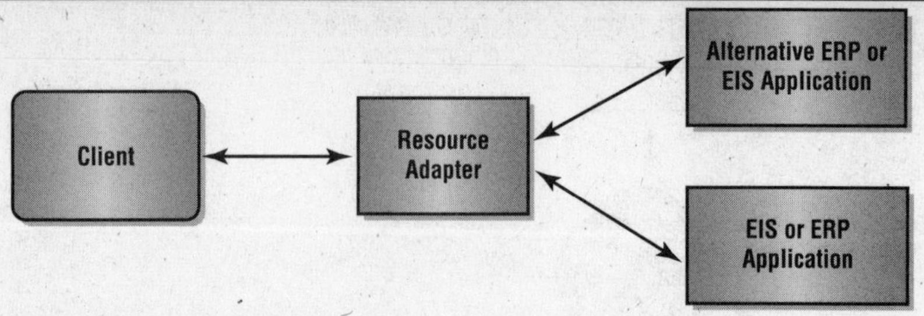

FIGURE 24.6: JCA resource adapters

The objective of a J2EE-based EAI strategy is to enable the building of applications using EJBs. Other clients can include JSPs and servlets; however, the true benefit comes from building up a new application using EJBs. This type of approach produces a new application that provides transaction and security services through the EJB container, thus simplifying the application code and providing a component-based layer for the new application. The resource adapters define contracts with the application and container to both enable the system to manage them, and to facilitate generic access from applications. Figure 24.7 shows the resource adapter contracts with the container and application.

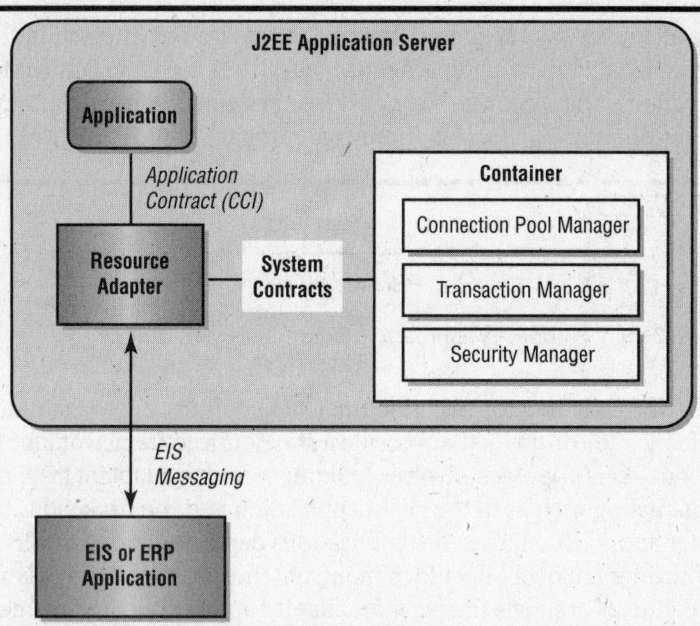

FIGURE 24.7: Resource adapter contracts

The end result is an environment in which existing Enterprise Information Systems can be accessed as transactional and secure components in an environment supporting Enterprise JavaBeans. The connections to these systems may be pooled, much like database connections, and accessed when needed within the system.

Contracts

The Java Connector Architecture is composed of several contracts that provide connection management, transaction and security management, and application support. The application contract is called the Common Client Interface (CCI), and is covered in the following section.

Connection Management Contract

Connection pooling and connection management are provided for by a connection management contract. This contract is provided by application server vendors and adapter providers. The application server uses this contract to create new connections to an EIS, configure connection factories, and find a matching physical connection from a set of pooled existing connections. Figure 24.8 shows the architecture of the connection management contract. The following steps are part of this contract:

1. The application looks up connection factory from JNDI.
2. The application uses factory to create connection to EIS.
3. The connection factory delegates the request to the application server. The application server attempts to use an existing pooled connection to EIS.
4. If no connection is available, the resource adapter is called to create a connection to the EIS which is added to the connection pool and then returned to the application component.
5. The application component uses the connection to the EIS.
6. When finished, the application component closes the handle to the connection.
7. The application server makes the connection available to other requestors.

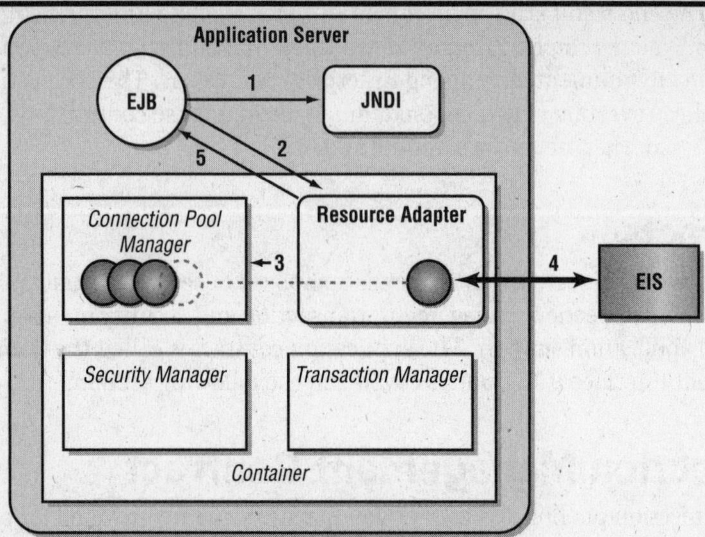

FIGURE 24.8: Connection Management Contract

The application programming model for the component requesting an EIS connection is fairly straightforward. Consider the following session EJB method for approving an employee's timesheet:

```
public void approve(Integer id)
    throws TimesheetException
  {
    try
      {
        Context jndi = new InitialContext();
        Javax.resource.cci.ConnectionFactory factory =
           (ConnectionFactory)jndi.lookup(
           "java:comp/env/eis/MainFrameCxFactory");
        Javax.resource.cci.Connection conn =
           factory.getConnection();
        ApproveTimesheetCommand command =
           new ApproveTSCommand(conn,
           factory.getRecordFactory());
        Command.setTimesheetId(id);
        Command.execute();
        Conn.close();
      }
```

```
        catch (Exception e)
          {
            throw new TimesheetException(e);
          }
      }
```

Much of the complexity of the EIS connection and its pooling is entirely removed from the client application. As the `conn.close()` statement executes, the application server leaves the connection open and makes it available to future requestors for connections to that EIS.

Transaction Management Contract

The JCA supports both local and distributed transactions (via the extended architecture/XA protocol).

NOTE

The XA protocol stands for Extended Architecture and is a standard protocol for managing distributed transactions.

Enterprise Information Systems vary in their support of transaction, and some do not support transactions or support only local transactions. The Java Transaction API enables distributed transactions on J2EE application servers by enabling transaction managers to manage multiple resource managers via the XA protocol. The JCA provides the interface for creating adapters so EIS systems can participate in JTA transactions as resource managers.

This approach of accessing EISs through an XA-compliant resource adapter provides the best transactional functionality. EISs may then participate in distributed transactions managed by the J2EE application server as regular resource adapters. For EISs that are non-transactional or support only local transactions, it is often necessary to use compensating transactions. This is a group of operations that undoes the work of a previously committed transaction. Unlike a rollback that occurs within the context of a transaction to ensure that all operations do get rolled back, a compensating transaction is a separate transaction. It does not provide any isolation from other transactions, and may itself fail. This is an effective method of enabling a non-transactional EIS to participate in a transactional J2EE application. But compensating transactions are not a perfect solution. They can fail, and cannot always undo the effect of a committed transaction. Figure 24.9 shows a compensating transaction.

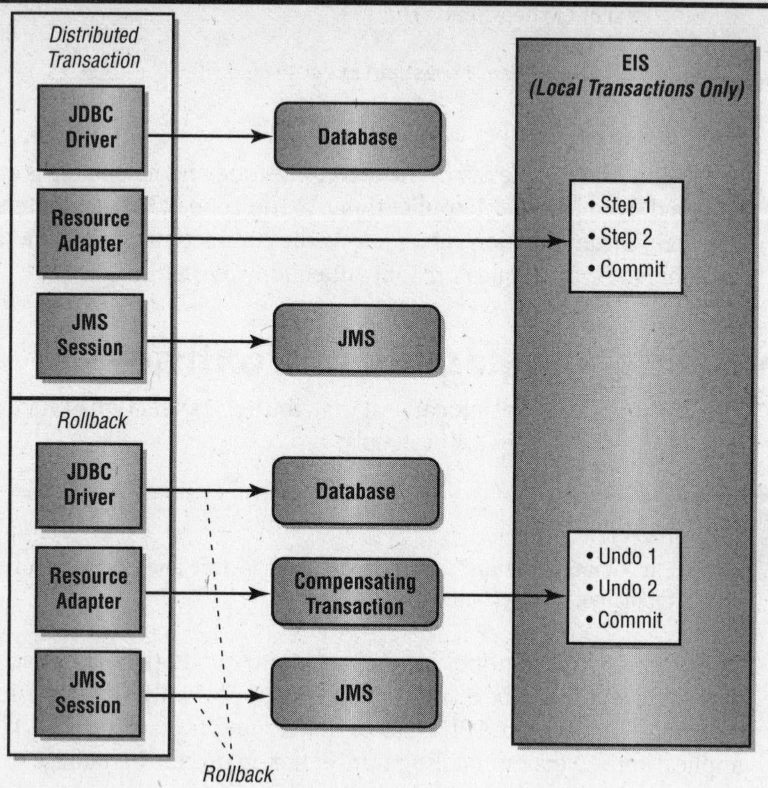

FIGURE 24.9: Compensating transaction

If a resource adapter supports the XA transaction protocol, the connection it provides to existing EISs can be used in distributed transactions along with TXDataSources, JMS sessions, and other XA-compliant resource managers. To support distributed transaction processing, the resource adapter must provide an implementation of the XAResource interface. The J2EE application server provides a transaction manager. This XAResource is a contract between the transaction manager and a resource manager, such as an EIS. The interface can be found in package javax.transaction.xa, and is as follows:

```
public interface javax.transaction.xa.XAResource
    {
    public void commit(Xid, boolean)
        throws XAException
    public void end(Xid, int) throws XAException
    public void forget(Xid) throws XAException
```

```
public int getTransactionTimeout()
    throws XAException
public boolean isSameRM(XAResource)
     throws XAException
public int prepare(Xid) throws XAException
public Xid[] recover(int) throws XAException
public void rollback(Xid) throws XAException
public boolean setTransactionTimeout(int)
     throws XAException
public void start(Xid, int)
     throws XAException
}
```

Implementing the XAResource interface allows the resource adapter to participate in global transactions with other resource managers. This is especially effective because it enables transactional J2EE applications to access multiple EISs without a breakdown of their transactional behavior. The alternative is to support local transactions only. This prevents the ability for transactions to span EJBs and EIS, producing a non-transactional integration environment.

Security Contract

Security is a rapidly growing aspect of all enterprise applications. It has always been at the core of EISs, but now that these EIS have the potential for reaching many more users, security has been put in the spotlight. The JCA security management contract enables support for different security mechanisms to protect an EIS from unauthorized access and loss of information. The objective of the JCA security contract is to enable JCA adapters to extend the J2EE security model.

Authentication is a straightforward process. A user presents a username and password or a signed certificate for proof of who they are, and the system then uses this to authorize access to resources in the application. Legacy EIS and ERP systems add some complexity, however, largely because they may have their own security functions in place. There are two basic methods for managing the client authentication to a resource adapter–container-managed and application-managed.

Container-Managed Authentication

Using container-managed authentication in a client to a resource adapter is similar to using container-managed security in an EJB. After you have a

ConnectionFactory from JNDI for the resource adapter, you call the no argument getConnection() method. The security information will be obtained by the container from the deployment descripter.

```
Context jndi = new InitialContext();
ConnectionFactory cf =
     (javax.resource.cci.ConnectionFactory)
Jndi.lookup("java:comp/env/eis/MyEISCxFactory");
javax.resource.cci.Connection cx = cf.getConnection();
```

Application-Managed Authentication

Application-managed authentication involves passing the security properties directly in the application code instead of placing these in the deployment descriptor. To do this, you will use an implementation of the ConnectionSpec interface. In this case, you have obtained this class using a factory class that you created for convenience.

```
Context jndi = new InitialContext();
ConnectionFactory cf = (javax.resource.cci.ConnectionFactory)
        Jndi.lookup("java:comp/env/eis/MyEISCxFactory");
ConnectionSpec properties =
    MyEISFactory.createConnectionSpec(username, password);
javax.resource.cci.Connection cx = cf.getConnection(properties);
```

EIS Authentication

So far you have learned how a J2EE application can pass authentication information to the resource adapter. But your security complexity occurs largely because by the time an application component authenticates with the resource adapter, that adapter already may have a pool of managed connections to the EIS. These connections have already authenticated with the EIS, and so you must somehow manage the possibly two different user identities to resolve this authentication difference. To do this you must start with a resource principal.

Resource and Initiating Principals

The resource principal is the user account or identity you will use to establish physical connection from the resource adapter to the EIS. The initiating principal is the calling principal (or user) in the J2EE application established on the getConnection() call to the resource adapter.

There are three approaches to resolving the initiating principal with the resource principal:

Configured identity approach This approach requires the resource principal be used for all interactions with the EIS, regardless of the initiating principal. This is a simple approach because there is no reconciling of the resource principal to the initiating principal, but the cost is that some flexibility in controlling authorization to the EIS is lost. To make sure that only authorized users can access the EIS, access to the resource adapter in its deployment descriptor must be restricted. From the EIS perspective, the identity of the caller is lost, as all of the J2EE principals access the EIS via one user account.

Principal mapping approach This approach involves mapping the initiating principal to the resource principal by the container. This method does not enable the inheritance of security properties from the initiating principal, but it does allow the resource principal to obtain properties from the principal mapping. As an example, principal "fred" might be mapped to (fred, inventory) and (fred, receiving) on two separate EIS systems.

Caller impersonation approach This approach involves the resource principal impersonating the initiating principal. The resource adapter accomplishes this by effectively logging in as the calling principal during that calling principal's use of the connection. This requires the EIS have the capability to handle temporary logins without breaking the physical connection, and then being able to log out of the calling principal's account to remain on a default login on the physical connection while between callers.

Resource Adapter Composition and Deployment

Resource adapters are bundled as a single archive file using the Java "jar" command. These archives are named with a .rar extension, standing for Resource ARchive. Each RAR file contains a deployment descriptor in XML format located at META-INF/ra.xml in the archive. The RAR also contains all the interfaces, classes, and files needed by the resource adapter. These files must be packaged in one or more jar–files. Each RAR file contains only one adapter. The jar files inside the RAR may vary from all files in one JAR, to multiple jar files perhaps separating client and implementation classes/interfaces.

Even though it is recommended that resource adapters use Java when possible, it is possible to put platform-specific libraries in a RAR file. If this is done, the RAR needs to be extracted manually and the application server configured to use the native library.

The resource adapter deployment descriptor provides for the configuration of resource adapter classes, as well as environment and security configurations. It is an XML file specified by the DTD found at `http://java.sun.com/j2ee/dtds/connector_1_0.dtd` (for JCA 1.0). Following is an example ra.xml:

```
<?xml version="1.0"?>
<!DOCTYPE connector PUBLIC '-//Sun Microsystems, Inc.//DTD
    Connector 1.0//EN' 'http://java.sun.com/j2ee/dtds/
    connector_1_0.dtd'>
<connector>
    <display-name>MainframeEIS</display-name>
    <vendor-name>Acme</vendor-name>
    <spec-version>1.0</spec-version>
    <eis-type>JDBC Database</eis-type>
    <version>1.0</version>
    <resourceadapter>
        <managedconnectionfactory-class>
            ...
        </managedconnectionfactory-class>
        <connectionfactory-interface>
            ...
        </connectionfactory-interface>
        <connectionfactory-impl-class>
            ...
        </connectionfactory-impl-class>
        <connection-interface>
            ...
        </connection-interface>
        <connection-impl-class>
            ...
        </connection-impl-class>
        <transaction-support>
            LocalTransaction
        </transaction-support>
        <config-property>
            <config-property-name>
                MainframeURL
            </config-property-name>
            <config-property-type>
        java.lang.String
            </config-property-type>
```

```
            <config-property-value>
                mainframeHost:1099
            </config-property-value>
        </config-property>
        <authentication-mechanism>
            <authentication-mechanism-type>
                BasicPassword
            </authentication-mechanism-type>
            <credential-interface>
                javax.resource.security.PasswordCredential
            </credential-interface>
        </authentication-mechanism>
        <reauthentication-support>
            false
        </reauthentication-support>
    </resourceadapter>
</connector>
```

Common Client Interface (CCI)

As discussed previously, the Java Connector Architecture (JCA) is composed of both application and system contracts that define how resource adapters interface with both applications and the servers in which they are running. The Common Client Interface (CCI) is a standard interface implementing the application contract that defines how resource adapters will interact with EIS applications.

A resource adapter must implement the system level contracts, but may choose which application interface to use. The CCI provides a common interface to the application contracts. A resource adapter developer may choose to use the CCI, or may choose to implement an EIS vendor's proprietary interface. Because each EIS is composed of a defined database and/or set of functions, a resource adapter is generally developed or configured for each specific EIS. The CCI is a framework for standardizing client access to the EIS, and therefore can turn what used to be repetitive custom code into common interfaces or classes. The CCI can also enable support for you're an EIS adapter from inside an Integrated Development Environment (IDE) that supports it.

The CCI is composed of several interfaces, including those for connection, interaction, and data. These interfaces are then implemented as classes by the JCA provider (usually the application server vendor), or implemented by the resource adapter vendor. Figure 24.10 shows the CCI class diagram.

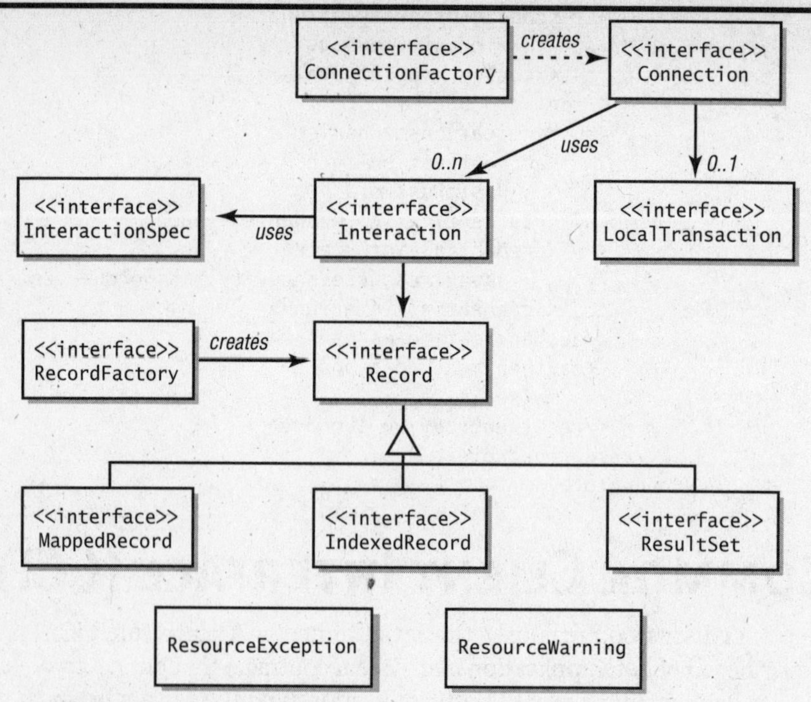

FIGURE 24.10: CCI class diagram

A simple example shows the basic usage of the CCI. A connection to the resource adapter (and therefore the EIS) is obtained inside a utility method (this could be a Java class or EJB). The user and password variables need to have been set up prior to the calls, largely because of the security model of the EIS.

```
Context jndi = new InitialContext();
ConnectionFactory cf = (ConnectionFactory)
        Jndi.lookup("java:comp/env/myEIS");
ConnectionSpec spec =
  new(CciConnectionSpec(user, password);
Conn = cf.getConnection(spec);
```

Now that a connection has been established, functions can be invoked to access and update the EIS. To avoid explicitly calling the EIS functions, which would lock interactions into a proprietary API, the Interaction interface can be used to decouple the client application from the EIS. An Interaction is obtained from the connection. Again a specification object is used for sending information to the interaction, except rather than a CciConnectionSpec, the CciInteractionSpec class is used. The specification object is the mechanism for indicating to a remote EIS which function call to make. A Record object also needs to be constructed to pass in the product to the catalog in this example. This is done via a RecordFactory object. The Record being sent contains the parameter information for the EIS function.

```
Interaction ix = conn.createInteraction();
CciInteractionSpec ispec = new CciInteractionSpec();
ispec.setCatalog("Power Tools");
ispec.setFunctionName("AddProduct");
RecordFactory rf = cf.getRecordFactory();
IndexedRecord irec =
     rf.createIndexedRecord("InputRecord");
irec.add(product);
irec.add(new Integer(productId));
ix.execute(ispec, irec);
```

In some cases, you may want to not only send records, but return information as well. The Interaction's `execute()` function will return a record containing information returned from the EIS.

```
Interaction ix = conn.createInteraction();
CciInteractionSpec ispec = new CciInteractionSpec();
ispec.setCatalog("Power Tools");
ispec.setFunctionName("GetProducts");
RecordFactory rf = cf.getRecordFactory();
IndexedRecord irec =
     rf.createIndexedRecord("InputRecord");
irec.add(search);
IndexedRecord result = (IndexedRecord)ix.execute(ispec,
      irec);
Iterator iter = result.iterator();
While (iter.hasNext())
{
 // ...
}
```

The following sections describe the various interfaces in detail.

Connection Interfaces

The connection interfaces are used to manage connections with the EIS. These include the ConnectionFactory for creating connections, the Connection itself, the ConnectionSpec, and the LocalTransaction.

An application component using a JCA resource adapter will begin by looking up the ConnectionFactory from JNDI.

ConnectionFactory

The ConnectionFactory is used to create a connection to the EIS:

```
public interface javax.resource.cci.ConnectionFactory
      extends java.io.Serializable,
      javax.resource.Referenceable
{
public Connection getConnection()
      throws ResourceException;
public Connection getConnection(ConnectionSpec props)
      throws ResourceException;
public ResourceAdapterMetaData getMetaData()
      throws ResourceException;
}
```

Connection

Connection provides the application a connection handle used to access the EIS:

```
public interface javax.resource.cci.Connection
{
public Interaction createInteraction()
       throws ResourceException;
public ConnectionMetaData getMetaData()
       throws ResourceException;
public ResultSetInfo getResultSetInfo()
       throws ResourceException;
public LocalTransaction getLocalTransaction()
       throws ResourceException;
public void close() throws ResourceException;
}
```

ConnectionSpec

ConnectionSpec provides an object for passing request-specific properties to the EIS:

```
public interface javax.resource.cci.ConnectionSpec
{
public void setUserName(String name)
       throws ResourceException;
public String getUserName()
       throws ResourceException;
```

```
public void setPassword(String password)
        throws ResourceException;
public String getPassword()
        throws ResourceException;
}
```

LocalTransaction

LocalTransaction is used to demarcate a local transaction around an EIS function request:

```
Public interface javax.resource.cci.LocalTransaction
{
public void begin() throws ResourceException;
public void commit() throws ResourceException;
public void rollback() throws ResourceException;
}
```

Interaction Interfaces

The interaction interfaces provide two interfaces that enable the execution of EIS operations, such as stored procedures. These are fairly simple interfaces that serve to decouple the calling application from any EIS-specific calling conventions.

Interaction

The primary purpose of the Interaction is to execute an EIS function. Prior to execution, an input (and possibly an output) Record may need to be set up (if you are passing any parameters to the EIS). The `getConnection()` method is used to obtain a connection. This connection should be closed when all immediate `execute()` invocations are complete. This does not close the connection, but rather returns it to the available pool.

```
public interface javax.resource.cci.Interaction
{
public Connection getConnection()
      throws ResourceException;
public void close() throws ResourceException;
public boolean execute(InteractionSpec ispec,
      Record input, Record output)
      throws ResourceException;
public Record execute(InteractionSpec ispec,
      Record input) throws ResourceException;
}
```

InteractionSpec

The InteractionSpec is used to pass function properties to the EIS. The standard properties defined by the CCI are functionName and interactionVerb. The interactionVerb is an integer that defines the mode of interaction as either synchronous or asynchronous. The default is synchronous.

```
public interface javax.resource.cci.InteractionSpec
    extends Serializable
{
public static final int SYNC_SEND = 0;
public static final int SYNC_SEND_RECEIVE = 1;
public static final int SYNC_RECEIVE = 2;
public void setFunctionName(String fname);
public String getFunctionName();
public void setInteractionVerb(int);
public int getInteractionVerb();
}
```

Data Representation Interfaces

The data representation interfaces encapsulate the information passed between a J2EE application component and an EIS. The objective is to prevent dependence in the application component on specific operation parameter types.

Record

This is the base Record interface, and is used to represent Interaction (EIS function) parameters being sent or returned from the EIS. This interface may be implemented in a CustomRecord, or the RecordFactory may be used to create an IndexedRecord or MappedRecord. The purpose of the Record is to decouple the parameters being sent to an EIS function and the function's implementation. In this way, the implementation can change without breaking the application, as would happen with tightly-coupled function calls.

```
public interface javax.resource.cci.Record
extends Cloneable
{
public String getRecordName();
public void setRecordName(String name);
public String getRecordShortDescription();
public void setRecordShortDescription(String desc);
public boolean equals(Object other);
public int hashcode();
```

```
public Object clone()
        throws CloneNotSupportedException;
}
```

RecordFactory

The RecordFactory is used to create Records and is available from the Interaction interface.

```
public interface javax.resource.cci.RecordFactory
{
public MappedRecord createMappedRecord() throws
   ResourceException;
public IndexedRecord createIndexedRecord(String recname)
   throws ResourceException;
}
```

IndexedRecord

The IndexedRecord represents an ordered set of parameters for the Interaction. This interface extends both the Record and java.util.List interfaces to effectively produce a record that may be accessed as a standard Java2 List. This includes accessing contents by their relative index, or via an iterator that can be used to walk the contents sequentially.

```
public interface javax.resource.cci.IndexedRecord
{
// List methods ...
public void add(int, Object);
public void add(Object);
public boolean addAll(Collection);
public boolean addAll(int, Collection);
public void clear();
public boolean contains(Object);
public boolean containsAll(Collection);
public Object get(int);
public int indexOf(Object key);
public boolean isEmpty();
public Iterator iterator();
public int lastIndexOf(Object key);
public ListIterator listIterator();
public ListIterator listIterator(int);
public Object remove(int);
public boolean remove(Object);
public boolean removeAll(Collection);
public boolean retainAll(Collection);
public Object set(int, Object);
```

```
public int size();
public List subList(int, int);
public Object[] toArray();
public Object[] toArray(Object[]);
// Record methods ...
public Object clone();
public String getRecordName();
public void setRecordName(String name);
public String getRecordShortDescription();
public void setRecordShortDescription(String desc);
}
```

MappedRecord

A MappedRecord is a key-value, map-based collection of record elements. It extends the Record interface as well as the java.util.Map interface.

```
public interface javax.resource.cci.MappedRecord
{
// Map methods ...
public void clear();
public boolean containsKey(Object key);
public boolean containsValue(Object key);
public Set entrySet();
public Object get(Object key);
public Set keySet();
public void put(Object key, Object value);
public void putAll(Map other);
public Object remove(Object key);
public int size();
public Collection values();
// Record methods ...
public Object clone();
public String getRecordName();
public void setRecordName(String name);
public String getRecordShortDescription();
public void setRecordShortDescription(String desc);
}
```

ResultSet

This interface represents tabular data, similar to the JDBC `java.sql.ResultSet` object. In fact, the `javax.resource.cci.ResultSet` does extend `java.sql.ResultSet`. The execute method on the Interaction interface may return a ResultSet instance, and this can then be used as a JDBC ResultSet.

```
public interface javax.resource.cci.ResultSet
extends Record, java.sql.ResultSet
{
public Connection getConnection()
        throws ResourceException;
public void close() throws ResourceException;
public boolean execute(InteractionSpec ispec,
        Record input, Record output)
        throws ResourceException;
public Record execute(InteractionSpec ispec,
        Record input) throws ResourceException;
}
```

MetaData Interfaces

CCI defines two interfaces for accessing and managing meta information. The ConnectionMetaData manages meta information for the connection to the EIS. The ResourceAdapterMetaData manages meta information regarding the resource adapter implementation. Notice that not all execute methods are implemented by all resource adapters. The ResourceAdapterMetaData calls can be used to check functionality from the J2EE application.

```
public javax.resource.cci.ConnectionMetaData
{
public String getEISProductName()
    throws ResourceException;
public String getEISProductVersion()
        throws ResourceException;
public String getUserName()
        throws ResourceException;
}

public javax.resource.cci.ResourceAdapterMetaData
{
public String getAdapterVersion();
public String getAdapterVendorName();
public String getAdapterName();
public String getAdapterShortDescription();
public String getSpecVersion();
public String[] getInteractionSpecsSupported();
public boolean
       supportsExecuteWithInputAndOutputRecord();
public boolean supportsExecuteWithInputRecordOnly();
public boolean supportsLocalTransactionDemarcation();
}
```

Exception Interfaces

Two exceptions are defined by the CCI. ResourceException is the base exception for the CCI hierarchy. It contains both an error code and string describing the error. The error codes are specific to the resource adapter or EIS. A ResourceWarning provides information related to warnings generated during execution. The first ResourceWarning instance can be obtained by calling `getWarning()` on the Interaction. If multiple Resource-Warnings exist for the interaction, they will be linked to the first warning and may be accessed from the `getLinkedWarning()` method inside of ResourceWarning.

CCI Client Example

CCI clients might be of various types, such as Java applications, applets, servlets, JSPs, and EJBs. Our example will be a stateless session EJB that accesses a remote EIS through CCI. Accessing CCI requires a specific routine. First we must obtain a ConnectionFactory, and establish a connection to the resource manager for the EIS. This is very much like obtaining a JDBC connection from a DataSource, but keep in mind that we are encapsulated from exactly "how" the EIS is implemented. This could allow us to access an existing SAP module for instance from our EJB, and minimize having to rebuild the EJB later if we were to switch ERP vendors or implement our own custom ERP application.

Since access to the EIS represents implementation all of the CCI access is done in the session bean class:

```
public class TimesheetMgrBean implements SessionBean
  {
  private final static String  JNDI_CF =
     "java:comp/env/CCIEIS";
  private final static String  JNDI_NAME =
     "java:comp/env/user";
  private final static String  JNDI_PASS =
     "java:comp/env/password";
  private ConnectionFactory  connfactory;
  private String  cciuser;
  private String  ccipass;
     ...
  public void ejbActivate
     ...
  public void ejbPassivate()
...
```

```
  public void ejbRemove()
...
  public void setSessionContext(SessionContext context)
...
  public Connection getCciConnection()
...
  private void closeCciConnection(Connection c)
...
  public void addTimesheet(String user, Date date, Timeheet ts)
...
  public Timesheet getTimesheet(String user, String date)
...
  }
```

The setSessionContext(SessionContext ctx) method is the first method called on the EJB by the container. It provides an opportunity to setup the ConnectionFactory. We are also grabbing the user and password used by the adapter as it connects to the EIS, largely because we already have a JNDI context from getting the ConnectionFactory. Here is the method:

```
public void setSessionContext(SessionContext context)
  {
  try
    {
    Context  jndi = new InitialContext();
    connfactory = (ConnectionFactory)jndi.lookup(JNDI_CF);
    cciuser = (String)jndi.lookup(JNDI_NAME);
    ccipass = (String)jndi.lookup(JNDI_PASS);
    }
  catch (NamingException e)
    {
    e.printStackTrace();
    throw new EJBException("Error setting context!!!");
    }
  }
```

Next we need a method to actually get a connection to the EIS. The CciConnection class actually uses a CciManagedConnection instance to implement our security strategy, but it encapsulates that complexity away from our client EJB. This method behaves very similarly to the `getConnection()` methods found in BMP entity beans. It will return a connection to the desired resource. The main difference is the addition of the CciConnectionSpec instance, used to pass information used for the connection. In this case the information setup in the CciConnectionSpec is the primary principal used to establish connection with the EIS.

```
public Connection getCciConnection()
  {
  Connection conn = null;
  try
    {
    ConnectionSpec spec =
new CciConnectionSpec (cciuser, ccipass);
    conn = _connfactory.getConnection(spec);
    }
  catch (ResourceException e)
    {
    e.printStackTrace();
    throw new EJBException("Error getting connection!!");
    }
  return conn;
  }
```

The next method is a private method used within the EJB to close the connection following its use. This is important because it returns the managed connection to the EIS back to the connection manager for other clients to use.

```
private void closeCciConnection(Connection c)
  {
  try
    {
    if (c != null)
      c.close();
    }
  catch (ResourceException e)
    {
    e.printStackTrace();
    }
  }
```

The addTimesheet(Timesheet) method is a business method on the EJB, exposed via the EJBs remote and/or local interface. This method represents the logical call on the TimesheetManager in the business model to add a Timesheet instance. The implementation here is to populate the InteractionSpec with information indicating the EIS procedure to call, and to create an InputRecord with the user, date, and Timesheet instance. These will propogate to the class implementing the javax.resource .cci.Interaction interface, which will call the EIS procedure. Your passing of the Timesheet instance does indicate that the CciInteraction class must know how to adapt this object to something that the EIS procedure knows how to handle. These business methods use the getCciConnection() and closeCciConnection() methods to obtain and return managed connections to the EIS.

```
public void addTimesheet(String user, Date date, TimeSheet ts)
  {
  Connection c = null;
  try
    {
    c = this.getCciConnection();
    Interaction ix = c.createInteraction();
    CciInteractionSpec ispec = new CciInteractionSpec();
    ispec.setSchema("TIMETRAK");
    ispec.setCatalog(null);
    ispec.setFunctionName("ADD_TIMESHEET");
    RecordFactory rf = connfactory.getRecordFactory();
    IndexedRecord irec = rf.createIndexedRecord
       ("InputRecord");
    irec.add(user);
    irec.add(date);
    irec.add(ts);
    ix.execute(ispec, irec);
    }
  catch (ResourceException e)
    {
    e.printStackTrace();
    throw new EJBException("Error adding timesheet!!");
    }
  finally
    {
    this.closeCciConnection(c);
    }
  }
```

The getTimesheet() method is also a business method on the TimesheetManager EJB. It passes the user and date, and returns the Timesheet instance for that user and date. In this method you see not only the InputRecord as in our last method, but also that the Interaction execute() method is returning an output record. This output record is also of type IndexedRecord, which supports a list of values. The interaction must populate this with the Timesheet instance retrieved from the EIS. Keep in mind that the EIS may not have any idea of what a Timesheet is, and that it is the resource adapter's responsibility to "adapt" these input and output records between the client and the EIS.

```
public TimeSheet getTimesheet(String user, Date date)
  {
  TimeSheet result = null;
  Connection c = null;
  try
    {
    c = this.getCciConnection();
    Interaction ix = c.createInteraction();
    CciInteractionSpec ispec = new CciInteractionSpec();
    ispec.setSchema("TIMETRAK");
    ispec.setCatalog(null);
    ispec.setFunctionName("GET_TIMESHEET");
    RecordFactory rf = connfactory.getRecordFactory();
    IndexedRecord irec =
       rf.createIndexedRecord("InputRecord");
    irec.add(user);
    Record orec = ix.execute(ispec, irec);
    Iterator iter = ((IndexedRecord)orec).iterator();
    if (iter.hasNext())
      {
      result = (TimeSheet)iter.next();
      }
    }
  catch (ResourceException e)
    {
    e.printStackTrace();
    throw new EJBException("Error getting timesheets!!");
    }
  finally
    {
    this.closeCciConnection(c);
    }
  return result;
  }
}
```

The resource adapter is responsible for mapping the InteractionSpec to the EIS procedures. This occurs largely in the implementation of the Interaction interface. The implementation of the CCI interfaces vary significantly based upon the type of EIS being accessed. An example of a JCA resource adapter implementation to JDBC remote procedure-based database can be found in the J2EE SDK from Sun.

NOTE

A tutorial to the JCA connector example can be found at `http://java.sun.com/j2ee/tutorial`**.**

JCA Messaging

Messaging between JCA resource adapters and EISs can be managed synchronously or asynchronously. Both messaging models are useful in different situations. Because the JCA is focused on managing logical connection to EISs, a look at messaging alternatives can be beneficial. The following sections look at both of these to provide better understand and manage the connection to the EIS.

Synchronous Messaging

Synchronous messaging is accomplished using the standard request/response model. This is the default messaging for JCA adapters. The adapter will send a request to the EIS and then wait for the response from the EIS before executing any further requests. After the response is received, the adapter may pass information back to the calling J2EE component via an output record and then wait for and process the next request. The JCA 1.0 specification supports only a synchronous messaging model. The synchronous messaging model leads to a tightly-coupled system where connection dependencies deteriorate maintainability, and where performance may be lost while systems wait for the completion of their tasks.

Asynchronous Messaging

Asynchronous messaging results in the sender being able to send a message without having to wait for a response. These asynchronous messages may use a point-to-point (or queued) model that allows only one receiver per message, or a publish-and-subscribe model in which each message can have many receivers. Chapter 17 covers the Java Messaging Service (JMS), which provides both point-to-point and publish-and-subscribe forms of asynchronous messaging. The benefit of asynchronous messaging is that the sender may trust the messaging system to deliver the message, freeing it to continue processing additional requests. In addition to the standard synchronous messaging in the 1.0 specification, the JCA 2.0 specification supports the following iteration modes:

- asynchronous inbound messages
- asynchrounous outbound messages
- synchronous inbound messages
- JMS-based messages

Asynchronous Inbound Messages

This involves the EIS sending an asynchronous message to the application via a message-driven EJB. The EIS sends the incoming message to the resource adapter that forwards the message asynchronously to a message-drive EJB within the J2EE application. The target message-driven bean destination is usually configured within the resource adapter deployment descriptor.

Asynchronous Outbound Messages

This involves a J2EE component sending an asynchronous message to the EIS. The message delivery is managed by the resource adapter. System-level contracts are used by the resource adapter in delivering the message to the EIS. During this delivery, the application continues processing rather than waiting for a reply.

Synchronous Inbound Messages

This is basically the opposite interaction from the basic synchronous messaging supported by the JCA 1.0 specification. The request originates with the EIS sending a request to the application again via a message-driven EJB. The resource adapter receives the request from the EIS and forwards it to an appropriate component target in the J2EE application such as a session or message-driven EJB.

JMS-Based Messages

If the EIS is able to access JMS, communciation between the application server and the EIS. There is currently no standard system-level contract supporting the JMS as a resource adapter. In this case, the JMS provider acts as the resource adapter between the J2EE application and the EIS.

Application Servers and ERP Adapters

To use the JCA, you must find a J2EE application server that supports it. Several application servers support JCA adapters, including HPAS, BEA Weblogic, Borland App Server, IBM, Websphere, JBoss, Oracle AS, and

Primati. Other J2EE application servers are adding this support. These server products provide excellent environments for your JCA-based EIA efforts. Several application servers are taking JCA even farther. As an example, BEA's Weblogic Integration server adds tools for visually building business processes as a way to tackle EAI development. The CCI provides a common client API that enables IDE vendors to provide generic JCA tools within their application for constructing the CCI-based elements.

Not all JCA adapters are custom built. You can find several vendors that provide JCA adapters for popular EIS and ERP products. These vendors include Insevo and Rai, and include adapters for products such as SAP, PeopleSoft, JD Edwards, Siebal, and more. These adapters often support bidirectional as well as both synchronous and asynchronous communication.

What's Next

JCA adapters provide a standard approach for building interaction with existing EISs. The objective is reuse and to provide a standard approach to integration. The result of a standard approach to integration projects results in EJBs that do not get locked into the specific interfaces of the EISs they integrate with. Over time this enables the "plugging in" of alternative EIS systems and easier migration to new EIS systems.

These adapters also provide a standard strategy and method for integrating vendor ERP products into your J2EE enterprise applications. They might possibly be the key to purchasing rather than implementing some functionality that has already been developed. The J2EE Connector Architecture is a simple yet indirect method of accessing your EISs. It doesn't try to do too much and those expecting loads of complexity may be dissappointed. However, it does produce a consistent approach for integrating EISs, and does help in producing EJBs that are not dependent on your existing EISs. The payoff many times comes down the road when migrating to new EIS or by enabling vendor ERP systems, such as SAP R/3, or products from PeopleSoft, Oracle or IBM, and others.

Part V
Spiders and Bots

Chapter 25

Building a Spider

Although this and the next two chapters do not cover J2EE specific features, they will be helpful and interesting to many J2EE web developers who want to track their own as well as other web sites.

This chapter demonstrates how to build a special type of bot called a spider. A *spider* is a type of bot that is capable of moving throughout the Web to search for new web pages, just as the arachnid moves about on the strands of its web looking for trapped food. The primary difference between a spider and a simple bot is that the spider is capable of moving to new pages not originally requested by its programmer.

Spiders proved to be useful to one of the first utility sites to appear on the Web—the search engine. Search engines function as indexes to the content of the web. As you know, you can type several keywords into a search engine and it will provide you with links to sites on the Web that match your search criteria. It does

Adapted from *Programming Spiders, Bots, and Aggregators in Java*™ by Jeff Heaton

ISBN 0-7821-4040-8 $59.99

this by drawing on its large databases that contain the indexed content of the Web. But how is this data gathered, and how do spiders fit into this?

It would be entirely too large a job for human workers to index and categorize the entire Web. This is a job that is almost always reserved for spiders that scan web sites and index their content. As the spider scans the site, it also looks at other pages to which the current site is linked. The spider keeps a list of these; when it is finished scanning the current site, it visits these linked sites. Due to the widespread use of hyperlinking on the Web, it can be assumed that by following this pattern a spider would eventually visit nearly every public page available on the Web; however, new sites are introduced daily, and it is unlikely that a spider would ever be able to visit every site on the Internet.

In addition to performing indexing functions for search engines, spiders can scan a web site looking for broken links, can download the entire contents of a web site to your hard drive, and can also create a visual map that shows the layout of a web site. Spiders prove useful whenever data must be retrieved from a site whose structure is not known beforehand by the programmer.

The Bot package presented in this book contains several classes designed to implement a spider. These classes take care of the more routine issues a spider deals with, such as tracking links and avoiding repetition. After explaining spiders and their functions in more detail, this chapter will show you how to uses these classes, and how they were constructed.

Featured in this chapter:

- Structure of a web site
- Examining the structure of a spider
- Following internal links
- Examining external links

Structure of Web Sites

A spider travels from web page to web page by locating the links stored on each page that it visits. The spider examines the web page's HTML code, and locates all the tags within it that facilitate some sort of link to another web page. Most tags that do link to other pages do this with a special type of attribute called a *hypertext reference (HREF)*. The different types of HREFs will be explored momentarily.

After discussing HREFs, but before going on to examine the structure of a spider, you must first look at the structure of a site on which the spider may be used. You will do this by examining a small web site that I created named `kimmswick.com`.

Types of Hypertext References (HREFs)

A spider must locate links to find other web pages. Web pages are linked together using HREFs, which are HTML attributes that specify links to other web pages.

All HTML links are contained in the `HREF` HTML attribute. `HREF` is not an HTML tag; it is just an attribute. As a result, you never see `HREF` as a tag on its own; instead, it is usually used in conjunction with an anchor tag. For the purposes of a spider, anchor tags and image maps do the same thing—they function as pointers to some other page the spider should explore. The spider only looks at the `HREF` attributes contained as part of an anchor tag or image map, however. To a spider, the following anchor tag just means that there is another page named `nextpage.html` to be examined; all other data is ignored.

```
<a href="nextpage.html" alt="Go Here">Click Here</a>
```

Similarly, the following HTML image map means the same thing to the spider as the anchor tag above. This is because the spider only cares about `HREF` attributes.

```
<map name="sample">
<area shape="rect" coords="20,27,82,111" href="nextpage.html">
<area shape="default" nohref>
</map>
```

Depending on the data contained in the `HREF`, there are three kinds of links that the spider will encounter. *Internal links* point to pages that are a part of the same web server as the page that contains the link. *External links* refer to pages that are contained on different web sites than the page that contained the link. There is also a third class of links, referred to as *other links*, which link to resources other than web pages. Each of these will now be explored in more detail.

Internal Links

An internal link is one that connects a web page to another web page that is on the same site. For example, if the document stored at `http://www.kimmswick.com/index.shtml` is linked to `http://www.kimmswick.com/attractions.shtml`, this would be considered an internal link.

A simplified view of the structure of the Kimmswick web site can be seen in Figure 25.1. This site, like many others, is made up of many interconnected web pages. The *root document*, called Kimmswick Information, is the page that is displayed when the user goes to the address `http://www.kimmswick.com`. From that root document, links are provided to other pages on the Kimmswick site. Figure 25.1 shows only some of the internal links found on this site.

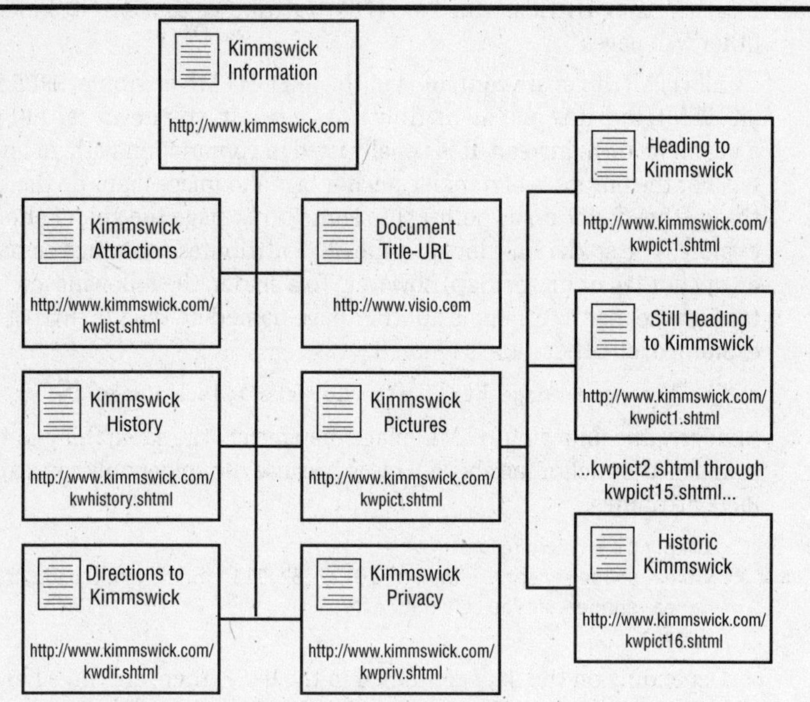

FIGURE 25.1: Structure of `kimmswick.com`

As implied earlier, visiting links, whether they are external or internal, is a recursive process. For instance, a spider visiting `kimmswick.com` would likely be given the URL of `http://www.kimmswick.com` as a starting point. This main page, as seen in Figure 25.1, contains internal links to six other pages. One of these six pages, Kimmswick Pictures, contains internal links to 16 pages. When the spider was sent to this URL, the Kimmswick Information page would be downloaded, the spider would encounter the first six links, and it would remember these for later exploration. When it visited each of these pages, the additional links that they contained would be found. This same process is replicated on a larger scale when a spider encounters external links.

External Links

To see how external links work, take a look at the following example. If you wanted to hyperlink the word Yahoo! to `http://www.yahoo.com` in your HTML, you would use the following tag:

```
<a href="http://www.yahoo.com">Yahoo</a>
```

The above HTML anchor tag works because it specifies an HREF. The result of this tag would be a web browser that would display the word Yahoo underlined. When the user clicked this link, the web browser would take them to `http://www.yahoo.com`.

This is an example of an *external link*. This link is external because it points to a web page that is external to your web site (unless your web site happens to be Yahoo!). Spiders are frequently programmed not to follow external links to prevent them from the near-infinite process of visiting entirely new web sites, which will in turn cause them to visit every site on the Internet. Spiders that are not restricted in this manner are often referred to as *voyagers* or *world spiders*.

Other Links

A link does not have to point to a web page. It is just as valid when it points to an e-mail address or another resource. Links that specify a scheme other than HTTP or HTTPS fall into this category as well. For example, the mailto scheme can be used to specify an e-mail address. A mailto link such as the following would be used to specify the e-mail address `webmaster@kimmswick.com`:

```
<a href="mailto:webmaster@kimmswick.com">[Email WebMaster]</a>
```

Sources of Links

Links come from many sources. The most common form of a link is the anchor tag that you already examined. A spider should not restrict itself merely to anchor tags, however. Instead, the spider should examine any HREF attribute present in any HTML tag. Table 25.1 summaries a few of these tags.

TABLE 25.1: Some HTML Tags with HREFs

HTML Tag	Example	Purpose
Base	`<base href="http://www.yahoo.com/">`	Establishes a new base for the web site. The base is usually the directory in which the HTML file is stored.
Area	`<area coords="0,0,52,52" href="page.html"/>`	Used to indicate a target for an image map.
A	`<a href="page.html">`	The anchor tag. This tag causes a portion of the HTML document to link to the specified page.

Structure of a Spider

There are two ways that a spider could be constructed. The first is by writing the spider as a recursive program. The second is by building a non-recursive spider that maintains a list of pages that it must ultimately visit. When you are trying to decide which approach to take, keep in mind that it must allow the spider to function properly with very large web sites.

The Recursive Program

Recursion is the programming technique in which a method calls itself. For some projects, constructing your spider to use recursion seems like a logical choice. It is particularly useful whenever the same basic task must be done repeatedly, or when the information for future tasks will be revealed as earlier tasks are processed. For instance, consider the following pseudocode:

```
void RecursiveSpider(String url)
{
  .... download URL ....
  .... parse URL ....
  for each URL found
    call RecursiveSpider(with found URL)
  end for
  .... process the page just downloaded...
}
```

In this piece of code, the task of looking at one single web page has been placed in a single method called `RecursiveSpider`. Here, the `RecursiveSpider` method is called to visit a URL. Instead, the method calls itself as it discovers links.

Though recursion seems like a logical choice for constructing a spider, it is not a suitable one unless there are relatively few pages to visit. This is because each iteration must be pushed onto the stack when a recursive program runs. If the recursive program must run many times, the stack can grow very large, which can consume the entire stack memory and prevent the program from running.

Another problem with recursion is encountered when you want to use multithreading, which allows many tasks to run at once. Multithreading is not compatible with recursion because with this process, each thread has its own stack. As the methods called themselves, they would need to use the same stack. This means that a recursive spider could not be extended to include multithreading.

The Non-Recursive Construction

The second way to construct a spider, and the one that you will be using, is to approach the problem non-recursively. By doing this, you will be writing a spider that uses a method that does not call itself as each new page is found. Instead, this approach uses a *queue*. A queue is much like the roped line at an amusement park. Individuals must wait in line to ride the roller coaster. Likewise, the non-recursive spider uses queues in which the newly discovered pages must wait to be processed by the spider.

The Spider's Queues

When the non-recursive approach is followed, the spider will be given a page to visit, and it will add this page to a queue of sites it should visit. As the spider finds new links, they too will be added to the queue. After the spider is finished with the current page, it will check the queue for the next page to process. (This differs from recursion, where a method to handle each page would immediately be called.)

Though only one queue was specified in this description, the spider will actually use a total of four queues, which are summarized momentarily. Each of these queues will hold URLs that are in some stage of being processed.

Waiting queue In this queue, URLs wait to be processed by the spider. New URLs are added to this queue as they are found.

Running queue URLs are transferred to this queue after the spider begins processing them. It is important that the same URL not be processed multiple times because this would be wasteful.

After the URL is processed, it moves to either the error queue or the complete queue.

Error queue If an error occurs while the page is being downloaded, its URL is added to the error queue. The URL does not move into another queue after it lands here. After moved to the error queue, a page will not be processed further by the spider.

Complete queue If no error occurs while the page is being downloaded, the URL is added to the complete queue. The URL does not move into another queue after it has been assigned here.

An individual URL will only be in one queue at a time. This is also called the *state* of the URL because computer programs are often described by state diagrams in which the program flows from one state to the next. Figure 25.2 shows how these states interrelate and how a page flows from one queue to another.

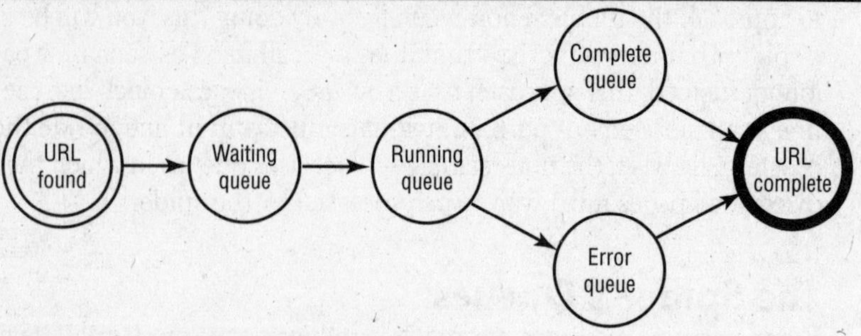

FIGURE 25.2: The flow of URL states

Figure 25.3 shows a simplification of what happens in one of the queues you saw in Figure 25.2. This figure only shows the flow of pages that did not result in an error. In this process, the spider is started when a single URL is added to the waiting queue. As long as there is a page in the waiting queue or the spider is processing a page, the spider will continue its job. When there is nothing in the waiting queue and no page is currently being processed, the spider will cease to function.

Now you will be shown how to construct a spider. You will see how the parts of a spider work together, and how you can extend the spider presented here. You will then be shown how to put this spider to some practical use. The example presented later in this chapter uses the spider to save the contents of the web site to a local disk.

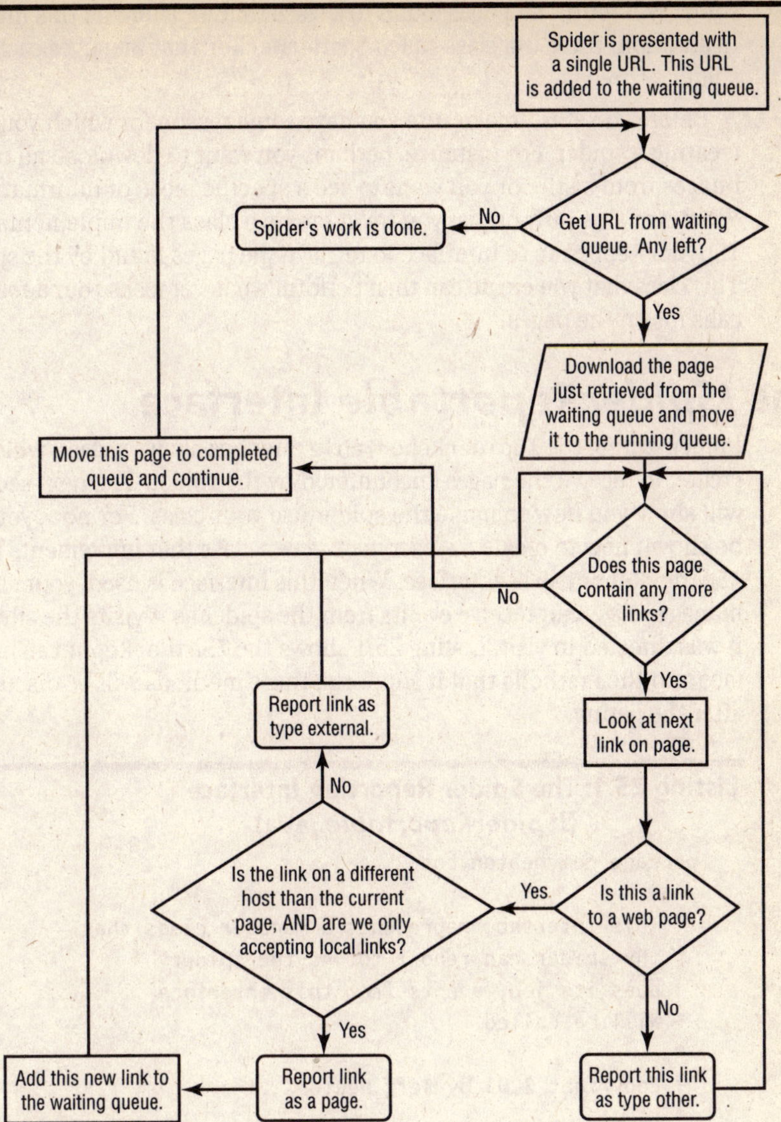

FIGURE 25.3: Typical spider flowchart

CONSTRUCTING A SPIDER

There are several classes and interfaces of which you must be aware to use the spider provided by the Bot package. First of all, there is an interface, named `IspiderReportable`, that you must implement. The Bot package spider will return all pages found to a class that implements this interface. In addition, there is a class called `SpiderWorker` that manages each of the spider's threads.

Before you start, make sure you have some reason for which you are creating a spider. For instance, perhaps you want to download all of the images from a site, or you want to see a specific piece of information. Whatever this purpose is, you must create a class the implements the `ISpiderReportable` interface to retrieve the pages found by the spider. This class that you create can then perform whatever tasks your application calls for on the pages.

The *ISpiderReportable* Interface

Implementing the `ISpiderReportable` interface allows a class, which you create, to receive the pages encountered by the spider. The next section will show you how to make the spider use your class. For now, you will be shown how to create a *spider manager*—a class that implements the `ISpiderReportable` interface. When this interface is used, your spider manager class can receive events from the spider as it visits the site that it was directed to visit. Listing 25.1 shows the `ISpiderReportable` interface and the methods that it supports; these methods will be discussed after the listing.

Listing 25.1: The Spider Reporting Interface (*ISpiderReportable.java*)

```
package com.heaton.bot;
/**
 * This interface represents a manager class that
 * the spider can report to. As the spider
 * does its job, events from this interface
 * will be called.
 *
 * Copyright 2001 by Jeff Heaton
 *
 * @author Jeff Heaton
 * @version 1.0
 */
public interface ISpiderReportable
{
   public boolean foundInternalLink(String url);
   public boolean foundExternalLink(String url);
```

```
    public boolean foundOtherLink(String url);
    public void processPage(HTTP page);
    public void completePage(HTTP page,boolean error);
    public boolean getRemoveQuery();
    public void spiderComplete();
}
```

The ISpiderReportable interface defines several events that the spider will send back to its controller. By providing handlers for each of these events, a wide variety of spiders can be created. The example program, shown later in this chapter, shows a spider that uses many of the methods described here. These methods are followed by a short description of their function and the code line in which they appear in Listing 25.1.

The `completePage` method Called to request that a page be processed. This page was just downloaded by the spider. The parameter page contains the page contents. The parameter `error` is true if this page resulted in an HTTP error.

```
public void completePage(HTTP page, boolean error)
```

The getRemoveQuery method Called by the spider to determine if query strings should be removed. If the query string is to be removed, this method should return true.

```
public boolean getRemoveQuery()
```

The `foundExternalLink` method Called when the spider finds an external link. An external link does not share the same host address as the URL from which the spider started its search. The `url` parameter specifies the URL that was found by the spider. If this method returns true, the spider should add this URL to the workload. If this method returns false, the spider should not add this URL to the workload.

```
public boolean foundExternalLink(String url)
```

The `foundInternalLink` method Called when the spider finds an internal link. An internal link shares the same host address as the URL that started the spider. The `url` parameter specifies the URL that was found by the spider. If this method returns true, the spider should add this URL to the workload. If this method returns false, the spider should not add this URL to the workload.

```
public boolean foundInternalLink(String url)
```

The foundOtherLink method Called when the spider finds another link. A link of type other does not point to an HTML page. Links of this type generally refer to e-mail address links. The url parameter specifies the URL that was found by the spider. If this method returns true, the spider should add this URL to the workload. If this method returns false, the spider should not add this URL to the workload.

```
public boolean foundOtherLink(String url)
```

The processPage method Called to process a page. This is where the work that is actually done by the spider is usually preformed. The page parameter contains the page contents.

```
public void processPage(HTTP page)
```

The spiderComplete method Called when the spider has no work remaining.

```
public void spiderComplete()
```

Using the *Spider* Class

The Bot package's spider is implemented through the Spider class. Though this class is considered the actual spider, it is not the only class that makes up the spider. The other classes that make up the spider will be explored in the next chapter, which explores how a high-volume spider can be constructed.

To use the Spider class in this chapter, you must first instantiate a Spider object. For this object to be instantiated, the constructor for the Spider class must be passed the initial URL, the spider manager, and the size of the thread pool. After these are specified, the spider may begin processing.

The Bot package's spider is multithreaded, which makes it more efficient because it can look at more than one web page at once as a result. You do not need to be aware of how this spider internally processes the pages to use it. Instead, you just need to focus on what a spider is and what it does. The following is a list of methods supported by the Spider class; each of these methods is followed by a description and an example of how they might appear in code.

NOTE

Because of the complexity of the spider classes, the next chapter is dedicated to explaining how a high-volume spider actually works. Think of the next chapter as the "Under the Hood" section for this chapter.

The `Spider` constructor This constructor prepares the spider so that it is ready to begin traversing a site. It also ensures that the basic information required to begin this journey is passed from the program using the spider. The constructor stores these values in the `Spider` class for later use.

In the following code, the parameters of this constructor function as noted. The `manager` parameter is the object to which this spider reports its findings. The `url` parameter is the URL at which the spider should begin. The `http` parameter is the HTTP handler used by this spider. The `poolsize` parameter specifies the size of the thread pool. The optional `w` parameter is a customized workload manager.

```
public Spider(ISpiderReportable manager,String url,HTTP http,
  int poolSize)
public Spider(ISpiderReportable manager,String url,HTTP http,
  int poolSize,IWorkloadStorable w)
```

The `addWorkload` method Called to add a workload to the workload manager. This method will release a thread that was waiting for a workload, but it will do nothing if the spider has been halted. The `url` parameter is the URL to be added to the workload.

```
synchronized public void addWorkload(String url)
```

The `completePage` method Called to request that a page be processed. This page was just downloaded by the spider. This method passes this call on to its manager. The page parameter of this method contains the page contents; the `error` parameter indicates if this page resulted in an error.

```
synchronized public void completePage(HTTP page,
  boolean error)
```

The `foundExternalLink` method Called when the spider finds an external link. This method hands the link off to the manager and adds the URL to the workload if necessary. If this is a world spider, external links are treated as internal links. The `url` parameter specifies the URL that was found by the spider. This method returns true if the spider should add this URL to the workload.

```
synchronized public boolean foundExternalLink(String url)
```

The `foundInternalLink` method Called when the spider finds an internal link. This method hands the link off to the manager and adds the URL to the workload if necessary. The `url` parameter specifies the URL that was found by the spider. This method returns true if the spider should add this URL to the workload.

```
synchronized public boolean foundInternalLink(String url)
```

The `foundOtherLink` method Called when the spider finds a type of link that does not point to another HTML page (for example a mailto link). This method hands the link off to the manager and adds the URL to the workload if necessary. The `url` parameter specifies the URL that was found by the spider. This method returns true if the spider should add this URL to the workload.

```
synchronized public boolean foundOtherLink(String url)
```

The `getMaxBody` method Called to return the maximum body size that will be downloaded. This method returns the body size, or −1 for unlimited.

```
public int getMaxBody()
```

The `getRemoveQuery` method Called by the spider to determine if query strings should be removed. By default, the spider always chooses to remove query strings, so true is returned. This method returns true if the query string should be removed.

```
synchronized public boolean getRemoveQuery()
```

The `getSpiderDone` method Called to get the `SpiderDone` object used by this spider to monitor its progress. The `SpiderDone` object is used to determine when the spider's work is complete.

```
public SpiderDone getSpiderDone()
```

The `getWorkload` method Called to get a workload from the workload manager. If no workload is available, this method will block until there is one. This method returns the next URL to be spidered.

```
synchronized public String getWorkload()
```

The `getWorldSpider` method Called to return true if this is a world spider. A world spider does not restrict itself to a single site, and will likely go on indefinitely.

```
public boolean getWorldSpider()
```

The `halt` method Called to cause the spider to halt. This will not happen immediately, but after the spider is halted, the `run` method will return.

```
synchronized public void halt()
```

The processPage method Called to process a page. This is where the work actually done by the spider is usually preformed. The page parameter contains the page contents.

```
synchronized public void processPage(HTTP page)
```

The run method Called to request the spider to begin processing. This can be called directly, or the `start` method can be called to run as a background thread. This method will not return until there is no work remaining for the spider.

```
public void run()
```

The setMaxBody method Called to set the maximum body size that will be downloaded. The `i` parameter specifies the maximum body size, or −1 for unlimited.

```
public void setMaxBody(int mx)
```

The setWorldSpider method Called to specify this spider as either a world or a site spider. See `getWorldSpider` for more information about what a world spider is. The b parameter is true if this is a world spider.

```
public void setWorldSpider(boolean b)
```

The spiderComplete method Called when the spider has no more work. This method just passes this event on to its manager.

```
synchronized public void spiderComplete()
```

GetSite Example

You will now examine an example spider, which will download all of the pages of the site that it is given. These files will be downloaded into a directory located on the local hard disk. Figure 25.4 shows this program running.

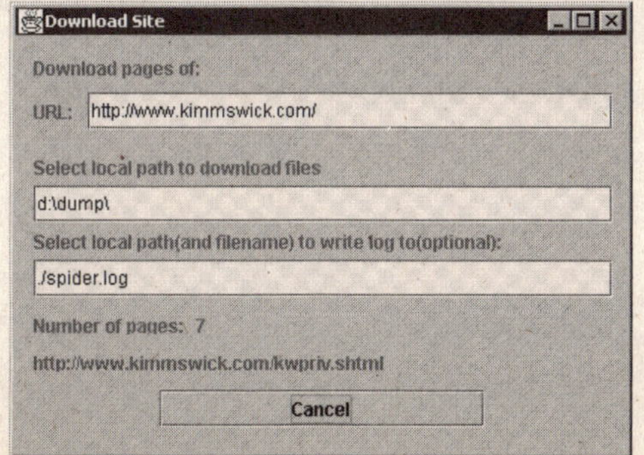

FIGURE 25.4: The `GetSite` spider example

To begin this process, you should select a URL from which the spider will download. You should also select a path to which the web pages should be downloaded. Optionally, you may specify a path to write a log file to as well. After you have entered this URL, you should click the Go button to begin the spider. After the spider is running, you can cancel the process by clicking the Cancel button, which does not appear until the spider begins.

The source code for the GetSite example is shown in Listing 25.2. After the Go button is clicked, the Go_actionPerformed method, which begins the spider threads, is called.

Listing 25.2: Downloading a Site (*GetSite.java*)

```
import java.awt.*;
import java.util.*;
import javax.swing.*;
import java.io.*;
import com.heaton.bot.*;

/**

 * This example program will download all of the HTML files
 * of a web site to a local drive. This shows how a spider can
 * be used to map/download a site.
 *
 * @author Jeff Heaton
 * @version 1.0
 */
public class GetSite extends javax.swing.JFrame implements
   ISpiderReportable
{

  /**
   * The underlying spider object.
   */
  Spider _spider = null;

  /**
   * The current page count.
   */
  int _pagesCount;
```

```
/**
 * The constructor. Set up the visual Swing
 * components that make up the user interface
 * for this program.
 */
public GetSite()
{
   //{{INIT_CONTROLS
   setTitle("Download Site");
   getContentPane().setLayout(null);
   setSize(405,268);
   setVisible(false);
   D.setHorizontalTextPosition(
     javax.swing.SwingConstants.LEFT);
   D.setVerticalTextPosition(
     javax.swing.SwingConstants.TOP);
   D.setVerticalAlignment(
     javax.swing.SwingConstants.TOP);
   D.setText("Download pages of:");
   getContentPane().add(D);
   D.setBounds(12,12,384,24);
   JLabel2.setText("URL:");
   getContentPane().add(JLabel2);
   JLabel2.setBounds(12,36,36,24);
   getContentPane().add(_url);
   _url.setBounds(48,36,348,24);
   JLabel3.setText("Select local path to download files");
   getContentPane().add(JLabel3);
   JLabel3.setBounds(12,72,384,24);
   getContentPane().add(_save);
   _save.setBounds(12,96,384,24);
   _go.setText("GO!");
   getContentPane().add(_go);
   _go.setBounds(96,228,216,24);
   getContentPane().add(_current);
   _current.setBounds(12,204,384,12);
   JLabel4.setText("Number of pages:");
   getContentPane().add(JLabel4);
   JLabel4.setBounds(12,180,120,12);
   _pages.setText("0");
   getContentPane().add(_pages);
   _pages.setBounds(120,180,108,12);
   JLabel6.setText(
```

```
"Select local path(and filename) to write log to(optional):");
        getContentPane().add(JLabel6);
        JLabel6.setBounds(12,120,384,24);
        _logPath.setText("./spider.log");
        getContentPane().add(_logPath);
        _logPath.setBounds(12,144,384,24);
        _go.setActionCommand("jbutton");
        //}}

        //{{INIT_MENUS
        //}}

        //{{REGISTER_LISTENERS
        SymAction lSymAction = new SymAction();
        _go.addActionListener(lSymAction);
        SymWindow aSymWindow = new SymWindow();
        this.addWindowListener(aSymWindow);
        //}}
    }

    /**
     * Added by Visual Cafe.
     *
     * @param b
     */
    public void setVisible(boolean b)
    {
        if (b)
            setLocation(50, 50);
        super.setVisible(b);
    }

    /**
     * Program entry point, causes the main
     * window to be displayed.
     *
     * @param args Command line arguments are not used.
     */
    static public void main(String args[])
    {
        (new GetSite()).setVisible(true);
    }
```

```
/**
 * Added by Visual Cafe.
 */
public void addNotify()
{
   // Record the size of the window prior
   // to calling parents addNotify.
   Dimension size = getSize();

   super.addNotify();

   if (frameSizeAdjusted)
      return;
   frameSizeAdjusted = true;

   // Adjust size of frame according to the insets and
      menu bar
   Insets insets = getInsets();
   javax.swing.JMenuBar menuBar =
     getRootPane().getJMenuBar();
   int menuBarHeight = 0;
   if (menuBar != null)
   menuBarHeight = menuBar.getPreferredSize().height;
   setSize(insets.left +
     insets.right +
     size.width,
     insets.top +
     insets.bottom +
     size.height + menuBarHeight);
}

// Used by addNotify
boolean frameSizeAdjusted = false;

//{{DECLARE_CONTROLS
javax.swing.JLabel D = new javax.swing.JLabel();
javax.swing.JLabel JLabel2 = new javax.swing.JLabel();

/**
 * The URL to spider.
 */
javax.swing.JTextField _url = new javax.swing.JTextField();
javax.swing.JLabel JLabel3 = new javax.swing.JLabel();
```

```
/**
 * The directory to save the files to.
 */
javax.swing.JTextField _save = new javax.swing.JTextField();

/**
 * The Go button.
 */
javax.swing.JButton _go = new javax.swing.JButton();

/**
 * Displays the current page.
 */
javax.swing.JLabel _current = new javax.swing.JLabel();
javax.swing.JLabel JLabel4 = new javax.swing.JLabel();

/**
 * A count of how many pages have been
 * downloaded.
 */
javax.swing.JLabel _pages = new javax.swing.JLabel();
javax.swing.JLabel JLabel6 = new javax.swing.JLabel();

/**
 * Used to specify the path to store the
 * log to.
 */
javax.swing.JTextField _logPath =
  new javax.swing.JTextField();
//}}

//{{DECLARE_MENUS
//}}


/**
 * An event handler class, generated by Visual Cafe.
 *
 * @author Visual Cafe
 */
class SymAction implements java.awt.event.ActionListener
{
```

```
    public void actionPerformed(java.awt.event.ActionEvent
      event)
    {
      Object object = event.getSource();
      if (object == _go)
        Go_actionPerformed(event);
    }
  }


/**
 * As the files of the web site are located,
 * this method is called to save them to disk.
 *
 * @param file The HTTP object corresponding to the page
 * just visited.
 */
protected void processFile(HTTP file)
{
  try
  {
    if(_save.getText().length()>0)
    {
      int i = file.getURL().lastIndexOf('/');

      if(i!=-1)
      {
        String filename = file.getURL().substring(i);
        if(filename.equals("/"))
          filename="root.html";
        FileOutputStream fso
          = new FileOutputStream(
          new File(_save.getText(),filename) );
        fso.write( file.getBody().getBytes("8859_1") );
        fso.close();
      }
    }
  }
  catch(Exception e)
  {
    Log.logException("Can't save output file: ",e);
  }
}
```

```
/**
 * This is where most of the action takes place. This
 * method is called when the Go button is pressed.
 *
 * @param event The event
 */
void Go_actionPerformed(java.awt.event.ActionEvent event)
{
  IWorkloadStorable wl = new SpiderInternalWorkload();
  if(_spider!=null)
  {

   Runnable doLater = new Runnable()
   {
     public void run()
     {
       _go.setText("Canceling...");
     }
   };
   SwingUtilities.invokeLater(doLater);

    _spider.halt();
    return;
  }

  try
  {
    if(_url.getText().length()>0)
    {
     HTTPSocket http = new HTTPSocket();
     http.send(_url.getText(),null);
   }
   else
   {
     _current.setText("<<distributed mode>>");
   }
  }
  catch(Exception e)
  {
   JOptionPane.showMessageDialog(this,
     e,
     "Error",
```

```
        JOptionPane.OK_CANCEL_OPTION,
        null );

      return;
    }

    Runnable doLater = new Runnable()
    {
      public void run()
      {
        _go.setText("Cancel");
        _current.setText("Loading....");
      }
    };
    SwingUtilities.invokeLater(doLater);

    // Prepare to start the spider
    _pagesCount = 0;
    if(_logPath.getText().length()>0)
    {
      File file = new File(_logPath.getText());
      file.delete();
      Log.setLevel(Log.LOG_LEVEL_NORMAL);
      Log.setFile(true);
      Log.setConsole(false);
      Log.setPath(_logPath.getText());
    }

// NOTE: To use SQL-based workload management,
// uncomment the following lines and include a
// valid data source.
/*
    try
    {
      wl = new SpiderSQLWorkload(
       "sun.jdbc.odbc.JdbcOdbcDriver",
       "jdbc:odbc:WORKLOAD");
    }
    catch(Exception e)
    {
     JOptionPane.showMessageDialog(this,
       e,
       "Error",
```

```
            JOptionPane.OK_CANCEL_OPTION,
            null );
        }
    */


        _spider
          = new Spider( this,
            _url.getText(),
            new HTTPSocket(),
            100,
            wl);
        _spider.setMaxBody(200);
        _spider.start();

      }

    /**
     * This method is called by the spider when an
     * internal link is found.
     *
     * @param url The URL of the link that was found. This
     * link is passed in fully resolved.
     * @return True if the spider should add this link to
     * its visitation list.
     */
    public boolean foundInternalLink(String url)
    {
      return true;
    }

    /**
     * This method is called by the spider when an
     * external link is found. An external link is
     * one that points to a different host.
     *
     * @param url The URL of the link that was found. This
     * link is passed in fully resolved.
     * @return True if the spider should add this link to
     * its visitation list.
     */
    public boolean foundExternalLink(String url)
```

```
{
  return false;
}

/**
 * This method is called by the spider when an
 * other type link is found. Links such as e-mail
 * addresses are sent to this method.
 *
 * @param url The URL of the link that was found. This
 * link is passed in fully resolved.
 * @return True if the spider should add this link to
 * its visitation list.
 */
public boolean foundOtherLink(String url)
{
  return false;
}

/**
 * A simple class used to update the current
 * URL target. This is necessary because Swing
 * only allows GUI components to be updated by the
 * main thread.
 *
 * @author Jeff Heaton
 * @version 1.0
 */

class UpdateTarget implements Runnable
{
  public String _t;
  public void run()
  {
    _current.setText(_t);
    _pages.setText( "" + _pagesCount );
  }
}

/**
 * Called by the spider when a page has been
 * loaded and should be processed. For
 * example, this method will save this file
```

```
 * to disk.
 *
 * @param page The HTTP object that corresponds to the
 * page just visited.
 */
public void processPage(HTTP page)
{
  _pagesCount++;
  UpdateTarget ut = new UpdateTarget();

  ut._t = page.getURL();
  SwingUtilities.invokeLater(ut);
  processFile(page);
}

/**
 * Not used. This must be implemented because
 * of the interface. Called when a page completes.
 *
 * @param page The page that just completed.
 * @param error True if the completion of this page
 * resulted in an error.
 */
public void completePage(HTTP page,boolean error)
{
}

/**
 * This method is called to determine if
 * query strings should be stripped.
 *
 * @return Returns true if query strings(the part of
 * the URL after the ?) should be stripped.
 */
public boolean getRemoveQuery()
{
  return true;
}

/**
 * This method is called once the spider
 * has no more work to do.
 */
```

```
public void spiderComplete()
{
  if(_spider.isHalted())
  {
  JOptionPane.showMessageDialog(this,
      "Download of site has been canceled. " +
      "Check log file for any errors.",
      "Done",
      JOptionPane.OK_CANCEL_OPTION,
      null );
  }
  else
  {
  JOptionPane.showMessageDialog(this,
      "Download of site is complete. " +
      "Check log file for any errors.",
      "Done",
      JOptionPane.OK_CANCEL_OPTION,
      null );
  }
  _spider=null;

  Runnable doLater = new Runnable()
  {
    public void run()
    {
      _go.setText("GO!!");
    }
  };
  SwingUtilities.invokeLater(doLater);
}


 /**
  * An event handler class generated by Visual Cafe.
  *
  * @author Visual Cafe
  */
 class SymWindow extends java.awt.event.WindowAdapter
 {
    public void windowClosed(java.awt.event.WindowEvent event)
    {
```

```
            Object object = event.getSource();
            if (object == GetSite.this)
               GetSite_windowClosed(event);
         }
      }
      /**
       * Called to close the window.
       *
       * @param event The event.
       */

      void GetSite_windowClosed(java.awt.event.WindowEvent event)
      {
         System.exit(0);
      }


   }
```

Examining the *GetSite* Example

The code just presented provides a simple spider that can be used to download every page from a site. You will now be shown how this example works. First several objects must be set up before the spider can begin.

Setting Up

In Listing 25.2 the `Go_actionPerformed` method begins by specifying that the spider will use an internal workload manager, which will use the computer's RAM to maintain the queues. (Refer to the next chapter to see how SQL database can be used to store these queues). The following code creates a memory resident workload storage system.

```
IWorkloadStorable wl = new SpiderInternalWorkload();
```

Canceling the Spider

There is only one push button on the spider's frame window. Its functionality alternates between starting and canceling the spider. Initially, it starts the spider; however, after the spider begins, the button becomes a Cancel button.

When this button is clicked, the `Go_actionPerformed` method is called. This method handles both canceling and starting the spider. To determine if it should perform a cancel or start procedure, the method checks to see if the spider is already running. If there is no spider running, the user is requesting that one should be started. If there is a spider running, the user is likely trying to cancel it.

To make this determination, you should check the `_spider` variable to see if a spider already exists. If one does, the user has attempted to cancel the spider download. If this is the case, the Go button's text is changed to the text "Canceling..." using the `invokeLater` method of Swing. This method must be used whenever there is a chance that a thread, other than the main thread, will be updating a GUI component. The text is changed to Canceling... because it will likely take a few seconds for all of the spider's threads to exit properly. The spider's shut down process is then initiated by calling `_spider.halt()`, as shown here.

```
if(_spider!=null)
{

 Runnable doLater = new Runnable()
 {
   public void run()
   {
     _go.setText("Canceling...");
   }
 };
 SwingUtilities.invokeLater(doLater);

  _spider.halt();
  return;
}
```

Starting the Spider

The `Go_actionPerformed` method can also start the spider. If this method was not called, you must find out why. To do this, first verify that a valid URL was entered. You can do this by opening an `HTTPSocket` connection to the specified URL. If the URL fails to load properly, or it is blank, an error message will be displayed, as is shown here:

```
try
{
  if(_url.getText().length()>0)
  {
   HTTPSocket http = new HTTPSocket();
   http.send(_url.getText(),null);
}
```

```
  else
  {
    _current.setText("<<distributed mode>>");
  }
}
catch(Exception e)
{
  JOptionPane.showMessageDialog(this,
    e,
    "Error",
    JOptionPane.OK_CANCEL_OPTION,
    null );

  return;
}
```

If no exception was generated, you have now verified that a valid URL has been entered. The spider can now be started. After the spider starts up the text, the Go button becomes a Cancel button. In code, you accomplish this change by using Java method `invokeLater`.

The following code is responsible for changing the current status indicator, which is a `JText` component, to Loading..... This is done to signify that the spider is about to start up and will soon be reporting pages. The code also changes the Go button to a Cancel button. These calls to change the status and button text are wrapped in a class to be passed to `invokeLater`. This is necessary when Swing components, such as buttons, are changed from inside secondary threads.

NOTE

As the program stands, the `invokeLater` calls used in this method are not required, but they are put in as a precaution because they are required in nearly every other method of this example. This placement ensures commutability in case the go method was called from a background thread.

```
Runnable doLater = new Runnable()
{
  public void run()
  {
     _go.setText("Cancel");
     _current.setText("Loading....");
  }
};
SwingUtilities.invokeLater(doLater);
```

After the button has been changed from Go to Cancel, logging is enabled if a log file path was specified. In this segment, normal level logging has been specified, with the output directed to a file.

```
// Prepare to start the spider
_pagesCount = 0;
if(_logPath.getText().length()>0)
{
  File file = new File(_logPath.getText());
  file.delete();
  Log.setLevel(Log.LOG_LEVEL_NORMAL);
  Log.setFile(true);
  Log.setConsole(false);
  Log.setPath(_logPath.getText());
}
```

Finally, the spider is constructed and started. In the following code, notice that the value 100 is used to specify that the thread pool will have 100 threads. A few lines later, the `wl` parameter specifies what workload manager this spider will be using; then the `setMaxBody` method specifies the largest page (in kilobytes) that can be downloaded. This prevents the spider from downloading huge multimedia files that it might encounter. Finally, the `start` method is called, which starts the spider up as a separate thread.

```
_spider
  = new Spider( this,
    _url.getText(),
    new HTTPSocket(),
    100,
    wl);
_spider.setMaxBody(200);
_spider.start();
```

Workload Management

As mentioned earlier in this chapter, the spider must track every URL that it encounters, and the management of this URL list referred to as *workload management*. By default, the spider uses the computer's RAM to store the workload. If the site is very large, it may be preferable to store the workload elsewhere, perhaps in a SQL database. Notice that the following code is commented out. This code can be uncommented to enable the spider to store its queues in a SQL database. This code is designed to use a DSN called WORKLOAD under the ODBC driver.

```
// NOTE: To use SQL-based workload management,
// uncomment the following lines and include a
// valid data source.
/*
     try
     {
       wl = new SpiderSQLWorkload(
         "sun.jdbc.odbc.JdbcOdbcDriver",
         "jdbc:odbc:WORKLOAD");
     }
     catch(Exception e)
     {
      JOptionPane.showMessageDialog(this,
        e,
        "Error",
        JOptionPane.OK_CANCEL_OPTION,
        null );
     }
*/
```

Monitoring the Spider's Progress

As the spider processes the sites, it calls the events methods of the `ISpiderReportable` interface (discussed earlier), which is implemented by the `GetSite` object (shown below). For example, the `processPage` method is called to save each page. Also, to update the GUI, the internal class `UpdateTarget` is used, and then it is invoked later. A small method named `processFile` is called to save the page to disk. Most of the work performed by a spider is done by the `processFile` method. This method is passed the page that was just downloaded. It simply saves the contents of the page to disk. The `processFile` method is shown in Listing 25.2.

What's Next

A spider is a specialized bot that follows links as it searches for pages. In this chapter, you explored the concept of a spider, built a spider that could download all of the HTML files for a web site, and learned of the most basic ways of using such a spider.

A spider is designed to take HTML output from a web site and trace its links. By using this process, the spider soon finds other links. This is a recursive operation because a spider is endlessly following these links. The spider in this chapter has been built without recursion, however.

Recursion would have stack requirements that are too great for a large site. The spider presented in this chapter maintains a list of links found. This list is then distributed amount several concurrent threads.

Another design consideration for spiders is making sure that they are doing something with the content they receive from sites. Simply looking at pages is not enough; most likely you will want to actually do something with the data encountered by the spider. The `ISpiderReportable` interface is a tool that can accomplish this by reporting back what the spider finds as it is navigating web pages. When you implement this interface you will receive events while the spider finds links, explores pages, and eventually finishes its search.

In the following chapter, you will look at what makes the spider that you created in this chapter processes data as fast is it does. In addition, you will learn how to create a high-volume spider.

Chapter 26

Building a High-Volume Spider

The job of a spider may seem never ending. As a spider visits pages, it locates other pages to visit; when it visits those new pages, still other sites pop up. As a result, the spider's workload begins to grow exponentially. Because of this, it is important that the spider is built as efficiently as possible.

The previous chapter showed how to use a couple of the Bot package classes to construct a spider. This chapter continues dealing with the construction of a spider, but it focuses more on why those classes were constructed the way that they were, and what performance considerations were taken during their development. It also spends a lot more time discussing how a spider can be programmed to be more efficient, which was not discussed in the previous chapter.

Adapted from *Programming Spiders, Bots, and Aggregators in Java*™ by Jeff Heaton

ISBN 0-7821-4040-8 $59.99

Multithreading, which is so important to the performance and efficiency of a spider, will be reviewed at the beginning of this chapter. Then thread synchronization, which shows how threads can work together to produce an aggregate result, will be discussed.

Workload management is also important to a high-performance spider because the spider must track thousands of web pages that it has visited. The spider described in the previous chapter stored its workloads in memory. This is effective for small sites, but it isn't effective for larger sites. This chapter will show you another approach—how to use Java Database Connectivity (JDBC) to make a SQL database to store the workload.

Using the techniques just described, a highly efficient spider will be developed. This chapter will begin by discussing how to use multithreading.

Featured in this chapter:

- Using threads
- Creating a high-volume spider

What Is Multithreading?

Before getting into the details of how to use threads, you must examine what exactly threads are. Basically, a *thread* is a path of execution through a program. Most programs written today run as a single thread, and thus they have just one path of execution; however, this can cause problems when multiple events or actions need to occur at the same time. For example, a single threaded program is not capable of downloading data from the network while it is also responding to mouse or keyboard input from the user. Instead, such a program must give its full attention to either the keyboard input or the network download. The ideal solution to this problem is the seamless execution of two or more sections of a program at the same time. This is the problem that giving a program multiple threads was designed to solve.

To explain how multithreading might help with efficiency, consider the following example. A spider has to download 10 pages. To do this, the spider must request and then receive those pages from a server. While the spider is awaiting a response, a bottleneck occurs. This happens because the spider has requested the page and now must wait for the request to travel through the Internet to the web server. It is in this type of situation that implementing multithreading can help. In this case, numerous threads would allow the wait times of these 10 pages to be combined, rather than having them be executed one after another. It is inefficient for the spider to be just waiting on one single page. Multithreading allows the spider to wait on a large number of pages simultaneously. Next you will be shown how to use multithreading in a Java application.

MULTITHREADING WITH JAVA

Threads are a feature supported by many different programming languages. Java has its own way of handling threads. Before you can create a spider that makes effective use of multithreading, you must first understand how to write a multithreaded program in Java. With a firm understanding of the fundamentals of Java thread programming, you will be able to create a spider that uses multithreading, but you must first learn how to create a thread in Java.

Creating Threads

A thread's job is to execute some part of the program in the background, while the rest of the program continues to run. When a thread is created in Java, that thread must be told exactly what code it should execute in the background. This code is isolated in one single method of the Java thread–the `run` method. Depending on where this `run` method is located within the code, Java handles multithreading in one of two ways.

The first way to handle multithreading is by subclassing the `Thread` object. The `Thread` object is the object that Java provides to encapsulate a thread. If you subclass the `Thread` class, you must override the `run` method in this class to provide the code that should be executed by this particular thread. If your class needs to subclass another class, you will not be able to subclass the `Thread` object.

The second way of handling multithreading is by implementing the `Runnable` interface that is provided by Java and then creating a `run` method in that class. A Java class can implement as many interfaces as needed, so this way does not have the limitations of the previous one; however, your `run` method is now no longer a descendant of the `Thread` class and, as a result, does not have direct access to the `Thread` methods.

It is important to understand both ways of handling multithreading with Java. The following section will continue by discussing the first way, which involves extending the `Thread` class.

NOTE

The `Thread` class is defined in the `java.lang` package, so it does not need to be imported (`java.lang` is always automatically imported by Java).

Subclassing the *Thread* Class

You can create a thread by directly subclassing the `Thread` class. This allows you to create a self-contained thread object that contains both your `run` method and the methods you need to control the execution of your `run` method. The following Java program demonstrates how to create a thread by extending the `Thread` class.

```
public class ExtendThread extends Thread
{
  public void run()
  {
    for(int i=0;i<=1000;i++)
    {
      System.out.println("Counting..." + i );
    }
  }

  public static void main(String args[])
  {
    ExtendThread t = new ExtendThread();
    t.start();
  }
}
```

The above program creates a thread that counts from 0 to 1000. The loop that actually does this work is placed in the `run` method. To begin execution, the `main` method instantiates our class of `ExecuteThread` and calls the `start` method, which was inherited from the `Thread` class. As previously stated, extending the `Thread` class does not allow you to extend from any other class. To alleviate this problem, Java includes a second way of creating a thread.

Implementing the *Runnable* Interface

The second way that Java allows threads to be created is by implementing the `Runnable` interface. The following code shows the same example as the one in the previous section, but in this case, a `Runnable` interface is being used instead of a `Thread` class.

```
public class ImplementRunnable implements Runnable
{
  public void run()
  {
    for(int i=0;i<=1000;i++)
    {
      System.out.println("Counting..." + i );
    }
  }

  public static void main(String args[])
  {
    ImplementRunnable runnable = new ImplementRunnable();
    Thread t = new Thread(runnable);
    t.start();
  }
}
```

In the code above, you can see that a thread that is created by implementing the `Runnable` interface is started slightly differently than a thread that subclassed with the `Thread` object. For such a thread to be created, the class that implements the `Runnable` interface must first be instantiated. After that task is completed, a `Thread` object must be instantiated. The `Thread` object is then passed the `runnable` object as an argument to its constructor. After the new `Thread` object has been instantiated, the thread can begin its work by calling the `start` method. It is important to note that the `run` method that is actually called is that of the class implementing the `Runnable` interface, not the `run` method of the `Thread` object.

Now that you know how to create a thread, you need to be shown how to control its execution; this includes knowing how to start, stop, and pause it.

Controlling the Thread's Execution

Now that you have examined the different ways to create an instance of a thread, ways to begin and end its execution will be discussed. You will also look at a short example program that uses several threads that remain synchronized.

For a thread to begin execution, the `start` method must be called.

```
public static void main(String args[])
{
  MyRunnable run = new MyRunnable();
  Thread t = new Thread(run);
  t.start();
}
```

Synchronizing Threads

Up to this point, you have only talked learned independent, asynchronous threads—those that are self contained and don't need any outside resources or methods to run. Instead, such threads may run at their own pace, and they don't need to be concerned with the state or activities of any other threads that may be running in the background.

This type of thread, however, is the exception rather than the rule. Most threads must usually work with other related threads. When such threads work together, they must not only share data, but they must also be aware of the state and activities of other threads. The threads used to create a multi-threaded spider share data this way. To make the spider run efficiently, the work of the spider (examining many web pages) is broken down into smaller subtasks, and these tasks are given to individual threads. These threads must communicate with each other to make sure that new work is obtained and no new work duplicates work already completed.

Object Locking

Java provides several mechanisms to facilitate this thread synchronization. Most Java synchronization centers around the mechanism of *object locking*. Every object in Java has its own lock, which allows it to be coordinated among threads to be shared.

Java uses the `synchronized` keyword to define sections of the program that require thread synchronization. The most basic operation performed by using the `synchronized` keyword is defining each section that needs such treatment as a *critical section*. In a critical section, only one thread can be executing at a time.

Most object orientated programs use `get` and `set` methods to get and set the values of properties. These methods are ideal candidates to use with the `synchronized` keyword. This is because the `get` method reads the internal state of any object and the `set` method changes the internal state of an object. You do not want the state changing right in the middle of a `get` operation. Likewise, you do not want the state to change while another thread is changing the state with the `set` operation. The following code shows just such an example.

```
public class MySynchronizedObject
{
  int myInt;
```

```
    public synchronized int getMyInt()
    {
      return myInt;
    }

    public synchronized void putMyInt(int value)
    {
      myInt = value;
    }
  }
```

In this code, the method declarations for both `putMyInt()` and `getMyInt()` make use of the `synchronized` keyword. As a result, the system creates a unique lock with every instantiation of `MySynchronizedObject`. Whenever a thread enters a `synchronized` method, all other threads must wait to access that method. No two threads can be inside of a `synchronized` method at the same time.

After a thread calls either `putMyInt()` or `getMyInt()`, that thread owns the lock of that instance of `MySynchronizedObject`, until the `putMyInt()` or `getMyInt()` method exits. Java automatically handles the acquisition and release of this lock.

NOTE

Each object only has one lock that is shared by all synchronized areas of that program. A common misconception is that each synchronized area contains its own lock.

Examining Thread Synchronization

You will now be shown an example of thread synchronization and object locking. In the next few sections, you will develop a simple object that uses object locking and synchronized sections to allow itself to be accessed by multiple threads. First, take a look at a conventional non-locking class to see why locking is needed.

A Non-Locking Example

The `MySynchronizedObject` stores its `contents` variable. A boolean variable, named `available`, is also declared. This variable has a value of true when the value has just been put but has not yet been gotten, and it is false when the value has been gotten but not yet put. First consider a simple implementation of synchronized `get` and `put` methods.

```
public synchronized int getMyInt()
{
  if (available == true)
  {
    available = false;
    return myInt;
  }
}
public synchronized void putMyInt(int value)
{
  if (available == false)
  {
    available = true;
    myInt = value;
  }
}
```

In the code above, these two methods will not work. First consider the `get` method. What happens if nothing has yet been put in the `MySynchronizedObject` and `available` isn't true? In this case, `get` doesn't do anything. Likewise, if something is put into the object before the `get` method was called, the `put` method does nothing.

In this case, what is needed is for the caller of the `get` method to wait until the there is something to read. Likewise, the caller of the `put` method should wait until there is no data, and it is safe to store its value. To allow this to work, the two methods must coordinate their actions. You will now be shown how to do this.

A Locking Example

Consider this new implementation in which both `get` and `put` wait on their class's lock and notify each other of their activities:

```
public synchronized int getMyInt()
{
  while (available == false)
  {
    try
    {
      // wait for a different thread to put a value
      wait();
    }
    catch (InterruptedException e)
    {
    }
  }
```

```
    available = false;
    // notify all remaining threads seeking this object that
       value has been retrieved
    notifyAll();
    return myInt;
  }

  public synchronized void putMyInt(int value)
  {
    while (available == true)
    {
      try
      {
        // wait for a different thread to get value
        wait();
      }
      catch (InterruptedException e)
      {
      }
    }
    myInt = value;
    available = true;
    // notify that value has been set
    notifyAll();
  }
```

Here, the get method loops until the put method has been called and there is data to read. The `wait` method is also called each time through this loop. When the `wait` method is called, the lock held on the `MySynchronizedObject` is relinquished (thereby allowing other threads to lock and update the `MySynchronizedObject`) as the thread waits for a `notify` method to be called. After something is put in the `MySynchronizedObject`, it notifies any waiting threads by calling `notifyAll()`. These waiting threads will then come out of the wait state, and the `available` variable will be set to true, causing the loop to exit. All of this will cause the get method to return the value in the `MySynchronizedObject`.

NOTE

The `put` method works in a similar fashion, waiting for a thread to consume the current value before allowing the other threads to add more values.

Calling the `notifyAll()` method, as mentioned above, will wake any threads that are waiting on the `MySynchronizedObject` that called notifyAll(). The code just demonstrated uses notifyAll() in both the get and set methods to release any threads that might have been waiting for these methods to finish. In addition to the notifyAll() method, there is a method named notify() that will select a single thread to release. You have no way to influence this selection, however. You may only release one seemingly random thread, or all the threads. As a result you cannot control exactly which thread will be released.

The High-Performance Spider

The example program for this chapter implements a spider that can use a SQL-based queue instead of a memory-based queue. This is the only difference between this example and the example program you saw in the last chapter. Both the SQL-based queue discussed here as well as the memory-based queue are useful; which you use depends on what you need for a particular situation. The memory-based queue spider of the last chapter is useful when you are running a program that may not have direct access to a SQL database. On the other hand, if your spider is to access large amounts of pages or many sites, the SQL-based spider is more effective.

TIP

From tests on my own computer I found that the memory-based spider becomes less effective on jobs that will cause such a spider to visit 10,000 pages or more. Jobs that require more than 10,000 pages should be handled by the SQL-based spider.

As stated, the changes to this program from the way it appeared in last chapter are minimal. This is because the source code that is necessary to use a SQL database for queue management was already contained in the last chapter's example in the form of commented text. These lines of code just need to be uncommented to produce a spider that uses a SQL DBMS rather than a memory-based one.

Because the GetSite.java file is nearly the same as that of the last chapter, it will not be reprinted here. Instead, you only need to take a look at the following lines of code, the ones that should be uncommented:

```
// NOTE: To use SQL based workload management,
// uncomment the following lines and include a
// valid data source.
```

```
try
{
  wl = new SpiderSQLWorkload(
    "sun.jdbc.odbc.JdbcOdbcDriver",
    "jdbc:odbc:WORKLOAD");
}
catch(Exception e)
{
 JOptionPane.showMessageDialog(this,
    e,
    "Error",
    JOptionPane.OK_CANCEL_OPTION,
    null );
}
```

By uncommenting this code, you are allowing this code to do several things. First, this code specifies that the `SpiderSQLWorkload` manager must use a SQL database to manage the queues. If a workload is not specified, the memory-based spider, implemented through the `SpiderInternalWorkload` class, will be used.

This code also asks that the constructor of `SpiderSQLWorkload` take two parameters. The first of these is the name of the JDBC driver. In this case, you are using the JDBC to ODBC bridge driver, which is denoted by the string `"sun.jdbc.odbc.JdbcOdbcDriver"`. The second parameter specifies the information to be used to open a connection; this is denoted by the string `"jdbc:odbc:WORKLOAD"`.

After this new workload manager has been specified, the spider will attempt to use a SQL DBMS to manage the queues. Before you go any farther, make sure that you have the database properly configured. Now that you have seen the high-performance spider in action and know how to use it, you will be shown how it was constructed.

Under the Hood

The high-performance spider makes extensive use of threads and its SQL database. You will now examine each of the classes that make up this spider in detail. In addition to these classes, the spider is designed to communicate with external classes provided by the programmer. In this section, you will see how all of this works. First, you will be presented with an overview of how the various classes fit together. Next, this section will explain the finer points of each class. Figure 26.1 shows how all of the spider related classes fit together.

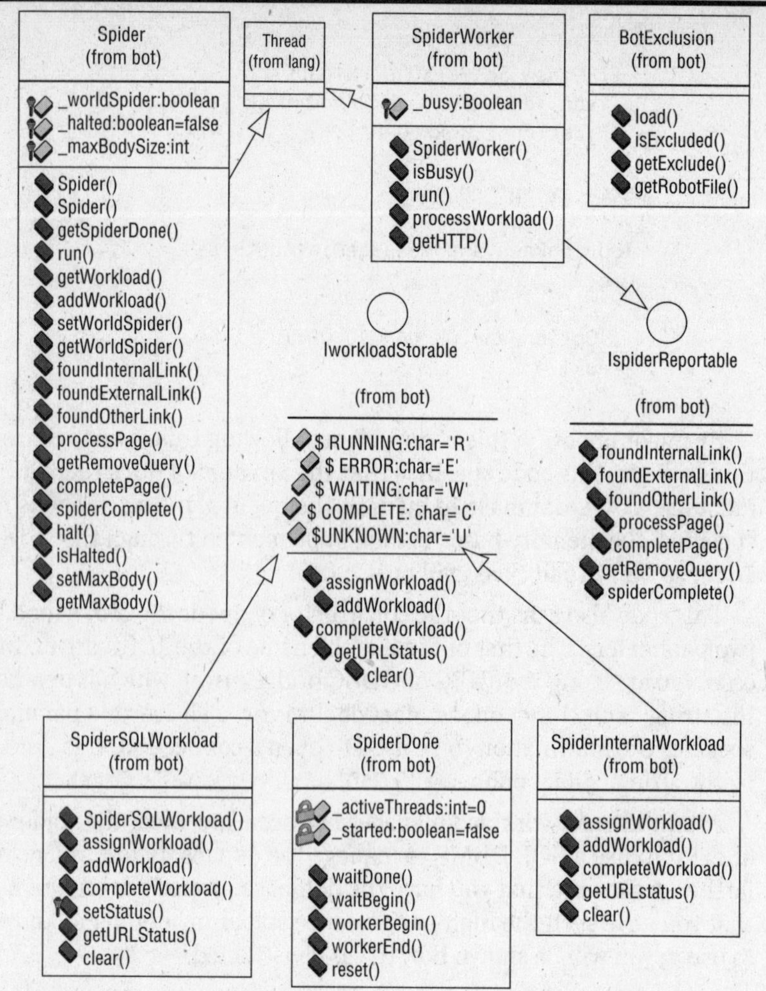

FIGURE 26.1: The spider classes

The Spider Class The `Spider` class is the class that you will work with as you create a spider of your own. This class contains many methods that act as the interface, through which you command the spider. The spider class allows two additional classes, defined by the `ISpiderReportable` and `IWorkloadStorable` interfaces, to be used to customize the operation of the spider.

The `ISpiderReportable` Interface This interface defines a consumer for web pages that the spider locates. A spider by itself simply traverses through web pages. This alone serves little purpose. The spider should actually do something with each page that it encounters. Any object that implements the `ISpiderReportable` interface can receive pages from the spider.

The `IWorkloadStorable` Interface The `IWorkloadStorable` interface is the second interface that allows you to customize the behavior of the spider. One major task for the spider is to organize the lists of sites visited, and those it has yet to visit. These lists are called the *workload*. This interface defines an object that can store and retrieve pages in the workload. The Bot package includes the following two workload managers: `SpiderSQLWorkload` and `SpiderInternalWorkload`.

The `SpiderSQLWorkload` Class The `SpiderSQLWorkload` class is one of the built-in workload managers. This workload manager can store the workload in a SQL database. Using a SQL database, this workload manager can handle large sites.

The `SpiderInternalWorkload` Class The `SpiderInternalWorkload` class is one of the built-in workload managers. This workload manager can store the workload in the computer's memory. Because it uses the computer's memory, this workload manager does not require a database to be set up. Though self contained, this approach may not work on extremely large sites.

The `SpiderWorker` Class The spider makes extensive use of multithreading, and must break the task into many smaller tasks. The basic task of the spider is to download a web site, and add any links that the page has to the workload. This `SpiderWorker` class implements this basic task. When the spider starts up, it creates a pool of `SpiderWorker` classes that will handle the pages found by the spider.

The `SpiderDone` Class With many concurrent threads, it is difficult to tell exactly when the spider is done. There needs to be an object that tracks exactly how many threads are still running, and one that provides an efficient way to wait for that count to reach zero. This is the purpose of the `SpiderDone` class.

The *Spider* Class

The `Spider` class is meant to serve three goals. It acts as the interface to the spider and provides methods for using the spider. In addition to this, this object manages the thread pool and it reports the findings of the spider back to the object that started the spider. (In this section, you will examine how the a `Spider` object communicates with the `SpiderWorker` objects.) Finally, it is the job of the `Spider` class to determine when the spider is done.

NOTE

This object's methods were documented in the last chapter, as was the interface between this class and an application using the spider.

The primary task that the `Spider` class provides for the `SpiderWorker` objects is management of the workload. The workload is the list of all URLs that the spider has interacted with so far.

The purpose of the `SpiderWorker` objects is to process URLs that the spider must visit. When a `SpiderWorker` object first starts up, it requires a URL process. The `SpiderWorker` objects call the `getWorkload()` method of the `Spider` object. The `getWorkload` method will return a new URL that was waiting to be checked. If no URL is waiting, the `getWorkload` method will wait for work to become available.

In addition to managing the workload, the `Spider` class must also keep track of when the spider is done. This task is delegated to the `SpiderDone` class. A `SpiderDone` object is made available to each of the `SpiderWorker` objects. This `SpiderDone` object keeps track of the `SpiderWorker` objects and can determine when the spider is done.

When you call the `Spider` object from another class, you expect to get back pages that the spider has found. The last task accomplished by the `Spider` class is the return of these pages. When the `Spider` object was first constructed, a `manager` object to which the pages would be handed off to was specified. This `manager` object, which must implement the `ISpiderReportable` interface, should be set up in your program to handle pages returned. The process for creating such a class was discussed in Chapter 25, "Building a Spider."

The following code shows such a spider manager (see Listing 26.1). This particular spider manager is used to download the contents of a site to files. For each page encountered by the spider, this manager will save that page to a file.

Listing 26.1: The Spider Manager (*Spider.java*)

```
/**
 * The Spider class is the main organizational class for
 * spidering. It delegates work to the SpiderWorker class.
 *
 * Copyright 2001 by Jeff Heaton
 *
 * @author Jeff Heaton
 * @version 1.0
 */
package com.heaton.bot;
import java.util.*;
import java.io.*;
import com.heaton.bot.*;

public class Spider extends Thread implements ISpiderReportable
{
    protected IWorkloadStorable _workload;
    protected SpiderWorker _pool[];
    protected boolean _worldSpider;
    protected ISpiderReportable _manager;
    protected boolean _halted = false;
    protected SpiderDone _done = new SpiderDone();
    protected int _maxBodySize;


    /**
     * This constructor prepares the spider to begin.
     * Basic information required to begin is passed.
     * This constructor uses the internal workload manager.
     *
     * @param manager The object to which this spider reports
        its findings.
     * @param url The URL at which the spider should begin.
     * @param http The HTTP handler used by this spider.
     * @param poolsize The size of the thread pool.
     */
    public Spider(ISpiderReportable manager,String url,HTTP
       http,int poolSize)
    {
```

```
    this(manager,url,http,poolSize,new
      SpiderInternalWorkload());
  }

  /**
   * This constructor prepares the spider to begin.
   * Basic information required to begin is passed.
   * This constructor allows the user to specify a
   * customized workload manager.
   *
   * @param manager The object to which this spider reports
       its findings.
   * @param url The URL at which the spider should begin.
   * @param http The HTTP handler used by this spider.
   * @param poolsize The size of the thread pool.
   * @param w A customized workload manager.
   */
  public Spider(ISpiderReportable manager,String url,HTTP
     http,int poolSize,IWorkloadStorable w)
  {
    _manager = manager;
    _worldSpider = false;

    _pool = new SpiderWorker[poolSize];
    for(int i=0;i<_pool.length;i++)
    {
      HTTP hc = http.copy();
      _pool[i] = new SpiderWorker( this,hc );
    }
    _workload = w;
    if(url.length()>0)
    {
      _workload.clear();
      addWorkload(url);
    }
  }

  /**
   * Get the SpiderDone object used by this spider
   * to determine when it is done.
   *
   * @return Returns SpiderDone object.
   */
```

```
public SpiderDone getSpiderDone()
{
  return _done;
}

/**
 * The main loop of the spider. This can be called
 * directly, or the start method can be called to
 * run as a background thread. This method will not
 * return until there is no work remaining for the
 * spider.
 */
public void run()
{
  if(_halted)
    return;
  for(int i=0;i<_pool.length;i++)
    _pool[i].start();

    try
    {
      _done.waitBegin();
        _done.waitDone();
        Log.log(Log.LOG_LEVEL_NORMAL,"Spider has no work.");
        spiderComplete();

        for(int i=0;i<_pool.length;i++)
        {
            _pool[i].interrupt();
            _pool[i].join();
            _pool[i] = null;
        }

    }
    catch(Exception e)
    {
      Log.logException("Exception while starting spider", e);
    }

}
```

```
/**
 * This method is called to get a workload
 * from the workload manager. If no workload
 * is available, this method will block until
 * there is one.
 *
 * @return Returns the next URL to be spidered.
 */
synchronized public String getWorkload()
{
  try
  {
    for(;;)
    {
      if(_halted)
        return null;
      String w = _workload.assignWorkload();
      if(w!=null)
        return w;
      wait();
    }
  }
  catch( java.lang.InterruptedException e)
  {
  }
  return null;
}

/**
 * Called to add a workload to the workload manager.
 * This method will release a thread that was waiting
 * for a workload. This method will do nothing if the
 * spider has been halted.
 *
 * @param url The URL to be added to the workload.
 */
synchronized public void addWorkload(String url)
{
  if(_halted)
    return;
    _workload.addWorkload(url);
    notify();
}
```

```
/**
 * Called to specify this spider as either a world
 * or site spider. See getWorldSpider for more information
 * about what a world spider is.
 *
 * @param b True to be a world spider.
 */
public void setWorldSpider(boolean b)
{
  _worldSpider = b;
}

/**
 * Returns true if this is a world spider; a world
 * spider does not restrict itself to a single site
 * and will likely go on "forever."
 *
 * @return Returns true if the spider is done.
 */
public boolean getWorldSpider()
{
  return _worldSpider;
}


/**
 * Called when the spider finds an internal
 * link. An internal link shares the same
 * host address as the URL that started
 * the spider. This method hands the link off
 * to the manager and adds the URL to the workload
 * if necessary.
 *
 * @param url The URL that was found by the spider.
 * @return true - The spider should add this URL to the
 *   workload.
 * false - The spider should not add this URL to the
 *   workload.
 */
synchronized public boolean foundInternalLink(String url)
{
```

```
    if(_manager.foundInternalLink(url))
      addWorkload(url);
    return true;
  }

  /**
   * Called when the spider finds an external
   * link. An external link does not share the
   * same host address as the URL that started
   * the spider. This method hands the link off
   * to the manager and adds the URL to the workload
   * if necessary. If this is a world spider, then
   * external links are treated as internal links.
   *
   * @param url The URL that was found by the spider.
   * @return true - The spider should add this URL to the
     workload.
   * false - The spider should not add this URL to the
     workload.
   */
  synchronized public boolean foundExternalLink(String url)
  {
    if(_worldSpider)
    {
      foundInternalLink(url);
      return true;
    }

    if(_manager.foundExternalLink(url))
      addWorkload(url);
    return true;
  }

  /**
   * Called when the spider finds a type of
   * link that does not point to another HTML
   * page (for example a mailto link). This method
   * hands the link off to the manager and adds
   * the URL to the workload if necessary.
   *
   * @param url The URL that was found by the spider.
   * @return true - The spider should add this URL to the
     workload.
```

```
 * false - The spider should not add this URL to the
   workload.
 */
synchronized public boolean foundOtherLink(String url)
{
  if(_manager.foundOtherLink(url))
    addWorkload(url);
  return true;
}

/**
 * Called to process a downloaded page.
 *
 * @param page The page contents.
 *
 */

synchronized public void processPage(HTTP page)
{
  _manager.processPage(page);    }


/**
 * This method is called by the spider to determine if
 * query strings should be removed. By default the spider
 * always chooses to remove query strings, so true is
 * returned.
 *
 * @return true - Query string should be removed.
 * false - Leave query strings as is.
 */
synchronized public boolean getRemoveQuery()
{
  return true;
}

/**
 * Called to request that a page be processed.
 * This page was just downloaded by the spider.
 * This message passes this call on to its
 * manager.
 *
 * @param page The page contents.
```

```
 * @param error true - This page resulted in an HTTP
   error.
 * false - This page downloaded correctly.
 */
synchronized public void completePage(HTTP page,boolean
  error)
{
  _workload.completeWorkload(page.getURL(),error);
}

/**
 * Called when the spider has no more work. This method
 * just passes this event on to its manager.
 */
synchronized public void spiderComplete()
{
  _manager.spiderComplete();
}

/**
 * Called to cause the spider to halt. The spider will
   not halt
 * immediately. Once the spider is halted, the run
   method will
 * return.
 */
synchronized public void halt()
{
  _halted = true;
  _workload.clear();
  notifyAll();
}

/**
 * Determines if the spider has been halted.
 *
 * @return Returns true if the spider has been halted.
 */
public boolean isHalted()
{
  return _halted;
}
```

```
  /**
   * This method will set the maximum body size
   * that will be downloaded.
   *
   * @param i The maximum body size, or -1 for unlimted.
   */
  public void setMaxBody(int mx)
  {
    _maxBodySize = mx;
    for(int i=0;i<_pool.length;i++)
      _pool[i].getHTTP().setMaxBody(mx);
  }

  /**
   * This method will return the maximum body size
   * that will be downloaded.
   *
   * @return The maximum body size, or -1 for unlimted.
   */
  public int getMaxBody()
  {
    return _maxBodySize;
  }

}
```

The *ISpiderReportable* Interface

The `ISpiderReportable` interface (discussed in detail in Chapter 25) is one of the two interfaces that you can use to customize the operation of the spider. This interface defines the methods used by the spider to report its findings. Listing 26.2 shows the source code for the `IspiderReportable` interface.

Listing 26.2: Reporting progress (*ISpiderReportable.java*)

```
package com.heaton.bot;

/**
 * This interface represents a class to which
 * the spider can report. As the spider
 * does its job, events from this interface
 * will be called.
```

```
 *
 * Copyright 2001 by Jeff Heaton
 *
 * @author Jeff Heaton
 * @version 1.0
 */
public interface ISpiderReportable {

  /**
   * Called when the spider finds an internal
   * link. An internal link shares the same
   * host address as the URL that started
   * the spider.
   *
   * @param url The URL that was found by the spider.
   * @return true - The spider should add this URL to the
       workload.
   * false - The spider should not add this URL to the
       workload.
   */
  public boolean foundInternalLink(String url);

  /**
   * Called when the spider finds an external
   * link. An external link does not share the
   * same host address as the URL that started
   * the spider.
   *
   * @param url The URL that was found by the spider.
   * @return true - The spider should add this URL to the
       workload.
   * false - The spider should not add this URL to the workload.
   */
  public boolean foundExternalLink(String url);

  /**
   * Called when the spider finds a type of
   * link that does not point to another HTML
   * page(for example a mailto link).
   *
   * @param url The URL that was found by the spider.
   * @return true - The spider should add this URL to the
       workload.
```

```
   * false - The spider should not add this URL to the workload.
   */
  public boolean foundOtherLink(String url);

  /**
   * Called to process a downloaded page.
   *
   * @param page The page contents.

   */
  public void processPage(HTTP page);

  /**
   * Called to request that a page be processed.
   * This page was just downloaded by the spider.
   *
   * @param page The page contents.
   * @param error true - This page resulted in an HTTP error.
   * false - This page downloaded correctly.
   */
  public void completePage(HTTP page,boolean error);

  /**
   * This method is called by the spider to determine if
   * query strings should be removed. A query string
   * is the text that follows a ? on a URL. For example:
   *
   * http://www.heat-on.com/cgi-bin/login.jsp?id=a;pwd=b
   *
   * Everything to the right of, and including, the ? is
   * considered part of the query string.
   *
   * @return true - Query string should be removed.
   * false - Leave query strings as is.
   */
  public boolean getRemoveQuery();

  /**
   * Called when the spider has no more work.
   */
  public void spiderComplete();
}
```

The *IWorkloadStorable* Interface

The `IWorkloadStorable` is the second interface that allows you to customize the operation of the spider. This interface implements the basic functionality required to store the four queues that manage the spider's workload. There are two implementations of the `IWorkloadStorable` interface provided by the Bot package.

`SpiderInternalWorkload` Stores the contents of the workload in memory.

`SpiderSQLWorkload` Stores the contents of the workload in a SQL database.

As the `IWorkloadStorable` interface stores and processes URLs, they are assigned status codes that specify which of the four queues a workload entity is currently in. These statuses are defined in Table 26.1.

TABLE 26.1: Spider Workload Statuses

Status Code	Description
RUNNING	A workload entry has a status of RUNNING if the spider worker is opening or downloading that page. This state usually goes to COMPLETE or ERROR.
ERROR	Processing this URL resulted in an error.
WAITING	This URL is waiting for a spider worker to take it on.
COMPLETE	This page is complete and should not be downloaded again.
UNKNOWN	The specified URL is not in any of the queues.

The following methods are defined by the `IWorkloadStorable` interface. Using these methods, URLs can be added and removed from the queues. After these methods are described, the listing for this interface will appears (see Listing 26.3).

The `addWorkload` method Adds a new URL to the workload and assigns it a status of `WAITING`. The `url` parameter specifies a new URL to be added.

```
public void addWorkload(String url);
```

The `assignWorkload` method Requests a URL to process. This method will return a `WAITING` URL and set that URL to a status of `RUNNING`.

```
public String assignWorkload();
```

The `completeWorkload` method Marks this URL as either `COMPLETE` or `ERROR`. The `url` parameter specifies the URL to complete. If the `error` parameter is true, this workload is assigned a status of `ERROR`; if it is false, this workload is assigned a status of `COMPLETE`.

```
public void completeWorkload(String url,boolean error);
```

The `clear` method Clears the contents of this workload store.

```
public void clear();
```

The `getURLStatus` method Gets the status of a URL. The `url` parameter specifies the URL. Returns either `RUNNING`, `ERROR`, `WAITING`, or `COMPLETE`. If the URL does not exist in the database, the value of `UNKNOWN` is returned.

```
public char getURLStatus(String url);
```

Listing 26.3: Storing the Workload (*IWorkloadStorable.java*)

```
package com.heaton.bot;

public interface IWorkloadStorable
{
  public static final char RUNNING = 'R';
  public static final char ERROR = 'E';
  public static final char WAITING = 'W';
  public static final char COMPLETE = 'C';
  public static final char UNKNOWN = 'U';

  public String assignWorkload();
  public void addWorkload(String url);
  public void completeWorkload(String url,boolean error);
  public char getURLStatus (String url);
  public void clear();
}
```

The *SpiderSQLWorkload* Class

The `SpiderSQLWorkload` class is an implementation of the `Ispider-WorkloadStorable` interface that stores the workload in a SQL database. When using this approach, the spider can use a SQL DBMS to maintain its store of queues. The `SpiderSQLWorkload` object, shown in Listing 26.4, does this. This object implements the `IWorkloadStorable` interface and provides all of the methods required by that interface.

The `SpiderSQLWorkload` object works by preparing several SQL statements that can be used to create, add, update, and delete workload entries. One internal method, `setURLStatus()`, is declared. This method will first check to see if any status exists for the specified URL. If no status exists, one will be created. If a status does exist, it will be updated. The following listing shows how an SQL based workload is managed.

Listing 26.4: Managing a SQL-based Workload (*SpiderSQLWorkload.java*)

```
package com.heaton.bot;
import java.util.*;
import java.sql.*;


/**
 * This class uses a JDBC database
 * to store a spider workload.
 *
 * @author Jeff Heaton
 * @version 1.0
 */
public class SpiderSQLWorkload implements IWorkloadStorable
{

  /**
   * The JDBC connection.
   */
  Connection _connection;

  /**
   * A prepared SQL statement to clear the workload.
   */
  PreparedStatement _prepClear;

  /**
   * A prepared SQL statement to assign a workload.
   */
  PreparedStatement _prepAssign;

  /**
   * A prepared SQL statement to get the status of
   * a URL.
```

```
 */
PreparedStatement _prepGetStatus;

/**
 * A prepared SQL statement to set the status.
 */
PreparedStatement _prepSetStatus1;

/**
 * A prepared SQL statement to set the status.
 */
PreparedStatement _prepSetStatus2;

/**
 * A prepared SQL statement to set the status.
 */
PreparedStatement _prepSetStatus3;

/**
 * Create a new SQL workload store and
 * connect to a database.
 *
 * @param driver The JDBC driver to use.
 * @param source The driver source name.
 * @exception java.sql.SQLException
 * @exception java.lang.ClassNotFoundException
 */
public SpiderSQLWorkload(String driver, String source)
  throws SQLException, ClassNotFoundException
{
  Class.forName(driver);
  _connection = DriverManager.getConnection(source);
  _prepClear = _connection.prepareStatement("DELETE FROM
     tblWorkload;");
  _prepAssign = _connection.prepareStatement("SELECT URL
     FROM tblWorkload WHERE Status = 'W';");
  _prepGetStatus = _connection.prepareStatement("SELECT
     Status FROM tblWorkload WHERE URL = ?;");
  _prepSetStatus1 = _connection.prepareStatement("SELECT
     count(*) as qty FROM tblWorkload WHERE URL = ?;");
  _prepSetStatus2 = _connection.prepareStatement("INSERT
     INTO tblWorkload(URL,Status) VALUES (?,?);");
```

```
    _prepSetStatus3 = _connection.prepareStatement("UPDATE
       tblWorkload SET Status = ? WHERE URL = ?;");
  }

  /**
   * Call this method to request a URL
   * to process. This method will return
   * a WAITING URL and mark it as RUNNING.
   *
   * @return The URL that was assigned.
   */
  synchronized public String assignWorkload()
  {
    ResultSet rs = null;

    try
    {
      rs = _prepAssign.executeQuery();

      if( !rs.next() )
        return null;
      String url = rs.getString("URL");
      setStatus(url,RUNNING);
      return url;
    }
    catch(SQLException e)
    {
      Log.logException("SQL Error: ",e );
    }
    finally
    {
      try
      {
        if(rs!=null)
          rs.close();
      }
      catch(Exception e){}
    }
    return null;
  }

  /**
   * Add a new URL to the workload, and
```

```
 * assign it a status of WAITING.
 *
 * @param url The URL to be added.
 */
synchronized public void addWorkload(String url)
{
  if(getURLStatus(url)!=UNKNOWN)
    return;
  setStatus(url,WAITING);

}

/**
 * Called to mark this URL as either
 * COMPLETE or ERROR.
 *
 * @param url The URL to complete.
 * @param error true - assign this workload a status
    of ERROR.
 * false - assign this workload a status of COMPLETE.
 */
synchronized public void completeWorkload(String
   url,boolean error)
{
  if(error)
    setStatus(url,ERROR);
  else
    setStatus(url,COMPLETE);

}


/**
 * This is an internal method used to set the status
 * of a given URL. This method will create a record
 * for the URL if one does not currently exist.
 *
 * @param url The URL for which to set the status.
 * @param status What status to set.
 */
protected void setStatus(String url,char status)
{
  ResultSet rs = null;
```

```
    try
    {
    // first see if one exists
      _prepSetStatus1.setString(1,url);
      rs = _prepSetStatus1.executeQuery();
      rs.next();
      int count = rs.getInt("qty");

      if( count<1)
      {// Create one
        _prepSetStatus2.setString(1,url);
        _prepSetStatus2.setString(2,(new
           Character(status)).toString());
        _prepSetStatus2.executeUpdate();
      }
      else
      {// Update it
        _prepSetStatus3.setString(1,(new
           Character(status)).toString());
        _prepSetStatus3.setString(2,url);
        _prepSetStatus3.executeUpdate();
      }
    }
    catch(SQLException e)
    {
      Log.logException("SQL Error: ",e );
    }
    finally
    {
      try
      {
        if(rs!=null)
          rs.close();
      }
      catch(Exception e){}
    }
  }


  /**
   * Get the status of a URL.
   *
   * @param url Returns either RUNNING, ERROR
```

```
 * WAITING, or COMPLETE. If the URL
 * does not exist in the database,
 * the value of UNKNOWN is returned.
 * @return Returns either RUNNING, ERROR,
 * WAITING, COMPLETE, or UNKNOWN.
 */
synchronized public char getURLStatus(String url)
{
  ResultSet rs = null;

  try
  {
  // first see if one exists
    _prepGetStatus.setString(1,url);
    rs = _prepGetStatus.executeQuery();

    if( !rs.next() )
      return UNKNOWN;

    return rs.getString("Status").charAt(0);
  }
  catch(SQLException e)
  {
    Log.logException("SQL Error: ",e );
  }
  finally
  {
    try
    {
      if(rs!=null)
        rs.close();
    }
    catch(Exception e){}
  }
  return UNKNOWN;
}

/**
 * Clear the contents of the workload store.
 */
synchronized public void clear()
{
  try
```

```
        {
          _prepClear.executeUpdate();
        }
        catch(SQLException e)
        {
          Log.logException("SQL Error: ",e );
        }
      }
    }
```

The *SpiderInternalWorkload* Class

The `SpiderInternalWorkload` class is an implementation of the `Ispider-WorkloadStorable` interface that stores the workload in memory. When using this approach, the spider does not require a SQL DBMS to maintain its store of queues. This allows the spider to operate as a completely self-contained unit. The `SpiderSInternalWorkload` object, shown in Listing 26.5, does this. This object implements the `IWorkloadStorable` interface and provides all of the methods required by that interface.

The `SpiderInternalWorkload` object works by preparing several Vectors that will contain each of the workload queues. As the methods defined by the `ISpiderWorkloadStorable` interface are called, the URLs are moved between the Vectors that represent the queues.

Listing 26.5: Handling the Internal Workload (*SpiderInternal-Workload.java*)

```
package com.heaton.bot;
import java.util.*;

/**
 * This class is used to maintain an internal,
 * memory-based workload store for a spider. This
 * workload store will be used by default if no
 * other is specified.
 *
 * Copyright 2001 by Jeff Heaton
 *
 * @author Jeff Heaton
 * @version 1.0
 */
public class SpiderInternalWorkload implements
   IWorkloadStorable {
```

```
/**
 * A list of complete workload items.
 */
Hashtable _complete = new Hashtable();

/**
 * A list of waiting workload items.
 */
Vector _waiting = new Vector();

/**
 * A list of running workload items.
 */
Vector _running = new Vector();

/**
 * Call this method to request a URL
 * to process. This method will return
 * a WAITING URL and mark it as RUNNING.
 *
 * @return The URL that was assigned.
 */
synchronized public String assignWorkload()
{
  if ( _waiting.size()<1 )
    return null;

  String w=(String)_waiting.firstElement();
  if ( w!=null ) {
    _waiting.remove(w);
    _running.addElement(w);
  }
  Log.log(Log.LOG_LEVEL_TRACE,"Spider workload
     assigned:" + w);
  return w;
}

/**
 * Add a new URL to the workload and
 * assign it a status of WAITING.
 *
 * @param url The URL to be added.
 */
```

```
synchronized public void addWorkload(String url)
{
  if ( getURLStatus(url) != IWorkloadStorable.UNKNOWN )
    return;
  _waiting.addElement(url);
  Log.log(Log.LOG_LEVEL_TRACE,"Spider workload added:"
     + url);
}

/**
 * Called to mark this URL as either
 * COMPLETE or ERROR.
 *
 * @param url The URL to complete.
 * @param error true - assign this workload a status
    of ERROR.
 * false - assign this workload a status of COMPLETE.
 */
synchronized public void completeWorkload(String
   url,boolean error)
{
  if ( _running.size()>0 ) {
    for ( Enumeration e = _running.elements() ;
       e.hasMoreElements() ; ) {
      String w = (String)e.nextElement();
      if ( w.equals(url) ) {
        _running.remove(w);
        if ( error ) {
          Log.log(Log.LOG_LEVEL_TRACE,"Spider workload
             ended in error:" + url);
          _complete.put(w,"e");
        } else {
          Log.log(Log.LOG_LEVEL_TRACE,"Spider workload
             complete:" + url);
          _complete.put(w,"c");
        }
        return;
      }
    }
  }
  Log.log(Log.LOG_LEVEL_ERROR,"Spider workload LOST:"
     + url);
```

```
}

/**
 * Get the status of a URL.
 *
 * @param url Returns either RUNNING, ERROR,
 * WAITING, or COMPLETE. If the URL
 * does not exist in the database,
 * the value of UNKNOWN is returned.
 * @return Returns either RUNNING, ERROR,
 * WAITING, COMPLETE or UNKNOWN.
 */
synchronized public char getURLStatus(String url)
{
  if ( _complete.get(url)!=null )
    return COMPLETE;

  if ( _waiting.size()>0 ) {
    for ( Enumeration e = _waiting.elements() ;
       e.hasMoreElements() ; ) {
      String w = (String)e.nextElement();
      if ( w.equals(url) )
        return WAITING;
    }
  }

  if ( _running.size()>0 ) {
    for ( Enumeration e = _running.elements() ;
       e.hasMoreElements() ; ) {
      String w = (String)e.nextElement();
      if ( w.equals(url) )
        return RUNNING;
    }
  }

  return UNKNOWN;
}

/**
 * Clear the contents of the workload store.
 */
```

```
    synchronized public void clear()
    {
      _waiting.clear();
      _complete.clear();
      _running.clear();
    }
  }
```

The *SpiderWorker* Class

Because the spider is multithreaded, it must have a way of dividing tasks up among different threads. The basic unit of work is the `SpiderWorker` object, as seen in Listing 26.6. After the listing, the code will be discussed.

Listing 26.6: The Worker Threads (*SpiderWorker.java*)

```
package com.heaton.bot;
import com.heaton.bot.*;
import java.net.*;

/**
 * The SpiderWorker class performs the actual work of
 * spidering pages. It is implemented as a thread
 * that is created by the spider class.
 *
 * Copyright 2001 by Jeff Heaton
 *
 * @author Jeff Heaton
 * @version 1.0
 */
public class SpiderWorker extends Thread
{

  /**
   * The URL that this spider worker
   * should be downloading.
   */
  protected String _target;

  /**
   * The owner of this spider worker class
   * should always be a Spider object.
   * This is the class to which this spider
```

```
 * worker will send its data.
 */
protected Spider _owner;

/**
 * Indicates if the SpiderWorker is busy or not.
 * true = busy
 * false = idle
 */
protected boolean _busy;

/**
 * A descendant of the HTTP object that
 * this class should be using for HTTP
 * communication. This is usually the
 * HTTPSocket class.
 */
protected HTTP _http;

/**
 * Constructs a spider worker object.
 *
 * @param owner The owner of this object, usually
 * a Spider object.
 * @param http
 */
public SpiderWorker(Spider owner,HTTP http)
{
  _http = http;
  _owner = owner;
}

/**
 * Returns true or false to indicate if
 * the SpiderWorker is busy or idle.
 *
 * @return true = busy
 * flase = idle
 */
public boolean isBusy()
{
    return _busy;
}
```

```
  /**
   * The run method causes this thread to go idle
   * and wait for a workload. Once a workload is
   * received, the processWorkload method is called
   * to handle the workload.
   */
  public void run()
  {
    for(;;)
    {
      _target = _owner.getWorkload();
      if(_target==null)
        return;
      _owner.getSpiderDone().workerBegin();
      processWorkload();
      _owner.getSpiderDone().workerEnd();
    }
  }

 protected void processWorkload()
 {
   try
   {
     _busy = true;
     Log.log(Log  /**
  * The run method actually performs the
  * the workload assigned to this object.
  */
.LOG_LEVEL_NORMAL,"Spidering " + _target );
     _http.send(_target,null);

     HTMLParser parse = new HTMLParser();
     parse._source = new StringBuffer(_http.getBody());
     _owner.processPage(_http);

     // find all the links
     while( !parse.eof() )
     {
       char ch = parse.get();
       if(ch==0)
       {
         HTMLTag tag = parse.getTag();
```

```
        Attribute href = tag.get("HREF");
        if(href==null)
          continue;

        URL target=null;
        try
        {
          target = new URL(new URL(_target),href.getValue());
        }
        catch(MalformedURLException e)
        {
          Log.log(Log.LOG_LEVEL_TRACE,
            "Spider found other link: " + href );
          _owner.foundOtherLink(href.getValue());
          continue;
        }

        if(_owner.getRemoveQuery())
          target = URLUtility.stripQuery(target);
        target = URLUtility.stripAnchor(target);


        if(target.getHost().equalsIgnoreCase(
          new URL(_target).getHost()))
        {
          Log.log(Log.LOG_LEVEL_NORMAL,
            "Spider found internal link: " + target
               .toString() );
          _owner.foundInternalLink(target.toString());
        }
        else
        {
          Log.log(Log.LOG_LEVEL_NORMAL,
            "Spider found external link: " + target
               .toString() );
          _owner.foundExternalLink(target.toString());
        }

        _owner.completePage(_http,false);
      }
    }
  }
```

```
    catch(java.io.IOException e)
    {
      Log.log(Log.LOG_LEVEL_ERROR,
        "Error loading file("+ _target +"): " + e );
    }
    catch(Exception e)
    {
      Log.logException(
        "Exception while processing file("+ _target +"): ", e );
    }
    finally
    {
      _owner.completePage(_http,true);
      _busy = false;

    }
  }

  /**
   * Returns the HTTP descendant that this
   * object should use for all HTTP communication.
   *
   * @return An HTTP descendant object.
   */
  public HTTP getHTTP()
  {
    return _http;
  }
}
```

Through this object, the spider maintains a *thread pool*, which alleviates the spider of the task of creating and destroying thread objects. In this code, you saw that each `SpiderWorker` object began in the `run` method of the `Spider` object as its `start()` method was called.

The `run` method then began a wait until there was a workload for it. After a workload had been acquired from the spider manager, the `SpiderDone` class was notified that the thread was no longer idle. At that point, the workload was passed off to the `processWorkload()` method to be handled.

In this code, the `processWorkload()` method did much of the work you would normally associate with a spider. The `processWorkload()` method began by downloading the specified page. If the download completed without error, the method would then parse the HTML and add every link to the waiting queue. Finally, the page was passed onto the manager object for this spider.

The *SpiderDone* Class

It's usually pretty easy for an application to tell when it is done. In the case of a multithreaded spider, however, this is not the case. There are two main criteria that must be met before the spider can consider itself done.

No Active Worker Threads There shouldn't be any threads that are currently downloading. If they are, they may very well add URLs to the waiting queue, which would cause the spider to continue searching.

No Waiting Queue There shouldn't be any data in the waiting queue. If there is, the worker threads will soon be processing it, in which case the spider cannot be considered finished.

The `SpiderDone` class is shown in Listing 26.7. After the code listing you will be shown how this class works.

Listing 26.7: Are We Done Yet? (*SpiderDone.java*)

```
package com.heaton.bot;

/**
 * This is a very simple object that
 * allows the spider to determine when
 * it is done. This object implements
 * a simple lock that the spider class
 * can wait on to determine completion.
 * Done is defined as the spider having
 * no more work to complete.
 *
 * Copyright 2001 by Jeff Heaton
 *
 * @author Jeff Heaton
 * @version 1.0
 */
class SpiderDone
{

  /**
   * The number of SpiderWorker object
   * threads that are currently working
```

```
   * on something.
   */
  private int _activeThreads = 0;

  /**
   * This Boolean keeps track of whether
   * the very first thread has started
   * or not. This prevents this object
   * from falsely reporting that the spider
   * is done, just because the first thread
   * has not yet started.
   */
  private boolean _started = false;
  /**
   * This method can be called to block
   * the current thread until the spider
   * is done.
   */

  synchronized public void waitDone()
  {
    try
    {
      while(_activeThreads>0)
      {
        wait();
      }
    }
    catch(InterruptedException e)
    {
    }
  }
  /**
   * Called to wait for the first thread to
   * start. Once this method returns, the
   * spidering process has begun.
   */

  synchronized public void waitBegin()
  {
    try
    {
```

```
      while(!_started)
      {
        wait();
      }
    }
    catch(InterruptedException e)
    {
    }
  }


  /**
   * Called by a SpiderWorker object
   * to indicate that it has begun
   * working on a workload.
   */
  synchronized public void workerBegin()
  {
    _activeThreads++;
    _started = true;
    notify();
  }

  /**
   * Called by a SpiderWorker object to
   * indicate that it has completed a
   * workload.
   */
  synchronized public void workerEnd()
  {
    _activeThreads--;
    notify();
  }

  /**
   * Called to reset this object to
   * its initial state.
   */
  synchronized public void reset()
  {
    _activeThreads = 0;
  }

}
```

The `SpiderDone` object is used to determine when there are no active threads and nothing is waiting to be processed. Often an object will want to wait for these two events to occur. By being in a separate object, the `SpiderDone` object will have its own lock, and thus objects can wait on the `SpiderDone` class. Because the `SpiderDone` object has its own lock, other objects are allowed to wait; this results in minimal CPU time being consumed until the spider is done.

The following methods make up the `SpiderDone` class.

The reset method The `reset` method will reset the `SpiderDone` object to its initial state—when no threads are running.

```
synchronized public void reset()
```

The `waitBegin` method The `waitBegin` method will wait for the spider to begin processing.

```
synchronized public void waitBegin()
```

The `waitDone` method The `waitDone` method will wait until the spider has no workload. Make sure you call the `waitBegin` method first so that you don't get a false Done reading because the spider has not been started yet.

```
synchronized public void waitDone()
```

The `workerBegin` method When a thread worker begins, it should call this method. Calling this method allows the `SpiderDone` object to keep an accurate count of how many threads are active.

```
synchronized public void workerBegin()
```

The `workerEnd` method When a thread worker ends, it should call this method. Calling this method allows the `SpiderDone` object to keep an accurate count of how many threads are active.

```
synchronized public void workerEnd()
```

What's Next

Threads allow a program to process more than one task at once. This is particularly useful for a spider because it may need to download multiple pages simultaneously. When the spider uses threads, a spider can execute more easily in the background and it does not need to consume unnecessary CPU cycles.

When you use threads, they must be synchronized. Synchronization can be achieved by using several built-in features of Java. Java provides support for object locking and critical sections. By making use of these tools, the programmer can cause portions of the spider to wait on others without having to enter idle loops so the spider does not consume unnecessary CPU cycles.

In addition to threads, a SQL database must also be used to create a more successful high-volume spider. JDBC allows Java to access such a database. Java also provides a JDBC to ODBC bridge that allows Java programs to access an ODBC data source as though it were a JDBC driver. This in turn allows JDBC to access SQL databases that only provide an ODBC driver.

By bringing together the technologies of threads, thread synchronization, and JDBC, you are able to create a high-performance spider. It may not be appropriate to use all of the high-performance features all of the time, however. For example, you may want to create a small spider that will not have access to a SQL database. The Bot package allows you to optionally use either a memory- or SQL-based queue store.

Now that you have seen how to create a spider, you will continue to build on this knowledge by creating more bots in the following chapter. Some of the more advanced bots introduced in the next chapter will use a spider-like process to seek out the specific information needed.

Chapter 27

Building a Bot

A *bot* is an Internet-aware program that can retrieve information for the user in an autonomous way. After summarizing the bot techniques already presented, this chapter goes one step further by showing how bots are designed to retrieve data from more than just one individual site.

To understand how many bots function, you should know that most bots are designed specifically to retrieve information from one specific web site. Basically, these bots are tied to the particular user-interface nuances that are built into this site. This chapter introduces a new type of bot, called a CatBot, which is designed to operate across an entire category of sites.

A normal bot is programmed with very intricate and specific information about a particular site; a *CatBot*, on the other hand, is programmed with broad general information about the type of site it will be examining. The Internet is filled with many such

Adapted from *Programming Spiders, Bots, and Aggregators in Java*™ by Jeff Heaton

ISBN 0-7821-4040-8 $59.99

site categories, including those sites that handle shipping packages, e-mail accounts, online banking information, or even weather information. A CatBot is designed to retrieve data from many sources that is based on the broad-ranging characteristics that all the sites in a particular category might share.

A CatBot also overcomes many of the limitations that are inherent in bots that are designed to work closely with the user interface of just one site. A common problem that such bots face is the volatility of the sites from which they are designed to retrieve information. (By volatility, I mean the constant state of flux most web sites seem to be in.) Because most bots look for specific features or landmarks, the bot will likely get lost if you remove one or more of these landmarks as they travel through their intended site.

This chapter will examine some of the characteristics of both regular bots and CatBots. It will begin by looking at how to construct a regular bot. It will then explore the limitations of this process, and then extend this normal bot into a CatBot. By doing so, you will develop a bot that works with a much larger set of web sites and is more responsive to changes in the underlying site.

Featured in this chapter:

- Using a traditional bot
- Weaknesses inherent in bots
- Recognizing common pages
- Creating an adaptive bot

Constructing a Typical Bot

Before you create an automated CatBot, you must first examine how to create a regular bot. Before you begin, remember that a regular bot is constructed specifically to access one type of site, and therefore, any changes to that underlying site will likely result in changes to the bot program.

Introducing the WatchBBS Bot

Many web sites operate bulletin boards to which users can post messages. These bulletin boards allow for ongoing discussions among the web site's visitors. My own web site has one such discussion area. To examine it, visit the URL `http://heat-on.com/cgi-bin/ubb/ultimatebb.cgi`, or take a look at Figure 27.1.

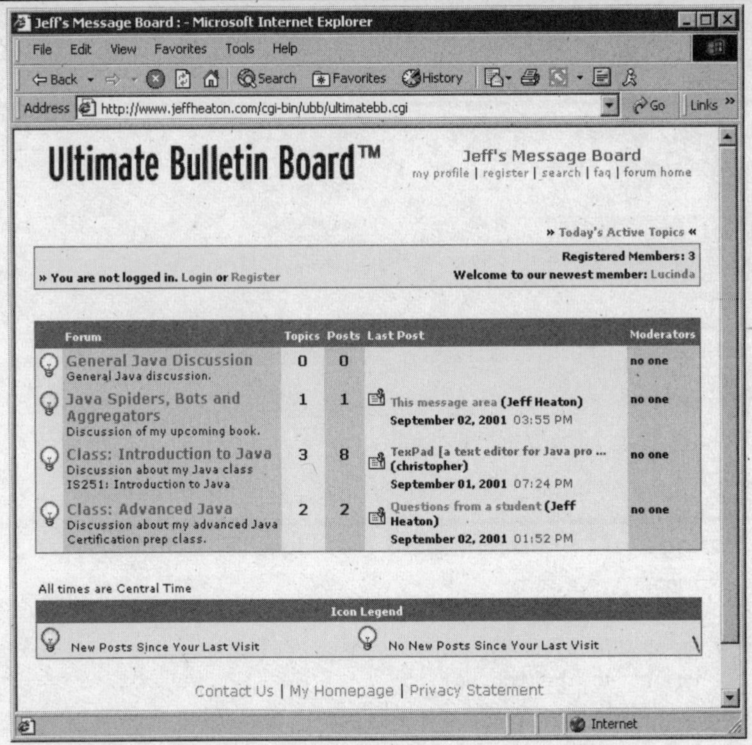

FIGURE 27.1: Discussion area at `JeffHeaton.com`

The first bot that you create will be designed to work with this bulletin board, which uses the Ultimate Bulletin Board system that was developed by the company InfoPop (`http://www.infopop.com`). Because this system is a common BBS package that is used by many web sites, it is the example bot that will be created here. In addition to working with my site, it should work with any site that uses the Ultimate Bulletin Board system.

This bot program has been designed to run in the background and monitor the bulletin board for a user to post a new message to the board. After the bot notices that a new message has been posted by one of the users, a pop-up window will alert the user that is running the bot. This program can be seen running in Figure 27.2, and its source code can be seen in Listing 27.1.

NOTE

This program does not use any new features of the Bot package; it simply uses the HTTP and HTML parsing classes, discussed in previous chapters, to look for new messages posted to the discussion board.

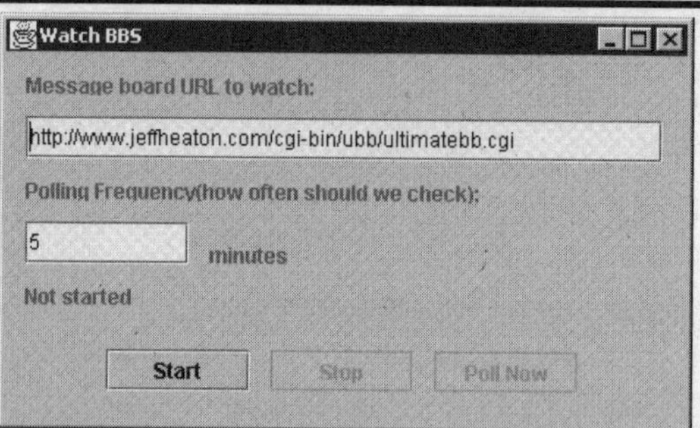

FIGURE 27.2: The WatchBBS application

Listing 27.1: Watching for Messages (*WatchBBS.java*)

```
import java.awt.*;
import java.util.*;
import javax.swing.*;
import com.heaton.bot.*;

/**
 * Example from Chapter 27
 *
 * This is a simple bot program that is designed
 * to work with one specific site. Later we will
 * see CatBots, which are designed to function across
 * an entire category of sites.
 *
 * This Bot is designed to scan the bulletin board hosted
 * at my site, http://www.jeffheaton.com, and look for new
 * messages. When a new message is located, the user is
 * informed that there are new messages waiting.
 *
 * @author Jeff Heaton
 * @version 1.0
 */
```

```
public class WatchBBS extends javax.swing.JFrame implements
  Runnable {

  /**
   * The time of the latest message posted.
   */
  Date _latest = null;

  /**
   * The time of the next poll.
   */
  Date _nextPoll;

  /**
   * The background thread.
   */
  Thread _thread;

  /**
   * The constructor. Used to setup all of the Swing
   * controls.
   */
  public WatchBBS()
  {
    //{{INIT_CONTROLS
    setTitle("Watch BBS");
    getContentPane().setLayout(null);
    setSize(398,210);
    setVisible(false);
    JLabel1.setText("Message board URL to watch:");
    getContentPane().add(JLabel1);
    JLabel1.setBounds(12,12,384,12);
    _url.setText(
    "http://www.jeffheaton.com/cgi-bin/ubb/ultimatebb.cgi");
    getContentPane().add(_url);
    _url.setBounds(12,36,372,24);
    JLabel2.setText("Polling Frequency(how often should we
       check):");
    getContentPane().add(JLabel2);
    JLabel2.setBounds(12,72,384,12);
    _minutes.setText("5");
    getContentPane().add(_minutes);
    _minutes.setBounds(12,96,96,24);
```

```
        JLabel3.setText("minutes");
        getContentPane().add(JLabel3);
        JLabel3.setBounds(120,108,240,12);
        _start.setText("Start");
        _start.setActionCommand("Start");
        getContentPane().add(_start);
        _start.setBounds(60,168,84,24);
        _stop.setText("Stop");
        _stop.setActionCommand("Stop");
        _stop.setEnabled(false);
        getContentPane().add(_stop);
        _stop.setBounds(156,168,84,24);
        _go.setText("Poll Now");
        _go.setActionCommand("Poll Now");
        _go.setEnabled(false);
        getContentPane().add(_go);
        _go.setBounds(252,168,84,24);
        _status.setText("Not started");
        getContentPane().add(_status);
        _status.setBounds(12,132,384,12);
        //}}

        //{{INIT_MENUS
        //}}

        //{{REGISTER_LISTENERS
        SymAction lSymAction = new SymAction();
        _start.addActionListener(lSymAction);
        _stop.addActionListener(lSymAction);
        _go.addActionListener(lSymAction);
        SymWindow aSymWindow = new SymWindow();
        this.addWindowListener(aSymWindow);
        //}}
    }

    /**
     * Added by Visual Cafe.
     *
     * @param b True if the window is visible.
     */
    public void setVisible(boolean b)
    {
        if ( b )
```

```
    setLocation(50, 50);
  super.setVisible(b);
}

/**
 * The program entry point.
 *
 * @param args Command line arguments are not used.
 */
static public void main(String args[])
{
  (new WatchBBS()).setVisible(true);
}

/**
 * Added by Visual Cafe.
 */
public void addNotify()
{
  // Record the size of the window prior to calling parents
     addNotify.
  Dimension size = getSize();

  super.addNotify();

  if ( frameSizeAdjusted )
    return;
  frameSizeAdjusted = true;

  // Adjust size of frame according to the insets and menu bar
  Insets insets = getInsets();
  javax.swing.JMenuBar menuBar =
     getRootPane().getJMenuBar();
  int menuBarHeight = 0;
  if ( menuBar != null )
    menuBarHeight = menuBar.getPreferredSize().height;
  setSize(insets.left
          + insets.right
          + size.width,
          insets.top + insets.bottom
          + size.height + menuBarHeight);
}
```

```
// Used by addNotify
boolean frameSizeAdjusted = false;

//{{DECLARE_CONTROLS
javax.swing.JLabel JLabel1 =
  new javax.swing.JLabel();

/**
 * The URL of the BBS to scan.
 */
javax.swing.JTextField _url =
  new javax.swing.JTextField();
javax.swing.JLabel JLabel2 =
  new javax.swing.JLabel();

/**
 * The polling frequency.
 */
javax.swing.JTextField _minutes =
  new javax.swing.JTextField();
javax.swing.JLabel JLabel3 =
  new javax.swing.JLabel();

/**
 * The Start button.
 */
javax.swing.JButton _start =
  new javax.swing.JButton();

/**
 * The Stop button.
 */
javax.swing.JButton _stop =
  new javax.swing.JButton();

/**
 * The "Poll Now" button.
 */
javax.swing.JButton _go =
  new javax.swing.JButton();

/**
 * The displayed status.
```

```
 */
javax.swing.JLabel _status =
  new javax.swing.JLabel();
//}}

//{{DECLARE_MENUS
//}}


/**
 * Added by Visual Cafe.
 *
 * @author Visual Cafe
 */
class SymAction implements java.awt.event.ActionListener {
  public void actionPerformed(java.awt.event.ActionEvent
     event)
  {
    Object object = event.getSource();
    if ( object == _start )
      Start_actionPerformed(event);
    else if ( object == _stop )
      Stop_actionPerformed(event);
    else if ( object == _go )
      Go_actionPerformed(event);
  }
}

/**
 * Called when the start button is clicked.
 * This method starts up the background thread
 * and determines the date of the latest post,
 * at this time. This time will later be used
 * as a refference to determine if there are any
 * new messages.
 *
 * @param event The event.
 */
void Start_actionPerformed(java.awt.event.ActionEvent
   event)
{
  if ( _latest==null ) {
    _latest = getLatestDate();
```

```
      if ( _latest==null )
        return;
    }
    if ( !setNextPoll() )
      return;
    _thread = new Thread(this);
    _thread.start();
    _start.setEnabled(false);
    _stop.setEnabled(true);
    _go.setEnabled(true);
  }

  /**
   * Called when the stop button is clicked.
   * This method stops the background thread.
   *
   * @param event
   */
  void Stop_actionPerformed(java.awt.event.ActionEvent event)
  {
    _thread.stop();
    _start.setEnabled(true);
    _stop.setEnabled(false);
    _go.setEnabled(false);
  }

  /**
   * Called when the Poll Now button is cliked. Also
   * called when the background thread determines that
   * it is time to poll again.
   *
   * @param event The event.
   */
  void Go_actionPerformed(java.awt.event.ActionEvent event)
  {
    setNextPoll();
    Date update = getLatestDate();
    if ( !update.toString().equalsIgnoreCase(_latest
        .toString()) ) {
      _latest = update;
      Runnable doit = new Runnable()
      {
        public void run()
```

```
        {
          JOptionPane.showMessageDialog(null,
            "There are new messages at:" + _url.getText(),
            "New Messages",
            JOptionPane.OK_CANCEL_OPTION,
            null );
        }
      };

      SwingUtilities.invokeLater(doit);

    }
  }

  /**
   * Added by Visual Cafe
   *
   * @author Visual Cafe
   */
  class SymWindow extends java.awt.event.WindowAdapter {
    public void windowClosed(java.awt.event.WindowEvent event)
    {
      Object object = event.getSource();
      if ( object == WatchBBS.this )
        WatchBBS_windowClosed(event);
    }
  }

  /**
   * Called when the window is closed.
   *
   * @param event The event.
   */
  void WatchBBS_windowClosed(java.awt.event.WindowEvent event)
  {
    System.exit(0);

  }

  /**
   * Called to get the latest date that
   * a message was posted at the specified
   * BBS.
```

```
   *
   * @return A Data class of the last message date.
   */
  protected Date getLatestDate()
  {
    HTTPSocket http;
    Date latest = new Date(0,0,0);
    try {
      http = new HTTPSocket();
      http.send(_url.getText(),null);
    } catch ( Exception e ) {
      JOptionPane.showMessageDialog(this,
        e,
        "Error",
        JOptionPane.OK_CANCEL_OPTION,
        null );
      return null;
    }
    HTMLParser parse = new HTMLParser();
    parse._source = new StringBuffer(http.getBody());

    int foundTag = 0;
    String date = "";


    // find all the links
    while ( !parse.eof() ) {
      char ch = parse.get();
      if ( ch==0 ) {
        HTMLTag tag = parse.getTag();
        if ( tag.getName().equalsIgnoreCase("B") ) {
          foundTag = 2;
          date="";
        } else if ( tag.getName().equalsIgnoreCase("/FONT") ) {
          foundTag--;
          if ( foundTag==0 ) {
            Date d = parseDate(date);
            if ( d!=null ) {
              if ( d.after(latest) )
                latest = d;
            }
          }
```

```
      }
    } else {
      if ( (ch=='\r') || (ch=='\n') )
        ch=' ';
      date+=ch;
    }
  }
  return latest;
}

/**
 * Parse a date of the form:
 *
 * September 2, 2001 5:30 PM
 *
 * @param str The string form of the date.
 * @return A Date object that was parsed.
 */
Date parseDate(String str)
{
  String months[] = {"jan","feb","mar","apr","may",
    "jun","jul","aug","sep","oct","nov","dec"};
  Date rtn;
  try {
    rtn = new Date();
    // month
    String mth = str.substring(0,str.indexOf(' '));
    for ( int i=0;i<months.length;i++ ) {
      if ( mth.toLowerCase().startsWith(months[i]) ) {
        rtn.setMonth(i);
        break;
      }
    }

    // day

    str = str.substring(str.indexOf(' ')+1);
    String day = str.substring(0,str.indexOf(','));
    rtn.setDate(Integer.parseInt(day));

    // Year
```

```
        str = str.substring(str.indexOf(',')+1).trim();
        String year = str.substring(0,str.indexOf(' '));
        rtn.setYear(Integer.parseInt(year)-1900);

        // Hour

        str = str.substring(str.indexOf(' ')+1).trim();
        String hour = str.substring(0,str.indexOf(':'));
        rtn.setHours(Integer.parseInt(hour));

        // Minute

        str = str.substring(str.indexOf(':')+1).trim();
        String minutes = str.substring(0,str.indexOf(' '));
        rtn.setMinutes(Integer.parseInt(minutes));
        rtn.setSeconds(0);

        // AM or PM
        str = str.substring(str.indexOf(' ')+1).trim();
        if ( str.toUpperCase().charAt(0)=='P' )
          rtn.setHours(rtn.getHours()+12);

        return rtn;
      } catch ( Exception e ) {
        return null;
      }
    }

    /**
     * This run method is called to execute
     * the background thread.
     */
    public void run()
    {
      while ( true ) {
        Runnable doit = new Runnable()
        {
          public void run()
          {
            Date d = new Date();
            long milli = (_nextPoll.getTime()-d.getTime())/1000;
            _status.setText("Will poll in " + milli + " seconds.");
```

```
      }
    };

    if ( _nextPoll.before(new Date()) ) {
      Go_actionPerformed(null);
    }

    SwingUtilities.invokeLater(doit);
    try {
      Thread.sleep(1000);
    } catch ( InterruptedException e ) {
    }
  }
}

/**
 * Called to determine the next time
 * that a poll will take place.
 *
 * @return True on success, false on failure.
 */
public boolean setNextPoll()
{
  try {
    int minutes = Integer.parseInt(_minutes.getText());
    Date d = new Date();
    d.setMinutes(d.getMinutes()+minutes);
    _nextPoll = d;
    return true;
  } catch ( Exception e ) {
    JOptionPane.showMessageDialog(this,
      e,
      "Invalid Polling Time",
      JOptionPane.OK_CANCEL_OPTION,
      null );
    return false;
  }
}
}
```

You will now examine how this program works and what limitations it has.

How the WatchBBS Bot Works

The WatchBBS example must sit in the background and scan the targeted BBS. To accomplish this, the program uses threads. As soon as the Start button is clicked, a background thread is started, and it begins scanning the BBS system. This thread continues until the Stop button is clicked, but the scanning is not continuous. A polling frequency is specified by the user to determine how often the bot should run.

The actual bot portion of this program can be found in the section of code that uses the `getLatestDate()` method. This method is called to determine the date on which the latest message was posted. By comparing this value taken at different times, the program can determine if any new messages have been posted since its last visit. As shown in the following code, this program begins by setting an internal variable, named `latest`, to a zero date, and then it opens a connection to the URL that is specified by the edit field. If any error occurs while this initial connection to the site is being made, the error will be displayed in a window.

```
HTTPSocket http;
Date latest = new Date(0,0,0);
try
{
 http = new HTTPSocket();
 http.send(_url.getText(),null);
}
catch(Exception e)
{
 JOptionPane.showMessageDialog(this,
   e,
   "Error",
   JOptionPane.OK_CANCEL_OPTION,
   null );
 return null;
}
```

Next, the data that was downloaded from the site must be parsed. To do this, an `HTMLParser` object is allocated. This will allow us to loop through all of the tags.

```
HTMLParser parse = new HTMLParser();
parse._source = new StringBuffer(http.getBody());

int foundTag = 0;
String date = "";
```

Now the code must loop through all of the tags, as is shown in the code segment below. If you refer back to Figure 27.1, you will notice that several dates are displayed. Each of the message areas maintains a separate time for the last posted message.

```
// find all the tags
while( !parse.eof() )
{
  char ch = parse.get();
  if(ch==0)
  {
    HTMLTag tag = parse.getTag();
```

One by one, the tags are read through until the date is reached.

If you look at the HTML for a date, you will see that it is of the following form:

```
<FONT size="1" face="Verdana, Helvetica, sans-serif">
  <B>September 03, 2001</B></FONT>
```

Items of text that match this pattern are located. As each is found, they are run through the `parseDate` method to determine if they are in a date format that is valid for the bulletin board.

```
    if(tag.getName().equalsIgnoreCase("B"))
    {
      foundTag = 2;
      date="";
    }
    else if(tag.getName().equalsIgnoreCase("/FONT"))
    {
      foundTag--;
      if(foundTag==0)
      {
        Date d = parseDate(date);
        if(d!=null)
        {
          if(d.after(latest))
            latest = d;
        }
      }
    }
}
```

This process results in a date displayed by the BBS that is in a form that cannot be parsed by `DateFormat`–Java's own date parsing class. (The BBS expresses dates in the form September 2, 2001 5:30 P.M.) Because of this, you must parse this date internally in the program. In this case, the code was set up so that the `parseDate()` method accepts a string containing a date formatted the way the BBS expresses it, and it then changes it into the format that the Java `Date` class uses.

As date after date is located, they are compared with previous dates, and from each of the message areas, the last date is located. Changes in these values will indicate that a user has posted a message. Whenever the date of the last posted message changes, it indicates that a new message has been posted to the discussion board.

Bot Weaknesses

The above bot may seem pretty effective, but there are several issues that it and other bots will face in their lifetimes that make them less than ideal. First is the reliability of the underlying sites that typical bots will be exploring. A bot must rely on a site to provide data in a reliable and consistent manner. If the site is down, the bot cannot retrieve its information. The bot must make adaptations so it doesn't crash when it experiences such events. If the bot is running unattended, it is unacceptable for it to crash if the target site fails to respond.

Another issue involves the volatility of site content. An event that can devastate a bot is a change, or redesign, of the underlying site. A bot, such as the `WatchBBS` bot that you just examined, is programmed to look for certain landmark features of the HTML code for a particular site. If these features are removed, or changed to the point where they are no longer recognizable, it is unlikely that the bot will succeed in finding its data. Because of this, it is important to build as much adaptability into the bot as possible. In the next section, you will examine a new type of bot, one that actually contains no data specific to the underlying site; this allows it to avoid the pitfalls mentioned here.

Using the CatBot

A CatBot, or category bot, is designed to be able to operate on an entire category of web sites. By using the CatBot classes, you can create CatBots for a wide variety of sites. The example that you will examine in this chapter is a shipping bot that retrieves status information about a package that has been shipped.

CatBot Recognizers

CatBots navigate a web site by using a series of classes called *recognizers*. A recognizer is a class specifically designed to recognize, and then interact with, a specific type of web page. If at least one recognizer is present for each type of page that the CatBot will encounter, the CatBot will be successful.

You will work with several kinds of recognizers to create the second example program for this chapter. First, consider the type of site that might benefit from such a CatBot.

There are many companies available that can ship packages. When you ship a package with one of these carriers, you are provided with a tracking number. By entering this tracking number into the carrier's web site, you can get the exact status of your package.

Though a bot that could obtain the status of a tracking number could be very useful, several design challenges may need to be considered. One potential challenge is that there are many different carriers available. Each of these carriers has their own web sites. Each of these web sites is likely laid out differently. This is a problem because a bot is normally only designed to handle one individual site. Also, many companies use a combination of the available carriers. It would be convenient to use one single bot for all carriers. It would be useful, therefore, to create a CatBot that can handle any carrier that likely to be encountered.

You may have to visit several different pages of a carrier's web site before you are actually allowed to enter the tracking number. Some carriers may even want to know what country you are accessing their site from first. But some carrier's have a box in which to enter your tracking number right on their home page. To be successful in navigating all of these possibilities, a shipping CatBot must contain a recognizer for each of these situations. First, examine the types of pages for which you are apt to need recognizers.

Pick your country (`RecognizeCountry`) The `RecognizeCountry` recognizer can recognize a page that typically displays a list of countries and asks you to identify yours. Some carriers use such a page on their site, but it is not necessarily just tied to shipping. Any page where you are presented with a list of countries and are made to choose one could be a candidate for this recognizer.

Find a link (`RecognizeLink`) The `RecognizeLink` recognizer can recognize a page that has a certain type of link on it. This link is of the type that leads you to the next page that you might be interested in. This is a very general recognizer that can be used any time you must seek out a text link that may take you to a new page. For instance, when you are tracking shipments, you might be seeking a link that contains the text "Click here to track shipment," or something similar.

Enter tracking number (`RecognizePackagePage`) The `RecognizePackagePage` recognizer can recognize a page in which you need to enter a tracking number. This page would only exist on a shipping site, and thus this recognizer is not very general. The shipping bot example that is examined later in this chapter, under the section "An Example CatBot" shows how this comes in to play.

Starting the CatBot

When the CatBot is first started, it is given three things. The CatBot is given a URL from which to begin its search. Also, the CatBot is given a series of recognizers with which to work. Finally, one of the recognizers is identified as the prime recognizer. The *prime recognizer* can recognize the type of data that is the ultimate goal of the CatBot. If the prime recognizer is satisfied, the CatBot considers its job done, regardless of whether the other recognizers were satisfied.

The CatBot begins at its starting URL. First, the prime recognizer is applied to the URL. If the data needed happens to be on the first page, it is gathered, and the job is done. If it isn't, all remaining recognizers are applied to the page. If none of them recognize it, the CatBot gives up and stops. If one recognizer does recognize the page, that recognizer is allowed to interact with that page. This recognizer knows how to move on to a new page, where the recognition process will start over again. The process will continue until the CatBot finds what it's looking for, or a page is reached that no recognizers recognize. This process is summarized in Figure 27.3.

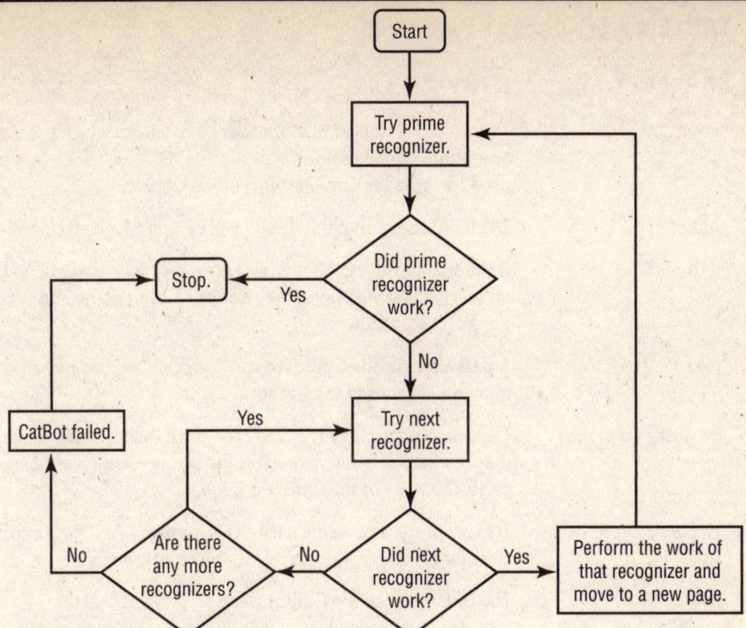

FIGURE 27.3: The recognition process flowchart

The *CatBot* Class

The `CatBot` class forms the foundation of any CatBot. This class contains several abstract methods and is therefore an abstract class. Because of this, you never work with an instance of the CatBot class; you use classes that are descendants of the `CatBot` class instead. The `CatBot` class only exists to provide a base class for other CatBots, such as the `ShipBot` that you will soon be examining.

CatBot Properties

The `CatBot` class contains several important properties, and any CatBot that you create will likely require you to use these. The class level properties of the `CatBot` class are summarized in Table 27.1.

TABLE 27.1: CatBot Properties

Property	Meaning
`_country`	This property is used to store the country from which the CatBot is operating. Usually some value such as "UK" or "USA". May not be used by some implementations of the CatBot.
`_http`	The HTTP object that this CatBot will be using for web communication.
`_uid`	If the site that the CatBot is accessing requires a user ID to be entered, it is stored here. May not be used by some implementations of the CatBot.
`_pwd`	A password for the CatBot to use. May not be used by some implementations of the CatBot.
`_primeRecognizer`	The prime recognizer that will recognize the ultimate information that the CatBot is seeking. After the prime recognizer recognizes a page, the work of the CatBot is done.
`_recognizers`	This property represents a list of recognizers. See the `Recognize` class for more information on what a recognizer is.
`_url`	The URL at which the CatBot starts.

CatBot Class Methods

The `CatBot` class also contains several methods. Some of these methods are marked as abstract and must be defined by child classes of this object. A complete list of the CatBot methods and the constructor for this class are summarized here.

The CatBot constructor Sets up the CatBot. The `http` parameter specifies an HTTP object that should be used for communication.

```
public CatBot(HTTP http)
```

The getCountry method Gets a country that the CatBot may have been using. This method returns the user ID that the CatBot was using.

```
public String getCountry()
```

The getHTTP method Returns the HTTP object being used by this CatBot.

```
public HTTP getHTTP()
```

The getPWD method Gets a password that the CatBot may have been using.

```
public String getPWD()
```

The getRecognizers method Gets the list of recognizers that should be used by this CatBot. This method will return the list of recognizers used by this CatBot.

```
public Vector getRecognizers()
```

The getUID method Gets a user ID that the CatBot may have been using.

```
public String getUID()
```

The setCountry method Sets a country for the CatBot to use. This parameter may or may not be used, depending on the type of CatBot. The uid parameter specifies a user ID for the CatBot to use.

```
public void setCountry(String country)
```

The setPWD method Sets a password for the CatBot to use. This parameter may or may not be used, depending on the type of CatBot. The pwd parameter specifies a password for the CatBot to use.

```
public void setPWD(String pwd)
```

The setUID method Sets a user ID for the CatBot to use. This parameter may or may not be used, depending on the type of CatBot. The uid parameter specifies a user ID for the CatBot to use.

```
public void setUID(String uid)
```

The setURL method Sets the URL that this CatBot should start on. The url parameter specifies this URL.

```
public void setURL(String url)
```

The standardRecognition method Causes the CatBot to begin moving through the site with a set of recognizers. The CatBot will continue until the prime recognizer recognizes something, or all recognizers have been exhausted. This method returns true if the recognition was successful.

```
protected HTMLPage standardRecognition
    throws java.io.IOException,
    javax.swing.text.BadLocationException
```

The *Recognize* Class

The `Recognize` class is the class from which all recognizers descend. As mentioned earlier in this chapter, the use of recognizers is an important concept for the CatBot. These classes can recognize and extract data from certain types of page, and can then provide these pages with the needed information so that the CatBot can continue. The following methods are provided by the `Recognize` class.

The `Recognize` constructor Stores the CatBot controller for this recognizer. The parameter `controller` specifies the CatBot controller for this object.

```
public Recognize(CatBot controller)
```

The `findOption` method Finds the specified option in an HTML select list. The `list` parameter specifies the component list to search. The `search` parameter specifies the search string. Only a partial match is needed.

```
public String findOption(AttributeList list,String
   search)
```

The `findPrompt` method Finds a form prompt based on a partial search string. The `form` parameter specifies the form to search. The `search` parameter specifies the form text that is being searched for.

```
public String findPrompt(HTMLForm form,String search)
```

The `has` method Returns true if the specified form has a component that matches the name passed to this method. The `form` parameter specifies the form object that is to be searched for. The `hasWhat` parameter specifies the search string. This method returns the component found.

```
public HTMLForm.FormElement has(HTMLForm form,String
   hasWhat)
```

The `internalPerform` method Performs the process of interacting with this page when called internally. This is an abstract method that must be implemented by child classes. The parameter page specifies the page to perform against. This method returns true if successful.

```
abstract protected boolean internalPerform
   (HTMLPage page)
  throws java.io.IOException,
  javax.swing.text.BadLocationException;
```

The `isRecognizable` method Returns true if this page is recognized. The parameter page specifies the page to look at. This method returns true if this page is recognized.

```
abstract public boolean isRecognizable(HTMLPage page);
```

The `isRecognized` method Returns true if this page has already been recognized.

```
abstract public boolean isRecognized();
```

The `perform` method Performs whatever task is done by this `Recognize` object.

```
public boolean perform(HTMLPage page)
```

An Example CatBot

Package delivery is an important business service. In the last few years, delivery companies have enabled their web sites to track the status of these packages. By logging on to your shipping company's web site and then entering your tracking number, you can see the exact status of your package. The example program you will examine here (called `ShipBot`) is designed to be given a package tracking number and return the status of that package.

This example program is implemented as a JSP page, which allows the user to enter a tracking number and the carrier's web site and then see the package status. Before you see ShipBot in action, you will first be shown how the JSP is structured.

WARNING

As always, you should verify that running a program such as this does not violate the *current* rules, regulations, and terms of service of the target company.

Running a JSP Page

The program that you will examine here is implemented as a JSP page. The example program can be seen running in Figure 27.4, and the code for the main JSP page can be seen at Listing 27.2.

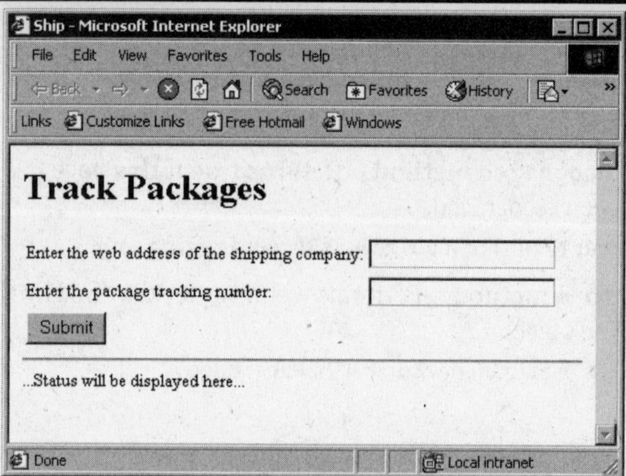

FIGURE 27.4: The package tracker running

Listing 27.2: Checking the Status of a Shipment (*ship.jsp*)

```
<%@page import="com.heaton.bot.ship.*" %>
<h1>Track Packages</h1>
<table border=0>
<form method=post>
<tr><td>Enter the web address of the shipping company:</td>
<td><input name="url"
   value="<%=request.getParameter("url")%>"></td></tr>
<tr><td>Enter the package tracking number:</td>
<td><input name="track"
   value="<%=request.getParameter("track")%>"></td></tr>
<tr><td colspan="2">
<input type="submit" value="Submit"></td></tr>
</form>
</table>
<hr>
<%
if(request.getParameter("url")==null)
{%>
...Status will be displayed here...
<%
}
else
{
```

```
    String str
      = FindPackage.findPackage(
        request.getParameter("url"),
        request.getParameter("track"),
        "U.S.A.");
     out.println(str);
}%>
```

This ship.jsp page will be displayed two times. The first time that the ship.jsp is called, it displays a form that allows a user to enter the tracking number, shipping carrier web address, and the country from which the package was sent. This is accomplished by the HTML seen at the top of Listing 27.2. The JSP seen near the bottom will not activate until the second time this JSP page is called, when the user completes the form and clicks Submit. As a result of this action, the contents of the form are posted right back to ship.jsp. When these contents are posted, the form is redisplayed, and the JSP code near the bottom begins to execute. First the JSP code checks to see if it should execute.

```
<%
if(request.getParameter("url")==null)
{%>
...Status will be displayed here...
<%
}
else
{
```

The above code checks to see if there is a value in the url parameter. If there is no value, the form has not yet been posted, and this is the first time the ship.jsp page has been displayed. This is because the parameters do not get filled until the form is posted. If there are no parameters, and this is the first time, ship.jsp simply reports "... status will be displayed here...."

If there is a value contained in the url parameter, the posted contents of the form will be evaluated. This is done with the following lines of code:

```
String str
  = FindPackage.findPackage(
    request.getParameter("url"),
    request.getParameter("track"),
    "U.S.A.");
 out.println(str);
```

Here, the `findPackage` method of the `FindPackage` class is called, and the URL, tracking number, and country of origin are all passed. This program defaults to U.S.A. for simplicity, but any nation could be entered here. The `findPackage` method will return a string that contains the status of that package, which is displayed below the form. Now that you have seen how the JSP works, you will now be shown how the `FindPackage` class works.

Connecting JSP to the Bot Package

As stated previously in this chapter, the `FindPackage` class allows the JSP to communicate with the Bot package. You will now be shown how the `FindPackage` class was constructed. (The `FindPackage` class can be seen in Listing 27.3.) This class contains a single static method called `findPackage()`; this method is called to start the `ShipBot` program. The `findPackage` method accepts three parameters—the URL of the shipping carrier, the tracking number, and the country from which the package was shipped. These are the same three parameters with which the JSP page passed with the `findPackage` method was called. The `findPackage` method does no more than instantiate a `ShipBot` object and call the `lookup` method from `ShipBot`. How `ShipBot` was constructed will be covered in the next section, "Recognizing HTML."

Listing 27.3: Finding the Status of a Tracking Number (*FindPackage.java*)

```
package com.heaton.bot.ship;
import com.heaton.bot.*;
import com.heaton.bot.catbot.*;

public class FindPackage
{
  public static String findPackage(String url,String
   code,String country)
  {
    try
    {
      ShipBot ship = new ShipBot(new HTTPSocket());
      ship.setURL(url);
      ship.setCountry(country);
      return ship.lookup(code);
    }
```

```
      catch(Exception e)
      {
        return e.toString();
      }
    }
  }
```

Recognizing HTML

The RecognizePackagePage recognizer class accomplishes a great deal of the ShipBot's work. This recognizer class, shown in Listing 27.4, is used to recognize an HTML page that is laid out to allow the entry of tracking numbers.

The two methods that are most active in this class are the isRecognizable() method and the interalPerform method. The isRecognizable() method that is called in the code determines if this page is actually a tracking entry page. It does this by looping through all forms and components on the page. After one is located that contains either the text number or track, that page is assumed to be a tracking number entry page. The internalPerform() method is called to interact with the page once it has been identified. This method will fill in the tracking number and submit the form. The resulting page is returned.

Listing 27.4: Identifying a Shipping Page (*RecognizePackagePage.java*)

```
package com.heaton.bot.ship;
import com.heaton.bot.*;
import com.heaton.bot.catbot.*;
import java.util.*;

public class RecognizePackagePage extends Recognize
{
  HTMLForm _targetForm = null;
  String _targetControl;

  public RecognizePackagePage(CatBot controller)
  {
    super(controller);
  }
```

```
public boolean isRecognized()
{
  return(_targetForm!=null);
}


public boolean isRecognizable(HTMLPage page)
{
  if(page.getForms()==null)
    return false;

  Vector forms = page.getForms();
  for (Enumeration e = forms.elements() ;
     e.hasMoreElements() ;)
  {
    HTMLForm form = (HTMLForm)e.nextElement();
    String target = findPrompt(form,"track");
    if(target!=null)
    {
      _targetForm = form;
      _targetControl = target;
      Log.log(Log.LOG_LEVEL_NORMAL,"Recognized a package
         page");
      return true;
    }
    target = findPrompt(form,"number");
    if(target!=null)
    {
      _targetForm = form;
      _targetControl = target;
      Log.log(Log.LOG_LEVEL_NORMAL,"Recognized a package
         page");
      return true;
    }
  }
  return false;
}

protected boolean internalPerform(HTMLPage page)
  throws java.io.IOException
{
  if(_targetForm==null)
    return false;
```

```
    _targetForm.set(_targetControl,
      ((ShipBot)_controller).getPackageID() );
    page.post(_targetForm);

    return true;
  }

}
```

The *ShipBot* Class

The `ShipBot` class (shown in Listing 27.5) provides the framework for the shipping bot, but there is little real work performed in this class.

The main method that is active in this class, the `lookup()` method, should be called to perform the actual lookup of shipping information. This method is then passed a tracking number, and with this information, it returns the status screen as HTML data. The status screen is the page that the shipping company provides in response to the given tracking number.

The `lookup()` method assembles the `link`, `country`, and `shipping` recognizers. The `shipping` recognizer is designated as the prime recognizer; then the `standardRecognition()` method is called to begin the process of searching for the shipping page.

Listing 27.5: ShipBot Framework (*ShipBot.java*)

```
package com.heaton.bot.ship;
import com.heaton.bot.*;
import com.heaton.bot.catbot.*;
import java.net.*;
import java.io.*;
import javax.swing.text.*;

import com.heaton.bot.*;

public class ShipBot extends CatBot
{
  protected String _packageID;
  public ShipBot(HTTP http)
  {
    super(http);
  }
```

```
  String getPackageID()
  {
    return _packageID;
  }

  public String lookup(String packageID)
    throws IOException, BadLocationException
  {
    _packageID = packageID;

    RecognizeCountry rcountry = new RecognizeCountry(this);
    RecognizeLink rlink = new RecognizeLink(this);
    rlink.setSearch("track");
    RecognizePackagePage rship = new
       RecognizePackagePage(this);
    _recognizers.addElement(_primeRecognizer=rship);
    _recognizers.addElement(rlink);
    _recognizers.addElement(rcountry);
    HTMLPage page = standardRecognition();
    if(page==null)
      return "Failed to understand site: " + _url;
    return page.getHTTP().getBody();

  }
}
```

Under the Hood

You will now examine how the more low-level classes of the CatBot function. The first one you will examine is the `CatBot` class itself. This class provides the framework for other CatBots. You will begin by examining the `CatBot` class. This class forms the framework for a `CatBot` and is the primary class that you will use in your own programs that will use a CatBot.

The *CatBot* Class

The `CatBot` class serves two primary purposes. It serves as a holder for many of the common properties that all CatBots will have. It holds such variables as the user ID, password, country, and starting URL.

The second main use for the CatBot class is to hold the standard-Recognition method. This method is used to loop through the web site and recognizers until the desired data is found. A prime recognizer (notated by the _primeRecognizer variable) must be designated. This prime recognizer can recognize the final page that the bot is looking for. After the primary recognizer's search is satisfied, the CatBot's run is complete. Figure 27.3, shown earlier in this chapter, is a flowchart of this process. Listing 27.6 shows the CatBot class.

Listing 27.6: The CatBot (*CatBot.java*)

```
package com.heaton.bot.catbot;
import java.util.*;
import com.heaton.bot.*;

/**
 * A CatBot is a bot that is designed to be able
 * to get information from a variety of sites in
 * the same category. This class lays the framework
 * for CatBots.
 *
 * @author Jeff Heaton
 * @version 1.0
 */
public class CatBot
{

  /**
   * A user ID for the CatBot to use.
   * May not be used by some implementations
   * of the CatBot.
   */
  protected String _uid = "";

  /**
   * A password for the CatBot to use.
   * May not be used by some implementations
   * of the CatBot.
   */
  protected String _pwd = "";

  /**
   * A country for the CatBot to use.
```

```
 * May not be used by some implementations
 * of the CatBot.
 */
protected String _country = "";

            protected String _state = "";


/**
 * The URL at which the CatBot starts.
 */
protected String _url = "";

/**
 * The HTTP object to be used by this
 * CatBot.
 */
protected HTTP _http;

/**
 * A list of recognizers. See the Recognize class
 * for more info on what a Recognizer is.
 */
protected Vector _recognizers = new Vector();

/**
 * The prime recognizer that will recognize the
 * ultimate information that the CatBot is
 * seeking.
 */
protected Recognize _primeRecognizer;

/**
 * The constructor. Sets up the CatBot.
 *
 * @param http An HTTP object that should be used for
 * communication.
 */
public CatBot(HTTP http)
{
  _http = http;
}
```

```
/**
 * Sets a user ID for the CatBot to use. This
 * parameter may or may not be used, depending
 * on the type of CatBot.
 *
 * @param uid A user ID for the CatBot to use.
 */
public void setUID(String uid)
{
  _uid = uid;
}

/**
 * Gets a user ID that the CatBot may have been
 * using.
 *
 * @return A user ID that the CatBot was using.
 */
public String getUID()
{
  return _uid;
}


/**
 * Sets a country for the CatBot to use. This
 * parameter may or may not be used, depending
 * on the type of CatBot.
 *
 * @param uid A user ID for the CatBot to use.
 */
public void setCountry(String country)
{
  _country = country;
}

/**
 * Gets a country that the CatBot may have been
 * using.
 *
 * @return A country that the CatBot was using.
 */
```

```
public String getCountry()
{
  return _country;
}


/**
 * Sets a password for the CatBot to use. This
 * parameter may or may not be used, depending
 * on the type of CatBot.
 *
 * @param pwd A password for the CatBot to use.
 */
public void setPWD(String pwd)
{
  _pwd = pwd;
}

/**
 * Gets a password that the CatBot may have been
 * using.
 *
 * @return A user ID that the CatBot was using.
 */
public String getPWD()
{
  return _pwd;
}

/**
 * Set the URL that this CatBot should start on.
 *
 * @param url The URL that this CatBot should start on.
 */
public void setURL(String url)
{
  _url = url;
}

/**
 * Get the HTTP object to use.
 *
 * @return The HTTP object being used by the
```

```
 * CatBot.
 */
public HTTP getHTTP()
{
  return _http;
}

/**
 * Get the list of recognizers that should
 * be used by this CatBot.
 *
 * @return The list of recoginzers used by this
 * CatBot.
 */
public Vector getRecognizers()
{
  return _recognizers;
}
/**
 * This method can be called to cause the CatBot
 * to begin moving through the site with a set of
 * recognizers. The CatBot will continue until the
 * prime recognizer recognizes something, or all
 * recognizers have been exhausted.
 *
 * @return HTMLPage reference if the recognition was
   successful, null if unsuccessful.
 * @exception java.io.IOException
 * @exception javax.swing.text.BadLocationException
 */

protected HTMLPage standardRecognition()
  throws java.io.IOException,
  javax.swing.text.BadLocationException
{
  boolean recognizedOne;

  HTMLPage page = new HTMLPage(_http);
  page.open(_url,null);

  // loop so long as the prime recognizer is not
  // satisfied and all other recognizers have
  // not been exhausted.
```

```
    do
    {
      recognizedOne = false;
      // first try the prime recognizer
      if(_primeRecognizer.perform(page))
        return page;
      for (Enumeration e = _recognizers.elements() ;
        e.hasMoreElements() ;)
      {
        Recognize rec = (Recognize)e.nextElement();
        if(!rec.isRecognized() && rec.perform(page))
        {
          // one was found, thats enough
          // the one that was just found moved
          // us to a new page so we must break
          // to restart the process.
          recognizedOne = true;
          break;
        }
      }
    } while( recognizedOne &&
   !_primeRecognizer.isRecognized() );

    // if successful return the page
    if( _primeRecognizer.isRecognized() )
      return page;
    else
      return null;
  }

}
```

Inside the *Recognize* Class

The `Recognize` class is the parent of all recognizer classes. This class contains many methods that you can use to recognize pages. This class also defines a common interface so that the recognition process, explained in the previous section "The `CatBot` Class," can execute new recognizers.

This class contains two important abstract methods that must be implemented. These two methods were discussed earlier in this chapter under the section "The `Recognize` Class." The first is the `isRecognizable()` method, which will return true if the specified page is recognizable. The second is the `internalPerform()` method, which must be implemented by a subclass of the `Recognize` class. The `internalPeform` method implemented in the subclass actually processes the current page.

In addition to these two abstract methods, the `Recognize` class also contains several useful utility methods. Many of these methods perform specialized searches for items such as option lists or user prompts. These methods are part of the public interface, and were documented earlier in this chapter under the "The `Recognize` Class." The base recognizer class is shown in Listing 27.7.

Listing 27.7: Recognizing a Page(*Recognize.java*)

```
package com.heaton.bot.catbot;

import com.heaton.bot.*;

/**
 * This class forms the base class for all
 * recognizers. Recognizers are an important
 * concept for the CatBot.
 * A recognizer is a class that can recognize
 * and extract data from certain types of page.
 * The recognizer will provide the page with the
 * needed information so that the CatBot can
 * continue.
 *
 * @author Jeff Heaton
 * @version 1.0
 */
abstract public class Recognize
{

  /**
   * The CatBot object that controls this object.
   */
  protected CatBot _controller;

  /**
   * Returns true if this page is recognized.
   *
   * @param page The page to look at.
   * @return Returns true if this page is recognized.
   */
```

```
abstract public boolean isRecognizable(HTMLPage page);

/**
 * This method is called internally to perform
 * the process of interacting with this page.
 * This is an abstract class that must be implemented
 * by child classes.
 *
 * @param page The page to perform against.
 * @return True if successful.
 * @exception java.io.IOException
 * @exception javax.swing.text.BadLocationException
 */
abstract protected boolean internalPerform(HTMLPage page)
  throws java.io.IOException,
  javax.swing.text.BadLocationException;

/**
 * Returns true if this page has already been
 * recognized.
 *
 * @return True if this page has already been recognized.
 */
abstract public boolean isRecognized();

/**
 * The constructor. This method stores the CatBot
 * controller for this recognizer.
 *
 * @param controller The CatBot controller for this object.
 */
public Recognize(CatBot controller)
{
  _controller = controller;
}

/**
 * Perform whatever task is done by this Recognize
 * object.
 *
 * @param page
 */
public boolean perform(HTMLPage page)
```

```
{
  try
  {
  if(!isRecognizable(page))
    return false;
  return internalPerform(page);
  }
  catch(java.io.IOException e)
  {
    Log.logException("CatBot IO exception during
       perform:",e);
    return false;
  }
  catch(javax.swing.text.BadLocationException e)
  {
    Log.logException("CatBot HTML Parse exception during
       perform:",e);
    return false;
  }
}

/**
 * Returns true if the specified form has
 * the specified type of component.
 *
 * @param form The form object that is to be searched.
 * @param hasWhat The search string
 * @return The component found.
 */
public HTMLForm.FormElement has(HTMLForm form,String
   hasWhat)
{
  if(form==null)
    return null;
  for(int i=0;i<form.length();i++)
  {
    HTMLForm.FormElement element =
       (HTMLForm.FormElement)form.get(i);
    if(element.getType().equalsIgnoreCase(hasWhat) )
      return element;
  }
  return null;
}
```

```
/**
 * Find the specified option in a select list.
 *
 * @param list The component list to search.
 * @param search The search string. Only a partial match is
 *   needed.
 */
public String findOption(AttributeList list,String search)
{
  if(list==null)
    return null;
  search = search.toUpperCase();
  for(int i=0;i<list.length();i++)
  {
    Attribute element = list.get(i);
    if( element.getName().toUpperCase().indexOf(search)!=-1 )
      return element.getValue();
  }
  return null;
}

/**
 * Find a form prompt based on a partial
 * search string.
 *
 * @param form The form to search.
 * @param search The form text we are searching for.
 */
public String findPrompt(HTMLForm form,String search)
{
  search = search.toUpperCase();
  for(int i=0;i<form.length();i++)
  {
    HTMLForm.FormElement element =
      (HTMLForm.FormElement)form.get(i);
    String name = element.getName();
    if(name==null)
      continue;
    if( name.toUpperCase().indexOf(search)!=-1 )
    {
      return element.getName();
    }
```

```
        }
        return null;
    }
}
```


Built-In Recognizers

There are a couple of built-in recognizers supported by the CatBot. These are the `RecognizeCountry` and `RecognizeLink` classes. This section will describe how these two classes were constructed.

The *RecognizeCountry* Recognizer

The `RecognizeCountry` class (shown in Listing 27.8) is used to recognize a page that contains a list of countries. From this list, the user must select their country. In addition to recognizing such a page, `RecognizeCountry` can complete it. You will now see how it works. Like any recognizer class, the `RecognizeCountry` class must implement two important methods: the `isRecognizeable` method must be implemented to determine if the current page is actually a country selection page, and the `internalPerform` method must also be implemented to actually request the correct country. It is the use of these two methods that makes this class a recognizer.

The `isRecognizable()` method does most of the work; it scans the forms on the page and looks for one that appears to be a list of countries. Several known countries' non-compound names are then chosen. (A *compound name* is a country such as the United States. It can be referred to as US, USA, United States, United States of America, or just America.) After such a list is found, it is remembered so that the `internalPerform` method can execute it.

The `internalPerform()` method is used to actually submit the country choice to the web site. The country choice is chosen by attempting to match the country that was selected earlier using the `CatBot.setCountry()` method.

Listing 27.8: Recognizing a Country Selection Page (*RecognizeCountry.java*)

```
package com.heaton.bot.catbot;

import java.io.*;
import java.util.*;
import com.heaton.bot.*;
```

```
/**
 * This recognizer is called to handle a page that
 * contains a large list of countries. The country
 * that was specified in the CatBot class will be
 * located and used.
 *
 * @author Jeff Heaton
 */
public class RecognizeCountry extends Recognize
{

  /**
   * The targeted form, if recognized.
   */
  protected HTMLForm _targetForm = null;

  /**
   * The target form component, if recognized.
   */
  protected HTMLForm.FormElement _targetElement = null;

  /**
   * The constructor. Passes the controller to the
   * parent constructor.
   *
   * @param controller The CatBot controller object.
   */
  public RecognizeCountry(CatBot controller)
  {
    super(controller);
  }

  /**
   * Used to indicate if this recognizer has
   * already recognized the country specified.
   *
   * @return Returns true if the country has been recognized.
   */
  public boolean isRecognized()
  {
    return(_targetForm!=null);
  }
```

```
/**
 * Returns true if the specified page can
 * be recognized to be a country page.
 *
 * @param page The page to look at.
 * @return Returns true if the page is recognized.
 */
public boolean isRecognizable(HTMLPage page)
{
  if(page.getForms()==null)
    return false;

  Vector forms = page.getForms();
  for (Enumeration e = forms.elements() ;
     e.hasMoreElements() ;)
  {
    HTMLForm form = (HTMLForm)e.nextElement();
    HTMLForm.FormElement element = has(form,"select");
    if(element!=null)
    {
      // look for a few known countries. USA is a bad example
      // is it USA? United States? America?
      // United States of America? We will use a few
         common ones
      // that do not have many name combinations:
      // Canada, France, Japan, Egypt.
      if( (findOption(element.getOptions(),"france")!
         =null ) ||
       (findOption(element.getOptions(),"canada")!=null ) ||
       (findOption(element.getOptions(),"japan")!=null ) ||
       (findOption(element.getOptions(),"egypt")!=null ) )
      {
        _targetForm = form;
        _targetElement = element;
        Log.log(Log.LOG_LEVEL_NORMAL,"Recognized a country
           page");
        return true;
      }
    }
  }
  return false;
}
```

```
  /**
   * The internalPerform method will transmit
   * our country choice back to the web server.
   *
   * @param page The page to look at.
   * @return True if successful.
   * @exception java.io.IOException
   */
  protected boolean internalPerform(HTMLPage page)
    throws java.io.IOException
  {
    if(_targetForm==null)
      return false;
    String code = findOption(
      _targetElement.getOptions(),
      _controller.getCountry());
    _targetForm.set(_targetElement.getName(),code);
    page.post(_targetForm);
    return true;
  }

}
```

The *RecognizeLink* Recognizer

The last provided recognizer is the `RecognizeLink` class (see Listing 27.9). This class attempts to find a link contained on the current page. This recognizer works on text links such as "Click here to read your e-mail" or "Click here to view your tracking numbers."

The link recognizer should be given a partial name to use to search links. Using the provided partial name, the `RecognizeLink` class will scan through all links on the current page looking for a partial or complete match. This is done with the following lines of code. Here, the program loops through ever link contained on the current page. The `ALT`, `HREF`, and prompt text are all obtained for comparison. (The *prompt* text is the text that you must click to activate the link.)

```
for(Enumeration e = page.getLinks().elements() ;
   e.hasMoreElements() ;)
{
  Link link = (Link)e.nextElement();
  String alt = link.getALT();
  String href = link.getHREF();
  String prompt = link.getPrompt();
```

```
    if(prompt==null)
      prompt="";
    if(alt==null)
      alt="";
    if(href==null)
      continue;
```

After the ALT, HREF, and prompt text are all obtained for the current link, these values are compared against the value you are searching for. This value is part of the prompt, for example the word "tracking."

```
  if( ( alt.toUpperCase().indexOf(_search)!=-1) ||
      ( prompt.toUpperCase().indexOf(_search)!=-1) ||
      ( href.toUpperCase().indexOf(_search)!=-1) )
  {
    _targetHREF = link.getHREF();
    Log.log(Log.LOG_LEVEL_NORMAL,"Recognized a link:" + _search);
    return true;
  }
```

The above code checks to see if the value being searched for (`_search`) is contained in any of the prompts. This is done with the `indexOf` calls contained in the `if` statement. After the link is located, the `_targetHREF` variable is set to contain the target of the link.

Listing 27.9: Finding a Link (*RecognizeLink.java*)

```
package com.heaton.bot.catbot;

import java.util.*;
import com.heaton.bot.*;

/**
 * The link recognizer is used to search for a specific
 * text or graphic link on the page. To locate this link
 * the recognizer uses alt tags, the text linked, and
 * even the HREF itself to establish the identity of
 * the link.
 *
 * @author Jeff Heaton
 * @version 1.0
 */
public class RecognizeLink extends Recognize
{
```

```
/**
 * The string that is being searched for.
 */
String _search;

/**
 * The HREF found in the target link.
 */
String _targetHREF;

/**
 * The constructor. Pass the controller on
 * to the parent.
 *
 * @param controller
 */
public RecognizeLink(CatBot controller)
{
  super(controller);
}

/**
 * Returns true if the link has already been
 * recognized.
 *
 * @return True if the link has already been recognized.
 */
public boolean isRecognized()
{
  return(_targetHREF!=null);
}

/**
 * Returns the search string being used to find
 * the link.
 *
 * @return The search string being used to find the
 * link.
 */
public String getSearch()
{
```

```
  return _search;
}

/**
 * Sets the search string being used to find the link.
 *
 * @param s The search string being used to find the link.
 */
public void setSearch(String s)
{
  _search = s.toUpperCase();
}


/**
 * Returns true if this page can be recognized.
 *
 * @param page The page to look at.
 * @return True if this page can be recognized.
 */
public boolean isRecognizable(HTMLPage page)
{
  for(Enumeration e = page.getLinks().elements() ;
     e.hasMoreElements() ;)
  {
    Link link = (Link)e.nextElement();
    String alt = link.getALT();
    String href = link.getHREF();
    String prompt = link.getPrompt();
    if(prompt==null)
      prompt="";
    if(alt==null)
      alt="";
    if(href==null)
      continue;

    if( ( alt.toUpperCase().indexOf(_search)!=-1) ||
        ( prompt.toUpperCase().indexOf(_search)!=-1) ||
        ( href.toUpperCase().indexOf(_search)!=-1) )
    {
      _targetHREF = link.getHREF();
      Log.log(Log.LOG_LEVEL_NORMAL,"Recognized a link:" +
         _search);
```

```
        return true;
      }
    }
    return false;
  }

  /**
   * The internal perform of this class will scan
   * all forms of links on the page searching for
   * the text specified by the setSearch method. This
   * is the method that actually performs the data
   * collection; because it is a protected method it is only
   * called internally.
   *
   * @param page The page to look at.
   * @return True if successful.
   * @exception java.io.IOException
   * @exception javax.swing.text.BadLocationException
   */
  protected boolean internalPerform(HTMLPage page)
    throws java.io.IOException,
      javax.swing.text.BadLocationException
  {
    if(_targetHREF!=null)
    {
      page.open(_targetHREF,null);
      return true;
    }
    else return false;
  }

}
```

What's Next

Standard bots are designed to retrieve data from specific web pages. By scanning the web page for HTML codes near the desired data, the bot can locate the data that it needs.

But there are several weaknesses that hinder most bots. Bots are particularly prone to problems arising from changes made to the underlying site. This is because a bot is typically programmed to look for landmarks from the underlying site. If these landmarks are changed or altered, this could cause the bot to not be able to handle the new site.

A CatBot (category bot) is a bot that can extract information from every site that is in the same category. It can look at a category of bots rather than one specific bot because no specific information about the underlying sites is programmed into the CatBot. CatBots are usually very accepting in their responses to changes that are made in the underlying sites.

As we conclude our tour of Java 2 Enterprise Edition, it is perhaps worth noting the tremendous breadth and depth of J2EE. We encourage the reader to keep this book handy as a reference manual as you begin to use each of the diverse technologies that make up J2EE. If you need to delve deeper into some of these topics, you may want to consider purchasing the books that these chapters were extracted from. We hope you have found this book to be a valuable learning tool.

Appendix

Setup

In this appendix, you will learn how to install containers to test servlets, JSP, EJB, and other J2EE technologies.

Adapted from *Mastering™ JSP™* by Todd Cook

ISBN 0-7821-2940-4 $49.99

Installing the Java 2 Standard Edition Software Development Kit (J2SE SDK)

Before you can begin developing J2EE applications, you must install the Java 2 Standard Edition Software Development Kit (J2SE SDK, or alternately JDK).

TIP

To get the most current version of J2SE SDK, visit `http://java.sun.com/j2se`**.**

Most operating systems install only the Java runtime environment for running applets on web pages.

After installing the J2SE SDK, the `JAVA_HOME` system variable should be set to the directory where Java was installed. That means that if you open a new Windows DOS prompt, typing `cd %JAVA_HOME%` should take you to the directory where Java was installed. In Unix, typing `cd ${JAVA_HOME}` should do the same thing. The PATH system variable should now include the `${JAVA_HOME}/bin` directory. The `${JAVA_HOME}/bin` directory contains several Java development tools, such as javac and jar. As a result of the changes to your path, you should be able to use any of the tools in `${JAVA_HOME}/bin` from any directory. If you have any problems with this, see the installation instructions on the page where you downloaded J2SE.

Installing the Java 2 Enterprise Edition Software Development Kit (J2EE SDK)

The web site for J2EE is `http://java.sun.com/j2ee/`. From here, you can download the J2EE SDK, J2EE documentation, J2EE tutorials, J2EE Blueprints, J2EE source code, J2EE specifications, as well as have access to a plethora of other related resources.

You should download the J2EE SDK from this site. After downloading it, run the executable file or setup script. After running the script, the `J2EE_HOME` environment variable should be set to the directory where J2EE was installed. In addition, the PATH system variable should have been appended to include the `${J2EE_HOME}/bin` directory. If you have any problems with this, see the installation instructions on the web page from where you downloaded the J2EE SDK.

After installing the J2EE SDK, you can explore the J2EE documentation in the `${J2EE_HOME}/doc` directory. Although J2EE SDK includes a complete reference implementation for J2EE, Apache Tomcat is the reference implementation for the servlet and JSP specifications. Using the J2EE SDK for EJB development will be discussed later in this appendix after examining Apache Tomcat for servlet and JSP development.

Installing a JSP/Servlet Environment

To run the servlet and JSP examples, you need to install a web server with a Java servlet and JSP server engine. There are many servlet and JSP engines from which to choose, ranging from the Apache Jakarta Tomcat project to large-scale enterprise application servers such as BEA WebLogic Server and iPlanet Application Server. Fortunately, Java is standardized, and any servlet and JSP engine that is compliant with the Servlet 2.3 and JSP 1.2 specifications should be compatible. Regardless of which of these products you choose to use, the code and deployment descriptors should require little, if any, changes. Because Apache Tomcat is free, of high quality, and is the official reference implementation for the servlet and JSP specifications, installation of it will be covered in this Appendix.

NOTE

You can find a complete updated list of specification-compliant servlet and JSP engines at `http://java.sun.com/products/servlet/industry.html`.

Installing Tomcat

Apache Tomcat version 4 is the reference implementation for the Java Servlet 2.3 and JSP 1.2 specifications.

TIP

To download the latest version of Apache's Tomcat, visit `http://jakarta.apache.org/tomcat`.

Tomcat 4 is a pure Java implementation that contains a web server in addition to the Java web server environment. Production systems usually use Tomcat with a separate web server, such as the Apache Web Server; however, for learning and testing purposes, the web server embedded in Tomcat is sufficient. To install Tomcat, simply download the compressed archive and then extract the files or run the installation script. If you navigate to the `/bin` subdirectory, you'll see a number of files, as shown in Figure A.1.

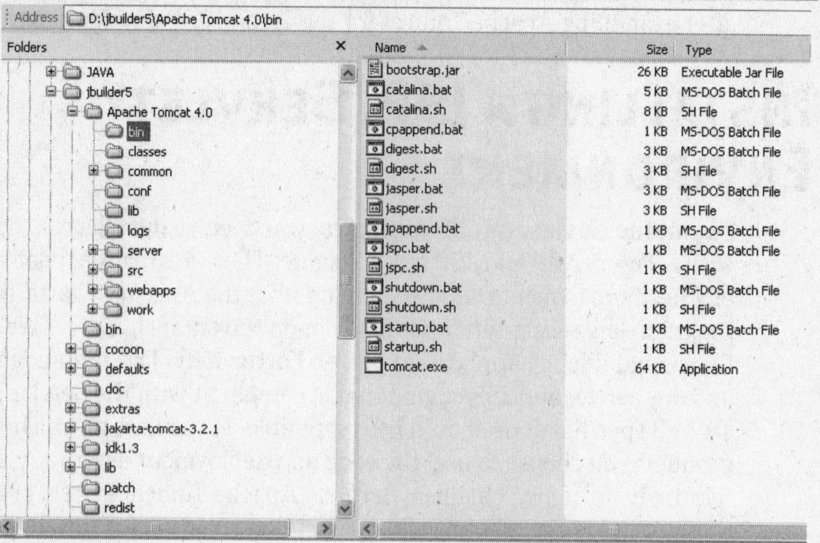

FIGURE A.1: The Tomcat directories, including the startup and shutdown scripts

The `.bat` scripts are for Windows, and the `.sh` scripts invoke Tomcat on Unix and Linux machines. In Windows, if the CLASSPATH and JAVA_HOME environment variables are set correctly, you can double-click the `startup.bat` file to display the Tomcat console, shown in Figure A.2.

The console will also appear when invoked from a command line, or when using a `.sh` script.

When Tomcat is started correctly, open your web browser and enter a URL of `http://localhost:8080` to display the default Tomcat configuration page, as shown in Figure A.3.

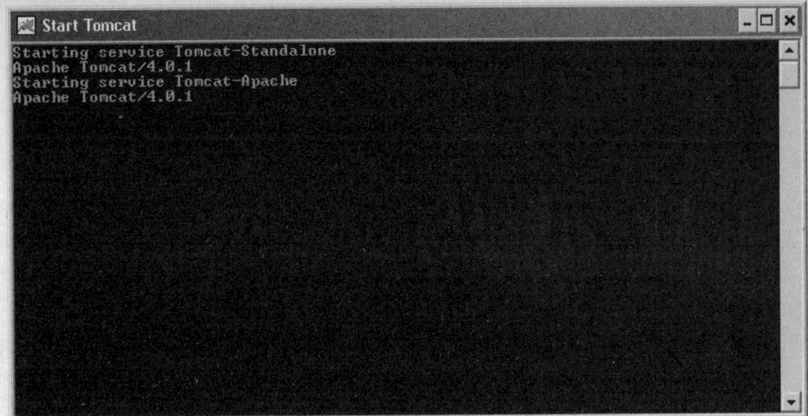

FIGURE A.2: The Tomcat console

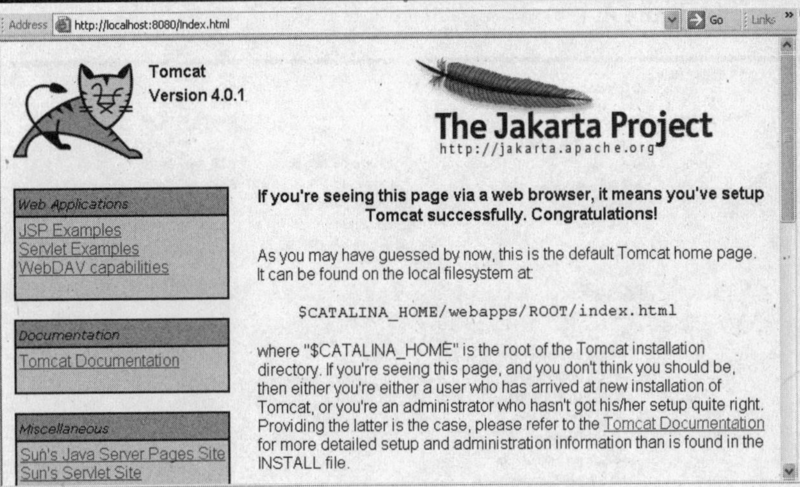

FIGURE A.3: Tomcat's default configuration page

DEFAULT WEB APPLICATION

Chapter 3 provides a detailed discussion of creating and deploying web applications. The following discussion provides a basic discussion of web applications to assist in the running of examples from Chapters 1 and 2; therefore, Chapter 3 should be read for more information.

In Java, a web application is a collection of servlets, JSP pages, and helper classes and files that are deployed in their own dedicated directory structure. By default, each application's directory structure in Tomcat is located in the /webapps subdirectory of the Tomcat installation. Different servlet engines place the web applications in different directories, so if you use servers other than Tomcat, you must see your server documentation for more information. The directory structure within each web application is mandated by the Servlet 2.3 and JSP 1.2 specifications. The following descriptions of these directory structures are the same for all specification compliant servers.

To create a new web application in Tomcat, you create a new directory within the webapps directory and then place the required sub-directories and files in it. This process is described in Chapter 3. Most servers, including Tomcat, come with a pre-made default web application that will be sufficient for the first two chapters of this book. In Tomcat, the default web application is called ROOT. The files in the ROOT directory are shown in Figure A.4.

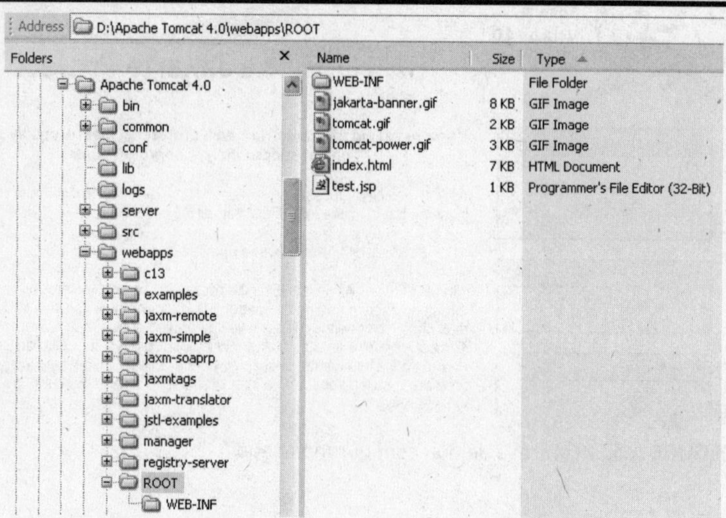

FIGURE A.4: The default configuration files in the /ROOT directory

JSP, HTML, and other general web files can be placed directly under the web application's directory. For example, if you have a filed called `TryMe.jsp` and you want to test it in Tomcat, you would place `TryMe.jsp` in the `webapps\ROOT` directory, ensure that Tomcat is running, and enter the URL `http://localhost:8080/TryMe.jsp` in your browser.

For testing purposes, Tomcat comes with an extra file, `test.jsp`, in the ROOT application. The file consists of a single snippet, shown in Listing A.1. The results of requesting this JSP are shown in Figure A.5.

Listing A.1 Test.jsp

```
<html>
<body>
Test.jsp <br>
Now is: <%= new java.util.Date()%>
</body>
</html>
```

You can view Test.jsp, as shown in Figure A.5.

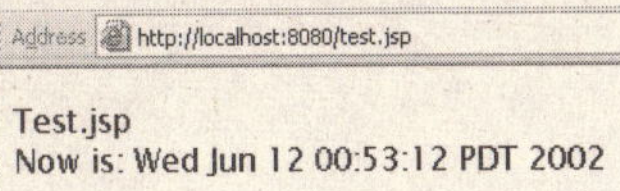

FIGURE A.5: The Test.jsp file shows that a new JSP can be added to the directory structure.

Every web application must have a sub-directory called `WEB-INF`. All files in this directory are protected from direct access by a browser or other client request.

To deploy a simple servlet, such as the ones shown in Chapter 1, you must do the following things:

1. Compile the source code.
2. If there is not already a directory under `WEB-INF` called `classes`, create it now.
3. Place the .class files in the `WEB-INF\classes` directory; if the servlet is in a package, replicate that directory structure under the `classes` directory and then place the servlet there. For example, if you are using Tomcat and deploying the `TryMe` servlet, which is in the `test.pack` package, you would place the `TryMe.class` file in the `webapps\ROOT\WEB-INF\classes\test\pack` directory.
4. Restart the servlet engine.
5. Request the servlet in a web browser. For the previously mentioned `TryMe` servlet deployed in Tomcat, you could use a URL of `http://localhost:8080/servlet/test.pack.TryMe`.

The WEB-INF directory must contain a file called web.xml. This file is the web application deployment descriptor that specifies deployment configuration for the web application. The location of the web.xml file for Tomcat's default web application is shown in Figure A.6.

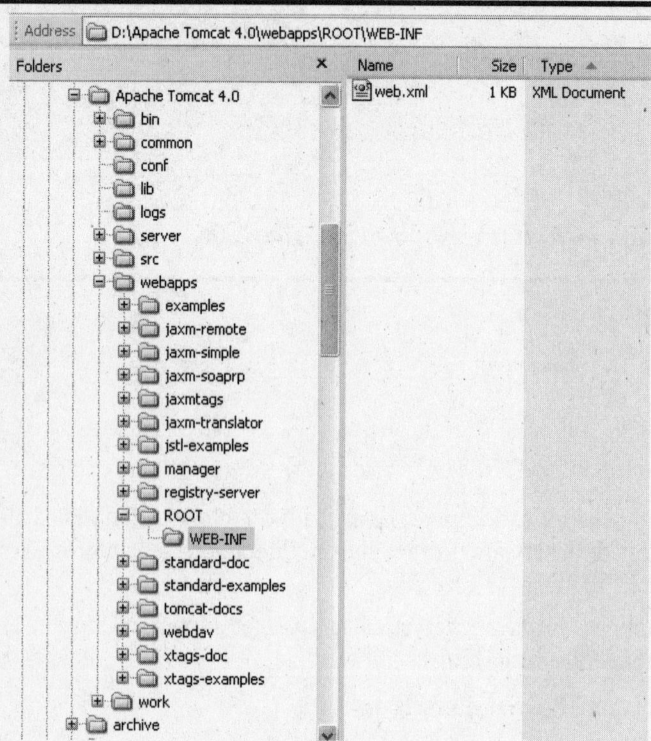

FIGURE A.6: Location of the web.xml configuration file

Tomcat's default web application's web.xml file is shown in Listing A.2.

Listing A.2: web.xml—The Default Deployment Descriptor for the Tomcat Setup

```
<?xml version="1.0" encoding="ISO-8859-1"?>
<!DOCTYPE web-app PUBLIC
 "-//Sun Microsystems, Inc.//DTD Web Application 2.3//EN"
 "http://java.sun.com/dtd/web-app_2_3.dtd">
<web-app/>
```

This most basic deployment descriptor merely indicates that a web application lives in the parent directory. Chapter 3 discusses the attributes that can be specified in this file to customize a deployment. For Chapters 1 and 2, you will not need to modify the `web.xml` file.

An EJB Environment

Apache Tomcat is an excellent environment for running servlets and JSP pages, but Tomcat is not a full J2EE server because it does not support all parts of J2EE such as Enterprise JavaBeans (EJB). For learning purposes, the J2EE Reference Implementation Server (J2EE RI) is a good choice because it is included in the J2EE SDK, it is free, and it follows the specification exactly. If you followed the instructions at the beginning of this appendix to install the J2EE SDK, you have already installed the J2EE RI. Part of the setup includes the `${J2EE_HOME}/bin` directory in the `PATH`, so you should be able to start the J2EE server from any directory using the commands in the `bin` directory.

NOTE

For an updated list of J2EE servers, go to `http://www.flashline.com/Components/appservermatrix.jsp`.

To start the J2EE server, type `j2ee -verbose`. This command should take several seconds, and end by printing `J2EE server startup complete.` The J2EE server remains running until you shut it down, so if you did not start this request as a background process you will have to open a new window to get a new prompt. As the server runs, it will display various logging messages in the window where you started it. When you are ready to shut down the J2EE server, type `j2ee -stop` in a new window.

Deploying an enterprise application that usually includes EJBs can be done using the J2EE deploy tool. After starting the J2EE server, type `deploytool` to start this graphical tool. You will now learn how to deploy the `MyExample` bean from Chapter 21. It is recommended that you read Chapters 20 and 21 before reading the following discussion. After starting the deploy tool, create a new enterprise application by selecting the `File`, `New`, `Application` to open the `New Application dialog` box, as shown in Figure A.7.

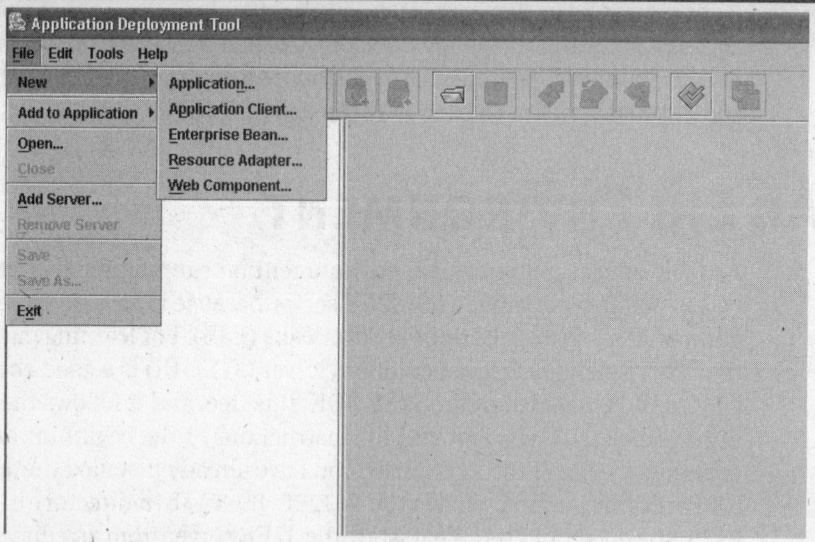

FIGURE A.7: New sub-menu of the File menu

In the New Application dialog box, choose a location and filename for this enterprise application's .ear file, as shown in Figure A.8.

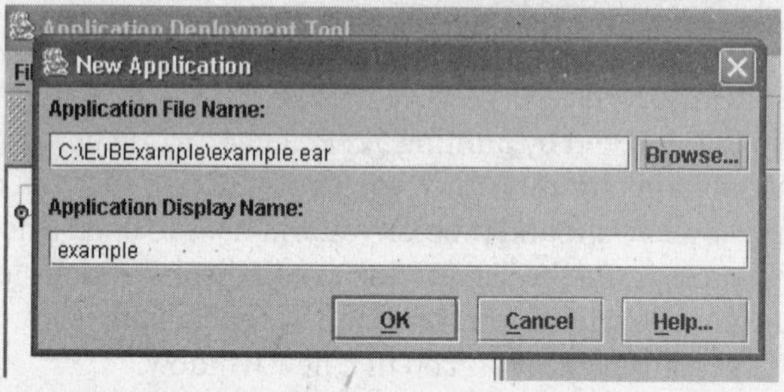

FIGURE A.8: New Application dialog window

To create a new enterprise bean to put in the new enterprise application, select the `File`, New, Enterprise Bean. The New Enterprise Bean Wizard will appear, as shown in Figure A.9.

Click Next to move to the next page of the wizard; then click the `Edit` button to browse your file system and add each .class file for the bean, its interfaces, and any other helper classes. The results are shown in Figure A.10.

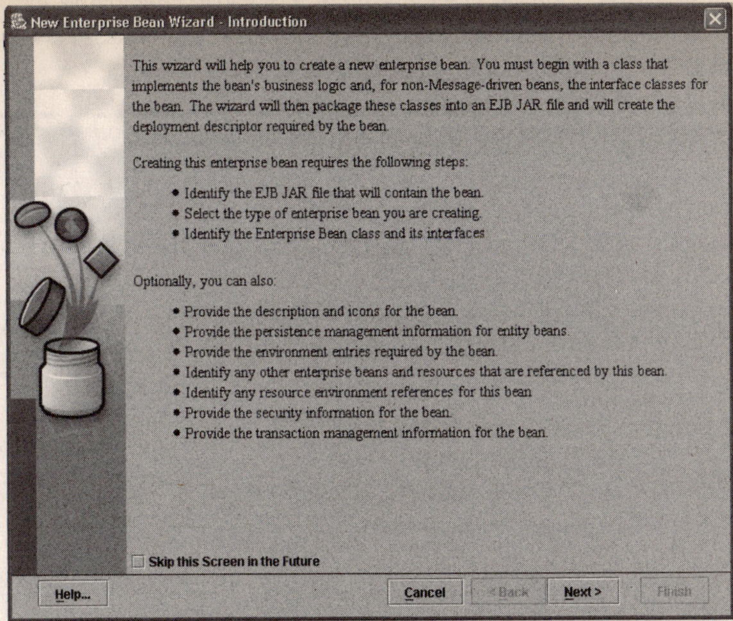

FIGURE A.9: New Enterprise Bean Wizard

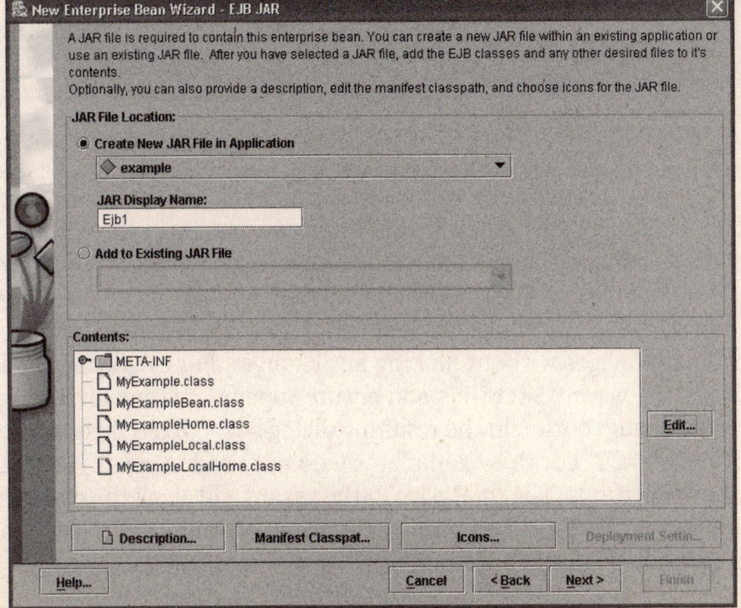

FIGURE A.10: New Enterprise Bean Wizard—EJB JAR page

Click Next; then select what kind of EJB you are deploying and select which .class files are the bean and which are the interfaces. The results are shown in Figure A.11.

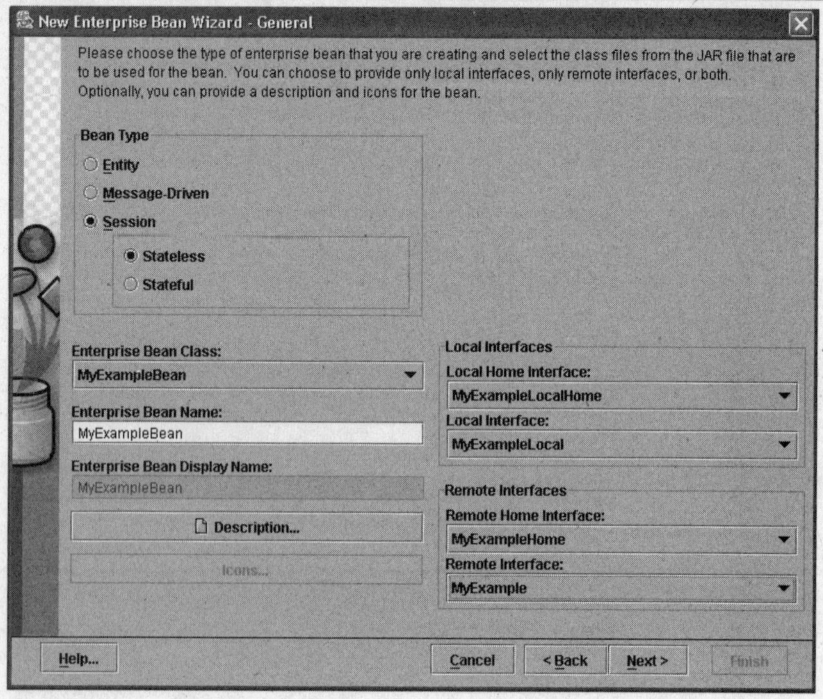

FIGURE A.11: Wizard general page

Click Next and then select your transaction attributes as explained in Chapter 22. For this example, you can move past this page without making any changes. The next four pages enable you to specify environment entries, referenced EJBs, resource factories, and resources used in your code. These are discussed in Chapter 23. For this example, you can skip these four pages without making any changes. For the Security page, click `Deployment Settings` and ensure `Support Client Choice` is the selected radio button in the resulting dialog box. EJB security is discussed in Chapter 22. For this example, you do not need to specify any other security settings. The final page in the wizard will show the deployment descriptor that the deploy tool has written based on your selections. This is shown in Figure A.12.

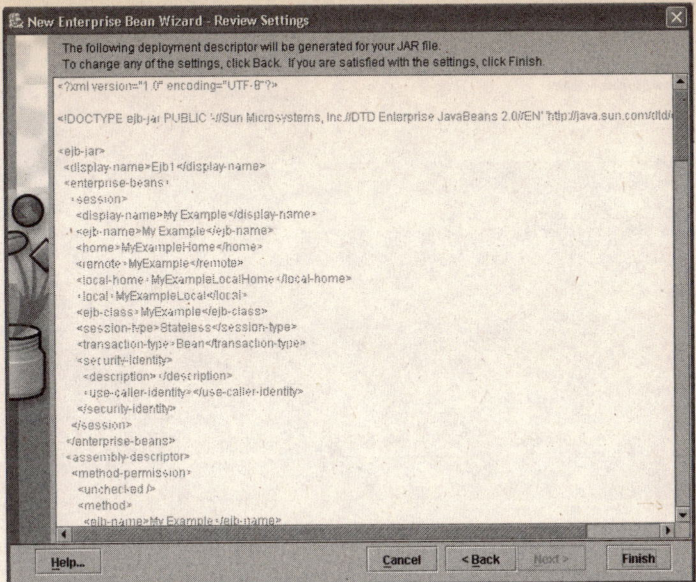

FIGURE A.12: Wizard Review Settings page

After completing the wizard, you should run the Verifier. Because the Java compiler can't catch EJB specific mistakes the programmer may have made, the Verifier runs a long series of additional checks on your code and deployment. To start the Verifier, select Tools, Verifier. Make sure your .ear file is selected and the click the `OK` button to start the verification. All successful and unsuccessful tests results are shown. To see if there are any problems, select `Failures and Warnings Only` to hide the successful tests. If all goes well, you should see no results displayed and the message `There were no failed tests`, as shown in Figure A.13. If there are errors or warnings, you can click on them for a more detailed error message. After fixing the problems, select `Tools, Update Files`; then select `File, Save`, and restart the verifier. If you believe the Verifier may be caching previous errors that you have already fixed, restart the deploy tool.

Finally, to deploy the application, select `Tools, Deploy to open the Deployment wizard`. In the first page, check `Return Client Jar` to make a jar file containing all the necessary class files for the client application. In the next page, enter a JNDI name for the EJB, such as `ejb/example`.

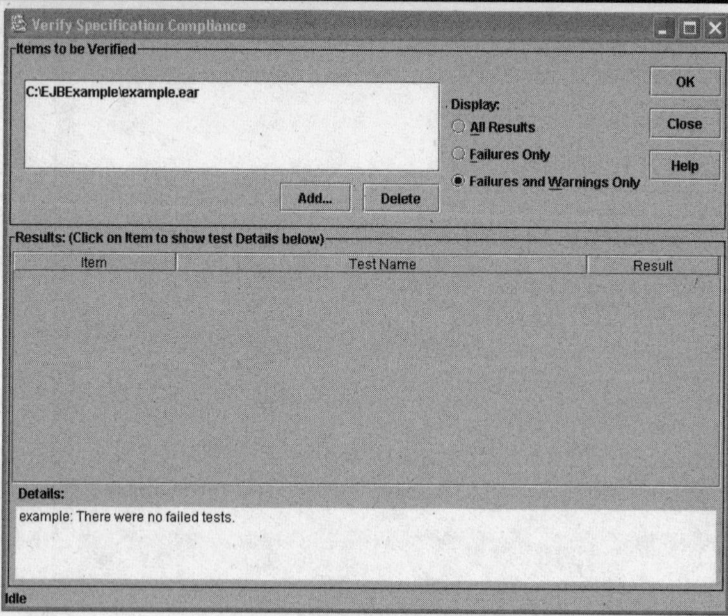

FIGURE A.13: Verifier showing no failed tests

This is the JNDI name that the client will use to look up this bean. Click `Finish`, and hold your breath while the green and blue bars rise to the top of the window. If these bars reach the top as shown in Figure A.14, your bean has been successfully deployed and you can now run a client application to access it.

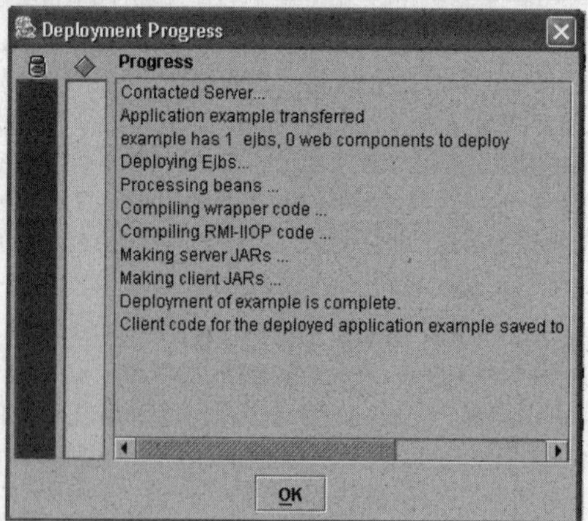

FIGURE A.14: Successful deployment

Glossary

Adapted from *Cocoon 2 Programming: Web Publishing with XML and Java*™ by Bill Brogden, Conrad D'Cruz, and Mark Gaither

ISBN 0-7821-4131-5 $39.99

100% Pure Java The designation for classes and applications that comply with Sun's criteria for total independence from the underlying operating system.

abstract A Java keyword describing classes or methods that define a runtime behavior, but don't provide a complete implementation. You can't create an object from an `abstract` class, but an object created from a class extending the `abstract` class can be referred to with the `abstract` class name.

Active Server Pages (ASP) Microsoft's technology for programmatically delivering HTML pages using embedded programming code written in VBScript, JScript, or the various Visual Studio .NET languages. ASP, JSP, PHP, and ColdFusion are competing technologies that do approximately the same thing in different ways.

algorithm A problem-solving operation that proceeds one step at a time to accomplish a specific program task.

alpha The typical designation given a program or application that is undergoing initial (internal) testing before being released for testing outside the company that developed it. *See also* beta.

American Standard Code for Information Interchange (ASCII) The ubiquitous computer industry standard for encoding text and control characters.

Apache Software Foundation The non-profit umbrella organization for many open source projects, such as Cocoon and Tomcat. The name comes from the original, informal project to build a web server.

API *See* application programming interface.

applet A Java program that operates within a Java Virtual Machine (JVM), supplied by the user's web browser. You can think of the browser as providing an applet container that lets it run on the client machine more or less independently of the underlying operating system.

application programming interface (API) Calling conventions or instruction set used by an application to access operating system and library services.

Application Service Provider (ASP) A firm that hosts applications at a remote data center and provides the required infrastructure and support services to a client on a subscription basis.

argument Java method call data item that can designate a Java primitive or object.

array Group of data items that share the same type, in which a 32-bit integer index addresses each data item uniquely.

ASCII *See* American Standard Code for Information Interchange.

ASP *See* Active Server Pages; *see* Application Service Provider.

attribute In XML, a name-value pair within the start tag of an element.

***automatic* (local) variable** Variable declared inside a method to which memory is automatically allocated when the method is called.

bean *See* Java bean.

beta The typical designation given a program or application that is under development and released for testing outside the company that developed it. *See also* alpha.

block A section of Java code that is contained within matching { and } characters.

byte An 8-bit Java integer-type primitive that is treated as a signed integer.

cache As a verb, to hold in memory the contents of a resource to speed access when the resource is needed. Also, the program mechanism that performs this function. Optimized caching can significantly improve Cocoon server response.

case-insensitive Programming language naming convention that does not distinguish between upper- and lowercase letters.

case-sensitive Programming language naming convention that distinguishes between upper- and lowercase letters; in other words, "Text" and "text" are read differently. Java and XML are case-sensitive.

catch Java keyword that declares specific exception type and creates a block of code or clause that executes when that exception contained in code with a `try` statement is thrown.

CGI *See* Common Gateway Interface.

char Java integer primitive variable that represents Unicode characters as 16-bit unsigned integers.

***Character* (class)** The Java wrapper class for `char` values.

character data The text contents of an element or attribute.

child In the context of object-oriented programming, any object that inherits from and obtains information from another object; a Java class that inherits from another class (parent or superclass).

In the context of XML documents, an element contained immediately inside another element is called a child.

class In general context of object-oriented programming, a method for grouping objects that share some characteristic or characteristics; all Java classes descend from the `Object` class.

***Class* (class)** The Java class (`java.lang.Class`) class that indicates the runtime type of any object.

class file The result of compiling a Java class is a class file containing byte codes.

class method Java method declared `static` and attached to an entire class, rather than to objects in the class.

***Collection* (interface)** Java interface (`java.util.Collection`) that defines basic behavior for Collections API objects.

Collections API Java 2 set of classes and interfaces that provide a number of methods for handling collections of objects.

***Collections* (class)** Java class (`java.util.Collections`) containing `static` methods applicable to collections.

Common Gateway Interface (CGI) The conventions governing communication between web servers and external applications. This was the first technology that supported dynamic interaction between users (via browsers) and web servers.

constructor Special kind of member function called on the creation of a class instance using `new`; initializes the object. Java classes can declare none, one, or many constructor methods.

container In Sun's terminology, the environment a Java applet, servlet, or EJB operates in is a specialized container that is required to provide specific services.

controller In the Model-View-Controller design pattern, the controller provides functions or services for communicating user input to the model and view(s).

cookie A small chunk of text data stored by a web browser as a consequence of visiting a website. This data is returned to the web server on subsequent visits to the site, and may be used to identify a user.

dbXML A project to create databases holding XML data. Recently donated to the Apache Software Foundation as the Xindice project. Supports the proposed XML:DB standard.

deprecated JDK (Java Developers' Kit) term that indicates a method whose use is no longer recommended. Deprecated methods may not be supported in future releases.

directives In JavaServer Pages, directives are tags that define general policies or conditions for a page or part of a page.

Document Object Model (DOM) An approach to processing an XML document in which the entire document is stored in memory as a parsed hierarchy of elements. Also, in web browsers, the hierarchical structure of the HTML document.

document type declaration A structure within an XML document that points to or contains markup declarations that describe a class of XML documents.

Document Type Definition (DTD) The markup declarations that describe a class of XML documents.

DOM *See* Document Object Model.

***double* (double precision)** Java 64-bit floating-point primitive type.

***Double* (class)** Java wrapper class for `double` primitive values.

DTD *See* Document Type Definition.

EJB *See* Enterprise Java Beans.

element An XML structural construct consisting of a start tag, an end tag, and information between the tags (contents).

encapsulation Term used in object-oriented programming for enclosing information and behavior within an object, hiding its structure and implementation from other objects. Encapsulation allows programmers to modify the way the object's internal functions without affecting any other code using the object.

Enterprise JavaBeans (EJB) A J2EE technology for creating distributed enterprise Java components. EJBs contain business logic and run inside an EJB server that provides services such as transaction management, security, and lifecycle maintenance.

entity An XML structural construct that associates character data or well-formed XML with a name. An entity can be referred to using an *entity reference*.

equals Java method that compares two object references and returns `true` when the objects' content is identical. The `Object` class default `equals` method returns `true` when both reference the same object.

***Error* (class)** Java class (`java.lang.Error`) that is the parent class of all Java error classes and a subclass of `Throwable`. Errors are typically conditions that a program cannot recover from, such as running out of memory.

***Exception* (class)** Java class (`java.lang.Exception`) that is the parent class of all Java exceptions and a subclass of `Throwable`. Exceptions generally signal conditions from which the program may be able to recover.

extends Java keyword used to define a new class that indicates the base class from which the new class will inherit.

Extensible Markup Language (XML) A simplified form of SGML that is the standard for creating custom markup languages. Its purpose is to permit the tags in a document to exactly describe the contents.

Extensible Stylesheet Language (XSL) A specification for transforming and presenting documents created with XML.

Extensible Stylesheet Language for Transformations (XSLT) One of two parts of the W3C XSL recommendation that addresses the transformation of documents from one XML language to another.

field Java variable that defines a particular class characteristic.

***Filter* (Java servlet sense)** An interface introduced with the servlet 2.3 API used to create objects that modify a servlet request or response.

final Java keyword that stipulates that a class cannot have subclasses. Applied to a member method, this stipulates that the method cannot be overridden by subclasses. Applied to a member variable, it stipulates the variable is a constant whose value cannot be changed after it is set.

finalize Object method executed by the Java garbage collection process when the memory that the object occupies is to be reclaimed. Typically used to ensure that system resources are recovered when an object is discarded.

float Java 32-bit floating-point primitive type.

***Float* (class)** Java wrapper class for `float` primitive values.

form A structure used in HTML pages to create elements that can accept user input and transmit it to a web server using CGI conventions.

forward A Java servlet or JSP handles a HTTP request by forwarding it to another servlet or JSP on the same server, which continues handling the request. This process is invisible to the requesting agent in contrast to redirection.

graphical user interface (GUI) A computer user interface that uses graphical elements, windows, and a pointing device; Mac OS, Windows, and X11 are examples of GUIs; supported by Java.

hashcode In a general computing context, a characteristic number derived from a data item's contents that allows a program or application to locate the item quickly by operating on the number.

hashCode The method in every Java object that generates an `int` primitive hashcode value characteristic of the object.

***Hashtable* (class)** Java class (`java.util.Hashtable`) object that stores Object references denoted by "key" objects using the key's hashcode.

hex (hexadecimal) Mathematical base 16 system used in computer programming that uses alphanumeric characters 0 through 9 and *A* through *F* or *a* through *f*.

hierarchical Logical arrangement of elements, also called a tree structure, in which every element, with the exception of the root object, has parents and might or might not have child objects (children). Examples of this structure can be found in the Java class library, XML documents, and computer file systems.

HTML *See* Hypertext Markup Language.

***HttpServlet* (class)** The base class in the `javax.servlet.http` package extended by servlets that need to respond to GET and POST operations.

Hypertext Markup Language (HTML) The document markup language used to create web pages and standardized by the W3C.

Hypertext Transfer Protocol (HTTP) The set of rules (protocols) based on TCP/IP that provides the foundation for communication between web clients and servers.

identifier Name given an item in a Java program or application.

implements Java keyword in class declarations that precedes a list of one or more interfaces for which the class supplies methods.

import Java source code file statement that informs the Java compiler which package holds classes used in the code.

inheritance In object-oriented programming, relationship among hierarchically arranged objects by which some objects (children) are granted attributes of another object (parent).

***init* (applet method)** By convention, a method that belongs to a Java applet's initial class, and that is called by a web browser's JVM after the applet object is created but before it is displayed.

***init* (servlet method)** A method that belongs to a Java servlet class, and is called by the servlet engine after the servlet object is created but before it services any user requests.

instance An object created from a specific class is said to be an instance of that class.

instance variable Java variable that is part of a class instance instead of the class itself (as opposed to a class or `static` variable).

int Java 32-bit integer primitive type that is always treated as a signed integer.

***Integer* (class)** Java wrapper class for `int` values.

interface Similar to a Java class definition, but provides only method declarations, not implementations. A Java class is free to implement as many interfaces as needed.

International Organization for Standardization (ISO) Group composed of national standards organizations from 89 countries that establishes international standards for telecommunications and technology.

J2EE *See* Java 2 Enterprise Edition.

J2SE *See* Java 2 Standard Edition.

Jakarta The Jakarta project is a major subdivision of the Apache Software Foundation's activities. Generally subprojects of Jakarta are concerned with server applications, but also contain utility projects such as the Ant utility.

JAR (Java ARchive) File format similar to Zip for collecting multiple resources (such as class files and Java class libraries) in a single file.

Java 2 Enterprise Edition (J2EE) An addition to Java 2 Standard Edition (J2SE) that provides the structure for creating multi-tier enterprise applications, such as web enabled applications. J2EE defines a set of specifications for various technologies, including servlets, JSP pages, and EJBs. J2EE also contains utilities, libraries, and reference implementations for these technologies.

Java 2 Standard Edition (J2SE) Sun's collection of Java utilities and libraries for core Java development. Enterprise Java developers use J2EE on top of J2SE.

Java API for XML Parsing (JAXP) Sun's API that provides a standardized way to specify operations on XML documents. This API is intended to be independent of the actual parser used.

Java bean *also* JavaBean Reusable software component written for a specific function or use, and meets the JavaBeans standard for getting and setting instance variable values. *Also see* Enterprise JavaBean.

Java Database Connectivity (JDBC) The collection of Java classes in several packages including the `java.sql` package that enables Java programs to connect to SQL-style databases.

Java Development Kit (JDK) Java package of development tools, utilities, a class library, and documentation that is downloadable from the `java.sun.com` website.

Java Message Service (JMS) The collection of Java classes in several packages including the javax.jms package that enables Java programs to connect to Message Oriented Middleware (MOM) servers for tasks such as asynchronous messaging.

Java Virtual Machine (JVM) Nonphysical (virtual) computer that is part of the Java runtime environment, and interprets Java bytecodes, providing the foundation for the cross-platform features of Java programs.

javadoc Java utility that allows automatic documentation by processing source code and producing reference pages in HTML format.

JavaScript Web page scripting language developed by Netscape (originally called LiveScript) that controls the way in which web pages appear in browsers. It is now found in both browser-side and server-side versions.

JavaServer Pages (JSP) The Java API that allows a programmer to combine HTML and Java code in a single document to create a dynamic web page. A JSP page is converted into a servlet automatically.

JAXP *See* Java API for XML Parsing.

JDBC *See* Java Database Connectivity.

JDK *See* Java Development Kit.

JMS *See* Java Message Service.

JSP *See* JavaServer Pages.

JVM *See* Java Virtual Machine.

***List* (interface)** Java interface (`java.util.List`) that supplies an ordered collection of object references. Not to be confused with the AWT component called List.

long Java 64-bit integer primitive type; always treated as signed integer. *See also* `double` (double precision).

***Long* (class)** Java wrapper class for `long` values.

method Java class function that is named and for which specific input parameters and return types are declared.

MIME, MIME type *See* Multipurpose Internet Mail Extensions.

Multipurpose Internet Mail Extensions (MIME) A standard way of denoting content type in a resource; originated for use with e-mail, but now widely used in network applications, including SOAP. A MIME type is a standardized string designating a particular type.

namespace 1. Complete set of class and method names as well as other program items that the Java compiler tracks to identify an item uniquely. 2. A way to resolve naming conflicts between elements from different vocabularies in an XML document.

null Java special literal value that is used for the value of an uninitialized reference variable.

object A class instance.

package Collection of associated Java classes and interfaces organized into distinct namespaces.

parent In a hierarchical system, any class that is the ancestor of another class.

primitive Java types (`boolean`, `char`, `byte`, `short`, `int`, `long`, `float`, and `double`) that are stored and accessed directly in binary form.

private Java keyword used to tag variables and methods that can be accessed only by methods declared within the same class.

protocol Rules that govern a transaction or data transmission between devices.

public Java keyword for modifying visibility of classes and members, making them accessible by all objects, regardless of package boundaries.

redirect In handling a HTTP request, a servlet may send a response that redirects to another resource. This terminates the request, and it is up to the requesting agent to generate a new request to the other resource. Compare to forwarding.

reference In Java, the process handled by the JVM by which a programmer works a "pointer" to an object (object reference) rather than directly with an object's physical memory address.

Remote Method Invocation (RMI) Java communications standard for distributed computing that allows a Java program to execute a method on an object that resides on another system or JVM as if it were a local object. RMI is a core technology for J2EE-based servers.

remote procedure call (RPC) The general term for executing a method on an application that resides on another system by means of some communication protocol.

RMI *See* Remote Method Invocation.

RPC *See* remote procedure call.

root The one item or object from which all others descend in a hierarchical system.

SAX *See* Simplified API for XML.

schema A formal specification of the structure of an XML document, including information on the types of content allowed in each element.

scope The identifier attribute that controls the identifier's accessibility to other parts of a program.

scripting language Generally speaking, scripting languages are designed for rapid development by linking together components from a powerful toolkit. They tend to have weak variable typing, and are interpreted rather than compiled. Examples include JavaScript, Python, and Perl.

serialize To convert a Java primitive value or object into a byte stream or character stream that is formatted in a way that allows reconstruction of the primitive value or object on the other end of a communication link.

server Network computer that supplies resources and services to client computers.

servlet Java program that runs in a servlet container on a web server and processes network requests (typically HTTP requests).

servlet container The environment in which a servlet runs. The servlet API defines a number of services that a servlet container must provide.

session In Java servlet and JSP applications, a session maintains information about a user during the course of interaction with an application.

***Set* (interface)** Java interface (`java.util.Set`) that is an extension of the `Collection` interface that holds object references, and is restricted to prevent duplication of references; hence, every reference is unique.

SGML *See* Standard Generalized Markup Language.

short Java 16-bit integer primitive variable type; always treated as signed integer.

***Short* (class)** Java wrapper class for `short` values.

signature Java method's name along with the type and order of parameters in its argument list.

Simple Object Access Protocol (SOAP) A standard way to transmit messages over networks using XML-formatted documents. The words "Object Access" are there to indicate that SOAP lends itself to object-oriented programming, typically in remote procedure calls (RPCs).

Simplified API for XML (SAX) An approach to processing XML documents in which the parser identifies and parses elements as it encounters them in a single pass through the document. The user of SAX must provide methods to process the parsed elements.

singleton Design pattern that allows the creation of only one instance of a class; a `static` class method controls access to the instance.

SOAP *See* Simple Object Access Protocol.

socket On computer networks, the combination of a computer address and a port number that provides a unique channel of communications.

***Socket* (class)** Java class object (`java.net.Socket`) representing a single network socket connection; can supply an `InputStream` and `OutputStream` for communication.

SQL *See* Structured Query Language.

stack trace Formatted text output that can provide the history of a `Thread`'s execution of a method that throws an exception or results in an error.

Standard Generalized Markup Language (SGML) A standard for annotating text documents with tags that express the structure of the document and how the content should be treated. SGML served as the basis for HTML and XML.

static Java method or variable tag that indicates the variable or method belongs to a class, rather than to a class instance.

Structured Query Language (SQL) A standard for programming and manipulating the contents of relational databases via text statements. Supported in Java by the JDBC API.

subclass Class that extends (indirectly or directly) another class; all Java classes (except `Object`) are subclasses of the `Object` class.

synchronized Java keyword that activates a method's or code block's monitor mechanism.

syntax Explicit rules for constructing code statements, including particular values and the order or placement of symbols.

***System* (Class)** Java class (`java.lang.System`) composed of `static` methods and variables that the JVM initializes when a program starts.

tag In markup languages such as HTML, XML, and JSP pages, a tag is a special character sequence that is not part of the document text, but defines additional information.

taglib In JSP technology, a programmer can define his own library of special purpose Java functions identified by tags. A special `taglib` directive tells JSP to use a particular library. XSP also uses the term for a library of functions.

TCP/IP *See* Transmission Control Protocol/Internet Protocol.

***Thread* (class)** Java class (`java.lang.Thread`) that encloses a single thread of control in the JVM and defines its behavior.

throw A Java statement that causes normal statement processing to halt and starts processing of an exception; must be associated with a `Throwable` object.

throws Java keyword that is employed in method declarations to introduce a list of the exceptions that method can throw.

Tomcat This is the servlet container developed by the Apache Foundation. It is the Reference Implementation of the Java Servlet and Java Server Pages technologies developed by Sun Microsystems, Inc.

toString Method possessed by all Java reference types that the compiler uses to evaluate statements that include `String` objects and the + operator.

Transmission Control Protocol/Internet Protocol (TCP/IP) Suite of communications protocols developed to support mixed network environments, such as the Internet.

try Java statement that constructs a code block in which an exception can occur; must be followed by at least one associated `catch` clause and/or a `finally` clause.

type A Java object's class or interface. In object-oriented programming in general, an object's interface is sometimes considered separately from its implementation, resulting in a further division into class and type.

Uniform Resource Identifier (URI) The generic set of all names and addresses that refer to resources.

Uniform Resource Locator (URL) The set of URI schemes that contains explicit instructions on how to access a resource on the Internet.

URI *See* Uniform Resource Identifier.

URL *See* Uniform Resource Locator.

***URL* (class)** Java class (`java.net.URL`) that represents a Uniform Resource Locator for a web server.

valid XML XML that conforms to the vocabulary specified in a DTD or schema.

view An object that creates a specific model data display in the Model-View-Controller design pattern. One model may have many views, but a view is always attached to a single model.

visibility Level of access a Java class grants to other Java classes.

W3C *See* World Wide Web Consortium.

Web application A collection of servlets, JSP pages, HTML files, image files, and other resources that exist in a structured hierarchy of directories on a server.

well-formed XML XML markup that meets the requirements of the W3C Recommendation for XML 1.0.

Wireless Markup Language (WML) A simplified variant of HTML designed for small wireless device displays.

World Wide Web Consortium (W3C) The organization that creates standards for the web (`www.w3.org`).

wrapper classes Java classes that correspond to each of the primitive types, providing related utility functions.

Xerces The Apache XML parser used in Cocoon. See the `xml.apache.org` website for the latest version.

XML *See* Extensible Markup Language.

XMLP Title of the XML Protocol project at the W3C that has taken over development of SOAP standards.

XPath This W3C recommendation language is designed to address subparts of an XML document, which can be used by XPointer and XSLT.

Xpointer The XML Pointer language defines constructs that can be used to address internal sections of an XML document.

XSL *See* Extensible Stylesheet Language.

XSLT *See* Extensible Stylesheet Language for Transformations.

INDEX

Note to the reader: Throughout this index **boldfaced** page numbers indicate primary discussions of a topic. *Italicized* page numbers indicate illustrations.

Symbols & Numbers

A

D

E

F

G

H

I

J

K

L

M

N

O

P

Q

R

S

T

U

V

X

About the Contributors

Some of the best–and best-selling–Sybex authors have contributed chapters from their books to *Enterprise Java 2, J2EE 1.3 Complete*.

Bill Brogden is a longtime computer programmer and wrote the best-selling *Java 2 Exam Cram* and *Java 2 Exam Prep* for Coriolis. He has also written for Sun's Advanced Technology Guides and the XML.com website. He is employed by LANWrights, Inc., where he has been using Java servlet technology for online courseware.

Todd Cook is a software developer with experience in Java, Web development, and Oracle. He has developed applications for Sun, the LAX airport in Los Angeles, and tickets.com, among others.

Conrad D'Cruz has 14 years' experience with programming, including Java and XML, and is also an instructor in web technologies.

Michael Ernest works with Inkling Research, a professional services group in the San Francisco Bay Area. He has roamed Silicon Valley for 10 years, designing storage systems, developing Java/J2EE applications, teaching Solaris kernel programming, and currently promoting Sun ONE architecture to his clients. He co-authored *The Complete Java 2 Certification Study Guide, 2nd Edition*.

Mark Gaither is a 10-year computer industry veteran who has built sophisticated web systems for the Texas Department of Commerce, TManage, Inc., Activerse, High End Systems, Instant Sports, and HTMLScript.

Jeff Heaton is an author, college instructor, programmer, and Internet entrepreneur. He has worked with many languages, including C++, Java, and Visual Basic. He co-authored SAMS' *Teach Yourself Visual C++ 6.0 Professional Reference Edition* and has written for *Java Developer's Journal*, *Windows Developer's Journal*, and *C++ Users Journal*. He teaches Java programming at St. Louis Community College and has served as a consultant programmer for Anheuser-Busch, MasterCard, and Boeing, among others.

Philip Heller is a software consultant, Java instructor, and novelist. He is the best-selling author of *Complete Java 2 Certification Study Guide* and a leading Sun certification instructor.

Natalie Levi is a Sun certified instructor and runs an educational testing service. She wrote the test questions for Sybex's Java 2 Virtual Test Center; she also contributed questions to *Complete Java 2 Certification Study Guide*.

Vince E. Marco is an independent J2EE consultant and owner of Enterprise Frameworks, Inc. Vince develops and teaches J2EE and XML courses for a wide range of companies including several Fortune 500 companies. Vince started software development with First Data Corporation in 1985, leading early development in C, C++, and Smalltalk before making his way out to Silicon Valley in 1993.

Chris Minnick is president of Minnick Web Services, which develops database-driven web applications for businesses. He has co-authored several Internet-related books and is a contributing editor for *Software Development* magazine.

Charles Mohnike develops in JSP, Perl, and ColdFusion. He currently runs a development shop specializing in porting print publications to the Web and writes for *Wired Webmonkey*, *Microsoft Bookshelf*, and *SmartTV*.

Victor Peters is an independent J2EE consultant and owner of Next Step Education & Software, Inc. He develops and teaches J2EE courses for a wide range of companies including several Fortune 500 companies. Victor began his career as a flight simulator programmer for MicroProse Entertainment, and several years ago, he leaped into J2EE as the architect and designer for a web survey tracking system that was used by several colleges across the country.

Simon Roberts is a Java course developer and software engineer for Sun. He began his computing career writing machine code and has been teaching programming for the past decade.

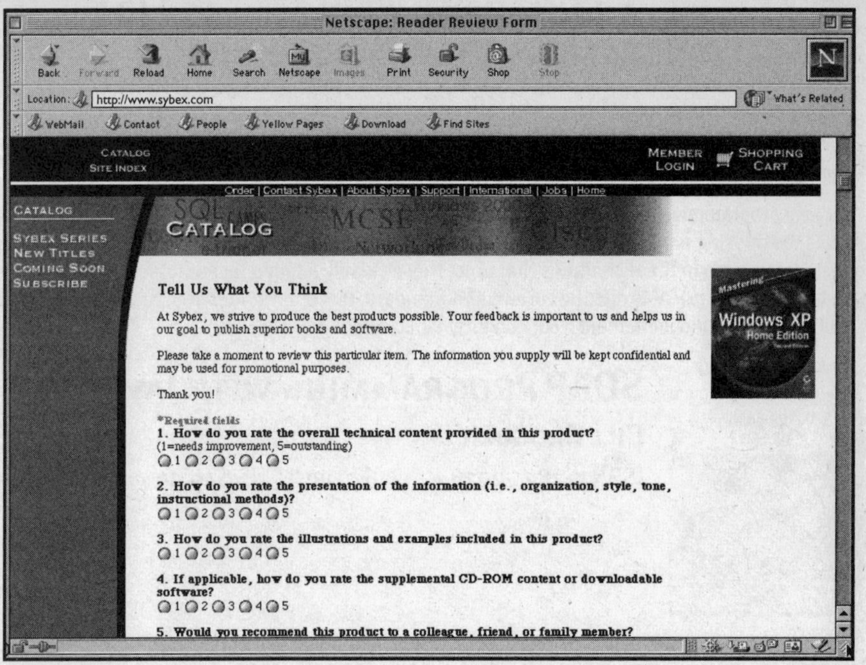